# Critical Strategies for Social Research

Critical Strategies for Social Research

Edited by William K. Carroll

Canadian Scholars' Press Inc.
Toronto

Critical Strategies for Social Research
Edited by William K. Carroll

First published in 2004 by
Canadian Scholars' Press Inc.
180 Bloor Street West, Suite 801
Toronto, Ontario
M5S 2V6

www.cspi.org

Every reasonable effort has been made to identify copyright holders. CSPI would be pleased to have any errors or omissions brought to its attention.

Canadian Scholars' Press gratefully acknowledges financial support for our publishing activities from the Government of Canada through the Book Publishing Industry Development Program (BPIDP).

Library and Archives Canada Cataloguing in Publication

Critical strategies for social research / edited by William K. Carroll.

Includes bibliographical references.
ISBN 1-55130-251-9

1. Social sciences--Research. 2. Social sciences--Methodology. I. Carroll, William K.

H62.C75 2004   300'.72   C2004-905173-3

Cover design by Zack Taylor: www.zacktaylor.com
Page design and layout by Brad Horning

04 05 06 07 08   5 4 3 2 1

Printed and bound in Canada by AGMV Marquis Imprimeur, Inc.

Canad**ä**

TABLE OF CONTENTS

Preface

This book stems from my experience in teaching a course entitled "Critical Research Strategies" at the University of Victoria. I designed the course as a core component in UVic Sociology's Social Justice undergraduate major program, established in 2001. The idea was to create a "different" kind of methods course, one that would complement standard offerings in qualitative and quantitative methods by addressing issues of knowledge, power, social justice, and social inquiry. Student reactions have been overwhelmingly favourable. When I was invited in the summer of 2002 to deliver the inaugural lecture for the University of Windsor's new Social Justice doctoral program in Sociology, I decided to base the lecture on the course. The compilation of an edited volume, building on both my inaugural lecture and the course as it has been evolving in the past two years, has been a natural next step. I hope the result will be of use to a great variety of students and activist-researchers.

Several people have made crucial contributions to this project. I am grateful to Barry Adam and other colleagues in the Department of Sociology and Anthropology at the University of Windsor for honouring me with the invitation to present a lecture that, as it turns out, launched both their doctoral program and this book. A host of generous colleagues at the University of Victoria have, in their styles of intellectual work and through various conversations with me, inspired and helped sustain this project. Within the Department of Sociology, they include Doug Baer, Cecilia Benoit, Ken Hatt, Sean Hier, Martha McMahon, Dorothy Smith, Alison Thomas, and Rennie Warburton, all of whom have been actively involved in creating and/or supporting our own social justice curriculum initiatives. Beyond the department, they include Marie Campbell, Evelyn Cobley, Radhika Desai, Budd Hall, Maeve Lydon, Warren Magnusson, Michael M'Gonigle, Marge Reitsma-Street, Rob Walker, and Bruce Wallace. My teaching assistants over the past three years—Kristin Atwood, Jean Hansen, Robyn Perry, and Kevin Walby—have been of tremendous help, both with the course on which this book is based and with background research for the book itself. Finally, I thank Megan Mueller, Senior Editor at Canadian Scholars' Press, Inc., for encouraging me to embark on this project and to complete it on time.

I dedicate this book to Bill Livant, friend, colleague, ace dialectician, and keen advocate for social justice.

William K. Carroll

NOTE FROM THE PUBLISHER

Thank you for selecting *Critical Strategies for Social Research*, edited by William K. Carroll.

The editor and publisher have devoted considerable time and careful development (including meticulous peer reviews) to this book. We appreciate your recognition of this effort and accomplishment.

Teaching Features

This reader distinguishes itself in many ways. One key feature is the book's well-written and comprehensive part openers, which help to make the readings all the more accessible to sociology and social research students.

The part openers feature a thorough summation and assessment of each reading. Here, the editor has added cohesion to the section and to the whole book by clearly articulating the need for each reading and the logic behind its inclusion. The themes of the book are clearly presented in the part openers.

The part openers are unusually rich in pedagogy. At the end of each section, there are critical thinking questions pertaining to each reading, annotated further readings, annotated relevant Web sites, and glossary terms.

DVD

Instructors and other interested readers are invited to order the DVD, titled "Sociology as Praxis," to accompany the book. Please contact Wreford Miller, Executive Director, Media for a Change, Communication Studies Productions, University of Windsor: Wreford@uwindsor.ca.

Unpacking and Contextualizing Critical Research Strategies

Since the 1960s, a plethora of textbooks has been published in the field of social science research methodology. This literature ranges from comprehensive "cookbooks" and manuals to specialized treatments of singular methodological approaches, and from the highly quantitative issues of measurement, statistical inference, and mathematical modelling to the highly qualitative concerns with meaning and concrete practice. The common denominator that unifies this otherwise disparate field is an overriding emphasis on *technique*. There is by now a well-established canon of methodological procedures for field research, for interviewing, for sampling, for textual analysis, and so on, and existing textbooks are effective means of communicating these techniques to students.

Yet in the same period—since the political ferment of the 1960s—important advances have been made, in and around the social sciences, in the broad praxis-oriented *strategies* of social inquiry. Emanating in great part from social and intellectual movements such as Marxism, feminism, post-colonialism, and post-structuralism, these critical research strategies question the detachment that has in the positivist tradition tended to produce a social science that reinforces status quo arrangements and understandings. But while their influence has grown, these strategies have to date remained scattered across the various disciplines of social science, the caring professions (particularly education and social work), and the humanities. This book draws together five critical strategies and explores their value for sociology and related disciplines.

WHY *CRITICAL STRATEGIES* FOR SOCIAL RESEARCH?

The term "critical" implies a critique of some sort. But why should one be *critical*, rather than *neutral*, or perhaps pragmatically cooperative? Personal whim—a cantankerous refusal to conform or a knee-jerk sympathy for the downtrodden—is not really a sufficient reason. Indeed, initiatives that stem from these sorts of motives are likely to be more dogmatic than critical in the sense I want to give that term. The key reason to be critical comes from a double recognition. On the one hand, the critic sees that our world is marked by extreme inequities and injustices, and that our knowledge of ourselves and that world is caught up in those very practices and structures of inequality and domination. Knowledge never floats free of its socio-political context, and if that context is organized around relations of power, then knowledge will be unavoidably implicated in those relations. On the other hand, the critic realizes that our social world—including our knowledge of that world—is not simply *given*, or the result of a natural process, but is an historical construction. It has been produced by the past actions of people, and therefore *can be remade* by future actions. If this is so then "social facts" can never have the same ontological status as "facts" pertaining to natural processes that are devoid of human agency. In the social field, domination and injustice are not inevitable; they can be undone and transcended. As an influential body of knowledge in the contemporary world, social science has a role to play in that ethical-political project.

Domination, of course, has many faces. It is evident

- in economic disparities that concentrate most of the world's wealth under the control of a tiny fragment of humanity, leaving a billion and a half people destitute,
- in the relations of dependency and isolation that keep many battered women in abusive relationships,
- in the ugliness of racism, not only as a learned pattern of attitude and action but as institutionalized practices that inferiorize those marked as racial minorities,
- in media representations that position viewers as passive consumers, whose fulfillment lies in possessing just the right accessories to fit the ideal of affluence,
- in the lack of control that most working people have over the conditions, process, and results of their labour,
- in the social vulnerability of refugees and migrant workers who are refused basic citizenship rights,
- in the declining quality of social services and the shrinking space for democratic discussion as corporate agendas come to displace (or impersonate) the public good,
- in the derogation of sexual minorities who do not fit within heterosexual assumptions about "normality,"
- in the legacy of colonization that has left much of the world without the organizational means and resources to build sustainable communities and economies, and
- in the ecological degradation that stems from the priority given to short-term private profits over the health of the earth.

If the inequities that presently trouble the world can, in principle, be undone, the critic must also recognize that creating social justice out of injustice is no small feat. One of the barriers to change lies in the role that social researchers themselves play in advising economic, political, and cultural elites on the most effective managerial strategies for accomplishing their organizational objectives. In the 1950s the maverick American sociologist C. Wright Mills referred to this as the role of *adviser to the king*. In its worst manifestations this reduces social science to a "functionally rational machine" wherein "the individual social scientist tends to lose his [*sic*] moral autonomy and his substantive rationality, and the role of reason in human affairs tends to become merely a refinement of techniques for administrative and manipulative uses" (1959: 180). Often, as Mills goes on to note, such advisers manage to avoid becoming ensconced within bureaucratic machinery. But even if consultants retain autonomy in their working conditions, the role of adviser to the king is difficult to fulfill in ways that retain moral and intellectual integrity. Clearly, this sort of social research is complicit with entrenched power, and cannot be expected to challenge the injustices that issue from that power.

Other social researchers maintain an arms-length relationship to entrenched power. Their inquiries are formulated from a detached, "neutral" place, typically in academe, and the knowledge they produce circulates within academic communities. One might describe this process of intellectual production and consumption as *benign*—neither directly critical of injustice nor complicit with it. However, to the extent that it ignores real issues of social injustice, academic neutrality produces sanitized and distorted representations of the social. Moreover, with corporate colonization of academe, the meaning of neutrality begins to shift, sometimes quite subtly, as private funding opportunities and "partnerships" present themselves, favouring the commercial application of social-scientific knowledge (Drakich et al., 2002: 251–252).[1]

The roles of adviser to the king and of scholarly neutrality in a detached scientific community tend to implicate social researchers, directly or indirectly, in the structures of domination that deprive so many people of the possibility to realize their human potential. To put the matter starkly, *in a socially unjust world, knowledge of the social that does not challenge injustice is likely to play a role in reproducing it*. Clearly there is a need for critical alternatives to the predominant roles that social researchers have tended to play in the production of social knowledge. But what does it actually mean to be "critical" in one's approach to research?

We may distinguish three overlapping images of the critical edge in social inquiry. There is first the notion of being *oppositional*, opposing the status quo arrangements that enforce and protect power. This means investigating and criticizing structures and practices of domination—class-based, gendered, racialized, and so on. Being oppositional means positioning oneself on the side of the oppressed or on the side of critical social movements,[2] taking up their standpoints and contesting dominant ideological accounts of social issues that legitimate entrenched power.

A second image of the critical edge is that of *radical* analysis. Within conservative thought, to be "radical" is to be extreme, and probably irrational, in one's thinking and action. What I mean by radical is quite different. Etymologically, radicality means getting at the *root* of matters: to grasp the deeper, systemic bases of the challenges we face, whether social, psychological, or ecological. This often means exploring the interconnections between issues, as in the intersections of race, class, and gender that constitute specific lived realities. The radical inquirer seeks to uncover the interconnections between problems that may, on first blush, seem unrelated—as in the way that corporations chasing higher profits can ruin local communities, create ecological messes, and leave people feeling hopeless and broken—all conjoint implications of the dominance of capital in human affairs (Ollman, 1978: 223).

A third image of the critical edge involves a strategy of *subversion*. The subversive critic disturbs the ordinary, taken-for-granted assumptions and understandings that position us in certain ways, narrowing a potentially wide range of human being to a limited set of identities and practices. By interrogating the common-sense binaries that normalize identities in fields such as gender/sexuality, race/ethnicity, and nationality/citizenship, the subversive unsettles what might otherwise appear as an obdurate reality, and opens a door to alternatives.

There is no one favoured way of enacting these oppositional, radical, and subversive roles, and this book is in any case not a "how-to" manual. Like any social science, critical social inquiry employs various techniques in gathering information, including ethnographic field work and participant observation, analysis of archives, documents and cultural texts, interviewing, questionnaires and surveys, and so on. And there are various qualitative and quantitative techniques for analyzing that information. Techniques of data collection and analysis are crucial in the conduct of research, and any aspiring researcher is well advised to study the techniques relevant to his or her field very thoroughly. Although in the conclusion I will comment briefly on techniques (particularly quantitative method), our concern here is with broader *strategies*, with general approaches to social inquiry that contribute to a project of social critique and social justice.

That said, it is also fair to say that the techniques that often predominate in conventional social research, and that are designed to a great extent for purposes of social surveillance, tend to play an ancillary role in critical research strategies. The forms that critical research takes are often quite different from mainstream media representations of "research," where scientists in lab coats oversee their experiments. What I mean by research is essentially the *production of new knowledge* that people can rely on to guide their actions. Critical research applies its oppositional, radical, and subversive concerns in a variety of knowledge-producing contexts, from the psychoanalysis that can produce new self-understandings and personal/political narratives clear through to macro-sociological investigations of the structures of social domination. In each context, the point of the research is to contribute to human emancipation—to help enlighten and empower people so that they can become active masters of their own lives. There is a strong democratic thrust to critical research.

CRITICAL SOCIAL RESEARCH AS A TRADITION

Sociology and social research have conservative—even reactionary—roots. When he first coined the term "sociology" in the 1820s, Auguste Comte envisaged his new discipline as a scientific response to the social crisis of post-revolutionary French society—a Eurocentric program for top-down social engineering in which the high priests of sociology would share power with the rising industrial bourgeoisie, furnish moral guidelines for the positive society, and "specify the duties, obligations, and social roles that have to be fulfilled in order for social harmony to prevail" (Seidman, 2004: 20). In the twentieth century, as its leading protagonists engaged in an inconclusive debate with the ghost of Marx (Zeitlin, 1968), sociology became aligned with the welfare state and the programming of society by way of top-down initiatives. If sociologists were denied the elite technocratic status envisaged by Comte, many did, as I have mentioned, take up the less prestigious role of adviser to the king. It is not that sociology is hopelessly compromised when it enters the terrain of the state. In Canada, for instance, as the welfare state and an expanded sense of social citizenship took root in the 1950s, 1960s, and 1970s, sociologists contributed to social reform, via public-policy venues that included Royal Commissions (Armstrong and Armstrong, 1992; McFarlane, 1992). Sociology continues to play a role in social programming, but with the shift in the 1980s to a neo-liberal policy paradigm emphasizing the free play of market forces over the regulation of social life by the state, the margin for pursuing social justice through state policies diminished (McBride, 2001). In the policy networks that surround and permeate the neo-liberal state sociologists are heavily outnumbered by economists, efficiency experts, risk-management consultants, and others whose world views incline them toward market-driven politics (Leys, 2001).

Critical research—aimed at contesting entrenched power—can also be traced back to the nineteenth century and to contemporaries of Auguste Comte. In 1844 Frederick Engels produced a detailed critical ethnography of *The Condition of the Working Class in England* (1952), which documented and reflected on the conditions of oppression that most of the English population knew at that time. Nearly four decades later, Karl Marx constructed a Workers' Questionnaire for the monthly *La Revue Socialists*, as a way of elucidating the economic demands of French factory workers.[3] In collaboration with Engels, Marx, an academically educated scholar who chose the life of an activist intellectual, developed a method of analysis and a critical theory of capitalism that has been a key inspiration for subsequent critics and activists. Marx's *dialectical social analysis* is the first critical strategy we consider at length in this book.

In the early decades of the twentieth century the Frankfurt Institute for Social Research became the first major academic site for interdisciplinary critical research that combined dialectical social analysis with psychoanalytic and other approaches. In the United States from the late nineteenth century we can also, with Joe Feagin (2001), trace a "countersystem" approach to sociology in the work of Jane Addams, W.E.B. Du Bois, and other activist sociologists whose efforts sought to build a grassroots base for social change.

By the early twentieth century then, both in Europe and North America, a tradition of critical social inquiry had been established. However, in the ensuing decades this tradition was marginalized, much in the way that other democratizing possibilities of modernity have tended to be submerged under the predominant logics of profit maximization, hierarchical state power, elite professionalization, and the like (Habermas, 1984). In Germany, the rise and consolidation of Nazism in the 1930s obliged Institute members to flee to the U.S. Although members of the Frankfurt School played a formative role in bringing survey-research methods to bear upon the problem of authoritarianism in the late 1940s (Jay, 1972: 219–252), with the demise of the Institute they turned away from a social research agenda (Morrow with Brown, 1994). In the U.S., Feagin tells us that already by the 1920s and 1930s, mainstream sociology's quest for professional respectability was pushing the critical tradition to the margins of the discipline. Indicatively, in his 1929 presidential address to the American Sociological Society, William F. Ogburn called for a sociology emphasizing statistical methods. He argued that sociologists should not be involved, as sociologists, in improving society. Instead, they should focus on efficiently discovering knowledge about society. "Whoever is in power 'some sterling executive,' might then apply this objective sociological research" (Feagin, 2001: 8).

With the rising affluence of the post-World War II years (mid-1940s to the mid-1960s), and in a Cold War context of state repression against left-wing dissidence, critical approaches to social analysis were further marginalized, particularly in the U.S. This period of *high modernism* (Jameson, 1991) also marked the high tide of positivist social science. Social research took on a neutral, scientific, and professional casting, especially within American academic and applied circles. With American cultural and political influence at its peak in the 1950s and 1960s, the paradigm of positivist research spread throughout much of the world. Positivist sociology, with its emphasis on quantifying social life into the language of variables and statistical relationships, gained the aura of universal, scientific truth.

Nevertheless, even in the period of positivist triumph, a counter-system tradition was maintained in the work of sociologists like C. Wright Mills, whose mappings of the power elite and other classes and strata raised searching questions about American society. It was Mills (1959) who delivered a scathing critique of positivist sociology in a book that we draw from at both the beginning and close of this collection. Other critiques followed (Horowitz, 1964; Reynolds and Reynolds, 1970; Lee, 1978), including in 1964 the exposure of Project Camelot (Horowitz,

1967), and with it, of the danger of social science research becoming a mere tool in the imperial designs of the American state. By the mid-1960s the hegemony of positivist detachment was being openly challenged, with prominent sociologists like Howard Becker asking, "Whose side are we all on?"

SOCIAL ACTIVISM AND CRITICAL INQUIRY: THE WATERSHED OF 1968

If we can trace, however sketchily for present purposes, a critical tradition that reaches back at least to the mid-19th century, it is nevertheless the case that most of the strategies featured in this book took shape in the late 20th century. In good measure, they arose out of the political ferment of the 1960s and first half of 1970s—a wave of intense social activism and political-cultural transformation. Immanuel Wallerstein (1989) has emphasized the world-historical ramifications of the protest wave that crested between 1968 and 1972 in what he calls the revolution of 1968. This was not a revolution in the classic sense of late 18th-century France or early 20th-century Russia. In 1968 no radical political party gained state power and proceeded to restructure society in accordance with an alternative vision. In fact, 1968 was distinctive for its skepticism about parties and states as the natural containers for politics. What the revolution did entail was a qualitative shift in the practices and understandings of politics, and with that a coming-to-voice of new political actors—new anti-systemic movements, in Wallerstein's terms—with new claims, perspectives, and strategies, both at the core of the capitalist world and on its periphery.[4]

The movements of the 1960s opened politics to the recognition that no one agent (e.g., "the working class") owns the franchise on social change and that cultural transformations and grassroots democracy are crucial elements of praxis. These new perspectives were worked out within a host of movements that serve as modernity's social laboratories for inventing and trying out new ways of life (Melucci, 1989), whether in the area of intimate relationships, ecological practice, or collective decision making. The wave of protest that began in the early 1960s was not uniform across different national contexts, but overall we can, with Snow and Benford (1992), discern a "master frame" of social justice that first informed civil rights, anti-colonial and student movements, and later was broadened to feminist, gay-lesbian, and ecological politics, and even to a rebirth of social unionism in sections of the labour movement. What is remarkable, though not actually surprising, is that these various movements emerged and grew in tandem, influencing each other's opportunities and sensibilities. It was their combination that made possible a shift in the definition of the political, to include the personal, the everyday, the cultural, and the environmental:

> The growth of a radical, intellectual subculture is the sometimes forgotten legacy of the 1960s. Many elements of this subculture—feminism, Western Marxism, post-structuralism, social ecology, critical political economy—converge with the themes of the new movements, which permeate not only the universities but also the high schools, media, art world, trade unions and even some municipal governments. (Boggs, 1995: 350)

But the intellectual legacy of the 1960s reaches beyond the *theoretical* innovations that Boggs rightly underscores. What I want to call attention to are the strategies for *research*—ways of producing knowledge of the social—that arose or were revived as part of the same political ferment.

Ron Eyerman and Andrew Jamison have emphasized how *cognitive praxis*—"the creation, articulation, formulation of new thoughts and ideas"—forms a core activity of social movements (1991: 55).[5] The anti-systemic movements of the late 1960s and early 1970s generated new *ways* of knowing, new *needs* for knowing, and new *interests* in knowing the social. As Jürgen Habermas (1971) has famously argued, humans seek knowledge for three reasons, that is, on the basis of three knowledge-constituting interests: (1) to control natural and social realities, (2) to qualitatively interpret and understand them, and (3) "to transform our individual and collective consciousness of reality in order to maximize the human potential for freedom and equality ..." (Morrow with Brown, 1994: 146). It was the third, "critical-emancipatory" interest that shaped the cognitive praxis of 1968, and that continues to shape the cognitive praxis of critical social movements.

This interest in creating social knowledge for the purposes of social change has been accentuated all the more by the *heightened reflexivity* concerning identity, culture, and life that the new movements brought with them (Giddens, 1991b: 14–15). For Giddens, "the reflexivity of modern social life consists in the fact that social practices are constantly examined and reformed in the light of incoming information about those very practices, thus constitutively altering their character" (1991a: 38). In modernity—and particularly in a modernity whose normative moorings are being continually scrutinized and periodically unsettled by a variety of critical movements—"the social" becomes an unstable object within a changing force-field of power and knowledge (Foucault, 1980). Whether in the form of Marxist ideology-critique, feminist consciousness-raising, the mind bombs of cultural radicalism,[6] the post-colonial critique of Western hegemony, or the call for a public sphere in which knowledge can be democratized, the currents of social activism that issued from the 1960s have been *carriers of a heightened reflexivity* about the nexus of knowledge and power. Their cognitive praxis has been formed around an interest in developing knowledge (and ways of knowing) that would empower the disempowered, challenge arbitrary authority, and promote democratic practice, whether in local communities or globally.

FIVE CRITICAL STRATEGIES AND THEIR PROXIMAL LINEAGES

All five of our critical research strategies share this emancipatory interest, but they do so in distinctive ways. Let us briefly consider each strategy, together with its proximal lineages in the confluent political currents of 1960s/70s activism (see Figure 1).

Dialectical social analysis (DSA) calls attention both to the systemic and deeply structured character of social injustice and to the potential for radical renovation of the social relations within which we realize our human possibilities, or suffer the thwarting of them. Although DSA is most immediately identified with the critical analysis of capital and class, it has been applied effectively in the analysis of other deeply structured relations such as those of gender (Hartsock, 1998) and ecology (Foster, 2000; Harvey, 1996). As a critical strategy, DSA invites us to view the social as always under construction, to uncover both the relations that constitute a social order and the sources of change within it, and to unmask ideologies that legitimate status quo arrangements. Marx's (1967) own critical analysis of the underlying social relations that constitute capitalism as form of class society is paradigmatic to this strategy, and in the initial revival of interest in dialectical social analysis the focus was very much on understanding the dynamics of capital and class, with an eye trained on the horizon of future possibilities for a world beyond class

Figure 1: Critical Strategies for Social Inquiry: Proximal Lineages

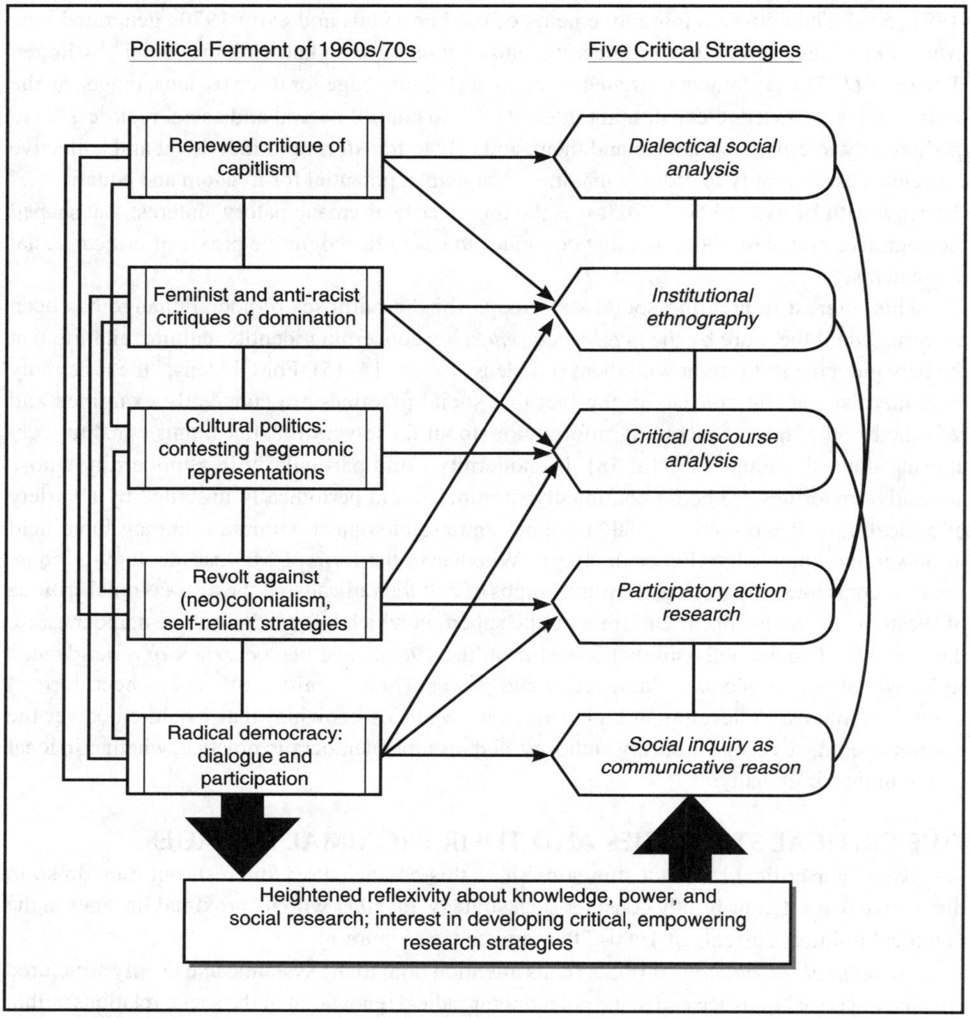

Political Ferment of 1960s/70s — Five Critical Strategies

- Renewed critique of capitlism → *Dialectical social analysis*
- Feminist and anti-racist critiques of domination → *Institutional ethnography*
- Cultural politics: contesting hegemonic representations → *Critical discourse analysis*
- Revolt against (neo)colonialism, self-reliant strategies → *Participatory action research*
- Radical democracy: dialogue and participation → *Social inquiry as communicative reason*

Heightened reflexivity about knowledge, power, and social research; interest in developing critical, empowering research strategies

inequality. In the North, this renewal was based partly on the recognition within the new left that consumer capitalism had brought material affluence yet social alienation to the industrialized heartland—epitomized in Marcuse's (1964) image of *One Dimensional Man*. Concomitantly, scholars and activists in Latin America, Africa, and Asia based their critiques on capitalism's apparent incapacity to foster anything more than a grossly uneven form of development in the Third World, combined with burgeoning poverty and misery (Amin, 1978). By the mid-1970s, as the world economy slipped into its first generalized downturn since the 1930s, a new generation had rediscovered Marxian social and political analysis, giving renewed vigour to a venerable tradition of critique that the further globalization of capitalism has only made more relevant in recent decades.

Institutional ethnography (IE), the most coherent and influential research strategy stemming from feminist and anti-racist activism of the 1970s, takes as its analytical starting point the actualities of everyday life as experienced by its practitioners. This is the same place from which women began in the micro-political consciousness-raising groups that were so integral to the practice of feminism in the late 1960s and early 1970s. In both cases, the point in beginning from direct experience is to develop a knowledge base outside of ruling ideological frameworks from which to *problematize* one's everyday world, to ask how it is that that world is put together in just the way that it is. By approaching everyday actualities as puzzles, a critical space is opened for exploration of how extra-local ruling relations reach into and shape the everyday. Originating in the 1970s in a series of articles by feminist sociologist Dorothy Smith (1987), IE is a project of "mapping social relations" (Campbell and Gregor, 2002) in such a way that those subjected to ruling relations gain the knowledge they need to subvert and challenge domination. Its lineage is very much centred in the practices of feminist and anti-racist politics that emphasize both the material injustices of male domination and racism as well as the cultural/psychological dimensions—the internalized oppressions that recommend strategies of consciousness-raising through which the oppressed come to name and understand their oppression and to rename themselves as people deserving dignity (De Vault, 1996: 30). But IE's lineage can also be traced to the renewed interest in Marx's critique of capital, which inspired Dorothy Smith's conception of extra-local ruling relations (Smith, 1977), and to the critique of colonization that also figured prominently in the wave of 1960s activism and that in Canadian intellectual circles took the form of a movement to "Canadianize" cultural production:

> In Canada at the University of British Columbia I discovered that I was teaching in what I came to think of as a colonized institution. So far as sociology was concerned, the University of British Columbia was a colony of the American sociological establishment ....
>
> The Canadianization critique of the social sciences and the humanities in Canada showed us the colonial character of the intellectual régime we practiced .... Canadianization began to free me for the possibilities of thinking from a different space in the society than I had been trained for. (Smith, 1992: 126)

Finally, IE offers a form of critical analysis of *texts*, since within this perspective texts of all sorts are seen to play a crucial role in social organization and extra-local practices of ruling. This concern with texts brings us to our third critical strategy.

Critical discourse analysis (CDA) focuses its lens on the discourses and texts that constitute our cultural environment and that come to structure our sense of self, identity, and human possibility. By showing how discourses work, how they *work on us*, and how they are articulated with other forms of power, CDA opens a space for reinventing who we are and for appreciating the different colours and hues in the human tapestry. Its most direct political lineage is to the *cultural politics* for which the 1960s are well known. Movements such as gay and lesbian liberation challenged the normalized images and messages that issue from dominant institutions and that stabilize identities and institutions. Movement-based critiques often started from an *affirmation* of received identities, as in "Black is Beautiful"; indeed, the lineage of CDA reaches back also to anti-racist and feminist critiques of domination. Yet if the cultural politics of the 1960s tended to essentialize racial, gender, sexual, and other identities as being stable with fixed attributes, by the 1980s and 1990s "social-constructionist perspectives held sway among movement-oriented academics" (Darnovsky et al., 1995: xiii), and activists themselves were incorporating more reflexive forms of critical discourse analysis into their own praxis, most notably with the queering of sexual politics (Phelan, 1993; Namaste, 1996). An institution of great relevance to CDA is the mass media. The activism of the 1960s was already deeply mass-mediated,[7] particularly in North America where television culture was consolidated in that decade, to be diffused globally in subsequent decades. As our world becomes increasingly permeated by a semiotics of everyday life, culture forms a vast terrain of contention over identity and meaning, and media literacy, which entails the capacity to engage in critical discourse analysis, becomes a crucial resource for activists and citizens.[8]

Participatory action research (PAR) is a critical strategy with deep roots in the colonized and impoverished periphery of global capitalism. It combines "social investigation, education and action designed to support those with less power in their organizational or community settings" (Hall, 2001: 171). At its inception in the 1960s, PAR was closely linked to the politics of decolonization and self-reliant development. Most dramatically in national liberation struggles (e.g., Cuba, Algeria, Viet Nam, South Africa), but also in local grassroots initiatives, the revolt against colonialism meant a refusal to be dominated from outside, by the colonizer. A politics of *self-reliance* was central to this revolt, founded in the recognition that genuine human development must be controlled by the participants in the development process (Wignaraja, 1993: 26–29). According to Orlando Fals Borda, one of PAR's pioneers, 1970 was a crucial year as important projects were undertaken or completed in India, Columbia, Tanzania, Brazil, and Mexico. By 1977, when 2,000 participants attended the first World Symposium of Action Research in Cartagena, Columbia, the quest for "a new type of scientific plus activist/emancipatory work" (2001: 30) was bearing tangible fruit. Inspired in part by Paulo Freire's (1970) dialogical approach to radical pedagogy (also a product of the 1960s), PAR sees the issues of people's participation, conscientization, and the building of countervailing power as "part of an ongoing social process: the long revolution towards social and structural change" (Wignaraja, 1993: 27). The emphasis is on democratic empowerment through participation in a process of knowledge production and social change—a goal that makes PAR useful in a wide variety of contexts, North and South.

Finally, what I have called *social inquiry as communicative reason* comprises a critical strategy whose lineage can be traced directly to the strongly *democratic* priorities that 1960s activism espoused. The student movement provides perhaps the best exemplar of what Eyerman and Jamison take to be the most central political accomplishment of the 1960s—"a re-cognition of direct democracy":

> Students organized themselves for a "democratic society" in the US and Germany, and their actions sought to rediscover what democratic behavior was all about. Industrial society had become in the eyes of many students a bureaucratic, mass society without ideology or any coherent value system. (1991: 90)

The vision of direct, participatory democracy presents a radical alternative to the hollowed-out representative democracies that now manage nearly all states, and the current wave of anti-corporate globalization activism draws deeply upon this same vision (McNally, 2002) as does contemporary ecological politics (Bookchin, 1991; Gale and M'Gonigle, 2000). When social inquiry is pursued as communicative reason, the objective of research is to produce knowledge that can contribute to a revitalized democratic society in which all may participate. This is precisely what C. Wright Mills (1959) considered the promise of sociology. It portends a reflexive, engaged "public sociology" (Seidman, 2004: 98), a sociology that spreads the critical capacity for social analysis widely among democratic publics, that helps reinvigorate a public sphere that has been cumulatively weakened by the incursions of bureaucracy and commodification, and that aligns itself with activists promoting more democratic ways of life, since they are the crucial agents of a potentially reconstituted public sphere.

We can glimpse in this last image of alignment the symbiotic relation that has existed between critical strategies for social inquiry and critical social movements. Just as activism both requires and generates *social knowledge*, critical strategies have *issued* from activism but they also *inform* activism. Because they have strong lineages in currents of radical and democratic activism they can provide leverage to social movements and to emancipatory politics in the here and now. As Giddens might say, critical strategies for social inquiry change the very object they are about. They are intrinsically reflexive approaches to understanding the social world while participating in its transformation.

What we also notice, at the close of these introductory sketches, is that there is by now a *plurality* of critical approaches to social inquiry, each of which can make distinctive contributions to a social science for social justice. These strategies need to be nurtured and developed, and made more widely accessible, in the academy and beyond the academy. This book is offered as a contribution to that effort.

NOTES

1. As my co-editors and I observed some years ago, in reflecting on the place of sociology and anthropology in Canadian society,

    the penetration of academe by corporate capital is by now itself an established reality. It is evident in the proliferation of direct institutional ties between business and universities, in the neoliberal state's shifting priorities for funding higher education, and in the new discourses and practices of corporate-style efficiency and productivity. "Value-for-money," "cost-effectiveness," and "accountability" are criteria central to the 'truth' of the marketplace. Whether they come to be centrally inscribed in the work of Canadian sociologists and anthropologists and to influence the content of social-scientific discourse is the focus of considerable struggle and anguish amongst practitioners of these disciplines. (Carroll et al., 1992: 10)

2. We can, with Magnusson and Walker (1988: 60) define *critical* movements as "open and experimental" movements engaged in a series of explorations—of new political spaces in which to act, including the local and personal spaces of civil society as well as the spaces of ecological regions and cultural networks; of political practices that often focus on small-scale actions, networking, lateral organization, self-transformation, and empowerment; of cultural horizons that foreground the politics of language and knowledge and that reinterpret such modern dichotomies as subject and object, self and other, male and female; of pluralistic political communities that refuse the monolithic boundaries of states.

3. An English translation of the questionnaire is available online at http://www.marxists.org/archive/marx/works/1880/04/20.htm.

4. David McNally (2002) provides a useful month-by-month overview of the events of 1968, noting how widely the spirit of revolt was in the air—from Paris through Prague, Saigon and Tokyo to Chicago and Mexico City, to name a few major venues.

5. Recently Janet Conway (2004) has shown the value of this insight in her study of knowledge production and identity construction in social movements contesting globalization.
6. On mind bombs, i.e., "the unanticipated disruption of settled patterns of thought," see Downing (2001: 159), who notes that this term comes out of the Greenpeace strategic vocabulary.
7. As the examples of the Students for a Democratic Society (Gitlin, 1980) and Greenpeace (Dale, 1996) vividly show.
8. Critical discourse analysis has relevance not only to the *critique* of hegemonic texts but to the *production* of alternative culture. The radical media discussed by Downing (2001), which pre-date the 1960s but gathered great force in that era, and which now extend to culture-jamming practices that critique and subvert dominant ideological images and messages, are part of a broad, reflexive questioning of culture as a social construct, and part of the inheritance of 1968.

REFERENCES

Amin, Samir. 1978. *The Law of Value and Historical Materialism*. New York: Monthly Review Press

Armstrong, Pat, and Hugh Armstrong. 1992. "Better Irreverent Than Irrelevant." In *Fragile Truths*, edited by William K. Carroll et al., 339–348. Ottawa: Carleton University Press.

Boggs, Carl. 1995. "Rethinking the Sixties Legacy: From New Left to New Social Movements." In *Social Movements: Critiques, Concepts, Case-Studies*, edited by Stanford M. Lyman, 331–355. London: Macmillan.

Bookchin, Murray. 1991. *The Ecology of Freedom: The Emergence and Dissolution of Hierarchy*, revised ed. Montreal: Black Rose Books.

Campbell, Marie, and Frances Gregor. 2002. *Mapping Social Relations*. Toronto: Garamond Press.

Carroll, William K., Linda Christiansen-Ruffman, Raymond F. Currie, and Deborah Harrison. 1992. "Introduction." In *Fragile Truths*, edited by W.K. Carroll, Linda Christiansen-Ruffman, Raymond F. Currie, and Deborah Harrison, 1–13. Ottawa: Carleton University Press.

Conway, Janet M. 2004. *Identity, Place, Knowledge: Social Movements Contesting Globalization*. Halifax: Fernwood Books.

Dale, Stephen. 1996. *McLuhan's Children*. Toronto: Between the Lines.

Darnovsky, Marcy, Barbara Epstein, and Richard Flacks. 1995. "Introduction." In *Cultural Politics and Social Movements*, edited by Marcy Darnovsky, Barbara Epstein, and Richard Flacks, vii–xxiii. Philadelphia: Temple University Press.

De Vault, Marjorie L. 1996. "Talking Back to Sociology: Distinctive Contributions of Feminist Methodology." *Annual Review of Sociology* 22: 29–50.

Downing, John D.H. 2001. *Radical Media: Rebellious Communication and Social Movements*. London: Sage.

Drakich, Janice, Karen R. Grant, and Penni Stewart. 2002. "The Academy in the 21st Century: Editors' Introduction." *Canadian Review of Sociology and Anthropology* 39(3): 249–260.

Engels, Frederick. 1952. *The Condition of the Working-Class in England in 1844*. London: Allen & Unwin.

Eyerman, Ron, and Andrew Jamison. 1991. *Social Movements: A Cognitive Approach*. University Park: Pennsylvania University Press.

Fals Borda, Orlando. 2001. "Participatory (Action) Research in Social Theory: Origins and Challenges." In *Handbook of Action Research*, edited by Peter Reason and Hilary Bradbury, 27–37. London: Sage.

Feagin, Joe R. 2001. "Social Justice and Sociology: Agendas for the Twenty-First Century." *American Sociological Review* 60(1): 1–20.

Foster, John Bellamy. 2000. *Marx's Ecology: Materialism and Nature*. New York: Monthly Review Press.

Foucault, Michel. 1980. *Power/Knowledge: Selected Interviews and Other Writings, 1972–1977*, edited by Colin Gordon. New York: Pantheon Books.

Freire, Paulo. 1970. *Pedagogy of the Oppressed*. New York: Seabury Press.

Gale, Fred, and R. Michael M'Gonigle. 2000. *Nature, Production, Power: Towards an Ecological Political Economy*. Northampton: E. Elgar.

Giddens, Anthony. 1991a. *The Consequences of Modernity*. Palo Alto: Stanford University Press.

_____. 1991b. *Modernity and Self-Identity*. Cambridge: Polity Press.

Gitlin, Tod. 1980. *The Whole World Is Watching: Mass Media in the Making and Unmaking of the New Left*. Berkeley: University of California Press.

Habermas, Jurgen. 1971. *Knowledge and Human Interests*. Boston: Beacon Press.

_____. 1984. *The Theory of Communicative Action*, vol. 1. Boston: Beacon Press.

Hall, Budd. 2001. "I Wish This Were a Poem of Practices of Participatory Research." In *Handbook of Action Research*, edited by Peter Reason and Hilary Bradbury, 171–178. London: Sage.

Hartsock, Nancy. 1998. "Marxist Feminist Dialectics for the 21st Century." *Science and Society* 62(3): 400–413.

Harvey, David. 1996. *Justice, Nature and the Geography of Difference*. Oxford: Blackwell.

Horowitz, Irving Louis. 1964. *The New Sociology*. New York: Oxford University Press.

Horowitz, Irving Louis, ed. 1967. *The Rise and Fall of Project Camelot: Studies in the Relationship between Social Science and Practical Politics.* Cambridge: The MIT Press.

Jameson, Fredric. 1991. *Postmodernism, or, the Cultural Logic of Late Capitalism.* Durham: Duke University Press.

Jay, Martin. 1972. *The Dialectical Imagination: A History of the Frankfurt School and the Institute of Social Research, 1923–1950*. Boston: Little, Brown.

Lee, Alfred McLung. 1978. *Sociology for Whom?* New York: Syracuse University Press.

Leys, Colin. 2001. *Market-Driven Politics*. London: Verso.

Magnusson, Warren, and Rob Walker. 1988. "De-Centring the State: Political Theory and Canadian Political Economy." *Studies in Political Economy* 26: 37–71.

Marcuse, Herbert. 1964. *One Dimensional Man: Studies in the Ideology of Advanced Industrial Society*. Boston: Beacon Press.

Marx, Karl. 1967. *Capital*, volumes 1–3. New York: International Publishers.

McBride, Stephen. 2001. *Paradigm Shift: Globalization and the Canadian State*. Halifax: Fernwood.

McFarlane, Bruce A. 1992. "Anthropologists and Sociologists, and Their Contributions to Policy in Canada." In *Fragile Truths*, edited by William K. Carroll et al., 281–294. Ottawa: Carleton University Press.

McNally, David. 2002. *Another World Is Possible: Globalization and Anti-Capitalism*. Winnipeg: Arbeiter Ring Publishing.

Melucci, Alberto. 1989. *Nomads of the Present*. Philadelphia: Temple University Press.

Mills, C. Wright. 1959. *The Sociological Imagination*. New York: Oxford University Press.

Morrow, Raymond A., with David D. Brown. 1994. *Critical Theory and Methodology*. London: Sage.

Namaste, Ki. 1996. "The Politics of Inside/Out: Queer Theory, Poststructuralism, and a Sociological Approach to Sexuality." In *Queer Theory/Sociology*, edited by Steven Seidman, 194–212. Oxford: Blackwell.

Ollman, Bertell. 1978. "On Teaching Marxism." In *Studies in Socialist Pedagogy*, edited by Theodore Mills Norton and Bertell Ollman, 215–253. New York: Monthly Review Press.

Phelan, Shane. 1993. "(Be)coming Out: Lesbian Identity and Politics." *Signs* 18: 765–790.

Reynolds, Larry T., and Janice M. Reynolds, eds. 1970. *The Sociology of Sociology: Analysis and Criticism of the Thought, Research, and Ethical Folkways of Sociology and its Practitioners*. New York: David McKay Company, Inc.

Seidman, Steven. 2004. *Contested Knowledge: Social Theory Today*, 3rd ed. Oxford: Blackwell.

Smith, Dorothy E. 1977. *Feminism and Marxism: A Place to Begin, a Way to Go*. Vancouver: New Star Books.

_____. 1987. *The Everyday World as Problematic: A Feminist Sociology*. Toronto: University of Toronto Press.

_____. 1992. "Remaking a Life, Remaking Sociology: Reflections of a Feminist." In *Fragile Truths*, edited by W.K. Carroll, Linda Christiansen-Ruffman, Raymond F. Currie, and Deborah Harrison, 125–134. Ottawa: Carleton University Press.

Snow, David A., and Robert D. Benford. 1992. "Master Frames and Cycles of Protest." In *Frontiers in Social Movement Theory*, edited by Aldon D. Morris and Carol McClurg Mueller, 133–155. New Haven: Yale University Press.

Wallerstein, Immanuel. 1989. "1968, Revolution in the World-System." *Theory and Society* 18: 431–449.

Wignaraja, Ponna. 1993. "Rethinking Development and Democracy." In *New Social Movements in the South: Empowering the People*, edited by Ponna Wignaraja, 4–35. London: Zed Books.

Zeitlin, Irving. 1968. *Ideology and the Development of Sociological Theory*. Englewood Cliffs: Prentice-Hall.

PART
1A

REDISCOVERING THE CRITICAL EDGE IN SOCIAL ANALYSIS

Although the years since the 1960s have seen a coming of age of reflexive, critical social inquiry, the critical edge in social science actually dates from the mid-19th century. The readings that follow provide us with three temporally sequenced takes—the first at the inception of critical social science, the second as the post-1940s hegemony of positivism was beginning to fall under challenge, and the third at the turn of the 21st century. It is instructive to consider the social position of each writer in the context of his day: Karl Marx, a political activist, exiled from Prussia and living in obscurity in Brussels; Howard Becker, a well-respected qualitative sociologist with a rather marginal position *vis-à-vis* the American sociological establishment of the mid-1960s; Joe Feagin, elected president of the American Sociological Association in 2000 and a leading sociologist. These three snapshots give us a very rough measure of the increasing influence of critical perspectives in sociology and related social sciences.

Marx's "Theses on Feuerbach," written in 1845 when at the age of 26 he renounced his Prussian nationality and declared himself "a citizen of the world" (Reiss, 1997: 3), are the perfect point of departure for critical research strategies. Marx wrote these epigrams simply as notes to himself, presumably to guide his own critical inquiry. More than a century and a half later they continue to be wise counsel for social analysts and activists alike.

The theses are perhaps the most concise expression available of the "philosophy of praxis" that Marx initiated. Most immediately, they criticize the materialist philosophy of Ludwig Feuerbach, whose *Essence of Christianity* (1957 [1841]) asserted the primacy of the material world (being) over the conceptual world (thought; Reiss, 1997: 84). More generally they oppose both the idealist absorption of reality into consciousness, interpretation, ideas, discourse, and the like and the (contemplative) materialist view that consciousness is no more than a reflection of the material conditions of existence. Idealism encourages a cultural politics inured to the need to transform social and material circumstances (see Thesis IV); contemplative materialism inhibits the possibilities of change by portraying people as passive effects of those circumstances (see Theses III, V, and IX). Against both positions, Marx calls for a materialism that *includes* human practice—activity-in-the-world—as integral to that world (Thesis I).

What Marx's theses give us is a view of the human condition as both natural (humans are objective beings in and of the natural world) and historical: human practice, particularly "revolutionary practice" transforms both the circumstance in which people are active and the people themselves (Thesis III). "All social life is essentially practical," Marx declares (Thesis VIII), and social inquiry, itself a practice, needs to reach a comprehension of practice if it is to avoid mystification. Even the "objective truth" of an idea is not an abstract question of theory, but "a *practical* question," to be proven in practice (Thesis II). For Marx, the social world has an open-ended but also a *relational* character. Indeed, what is *essential* about the human condition is not any abstract trait shared by all individuals but rather the concrete social relationality of people living their lives and making history as they do so (Thesis VI).[1] Thus, in contrast to the "old materialism," which included not only Feuerbach but classical economists like Adam Smith, the *standpoint* of Marx's materialism is not that of "single individuals" in "civil society" but that of "social humanity" (Theses IX and X).

Yet, as Marx well knew, the very practices and relations of capitalist society—the dominance of capital over labour and the grievous inequities contained therein, the amoral pursuit of profit over public good, the commodification of the world, and the debasement of human relations to market relations—encourage people to see themselves as social fragments—as single individuals in civil society. In this early statement, and all the more in his later work (see Larrain, 1986), Marx realized that even as capitalism creates an integrated global order in which our fates are intertwined, it also fragments human sociality, inserting each person as an isolated individual into the competitive market system. By implication, a social science content merely to describe and interpret the extant reality of such a social order will reproduce in its knowledge the same limited and ultimately erroneous standpoint, that of the "abstract—*isolated*—human individual" (Thesis VI). In this we can recognize the importance of Thesis XI (which, incidentally, is inscribed on Marx's tomb): "the philosophers have only *interpreted* the world, in various ways; the point is to *change* it." It is not enough to show, as Feuerbach did, that traditional Christianity legitimates a certain form of the family (which today we might call patriarchal and authoritarian). From the standpoint of social humanity, that family form must itself be criticized in theory and revolutionized in practice (Thesis IV). This conjunction of critical theory and transformative practice, so central to Marx's method, is called "praxis."

Ultimately it is through praxis that the standpoint of social humanity gains visibility and credibility. As Cyril Smith points out, "what matters is how we ourselves *act* in relation to each other and to nature, and how we can transform our way of life. What actions will enable us consciously and purposively to remake the relations between us, so that we become what we really are: all-sided, social, free individuals?" (1996: 64). This last question gives us one criterion on which to begin honing the critical edge of social analysis. As Patti Lather has put matters, "an emancipatory, critical social science must be premised upon the development of research approaches which empower those involved to change as well as understand the world" (1991: 3). Our inquiries should contribute to the praxis of social justice, enabling people consciously and purposively to remake their way of life, to actualize the full range of their possibilities as creative, multifaceted human beings.

In "Whose Side Are We On?" Howard Becker provides us with our first take on knowledge and power as they bear upon social research. Becker's is a classic critique of "value-free sociology"—the misleading notion that the social analyst can simply opt out of the real relations of power and politics in which all humans are implicated. Becker argues that since social institutions—workplaces, schools, prisons, etc.—are hierarchically arranged, those at the top of each structure have the prerogative to define the way things "really are." Effective socialization means that all participants in the system learn to accept this definition of the situation as legitimate. Although he does not use the term, what Becker is describing is a situation of *hegemony*: the prestige and authority of ruling groups, which itself derives in part from their control of resources and their capacity to exercise decisive agency, making their viewpoint culturally dominant. The dominant groups are the ones with access to the full range of information; members of subordinate groups will have only partial and thus distorted knowledge. Well-socialized members of such a social order will therefore put their trust in the managers, officials, and professionals who occupy the higher echelons of the system. In this way, social knowledge and social power are tightly interlaced in what Becker calls a *hierarchy of credibility*.

As long as sociologists fashion their accounts from this superordinate, or hegemonic, standpoint, their work is accepted by the powers that be as "objective"—that is to say, value-free. There is no charge of bias, since the knowledge they produce reinforces the dominant point of view, which is already widely held common sense. It is when sociologists give credence to subordinate perspectives and experiences, thereby challenging the hierarchy of credibility, that they may be charged with bias. A good example is the media hysteria that greeted Sunera Thobani's remarks about American imperialism at a feminist conference shortly after U.S. President George W. Bush declared his "war on terrorism" in the wake of the events of September 11, 2001. Dr. Thobani, a sociologist at the University of British Columbia, was subjected to public ridicule and censure in major newspapers and even in the Parliament of Canada because she directly contested the authority of the imperial American state, criticizing the brutality of American foreign policy. What frustrated Thobani most about the reaction to her speech was the lack of discussion in the mainstream media about the speech's actual content: "the really serious issues were not being discussed and instead it was a kind of personal vilification and humiliation that many journalists and editors across the country resorted to" (quoted in Croft, 2002). Thobani's critical analysis of American imperial power in the world raised a direct challenge to the hierarchy of credibility within which the media and political establishment operate. The ensuing charge of "bias" was, in this case, particularly strident.

Becker's point is that "there is no position from which sociological research can be done that is not biased in one way or another." We must always look at the world from someone's point of view. We must, in hierarchical situations, take sides. Thus the question "Whose side are we on?" is always pertinent. Social researchers must recognize the hierarchy of credibility and its implications for the production of knowledge. One implication is that it is generally easier, and typically more financially lucrative, to produce conservative knowledge that reinforces existing common sense and legitimates existing hierarchies. Critical inquiry takes great effort and sometimes great courage.

Joe Feagin took full advantage of his position as president of the American Sociological Association in 2000 to express the keen interest that many sociologists now have in practising a sociology for social justice, and to suggest some agendas for such work in the 21st century. His essay begins with an account of the disparities, injustices, and ecological crises that mark our world and that impose increasing and unrelenting hardships on a majority of its people. Centring his analysis around a critique of global capitalism, Feagin emphasizes the interconnected character of both the biosphere and the "sociosphere"—the global web of social relationships. Although the sociosphere is increasingly integrated, it remains highly stratified, with most benefits accruing to the dominant classes and strata of international capitalism. Yet movements opposed to capitalism's injustices and ecological unsustainability are proliferating, politicizing our knowledge of the social and disturbing hierarchies of credibility. As social justice becomes a recurring concern globally, "sociologists must vigorously engage issues of social justice or become largely irrelevant to the present and future course of human history" (p. 33). To side with entrenched power, to produce knowledge that simply reinforces existing hierarchies and the common-sense beliefs that legitimate them, is a formula not for scientific advancement but for irrelevance.

Feagin looks to the past to find the solutions to present challenges in American sociology. He excavates a "robust 'counter-system' tradition," reaching back to the late 19th century, and dedicated to reducing or eliminating social injustice. In the counter-system approach, the social analyst steps outside mainstream understandings to critique existing society. This was very much Marx's project, but it is also the project of many feminist, anti-racist, ecological, and other praxis-oriented researchers. From the vantage point of this long tradition, the positivist dominance of American sociology that began to gather force in the 1920s and that reached its apex in the 1950s and 1960s has been perhaps little more than an interlude, although, as Feagin notes, the detached-science perspective of positivist sociology retains considerable institutional advantages and centrality.[2]

Looking ahead, five items appear on sociology's agenda for the new century, and with these we have another means of sharpening the critical edge of our research strategies. Feagin urges sociologists

- to bring social justice back to the centre of the discipline;
- to nurture the counter-system tradition by documenting social injustice, by helping to build the power base for grassroots activism through collaborative research, and by posing alternatives to the prevailing "bureaucratic-capitalist morality";
- to be more self-critical in reflecting on the practices of power and prestige within the social sciences that shape and limit our knowledge of the social;
- to recognize the importance of teaching sociology in ways that inspire students to "think critically about their own lives and about building a better society"; and
- to take on the big social questions, the key public issues that matter in people's lives such as the enormous transfer of wealth from the working classes to the rich, the human costs of racism, sexism, and other oppressions, and the social impact of environmental crises.

This is an agenda for social inquiry that makes good on Marx's Thesis XI.

NOTES

1.   Etienne Balibar has expressed this sense of manifold relationality quite succinctly. In his interpretation of Thesis VI, Balibar suggests that what is essential in human existence is "the

multiple and active *relations* which individuals establish with each other (whether of language, labour, love, reproduction, domination, conflict, etc.), and the fact that it is these relations which define what they have in common, the 'genus'" (1995: 30).
2. The situation in Canada and elsewhere beyond North America is somewhat different. It was particularly in the U.S. that the sort of "value-free" positivist sociology criticized by Becker established itself as hegemonic by the middle decades of the twentieth century. In other countries there has generally been more diversity in sociological practice and more space for critical strategies to flourish (for Canada, see Carroll et al., 1992).

REFERENCES

Balibar, Etienne. 1995. *The Philosophy of Marx*. London: Verso.

Carroll, William K., Linda Christiansen-Ruffman, Raymond F. Currie, and Deborah Harrison. 1992. "Introduction." In *Fragile Truths*, edited by W.K. Carroll, Linda Christiansen-Ruffman, Raymond F. Currie, and Deborah Harrison, 1–13. Ottawa: Carleton University Press.

Croft, Stephanie. 2002. "Thobani Speech Prompts Outpouring of Support." *Herizons* 15(3) (Winter): 6–7.

Feuerbach, Ludwig. 1957 [1841]. *Essence of Christianity*. New York: Harper & Row.

Larrain, Jorge. 1986. *A Reconstruction of Historical Materialism*. London: Allen & Unwin.

Lather, Patti. 1991. *Getting Smart: Feminist Research and Pedagogy with/in the Postmodern*. New York: Routledge.

Reiss, Edward. 1997. *Marx: A Clear Guide*. London: Pluto Press.

Smith, Cyril. 1996. *Marx at the Millennium*. London: Pluto Press.

CHAPTER 1

Theses on Feuerbach

K**ARL** M**ARX**

I

The chief defect of all hitherto existing materialism—that of Feuerbach included—is that the thing, reality, sensuousness, is conceived only in the form of the *object or of contemplation*, but not as *sensuous human activity, practice*, not subjectively. Hence, in contradistinction to materialism, the *active* side was developed abstractly by idealism—which, of course, does not know real, sensuous activity as such.

Feuerbach wants sensuous objects, really distinct from the thought objects, but he does not conceive human activity itself as *objective* activity. Hence, in *The Essence of Christianity*, he regards the theoretical attitude as the only genuinely human attitude, while practice is conceived and fixed only in its dirty-judaical manifestation. Hence he does not grasp the significance of "revolutionary," of "practical-critical," activity.

II

The question whether objective truth can be attributed to human thinking is not a question of theory but is a *practical* question. Man must prove the truth—i.e., the reality and power, the this-sidedness of his thinking in practice. The dispute over the reality or non-reality of thinking that is isolated from practice is a purely *scholastic* question.

III

The materialist doctrine concerning the changing of circumstances and upbringing forgets that circumstances are changed by men and that it is essential to educate the educator himself. This doctrine must, therefore, divide society into two parts, one of which is superior to society.

The coincidence of the changing of circumstances and of human activity or self-changing can be conceived and rationally understood only as *revolutionary practice*.

IV

Feuerbach starts out from the fact of religious self-alienation, of the duplication of the world into a religious world and a secular one. His work consists in resolving the religious world into its secular basis.

But that the secular basis detaches itself from itself and establishes itself as an independent realm in the clouds can only be explained by the cleavages and self-contradictions within this secular basis. The latter must, therefore, in itself be both understood in its contradiction and revolutionized in practice. Thus, for instance, after the earthly family is discovered to be the secret of the holy family, the former must then itself be destroyed in theory and in practice.

V

Feuerbach, not satisfied with abstract thinking, wants contemplation; but he does not conceive sensuousness as practical, human-sensuous activity.

VI

Feuerbach resolves the religious essence into the human essence. But the human essence is no abstraction inherent in each single individual. In its reality it is the ensemble of the social relations.

Feuerbach, who does not enter upon a criticism of this real essence, is consequently compelled:

To abstract from the historical process and to fix the religious sentiment as something by itself and to presuppose an abstract—isolated—human individual.

Essence, therefore, can be comprehended only as "genus," as an internal, dumb generality which naturally unites the many individuals.

VII

Feuerbach, consequently, does not see that the "religious sentiment" is itself a social product, and that the abstract individual whom he analyses belongs to a particular form of society.

VIII

All social life is essentially practical. All mysteries which lead theory to mysticism find their rational solution in human practice and in the comprehension of this practice.

IX

The highest point reached by contemplative materialism, that is, materialism which does not comprehend sensuousness as practical activity, is contemplation of single individuals and of civil society.

X

The standpoint of the old materialism is civil society; the standpoint of the new is human society, or social humanity.

XI

The philosophers have only interpreted the world, in various ways; the point is to change it.

CHAPTER 2

Whose Side Are We On?[1]

HOWARD S. BECKER

To have values or not to have values: the question is always with us. When sociologists undertake to study problems that have relevance to the world we live in, they find themselves caught in a crossfire. Some urge them not to take sides, to be neutral, and do research that is technically correct and value free. Others tell them their work is shallow and useless if it does not express a deep commitment to a value position.

This dilemma, which seems so painful to so many, actually does not exist, for one of its horns is imaginary. For it to exist, one would have to assume, as some apparently do, that it is indeed possible to do research that is uncontaminated by personal and political sympathies. I propose to argue that it is not possible and, therefore, that the question is not whether we should take sides, since we inevitably will, but rather whose side we are on.

* * * * *

When do we accuse ourselves and our fellow sociologists of bias? I think an inspection of representative instances would show that the accusation arises, in one important class of cases, when the research gives credence, in any serious way, to the perspective of the subordinate group in some hierarchical relationship. In the case of deviance, the

hierarchical relationship is a moral one. The superordinate parties in the relationship are those who represent the forces of approved and official morality; the subordinate parties are those who, it is alleged, have violated that morality.

Though deviance is a typical case, it is by no means the only one. Similar situations, and similar feelings that our work is biased, occur in the study of schools, hospitals, asylums, and prisons, in the study of physical as well as mental illness, in the study of both "normal" and delinquent youth. In these situations, the superordinate parties are usually the official and professional authorities in charge of some important institution, while the subordinates are those who make use of the services of that institution. Thus, the police are the superordinates, drug addicts are the subordinates; professors and administrators, principals and teachers, are the superordinates, while students and pupils are the subordinates; physicians are the superordinates, their patients the subordinates.

All of these cases represent one of the typical situations in which researchers accuse themselves and are accused of bias. It is a situation in which, while conflict and tension exist in the hierarchy, the conflict has not become openly political. The conflicting segments or ranks are not organized for conflict; no one attempts to alter the shape

23

of the hierarchy. While subordinates may complain about the treatment they receive from those above them, they do not propose to move to a position of equality with them, or to reverse positions in the hierarchy. Thus, no one proposes that addicts should make and enforce laws for policemen, that patients should prescribe for doctors, or that adolescents should give orders to adults. We can call this the *apolitical* case.

In the second case, the accusation of bias is made in a situation that is frankly political. The parties to the hierarchical relationship engage in organized conflict, attempting either to maintain or change existing relations of power and authority. Whereas in the first case subordinates are typically unorganized and thus have, as we shall see, little to fear from a researcher, subordinate parties in a political situation may have much to lose. When the situation is political, the researcher may accuse himself or be accused of bias by someone else when he gives credence to the perspective of either party to the political conflict. I leave the political for later and turn now to the problem of bias in apolitical situations.[2]

We provoke the suspicion that we are biased in favor of the subordinate parties in an apolitical arrangement when we tell the story from their point of view. We may, for instance, investigate their complaints, even though they are subordinates, about the way things are run just as though one ought to give their complaints as much credence as the statements of responsible officials. We provoke the charge when we assume, for the purposes of our research, that subordinates have as much right to be heard as superordinates, that they are as likely to be telling the truth as they see it as superordinates, that what they say about the institution has a right to be investigated and have its truth or falsity established, even though responsible officials assure us that it is unnecessary because the charges are false.

We can use the notion of a *hierarchy of credibility* to understand this phenomenon. In any system of ranked groups, participants take it as given that members of the highest group have the right to define the way things really are. In any organization, no matter what the rest of the organization chart shows, the arrows indicating the flow of information point up, thus demonstrating (at least formally) that those at the top have access to a more complete picture of what is going on than anyone else. Members of lower groups will have incomplete information, and their view of reality will be partial and distorted in consequence. Therefore, from the point of view of a well socialized participant in the system, any tale told by those at the top intrinsically deserves to be regarded as the most credible account obtainable of the organizations' workings. And since, as Sumner pointed out, matters of rank and status are contained in the mores,[3] this belief has a moral quality. We are, if we are proper members of the group, morally bound to accept the definition imposed on reality by a superordinate group in preference to the definitions espoused by subordinates. (By analogy, the same argument holds for the social classes of a community.) Thus, credibility and the right to be heard are differentially distributed through the ranks of the system.

As sociologists, we provoke the charge of bias, in ourselves and others, by refusing to give credence and deference to an established status order, in which knowledge of truth and the right to be heard are not equally distributed. "Everyone knows" that responsible professionals know more about things than laymen, that police are more respectable and their words ought to be taken more seriously than those of the deviants and criminals with whom they deal. By refusing to accept the hierarchy of credibility, we express disrespect for the entire established order.

We compound our sin and further provoke charges of bias by not giving immediate attention and "equal time" to the apologies and explanations of official authority. If, for instance, we are concerned with studying the way of life inmates in a mental hospital build up for themselves, we will naturally be concerned with the constraints and conditions created by the actions of the administrators and physicians who run the hospital. But, unless we also make the administrators and physicians the object of our study (a possibility I will consider later), we will not inquire into why those conditions and constraints are present. We will not give responsible officials a chance to explain themselves and give their reasons for acting as they do, a chance to show why the complaints of inmates are not justified.

It is odd that, when we perceive bias, we usually see it in these circumstances. It is odd because it is easily ascertained that a great many more studies are biased in the direction of the interests of responsible officials than the other way around. We may accuse an occasional student of medical sociology of having given too much emphasis to the complaints of patients. But is it not obvious that most medical sociologists look at things from the point of view of the doctors? A few sociologists may be sufficiently biased in favor of youth to grant credibility to their account of how the adult world treats them. But why do we not accuse other sociologists who study youth of being biased in favor of adults? Most research on youth, after all, is clearly designed to find out why youth are so troublesome for adults, rather than asking the equally interesting sociological question: "Why do adults make so much trouble for youth?" Similarly, we accuse those who take the complaints of mental patients seriously of bias; what about those sociologists who only take seriously the complaints of physicians, families and others about mental patients?

Why this disproportion in the direction of accusations of bias? Why do we more often accuse those who are on the side of subordinates than those who are on the side of superordinates? Because, when we make the former accusation, we have, like the well socialized members of our society most of us are, accepted the hierarchy of credibility and taken over the accusation made by responsible officials.

The reason responsible officials make the accusation so frequently is precisely because they are responsible. They have been entrusted with the care and operation of one or another of our important institutions: schools, hospitals, law enforcement, or whatever. They are the ones who, by virtue of their official position and the authority that goes with it, are in a position to "do something" when things are not what they should be and, similarly, are the ones who will be held to account if they fail to "do something" or if what they do is, for whatever reason, inadequate.

Because they are responsible in this way, officials usually have to lie. That is a gross way of putting it, but not inaccurate. Officials must lie because things are seldom as they ought to be. For a great variety of reasons, well known to sociologists, institutions are refractory. They do not perform as society would like them to. Hospitals do not cure people; prisons do not rehabilitate prisoners; schools do not educate students. Since they are supposed to, officials develop ways both of denying the failure or the institution to perform as it should and explaining those failures which cannot be hidden. An account of an institution's operation from the point of view of subordinates therefore casts doubt on the official line and may possibly expose it as a lie.[4]

For reasons that are a mirror image of those of officials, subordinates in an apolitical hierarchical relationship have no reason to complain of the bias of sociological research oriented toward the interests of superordinates. Subordinates typically are not organized in such a fashion as to be responsible for the overall operation of an institution. What happens in a school is credited or debited to the faculty and administrators; they can be identified and held to account. Even though the failure of a school may be the fault of the pupils, they are not so organized that any one of them is responsible for any failure but his own. If he does well, while others all around him flounder, cheat, and steal, that is none of his affair, despite the attempt of honor codes to make it so. As long as the sociological report on his school says that every student there but one is a liar and a cheat, all the students will feel complacent, knowing they are the one exception. More likely, they will never hear of the report at all or, if they do, will reason that they will be gone before long, so what difference does it make? The lack of organization among subordinate members of an institutionalized relationship means that, having no responsibility for the group's welfare, they likewise have no complaints if someone maligns it. The sociologist who favors officialdom will be spared the accusation of bias.

And thus we see why we accuse ourselves of bias only when we take the side of the subordinate. It is because, in a situation that is not openly political, with the major issues defined as arguable, we join responsible officials and the man in the street in an unthinking acceptance of the hierarchy of credibility. We assume with them that the man at the top knows best. We do not realize that there are sides to be taken and that we are taking one of them.

The same reasoning allows us to understand why the researcher has the same worry about the effect of his sympathies on his work as his uninvolved colleague. The hierarchy of credibility is a feature of society whose existence we cannot deny, even if we disagree with its injunction to believe the man at the top. When we acquire sufficient sympathy with subordinates to see things from their perspective, we know that we are flying in the face of what "everyone knows." The knowledge gives us pause and causes us to share, however briefly, the doubt of our colleagues.

When a situation has been defined politically, the second type of case I want to discuss, matters are quite different. Subordinates have some degree of organization and, with that, spokesmen, their equivalent of responsible officials. Spokesmen, while they cannot actually be held responsible for what members of their group do, make assertions on their behalf and are held responsible for the truth of those assertions. The group engages in political activity designed to change existing hierarchical relationships and the credibility of its spokesmen directly affects its political fortunes. Credibility is not the only influence, but the group can ill-afford having the definition or reality proposed by its spokesmen discredited, for the immediate consequence will be some loss of political power.

Superordinate groups have their spokesmen too, and they are confronted with the same problem: to make statements about reality that are politically effective without being easily discredited. The political fortunes of the superordinate group—its ability to hold the status changes demanded by lower groups to a minimum—do not depend as much on credibility, for the group has other kinds of power available as well.

When we do research in a political situation we are in double jeopardy, for the spokesmen of both involved groups will be sensitive to the implications of our work. Since they propose openly conflicting definitions of reality, our statement of our problem is in itself likely to call into question and make problematic, at least for the purposes of our research, one or the other definition. And our results will do the same.

The hierarchy of credibility operates in a different way in the political situation than it does in the apolitical one. In the political situation, it is precisely one of the things at issue. Since the political struggle calls into question the legitimacy of the existing rank system, it necessarily calls into question at the same time the legitimacy of the associated judgments of credibility. Judgments of who has a right to define the nature of reality that are taken for granted in an apolitical situation become matters of argument.

Oddly enough, we are, I think, less likely to accuse ourselves and one another of bias in a political than in an apolitical situation, for at least two reasons. First, because the hierarchy of credibility has been openly called into question, we are aware that there are at least two sides to the story and so do not think it unseemly to investigate the situation from one or another of the contending points of view. We know, for instance, that we must grasp the perspectives of both the resident of Watts and of the Los Angeles policeman if we are to understand what went on in that outbreak.

Second, it is no secret that most sociologists are politically liberal to one degree or another. Our political preferences dictate the side we will be on and, since those preferences are shared by most of our colleagues, few are ready to throw the first stone or are even aware that stone-throwing is a possibility. We usually take the side of the underdog; we are for Negroes and against Fascists. We do not think anyone biased who does research designed to prove that the former are not as bad as people think or that the latter are worse. In fact, in these circumstances we are quite willing to regard the question of bias as a matter to be dealt with by the use of technical safeguards.

We are thus apt to take sides with equal innocence and lack of thought, though for different reasons, in both apolitical and political situations. In the first, we adopt the commonsense view, which awards unquestioned credibility to the responsible official. (This is not to deny that a few of us, because something in our experience has alerted them to the possibility, may question the conventional hierarchy of credibility in the special area of our expertise.) In the second case, we take our politics so for granted that it supplants convention in dictating whose side we will be on. (I do not deny, either, that some few sociologists may deviate politically from their liberal colleagues, either to the right or the left, and thus be more liable to question that convention.)

In any event, even if our colleagues do not accuse us of bias in research in a political situation, the interested parties will. [...] They base the accusation not on failures of technique or method, but on conceptual defects. They accuse the sociologist not of getting false data but of not getting all the data relevant to the problem. They accuse him, in other words, of seeing things from the perspective of only one party to the conflict. But the accusation is likely to be made by interested parties and not by sociologists themselves.

What I have said so far is all sociology of knowledge, suggesting by whom, in what situations and for what reasons sociologists will be accused of bias and distortion. I have not yet addressed the question of the truth of the accusations, of whether our findings are distorted by our sympathy for those we study. I have implied a partial answer, namely, that there is no position from which sociological research can be done that is not biased in one or another way.

We must always look at the matter from someone's point of view. The scientist who proposes to understand society must, as Mead long ago pointed out, get into the situation enough to have a perspective on it. And it is likely that his perspective will be greatly affected by whatever positions are taken by any or all of the other participants in that varied situation. Even if his participation is limited to reading in the field, he will necessarily read the arguments of partisans of one or another side to a relationship and will thus be affected, at least, by having suggested to him what the relevant arguments and issues are. A student of medical sociology may decide that he will take neither the perspective of the patient nor the perspective of the physician, but he will necessarily take a perspective that impinges on the many questions that arise between physicians and patients; no matter what perspective he takes, his work either will take into account the attitude of subordinates, or it will not. If he fails to consider the questions they raise, he will be working on the side of the officials. If he does raise those questions seriously and does find, as he may, that there is some merit in them, he will then expose himself to the outrage of the officials and of all those sociologists who award them the top spot in the hierarchy of credibility. Almost all the topics that sociologists study, at least those that have some relation to the real world around us, are seen by society as morality plays and we shall find ourselves, willy-nilly, taking part in those plays on one side or the other.

* * * * *

We can never avoid taking sides. So we are left with the question of whether taking sides means that some distortion is introduced into our work so great as to make it useless. Or, less drastically, whether some distortion is introduced that must be taken into account before the results of our work can be used. I do not refer here to feeling that the picture given by the research is not "balanced," the indignation aroused by having a conventionally discredited definition of reality given priority or equality with what "everyone knows," for it is clear that we cannot avoid that. That is the problem of officials, spokesmen, and interested parties, not ours. Our problem is to make sure that, whatever point of view we take, our research meets the standards of good scientific work, that our unavoidable sympathies do not render our results invalid.

* * * * *

NOTES

1. Presidential address, delivered at the annual meeting of the Society for the Study of Social Problems, Miami Beach, August 1966.
2. No situation is necessarily political or apolitical. An apolitical situation can be transformed into a political one by the open rebellion of subordinate ranks, and a political situation can subside into one in which an accommodation has been reached and a new hierarchy been accepted by the participants. The categories, while analytically useful, do not represent a fixed division existing in real life.
3. William Graham Sumner, "Status in the Folkways," in *Folkways* (New York: New American Library, 1960), 72–73.
4. I have stated a portion of this argument more briefly in "Problems of Publication of Field Studies," in Arthur Vidich, Joseph Bensman, and Maurice Stein (Eds.), *Reflections on Community Studies* (New York: John Wiley and Sons, 1964), 267–284.

CHAPTER 3

Social Justice and Sociology: Agendas for the Twenty-First Century

JOE R. FEAGIN

We stand today at the beginning of a challenging new century. Like ASA Presidents before me, I am conscious of the honor and the responsibility that this address carries with it, and I feel a special obligation to speak about the role of sociology and sociologists in the twenty-first century. As we look forward, let me quote W.E.B. Du Bois, a pathbreaking U.S. sociologist. In his last autobiographical statement, Du Bois (1968) wrote:

> [T]oday the contradictions of American civilization are tremendous. Freedom of political discussion is difficult; elections are not free and fair .... The greatest power in the land is not thought or ethics, but wealth .... Present profit is valued higher than future need .... I know the United States. It is my country and the land of my fathers. It is still a land of magnificent possibilities. It is still the home of noble souls and generous people. But it is selling its birthright. It is betraying its mighty destiny. (418–19)

Today the social contradictions of American and global civilizations are still immense. Many prominent voices tell us that it is the best of times; other voices insist that it is the worst of times. Consider how the apologists for modern capitalism now celebrate the "free market" and the global capitalistic economy. Some of these analysts even see modern capitalism as the last and best economic system, as the "end of history" (Fukuyama, 1992). In contrast, from the late 1930s to the 1950s many influential economists and public leaders were committed to government intervention (Keynesianism) as the way to counter the negative effects of capitalist markets in the United States and other countries—effects clearly seen in the Great Depression of the 1930s. The view that a capitalistic market alone should be allowed to make major social and economic decisions would then have been met with incredulity or derision (George, 1999; also see Block, 1990). Half a century ago, Karl Polanyi ([1944] 1957), a prescient economic historian, critically reviewed the history of the free-market idea: "To allow the market mechanism to be sole director of the fate of human beings and their natural environment, indeed, even of the amount and use of purchasing power, would result in the demolition of society" (73).

Since the 1960s, conservative business groups have pressed upon the world's political leaders, and upon the public generally, the idea of a self-regulating market mechanism, thereby organizing a successful counter-attack against Keynesian ideas (Steinfels, 1979). These new apologists for capitalism have heralded the beneficial aspects of a globalizing capitalism and have exported the free-market model in an economic proselytizing project of grand scope. [...]

THE DOWNSIDE OF A CAPITALISTIC WORLD

Nonetheless, many people in the United States and across the globe insist that this is *not* the best of times. Karl Marx long ago underscored the point that modern capitalism creates bad economic times that encompass both social injustice and inequality. Looking at the present day, I will briefly describe a few examples of the troubling conditions currently being created or aggravated by modern capitalism:

Many of the World's People Still Live in Misery

First, while it may be the best of times for those at the top of the global economy, it is not so for the majority of the world's peoples. The pro-capitalist policies of many national governments and international organizations have fostered a substantial transfer of wealth from the world's poor and working classes to the world's rich and affluent social classes. Social injustice in the form of major, and sometimes increasing, inequalities in income and wealth can be observed across the globe. Thus, in the United States, income inequality has reached a record level for the period during which such data have been collected: The top one-fifth of households now has nearly half the income; the bottom one-fifth has less than 4 percent. [...] In recent decades the number of millionaires and billionaires has grown dramatically. Yet many ordinary workers have seen their real wages decline—even while the costs of housing, transportation, and medical care have increased significantly in real terms.

Of the six billion people on earth, a large proportion live in or near poverty and destitution, with 1.2 billion living on less than one dollar a day. The numbers living in poverty are increasing in areas of South Asia, Africa, and Latin America. Today one-fifth of the world's people, those in the developed countries, garner 86 percent of the world's gross domestic product, with the bottom fifth garnering just one percent. In recent years the world's richest 200 people, as a group, have doubled their wealth, to more than 1 trillion dollars for the year 2000 (Oxfam, 1999). While there has been much boasting about economic growth among those pushing global capitalism, between 1980 and the late 1990s most of the world's countries saw sustained annual growth rates of less than 3 percent per capita, and 59 countries actually experienced economic declines *(Toward Freedom,* 1999). Moreover, in most countries great income and wealth inequalities create major related injustices, including sharp differentials in hunger, housing, life satisfaction, life expectancy, and political power.

Viewed from a long-term perspective, the high levels of wealth and income inequality, and the increase in that inequality, signal yet another critical point in human history where there is a major foregrounding of social justice issues.

Working Families Are Exploited and Marginalized

Second, global capitalism may bring the best of times for corporate executives and the well-off, yet for many of the world's people it brings recurring economic disruption, exploitation, marginalization, and immiseration. The international scene is increasingly dominated by highly bureaucratized multinational corporations, which often operate independently of nation states. Working for their own economic interests, these transnational corporations routinely "develop" their markets—and destroy and discard regions, countries, peoples, cultures, and natural environments. For example, transnational corporations now control much of the world's agricultural system. In developing countries small farmers are shoved aside by large agribusiness corporations or are pressured to produce crops for an international market controlled by big transnational corporations— thereby reducing the production of essential foodstuffs for local populations (Sjoberg, 1996: 287).

Today there are an estimated 1 billion un-employed or underemployed workers around the world, with 50 million unemployed in the European countries alone. Hundreds of millions, including many millions of children, work in onerous or dangerous workplaces. Some 30 million people die from hunger annually in a world whose large agricultural enterprises produce more than enough food for every person (Ramonet, 1999). The real effects of expanding capitalism for a large proportion of the planet's inhabitants are not only greater inequality but also job restructuring, unsafe working conditions, low wages, underemployment or unemployment, loss of land, and forced migration. Ordinary working people and their families—in most nationality, racial, and ethnic groups across the globe—face significant negative social impacts from an encircling capitalism.

Capitalism Imposes Huge Environmental Costs

Third, the global capitalistic economy generates profits at the huge cost of increasing environmental degradation. Since the 1970s, the levels of some greenhouse gases (e.g., carbon dioxide) in the earth's atmosphere have grown significantly because of the increasing use of fossil fuels, widespread deforestation, and industrial pollution. Global warming, which results from this increase in greenhouse gases, is melting polar ice packs, increasing coastal flooding, generating severe weather, creating droughts and reshaping agriculture, and facilitating the spread of disease. In addition, as a result of human actions, the earth's ozone layer is severely depleted in some areas. This alone results in a range of

negative effects, including increases in skin cancer incidence and major threats to essential species, such as phytoplankton in the oceans (M. Bell, 1998; Hawken et al., 1999).

A lack of sufficient water and poor water quality are large-scale problems in many countries. Half the world's wetlands and nearly half the forests have been destroyed in just the last century. The destruction of forests is killing off many plant species, including some supplying the oxygen we breathe. The consequences of these environmental changes will be the greatest for the world's poorest countries, many of which are in areas where the increasing heat of global warming is already having a serious impact on water availability, soil erosion, destruction of forests, agriculture, and the spread of disease (Sachs, 1999).

Today, some environmental experts are seriously discussing the possibility that most of the planet's plant and animal species will be gone by the twenty-second century. Jared Diamond, a leading physical scientist, has reviewed the evidence and concludes that movement toward an environmental catastrophe is accelerating. The only question, in his view, is whether it is likely to "strike our children or our grandchildren, and whether we choose to adopt now the many obvious countermeasures" (Diamond, 1992: 362). And there are yet other related problems facing humanity, such as those arising out of the new technologies associated with worldwide, capitalist-led economic development.

Global Capitalism Reinforces Other Injustice and Inequality

Fourth, in addition to the economic and environmental inequalities generated or aggravated by contemporary capitalism, other forms of social injustice and inequality remain central to the United States and other societies. I only have space here to note briefly such major societal realities as racial and ethnic oppression, patriarchy, homophobia, bureaucratic authoritarianism, violence against children, and discrimination against the aged and the disabled. These persisting forms of discrimination and oppression generally have their own independent social dynamics, yet they too are often reinforced or exacerbated by the processes of modern capitalism.

WHAT KIND OF A WORLD DO WE WANT?

The world's majority now live, or soon will live, in difficult economic and environmental times. By the end of the twenty-first century, it is likely that there will be sustained and inexorable pressures to replace the social institutions associated with corporate capitalism and its supporting governments. Why? Because the latter will not have provided humanity with just and sustainable societies. Such pressures are already building in the form of grassroots social movements in many countries.

A few of the world's premier capitalists already see the handwriting on the wall. The billionaire investor George Soros (1998), for instance, has come to the conclusion that free markets do *not* lead to healthy societies:

> Markets reduce everything, including human beings (labor) and nature (land), to commodities. We can have a market economy, but we cannot have a market society. In addition to markets, society needs institutions to serve such social goals as political freedom and social justice. (24)

As Soros sees it, without a more egalitarian global society, capitalism cannot survive.

* * * * *

As I see it, social justice requires resource equity, fairness, and respect for diversity,

as well as the eradication of existing forms of social oppression. Social justice entails a redistribution of resources from those who have unjustly gained them to those who justly deserve them, and it also means creating and ensuring the processes of truly democratic participation in decision-making. A common view in Western political theory is that, while "the people" have a right to self-rule, they delegate this right to their representatives—to the government leaders who supposedly act in the public interest and under the guidance of impartial laws (Young, 1990: 91–92). However, there is no impartial legal and political system in countries like the United States, for in such hierarchically arranged societies those at the top create and maintain over time a socio-legal framework and political structure that strongly support their group interests. It seems clear that only a decisive redistribution of resources and decision making power can ensure social justice and authentic democracy.

[...] For some decades now central ideas in physics and biology have stressed the interconnectedness of what were once thought to be discrete phenomena. Thus, the "gaia theory" in biology suggests, according to Lovelock (1987), that

> ... the entire range of living matter on Earth, from whales to viruses, and from oaks to algae, could be regarded as constituting a single living entity, capable of manipulating the Earth's atmosphere to suit its overall needs and endowed with faculties and powers far beyond those of its constituent parts. (9)

This is more than a metaphorical description, for in fact we live on a planet that, we are increasingly realizing, is truly interwoven. All of earth's aspects—from biosphere, to soils and oceans, to atmosphere—are seen as parts of one interconnected living system with important cybernetic features. Thus, environmental irresponsibility in one place, such as the excessive burning of fossil fuels in the United States, contributes to negative effects elsewhere, such as to global warming in Australia.

Perhaps there are clues in the gaia theory for a broader sociological framework for viewing the development of human societies. We human beings are not just part of an interconnected biosphere, but are also linked in an increasingly integrated and global web of structured social relationships. This complex "sociosphere" consists of some 6 billion people living in many families and communities in numerous nation states. Nation states and their internal organizations are linked across an international web. Indeed, we human beings have long been more interconnected than we might think. According to current archaeological assessments, we all descended from ancestors who migrated out of Africa some millennia in the past. Today, most human beings speak related languages; about half the world's people speak an Indo-European language. In recent decades the expansion of telecommunication technologies has placed more people in potential or actual contact with one another than ever before. For the first time in human history, these technologies are rapidly creating one integrated body of humanity (Sahtouris, 1996).

Yet, this increasingly interconnected sociosphere remains highly stratified: Great benefits accrue to those classes dominant in international capitalism. Today most of the globe's political and business leaders, as well as many of its academic experts, have come to accept capitalism as the more or less inevitable economic system for all countries. However, at the same time, growing numbers of people are recognizing that, because of globalizing capitalism, the earth is facing a massive environmental crisis, one that has the potential to destroy the basic conditions for human societies within a century or two.

Issues of ecological destruction—as well as broader issues of social inequality and injustice—are being forced to the forefront not by corporate executives but by some 30,000 people's groups and movements around the globe. These include environmental groups, indigenous movements, labor movements, health-policy groups, feminist groups, anti-racist organizations, and anti-corporate groups (Klein, 2000). [...]

* * * * *

Unquestionably, social justice appears as a recurring concern around the globe. For that reason alone, we sociologists must vigorously engage issues of social justice or become largely irrelevant to the present and future course of human history.

A LONG TRADITION: SOCIOLOGY AND SOCIAL JUSTICE

Given impending national and international crises, sociology appears to be the right discipline for the time. Sociology is a broad interdisciplinary field that draws on ideas from other social sciences, the humanities, and the physical sciences. Our intellectual and methodological pluralism, as well as our diversity of practitioners, are major virtues. Such richness gives sociology a particularly good position as a science to examine the complexities and crises of a socially interconnected world. Those sciences with diverse viewpoints and constructive conflicts over ideas and issues have often been the most intellectually healthy. As P.H. Collins (1998) has put it, "Sociology's unique social location as a contested space of knowledge construction allows us to think through new ways of doing science" (10; also see Burawoy, 1998).

Views of sociology's goals have long reflected a dialectical tension between a commitment to remedy social injustice and the desire to be accepted as a fully legitimate discipline in the larger society, especially by powerful elites. [...]

Moreover, from the beginning there has been a robust "countersystem" tradition within U.S. sociology—a tradition whose participants have intentionally undertaken research aimed at significantly reducing or eliminating societal injustice. The counter-system approach is one in which social scientists step outside mainstream thought patterns to critique existing society (Sjoberg and Cain, 1971). From the perspective of this research tradition, social scientists have all too often accepted the status quo as their standard. It is noteworthy too that much countersystem analysis develops ideas about alternative social systems. For instance, any serious exploration of the countersystem tradition must acknowledge the past and current influence of Marx's critical analysis of capitalism, which included ideas about an alternative social system. Marx's countersystem analysis has, directly or indirectly, influenced many social scientists, including several of the sociologists to whom I now turn.

In the late nineteenth and early twentieth centuries, a number of white women, black men, and black women sociologists—as well as a few white male sociologists—did much innovative sociological research and at the same time took strong informed positions in regard to ending the oppression of women, black Americans, the poor, and immigrants. Among the now forgotten women and black male sociologists were Jane Addams, Florence Kelley, Emily Greene Balch, Ida B. Wells-Barnett, Charlotte Perkins Gilman, and W.E.B. Du Bois. All were practicing sociologists, and all developed important sociological ideas and research projects. [...]

* * * * *

By the 1930s and 1940s the critical, countersystem approaches of sociologists like Addams and Du Bois were losing out to a politically safe, academic, and distancing sociology. Sociology was increasingly be-coming a discipline whose college and university departments were dominated by White male sociologists and often linked to elite interests—including ties such as grants from corporate foundations and government agencies. As Deegan (1988) has noted regarding the dominant sociologists at the University of Chicago,

> These later men therefore condemned political action for sociologists, while the ideas of the elite, in fact, permeated their work .... Rather than condemn the exploitation and oppression of daily life, the later Chicago men described it. They justified it through their acceptance of it. (304)

In the decades after World War II, many mainstream sociologists continued the move toward the pure-science ideal and away from the concerns for social justice and the making of a better society. There was a great expansion of federally funded research in the physical sciences, and leading sociologists worked aggressively to grasp a share of the new federal money, often by stressing an instrumental positivist sociology that attempted to imitate those physical sciences. [...]

* * * * *

[...] Not surprisingly, social scientists who have secured major funding from federal government agencies and large corporate foundations have rarely done research that draws on the countersystem tradition and is strongly critical of established institutions in the corporate or governmental realms. From the 1930s to the present, the accent on academic grant-getting, the heavy emphasis on certain types of quantitatively oriented research, and the movement away from the social justice concerns of earlier sociologists have been associated trends (see Cancian, 1995).

A detached-science perspective has been influential in many areas of sociology for some decades now, but not without strong countering perspectives (e.g., see Vaughan, 1993). Since the late 1960s there has been a periodic resurgence of interest in an activist sociology, including an increased concern with research on (and the eradication of) institutional discrimination and other forms of social oppression (e.g., see Omi and Winant, 1994). Significantly, the recent history of sociology has been dialectical, with supporters of the detached-science perspective often being central, yet regularly challenged by those advocating a sociology committed to both excellent sociological research and social justice.

AGENDAS FOR SOCIOLOGY: THE NEW CENTURY

Looking toward the next few decades, I see important conceptual, empirical, policy, and activist tasks for which the rich diversity of contemporary sociology can help prepare us. These tasks often relate to questions of social justice. Indeed, one major reason that some subfields of sociology are periodically attacked by conservative, and often ill-informed, journalists and media commentators is that analyses of discrimination, domination, and social justice are generally threatening to those who desire to maintain the status quo. Moreover, we should keep in mind that sociologists have already had a broad impact. Sociological ideas and research are frequently used in public discourse by those grappling with societal problems, and sociology books are more widely reviewed (and perhaps even read) outside the discipline than any other social science books except history books (Bressler, 1999: 718).

Let us now consider a few of the socially relevant agendas for the twenty-first century that can be inaugurated or accelerated by sociologists with many different research perspectives and methods.

Bring Social Justice Back to the Center

First, it is time for the discipline to fully recover and celebrate its historical roots in a sociology committed to social justice in ideals and practice. In recent decades no sociologist has published even one substantial article in a major sociology journal (e.g., the *American Journal of Sociology, American Sociological Review,* and *Sociological Theory*) on the sociological ideas of the women sociologists in the founding generation (Lengermann and Niebrugge-Brantley, 2001). It is time for us sociologists to remedy this neglect and help to reclaim the important ideas of those women sociologists and sociologists of color who are among the founders of our discipline.

* * * * *

[...] The work of the early women and African American sociologists, as well as that of progressive white men, may well point us toward a new conceptual paradigm for sociology. Such a paradigm would accent the centrality of differences, oppressions, and inequalities—as well as recurring movements for social justice—within societies like the United States.

* * * * *

Nurture the Countersystem Approach

Second, contemporary sociologists need to enlarge and cultivate the long-standing countersystem approach, not only in regard to investigating social inequality and injustice but also in regard to assessing alternative social systems that may be more just.

Today, the sociology handbooks and encyclopedias on my bookshelves have little to say about the concept of social justice. One significant task for social scientists is to document empirically, and ever more thoroughly, the character of major social injustices, both nationally and internationally. We also need more conceptual work that develops and enriches the concepts of social justice and equality. In my view, social justice is not only a fundamental human right but is also essential for a society to be sustainable in the long term. [...]

As I have suggested above, social injustice can be examined not only in terms of the maldistribution of goods and services, but also in regard to the social relations responsible for that maldistribution. These social relations, which can range from centrally oppressive power relations to less central mechanisms of discrimination, determine whether individuals, families, and other groups are excluded from society's important resources and decision making processes. They shape the development of group and individual identities and the sense of personal dignity. In the end, social justice entails a restructuring of the larger frameworks of social relations generally (Feagin and Vera, 2001).

We sociologists have made a good start toward understanding certain types of social injustice and inequality. Some of us have done considerable work to document the character and impact of class, racial, and gender subordination. In the United States and in Latin America some sociologists using participatory-action-research strategies have honed countersystem ideas and methods and worked interactively with people at the grassroots level seeking assessments of, and alternatives to, an onerous status quo (e.g., Fals-Borda, 1960). The commitment here is to get out of the ivory tower and to help build a resource and power base for the disenfranchised in their communities. The legitimacy of this type of sociological research must be enhanced. [...] Collaborative research between sociologists and community groups seeking solutions to serious local problems of housing, work, education, poverty, discrimination, and environmental pollution should not be shoved aside, as it sometimes is, with cavalier comments about sociological "do-goodism," but should be placed in the respected core of sociological research—where it was at the birth of U.S. sociology.[1]

In everyday practice all sociology is a moral activity, whether this is recognized or not. In a society deeply pervaded and structured by social oppressions, most sociological research will reflect these realities to some degree, and attempts to deny these realities or their impact on research are misguided at best. All social science perspectives have an underlying view of what the world ought to be. As Moore (1971) noted,

[Questions] that arouse human passions, especially in a time of change, have had to do with the forms of authority and justice, and the purposes of human life .... It is impossible therefore to avoid taking some kind of a moral position, not only in writing about politics but also in *not* writing about them. (3)

A countersystem approach attempts to assess the status quo from a viewpoint at least somewhat outside the frame of the existing society and/or nation state. In practice, social scientists can accept the prevailing nation-state or bureaucratic-capitalistic morality or they can resist this morality by making a commitment to social justice and human rights. Contemporary countersystem approaches often accent a broad human rights framework in which each person is entitled to fair treatment and justice simply because they are human beings, not because they are members of a particular nation-state. Moreover, some social scientists (e.g., Sjoberg, 1996) have suggested that the United Nation's Universal Declaration of Human Rights—with its strong array of social, political, and economic rights—may be a good starting place for developing a robust human rights framework for social science research.

We should seek a sociology that is grounded in empirical and theoretical research *and* that hones a critical perspective less restricted by established institutions. Careful data collection, reasoned argument, and critical moral judgments are *not* incompatible. The great sociologist of race and class, Oliver C. Cox, underscored this point:

> Clearly, the social scientist should be accurate and objective but not neutral; he [or she] should be passionately partisan in favor of the welfare of the people and against the interests of the few when they seem to submerge that welfare. (Cox, 1948: xvi)

Numerous sociologists, from Jane Addams and W.E.B. Du Bois, to Robert and Helen Lynd and Gunnar Myrdal, to more contemporary scholars as diverse as Alfred McClung Lee, Jessie Bernard, James Blackwell, Robert Bellah, and Orlando Fals-Borda have accented the importance of bringing moral discourse and research on "what is the good society" into the center of sociological debate and analysis. Even more, today we need to look beyond the borders of the nation-state to address the possibility of a world moral community.

Be More Self-Critical

Third, as part of an ongoing self-renewal process, I see the need for accelerated self-reflection in sociology. This is a task closely related to my last point. The communities, colleges, universities, agencies, companies, and other settings in which we practice sociology are shaped in part by the oppressive social relations of the larger society. We need a liberating and emancipating sociology that takes risks to counter these oppressive social relations in our own bailiwicks.

As social scientists, we should regularly examine our research environments, including our metascientific underpinnings and commitments. Critical social perspectives, such as those of feminists, gay/lesbian scholars, critical theorists, anti-racist scholars, and Marxist researchers, among others, have been resurgent since the 1960s. Scholars researching from these perspectives, as well as symbolic interactionists and ethnomethodologists, have called for more internal reflection in the social sciences. In one such disciplinary reflection, feminist sociologists Stacey and Thorne (1996: 1–3) argue that, while anthropology and history have incorporated feminist ideas better than sociology, the questioning of androcentric concepts and structures is finally beginning to have a broader impact in sociology. In an earlier critical reflection, Dorothy Smith (1987) argues that mainstream sociology has historically been part of the dominant ideological apparatus, which focuses on issues primarily of concern to men. Mainstream sociology's central themes are "organized by and articulate the perspectives of men—not as individuals ... but as persons playing determinate parts in the social relations of this form of society ..." (56). Feminist sociologists have pressured the discipline to view and research the social world from the perspective of women and thereby greatly expand its fund of knowledge.

* * * * *

Hopefully, more self-reflection among sociologists can also lead us and other social scientists to destroy the insidious boundaries we often draw around ourselves, such as the artificial dichotomy of quantitative versus qualitative research, the ranking of basic over applied research, and the valuing of research over teaching.

Recognize and Stress the Importance of Teaching Sociology

Fourth, we need to recognize and accent the importance of teaching sociology—especially the kind of quality teaching that will prepare present and future generations for the coming social, economic, technological, and environmental challenges. [...]

The majority of undergraduate and graduate students in sociology are looking for meaningful ways to contribute to making a better society. Thus, it is disturbing to hear reports from some of these students at various colleges and universities that their professors are asserting that there is no room in sociology for idealism and activism. Social scientists who attempt to avoid social betterment issues often defend themselves with phrases like, "We are not out to save the world." C. Wright Mills (1958) once suggested,

> Sometimes this is the disclaimer of a modest scholar; sometimes it is the cynical contempt of a specialist for all issues of larger concern; sometimes it is the disillusionment of youthful expectations; often it is the posture of men who seek to borrow the prestige of The Scientist, imagined as a pure and disembodied intellect. (133)

As teachers of sociology, we should make clear to the coming generations of sociologists not only that there is plenty of room for idealism and activism in the field but that these qualities might be required for humanity to survive the next century or so. We need to communicate the excitement and importance of doing sociology. Alfred McClung Lee (1978) was eloquent in this regard:

The wonder and mysteries of human creativity, love, and venturesomeness and the threatening problems of human oppression and of sheer persistence beckon and involve those with the curiosity and courage to be called sociologists. Only those who choose to serve humanity rather than to get caught up in the scramble for all the immediate rewards of finance and status can know the pleasures and lasting rewards of such a pursuit. (16–17)

In my view, sociology students should be shown how the diversity of theories, methods, debates, and practitioners in sociology is generally healthy for the field and for society. We also should strive to help our students think critically about their social lives and about building a better society. Wendell Bell (1998) has underscored the importance of showing social science students how to engage in debates about important issues, critically assess necessary moral judgments, and explore possible social futures for themselves and their societies.

Study the Big Social Questions

Finally, contemporary sociologists need to spend much more effort studying the big social questions of the twenty-first century. Interestingly, Kai Erikson (1984: 306; also see Wilner, 1985) once suggested that a review of leading sociology journals over several decades would likely find that many decisive events had been ignored there by sociologists. When social scientists become too professionalized and too narrowly committed to a discipline or area of study, research issues tend to be defined from within their dominant professional paradigm. They rely heavily on a narrow range of theories and methods. Only those research topics and interpretations are accepted that do not threaten the basis of the profession and its established intellectual capital. However, technological and other knowledge developments are now moving so fast that a social scientist who is too narrowly trained or focused may be incapable of making sense out of the ongoing currents of change.

In many U.S. colleges and universities the administratively sanctioned goal of generating grant money—often for its own sake—still distorts too much social science research in the direction of relatively minor social issues. This heavy focus on grant money reduces the amount of research on key public issues and diminishes the potential for colleges and universities to be arenas for critical debate and discussion of those issues (Black, 1999).

C. Wright Mills (1958) called for social scientists to challenge dominant ideas:

> If truly independent ideas are not even for-mulated, if we do not set forth alternatives, then we are foolishly trapped by the diffi-culties those now at the top have gotten us into. (137)

Sociologists need to formulate more original and independent ideas, and to illuminate and directly and critically address recurring national and global crises. We need to implement Gans's (1989) call for more sociologists to become public intellectuals who will speak critically, and from data, about major societal issues. Especially in our journals, many social scientists need to break from the conventional style of research presentation and jargonistic writing that targets a specialized audience and move to a style accessible to broad audiences and to an approach that addresses the big social questions and the implications of research for society. At the same time, we should recognize that there are numerous sociologists who write well and accessibly, yet often face the censorship of ideas that are seen as too critical—an experience still common in this society. Thus, we also should insist that the relevant publishing outlets consider and publish important critical analyses of

momentous social issues, and not rule them out as "too controversial" or as "only thought pieces" (Agger, 1989: 220).

Yes, some sociologists do work on the big and tough questions; yet we need many more to ask major questions about such societal trends as the huge and ongoing wealth transfers from the working classes to the rich, the social impact of environmental crises, the impact of globalizing capitalism on local communities, and the human costs of racism, sexism, and other social oppressions.

One major research question requiring much attention relates to the international impact of multinational capitalism and its "free markets." We hear much today about the global capitalistic economy, but all too little social science research is examining its deep structure and broad range of human consequences. Half a century ago, in a foreword to Polanyi's book, *The Great Transformation,* sociologist Robert M. MacIver ([1944] 1957) noted that some research on capitalistic markets already indicated that formulas like "world peace through world trade" were dangerous simplifications:

> Neither a national nor an international sys-tem can depend on the automatic regulants. Balanced budgets and free enterprise and world commerce and international clearinghouses ... will not guarantee an international order. Society alone can guarantee it; international society must also be discovered. (xi)

Other major research questions deserving more attention from sociologists center on the character, costs, and future of contemporary racism. While some sociologists have pressed forward in researching the white-generated oppression targeting Americans of color, more researchers should address the ways in which racial oppression becomes disguised or subtle in its character and practice, the ideological defense of that oppression, and the social costs for its targets and the larger society.

We should also encourage similar sociological research on other major forms of social oppression that pervade this and other contemporary societies. In recent years sociologists and other social scientists have undertaken significant empirical and theoretical work on sexism, homophobia, ageism, and discrimination against the disabled, yet today these areas cry out for much more research and analysis.

In addition, more sociologists should study societal futures, including the alternative social futures of just and egalitarian societies. [...] Social scientists can extrapolate critically from understandings of the trends and possibilities already apparent in various societal arenas, as well as probe an array of societal alternatives with imaginative research approaches.

Major societal transformations loom ahead of us. There are, for example, the demographic changes well described by some sociologists, such as the graying of societies. Such trends will likely be associated with other societal changes: Aging societies, for example, may have less interest in war, experience less street crime, and focus themselves more on issues of health care, social services, and euthanasia. Another demographic shift already underway is an increasing racial and ethnic diversity in some national populations. [...] There is ample opportunity right now for sociological research into the possible or likely societal futures associated with trends such as these, particularly assessments from a countersystem framework accenting the goals of social justice and multiracial democracy.

* * * * *

CONCLUSION

In an 1843 letter, the young Karl Marx suggested that critical social analysis should lay bare the hidden societal realities. The goal must be the "reform of consciousness not through dogmas but by analyzing mystical consciousness obscure to itself, whether ... in religious or political form" (Marx, [1843] 1975: 209). Marx added that the task for involved social scientists, as for other citizens of the world, was the clarification of the "struggles and wishes of the age" (209).

For many millennia human beings have been tool-makers, yet in just a few decades we have created economies and technologies—such as polluting industries, fossil-fuel consuming engines, and nuclear weapons—that may well threaten the survival of our species and of our living planet itself. It seems likely that the fate of our planet and its many species will be decided within the next few generations by just one of its species. As moral beings, we need to ask insistently: What would alternatives to our self-destructive societies look like? And how do we get there?

Much of humanity might agree on a new global social system that reduces injustice, is democratically accountable to all people, offers a decent standard of living for all, and operates in a sustainable relation to earth's other living systems (e.g., see Korten, 1999; Sahtouris, 1996). Determining whether this is the case and how such a just global society might be developed are enormous questions that sociologists—and other citizens of the world—should be tackling.[2] [...]

* * * * *

NOTES

1. Interestingly, one 1990s survey of 12,000 Ph.D. sociologists revealed that over half spent at least 10 hours a week doing what they view as "applied" research (Dotzler and Koppel, 1999: 79).
2. For example, visualizing the path to a better future for the world's poor is not difficult. The 1997 *Human Development Report* of the United Nations indicated that for about 15 percent of the U.S. defense budget, or about $40 billion a year, the basic needs for health, nutrition, education, reproductive health, safe water, and sanitation could be met for the entire population of the planet. Another $40 billion would be enough to bring the poorest residents of the planet out of extreme poverty (Williamson, 2000).

REFERENCES

Agger, Ben. 1989. *Reading Science: A Literary, Political, and Sociological Analysis.* Dix Hills: General Hall.

Bell, Michael M. 1998. *An Invitation to Environmental Sociology.* Thousand Oaks: Pine Forge.

Bell, Wendell. 1998. "Making People Responsible: The Possible, the Probable, and the Preferable." *American Behavioral Scientist* 42: 323–339.

Black, Timothy. 1999. "Going Public: How Sociology Might Matter Again." *Sociological Inquiry* 69: 257–275.

Block, Fred. 1990. *Postindustrial Possibilities: A Critique of Economic Discourse.* Berkeley: University of California Press.

Bressler, Marvin. 1999. "Contemporary Sociology: A Quarter Century of Book Reviews." *Sociological Forum* 14: 707–720.

Burawoy, Michael. 1998. "Critical Sociology: A Dialogue between Two Sciences." *Contemporary Sociology* 27: 12–20.

Cancian, Francesca M. 1995. "Truth and Goodness: Does the Sociology of Inequality Promote Social Betterment." *Sociological Perspectives* 38: 339–356.

Collins, Patricia Hill. 1998. "On Book Exhibits and New Complexities: Reflections on Sociology as Science." *Contemporary Sociology* 27: 7–11.

Cox, Oliver C. 1948. *Caste, Class, and Race: A Study in Social Dynamics.* New York: McGraw-Hill.

Deegan, Mary Jo. 1998. *Jane Addams and the Men of the Chicago School, 1892–1918.* New Brunswick: Transaction Books.

Diamond, Jared. 1992. *The Third Chimpanzee: The Evolution and Future of the Human Animal.* New York: HarperCollins.

Dotzler, Robert J., and Ross Koppel. 1999. "What Sociologists Do and Where They Do It—The NSF Survey on Sociologists's Work Activities and Workplaces." *Sociological Practice* 1: 71–83.

Du Bois, W.E.B. 1968. *The Autobiography of W.E.B. Du Bois: A Soliloquy on Viewing My Life from the Last Decade of Its First Century.* New York: International Publishers.

Erikson, Kai. 1984. "Sociology and Contemporary Events." In *Conflict and Consensus: A Festscrift in Honor of Lewis A. Coser,* edited by W.W. Powell and R. Robbins, 303–310. New York: Free Press.

Fals-Borda, Orlando. 1960. *Accion Comunal en Una Vereda Colombiana: Su Applicacion, Sus Resultados y Su Interpretacion* (Communal Action in a Columbian Area: Its Application, Its Results, and Its Interpretation). Bogota: Universidad

Nacional de Colombia, Departamento de Sociologia.

Feagin, Joe R., and Hernan Vera. 2001. *Liberation Sociology.* Boulder: Westview.

Fukuyama, Francis. 1992. *The End of History and the Last Man.* New York: Free Press.

Gans, Herbert J. 1989. "Sociology in America: The Discipline and the Public." *American Sociological Review* 54: 1–16.

George, Susan. 1999. "A Short History of Neo-Liberalism." Paper presented at the Conference on Economic Sovereignty in a Globalizing World, March 24, Bangkok, Thailand. Retrieved December 21, 1999 (http://www. zmag.org).

Hawken, Paul, Amory Lovins, and L. Hunter Lovins. 1999. *Natural Capitalism: Creating the Next Industrial Revolution.* Boston: Little, Brown.

Klein, Naomi. 2000. *No Space, No Choice, No Jobs, No Logo: Taking Aim at the Brand Bullies.* New York: Picador.

Korten, David. 1999. *The Post-Corporate World: Life after Capitalism.* San Francisco: Berrett-Koehler Publishers and Kumarian Press.

Lee, Alfred McClung. 1978. *Sociology for Whom?* New York: Oxford University Press.

Lengermann, Patricia Madoo, and Jill Niebrugge. 2001. "The Meaning of 'Things': Theory and Method in Harriet Martineau's *How to Observe Morals and Manners* and Emile Durkheim's *The Rules of Sociological Method.*" In *Harriet Martineau: Theoretical and Methodological Perspectives,* edited by M.R. Hill and S. Hoecker-Drysdale, 212–237. New York: Garland.

Lovelock, James E. 1987. *Gaia: A New Look at Life on Earth.* Oxford: Oxford University Press.

MacIver, Robert M. [1944] 1957. "Foreword." In *The Great Transformation: The Political and Economic Origins of Our Time,* by K. Polanyi, ix–xxi. Boston: Beacon.

Marx, Karl. [1843] 1975. "Letters from the *Franco-German Yearbooks.*" 1843 letter to A. Ruge. In *Early Writings [of] Marx,* introduced by L. Colletti, translated by R. Livingstone and G. Benton, 206–209. London: Penguin Books.

Mills, C. Wright. 1958. *The Causes of World War III.* New York: Simon and Schuster.

Moore, Barrington. 1971. *Reflections on the Causes of Human Misery, and upon Certain Proposals to Eliminate Them.* Boston: Beacon.

Omi, Michael, and Howard Winant. 1994. *Racial Formation in the United States: From the 1960s to the 1990s,* 2nd ed. New York: Routledge.

Oxfam. 1999. "New Millennium—Two Futures." Oxfam Policy Papers. Retrieved December 30, 1999 (http://www.oxfam.org.uk/policy/papers).

Polanyi, Karl. [1944] 1957. *The Great Transformation: The Political and Economic Origins of Our Time.* Boston: Beacon.

Ramonet, Ignacio. 1999. "The Year 2000." *La Monte Diplomatique,* December 15. Retrieved December 1999 (http://www.monde-diplomatique.fr/en/1999/12?c=011eader).

Sachs, Jeffrey. 1999. "Apocalypse Soon." *Boston Magazine.* Retrieved December 21, 1999 (http://www.alternet.org/PublicArchive/Sachsl217.html).

Sahtouris, Elisabet. 1996. *Earthdance: Living Systems in Evolution.* Alameda: Metalog Books.

Sjoberg, Gideon. 1996. "The Human Rights Challenge to Communitarianism: Formal Organizations and Race and Ethnicity." In *Macro Socio-Economics: From Theory to Activism,* edited by D. Sciulli, 273–293. Armonk: M.E. Sharpe.

Sjoberg, Gideon, and Leonard D. Cain. 1971. "Negative Values, Countersystem Models, and the Analysis of Social Systems." In *Institutions and Social Exchange: The Sociologies of Talcott Parsons and George C. Homans,* edited by H. Turk and R.L.

Simpson, 212–229. Indianapolis: Bobbs-Merrill.

Smith, Dorothy E. 1987. *The Everyday World as Problematic: A Feminist Sociology.* Boston: Northeastern University Press.

Soros, George. 1998. "Toward a Global Open Society." *Atlantic Monthly* (January): 20–24, 32.

Stacey, Judith, and Barrie Thorne. 1996. "Is Sociology Still Missing Its Feminist Revolution?" *Perspectives: The ASA Theory Section Newsletter* 18: 1–3.

Steinfels, Peter. 1979. *The Neoconservatives: The Men Who Are Changing America's Politics.* New York: Touchstone.

Toward Freedom. 1999. "What a World! Ten Troubling Faces from the 1999 UN Development Report." *Toward Freedom.* Retrieved March 2, 2000 (http://www.undp.org/hdro/99.htm).

Vaughan, Ted R. 1993. "The Crisis in Contemporary American Sociology: A Critique of the Discipline's Dominant Paradigm." In *A Critique of Contemporary American Sociology,* edited by T.R. Vaughan, G. Sjoberg, and L.T. Reynolds, 10–53. New York: General Hall.

Williamson, Thad. 2000. "Global Economic In-equality." *Dollars and Sense* (January–February). Retrieved March 2000 (atwww.igc.org/ dollars/2000/0100econin.html).

Wilner, Patricia. 1985. "The Main Drift of Sociology between 1936 and 1984." *Journal of the History of Sociology* 5: 1–20.

Young, Iris Marion. 1990. *Justice and the Politics of Difference.* Princeton: Princeton University Press.

Rethinking Part 1A: Rediscovering the Critical Edge in Social Analysis

CRITICAL THINKING QUESTIONS

Chapter 1: Theses on Feuerbach

1. What are the main criticisms Marx registers against Feuerbach's "contemplative materialism"? How does Marx's emphasis on *practice* mark an improvement?
2. What is meant by Marx's statement that "the human essence is ... the ensemble of the social relations" (Thesis VI), and what might be its implications for social inquiry?
3. How can we understand the human condition as both *natural* and *historical*, and what might be the implications of this understanding for how we inquire into social reality?

Chapter 2: Whose Side Are We On?

1. What sorts of *hierarchies of credibility* organize conventional knowledge of "the economy," "the family," and "crime"? Can you in each case think of an example of social scientific thought taking the side of superordinates, and another example of social scientific thought taking the side of subordinates?
2. Becker maintains that when a situation has been defined politically, matters are quite different from instances of entrenched hegemony when the hierarchy of credibility is uncontested. What would be a good example of a contemporary situation that has been defined politically; of a contemporary situation in which the hierarchy of credibility is largely uncontested? Does social inquiry take a different form in these differing situations?
3. Becker concludes that we can never avoid taking sides, but does he provide enough guidance as to whose side we should take, or is his own stance simply relativistic?

Chapter 3: Social Justice and Sociology: Agendas for the Twenty-First Century

1. Joe Feagin predicts that "by the end of the twenty-first century there will be sustained and inexorable pressures to replace the social institutions associated with corporate capitalism and its supporting governments." From what sources and agents are the pressures likely to come, and what role can social scientists and researchers play in the change process?
2. What is the significance of the "countersystem tradition" in enabling a sociology for social justice?
3. Joe Feagin views sociology as "a broad interdisciplinary field that draws on ideas from other social sciences, the humanities, and the physical sciences." Is

sociology uniquely an interdiscipline, or could the same be said of other social sciences? Are the disciplinary boundaries among the social sciences helpful to social inquiry, or do they often hamper inquiry by unduly narrowing its focus?

GLOSSARY TERMS

Countersystem tradition: A tradition in sociology whose participants have intentionally undertaken research aimed at reducing or eliminating social injustice.

Hegemony: A situation of hierarchy in which the dominant group rules with the active consent of the dominated. With hegemony, the dominant group enjoys widespread prestige and authority, and its viewpoint is culturally dominant, minimizing the need for coercion in maintaining hierarchy. What Becker calls the "apolitical case," in which an established hierarchy is not challenged but is accepted by dominants and subordinates alike, is an instance of hegemony.

Hierarchy of credibility: An interlacing of knowledge and power in which the socially recognized credibility of knowledge increases as one moves up the hierarchy of power. Thus, knowledge claims that contest the viewpoint of the dominant group tend to be dismissed as "biased."

Practice: Human sensuous activity; action in the world, which is part of the world.

Praxis: The conjunction of critical theory and transformative practice that changes both the circumstances in which people are active and the people themselves.

Public intellectuals: Social scientists and others who speak and write critically about major societal issues in styles that are accessible to broad audiences.

Sociosphere: An increasingly integrated global web of structured social relationships that is embedded within the biosphere.

Value-free sociology: The notion that the social analyst can opt out of the relations of power and politics in which all people are implicated, and create knowledge of the social based on a view from nowhere.

FURTHER READING

Fay, Brian. 1987. *Critical Social Science*. Cambridge: Polity Press.
Defining critical social science as "an attempt to understand in a rationally responsible manner the oppressive features of a society such that this understanding stimulates its audience to transform their society and thereby liberate themselves" (4), Fay discusses at length the ontology, values, and politics of critical social science.

Hammersley, Martyn. 2001. "Which Side Was Becker on? Questioning Political and Epistemological Radicalism." *Qualitative Research* 1(1): 91–110.
A re-examination of Becker's classic article, excerpted in this volume, which questions the degree to which Becker took an epistemologically or politically radical position but accepts that Becker put forward the view that systematic and rigorous social research inevitably tends to have radical political implications.

Johnson, Alan. 2001. *Privilege, Power, and Difference*. New York: McGraw-Hill.
  Presents a very accessible theoretical framework for thinking about systems of
  privilege, domination, and oppression as social constructions in which we are
  all implicated.

Perrucci, Robert. 2001. "Inventing Social Justice: SSSP and the Twenty-First
  Century." *Social Problems* 48(2): 159–167.
  Revised version of a presidential address to the Society for the Study of Social
  Problems (SSSP). Perrucci traces the history of SSSP from its 1951 emergence
  in opposition to a scientific model of sociology, and urges members to make
  their knowledge available to the general public. He holds that social change can
  occur only when intellectuals offer useful interpretations of shared problems to
  people in the real world, who can then construct alternatives to the present. The
  article contains a proposed "Agenda for Social Justice."

Thomson, Ernie. 1994. "The Sparks That Dazzle Rather Than Illuminate: A New
  Look at Marx's 'Theses on Feuerbach.'" *Nature, Society, and Thought* 7(3):
  299–323.
  A discussion that probes the meaning of Marx's theses by placing them within
  the context of philosophical debate in 1840s Germany.

RELEVANT WEB SITES

Sociologists without Borders

http://www.sociologistswithoutborders.org/

  The English-language Web page of an organization of sociologists committed
  to global social justice, formed in 2002. Contains articles, curriculum material,
  commentary, and links.

SocioSite

http://www2.fmg.uva.nl/sociosite/

  Based at the University of Amsterdam, this "social science information
  system" contains a remarkable and well-organized set of links to associations,
  departments, journals, research institutes, prominent sociologists, and other
  resources.

Study Guide for Marx's Theses on Feuerbach

http://www.marxists.org/archive/marx/works/1845/theses/guide.htm

  A very useful set of questions meant to aid in your engagement with these
  classic assertions on theory, practice, and social/material reality.

World Social Forum

http://www.forumsocialmundial.org.br/home.asp

  An "open meeting place where groups and movements of civil society
  opposed to neo-liberalism and a world dominated by capital or by any form of
  imperialism, but engaged in building a planetary society centred on the human
  person, come together to pursue their thinking, to debate ideas democratically,
  for formulate proposals, share their experiences freely and network for effective

action." The Forum meets annually and its website is regularly updated with news and analysis.

ZNet
http://www.zmag.org
A large Web site updated regularly and designed to convey critical analyses of a wide range of social and political issues.

1B

STEPS TOWARD
CRITICAL INQUIRY

If Marx's "Theses on Feuerbach" are a good point of entry to the critical tradition in social science, C. Wright Mills's essay on intellectual craftsmanship guides us in some initial steps toward actual strategies for critical inquiry. Drafted in 1952 as lecture notes (Mills, 1980 [1952]), Mills's essay was published seven years later as the appendix to *The Sociological Imagination*, a scathing critique of positivist sociology's complicity with entrenched power but also a call for a public sociology geared toward revitalizing democracy.

Mills depicted mainstream sociology as organized around two problematical styles of inquiry. "Grand theory," exemplified by Talcott Parsons's *The Social System* (1951), turns away from the pursuit of socio-historical knowledge in favour of "the associating and dissociating of concepts" (1959: 26): the construction of needlessly abstract, obscure, and decontextualized formulations that have no discernible connection to substantive problems of human affairs, but that elevate sociological theorists to an elite priesthood bound together by an exclusivist language.

Although grand theory severs the relation between sociology and social justice, Mills understood its impact to be less pernicious than that of the second predominant research style in his time. With "abstracted empiricism" it is not concepts but variables—columns of quantitative data—that are associated and dissociated through correlational analysis. Mills, who recognized the value of quantitative analysis,[1] also noticed the inhibiting impact of tailoring one's social analysis to what he called the "Statistical Ritual." What troubled him was the ritualized way in which quantitative researchers would approach inquiry, often reducing complex configurations of biography, history, and social structure to the quantitative indicators required by their statistical techniques. He wondered "how much exactitude, or even pseudo-precision, is here confused with 'truth,' and how much abstracted empiricism is taken as the only 'empirical' manner of work" (1959: 72). He doubted that the piling up of "facts" from a succession of atheoretical quantitative studies would produce an integrated social science. However, Mills did note that abstracted empiricism generates knowledge that is compatible with the "bureaucratic forms of domination in modern society" (1959: 101). When detached from firm connection to substantive problems, the techniques of quantitative sociology can be readily pressed into service by corporate and state clients, whose agendas are anything but neutral. The positivist goals for social science—"the prediction and control of human behavior"—are, after all, also the goals of entrenched power (1959: 113). Mills viewed the bureaucratization of social science as a trend that threatened to reduce sociologists from engaged intellectuals addressing "the public" to technicians serving powerful clients (1959: 102). Decades later, asking the question, "can sociologists do critical research?" Reece Walters has observed an accentuation of the same threat:

> We are witnessing an unprecedented volume of "private research" or consultancies where the researcher enters into a transaction as "service provider" to a designated client. These contractual arrangements continue to blossom as government and private industries seek expertise or aim to demonstrate accountability, and with them they bring a range of regulations over the scope of the research as well as legal controls over the way the research findings are reported and disseminated. (2003: 227)

This absorption of social inquiry into the machinery of domination is no more inevitable today than it was in Mills's time. Mills, indeed all the authors featured in this section, grappled with the key question of how researchers can define for themselves a critical and emancipatory role in the production of social knowledge. His alternative to abstracted empiricism (and also to grand theorizing) was the cultivation of intellectual craftsmanship.[2] The intellectual craftsman, or craftswoman, gives us one vivid image of the practice of critical social analysis. She or he does not separate life and work but integrates personal experience and professional activities by keeping an elaborate file of ideas, notes, plans, outlines, and the like—all of which enables an ongoing, self-reflective project of independent intellectual production. Central to the practise of this craft is what Mills called the sociological imagination, which requires "the capacity to shift from one perspective to another, and in the process to build up an adequate view of a total society and its components." This imagination is not a gift but neither is it a technical skill. Rather, it is the quality of a self-conscious thinker who is keen to understand people as "historical and social actors ... intricately formed by the variety of human societies." Such a quality of mind is integral to critical social inquiry, and Mills's extensive suggestions as to how the sociological imagination can be released are worth heeding. Rearranging one's file, playing with the semantics of terminology, working up typologies and cross-classifications, shifting from one disciplinary perspective to another, and so on—these are reflexive ways of generating the fresh, creative, and sometimes unorthodox ideas that fuel critical social inquiry. Finally, Mills advises the intellectual craftsman to avoid the indulgence in "socspeak" (the most Byzantine instance of which was grand theory), but to present one's work in clear language, without pretentious academic claims and in a voice that emanates from oneself as a centre of experience and reasoning.

Sandra Kirby and Kate McKenna, in the introductory chapter to their influential 1989 text, *Experience, Research, Social Change*, build on Mills's insights but incorporate important lessons from three decades of critical scholarship and activism that followed in the wake of *The Sociological Imagination*. They view research not as a specialized, technical activity but as a form of literacy that can transform social relations by breaking the monopoly that dominant groups hold over information. Like Howard Becker, these authors recognize that social hierarchies validate certain knowledge claims over others, but they go further than Becker in advocating "methods from the margins." These methods enable those on the margins of intellectual production "to create knowledge that will describe, explain and help change the world in which they live." Like Mills's intellectual crafts(wo)man, the researcher from the margins does not command extensive funding and paid staff, is typically positioned outside the ruling apparatus, and engages in a multifaceted and reflexive exploration of the social world.

Methods from the margins are in fact doubly reflexive in the ways that they construct knowledge of the social. This can be seen by contrasting them with a somewhat stylized version of traditional positivist method (see Table 1B.1).

In the first place, positivist research is research *"on"* a particular group or social category: the relation between the researcher and the subjects of the study is one of *objectification* (subjects are treated as cases to be observed) and *appropriation* (knowledge is transferred from the subjects to the researcher, who is the sovereign authority). The relationship between researcher and researched is one-sided and non-reflexive. In contrast, the practitioner of methods from the margins does research *with, by and for* marginalized people: she or he constructs an intersubjective relationship with the subjects of the study, who become *participants* and *collaborators* in an authentic dialogue. Research from the margins thus becomes a resource for the oppressed to study themselves and to share their truths in ways that can inform processes of change.

In the second place, positivism does not reflect deeply on the personal and political context in which research occurs, except as it might interfere with proper measurement of variables. For the researcher from the margins, this context requires critical reflection throughout the project—a questioning of the preconceptions, motives, interests, power dynamics, and so on that shape the definition of the research problem and the production and circulation of new knowledge. This reflection enables the researcher to contextualize herself in the research as a *subject* in the study, and therefore subverts the researcher/researched division from the other side.[3] This double-sided reflexivity gives us another specification of the term "praxis," which Kirby and McKenna define elsewhere in their book as "thoughtful reflection and action that occurs simultaneously ... the integration of knowing and doing" (1989: 34).

Table 1B.1: Comparison of Methods: Traditional Positivism vs. Methods from the Margins

Relations of Knowledge Production	Traditional Positivism	Methods from the Margins
Between researcher and *subjects* of research	Subjects are treated as cases to be observed: objectification and appropriation. "Research *on*"	Subjects are participants and collaborators: authentic dialogue. "Research *by, for and with*"
Between researcher and the *context* of research	The personal and political context from which knowledge springs is not deemed relevant.	Ongoing critical reflection on personal and political dynamics within the context of research.

A compelling example of methods from the margins can be seen in Linda Tuhiwai Smith's landmark text *Decolonizing Methodologies*, a chapter of which is reprinted as our third reading in this section. Part of a social and intellectual movement to critique and transcend the oppressive legacy that Western colonialism/imperialism has bequeathed to many of the world's peoples, Tuhiwai Smith's post-colonial analysis begins from Edward Said's (1978) premise that colonialism/imperialism was a system not only of material and cultural appropriation but of "positional superiority" in which knowledge of the non-western Other was "discovered," extracted, and distributed. The result was not only a misrepresentation of Aboriginal communities within Western discourses but a colonization of the minds of Aboriginal peoples. For the West—Europe and North America—knowing the Other meant classifying, categorizing, and commodifying: unilateral processes of knowledge/power that fit the template of traditional positivist research. An integral aspect of the colonizing project, the Western research program to know the non-Western Other was driven by an interest in social control. Within such a research paradigm, "the objects of research do not have a voice and do not contribute to research" (Smith, 1999: 61); rather, indigenous ways of knowing were excluded and marginalized, and colonized people were often forced to adopt the languages and customs of the occupying power, a particularly horrific example being the Canadian residential schools in which many First Nations children were incarcerated until not long ago.

For indigenous communities, whose extreme marginalization from intellectual production has coincided with other economic, political, and cultural forms of inferiorization, the need for innovative and empowering research strategies is urgent. Toward the close of her book, in the essay reprinted below, Tuhiwai Smith discusses 25 indigenous projects that attempt to decolonize methodology. She notes that "the acts of reclaiming, reformulating and reconstituting indigenous cultures and languages have required the mounting of an ambitious research programme, one that is very strategic in its purpose and activities and relentless in its pursuit of social justice" (p. 75). The projects she sketches interpenetrate, and they involve a variety of agents—indigenous lawyers, community leaders, social workers, etc. As we reflect on these projects, we notice that, although they all entail a piecing-together of knowledge as a crucial element in empowerment, not all of them fall within the domain of empirical research. For instance, *celebrating survival* (project 4) affirms indigenous identities by mobilizing the truths of cultures that have resisted and persisted in the face of overwhelming adversity. *Reading* (project 10) reinterprets the White imperial story of Western history and opens up alternative narratives—a history "through the eyes of indigenous and colonized peoples" (p. 80). *Naming* (project 20)—restoring the original indigenous names for landscape, people, and events—"is about retaining as much control over meaning as possible. By 'naming the world' people name their realities" (p. 86). *Sharing* (project 25) communicates the new knowledge across networks and around the world of indigenous peoples in ways that are inclusive and dialogical rather than elitist.

Clearly, Tuhiwai Smith is describing forms of research from the margins, intended to challenge entrenched power and to empower the oppressed. Some of the projects are more focused on political action and cultural renewal than on social analysis per se; indeed, these decolonized methodologies seem to subvert the very boundary that separates understanding the world from changing it. In decolonizing methodologies, the knowledge/power relation is especially taut. Just as colonizing knowledge of the Other was constructed as part and parcel of the domination that reshaped indigenous worlds and peoples, decolonizing knowledge is being constructed as indigenous communities act to transform their worlds. Knowledge and its object are in motion, as praxis.

Abigail Fuller takes us a few steps further toward critical research strategies in her essay, "Toward an Emancipatory Methodology for Peace Research." Not many years ago, as the Cold War was coming to a close with the collapse of the Soviet Union, the notion of a "peace dividend"—a redirection of resources toward human development—was widely mooted. In fact, the reverse occurred as regional wars have continued to proliferate and as a bellicose American administration has pursued a dangerous project of imperial expansion under the cover of a seemingly endless "war on terrorism." The need for a vibrant peace movement worldwide can hardly be overstated.

Fuller, writing in the early 1990s, begins by noting two debilitating flaws in the practice of peace research. Substantively, peace research focuses on issues of relevance to dominant groups and thereby validates the hierarchy of credibility rather than challenging it; methodologically, peace research excludes subordinate groups from the research process, except as passive objects of knowledge. In some respects Fuller's emancipatory methodology anticipates the extensive treatment of institutional ethnography that the reader will find later in this volume. Both rely on an epistemology, a theory of knowledge, called *standpoint theory*. Fuller's version of this theory turns on two claims: (1) knowledge is socially situated, and in a hierarchical society one's perspective is shaped by one's position within social hierarchies; and (2) the perspective of those in a subordinate position, actively struggling to transform structures of domination, is "epistemologically advantageous"—it contains insights not available to those in dominant positions (cf. Hartsock, 1998). This advantage derives from praxis. It is only when people "push up against" oppressive social structures in a process of struggle that the structures themselves become visible. If, for instance, Nelson Mandela and other radicals had not conducted a broad movement of resistance to the system of apartheid in South Africa from the 1950s to the 1990s, the reality of that system, including its violence, would have likely remained obscured behind a façade of official discourse and deceit, in which the apartheid state's major trading partners—the United States, Britain, Germany, and Japan—were active participants.

By implication, the epistemological advantage of taking up the standpoint of subordinate groups is not an automatic effect of social positioning, but is gained only through the sort of transformative practice that Marx wrote of in his "Theses on Feuerbach." "The standpoint of a subordinate group is available to those who would engage in the struggle for its emancipation" (p. 100).[4] Out of this struggle comes knowledge that is actually *more* scientifically valid (i.e., a better representation of reality) than top-down perspectives, which, like the master in Hegel's master-slave relationship, take for granted the social and material premises of their own existence.

Part of the enhanced validity comes from a broadening of the research agenda as one moves away from the concerns of dominant groups whose interests tend to preclude serious challenges to the hierarchical structures they subtend. When peace researchers adopt the standpoint of subordinates, their own concepts and priorities become broadened beyond the narrow framing of "peace as the absence of international violence." As Third World activists struggled against the violence of colonialism in the 1970s and as feminists struggled against militarism and masculinized violence in the 1980s, the very concept of "peace" was transformed to mean "the absence of structural violence, or the presence of justice" (p. 98). Peace activists and researchers came to view violence as *structural*, perpetrated not only through war but through oppressive social structures. More people die each year from the structural violence of starvation and other economic injustices of global capitalism than on the battlefield. With a broadened perspective on peace, the researcher becomes more reflexive as to whether the research process promotes justice or reinforces structural violence. By taking up the standpoint of subordinates, the peace researcher can avoid reproducing, within the relationship between researcher and researched, the four components of structural violence—exploitation, penetration, fragmentation, and marginalization—that peace activism challenges. Like Kirby and McKenna's methods from the margins, Fuller's emancipatory methodology commits us ultimately to "a democratization of the production of knowledge such that anyone who so desires can gain the skills and knowledge necessary for research" (p. 97).

NOTES

1. Mills wrote, "if the problems upon which one is at work are readily amenable to statistical procedures, one should always try to use them" (Mills, 1959: 73).
2. Mills uses gender-coded language throughout his essay, subsuming all people under the male pronoun. I have avoided the sexist use of language in my own rendition, but retain the term "craftsmanship" in the interests of concision.
3. As Kirby and McKenna state elsewhere in their book, by contextualizing yourself in the research, "you change the traditional power dynamics or the hierarchy which tends to exist between the researcher and those who are researched. The researcher becomes another subject in the research process, and another dimension is added to the data" (1989: 53).
4. For this reason standpoint theory is not an "essentialist" formulation. The most compelling proof of this comes from the life of Frederick Engels, who, with Karl Marx, developed the first version of standpoint theory in critical social science. Engels was a member of a capitalist family and had experience in managing the factories his family owned. With Marx, he took up the standpoint of the proletariat not as a reflex of his "class position" but as an aspect of his emancipatory political practice. For further discussion of standpoint theory, see Hartsock (1998) and New (1998).

REFERENCES

Hartsock, Nancy. 1998. "Marxist Feminist Dialectics for the 21st Century." *Science and Society* 62(3): 400–413.

Kirby, Sandra, and Kate McKenna. 1989. *Experience, Research, Social Change*. Toronto: Garamond Press.

Mills, C. Wright. 1959. *The Sociological Imagination*. New York: Oxford University Press
_____. 1980 [1952]. "On intellectual craftsmanship." *Society* 17(2): 63–70.

New, Caroline. 1998. "Realism, Deconstruction and the Feminist Standpoint." *Journal for the Theory of Social Behaviour* 28(4): 349–372.

Parsons, Talcott. 1951. *The Social System*. New York: Free Press.

Said, Edward W. 1978. *Orientalism*. New York: Pantheon Books.

Smith, Linda Tuhiwai. 1999. *Decolonizing Methodologies*. London: Zed Books.

Walters, Reece. 2003. "Can Sociologists Do Critical Research?" In *Sociology for the Asking*, edited by Myra Hird and George Pavlich, 221–231. Auckland: Oxford University Press.

CHAPTER 4

On Intellectual Craftsmanship

C. Wright Mills

To the individual social scientist who feels himself a part of the classic tradition, social science is the practice of a craft. A man at work on problems of substance, he is among those who are quickly made impatient and weary by elaborate discussions of method-and-theory-in-general; so much of it interrupts his proper studies. It is much better, he believes, to have one account by a working student of how he is going about his work than a dozen "codifications of procedure" by specialists who as often as not have never done much work of consequence. Only by conversations in which experienced thinkers exchange information about their actual ways of working can a useful sense of method and theory be imparted to the beginning student. I feel it useful, therefore, to report in some detail how I go about my craft. This is necessarily a personal statement, but it is written with the hope that others, especially those beginning independent work, will make it less personal by the facts of their own experience.

1

It is best to begin, I think, by reminding you, the beginning student, that the most admirable thinkers within the scholarly community you have chosen to join do not split their work from their lives. They seem to take both too seriously to allow such dissociation, and they want to use each for the enrichment of the other. Of course, such a split is the prevailing convention among men in general, deriving, I suppose, from the hollowness of the work which men in general now do. But you will have recognized that as a scholar you have the exceptional opportunity of designing a way of living which will encourage the habits of good workmanship. Scholarship is a choice of how to live as well as a choice of career; whether he knows it or not, the intellectual workman forms his own self as he works toward the perfection of his craft; to realize his own potentialities, and any opportunities that come his way, he constructs a character which has as its core the qualities of the good workman.

What this means is that you must learn to use your life experience in your intellectual work: continually to examine and interpret it. In this sense craftsmanship is the center of yourself and you are personally involved in every intellectual product upon which you may work. To say that you can "have experience," means, for one thing, that your past plays into and affects your present, and that it defines your capacity for future experience. As a social scientist, you have to control this rather elaborate interplay, to capture what you experience and sort it out; only in this way can you hope to use it to guide and test your reflection, and in the process shape yourself as an intellectual craftsman. But how can you do this? One answer is: you must set up a file, which is, I suppose, a sociologist's way of saying: keep a journal. Many creative writers keep journals; the sociologist's need for systematic reflection demands it.

In such a file as I am going to describe, there is joined personal experience and professional activities, studies under way and studies planned. In this file, you, as an intellectual craftsman, will try to get together what you are doing intellectually and what you are experiencing as a person. Here you will not be afraid to use your experience and relate it directly to various work in progress. By serving as a check on repetitive work, your file also enables you to conserve your energy. It also encourages you to capture "fringe-thoughts": various ideas which may be byproducts of everyday life, snatches of conversation overheard on the street, or, for that matter, dreams. Once noted, these may lead to more systematic thinking, as well as lend intellectual relevance to more directed experience.

* * * * *

By keeping an adequate file and thus developing self-reflective habits, you learn how to keep your inner world awake. Whenever you feel strongly about events or ideas you must try not to let them pass from your mind, but instead to formulate them for your files and in so doing draw out their implications, show yourself either how foolish these feelings or ideas are, or how they might be articulated into productive shape. The file also helps you build up the habit of writing. You cannot "keep your hand in" if you do not write something at least every week. In developing the file, you can experiment as a writer and thus, as they say, develop your powers of expression. To maintain a file is to engage in the controlled experience.

One of the very worst things that happens to social scientists is that they feel the need to write of their "plans" on only one occasion: when they are going to ask for money for a specific piece of research or "a project." It is as a request for funds that most "planning" is done, or at least carefully written about. However standard the practice, I think this very bad: It is bound in some degree to be salesmanship, and, given prevailing expectations, very likely to result in painstaking pretensions; the project is likely to be "presented," rounded out in some arbitrary manner long before it ought to be; it is often a contrived thing, aimed at getting the money for ulterior purposes, however valuable, as well as for the research presented.

* * * * *

Any working social scientist who is well on his way ought at all times to have so many plans, which is to say ideas, that the question is always, which of them am I, ought I, to work on next? And he should keep a special little file for his master agenda, which he writes and rewrites just for himself and perhaps for discussion with friends. From time to time he ought to review this very carefully and purposefully, and sometimes too, when he is relaxed.

* * * * *

Under various topics in your file there are ideas, personal notes, excerpts from books, bibliographical items, and outlines of projects. It is, I suppose, a matter of arbitrary habit, but I think you will find it well to sort all these items into a master file of "projects," with many subdivisions. The topics, of course, change, sometimes quite frequently. For instance, as a student working toward the preliminary examination, writing a thesis, and, at the same time, doing term papers, your files will be arranged in those three areas of endeavor. But after a year or so of graduate work, you will begin to re-organize the whole file in relation to the main project of your thesis. Then as you pursue your work you will notice that no one project ever dominates it, or sets the master categories in which it is arranged. In fact, the use of the file encourages expansion of the categories which you use in your thinking. And the way in which these categories change, some being dropped and others being added— is an index of your intellectual progress and breadth. Eventually, the files will come to be arranged according to several large projects, having many sub-projects that change from year to year.

All this involves the taking of notes. You will have to acquire the habit of taking a large volume of notes from any worth-while book you read—although, I have to say, you may get better work out of yourself when you read really bad books. The first step in translating experience, either of other men's writing, or of your own life, into the intellectual sphere, is to give it form. Merely to name an item of experience often invites you to explain it; the mere taking of a note from a book is often a prod to reflection. At the same time, of course, the taking of a note is a great aid in comprehending what you are reading.

Your notes may turn out, as mine do, to be of two sorts: in reading certain very important books you try to grasp the structure of the writer's argument, and take notes accordingly; but more frequently, and after a few years of independent work, rather than read entire books, you will very often read parts of many books from the point of view of some particular theme or topic in which you are interested and concerning which you have plans in your file. Therefore, you will take notes which do not fairly represent the books you read. You are using this particular idea, this particular fact, for the realization of your own projects.

2

But how is this file—which so far must seem to you more like a curious sort of "literary"

journal—used in intellectual production? The maintenance of such a file is intellectual production. It is a continually growing store of facts and ideas, from the most vague to the most finished. For example, the first thing I did upon deciding on a study of the elite was to make a crude outline based on a listing of the types of people that I wished to understand.

Just how and why I decided to do such a study may suggest one way in which one's life experiences feed one's intellectual work. I forget just when I became technically concerned with "stratification," but I think it must have been on first reading Veblen. He had always seemed to me very loose, even vague, about his "business" and "industrial" employments, which are a kind of translation of Marx for the academic American public. At any rate, I wrote a book on labor organizations and labor leaders—a politically motivated task; then a book on the middle classes—a task primarily motivated by the desire to articulate my own experience in New York City since 1945. It was thereupon suggested by friends that I ought to round out a trilogy by writing a book on the upper classes. I think the possibility had been in my mind; I had read Balzac off and on especially during the 'forties, and had been much taken with his self-appointed task of "covering" all the major classes and types in the society of the era he wished to make his own. I had also written a paper on "The Business Elite," and had collected and arranged statistics about the careers of the topmost men in American politics since the Constitution. These two tasks were primarily inspired by seminar work in American history.

In doing these several articles and books and in preparing courses in stratification, there was of course a residue of ideas and facts about the upper classes. Especially in the study of social stratification is it difficult to avoid going beyond one's immediate subject, because "the reality" of any one stratum is in large part its relations to the rest. Accordingly, I began to think of a book on the elite.

And yet that is not "really" how "the project" arose; what really happened is (1) that the idea and the plan came out of my files, for all projects with me begin and end with them, and books are simply organized releases from the continuous work that goes into them; (2) that after a while, the whole set of problems involved came to dominate me.

After making my crude outline I examined my entire file, not only those parts of it that obviously bore on my topic, but also those which seemed to have no relevance whatsoever. Imagination is often successfully invited by putting together hitherto isolated items, by finding unsuspected connections. I made new units in the file for this particular range of problems, which of course, led to new arrangements of other parts of the file.

As you re-arrange a filing system, you often find that you are, as it were, loosening your imagination. Apparently this occurs by means of your attempt to combine various ideas and notes on different topics. It is a sort of logic of combination, and "chance" sometimes plays a curiously large part in it. In a relaxed way, you try to engage your intellectual resources, as exemplified in the file, with the new themes.

In the present case, I also began to use my observations and daily experiences. I thought first of experiences I had had which bore upon elite problems, and then I went and talked with those who, I thought, might have experienced or considered the issues. As a matter of fact, I now began to alter the character of my routine so as to include in it (1) people who were among those whom I wanted to study, (2) people in close contact with them, and (3) people interested in them usually in some professional way.

I do not know the full social conditions of the best intellectual workmanship, but certainly surrounding oneself by a circle of people who will listen and talk—and at times they have to be imaginary characters—is one of them. At any rate I try to surround myself; with all the relevant environment—social and intellectual—that I think might lead me into thinking well along the lines of my work. That is one meaning of my remarks above about the fusion of personal and intellectual life.

Good work in social science today is not, and usually cannot be, made up of one clear-cut empirical "research." It is, rather, composed of a good many studies which at key points anchor general statements about the shape and the trend of the subject. So the decision—what are these anchor points?—cannot be made until existing materials are re-worked and general hypothetical statements constructed.

Now, among "existing materials," I found in the files three types relevant to my study of the elite: several theories having to do with the topic; materials already worked up by others as evidence for those theories; and materials already gathered and in various stages of accessible centralization, but not yet made theoretically relevant. Only after completing a first draft of a theory with the aid of such existing materials as these can I efficiently locate my own pivotal assertions and hunches and design researches to test them—and maybe I will not have to, although of course I know I will later have to shuttle back and forth between existing materials and my own research. Any final statement must not only "cover the data" so far as the data are available and known to me, but must also in some way, positively or negatively, take into account the available theories. Sometimes this "taking into account" of an idea is easily done by a simple confrontation of the idea with overturning or supporting fact; sometimes a detailed analysis or qualification is needed. [...] At any rate, in the book on the elite I had to take into account the work of such men as Mosca, Schumpeter, Veblen, Marx, Lasswell, Michel, Weber, and Pareto.

In looking over some of the notes on these writers, I find that they offer three types of statement: (a) from some, you learn directly by restating systematically what the man says on given points or as a whole; (b) some you accept or refute, giving reasons and arguments; (c) others you use as a source of suggestions for your own elaborations and projects. This involves grasping a point and then asking: How can I put this into testable shape, and how can I test it? How can I use this as a center from which to elaborate—as a perspective from which descriptive details emerge as relevant? It is in this handling of existing ideas, of course, that you feel yourself in continuity with previous work. [...]

* * * * *

3

There comes a time in the course of your work when you are through with other books. Whatever you want from them is down in your notes and abstracts; and on the margins of these notes, as well as in a separate file, are ideas for empirical studies.

Now I do not like to do empirical work if I can possibly avoid it. If one has no staff it is a great deal of trouble; if one does employ a staff, then the staff is often even more trouble.

[...] There is no more virtue in empirical inquiry as such than in reading as such. The purpose of empirical inquiry is to settle disagreements and doubts about facts, and thus to make arguments more fruitful by basing all sides more substantively. Facts discipline reason; but reason is the advance guard in any field of learning.

Although you will never be able to get the money with which to do many of the empirical studies you design, it is necessary that you continue designing them. For once you lay out an empirical study, even if you do not follow it through, it leads you to a new search for data, which often turn out to have unsuspected

relevance to your problems. Just as it is foolish to design a field study if the answer can be found in a library, it is foolish to think you have exhausted the books before you have translated them into appropriate empirical studies, which merely means into questions of fact.

Empirical projects necessary to my kind of work must promise, first, to have relevance for the first draft, of which I wrote above; they have to confirm it in its original form or they have to cause its modification. Or to put it more pretentiously, they must have implications for theoretical constructions. Second, the projects must be efficient and neat and, if possible, ingenious. By this I mean that they must promise to yield a great deal of material in proportion to the time and effort they involve.

* * * * *

In the course of the reading and analyzing of others' theories, designing ideal research, and perusing the files, you will begin to draw up a list of specific studies. Some of them are too big to handle, and will in time be regretfully given up; some will end as materials for a paragraph, a section, a sentence, a chapter; some will become pervading themes to be woven into an entire book. Here are initial notes for several such projects:

(1) A time-budget analysis of a typical working day of ten top executives of large corporations, and the same for ten federal administrators. These observations will be combined with detailed "life history" interviews. The aim here is to describe the major routines and decisions, partly at least in terms of time devoted to them, and to gain an insight into the factors relevant to the decisions made. The procedure will naturally vary with the degree of co-operation secured, but ideally will involve first, an interview in which the life history and present situation of the man is made clear; second, observations

of the day, actually sitting in a corner of the man's office, and following him around; third, a longish interview that evening or the next day in which we go over the whole day and probe the subjective processes involved in the external behavior we've observed.

(2) An analysis of upper-class week ends, in which the routines are closely observed and followed by probing interviews with the man and other members of the family on the Monday following.

For both these tasks I've fairly good contacts and of course good contacts, if handled properly, lead to better ones. [added 1957: this turned; out to be an illusion.]

(3) A study of the expense account and other privileges which, along with salaries and other incomes, form the standard and the style of living of the top levels. The idea here is to get something concrete on "the bureaucratization of consumption," the transfer of private expenses to business accounts.

(4) Bring up to date the type of information contained in such books as Lundberg's America's Sixty Families, which is dated as of the tax returns for 1923.

(5) Gather and systematize, from treasury records and other government sources, the distribution of various types of private property by amounts held.

(6) A career-line study of the Presidents, all cabinet members, and all members of the Supreme Court. This I already have on IBM cards from the Constitutional period through Truman's second term, but I want to expand the items used and analyze it afresh.

* * * * *

After these designs were written down, I began to read historical works on top groups, taking random (and unfiled) notes and interpreting the reading. You do not really have to study a topic you are working on; for as I have said, once you are into it, it is everywhere. You are sensible to its themes; you see and hear them everywhere in your experience, especially, it always seems to me, in apparently unrelated areas. Even the mass media, especially bad movies and cheap novels and picture magazines and night radio, are disclosed in fresh importance to you.

4

But, you may ask, how do ideas come? How is the imagination spurred to put all the images and facts together, to make images relevant and lend meaning to facts? I do not think I can really answer that; all I can do is talk about the general conditions and a few simple techniques which have seemed to increase my chances to come out with something.

The sociological imagination [...] in considerable part consists of the capacity to shift from one perspective to another, and in the process to build up an adequate view of a total society and of its components. It is this imagination, of course, that sets off the social scientist from the mere technician. Adequate technicians can be trained in a few years. The sociological imagination can also be cultivated; certainly it seldom occurs without a great deal of often routine work.[1] Yet there is an unexpected quality about it, perhaps because its essence is the combination of ideas that no one expected were combinable— say, a mess of ideas from German philosophy and British economics. There is a playfulness of mind back of such combining as well as a truly fierce drive to make sense of the world, which the technician as such usually lacks. Perhaps he is too well trained, too precisely trained. Since one can be *trained* only in what is already known, training sometimes incapacitates one from learning new ways; it makes one rebel against what is bound to be at first loose and even sloppy. But you must cling to such vague images and notions, if they are yours, and you must work them out for it is in such forms that original ideas, if any, almost always first appear.

There are definite ways, I believe, of stimulating the sociological imagination:

(1) On the most concrete level, the re-arranging of the file, as I have already said, is one way to invite imagination. You simply dump out heretofore disconnected folders, mixing up their contents, and then re-sort them. You try to do it in a more or less relaxed way. How often and how extensively you re-arrange the files will of course vary with different problems and with how well they are developing. But the mechanics of it are as simple as that. Of course, you will have in mind the several problems on which you are actively working, but you will also try to be passively receptive to unforeseen and unplanned linkages.

(2) An attitude of playfulness toward the phrases and words with which various issues are defined often loosens up the imagination. Look up synonyms for each of your key terms in dictionaries as well as in technical books, in order to know the full range of their connotations. [...] But such an interest in words goes further than that. In all work, but especially in examining theoretical statements, you will try to keep close watch on the level of generality of every key term, and you will often find it useful to break down a high-level statement into more concrete meanings. When that is done, the statement often falls into two or three components, each lying along different dimensions. You will also try to move up the level of generality: remove the specific qualifiers and examine the re-formed statement or inference more abstractly, to see if you can stretch it or elaborate it. So from above and from below, you will try to probe, in search of clarified meaning, into every aspect and implication of the idea.

(3) Many of the general notions you come upon, as you think about them, will be cast into types. A new classification is the usual beginning of fruitful developments. The skill to make up types and then to search for the conditions and consequences of each type will, in short, become an automatic procedure with you. Rather than rest content with existing classifications, in particular, common-sense ones, you will search for their common denominators and for differentiating factors within and between them. Good types require that the criteria of classification be explicit and systematic. To make them so you must develop the habit of cross-classification.

The technique of cross-classifying is not of course limited to quantitative materials; as a matter of fact, it is the best way to imagine and to get hold of new types as well as to criticize and clarify old ones. Charts, tables, and diagrams of a qualitative sort are not only ways to display work already done; they are very often genuine tools of production. They clarify the "dimensions" of the types, which they also help you to imagine and build. As a matter of fact, in the past fifteen years, I do not believe I have written more than a dozen pages first-draft without some little cross-classification—although, of course, I do not always or even usually display such diagrams. Most of them flop, in which case you have still learned something. When they work, they help you to think more clearly and to write more explicitly. They enable you to discover the range and the full relationships of the very terms with which you are thinking and of the facts with which you are dealing.

For a working sociologist, cross-classification is what diagramming a sentence is for a diligent grammarian. In many ways, cross-classification is the very grammar of the sociological imagination. Like all grammar, it must be controlled and not allowed to run away from its purposes.

(4) Often you get the best insights by considering extremes—by thinking of the opposite of that with which you are directly concerned. If you think about despair, then also think about elation; if you study the miser, then also the spendthrift. The hardest thing in

the world is to study one object; when you try to contrast objects, you get a better grip on the materials and you can then sort out the dimensions in terms of which the comparisons are made. You will find that shuttling between attention to these dimensions and to the concrete types is very illuminating. […]

The idea is to use a variety of viewpoints: you will, for instance, ask yourself how would a political scientist whom you have recently read approach this, and how would that experimental psychologist, or this historian? You try to think in terms of a variety of viewpoints and in this way to let your mind become a moving prism catching light from as many angles as possible. In this connection, the writing of dialogues is often very useful. You will quite often find yourself thinking against something, and in trying to understand a new intellectual field, one of the first things you might well do is to lay out the major arguments. One of the things meant by "being soaked in the literature" is being able to locate the opponents and the friends of every available viewpoint. […]

(5) The fact that, for the sake of simplicity, in cross-classification, you first work in terms of yes-or-no, encourages you to think of extreme opposites. That is generally good, for qualitative analysis cannot of course provide you with frequencies or magnitudes. Its technique and its end is to give you the range of types. For many purposes you need no more than that, although for some, of course, you do need to get a more precise idea of the proportions involved.

The release of imagination can sometimes be achieved by deliberately inverting your sense of proportion.[2] If something seems very minute, imagine it to be simply enormous, and ask yourself: What difference might that make? And vice versa, for gigantic phenomena. What would pre-literate villages look like with populations of 30 millions? Nowadays at least, I should never think of actually counting or measuring anything, before I had played

with each of its elements and conditions and consequences in an imagined world in which I control the scale of everything. […]

(6) Whatever the problem with which you are concerned, you will find it helpful to try to get a comparative grip on the materials. The search for comparable cases, either in one civilization and historical period or in several, gives you leads. […] In time you will come almost to automatically orient your reflection historically. One reason for doing so is that often what you are examining is limited in number: to get a comparative grip on it, you have to place it inside an historical frame. To put it another way, the contrasting-type approach often requires the examination of historical materials. This sometimes results in points useful for a trend analysis, or it leads to a typology of phases. You will use historical materials, then, because of the desire for a fuller range, or for a more convenient range of some phenomenon—by which I mean a range that includes the variations along some known set of dimensions. Some knowledge of world history is indispensable to the sociologist; without such knowledge, no matter what else he knows, he is simply crippled.

(7) There is, finally, a point which has more to do with the craft of putting a book together than with the release of the imagination. Yet these two are often one: how you go about arranging materials for presentation always affects the content of your work. The idea I have in mind […] is the distinction between theme and topic.

A topic is a subject, like "the careers of corporation executives" or "the increased power of military officials," or "the decline of society matrons." Usually most of what you have to say about a topic can readily be put into one chapter or a section of a chapter. But the order in which all your topics are arranged often brings you into the realm of themes.

A theme is an idea, usually of some signal trend, some master conception, or a key distinction, like rationality and reason, for example. In working out the construction of a book, when you come to realize the two or three, or, as the case may be, the six or seven themes, then you will know that you are on top of the job. You will recognize these themes because they keep insisting upon being dragged into all sorts of topics and perhaps you will feel that they are mere repetitions. [...]

What you must do is sort them out and state them in a general way as clearly and briefly as you can. Then, quite systematically, you must cross-classify them with the full range of your topics. This means that you will ask of each topic: Just how is it affected by each of these themes? And again: Just what is the meaning, if any, for each of these themes of each of the topics?

Sometimes a theme requires a chapter or a section for itself, perhaps when it is first introduced or perhaps in a summary statement toward the end. In general, I think most writers—as well as most systematic thinkers—would agree that at some point all the themes ought to appear together, in relation to one another. Often, although not always, it is possible to do this at the beginning of a book. Usually, in any well-constructed book, it must be done near the end. And, of course, all the way through you ought at least to try to relate the themes to each topic. [...]

Sometimes, by the way, you may find that a book does not really have any themes. It is just a string of topics, surrounded, of course, by methodological introductions to methodology, and theoretical introductions to theory. These are indeed quite indispensable to the writing of books by men without ideas. And so is lack of intelligibility.

5

I know you will agree that you should present your work in as clear and simple language as your subject and your thought about it permit. But as you may have noticed, a turgid and polysyllabic prose does seem to prevail in the social sciences. [...] Is this peculiar language due to the fact that profound and subtle issues, concepts, methods, are being discussed? If not, then what are the reasons for what Malcolm Cowley aptly calls "socspeak"?[3] Is it really necessary to your proper work? If it is, there is nothing you can do about it; if it is not, then how can you avoid it?

Such lack of ready intelligibility, I believe, usually has little or nothing to do with the complexity of subject matter, and nothing at all with profundity of thought. It has to do almost entirely with certain confusions of the academic writer about his own status.

In many academic circles today anyone who tries to write in a widely intelligible way is liable to be condemned as a "mere literary man" or, worse still, "a mere journalist."

* * * * *

To write is to raise a claim for the attention of readers. That is part of any style. To write is also to claim for oneself at least status enough to be read. [...] Desire for status is one reason why academic men slip so readily into unintelligibility. And that, in turn, is one reason why they do not have the status they desire. A truly vicious circle—but one out of which any scholar can easily break.

To overcome the academic prose you have first to overcome the academic pose. It is much less important to study grammar and Anglo-Saxon roots than to clarify your own answers to these three questions: (1) How difficult and complex after all is my subject? (2) When I write, what status am I claiming for myself? (3) For whom am I trying to write?

(1) The usual answer to the first question is: Not so difficult and complex as the way in which you are writing about it. Proof of that is everywhere available: it is revealed by the ease with which 95 per cent of the books of social science can be translated into English.[4]

But, you may ask, do we not sometimes need technical terms? Of course we do, but "technical" does not necessarily mean cult, and certainly it does not mean jargon: If such technical terms are really necessary and also clear and precise, it is not difficult to use them in a context of plain English and thus introduce them meaningfully to the reader.

Perhaps you may object that the ordinary words of common usage are often loaded with feelings and values, and that accordingly might be well to avoid them in favor of new words or technical terms. Here is my answer: it is true that ordinary words are often so loaded. But many technical terms in common use in social science are also loaded. To write clearly is to control these loads, to say exactly what you mean in such a way that this meaning and only this will be understood by others. [...]

My first point, then, is that most "socspeak" is unrelated to any complexity of subject matter or thought. It is used—I think almost entirely—to establish academic claims for one's self; to write in this way is to say to the reader (often I am sure without knowing it): "I know something that is so difficult you can understand it only if you first learn my difficult language. In the meantime, you are merely a journalist, a layman, or some other sort of underdeveloped type."

(2) To answer the second question, we must distinguish two ways of presenting the work of social science according to the idea the writer has of himself, and the voice with which he speaks. One way results from the idea that he is a man who may shout, whisper, or chuckle—but who is always there. It is also clear what sort of man he is: whether confident or neurotic, direct, or involuted, he is a center of experience and reasoning; now he has found out something, and he is telling us about it, and how he found it out. This is the voice behind the best expositions available in the English language.

The other way of presenting work does not use any voice of any man. Such writing is not a "voice" at all. It is an autonomous sound. It is a prose manufactured by a machine. That it is full of jargon is not as noteworthy as that it is strongly mannered: it is not only impersonal; it is pretentiously impersonal. Government bulletins are sometimes written in this way. Business letters also. And a great deal of social science. Any writing—perhaps apart from that of certain truly great stylists—that is not imaginable as human speech is bad writing.

(3) But finally there is the question of those who are to hear the voice—thinking about that also leads to characteristics of style. It is very important for any writer to have in mind just what kinds of people he is trying to speak to—and also what he really thinks of them. These are not easy questions: to answer them well requires decisions about oneself as well as knowledge of reading publics. To write is to raise a claim to be read, but by whom?

One answer has been suggested by my colleague, Lionel Trilling, who has given me permission to pass it on. You are to assume that you have been asked to give a lecture on some subject you know well, before an audience of teachers and students from all departments of a leading university, as well as an assortment of interested people from a near-by city. Assume that such an audience is before you and that they have a right to know; assume that you want to let them know. Now write.

* * * * *

There is one last point, which has to do with the interplay of writing and thinking. If you write solely with reference to what Hans Reichenbach has called the "context of discovery" you will be understood by very few people; moreover you will tend to be quite subjective in statement. To make whatever you think more objective, you must work in the context of presentation. At first, you "present" your thought to yourself, which is often called "thinking clearly." Then when you feel that you have it straight, you present it to others—and often find that you have not made it clear. Now you are in the "context of presentation." Sometimes you will notice that as you try to present your thinking, you will modify it—not only in its form of statement but often in its content as well. You will get new ideas as you work in the context of presentation. In short, it will become a new context of discovery, different from the original one, on a higher level I think, because more socially objective. Here again, you cannot divorce how you think from how you write. You have to move back and forth between these two contexts, and whenever you move it is well to know where you might be going.

6

From what I have said, you will understand that in practice you never "start working on a project"; you are already "working," either in a personal vein, in the files, in taking notes after browsing, or in guided endeavors. Following this way of living and working, you will always have many topics that you want to work out further. After you decide on some "release," you will try to use your entire file, your browsing in libraries, your conversation, your selections of people—all for this topic or theme. You are trying to build a little world containing all the key elements which enter into the work at hand, to put each in its place in a systematic way, continually to readjust this framework around developments in each part of it. Merely to live in such a constructed world is to know what is needed: ideas, facts, ideas, figures, ideas.

So you will discover and describe, setting up types, for the ordering of what you have found out, focusing and organizing experience by distinguishing items by name. This search for order will cause you to seek patterns and trends, to find relations that may be typical and causal. You will search, in short, for the meanings of what you come upon, for what may

be interpreted as a visible token of something else that is not visible. You will make an inventory of everything that seems involved in whatever you are trying to understand; you will pare it down to essentials; then carefully and systematically you will relate these items to one another in order to form a sort of working model. And then you will relate this model to whatever it is you are trying to explain. Sometimes it is that easy; often it just will not come.

* * * * *

Thinking is a struggle for order and at the same time for comprehensiveness. You must not stop thinking too soon—or you will fail to know all that you should; you cannot leave it to go on forever, or you yourself will burst. It is this dilemma, I suppose, that makes reflection, on those rare occasions when it is more or less successful, the most passionate endeavor of which the human being is capable.

Perhaps I can best summarize what I have been trying to say in the form of a few precepts and cautions:

(1) Be a good craftsman: Avoid any rigid set of procedures. Above all, seek to develop and to use the sociological imagination. Avoid the fetishism of method and technique. Urge the rehabilitation of the unpretentious intellectual craftsman, and try to become such a craftsman yourself. Let every man be his own methodologist; let every man be his own theorist; let theory and method again become part of the practice of a craft. Stand for the primacy of the individual scholar; stand opposed to the ascendancy of research teams of technicians. Be one mind that is on its own confronting the problems of man and society.

(2) Avoid the Byzantine oddity of associated and disassociated Concepts, the mannerism of verbiage. Urge upon yourself and upon others the simplicity of clear statement. Use more elaborated terms only when you

believe firmly that their use enlarges the scope of your sensibilities, the precision of your references, the depth of your reasoning. Avoid using unintelligibility as a means of evading the making of judgments upon society—and as a means of escaping your readers' judgments upon your own work.

(3) Make any trans-historical constructions you think your work requires; also delve into sub-historical minutiae. Make up quite formal theory and build models as well as you can. Examine in detail little facts and their relations, and big unique events as well. But do not be fanatic: relate all such work, continuously and closely, to the level of historical reality. [...] Take as your task the defining of this reality; formulate your problems in its terms; on its level try to solve these problems and thus resolve the issues and the troubles they incorporate. And never write more than three pages without at least having in mind a solid example.

(4) Do not study merely one small milieu after another; study the social structures in which milieux are organized. In terms of these studies of larger structures, select the milieux you need to study in detail, and study them in such a way as to understand the interplay of milieux with structure. Proceed in a similar way in so far as the span of time is concerned. [...] So do not merely report minute researches into static knife-edge moments, or very short-term runs of time. Take as your time-span the course of human history, and locate within it the weeks, years, epochs you examine.

(5) Realize that your aim is a fully comparative understanding of the social structures that have appeared and that do now exist in world history. Realize that to carry it out you must avoid the arbitrary specialization of prevailing academic departments. Specialize your work variously, according to topic, and above all according to significant problem. In formulating and in trying to solve these problems, do not hesitate, indeed seek, continu-ally and imaginatively, to draw upon the perspectives and materials, the ideas and methods, of any and all sensible studies of man and society, They are *your* studies; they are part of what you are a part of; do not let them be taken from you by those who would close them off by weird jargon and pretensions of *expertise*.

(6) Always keep your eyes open to the image of man—the generic notion of his human nature—which by your work you are assuming and implying; and also to the image of history—your notion of how history is being made. In a word, continually work out and revise your views of the problems of history, the problems of biography, and the problems of social structure in which biography and history intersect. Keep your eyes open to the varieties of individuality, and to the modes of epochal change. Use what you see and what you imagine, as the clues to your study of the human variety.

(7) Know that you inherit and are carrying on the tradition of classic social analysis; so try to understand man not as an isolated fragment, not as an intelligible field or system in and of itself. Try to understand men and women as historical and social actors, and the ways in which the variety of men and women are intricately selected and intricately formed by the variety of human societies. Before you are through with any piece of work, no matter how indirectly on occasion, orient it to the central and continuing task of understanding the structure and the drift, the shaping and the meanings, of your own period, the terrible and magnificent world of human society in the second half of the twentieth century.

(8) Do not allow public issues as they are officially formulated or troubles as they are privately felt, to determine the problems that you take up for study. Above all, do not give up your moral and political autonomy by accepting in somebody else's terms the illiberal practicality of the bureaucratic ethos

or the liberal practicality of the moral scatter. Know that many personal troubles cannot be solved merely as troubles, but must be understood in terms of public issues—and in terms of the problems of history-making. Know that the human meaning of public issues must be revealed by relating them to personal troubles—and to the problems of the individual life. Know that the problems of social science, when adequately formulated, must include both troubles and issues, both biography and history, and the range of their intricate relations. Within that range the life of the individual and the making of societies occur; and within that range the sociological imagination has its chance to make a difference in the quality of human life in our time.

NOTES

1. See the excellent articles on "insight" and "creative endeavor" by Hutchinson in *Study of Interpersonal Relations*, edited by Patrick Mullahy, New York, Nelson, 1949.

2. By the way, some of this is what Kenneth Burke, in discussing Nietzsche, has called "perspective by incongruity." See, by all means, Burke, *Permanence and Change*, New York, New Republic Books, 1936.

3. Malcolm Cowley, "Sociological Habit Patterns in Linguistic Transmogrification," *The Reporter*, 20 September 1956, pp. 41 ff.

4. By the way, on writing, the best book I know is Robert Graves and Alan Hodge, *The Reader Over Your Shoulder*, New York, Macmillan, 1944. See also the excellent discussions by Barzun and Graff, *The Modem Researcher*, op. cit., G.E. Montague, *A Writer's Notes on His Trade*, London, Pelican Books, 1930–1949, and Bonamy Dobree, *Modern Prose Style*, Oxford, Clarendon Press, 1934–1950.

CHAPTER 5
Methods from the Margins

SANDRA KIRBY AND KATE MCKENNA

We live in a world in which knowledge is used to maintain oppressive relations. Information is interpreted and organized in such a way that the views of a small group of people are presented as objective knowledge, as "The Truth." We believe that Maria Mies is right when she says that "Research, which so far has been largely the instrument of dominance and legitimation of power elites, must be brought to serve the interests of dominated, exploited and oppressed groups" (1983: 123). It is our hope that the content and process we describe will contribute to this effort.

People have begun to challenge the way language, research, and knowledge are used as instruments of power that impose form and order for the purpose of control. Whether it be calls from the governments of third world countries demanding what they have called a New World Information Order,[1] progressive literacy workers and popular educators using the context of learning as a means of transforming social relations, or feminists challenging the way knowledge is produced and whose view of the world it represents, they are all questioning the monopoly that certain powerful groups hold over information.

Because many people cannot read or write they do not have access to information that could affect the quality of their daily lives, and in some instances, their actual survival. Many literacy workers have pointed to the connection between cultural domination and illiteracy.

Most of us have not had the opportunity to research, to create knowledge which is rooted in and representative of our experience. We have been excluded from participating in, describing, and analyzing our own understanding of reality.

If we think of research as a form of literacy, some of the insights which have grown out of progressive literacy work become helpful in understanding research from the margins. Progressive literacy workers stress that "the only valid form of literacy training is one which enables the learner to intervene in reality;" literacy education "must serve the purpose of teaching people how to demythologize and decode their culture" (Bee, 1980: 50). Without analysis of the social context, the workers argue, literacy remains merely functional, enabling people to function within the status quo rather than allowing them to interact with and change society (Bee, 1980; Darville, forthcoming). And so it is with research; research that does not reflect on and analyze the social context from which it springs serves only the status quo and does not enable us to interact with and change society.

Reading and writing are skills that are context dependent. Many of us have at times found ourselves feeling either hesitation, frustration, insecurity, or anger as we have tried to understand written information. Our hesitation involves more than simple lack of skill. It occurs "when [we] encounter an unfamiliar form of literacy, and the skills [we] do have seem 'out of place'" (Darville, forthcoming).

One of the major themes in discussions of literacy is the assertion that literacy has more than one form, that no single definition is sufficient since "literacy is more than a mechanical set of skills ... practices of reading and writing are bound within specific uses by particular actors from their different positions in the social order" (Weinstein, 1984: 480). What this means is that whether people are literate or illiterate depends on the specific context in which they find themselves. Literacy can only be determined with reference to particular needs and uses for those skills which themselves vary and change over time and place.

We would argue that research needs are also context dependent. Although some people claim that research is capable of representing everyone equally because it is done in an objective, non-involved manner, women and people from various oppressed groups have been challenging such positivist claims. They say that in fact research has not been objective and that it does not represent their experience. Rather, they argue, research and knowledge are produced in a manner which represents the political and social interests of a particular group. They point out that research has often been a tool of domination which has helped perpetuate and maintain current power relations of inequality. Too often the experts who do research have been well trained in patterns of thinking which not only conflict with their understanding, but explain and justify a world many are actually interested in changing.

It is important that the process of investigating the world not remain a specialized activity. Our everyday lives teach us skills which we use to observe and reflect on our experience. We focus on problems, ask questions, collect information and analyze and interpret "data." We already "do research" as we interact with the everyday world.

When we talk about doing research from the margins we are talking about being on the margins of the production of knowledge. In researching from the margins we are concerned with how research skills can enable people to create knowledge that will describe, explain, and help change the world in which they live.

> We need to reclaim, name and re-name our experience and thus our knowledge of this social world we live in and daily help to construct, because only by doing so will it become truly ours, ours to use and do with as we will. (Stanley and Wise, 1983: 205)

Think of the way in which graffiti is sometimes used as social comment, a sort of advertising from the margins, for example:

> If voting could change the system it would be illegal
> Too many causes without a rebel
> Get your ads off my body
> We're poor and we know why

These comments are made by individuals who are "making sense of" or analyzing their experience from the margins. These people are not only making sense but taking action by claiming public space to express their analysis, space normally monopolized by mainstream comment.

Researching from the margins shares some characteristics with advertising from the margins in that:

- it can be done without a great deal of money;
- it can be collaborative and creative;

- it carries an alternative viewpoint;
- it can highlight the ways in which information is controlled;
- it can turn the language of the status quo back on itself;
- it often uses rage and humour to critique the status quo;
- it most often is not institution-alized.

We seek to describe a way of researching that incorporates an understanding of living in an antagonistic world and the need to act on such knowledge. Through research, we can begin to take control of the information we present and that which is presented on our behalf.

* * * * *

There is a need to move beyond the traditional academic understanding that knowledge can be created in a vacuum, and begin to claim and incorporate the personal and political context from which the knowledge springs as part of the data-gathering process.

Becky, a graduate theology student, told us:

> In my classes we have been critiquing research that claims to have been done in an objective fashion. Women and people from various minority groups are saying that it's not objective, that it's coming from a particular group who have specific political and social interests .... I want to research something I'm really interested in and that does have a stake in my life and other people's lives. I want to know how research can be done differently, but I'm not sure what that means.

We believe research must begin to reflect the experience and concerns of people who have traditionally been marginalized by the research process and by what gets counted as knowledge.

It is impossible to discuss research without talking about power and influence. Differences in wealth and power separate people into identifiable groups, separate the "haves" from the "have nots": the rich from the poor; men from women; white people from people of colour; the overdeveloped countries of the world from the exploited countries. The list is endless.

We have all heard the expression "knowledge is power." One of the basic elements of power is that those who have positions of power are able to manufacture ideas. Another is being able to place ideas that have been created into the public agenda. Edward Bernays, a spokesperson for the public relations industry and the recipient of academic honours for his contributions to applied psychology, introduced the term "engineering of consent." The term describes the "freedom to persuade and suggest," which he charac-terizes as "the very essence of the democratic process." In a democracy, consent is not often achieved through force, but through the "domination of the flow of information and the means for expressing opinion or analysis" (Chomsky, 1981: 140).

Because research is done by particular people in specific social and historical contexts, these have implications which need to be acknowledged.

> All knowledge that is about human society, and not about the natural world, is historical knowledge, and therefore rests upon judg-ment and interpretation. That is not to say that facts and data are nonexistent, but that facts and data get their importance from what is made of them in interpretation. (Said, 1981: 154–156)

The act of interpretation underlies the entire research process. The act of interpretation is not something which occurs only at one specific point in the research after the data has been gathered; rather, interpretation exists at the beginning and continues throughout the entire process. What kind of data and facts you are able to gather will depend on the kind of questions you think are important to ask and the way in which you go about asking them. The research process is a social activity which is located in a specific historical and social context, and involves intentional activity.

Power is used to perpetuate and extend existing inequalities. Those in positions of power are able to decide what news is fit to print or air, and what parameters are available for interpreting such news. They decide what books get published, what research is funded, and what knowledge is legitimated. Information about people who live in the margins is limited and often distorted through this control.

Brenda T.: I use quotation marks around the word "welfare" because of the way the word is used by the media and other ignorant people to describe us. The word "welfare" when placed in front of "mother" taints our motherhood, makes us less than human, and less than deserving in the opinion of so many people.

The major institutions, such as the media, educational institutions, and government agencies, interpret and choose facts in such a way as to enable them to construct an image of the world that suits their needs. As a result, the facts and interpretations that exist in the public record are restricted and exclusive.

We want to demystify the research process and get the word out about the different kinds of knowledge and understanding that methods from the margins can begin to make publicly accessible.

Andrea was hired as a researcher, to study the funding needs of women's centres in Nova Scotia. She was given a research

focus which she did not think was the most appropriate for getting at the issues. After discussing this with Sandi, she found a way to change the focus so that it was better able to address the needs of the groups she was investigating while still meeting the goals of those who were funding the project.

During her visits to different communities, women talked with Andrea about the way she was doing the research and expressed interest in gaining access to similar research skills.

Demystifying the research process is the first step in decoding and demythologizing the way knowledge is created. It helps make research skills accessible to those who need them, and enables us to develop a better understanding of the actual social relations and practices that are broadly labelled ideology or culture (Smith, 1984).

We believe that researching from the margins is a necessary part of action for change. One student of women's studies wrote:

We have a common belief that there is a lie and that lie is about us. Our struggle is to realize this, to understand this and change this.

One of the characteristics of oppressed people is that they are often required to perform a kind of doublethink/doublespeak; lies are needed because the truth is not allowed. We believe that research from the margins is necessary in order to begin to share our truths and expose the hidden side of a society that only professes to be democratic and peaceful.

For example, Catherine used the research process as an opportunity to understand her own experience of childhood sexual abuse. At the end of her very personal research project she suggested the possibility of action.

I think I have to make room to turn this topic into action ... the data and myself are begging for such a release. I have a vague picture of myself working with other incest survivors doing research together to help heal ourselves.

* * * * *

Over and over again activists ask, "Where is the work that looks at how social change is brought about?" They point out that although

how-to-do-it manuals provide step-by-step guidelines for doing almost every human activity, from baking a cake and playing tennis to having a happy relationship and running a war ... there are no such model frameworks available to help activists understand and organize social movements. The lack of a practical how-to-do-it model framework has contributed to some of the most critical common problems of activists and their movements. (Moyer, 1986)

Maria Mies has suggested that "separation from praxis" is "one of the most important structural prerequisites" of the academic paradigm (1983: 124). What is particularly noteworthy is that while descriptions of the research process emphasize data gathering and analysis, rarely is there any discussion of responsibility to act on what is known. In fact, the opposite seems to be the case. Within the institutions of Western education we are trained as spectators or commentators, to absorb experience, not to act on it. This disdain for the practical, an academic paradigm that is particularly strong within the social sciences, has resulted in a kind of paralysis.

There has recently been a great deal of discussion about the political nature of knowledge creation. However, there has been little discussion about how these insights could be translated into actual research practices.

Doing research is a human activity. When we engage in research we involve ourselves

in a process in which we construct meaning. Because the social world is multifaceted (i.e., the same situation or experience is able to give us many different kinds of knowledge), when we "do research" we involve ourselves in a process of revealing "possible knowledges" (Morgan, 1983). What knowledge we are able to observe and reveal is directly related to our vantage point, to where we stand in the world. Our interaction with the social world is affected by such variables as gender, race, class, sexuality, age, physical ability, etc. This does not mean that facts about the social world do not exist, but that what we see and how we go about constructing meaning is a matter of interpretation.

For example: quantum physicists have shown, in relation to the study of light, that it is possible to look at light as either a wave or a particle, and that whether light is seen to behave as a wave or as a particle depends on the way it is studied. What is interesting is that if we think about light in the form of a wave we cannot see it in the form of particles. They are mutually exclusive views. "Hence in attempting to study light in one way the scientist precludes the possibility of knowing it in another" (Morgan, 1983: 389).

Researching from the margins accepts that:

1. knowledge is socially constructed;
2. social interactions form the basis of social knowledge;
3. different people experience the world differently;
4. because they have different experience people have different knowledge;
5. knowledge changes over time;
6. differences in power have resulted in the commodification of knowledge and a monopoly on knowledge production.

Research from the margins involves more than just learning and then using a set of mechanical skills. While some researchers may argue that research methodologies are like a set of tools from which you can pick and choose depending on the circumstances, we believe that different methodologies carry with them specific underlying assumptions which will shape the way information is gathered and the kind of knowledge created. Dorothy Smith has made an analogy that captures this well. She draws a comparison between those who work "within established methods of thinking and inquiry" and the driver of a car: "It is true that we can do the driving and can choose the direction and destination; but the way the car is put together, how it works, and how and where it will travel structures our relation to the world we travel in" (Smith, 1979: 158).

In the conclusion of their book *Making the Difference*, a report on research about educational inequality, Connell et al. stress the need for research to be "organized in a fundamentally different way—by and with the people it is ultimately supposed to benefit." While they acknowledge the very real constraints which hinder such a development (funding, professional commitments, information control), they go on to suggest:

... the goal of a different model of research is clear. It should empower the people who are normally just the objects of research, to develop their capacity to research their own situations and evolve their own solutions. It should embody a relationship where expertise is a resource available to all rather than a form of power for a few. (Connell et al., 1982: 216)

* * * * *

Part of what it means to do research from the margins is that as different people use the method they contribute to the way in which it is developed. We think of research from the margins as method in process; it is continually unfolding. [...]

The right to free expression of ideas and free access to information is a basic human right, and in principle it is available to all, though in practice only to the extent that one has the special privilege, power, training and facilities to exercise these rights in a meaningful way. (Chomsky, 1981: 139)

A [key] theme is that of the construction of knowledge as a political process. The fact that universities and research institutes are still largely the domain of white, middle and upper class males can be perceived as a clear manifestation of inequality. However, what may be less obvious is the way choice of research areas, research "rules of the road," and control of research methodology and funding help to construct and legitimate their power and maintain current social relations. The institutionalization of the research process has, in effect, put a monopoly on the creation of certain kinds of knowledge. Demystifying the research process is a way of challenging this monopoly.

It is important to be conscious, throughout the entire research process, of any potential threat the research could pose to the research participants or other marginalized people. Because of their vulnerability and the real possibilities that research information could be used against them, researchers like Susan George argue that research concerned with social change should focus on the rich and powerful and not on those on the margins. She says: "Let the poor study themselves. They already know what is wrong with their lives and if you truly want to help them, the best you can do is give them an idea of how their oppressors are working now and can be expected to work in the future" (1976: 289).

While we agree that research on the rich and powerful is essential, we argue that subordinate groups have been structurally blocked from the process of selecting, naming, disseminating, and evaluating knowledge. Knowledge production "reflects both the distribution of power and the principles of social control" (Bernstein, quoted in Spender, 1981: 3); this process helps to construct and perpetuate current power relations. Researching from the margins is a resource for the oppressed to study themselves. By beginning with the experience and research needs of those who have been silenced, the process of knowledge production is transformed and the ideological power base is challenged.

It has been our experience that people on the margins often know something is wrong, but their concerns are interpreted as a personal problem or failing rather than as a public issue. The method of researching from the margins involves two interrelated processes which connect the personal and political.

First, research from the margins requires intersubjectivity: an authentic dialogue between all participants in the research process in which all are respected as equally knowing subjects. And second, it requires critical reflection. Critical reflection involves an examination of people's social reality, for as Freire has pointed out, this is "the real, concrete context of facts" (1985: 51).

Research from the margins is not research *on* people from the margins, but research *by*, *for*, and *with* them. Research from the perspective of the margins will often focus on the oppressors. This can be particularly useful work for those who do not share the experience, but want to act in solidarity with a specific group on the margins. If you undertake such a project, we would stress that it is essential to collaborate with those people on the margins who may benefit from or who may be affected by your research. The insights and direction they can give are invaluable.

* * * * *

NOTE

1. For more information on the New World Information Order, see "The Politics of Information," CBC-Radio *Ideas*, May 1983.

REFERENCES

Bee, Barbara. 1980. "The Politics of Literacy." In *Literacy and Revolution*, edited by R. Mackie. London: Pluto Press.

CBC. 1983. "The Politics of Information," *Ideas* (May). Toronto: CBC Radio.

Chomsky, Noam. 1981. *Radical Priorities*. Montreal: Black Rose Books.

Connell, R.W., D.J. Ashenden, S. Kessler, and G.W. Dowsett. 1982. *Making the Difference*. Sydney: George Allen & Unwin.

Darville, Richard. Forthcoming. "The Language of Experience and the Literacy of Power." In *Adult Basic Education: A Field of Practice*, edited by J. Draper and M. Taylor. Culture Concepts Inc.

Freire, Paulo. 1985. *The Politics of Education*. South Hadley: Bergin and Garvey Publishers.

George, Susan. 1976. *How the Other Half Dies*. New York: Penguin Books.

Mies, Maria. 1983. "Towards a Methodology for Feminist Research." In *Theories of Women's Studies*, edited by G. Bowles and R. Duelli Klein. London: Routledge & Kegan Paul.

Morgan, Gareth. 1983. *Beyond Method*. Beverly Hills, Calif.: Sage Publications.

Moyer, Bill. 1986. "The Movement Action Plan." *The Dandelion* (Fall).

Said, Edward W. 1981. *Covering Islam: How the Media and the Experts Determine How We See the Rest of the World*. New York: Pantheon Books.

Smith, Dorothy. 1979. "A Sociology for Women." In *The Prism of Sex: Essays in Sociology of Knowledge*, edited by Julia Sherman and Evelyn T. Beck. Madison: University of Wisconsin Press.

———. 1984. "Textually Mediated Social Organization." *International Social Science Journal*, 36(1): 59–75.

Spender, Dale. 1981. *Men's Studies Modified*. Oxford: Pergamon Press.

Stanley, Liz, and Sue Wise. 1983. *Breaking Out: Feminist Consciousness and Feminist Research*. London: Routledge & Kegan Paul.

Weinstein, Gail. 1984. "Literacy and Second Language Acquisition: Issues and Perspectives." *TESOL Quarterly*, 18(3): 471–484.

CHAPTER 6
Twenty-Five Indigenous Projects

LINDA TUHIWAI SMITH

The implications for indigenous research which have been derived from the imperatives inside the struggles of the 1970s seem to be clear and straightforward: the survival of peoples, cultures, and languages; the struggle to become self-determining, the need to take back control of our destinies. These imperatives have demanded more than rhetoric and acts of defiance. The acts of reclaiming, reformulating, and reconstituting indigenous cultures and languages have required the mounting of an ambitious research programme, one that is very strategic in its purpose and activities and relentless in its pursuit of social justice. Within the programme are a number of very distinct projects. Themes such as cultural survival, self-determination, healing, restoration, and social justice are engaging indigenous researchers and indigenous communities in a diverse array of projects. The projects intersect with each other in various ways. They have multiple goals and involve different indigenous communities of interest. Some projects, for example, have been driven by indigenous lawyers and constitutional experts, others by indigenous women and health workers, or by social workers and policy analysts. This chapter sets out 25 different projects currently being pursued by indigenous communities. The projects constitute a very complex research programme. [...] Each project is outlined to give a bare indication of the parameters offered

within it and how these may link in with some of the others.

The projects are not claimed to be entirely indigenous or to have been created by indigenous researchers. Some approaches have arisen out of social science methodologies, which in turn have arisen out of methodological issues raised by research with various oppressed groups. Some projects invite multidisciplinary research approaches. Others have arisen more directly out of indigenous practices. There are two technical points to make here. First, while most projects fall well within what will be recognized as empirical research, not all do. Some important work is related to theorizing indigenous issues at the level of ideas, policy analysis, and critical debate, and to setting out in writing indigenous spiritual beliefs and world views. Second, the focus is primarily on social science research projects rather than what may be happening in the natural or physical sciences or technology. There is one technical distinction to clarify. In the chapter I draw on Sandra Harding's very simple distinction between methodology and method, that is, "A research methodology is a theory and analysis of how research does or should proceed ..." and, "A research method is a technique for (or way of proceeding in) gathering evidence."[1] Methodology is important because it frames the questions being asked, determines the set of instruments and methods to be employed, and shapes the analyses. Within an indigenous framework, methodological debates are ones concerned with the broader politics and strategic goals of indigenous research. It is at this level that researchers have to clarify and justify their intentions. Methods become the means and procedures through which the central problems of the research are addressed. Indigenous methodologies are often a mix of existing methodological approaches and indigenous practices. The mix reflects the training of indigenous researchers which continues to be within the academy, and the parameters and common sense understandings of research which govern how indigenous communities and researchers define their activities.

THE PROJECTS

The following projects are not ranked or listed in any particular order.

1. Claiming

In a sense colonialism has reduced indigenous peoples to making claims and assertions about our rights and dues. It is an approach that has a certain noisiness to it. Indigenous peoples, however, have transformed claiming into an interesting and dynamic process. Considerable work and energy has gone into developing the methodologies which relate to "claiming" and "reclaiming." For some indigenous groups the formal claims process demanded by tribunals, courts, and governments has required the conducting of intensive research projects resulting in the writing of nation, tribe and family histories. These "histories" have a focus and purpose, that is, to establish the legitimacy of the claims being asserted for the rest of time. Because they have been written to support claims to territories and resources or about past injustices, they have been constructed around selected stories. These claiming histories have also been written for different audiences. One audience is the formal court or tribunal

audience, who are generally non-indigenous, another the general non-indigenous population, and a third the people themselves. For this last audience the histories are also important teaching histories. They teach both the non-indigenous audience and the new generations of indigenous peoples an official account of their collective story. But, importantly, it is a history which has no ending because it assumes that once justice has been done the people will continue their journey. It may be that in time the histories have to be rewritten around other priorities.

2. Testimonies

> "My Name is Rigoberta Menchu, I am twenty-three years old, and this is my testimony."[2]

Testimonies intersect with claiming because they are a means through which oral evidence is presented to a particular type of audience. There is a formality to testimonies and a notion that truth is being revealed "under oath." Indigenous testimonies are a way of talking about an extremely painful event or series of events.[3] The formality of testimony provides a structure within which events can be related and feelings expressed.[4] A testimony is also a form through which the voice of a "witness" is accorded space and protection. It can be constructed as a monologue and as a public performance. The structure of testimony—its formality, context, and sense of immediacy appeals to many indigenous participants, particularly elders. It is an approach that translates well to a formal written document. While the listener may ask questions, testimonies structure the responses, silencing certain types of questions and formalizing others.

3. Story Telling

Story telling, oral histories, the perspectives of elders and of women have become an integral part of all indigenous research. Each individual story is powerful. But the point about the stories is not that they simply tell a story, or tell a story simply. These new stories contribute to a collective story in which every indigenous person has a place. In a book called *The Wailing: A National Black Oral History*, Stuart Rintoul has called the oral histories he gathered "stories handed down in the homes of Black Australians, told to new generations, taught in explanation of racism and mistreatment, recited with rage and dignity and sorrow."[5] Rintoul writes further that the stories are also "memories of injustice ... an avalanche of voices crying out in hundreds of countries across innumerable Dreamings."[6] For many indigenous writers stories are ways of passing down the beliefs and values of a culture in the hope that the new generations will treasure them and pass the story down further. The story and the story teller both serve to connect the past with the future, one generation with the other, the land with the people, and the people with the story. As a research tool, Russell Bishop suggests, story telling is a useful and culturally appropriate way of representing the "diversities of truth" within which the story teller rather than the researcher retains control.[7] Bishop also suggests that "the indigenous community becomes a story that is a collection of individual stories, ever unfolding through the lives of the people who share the life of that community."[8]

Intrinsic in story telling is a focus on dialogue and conversations amongst ourselves as indigenous peoples, to ourselves and for ourselves. Such approaches fit well with the oral traditions which are still a reality in day-to-day indigenous lives. Importantly, story telling is also about humour and gossip and creativity. Stories tell of love and sexual encounters, of war and revenge. Their themes tell us about our cultures. Stories employ familiar characters and motifs which can reassure as well as challenge. Familiar characters can be invested

with the qualities of an individual or can be used to invoke a set of shared understandings and histories.

4. Celebrating Survival

Celebrating survival is a particular sort of approach. While non-indigenous research has been intent on documenting the demise and cultural assimilation of indigenous peoples, celebrating survival accentuates not so much our demise but the degree to which indigenous peoples and communities have successfully retained cultural and spiritual values and authenticity. The approach is reflected sometimes in story form, sometimes in popular music, and sometimes as an event in which artists and story tellers come together to celebrate collectively a sense of life and diversity and connectedness. Events and accounts which focus on the positive are important not just because they speak to our survival, but because they celebrate our resistances at an ordinary human level and they affirm our identities as indigenous women and men. Celebrating survival as an approach is also a theme running through the collections of elders' stories. In one such collection told to Sandy Johnson she writes of the way in which "[the elders] speak openly of their personal struggles to stay on the path against impossible odds. Their stories of what they have lost and what they have fought to save are both tragic and heroic."[9] Gregory Cajete writes that "celebrating is a natural outcome of spiritual sharing and it too can take a diversity of forms. It is an individual and communal process that celebrates the mystery of life and the journey that each of us takes. Celebration is a way of spreading the lights around."[10]

5. Remembering

The remembering of a people relates not so much to an idealized remembering of a golden past but more specifically to the remembering of a painful past and, importantly, people's responses to that pain. While collectively indigenous communities can talk through the history of painful events, there are frequent silences and intervals in the stories about what happened after the event. Often there is no collective remembering as communities were systematically ripped apart, children were removed for adoption, extended families separated across different reserves and national boundaries. The aftermath of such pain was borne by individuals or smaller family units, sometimes unconsciously or consciously obliterated through alcohol, violence, and self-destruction. Communities often turned inward and let their suffering give way to a desire to be dead. Violence and family abuse became entrenched in communities which had no hope. White society did not see and did not care. This form of remembering is painful because it involves remembering not just what colonization was about but what being dehumanized meant for our own cultural practices. Both healing and transformation become crucial strategies in any approach which asks a community to remember what they may have decided unconsciously or consciously to forget.

6. Indigenizing

This project has two dimensions. The first one is similar to that which has occurred in literature with a centering of the landscapes, images, languages, themes, metaphors, and stories in the indigenous world and the disconnecting of many of the cultural ties between the settler society and its metropolitan homeland. This project involves non-indigenous activists and intellectuals. The second aspect is more of an indigenous project. The term is used more frequently in South and Central America. The concept of indigenist, says Ward Churchill, means "that I am one who not only takes the rights of indigenous peoples as the highest priority of my political life, but who draws upon the traditions—the bodies of knowledge and corresponding codes

of values—evolved over many thousands of years by native peoples the world over."[11] The term centres a politics of indigenous identity and indigenous cultural action. M. Annette Jaimes refers to indigenism as being grounded in the alternative conceptions of world view and value systems. "These differences provide a basis for a conceptualisation of Indigenism that counters the negative connotations of its meanings in third world countries, where it has become synonymous with the 'primitive,' or with backwardness among superstitious peoples."[12] Lester Rigney, an Aborigine researcher in New South Wales, names the approach he takes as indigenist research, an approach which borrows freely from feminist research and critical approaches to research, but privileges indigenous voices.

7. Intervening

Intervening takes action research to mean literally the process of being proactive and of becoming involved as an interested worker for change. Intervention-based projects are usually designed around making structural and cultural changes. Graham Smith describes this approach as a necessary approach when faced with crisis conditions. Smith argues

firstly, that Maori educational crises continue—this points to a failure of educational policy reforms, research and researchers. Secondly, educational researchers have continued to fail to intervene because of the lack of responsibility and accountability placed on researchers and policy makers. Thirdly much of research has been counter productive to Maori interests, and has merely served the dominant Pakeha group interests, by maintaining the status quo of unequal power distribution.[13]

It is not ethical to walk away, or simply to carry out projects which describe what is already known. State policies for indigenous peoples were also interventionist in profoundly destructive ways. The indigenous intervening project carries with it some working principles. For example, the community itself invites the project in and sets out its parameters. The various departments and agencies involved in such a project are also expected to be willing to change themselves in some way, redirect policy, design new programmes, or train staff differently. Intervening is directed then at changing institutions which deal with indigenous peoples and not at changing indigenous peoples to fit the structures.

8. Revitalizing

Indigenous languages, their arts, and their cultural practices are in various states of crisis. Many indigenous languages are officially "dead" with fewer than a hundred speakers. Others are in the last stages before what is described by linguists as "language death." Revitalization initiatives in languages encompass education, broadcasting, publishing, and community-based programmes. While the Welsh people are not formally part of the indigenous peoples' movements, their programmes are often studied as examples of indigenous achievement. The Welsh language programme is promoted as a model for language revitalization. Welsh schools, from kindergarten to secondary schools, offer teaching through the medium of Welsh. This is supported officially through government funding. Television and newspapers in the medium of Welsh—which include children's programming, drama, documentaries, news, and sports—provide a comprehensive approach to language revitalization. The European Bureau of Lesser Languages has a role of supporting the diverse minority languages of Europe. Maori language development has followed a similar pattern to the Welsh language example, with an official Language Act and associated educational programmes. In the case of Maori

and Welsh language, there is a clear singular language. Many places have to battle for the survival of several languages spoken by small populations. In Canada, for example, most of the indigenous languages could be categorized as being on the verge of extinction. British Columbia has a diverse range of indigenous languages, all of which require support. The Squamish language, for example, has few native speakers. The Squamish Nation helped co-host a conference on indigenous languages in 1989 in order to stimulate discussions and seek solutions to the language crisis. Their Nation's Band Office has an education centre whose staff develop resources for schools and encourage the use of the language by their remaining native speakers. For much of the indigenous world there is little proactive coordination or support. Literacy campaigns tend to frame language survival programmes. Such campaigns are designed around either official languages or one or two dominant languages. The indigenous language is often regarded as being subversive to national interests and national literacy campaigns.

9. Connecting

The importance of making connections and affirming connectedness has been noted also by other minority group researchers. Connectedness positions individuals in sets of relationships with other people and with the environment. Many indigenous creation stories link people through genealogy to the land, to stars and other places in the universe, to birds and fish, animals, insects, and plants. To be connected is to be whole. The project of connecting is pursued in New South Wales in one form as literally connecting members of families with each other. A link programme has been designed to restore the descendants of "stolen children," ones forcibly taken from their families and adopted, to their family connections. Forced adoption and dehumanizing child welfare practices were carried out in many indigenous contexts. Being reconnected to their families and their culture has been a painful journey for many of these children, now adults. Connecting also involves connecting people to their traditional lands through the restoration of specific rituals and practices. In New Zealand one example of this is the practice of burying the afterbirth in the land. The word for afterbirth is the same as the word for land, *whenua*. The practice was prohibited as Maori mothers were forced to have their babies in hospitals rather than at home. The policies and hospital practices have now changed and Maori parents have reinstituted the practice of taking the afterbirth and burying it in traditional territory. Connecting children to their land and their genealogies through this process is also part of a larger health project designed to encourage young Maori mothers to take better care of themselves and their babies through stronger cultural supports. Connecting is related to issues of identity and place, to spiritual relationships and community well-being.

There are other challenges in relation to the project of connecting. Researchers, policy makers, educators, and social service providers who work with or whose work impacts on indigenous communities need to have a critical conscience about ensuring that their activities connect in humanizing ways with indigenous communities. It is a very common experience to hear indigenous communities outline the multiple ways in which agencies and individuals treat them with disrespect and disregard. Connecting is about establishing good relations.

10. Reading

Critical rereading of Western history and the indigenous presence in the making of that history has taken on a different impetus from what was once a school curriculum designed to assimilate indigenous children. The new reading programme is motivated partly by

a research drive to establish and support claims, but also by a need to understand what has informed both internal colonialism and new forms of colonization. The genealogy of colonialism is being mapped and used as a way to locate a different sort of origin story, the origins of imperial policies and practices, the origins of the imperial visions, the origins of ideas and values. These origin stories are deconstructed accounts of the West, its history through the eyes of indigenous and colonized peoples. The rereading of imperial history by post-colonial and cultural studies scholars provides a different, much more critical approach to history than was previously acceptable. It is no longer the single narrative story of important white imperial figures, adventurers, and heroes who fought their way through undiscovered lands to establish imperial rule and bring civilization and salvation to "barbaric savages" who lived in "utter degradation."

11. Writing

Indigenous people are writing. [...] Maori author Witi Ihimaera has assembled a five-volume anthology of Maori literature which he argues represents the "crossroads ... of a literature of a past and a literature of a present and future."[14] The title of an anthology of Native Women's writings of North America, *Reinventing the Enemy's Language*, gives a sense of the issues being explored through writing.[15] Similar anthologies and works of indigenous literature are being published around the world by indigenous writers for indigenous reading audiences.[16] The boundaries of poetry, plays, song writing, fiction, and non-fiction are blurred as indigenous writers seek to use language in ways which capture the messages, nuances, and flavour of indigenous lives. The activity of writing has produced the related activity of publishing. Maori newspapers, which were quite common in the nineteenth century, have been revived as different organizations and tribes seek to provide better information than is available in the mainstream media. Language revitalization initiatives have created a demand for multi-media language resources for children. In the Western Isles of Scotland, a Stornaway publishing house called Acair has produced children's comic books in Scottish Gaelic and cookbooks and other material which support the Gaelic language. Similar small publishing groups are operating across the indigenous world. Writing workshops and writing courses offered by indigenous writers for indigenous people who want to write are held in many places. The work of authors such as Patricia Grace, Paula Gunn Allen, Louise Erdrich, Witi Ihimaera, and Sally Morgan is read by both indigenous and non-indigenous audiences. Biographies and autobiographies including those which are accounts "told to a non-indigenous person," are sought after by a new reading audience of indigenous people.

12. Representing

Indigenous communities have struggled since colonization to be able to exercise what is viewed as a fundamental right, that is to represent ourselves. The representing project spans both the notion of representation as a political concept and representation as a form of voice and expression. In the political sense colonialism specifically excluded indigenous peoples from any form of decision making. States and governments have long made decisions hostile to the interests of indigenous communities but justified by a paternalistic view that indigenous peoples were like children who needed others to protect them and decide what was in their best interests. Paternalism is still present in many forms in the way governments, local bodies, and non-government agencies decide on issues which have an impact on indigenous communities. Being able as a minimum right to voice the views and opinions of indigenous communities

in various decision-making bodies is still being struggled over. Even at the minimal level of representation indigenous communities are often "thrown in" with all other minorities as one voice amongst many. The politics of sovereignty and self-determination have been about resisting being thrown in with every other minority group by making claims on the basis of prior rights.

Representation is also a project of indigenous artists, writers, poets, film makers, and others who attempt to express an indigenous spirit, experience or world view. Representation of indigenous peoples by indigenous people is about countering the dominant society's image of indigenous peoples, their lifestyles, and belief systems. It is also about proposing solutions to the real-life dilemmas that indigenous communities confront and trying to capture the complexities of being indigenous. Many of the dilemmas are internalized stress factors in community life which are never named or voiced because they are either taken for granted or hidden by a community. There is an element of the raw, tough, and unsympathetic representation of indigenous life by a writer such as Allen Duff who wrote the novel *Once Were Warriors*. And there is the humour of Alexie Sherman who wrote *Reservation Blues*. Film makers such as Merata Mita have a very clear purpose in their work which locates it firmly within a decolonization framework. She says that,

> Not surprisingly, when my obsessive struggle with filmmaking began, it was with the issues that most concerned us as Maori women that I became pre-occupied—the issues of injustice, land, te reo Maori [Maori language], the Treaty, and racism. Add to that women and gender issues, and for those who don't know, these are the things that consume us, consume our energy, beset us every moment of our daily lives, they are brutalising, violent, and some of us die because of them.[17]

13. Gendering

Gendering indigenous debates, whether they are related to the politics of self-determination or the politics of the family, is concerned with issues related to the relations between indigenous men and women. Colonization is recognized as having had a destructive effect on indigenous gender relations which reached out across all spheres of indigenous society. Family organization, child rearing, political and spiritual life, work, and social activities were all disordered by a colonial system which positioned its own women as the property of men with roles which were primarily domestic. Indigenous women across many different indigenous societies claim an entirely different relationship, one embedded in beliefs about the land and the universe, about the spiritual significance of women, and about the collective endeavours that were required in the organization of society. Indigenous women would argue that their traditional roles included full participation in many aspects of political decision making and marked gender separations which were complementary in order to maintain harmony and stability. Gendering contemporary indigenous debates occurs inside indigenous communities and while it is debated in other contexts, such as in Western feminist debates, indigenous women hold an analysis of colonialism as a central tenet of an indigenous feminism. A key issue for indigenous women in any challenge of contemporary indigenous politics is the restoration to women of what are seen as their traditional roles, rights, and responsibilities. Aroha Mead gives an account of a statement delivered by two Maori women to the Twelfth Session (1994) of the United Nations Working Group on Indigenous Peoples which addressed the way colonialism has influenced indigenous men and had a detrimental affect on indigenous gender relations. She says that

never before have I witnessed what occurred while the full statement was being read out. Indigenous women sitting within their delegations were visibly moved—some looked around to see who was talking about their pain—some gave victory signals and physical signs of agreement, and many, perhaps even the majority, sat stoically, with tears swelling in their eyes. The words broke through the barriers of language and regionalism. A raw wound was clearly touched.[18]

14. Envisioning

One of the strategies which indigenous peoples have employed effectively to bind people together politically is a strategy which asks that people imagine a future, that they rise above present day situations which are generally depressing, dream a new dream, and set a new vision. The confidence of knowing that we have survived and can only go forward provides some impetus to a process of envisioning. In New Zealand, for example, tribes which began their grievance claims against the Crown last century have not only had their claims heard but are negotiating a settlement. For the people who began the process these settlements were simply dreams. If they had listened to politicians, taken the mainstream media seriously, taken heed of scholars and commentators, they would not have begun. Similarly, communities who have worked to revitalise their language or build a new economic base or renegotiate arrangements with governments have worked on the basis of a shared vision. The power of indigenous peoples to change their own lives and set new directions despite their impoverished and oppressed conditions speaks to the politics of resistance.

Sometimes the visions which bind people were set a long time ago and have been passed down the generations as poems, songs, stories, proverbs, or sayings. Every indigenous community probably has special sayings, predictions, riddles, and proverbs which are debated frequently and raised both informally and formally. Children are socialized into these sayings and pass them down to their own children. The profound statements of indigenous leaders from the last century and the centuries before are often written in diaries and notebooks, carved into stone, distributed by T-shirt and poster. Often the original source of the comment has been forgotten but the power of the words remain. They make our spirits soar and give us hope. Indigenous people have borrowed freely from each other and it is not uncommon to find the saying of an Indian chief stuck to the kitchen wall in a Maori home, or the saying of a Maori chief embroidered into a wall hanging in an Aborigine home. These sayings have acted like resistance codes which can be passed down by word of mouth to the next person, to the next generation.

15. Reframing

Reframing is about taking much greater control over the ways in which indigenous issues and social problems are discussed and handled. One of the reasons why so many of the social problems which beset indigenous communities are never solved is that the issues have been framed in a particular way. For example, governments and social agencies have failed to see many indigenous social problems as being related to any sort of history. They have framed indigenous issues in "the indigenous problem" basket, to be handled in the usual cynical and paternalistic manner. The framing of an issue is about making decisions about its parameters, about what is in the foreground, what is in the background, and what shadings or complexities exist within the frame. The project of reframing is related to defining the problem or issue and determining how best to solve that problem. Many indigenous activists have argued that such things as mental illness,

alcoholism, and suicide, for example, are not about psychological and individualized failure but about colonization or lack of collective self-determination. Many community health initiatives address the whole community, its history, and its wider context as part of the problem and part of the solution.

Reframing occurs in other contexts where indigenous people resist being boxed and labelled according to categories which do not fit. This is particularly pertinent in relation to various development programmes, government and non-government. In the case of Maori, for example, a Maori language initiative for young children from birth to school age—known as Te Kohanga Reo, or Maori language nests—constantly has to explain why it is not a child-care centre but a language and culture initiative for young children. The problem of definition is important in this case because it affects funding, but the constant need to justify difference is experienced by many other communities whose initiatives are about changing things on a holistic basis rather than endorsing the individualized programme emphasis of government models. The need to reframe is about retaining the strengths of a vision and the participation of a whole community.

Reframing occurs also within the way indigenous people write or engage with theories and accounts of what it means to be indigenous. In the politics of indigenous women, for example, there is continuing resistance to the way Western feminists have attempted to define the issues for indigenous women and categorize the positions in which indigenous women should be located. Moves to discuss patriarchy without addressing imperialism and racism are always reframed by indigenous women, and of course other minority women, as inadequate analyses. Similarly moves to attack indigenous culture or indigenous men "as a group" are also resisted because for indigenous women the issues are far more complex and the objective of analysis is always focused on solving problems. In the end indigenous men and women have to live together in a world in which both genders are under attack.

16. Restoring

Indigenous peoples across the world have disproportionately high rates of imprisonment, suicide, and alcoholism. Some indigenous activists regard these rates as the continuation of a war. Says Bobbi Sykes, "The main question, which has not been addressed by government, is the legitimacy or otherwise of the assumption that white domination of Aboriginal people is in itself a concept of justice."[19] For Aborigines the high rates of black deaths in custody eventually provoked the establishment of a Royal Commission of Inquiry in 1987 into a problem which had been hidden for many years. The Aborigine rates of death in custody was said to be higher than the rate in South Africa. Inside the incarceration rates for indigenous peoples are similar rates for youth offending and for indigenous women. In the health arena indigenous people have high rates of morbidity and mortality. Maori women have one of the highest rates of lung cancer in the world. Maori suicide rates, both male and female, have risen sharply over the last decade, with New Zealand rates amongst the highest in OECD countries. Aborigine rates of illness have frequently been cited as examples of the Fourth World, rates, which are worse than the rates in developing Third World states, and are made more horrific by the fact that these communities live in nations that have the highest standards of living. At a recent gathering of Pacific leaders, for example, the Australian Prime Minister John Howard was reported to have been reluctant to agree on helping to counter the effects of global warming, citing his duty to put the standard of living of Australians first. He was not talking about indigenous Australians.

The restoring of well-being spiritually, emotionally, physically, and materially has involved social workers and health workers in a range of initiatives, some of which have been incorporated into mainstream programmes. Restorative justice in Canada, for example, applies concepts of the "healing circle" and victim restoration which are based on indigenous processes. These systems have been discussed widely and used to motivate other societies to develop better ways of dealing with offenders and victims. In New Zealand adoption policies and programmes for dealing with children have similarly co-opted indigenous practices. Restoring is a project which is conceived as a holistic approach to problem solving. It is holistic in terms of the emotional, spiritual, and physical nexus, and also in terms of the individual and the collective, the political, and the cultural. Restorative programmes are based on a model of healing rather than of punishing. They sometimes employ concepts such as public shaming as a way of provoking individual accountability and collective problem solving. Health programmes addressing basic health issues have begun to seek ways to connect with indigenous communities through appropriate public health policy and practice models. The failure of public health programmes to improve the health of indigenous communities significantly has motivated a self-help approach by communities. It is especially infuriating when projects such as the Human Genome Project are justified on the grounds that knowledge about genetic resistances to various diseases will "benefit mankind" when Western health has failed to benefit indigenous human beings.

17. Returning

This project intersects with that of claiming. It involves the returning of lands, rivers, and mountains to their indigenous owners. It involves the repatriation of artefacts, remains, and other cultural materials stolen or removed and taken overseas. Sykes lists the following examples: "pickled heads, human gloves, scrotum tobacco pouches, dried scalps, pickled foetus, cicatured skins, complete stuffed, mummified children's bodies and women with child."[20] In New Zealand the current Minister of Maori Affairs, who is a Maori, has set out a plan to return all tattooed Maori heads which are housed in museums and other collections across the world. They apparently number in the hundreds.

Returning also involves the living. One major tribe in New Zealand has negotiated the return of traditional food gathering sites which will be marked out for their exclusive use by tribal members. Other programmes have been initiated to repatriate people either through ensuring their membership in official tribal registers or by physically reclaiming them. Adopted children, for example, are encouraged to seek their birth families and return to their original communities.

18. Democratizing

Although indigenous communities claim a model of democracy in their traditional ways of decision making, many contemporary indigenous organizations were formed through the direct involvement of states and governments. Legislation was used to establish and regulate indigenous councils and committees, indigenous forms of representation, and indigenous titles to lands. They are colonial constructions that have been taken for granted as authentic indigenous formations. Furthermore many such councils, because they were established through colonialism, have privileged particular families and elite groups over other indigenous families from the same communities. Needless to say, many councils were created as exclusively male domains while the health and welfare programmes were assigned to the women. Maori lawyer Annette Sykes argues, for example, in relation

to a claim being made by Maori women to the Waitangi Tribunal, that

> The essence of the claim is to bring to the forefront of the current Treaty jurisprudence, the need to look at notions of governance in Aotearoa and the exclusionary practices that exist, which inhibit and prevent participation by Maori women in the tribal models for self-determination, that have been erected under New Zealand legislation, and the erosion that this in itself has had on Te Mana Wahine in Te Ao Maori [the mana of women in the Maori World].[21]

Democratizing in indigenous terms is a process of extending participation outwards through reinstating indigenous principles of collectivity and public debate.

19. Networking

Networking has become an efficient medium for stimulating information flows, educating people quickly about issues, and creating extensive international talking circles. Building networks is about building knowledge and data bases which are based on the principles of relationships and connections. Relationships are initiated on a face to face basis and then maintained over many years often without any direct contact. People's names are passed on and introductions are used to bring new members into the network. The face to face encounter is about checking out an individual's credentials, not just their political credentials but their personalities and spirit. Networking by indigenous peoples is a form of resistance. People are expected to position themselves clearly and state their purposes. Establishing trust is an important feature. In many states police surveillance of indigenous activists and their families is common practice. In some states, such as Guatemala, the disappearance of indigenous peoples has also been common practice. In these contexts networking is dangerous.

Networking is a way of making contacts between marginalized communities. By definition their marginalization excludes them from participation in the activities of the dominant non-indigenous society, which controls most forms of communication. Issues such as the Conventions on Biodiversity or GATT, for example, which have a direct impact on indigenous communities, are not addressed by mainstream media for an indigenous audience. Indigenous peoples would not know of such agreements and their impact on indigenous cultural knowledge if it were not for the power of networking. The project of networking is about process. Networking is a process which indigenous peoples have used effectively to build relationships and disseminate knowledge and information.

20. Naming

This project takes its name from Brazilian educator Paulo Freire whose saying, "name the word, name the world" (which was about literacy programmes), has been applied in the indigenous context to literally rename the landscape. This means renaming the world using the original indigenous names. Naming as a project of Maori people can be seen in the struggles over the geographical names of some of New Zealand's mountains and significant sites which were renamed randomly after British people and places. Many of the Maori names have now been restored. Naming can also be seen in the naming of children. Indigenous names carried histories of people, places, and events. As a result of Christian baptism practices, which introduced Christian names and family names, and schooling practices, where teachers shortened names or introduced either generic names or nicknames, many indigenous communities hid their indigenous names either by using them only in indigenous ceremonies or by positioning

them as second names. A more recent assertion in Maori naming practices has been to name children again with long ancestral names and to take on new names through life, both of which were once traditional practices. Children quite literally wear their history in their names.

Naming applies to other things as well. It is about retaining as much control over meanings as possible. By "naming the world" people name their realities. For communities there are realities which can only be found in the indigenous language; the concepts which are self-evident in the indigenous language can never be captured by another language.

21. Protecting

This project is multifaceted. It is concerned with protecting peoples, communities, languages, customs and beliefs, art and ideas, natural resources, and the things indigenous peoples produce. The scale of protecting can be as enormous as the Pacific Ocean and the Amazon rainforest or as small as an infant. It can be as real as land and as abstract as a belief about the spiritual essence of the land. Every indigenous community is attempting to protect several different things simultaneously. In some areas alliances with non-indigenous organizations have been beneficial in terms of rallying international support. In other areas a community is trying to protect itself by staying alive or staying off alcohol.

Some countries have identified sacred sites and have designated protected areas. Many of these, unfortunately, become tourist spots. Issues about the protection of indigenous knowledge have been discussed at various indigenous conferences which have produced charters and conventions aimed at signalling to the world at large that indigenous knowledges ought to be protected. History seems to suggest that many of these calls for international adherence to such charters will be at best highly selective. The need to protect a way of life, a language, and the right to make our own history is a deep need linked to the survival of indigenous peoples.

22. Creating

The project of creating is about transcending the basic survival mode through using a resource or capability which every indigenous community has retained throughout colonization—the ability to create and be creative. The project of creating is not just about the artistic endeavours of individuals but about the spirit of creating which indigenous communities have exercised over thousands of years. Imagination enables people to rise above their own circumstances, to dream new visions, and to hold on to old ones. It fosters inventions and discoveries, facilitates simple improvements to people's lives, and uplifts our spirits. Creating is not the exclusive domain of the rich nor of the technologically superior, but of the imaginative. Creating is about channelling collective creativity in order to produce solutions to indigenous problems. Every indigenous community has considered and come up with various innovative solutions to problems. That was before colonialism. Throughout the period of colonization indigenous peoples survived because of their imaginative spirit, their ability to adapt, and to think around a problem.

Indigenous communities also have something to offer the non-indigenous world. There are many programmes incorporating indigenous elements, which on that account are viewed on the international scene as "innovative" and unique. Indigenous peoples' ideas and beliefs about the origins of the world, their explanations of the environment, often embedded in complicated metaphors and mythic tales, are now being sought as the basis for thinking more laterally about current theories about the environment, the earth, and the universe.

Communities are the ones who know the answers to their own problems, although their ideas tend to be dismissed when suggested to various agencies and governments. Visits to communities which have developed their own programmes demonstrate both the creativity alive and well at the community level and the strength of commitment shown when the programme is owned by the community.

23. Negotiating

Negotiating is about thinking and acting strategically. It is about recognizing and working towards long-term goals. Patience is a quality which indigenous communities have possessed in abundance. Patience and negotiation are linked to a very long view of our survival. When one reads of the decisions made by various indigenous leaders to accept the terms and conditions of colonization, what emerges from those stories is the concern shown by leaders for the long-term survival chances of the collective, of their own people. That was the basis of their courage and, despite the outrage younger generations of indigenous people might feel about the deal which some leaders accepted, the broader picture across several indigenous contexts is one of dignity and acceptance of a specific reality. Their negotiations were undertaken quite literally with guns held at their heads, with their people starving and with death around them.

In today's environment negotiation is still about deal making and it is still about concepts of leadership. Negotiations are also about respect, self-respect, and respect for the opposition. Indigenous rules of negotiation usually contain both rituals of respect and protocols for discussion. The protocols and procedures are integral to the actual negotiation and neglect or failure to acknowledge or take seriously such protocols can be read as a lack of commitment to both the process and the outcome. Many indigenous societies are socialized into some forms of negotiation because they are part of trading practices or basic communication styles. The contemporary negotiation project is related to self-determination, in that indigenous nations are negotiating terms for settlements, which often mean semi-autonomous government or statutory representation or control over key resources, such as natural resources within their own territories. Negotiation also occurs where small gains are at stake, however, such as when local communities have worked out an agreement with a local government or agency or another local community. The formality of negotiation is important in protecting the sanctity of the agreement which emerges from a negotiation. Indigenous peoples know and understand what it means for agreements to be dishonoured. The continued faith in the process of negotiating is about retaining a faith in the humanity of indigenous beliefs, values, and customary practices.

24. Discovering

This project is about discovering Western science and technology and making science work for indigenous development. There are very few indigenous scientists who remain closely connected to their own indigenous communities. Indigenous students across many contexts have struggled with Western science as it has been taught to them in schools. Science has been traditionally hostile to indigenous ways of knowing. Science teaching in schools has also been fraught with hostile attitudes towards indigenous cultures, and the way indigenous students learn. There are huge debates within the scientific community about the nature of science and how it ought to be taught. This debate is over the notion of constructivism, and concerns the extent to which knowledge is socially constructed or exists "out there" as a body of knowledge which students simply learn. The development of ethno-science and the application of science to matters which interest indigenous peoples such as environmental and resource management or biodiversity offer some new possibilities for

indigenous people to engage with the sciences which they decide are most relevant.

25. Sharing

The final project discussed here is about sharing knowledge between indigenous peoples, around networks, and across the world of indigenous peoples. Sharing contains views about knowledge being a collective benefit and knowledge being a form of resistance. Like networking, sharing is a process which is responsive to the marginalized contexts in which indigenous communities exist. Even in the context of New Zealand—a small country, relatively well-off in terms of televisions and communications—Maori people learn more about the issues which affect them at one of the many community gatherings which are held on *marae* then they do from the mainstream media. These gatherings may be for weddings or funerals but they are also used as opportunities to keep the community informed about a wide range of things. The face-to-face nature of sharing is supplemented with local newspapers, which focus on indigenous issues and local radio stations, which specialize in indigenous news and music. Sharing is also related to the failure of education systems to educate indigenous people adequately or appropriately. It is important for keeping people informed about issues and events which will impact on them. It is a form of oral literacy, which connects with the story telling and formal occasions that feature in indigenous life.

Sharing is a responsibility of research. The technical term for this is the dissemination of results, usually very boring to non-researchers, very technical, and very cold. For indigenous researchers sharing is about demystifying knowledge and information and speaking in plain terms to the community. Community gatherings provide a very daunting forum in which to speak about research. Oral presentations conform to cultural protocols and expectations. Often the audience may need to be involved emotionally with laughter, deep reflection, sadness, anger, challenges, and debate. It is a very skilled speaker who can share openly at this level within the rules of the community.

SUMMARY

The projects touched on in this chapter are not offered as the definitive list of activities in which indigenous communities are engaged. There are numerous collaborative projects being undertaken with non-indigenous researchers and organizations. Many of these research partnerships help to develop a trained workforce through the mentoring and guidance provided by the non-indigenous researchers. There are also the more standard types of research projects and methodologies in the social sciences that have not been mentioned here. Some of these approaches, for example those in critical ethnography, have been written about and theorized by scholars working in those disciplines. The naming of the projects listed in this chapter was deliberate. I hope the message it gives to communities is that they have issues that matter and processes and methodologies which can work for them.

NOTES

1. S. Harding, *Feminism and Methodology* (Bloomington: Indiana University Press, 1987), 2–3.

2. R. Menchu, *I, Rigoberta Menchu: An Indian Woman in Guatamala*, translated by A. Wright (London: Verso, 1984).

3. See, for example, S. Jonas, E. McCaughan, and E. Martinez, *Guatemala: Tyranny on Trial* (San Francisco: Synthesis Publications, 1984); and J. Beverley, "The Margin at the Centre: On Testimonies," in *De/Colonizing the Subject: The Politics of Gender in Women's Autobiography*, edited by S. Smith and J. Watson (Minneapolis: University of Minneapolis Press, 1992); and G. Yudice, "Testimonies and Post Modernism," in *Latin American Perspectives: A Journal on Capitalism and Socialism* 18(3–4): 15–31.

4. See also P. Nabokov, *Native American Testimony* (New York: Penguin Books, 1992).

5. S. Rintoul, *The Waiting: A National Black Oral History* (Australia: Heinemann, 1993), 8.

6. Ibid., 8.

7. R. Bishop, *Collaborative Research Stories* (Palmerston North: Dunmore Press, 1996), 24.

8. Ibid., 169.

9. S. Johnson and D. Budnik, *The Book of Elders* (San Francisco: Harper, 1994), 7.

10. G. Cajete, *Look to the Mountain. An Ecology of Indigenous Education* (Colorado: Kivaki Press, 1994), 73.

11. W. Churchill, "I Am Indigenist," in *Struggle for the Land*, edited by Ward Churchill (Monroe: Common Courage Press, 1993), 403–451.

12. M.A. Jaimes, "Native American Identity and Survival: Indigenism and Environmental Ethics," in *Issues in Native American Cultural Identity*, edited by M.K. Green (New York: Peter Lang Publishers, 1995).

13. G.H. Smith, "Research Issues Related to Maori," in *The Issue of Research and Maori*, edited by G.H. Smith and M. Hohepa, Monograph 9 (Auckland: Research Unit for Maori Education, University of Auckland, 1990), 14–22.

14. W. Ihimaera, *Te Ao Marama*, vol. 1 (Auckland: Reed Books, 1990).

15. J. Harjo and G. Bird, eds, *Reinventing the Enemy's Language. Contemporary Native Women's Writings of North America* (New York: W.W. Norton and Company, 1997).

16. See, for example, D.D. Moses and T. Goldie, eds., *An Anthology of Canadian Native Literature in English* (Toronto: Oxford University Press, 1992).

17. M. Mita, "Trick or Treat Issues of Feminism and Post-colonialism in Relation to the Arts," in *Te Pua Journal of Maori Women's Writing* 3(1): 27–41.

18. A. Mead, "Maori Leadership," in *Te Pua Journal of Maori Women's Writing, Research Unit for Maori Education* 3(1): 11–20.

19. R.B. Sykes, *Black Majority* (Melbourne: Hudson Hawthorn, 1989), 146.

20. Ibid., 226.

21. A. Sykes, "Constitutional Reform and Mana Wahine," in *Te Pua Journal of Maori Women's Writing* 3(2): 15–20.

CHAPTER 7

Toward an Emancipatory Methodology for Peace Research

ABIGAIL A. FULLER

The work that peace researchers generate is meant to foster the development of a more peaceful world. Yet, while the field of peace research has grown in recent decades, insufficient attention has been paid to whether peace research actually helps build peace. No research ever changes society in and of itself: it does so only through its effects on the actions of people. Thought must be translated into action. For peace research, in particular, to be true to its mission requires that it be useful to and used by people in their efforts to build a peaceful society.

There are two ways in which peace research can aid individuals and groups in their efforts toward peace. First, it can do so in its substantive focus: by contributing to the body of theoretical and concrete knowledge of the causes, consequences, and dynamics of different types of violence, peace research can aid actors in preventing and resolving violent conflicts. Second, it can do so in its methodology: peace research can contribute to peace by utilizing research methodologies that in themselves help those struggling for peace and justice.

Current peace research falls short of its potential in both these respects. In its selection of research problems, most peace research focuses (implicitly or explicitly) on issues of relevance to dominant groups—those at the top of the various structures of social stratification—and neglects the perspective and concerns of subordinate groups—those at the bottom of stratification systems. Peace research that does focus on subordinate groups uses them as objects of knowledge in a research process that mirrors hierarchical relations in society, rather than engaging them as coinvestigators in a mutually beneficial relationship that contributes to the effectiveness of their efforts at change. The consequence of excluding subordinate groups from the research process is the compromising both of the validity of the research, because important (perhaps the most important) perspectives are excluded, and of its potential to assist struggles for peace and justice, because subordinates are not aided in gaining a greater understanding themselves of social reality. In this article I argue that for peace research to be true to its professed mission demands a research methodology that starts from the lives of, and includes in the research process, people engaged in the struggles of subordinate groups to transform structures of social stratification.

THE SUBSTANTIVE FOCUS AND METHODOLOGY OF PEACE RESEARCH

Peace Research as Research for Dominant Groups

In 1972, Berenice Carroll wrote an article titled "Peace Research: The Cult of Power."[1] In it she warned against the "uncritical acceptance of prevailing conceptions of power" and the preoccupation and identification of peace researchers with those "institutions, groups, or persons conceived to be powerful" in our society, which "appears in some respects to run altogether contrary to the basic objectives of peace research."[2] According to Carroll, the acceptance by peace researchers of a conception of power as dominance—the type of power possessed by nation-states—rather than of power as "independent strength, ability, autonomy, self-determination, control over one's own life, rather than the lives of others, competence to deal with one's environment out of one's own energies and resources, rather than on the basis of dependence"—the type of power possessed by the "powerless"—results in an uncritical acceptance of the nation-state as the unit of analysis and in a concern with being listened to by the powerful.[3]

Other researchers agreed. Herman Schmid analyzed twenty-one articles with policy implications and found "that mostly they presuppose governments as agents."[4] Michael Wallace concurred, observing that "the very use of the term 'policy research' or 'policy implications' betrays the extent to which an official clientele is taken for granted" and warning that researchers will adopt values of their clientele, which for the state is how to maintain its power.[5] Nearly twenty years since these early criticisms, the field has changed little, as supported by Chadwick Alger's more recent remark that for peace researchers "the public may have 'opinions,' if asked for them by scientifically valid procedures, but they

are not viewed as participants. The 'actors' are to be found in selected government offices at the places where stars appear on the world map."[6]

* * * * *

Since the state is the primary vehicle for the maintenance of the power of dominant groups in the modern world, a focus on the concerns of dominant groups translates into a focus on international conflict. In the early days of peace research, the concept of structural violence was introduced in an effort to broaden the agenda of the field beyond the study of war. Whereas peace researchers in industrialized countries tended to be concerned with war, particularly superpower relations, in Third World countries the primary concern of peace researchers has been development. Johan Galtung and others have sought to include the concerns of the latter in peace research, arguing that violence is perpetuated not only directly, as in war, but through social structures as well.[7] For example, while war injures and kills immediately, an unjust economic structure injures and also kills. The only difference is that people starve more slowly than they are slain in battle.

More recently, others have brought to the attention of peace researchers that in addition to structural violence, there are forms of direct violence besides war that merit the attention of peace researchers. For example, feminists have argued that for women, the violence of rape and spouse abuse is at least as injurious, and so of at least as great concern, as war. Andrea Dworkin has advised women to be wary of those who profess a commitment to nonviolence but do not struggle to end violence against women.[8] Alice Walker, a noted black feminist, wrote that from the viewpoint of black people suffering under racism, a nuclear war that wiped out a white-dominated society might not be so bad.[9] Walker's remark serves as a response to those (generally white, Western, and male) who argue that nuclear war should be the primary concern of peace research because it is the most potentially destructive form of violence.

Today, almost no peace researcher would argue that the field should confine itself to the study of war. [...] Yet the evidence indicates that (at least for Western peace researchers) the acceptance of a broad definition of peace is still more nominal than actual. In the peace research journals, the overwhelming majority of articles are about war and international relations or include other forms of violence only as they relate to war (for example, the connection between sexism and militarism).[10] [...] Similarly, the "peace movement" is still commonly understood to be composed of organizations working against wars or nuclear weapons, but not as including women's organizations, antiracist organizations, environmental organizations, and the like.

When peace researchers introduced the concept of structural violence, they argued for its inclusion in the peace research agenda both on principle—"violence is violence ... regardless of how it is exercised"[11]—and for practical reasons—structural violence and direct violence are causally connected. One reason why a substantive focus on dominant groups and their concerns is problematic is ethical: peace researchers ought to be concerned with the needs of all people, not just the powerful. The adage that a society is only as good as how it treats its least fortunate members might be applied to peace research: peace research is only as good as the extent to which it focuses on the concerns of subordinate groups.

On a practical level, research directed toward the concerns of dominant groups contains the implicit assumption that the way to achieve peace is to influence the powerful. The problem with this assumption is that given the existence of structural violence, genuine peace requires the transformation of structures of social stratification (economic, social, or political) to achieve a redistribution of power, yet historically those with power have not been known to relinquish it. This issue was debated among peace researchers in the late 1960s and the 1970s. Some argued that it is most effective to gear their work toward influencing state policymakers, because it is the state that has the bulk of violence-inflicting mechanisms at its disposal. In contrast, others argued that given that the state is the major perpetrator of violence in the modern world, peace researchers ought to aim for their work to be helpful to grassroots efforts against state violence, such as antinuclear weapons organizations. Schmid stated that peace research "should formulate its problems not in terms meaningful to international and supranational institutions, but in terms meaningful to suppressed and exploited groups and nations."[12]

* * * * *

Because the powerful benefit from the violence perpetrated against subordinate groups, objectively they do not have an interest in eradicating it. For example, an analysis of the workings of capitalism reveals that wealth is accumulated at the expense of those whose labor is exploited, so poverty cannot be eradicated without the wealthy giving up some of their privilege. Violence against women helps maintain the system of sexual stratification in which men enjoy dominance.[13] For dominant groups to work against these types of violence would mean to undercut their privilege. Peace researchers have pointed out that their conclusions are unlikely to be heeded by dominant groups because the latter are interested in peace only to the extent that it does not threaten their power.[14] [...]

PEACE RESEARCH AS RESEARCH ABOUT SUBORDINATES

Some peace researchers do conduct studies of subordinate groups and their efforts at change, such as research on nonviolent social movements. Yet this research is generally not conducted so as to include the subordinate groups in the research process.[15] As a result, an opportunity is lost for subordinates to develop a more profound understanding of their social reality that would increase the effectiveness of their efforts at change. While it is important that peace researchers study grass-roots movements, it is contrary to the emancipatory project to utilize grass-roots movements merely as data for research. Paulo Freire writes about the conscientization that is possible when subordinate groups are included in an interactive learning process in which they are not objects of knowledge, but subjects who are involved in knowledge creation.[16] Conscientization involves developing an awareness of the forces of violence and their causal connections and a concrete understanding of how violence is rooted in social structures. Mushakoji refers to this process as "endogenous peace learning."[17]

* * * * *

Alger notes that some peace researchers are calling for new methodologies to generate research that aids grass-roots efforts.[18] He cites D.L. Sheth's conclusion that "a macro-vision is the prime need of these groups and movements, and this can be satisfied only by a growing partnership between activists and intellectuals in the process of social transformation."[19] Catalin Mamali is also cited by Alger as asserting that a knowledge of the social reality within which people live is necessary for the "conscious participation" of members of a community in processes of change, and that such knowledge is attainable only through the democratization of the process of the production of knowledge.[20] Mushakoji agrees that research on grass-roots movements must be based on the values of the people in those communities; he advises

peace researchers to engage peace activists in the research process.[21]

* * * * *

THE EPISTEMOLOGICAL BASIS FOR AN EMANCIPATORY METHODOLOGY

The examples in the previous section provide evidence that the exclusion of subordinate groups from the research process both forgoes opportunities to help increase the effectiveness of such groups in their emancipatory efforts and results in findings that reflect a less comprehensive understanding of peace and violence. Thus for peace research to be effective two questions concerning methodology must be answered. One is a scientific question: how can the most valid results be obtained concerning the causes, dynamics, and consequences of violence and conditions for its eradication (peace)? The other is a political question: what research methodology is most effective for aiding subordinate groups in their struggles for peace and justice?

Every research methodology contains an underlying epistemology or theory of knowledge. From a theory of what categories of things it is possible to know and how we come to know them, a corresponding research strategy is created. It is necessary, then, to explicate the epistemology that justifies including subordinate groups in the research process. One such epistemology is standpoint theory.

Standpoint Theory

Standpoint theory is a theory of knowledge that makes two general claims: (1) in a stratified society, one's perspective on social reality is affected by one's position within structures of social stratification, and (2) the perspective of those in a subordinate position actively struggling to transform those structures is "epistemologically advantageous"—less perverse and less partial—relative to that of those in the corresponding dominant group.

While it is feminist scholars who coined the term standpoint theory, the theory can be traced back to Karl Marx.[22] Marx postulated that an individual's perspective on social reality is influenced by her or his class position. For Marx, the most fundamental division in society is that of class, defined in terms of one's relation to the mode of production. In a class society, a dominant ideology arises that obscures the underlying structural mechanisms and justifies the status quo. The concept of an epistemological standpoint refers to the idea that subordinate groups (for Marx, the proletariat) are more likely than dominant groups (the bourgeoisie) to see through the illusions of the dominant ideology because unlike the latter they do not have an objective interest in maintaining such illusions.

In an effort to explain why this is so, Charles Mills usefully distinguishes four mechanisms identified by Marx through which the dominant ideology is perpetuated.[23]

1. *Class domination:* This refers not to a conscious intent on the part of members of a ruling class to dominate others, but to the way in which a class system itself perpetuates the dominant ideology. For example, under capitalism the media and the educational system are controlled by the ruling class, but they rarely employ blatant censorship of dissent; rather, while there is debate, it takes place within procapitalist assumptions. Also, individuals are discouraged from dissenting by the costs imposed on them if they do.

2. *Societal appearance:* Marx theorized that capitalism itself generates illusions that inhibit people from seeing the structural mechanisms underlying social reality. This was Marx's realist stance: he distinguished the outward appearances of social phenomena from the underlying structures that give rise to them. Hence the dominant ideology is perpetuated, quite apart from the actions of the ruling class, by the very nature of capitalism. [...] Of course, the dominant ideology is believable because it fits the reality of the underlying structure in which societal appearance "buttresses" class domination.

3. *Class interest:* This [...] refers to the propensity of members of the dominant class to accept the dominant ideology because of their class position and the propensity of members of subordinate classes to question the dominant ideology. Mills takes care to note that class interest does not generate illusory beliefs but, rather, contributes to their acceptance.

4. *Class position:* Different class positions give rise to divergent experiences of social reality. Hence the working class, because its experiences contradict the dominant ideology, is in a better position to see through the illusions. Mills emphasizes that this is a tendency, not a law. Hence he asks who is more likely to have the greater understanding of the functioning of social structures: a white resident of Johannesburg who attends cocktail parties and plays golf, or a black who lives in Soweto and commutes to work.

These causal mechanisms lead only to the tendency for members of the proletariat but not members of the ruling class to see through the illusions of dominant ideology.

It is still necessary to explain both why it is that not all workers see through such illusions and why some members of the bourgeoisie do. The answer is that a "veridical"[24] insight into social reality (or, as Marx called it, "revolutionary consciousness") is achieved through active struggle against oppressive structures. In principle, anyone from any class is capable of engaging in such struggle and achieving this insight. However, because of the mechanisms explained above, in practice members of the proletariat are more likely to engage in active struggle against oppressive structures than are members of the bourgeoisie are.

This brings us to the notion of praxis. The reason that individuals cannot attain a revolutionary consciousness without engaging in active struggle against oppressive structures is that social structures become visible only when one pushes up against them in struggle. As Sandra Harding notes, "Members of marginalized groups must struggle to name their own experience *for* themselves in order to claim the subjectivity that is given to members of dominant groups 'at birth' .... Achieving publicly self-named 'experience' is a precondition for generating knowledge"[25] (emphasis in original). It is through this struggle that the structures of social stratification and their dynamics are revealed: "In a socially stratified society, the objectivity of the results of research is increased by political activism by and on behalf of the oppressed, exploited and dominated groups."[26]

Feminist Standpoint Theory

Standpoint theory has been advanced by feminist scholars in their justifications of a unique feminist perspective on social reality. Feminists have, however, contributed to and changed Marx's theory of knowledge. There has been much fruitful debate in the feminist movement on the proper relation between feminist research, or academic feminism, and feminist activism. Central to this debate has been the development of feminist research methods to guide the work of researchers. Feminists have asked the question, How can research be conducted so as to maximize its emancipatory potential for women? Feminist theorists have adapted and developed the Marxist theory of knowledge to explain why it is that the inclusion of feminist perspectives leads to "more empirically accurate and theoretically richer explanations than the conventional research."[27]

Feminists have taken issue with Marx's assertion that the proletariat is the only group in a position to see through the dominant ideology. They argue that because of their position in the social structure of gender stratification, women also have an epistemologically advantageous standpoint. Feminist research has uncovered empirical evidence for a unique women's standpoint; for example, psychological research regarding women's different perceptions of reality.[28] Feminists have also begun to investigate the specific resources that women as a subordinate group bring to an analysis of social reality. These resources stem from the characteristics of women's subordination. For instance, because of their role as the physical and emotional caretakers of men and children, women have a more complete view of the daily "production" of human beings than do men.

Other Standpoint Theories

Although standpoint theory has been most highly developed by feminists, in principle any subordinate group within a social stratification system has a unique standpoint. Each group will have different "distinctive resources" that have been neglected or devalued by mainstream researchers, resulting in a unique standpoint. For example, white women are more apt than white men to understand patriarchal social structures clearly, but white women are less apt to have the same degree of insight into racist social structures as black women have. Mills cites black philosophers who argue for a black standpoint, asserting that "philosophy has not been immune to the racism that has pervaded so much of Western thought about non-European peoples."[29] As Harding concludes, "Knowledge is always socially situated; but the insights of standpoint theory enable us to see how nevertheless we can find rationally justifiable and competent criteria to distinguish less false from more false assumptions and claims."[30]

In summary, standpoint theory offers an epistemological justification for starting research from the standpoint of those actively working with subordinate groups to transform social structures: research so done is actually more scientifically valid. Such research will then be more effective in aiding work for peace and justice. Engaging those working for peace and justice as coinvestigators in the research process also increases its emancipatory potential.

THE SPECIFICS OF AN EMANCIPATORY RESEARCH METHODOLOGY

A research methodology based in standpoint epistemology starts from the lives of those actively struggling with subordinate groups for peace and justice and involves them interactively in the research process. It should be noted that to speak of "involving" others implies that the researcher remains in control of who participates and who does not, which is contrary to the self-determination that is an essential element of emancipatory research. Galtung concludes that "every profession is in and by itself some form of structural violence," because by definition a professional has a monopoly on some type of competence.[31] Ideally, those working for peace and justice would possess the skills and knowledge necessary to conduct research themselves; at the very least, they would initiate research projects and enlist trained researchers as coinvestigators. At the present time, however,

the professional social science researcher does exist: the requisite knowledge and skills for research are taught in the university, to which members of subordinate groups have relatively less access. What needs to occur is a democratization of the production of knowledge such that anyone who so desires can gain the skills and knowledge necessary for research. In the meantime, peace researchers will probably need to "invite" the collaboration of subordinate groups.

Peace researchers have been largely silent on the issue of the appropriateness of their research methodologies to the promotion of peace. A notable exception to the paucity of discussion on peace research methodology is Galtung's application of the concept of structural violence to social science research.[32] Galtung illustrates how the four components of structural violence are found in the relationship between the researcher and the researched in traditional social science methodology:

1. *exploitation:* the research is characterized by a vertical division of labor in which the researcher uses the researched for her or his own interests, without tangible benefit for the researched;
2. *penetration:* the autonomy of the researched is violated when she or he does not know what the research is about while the researcher does know;
3. *fragmentation:* the researched are separated from each other by the researcher, this is done in traditional research in order to increase the validity of the research by avoiding "contamination"; and
4. *marginalization:* the researcher is the (supposedly) objective and knowledgeable observer, and the researched become a "scientific proletariat."

Inexplicably, there is no evidence in the literature that Galtung's article provoked any discussion among peace researchers. The author himself, however, did follow up on his ideas about social science research in his work *The True Worlds*.[33] In the last chapter of the book, Galtung notes that proposals about what should be done to achieve a more peaceful world are incomplete without an "operational part" that delineates "who," "how," "when," and "where." As to who, Galtung notes that in a stratified society, the individuals most capable of implementing change—those at the top—are unlikely to possess much motivation to do so. We need to look at how those most motivated—those at the bottom—can become more capable of making change.

Galtung warns of such theories that a priori designate a specific category of people as the agent of change and categorize all others as the enemy. (He specifically mentions Marxism, noting that it may be either the theory itself or the use of the theory that is problematic.) I would argue that it is important to identify that category or categories of people who, because of their objective position within a social structure, are potential agents of structural change. Standpoint theory stresses that doing so does not entail the a priori inclusion or exclusion of anyone in the group of agents of social change: while an individual's objective structural position indicates her or his relative tendency to resist or promote social change, it is individual volition that finally determines whether a person becomes an agent of change or not.

The way to create new social structures is, for Galtung, through the promotion of self-reliance. Although Galtung does not mention his earlier article, it is obvious that in the context of social science research, self-reliance entails not being "researched" by professional researchers, but learning the skills and acquiring the knowledge to conduct research oneself. Galtung discusses the emancipatory potential of self-reliance,

noting that an "expert" on conflict who offers to solve the problems of others "is, structurally speaking, a thief, for he takes away from others a possibility for personal, and thereby social, growth."[34]

* * * * *

SOME IMPLICATIONS OF STANDPOINT THEORY FOR PEACE RESEARCH

The Definition of Peace

Since the inception of the field, the definition of what constitutes peace and consequently the proper focus of peace research has never been taken for granted in the peace research community. As has been suggested, the debate has engaged those who would adopt a "narrow" definition of peace as the absence of international violence with those who argue for a "broad" definition that includes the absence of structural violence, or the presence of justice. Standpoint theory offers an explanation of why this debate has occurred. According to standpoint theory, it is the social structural positions of the actors in this debate that form the basis for their positions. This becomes obvious when we note, for instance, that it was the growing protest of Third World peoples against colonialism and its consequences that led to the inclusion of structural violence in the peace research agenda in the 1970s. Similarly, it is largely women peace researchers who have argued for the inclusion of feminist concerns in peace research. Conversely, it tends to be white, Western, male peace researchers who confine their scholarship to analyses of the causes and prevention of international conflict. Mills suggests that "certain issues have only historically been seen as problems in the first place because of the privileged universalization of the experience and outlook of a very limited (particularistic) sector of humanity—largely white, male, and propertied."[35] As more disenfranchised groups are included in the peace research community, how that community defines peace is likely to change further. Galtung notes that history is a process, such that our goals are not constant or fixed; "we shall always be under way."[36]

This is not to say that the study of war is not important. But a fundamental tenet of peace research is that we are global citizens. From this follows the obligation to counter not only the violence to which we are personally vulnerable but all types of violence that affect people globally. As argued above, fulfilling this obligation results in better research: we gain a better understanding of how poverty, war, racism, militarism, sexism, economic exploitation, and the like are interconnected.

* * * * *

CONCLUSION: PROSPECTS FOR THE ADOPTION OF AN EMANCIPATORY METHODOLOGY

Whether an emancipatory research methodology can or will be practiced by peace researchers has much to do with the institutional milieu within which peace research is conducted. Peace research, like any other kind of research, does not take place in a social vacuum. In the United States, most peace researchers are faculty at colleges and universities, so the context of the production of peace research is the academy. This creates a contradiction. On the one hand, as argued here, genuine peace involves the redistribution of power in society. On the other hand, the educational system is itself one of the major institutions for the perpetuation of social stratification.[37] It should come as no surprise, then, that the academy does not generally reward the production of research aimed explicitly at creating egalitarian social structures. In decisions regarding hiring, tenure, and promotion of faculty, the fact that a researcher has attempted to make her or his work of practical use to anyone outside academia generally does not count in their favor.

This is likely to be especially true if those for whom the research is meant to be useful are not dominant groups (such as corporations or the government) but groups challenging the economic, political, or social status quo. Furthermore, doing research about subordinate groups is likely to be more acceptable than doing research for (or with) subordinate groups. What researchers are rewarded for is procuring research grants and disseminating their research findings to colleagues through publication in scholarly journals or presentation at professional meetings. And those in a position to offer research grants are, of course, not subordinate groups, but government and private foundations that are controlled by and reflect the interests of the powerful.

On the other side of the equation, engaging subordinate groups as coinvestigators in peace research means the latter must overcome their distrust of academic scholars as "arm-chair intellectuals." This distrust is at least partly justified. Historically, academicians have not generally involved themselves in the struggles of such groups. As described above, social scientists studying subordinate groups have most often simply exploited the latter as a source of research data, useful for future publications to secure tenure and promotions.

The task for peace researchers is to take seriously that "an emancipatory intent is no guarantee of an emancipatory outcome."[38] During the 1970s, peace researchers reacted against the assertion that scholarly research can or should be value-free. But repudiating the myth of value-free research does not mean giving up the quest for scientific knowledge and for the research methodologies that will best generate such knowledge. Certainly we want peace research to be effective at its task, which means that scientifically it must be valid. At the same time, it should be ethically emancipatory.

I am not arguing for methodological monism. What has been put forth here is meant as a corrective to peace research as it is currently practiced, not as a new orthodoxy. The point is that peace researchers need to be more aware of the ethical and strategic implications of their selection of research problems and of how they study them. We may in fact need some researchers to continue to try to influence state policymakers, for example. But such researchers would be wise to remember the dilemmas of their task and to exercise vigilance against feeling too comfortable within circles of power.

Neither am I arguing that white, Western, males cannot do good peace research. Standpoint theory is emphatically not an essentialist theory. The standpoint of a subordinate group is available to those who would engage in the struggle for its emancipation. It is not, however, available simply from reading or writing books or journal articles. Perhaps being a good peace researcher means getting out of the "ivory tower" and struggling alongside subordinate groups. As peace researchers, we need to take a hard look not only at the institutional milieu within which we conduct our research but also inside ourselves to discover what are the obstacles to producing peace research that meets the "challenge of authenticity"[39]—the challenge to be what we claim to be.

NOTES

1. Berenice A. Carroll, "Peace Research: The Cult of Power," *Journal of Conflict Resolution* 16 (1972): 585–616.
2. Ibid., 585.
3. Ibid, 607.
4. Herman Schmid, "Peace Research, Peace Action and Action Research" (Paper presented at the 139th meeting of the American Association for the Advancement of Science, December 30,1972).
5. Michael D. Wallace, "The Radical Critique of Peace Research: An Exposition and Interpretation," *Peace Research Reviews* 4(4) (1972): 37.
6. Chadwick F. Alger, "Peace Studies at the Crossroads: Where Else?" *Annals of the American Academy of Political and Social Science* 504 (July 1989): 124
7. Johan Galtung, "Violence, Peace, and Peace Research," *Journal of Peace Research* 6 (1969): 167–191.
8. Andrea Dworkin, *Our Blood: Prophecies and Discourse on Sexual Politics* (New York: Harper & Row, 1976).
9. Alice Walker, *Living by the Word: Selected Writings, 1973–1987* (San Diego: Harcourt Brace Jovanovich, 1988).
10. A cursory review of the articles published in the last several years in the *Journal of Peace Research*, the *Bulletin of Peace Proposals*, and *Peace and Change* bears out this conclusion. In all three journals, the great majority of articles (approximately 75% to 90%) take the nation-state to be the primary actor, focusing on such topics as war, arms races, nuclear weapons, conventional weapons, militarism, military service, military spending, national civilian-based defense, arms control, international relations, international law, and international organizations (e.g., the United Nations). The other articles focus on such topics as the environment, culture and conflict resolution, gender and conflict resolution, transnational organizations (e.g., the Red Cross), nonviolence, peace education, peace action, and the global economy.

Similarly, the *UNESCO Yearbook on Conflict and Peace Studies, 1988* (Paris:

UNESCO and Westport: Greenwood, 1990) contains four articles, all of which assume the nation-state, or its leaders, as primary actor.

11. Johan Galtung, "Twenty-Five Years of Peace Research: Ten Challenges and Some Responses," *Journal of Peace Research* 22(2) (1985): 146.

12. Herman Schmid, "Peace Research and Politics," *Journal of Peace Research* 5(3) (1968): 217–232.

13. See, for example, Susan Brownmiller, *Against Our Will: Men, Women and Rape* (New York: Simon and Schuster, 1975).

14. See Schmid, "Peace Research, Peace Action and Action Research"; Thomas S. Lough, "Peace Researchers and the Movement: No Meeting Place?" *Peace and Change* 1(1) (1972): 55–62; Mark Pilisuk and Thomas Hayden, "Is There a Military-Industrial Complex Which Prevents Peace?" *Journal of Social Issues* 21(3) (1965): 67–117.

15. As stated in note 10, none of the articles in the *UNESCO Yearbook on Conflict and Peace Studies, 1988*, assume subordinate groups as primary actors. Of the thirty-six articles in *A Just Peace through Transformation* (the proceedings of the Eleventh Conference of the International Peace Research Association, published in 1988), about one-third focus on the concerns of subordinate groups. However, the only one that shows evidence of having included the researched groups in the research process is Wehr and Fitzsimmons's study. For example, Rawlinson's article comparing three nonviolent campaigns makes no mention of any participation by the campaigners in his research process or of his making his research results available to them.

16. Paulo Freire, *Pedagogy of the Oppressed* (New York: Herder & Herder, 1970).

17. Kinihide Mushakoji, "Peace Research as an International Learning Process: A New Meta-Paradigm," *International Studies Quarterly* 22(2) (June 1978): 184, cited in Alger, "Peace Studies at the Crossroads."

18. Alger, "Peace Studies at the Crossroads."

19. D.L. Sheth, "Grass-Roots Stirrings and the Future of Politics," *Alternatives* 9 (Summer 1983): 386.

20. Catalin Mamali, *Societal Learning and Democratization of the Social Research Process* (Bucharest: Bucharest Research Center for Youth Problems, 1979).

21. Mushakoji. "Peace Research as an International Learning Process."

22. Karl Marx, *The German Ideology* (London: Lawrence & Wisbart, 1965).

23. Charles W. Mills, "Determination and Consciousness in Marx," *Canadian Journal of Philosophy* 19(3) (1989): 421–446.

24. Mills, "Determination and Consciousness in Marx," 443.

25. Sandra Harding, "Starting Thought from Women's Lives: Eight Resources for Maximizing Objectivity," *Journal of Social Philosophy* 21(2, 3) (Fall/Winter 1990): 9.

26. Ibid., 15.

27. Ibid., 2. See also Alison Jaggar, *Feminist Politics and Human Nature* (Totowa: Rowman & Allanheld, 1983); Nancy Hartsock, "The Feminist Standpoint: Developing the Ground for a Specifically Feminist Historical Materialism," in *Discovering Reality*, edited by Sandra Harding and M. Hintikka (Dordrecht: Reidel, 1983); Hilary Rose, "Hand, Brain, and Heart: A Feminist Epistemology for the Natural Sciences," *Signs* 9(1) (1983): 73–90; Dorothy Smith, *The Everyday World as Problematic* (Boston: Northeastern University Press, 1987).

28. See, for example, Jaggar, *Feminist Politics and Human Nature*; Carol Gilligan, *In a Different Voice: Psychological Theory and Women's Development* (Cambridge: Harvard University Press, 1982).

29. Charles W. Mills, "Alternative Epistemologies," *Social Theory and Practice*

14(3) (1988): 237. Mills cites a special issue of *Philosophical Forum* (9 [Winter-Spring 1977–1978]) titled "Philosophy and the Black Experience"; Leonard Harris, ed., *Philosophy Born of Struggle: Anthology of Afro-American Philosophy* (Dubuque: Kendall/Hunt, 1983); Howard McGary, Jr., "Teaching Black Philosophy," *Teaching Philosophy* 7(2) (1984): 129–137.

30. Harding, "Starting Thought from Woman's Lives," 23.

31. Johan Galtung, *The True Worlds* (New York: Free Press, 1980), 415.

32. Johan Galtung, "Is Peaceful Research Possible? On the Methodology of Peace Research," chapter 12 in *Essays in Peace Research*, vol. 1 (Copenhagen: Christian Ejlers, 1975): 263–279.

33. Galtung, *True Worlds*.

34. Ibid., 417.

35. Mills, "Alternative Epistemologies," 238.

36. Galtung, *True Worlds*, 413.

37. See, for example, Henry A. Giroux, *Schooling and the Struggle for Public Life* (Minneapolis: University of Minnesota, 1988).

38. J. Acker, K. Barry, and J. Esseveld, "Objectivity and Truth: Problems in Doing Feminist Research," *Women's Studies International Forum* 6(4): 431, cited in Lather, "Research as Praxis," 267.

39. Betty Reardon, "Are the Walls Coming Down?" (Panel presentation at the Second Annual Meeting of the Peace Studies Association, March 10, 1990, Eugene, OR).

Rethinking Part 1B: Steps toward Critical Inquiry

CRITICAL THINKING QUESTIONS

Chapter 4: On Intellectual Craftsmanship

1. What is the purpose and value of setting up a file that joins personal experience and professional activities? How can such a file *be* "intellectual production"; how does it enable intellectual craftsmanship?
2. What does Mills mean when he states, "To overcome the academic *prose* you have first to overcome the academic *pose*"?
3. In the final paragraphs of his essay, Mills summarizes in a few precepts what he means by "carrying on the tradition of classic social analysis." How relevant and viable is this tradition in the 21st century?

Chapter 5: Methods from the Margins

1. In introducing methods from the margins, Kirby and McKenna discuss literacy training as a form of empowerment. How would you compare methods from the margins with literacy training as approaches to dealing with language, knowledge, and power?
2. "Demystifying the research process" is a way of challenging existing monopolies of knowledge. How do Kirby and McKenna suggest that this demystification occur?
3. In the dominant institutions of Western education, a disdain for the practical has resulted in a kind of paralysis. How do methods from the margins break from this paradigm?

Chapter 6: Twenty-Five Indigenous Projects

1. Many of the projects that Linda Tuhiwai Smith describes have no obvious connection to conventional forms of social-scientific research. Does this make them "unscientific" or does it indicate a need to broaden and contextualize our understanding of what "counts" as research?
2. Tuhiwai Smith holds that in naming the world, people name their realities. What are the implications of this for critical research strategies?
3. Science, as Tuhiwai Smith observes, has traditionally been hostile to indigenous ways of knowing. Yet the emergence of ethno-science offers hope for new possibilities of indigenous engagement with science. What might be the parallels for this engagement in the field of social science?

Chapter 7: Toward an Emancipatory Methodology for Peace Research

1. Consider a particular social issue, such as that of militarism/peace, or health or urban life. What kinds of research questions might be posed about that issue from the standpoint of dominant groups? From the standpoint of subordinate groups?
2. Fuller argues that it is only when people, through their struggles, push up against structures of oppression that the structures become visible. What are the implications of this proposition for our knowledge of the social?
3. According to Johan Galtung, the four components of structural violence—exploitation, penetration, fragmentation, and marginalization—are contained within the relationship between researcher and subject in traditional social science methodology. How can the promotion of "self-reliance" in the construction of social knowledge avoid these problems?

GLOSSARY TERMS

Abstracted empiricism: A style of social research that is overly concerned with methodological technique and quantitative analysis, and not sufficiently attuned to the need for historically contextualized and properly theorized inquiry.

Critical reflection: Examination of people's social reality in a manner that places that reality in a broad social context while connecting the personal with the political. One integral aspect of research from the margins.

Decolonizing methodology: An effort, spearheaded by indigenous people, to critique the legacy of colonial domination in the forms of contemporary knowledge and culture and to construct empowering alternatives based on the needs of indigenous communities.

Intellectual craftsmanship: The style of social research, favoured by Mills, emphasizing the interdisciplinary integration of available knowledge from all relevant sources in a reflective, historical-comparative analysis of social structure and individual biography. For Mills, intellectual craftsmanship is the best way of cultivating the sociological imagination.

Intersubjectivity: An authentic dialogue between all participants in the research process, in which all are respected as equally knowledgeable subjects. The other integral aspect of research from the margins.

Peace research: Research intended to foster the development of a more peaceful world. This goal requires that peace research be useful to activists in their efforts to build peace and justice.

Positional superiority: A term coined by Edward Said that conveys how Western colonialism and imperialism positioned the colonizers culturally as the dominant knowers of the non-Western Other, enabling them to "discover," appropriate, and distribute knowledge of non-Western people who were treated as voiceless objects of the Western gaze.

Reframing: One of 25 indigenous projects described by Tuhiwai Smith, reframing occurs when indigenous people resist being labelled and boxed according to categories that do not fit. It involves taking control of the ways in which indigenous issues and problems are framed, and provides one instance of how decolonizing methodologies are modes of struggle in the production of knowledge.

Research from the margins: Research by, for, and with people on the margins of knowledge/power hierarchies. Such research enables marginalized people to create knowledge that will describe, explain, and help to change their world.

Socspeak: Turgid, polysyllabic prose common in the social sciences. Jargon that seeks to establish the scientific status of the writer by excluding lay readers from the conversation.

Standpoint theory: A theory of knowledge, introduced by Karl Marx and developed by feminist scholars, that asserts the "epistemological advantage" that subordinate groups struggling to transform oppressive structures have over dominant groups whose interests lie in maintaining both the structures and the ideological illusions that naturalize and legitimate them. This theory offers a rationale for beginning research from the standpoint of those actively working to transform social structures.

Structural violence: Violence, i.e., material harm to people, caused not by war but through oppressive social structures, such as unjust economic arrangements. Each year more people die slowly from starvation than are killed in battle.

FURTHER READING

Cormack, Patricia. 1999. "Making the Sociological Promise: A Case Study of Rosemary Brown's Autobiography." *Canadian Review of Sociology and Anthropology* 36(3): 355–369

Discusses C. Wright Mills's formulations of sociological analysis, arguing that for Mills sociological thought is a matter of biographical and historiographical storytelling. Drawing on the autobiography of Canadian politician and activist Rosemary Brown, Cormack finds a creative sociological imagination in Brown's writing. Cormack recommends that sociologists study popular narratives such as Brown's to draw out the sociological insights that they often implicitly embody.

DeVault, Marjorie L. 1996. "Talking Back to Sociology: Distinctive Contributions of Feminist Methodology." *Annual Review of Sociology* 22: 29–50.

DeVault presents an overview of feminist methodology as having emerged with the second wave of feminist activism in the 1960s–1970s. Despite its diversity, feminist methodology is unified by "a sense of accountability to a movement that is best conceived as a changing and contested discourse" (31); thus feminist method is a good example of praxis-oriented inquiry.

Hughes, Donna M. 1995. "Significant Differences: The Construction of Knowledge, Objectivity, and Dominance." *Women's Studies International Forum* 18(4): 395–406.

A trenchant feminist critique of statistics as an objectifying practice in social science. Hughes traces the history of statistics, emphasizing its racist origins in the eugenic movement of the 19th century, and presents a five-step model of how statistical analysis amounts to a scientific construction of the Other. Hughes's argument is overstated at points but worth considering.

Lather, Patti. 1991. *Getting Smart: Feminist Research and Pedagogy with/in the Postmodern*. New York: Routledge.

An important analysis of the methodological implications of various critical theories, including feminist, neo-Marxist, Freirian. and poststructural formulations. Lather places praxis at the heart of her project and explores links between knowledge and power.

RELEVANT WEB SITES

Canadian Centre for Policy Alternatives
http://www.policyalternatives.ca/

The CCPA undertakes and promotes research on issues of social and economic justice. It produces research reports, books, opinion pieces, fact sheets, and other publications, including *The Monitor*, a monthly digest of progressive research and opinion. Many of these resources are available from the Web site.

Communications for a Sustainable Future
http://csf.colorado.edu

A site founded on the idea that "computer networking could be used to enhance communications with the objective of working through disparate views and ideologies to secure a more promising future." Hosts or links to a great number of interesting Web pages dedicated to progressive sociology, peace and conflict studies, ecology and environment, international studies, and heterodox economics.

The Critical Methods Collective
http://www.criticalmethods.org/

A South Africa-based association "interested in the critical possibilities of social science methodologies and in ways of understanding and disrupting knowledge production processes inside and beyond the academy." The group arranges conferences about the politics of knowledge production and supports critical research, guerilla publishing and radical teaching initiatives. This site contains extensive links to various qualitative method Web sites.

The Global Site: Critical Gateway to World Politics, Society and Culture
http://www.theglobalsite.ac.uk/index.html

An interdisciplinary site that features the work of critical social scientists. Includes original articles and book-length works, reviews, and commentary.

Radical Statistics
http://www.radstats.org.uk/

Site of the UK-based Radical Statistics Group, which believes that "statistics can be used to support radical campaigns for progressive social change. Statistics should inform, not drive policies. Social problems should not be disguised by technical language." Contains various articles on the use of statistics and statistical analysis as well as links to mainly European-based sites.

2 FIVE CRITICAL RESEARCH STRATEGIES

PART 2A: MAKING CONNECTIONS, UNMASKING RELATIONS: DIALECTICAL SOCIAL ANALYSIS

Chapter 8
Getting Started on Social Analysis in Canada
Jamie Swift, Jacqueline M. Davies, Robert G. Clarke,
and Michael S.J. Czerny

Chapter 9
The Principles of Dialectics
David Harvey

Chapter 10
Why Dialectics? Why Now? Or, How to Study the
Communist Future inside the Capitalist Present
Bertell Ollman

Chapter 11
Explaining Global Poverty: A Realist Critique of the
Orthodox Approach
Branwen Gruffydd Jones

PART 2B: PROBLEMATIZING THE EVERYDAY WORLD: INSTITUTIONAL ETHNOGRAPHY

Chapter 12
Theory "in" Everyday Life
Marie Campbell and Frances Gregor

Chapter 13
Ethnography, Institutions, and the Problematic of the
Everyday World
Peter R. Grahame

PART 2E: SOCIAL INQUIRY AS COMMUNICATIVE REASON: TOWARD A PUBLIC SOCIOLOGY

Chapter 24
The Promise
C. Wright Mills

Chapter 25
Exploring the Relevance of Critical Theory for Action Research: Emancipatory Action Research in the Footsteps of Jürgen Habermas
Stephen Kemmis

Chapter 26
The "Project of Modernity" and the Parameters for a Critical Sociology: An Argument with Illustrations from Medical Sociology
Graham Scambler

Chapter 27
Emancipatory Politics, Critical Evaluation, and Government Policy
Madine VanderPlaat

PART 2A MAKING CONNECTIONS, UNMASKING RELATIONS: DIALECTICAL SOCIAL ANALYSIS

Although the four readings that make up this part were published in the past decade, dialectical social analysis has a much longer and somewhat checkered history. Jorge Larrain (1986) has given a good account of how in the era of Stalinist dictatorship in the U.S.S.R. (1930s–1950s) one interpretation of Marx's critical method was codified into a dogmatic orthodoxy and promulgated internationally within the Communist left. That orthodoxy presented "dialectical materialism" or *diamat* as a closed system purporting to answer all questions about the natural and social world (e.g., Stalin, 1940)—a position irreconcilable with empirical social science research (Vaillancourt, 1986: 86).

Marx's own method, which we feature below, was very much the reverse. As Sherman (1995: 230) suggests, dialectics as a critical method amounts to a set of *questions*—not answers—that guide social research by directing our gaze toward the historical, relational, and emergent character of reality. Marx famously claimed that "men make their own history, but they do not make it just as they please; they do not make it under circumstances chosen by themselves, but under circumstances directly encountered, given and transmitted from the past" (Marx, 1968 [1852]: 97). From the perspective of dialectical analysis, social reality is always in the process of being created through the practices of people whose human capacities, material technologies, and social relations have been shaped in the past. Viewed this way, social life always presents openings for change. The present world is a construction site for various possible futures. Part of the task of dialectical social analysis is to discern those possibilities through careful study of present and past practice.

In two excerpts from their 2003 book, *Getting Started on Social Analysis in Canada*, Swift, Davies, Clarke, and Czerny offer an especially accessible introduction to this critical research strategy. They begin with a simple cup of coffee, the entry point to exploring an extended range of social relations in which the cup of coffee is implicated. As we place the object in its full context, a raft of questions and social issues comes up, all relating either to its *history* as the embedded product of labour, international trade, and so on, or to the *future* implications of its use (as in the ecological effects of bleached coffee filters and styrofoam cups). A cup of coffee, or any other object we might take for granted, does not just happen. Rather, the object is a resumé of a whole range of social activities and relations, just as it enables other activities to occur, which have their own ramifications. Dialectical social analysis begins by questioning the world around us. How has that world been put together—by people "making their own history"—in ways that enable yet constrain us to live our lives as we do?

For Swift and his colleagues, raising questions about society and seeking answers set a process in motion that develops the critical awareness that can lead to social justice. As questions are raised and pursued, the connections between social issues—of coffee production, international trade, the food industry, the effects of coffee whiteners on human health, etc.—are made evident. Inevitably, the process begins to uncover "the deep inequities and structural problems" (p. 119) that characterize contemporary societies. What Swift and his coauthors attempt to provide are "elements of the grammar of social literacy" (p. 119)—the means by which people can learn to read social reality and thus participate fully in social and political life. One key element is social structure. Institutionalized arrangements, invisible to the eye, define the meaning and set the limits of daily life, and too frequently favour a few and harm the many. Dialectical social analysis involves "discovering, describing, explaining, and ultimately challenging" the underlying structures that define our social existence (p. 121). Such praxis obliges the social analyst to question and criticize commonly accepted beliefs and official "truths," to trace the history of the social issue at hand, to identify the key players who make decisions or benefit from decisions or pay the costs of the decisions, to move with agility between the individual and collective aspects of the issue, and to view any given issue in the broader context of the "system" within which social, political, economic, and cultural structures overlap and interweave.

In our second reading David Harvey takes a more philosophical line in enumerating 11 principles of dialectical analysis and exploring some implications for critical inquiry. In the book from which this reading has been excerpted, *Justice, Nature and the Geography of Difference*, Harvey weaves the various social sciences together with normative philosophical theory and ecological analysis. The result is a compelling series of reflections on the contemporary condition of humanity and the possibilities for emancipation. For present purposes, Harvey's contribution is particularly helpful for its engagement with ecological thought and natural science—knowledges that are all too often bracketed off from social and cultural studies. His account of dialectics begins with a "deep ontological principle"—that the entities making up the world do not exist outside of or prior to the processes that create, maintain, or subvert them. There are not "things" *here* and "processes" generating change *there*; rather the world is inherently in motion—"change is here to stay," as the saying goes. Methodologically this implies that our comprehension of reality must be attuned to its intrinsic movement and transformation. The "things" that compose the natural world (and the social world embedded within it) are constituted of multiple flows, processes, and relations that render them internally heterogeneous, i.e., contradictory.[1] Change stems from this heterogeneity and is characteristic of all systems, including, of course, social structures and institutions. Space and time do not stand "outside" this dynamic reality; they are contained within the processes that constitute it, as are the parts and wholes (e.g., the individual and the social field) that mutually constitute each other. For Harvey, "the theoretical and empirical research task is to identify those characteristic 'moments' and 'forms' (i.e., 'things') embedded within continuous flows which can produce radical transformations," or conversely, to identify "gatekeeping" or other mechanisms that "give a 'thing' or a system (such as a person, a city, a region, a nation state) qualities of identity, integrity, and relative stability" (p. 130).

Harvey's final two principles are particularly well taken by critical researchers. The relationship between researcher and researched is viewed as one between "two active subjects," each of whom internalizes something from the other by virtue of the processes linking them. In the process of European colonization, the positional superiority assumed by the colonizers—the assumption that they could "know the oriental" without changing either themselves or the object of their gaze (p. 131)—was never anything more than an ideological fiction. Both colonized and colonizers were changed by virtue of the processes linking them. This means more generally that it is not possible to understand the world without at the same time changing it and ourselves (for better or worse). However, and secondly, since our world is dynamic, contradictory, and emergent, *knowledge that limits itself to "the facts"*—to formulating general laws regulating what already exists—*will be inherently flawed.* "The exploration of potentialities for change, for self-realization, for the construction of new collective identities and social orders"—an exploration that builds into its own process moral, ethical, and political choices—is integral to dialectical analysis (p. 131).

Probably the clearest and most detailed accounts of dialectical social analysis as a critical method have been those of Bertell Ollman, beginning with his classic text *Alienation: Marx's Concept of Man in Capitalist Society* (1976) and continuing through a long series of articles that have been collected into two volumes (Ollman, 1993, 2003). Our third selection, a chapter from the more recent collection, *Dance of the Dialectic*, asks why dialectical social analysis is important, and why, in contemporary times, it is all the more so. Dialectical analysis of the social provides a means of grasping the many-sided character of a world that is fundamentally relational, practical, and open to various futures. This method is indispensable in a world more integrated than ever around a highly dynamic and globalized form of capitalism. Ollman tells us that the fundamental assumption underlying Marx's method is that "reality is an internally related whole with temporal as well as spatial dimensions" (p. 138). To understand one social issue, such as poverty, one must uncover the ways in which it is implicated in other issues and relations. If dialectical analysis is holistic, it is also historical. Marx's method rejects metaphysical conceptions that view the present as "walled off" from either the past or the future. Such conceptions, all too common in social science and policy discourses, can become "a prison for thinking," as the present form of something—"the family," "the economy," "retirement"—is mistaken for "what it is in full, and what it could only be" (p. 136). Marx's historical appreciation of the *internal relations* that constitute our world extends not only from past to present but also into the future. Just as the present is a resumé of past practice, the future, as potential, already inhabits the present. Thus, a careful analysis of contemporary social contradictions, emergent practices and relations, and forms of collective agency can help identify ways forward for social justice initiatives, as in possibilities for a widening and deepening of democracy, or for the appropriate use of new technologies.

Such projections, however, are no more than probable eventualities. For Marx, the future is radically contingent: it depends upon what people do, how they make history. Ollman's "dance of the dialectic," reproduced in Figure 10.1, suggests how Marx's method can be used to "unlock the future":

1.   Trace the main lines of the interactions and relations that make (capitalist) society what it is. Do this analysis from various perspectives—economic, cultural, psychological,

etc.—in each case drawing out the relational character of social reality. Do not reify the elements of reality into simple "things," but keep the internal relations between "objective" conditions and "subjective" agency fully in view. View the present as history in the making.

2. Consider what the preconditions in the past were for this present to develop as it has. How, for instance, did capitalism—which has only existed for a short time in the broad sweep of history—grow out of previous forms of society? How did today's globalized corporate capitalism emerge out of the competitive capitalism of the 19th century? How did neo-liberal regimes, whether in Britain or in British Columbia, grow out of the contradictions of Keynesian approaches to governing capitalism, etc.?

3. Having examined the past and its internal relations to the present, consider the *contradictions* that organize that present, including the people involved in them, to highlight the potentialities for a different future. Given that the future, as potential, inhabits the present, project these contradictions forward: how might they be resolved through the practical interventions of human beings? For instance, capitalism, in harnessing science and technology into the project of accumulating wealth under private control (as capital), produces enormous material advances ("forces of production"), yet capitalism's class relations restrict social wealth to a small fraction of the entire population. Hence, disparities intensify as brutalizing poverty necessarily coexists with unprecedented opulence on a global scale. As they intensify, capitalism's contradictions prefigure two possible futures: one in which they are resolved by moving beyond capital (to what Marx calls socialism), another in which the contradictions exhaust the system's human and ecological infrastructure (i.e., barbarism; see Van der Pijl, 1998).

4. Having made reasonable projections of a future in which the contradictions of a problematic way of life are resolved, return to the present to seek out the preconditions for such a future. In this way, develop political strategy based on analysis of the immanent possibilities for social justice and ecological health.

In our final reading, Branwen Jones applies a contemporary variant of dialectical social analysis to the explanation of global poverty. "Critical realism," a perspective on science pioneered in the 1970s by Roy Bhaskar (1979, 1993), and heavily indebted to Marx's method as deployed in *Capital*, has become an influential tradition within British social science. It espouses a relational and dynamic view of social phenomena, and a view of human beings as "complex, stratified natural beings" with emergent powers (e.g., conceptual functioning, symbolic communication, labour) and needs (emotional, aesthetic, etc.) rooted in their social milieux. It follows that to explain the phenomenon of poverty—a condition of inadequate need satisfaction given the possibilities prevailing in a particular societal context—we must examine "the social relations that determine the production and distribution of social powers in society" (p. 150).

This starting point in historically produced structures differs fundamentally from the World Bank's explanation of global poverty, an approach reminiscent of what C. Wright Mills called abstracted empiricism (see Part 1B). In the World Bank's account, poverty is an attribute of certain individuals with certain observable characteristics. By measurement and analysis of relevant variables and their statistical relationships, one can build up both a description of poverty and an *explanation* that derives from the correlation of poverty with various measured "determinants." A major report by the World Bank thereby concludes that lack of access to income-earning opportunities and the incapacity to respond to those opportunities are the major determinants of poverty.

As an empiricist account, the World Bank explanation reduces what exists to what is empirically observable. The result is an analysis accurate at the descriptive level of surface appearances but blind to the underlying relations that generate those appearances. For Jones, as for Marx, these underlying relations are just as real as what people experience immediately: reality has a *depth*; it is stratified (Sayer, 2000: 12–13). Part of the mission of critical social science is to penetrate beneath the surface, to *unmask* underlying relations such as class exploitation that generate phenomena such as global poverty.[2] Jones proceeds to give an account of how global capitalist production relations, the interstate system through which capitalist accumulation is organized, and local modes of production in much of the Third World are articulated together in generating global poverty.

The two perspectives differ dramatically in their political implications. The World Bank takes for granted, and *reifies* what are historically specific features of contemporary society. Its ahistorical empiricism and social atomism lead to the conclusion that the poor need to earn more money—i.e., become more fully integrated in global market relations—so that they can satisfy their needs. This inference is both *conservative* and *ideological*: it fails to challenge or even acknowledge existing social relations and thereby functions in the interest of the established order. In contrast, a dialectical—and realist—analysis, attuned to reality's historical, relational, stratified, and emergent character—leads to the conclusion that "problems of poverty and inequality demand a transformation in the social relations through which production is organised and which determine the distribution of powers in society" (p. 156).

As a critical research strategy, dialectical social analysis has two main strengths: (1) it enables the researcher to "make connections," to grasp the many-sided character of a social/natural world that is fundamentally *relational, practical*, and *emergent*; (2) it enables the researcher to "unmask" both the underlying relations that generate social injustices and ecological maladies and the ideologies that legitimate entrenched power by attending only to surface-level appearances.[3] "Making connections" and "unmasking" are strategies well suited not only to interpreting the world, but to *changing* it.

NOTES

1. As Ollman explains, by contradictions Marx means the main tendencies at work in a system, viewed as interacting processes "that are simultaneously mutually supporting and mutually undermining one another" (p. 138).
2. Indeed, as Marx held, "all science would be superfluous if the outward appearance and the essence of things directly coincided" (quoted in Ollman, 1976: 64).
3. The latter sort of unmasking is termed ideology critique. For a very clear account of Marx's critique of liberal ideology as a world view that celebrates the freedoms and equal opportunities offered by the market—capitalism's most evident surface reality—while denying the deeper relations of class exploitation and alienation that are integral to capitalism, see Larrain (1983: Chapter 1).

REFERENCES

Bhaskar, Roy. 1979. *The Possibility of Naturalism*. Brighton: Harvester Press.

_____. 1993. *Dialectic: The Pulse of Freedom*. London: Verso.

Larrain, Jorge. 1983. *Marxism and Ideology*. London: Macmillan.

_____. 1986. *A Reconstruction of Historical Materialism*. London: Allen & Unwin.

Marx, Karl. 1968 [1852]. "The Eighteenth Brumaire of Louis Bonaparte." In *Karl Marx and Frederick Engels, Selected Works*, 97–180. New York: International Publishers.

Ollman, Bertell. 1976. *Alienation: Marx's Conception of Man in Capitalist Society*, 2nd ed. Cambridge: Cambridge University Press.

_____. 1993. *Dialectical Investigations*. New York: Routledge.

Sayer, Andrew. 2000. *Realism and Social Science*. London: Sage.

Sherman, Howard J. 1995. *Reinventing Marxism*. Baltimore: Johns Hopkins University Press.

Stalin, Joseph. 1940. *Dialectical and Historical Materialism*. New York: International Publishers.

Vaillancourt, Pauline M. 1986. "Dialectics, Marxism and Social Science Research." *Bulletin de Methodologie Sociologique* 11(July): 83–100.

Van der Pijl, Kees. 1998. *Transnational Classes and International Relations*. New York: Routledge.

CHAPTER 8

Getting Started on Social Analysis in Canada

JAMIE SWIFT, JACQUELINE M. DAVIES,
ROBERT G. CLARKE, AND MICHAEL S.J. CZERNY

WELCOME TO SOCIAL ANALYSIS

"Let's have another cup of coffee."

A friendly way to carry on a conversation ... and a good way to begin social analysis. Most of us probably don't think twice about having a cup of coffee (unless it's to heed the warnings about too much caffeine). But if we stop to think about it, a coffee can quickly get some questions going.

- "Yes, I'd like a cup." The coffee beans may come from one of those small Central American countries that drift in and out of the news. Do you know what the local producers get paid for their work? What happens as the coffee beans make their way to us?
- "How much do I owe you for that?" Now and then we hear about a slump in coffee prices, like the one in 2001, when producer prices reached a 30-year low.[1] It seems coffee prices have been in a continuing downward spiral (which is not reflected at the cash register of trendy cafés). What does news like this have to do with Canada?
- "Let me fill the kettle." With tap water? Is the water filtered? Is it safe? Given the tainted water scandals of Walkerton, Ontario, and North Battleford, Saskatchewan—and doubts in many other communities across the country—you might prefer to use bottled water. But does this option carry a cost to the environment as well as at the check-out counter?
- "I'll put on a pot." If the coffee is filtered, check the paper filter. Did its material originate with a logging company embroiled in a land dispute like the one that has frustrated Alberta's Lubicon Cree for decades? Is the filter "whiter than white"? According to one study, "The principal agent of paper's dazzling whiteness—chlorine—is guilty of creating some of the most toxic pollutants ever discharged into our environment."[2]
- "A coffee to go." The drink could come in a cheap, disposable styrofoam cup fashioned from petroleum (there may be a shortage or a glut). The styrofoam might have been manufactured using chemicals that contribute to the depletion of the ozone layer. You'll probably get a plastic stir-stick. When you throw these things away, where do they go?

- "A spoonful of instant." The makings of that coffee may have come from a dozen different countries, but where was it processed? What is the nationality of the company that processed and markets the instant? What else does it sell? Who controls the "coffee market"? Does it make any difference?

- "Do you take sugar?" Sugar (which is apparently not all that good for us) is produced in about 120 countries around the world, including Canada. But 85 per cent of the sugar consumed in Canada is imported, much of it from Third World countries. The aid agency Oxfam has linked the agricultural policies of the European Union—which subsidizes sugar production, leading to low prices—with the plight of farmers in poorer countries who rely on sugar for their livelihoods.[3]

- "Would you like cream?" Dairy farms have gone the way of other small farms in Canada—they either grow larger or they have trouble surviving, and disappear. What impact does the trend towards agribusiness have on the quality of farm products, especially as reliance on growth hormones and antibiotics increases in the production process?

- "We're out of milk—here's a whitener." What's on the list of ingredients? Is the whitener an edible oil product? Do you have any idea what the ingredients do to your health?

- "Good to the last drop." A cup of coffee does not just happen. Many people are involved in getting it ready, from planting the seedling and maintaining the clean water supply, through all the stages of processing, to serving the coffee and washing the cup: owner, planter, picker, shipper, buyer, insurer, processor, packer, advertiser, seller, shopper, consumer, dishwasher. How are all these people—and jobs—related to each other, to their communities, and to the natural environment? Which leads to our final question:

- Is there any fair trade coffee around here? Fairly traded foods ensure that producers are paid a decent price for their work. Fair trade links producers more closely with consumers, reducing the need for middle people and guaranteeing a minimum price to the workers. You can look for a fair trade label on produce, coffee, tea, paper products, and clothing.

A QUESTIONING AWARENESS

Social analysis begins with *questions* like these. As they surface, they start us thinking about a particular issue, like Third World exports, or our health, or a whole cluster of issues like the coffee cycle. Similar questions can prompt us to think about Canadian society. This is what social analysis means—acquiring the habit of questioning the world around us and looking for patterns that raise new questions. There are many different approaches to social analysis, and many theories. [...]

Social analysis, as we are using the term, means *raising questions* about society and *seeking answers*. Its purpose is not only to *develop a critical awareness of the world* but also *to lead towards social justice.*

The process of social analysis also gives rise to further questions about what is going on and who is benefiting and who is getting hurt. This leads to further research. The process brings out the links or connections between different social issues. It helps us find out what is really going on beneath the surface of society, or beyond the appearances. It encourages group discussion.

Social analysis helps people become *critical*. Critical does not mean being negative, or condemning the society we live in, or showing a lack of gratitude for the good things it has to offer. Critical means becoming conscious, aware, questioning. It means developing a discerning attitude, a habit of trying to get to the bottom of things.

All the questions that arise from this process cannot be answered right away. Some open up topics that require *research*. This means taking time to pursue the questions as far as we possibly can. For example, after a discussion of the coffee cycle, we might want to look for additional information about the health hazards of caffeine, sugar, or whitener; the system that ensures the purity of the water we drink; the workings of the international coffee and sugar markets and the possibilities of fair trade; or the situation of coffee-producing peoples and their needs. It is also important to question the information we gather—to make sure it is accurate and thorough.

Critical questions lead to an awareness of previously unsuspected *connections* between issues. For example, thinking about where a cup of coffee comes from and how its ingredients get to us can quickly lead to questions about the international balance of trade, the structure of the food industry, the science, economics, and politics of maintaining a clean water supply, and the effects of caffeine and sugar on health.

Or take another example: a comparative analysis of a particular industry in Canada and a Third World country might soon uncover a common tendency to export relatively unprocessed raw materials. Social analysis tries to trace the links connecting issues, in order to understand how society works and fails to work.

Why raise questions, become critical, do research, and trace connections? Social analysis is not motivated merely by intellectual or scientific curiosity. The purpose is to seek the truth of a situation—whether it is the coffee cycle or unemployment in Canada—in order to lay bare any injustice that characterizes the situation. Social analysis is oriented towards *social justice*—towards taking some action, towards promoting change where this is judged necessary. It hopes to contribute effectively to the quest for greater social justice.

Social analysis is preferably done *in a group,* where one comment can spark new thoughts and people's opinions can get refined by coming up against other points of view. As the members of a group gain a picture of an issue, they move from analysis of a problem that has been identified, through a discussion of possible action, to making decisions, distributing tasks, contacting other groups, and taking action.

* * * * *

Some people say, "I have other things to do." Or, "I can't be bothered about dealing with that. Let other people—politicians, experts—figure it out." But the alternative to social analysis is to accept the surface meanings; to think what we are told to think; to consume, not only goods and services, but also the slogans, meanings, and values of society that go along with them. If we leave all the interpretation and direction of society in the hands of a few people, we may not like the results.

One day, seeing that things have gone too far, we might object, "I wasn't consulted!" By then it may be too late.

TOWARDS SOCIAL JUSTICE

Social analysis leads to action on behalf of justice. Such action may entail looking up more information, organizing a group to take action about an issue, making a small gesture of protest, or contributing to a national campaign that is tackling an important issue. Whatever the action, it will in turn raise new questions and once again involve people more deeply in the process of social analysis.

It doesn't take long for social analysis to begin uncovering the deep inequities and structural problems that characterize Canadian society. These matters can be stated starkly, even simply. But practical solutions are rarely black or white, and usually they are quite messy. They need to be hammered out in an often difficult process of compromise. [...]

* * * * *

LEARNING TO READ

* * * * *

Reading and writing are, without question, critical to active participation in our society today. Illiteracy can present a barrier to full participation in life.

There is another, even more common, form of illiteracy that also prevents people from participating in society, and that is social illiteracy. For example, given the shortage of affordable housing in Canada:

- How did the shortage arise?
- What is its impact?
- Why does it continue?
- What can be done about it?

A person might recognize that the questions are important, but not know where to begin, what to ask, or think, or say. Not knowing where to begin is an experience of social illiteracy.

Social illiteracy means being unable to read—to interpret—the events that are going on in society. Unfortunately, few institutions teach Canadians to read social reality. A good percentage of our population remains unaware of how society works or where it is headed.

There is another interesting parallel between the understanding of language and society. Once upon a time, people thought of language as something forever fixed and unchanging, "a gift of the gods." But the study of linguistics makes it clear that every word is a human creation; language is inherited, and it evolves as it is used.

Similarly, people also used to think of human society as something God-given or eternal, as divinely created or the result of an age-old and unchangeable social contract. Today nearly everyone agrees that social institutions are human creations: the deliberate product of human ideas and the result of habitual human action. As evolving human creations, social structures and institutions are something people can learn about and understand—and change.

Learning to read—whether you are using a native language or a foreign one—is a somewhat mysterious process. What's involved? Certainly it doesn't mean memorizing a grammar text or dictionary. First of all, it means connecting sounds with letters, pictures with words. The learner grasps individual words, builds up a vocabulary, starts recognizing new words from their context. With time this process develops into expertise, which allows the newly literate person to understand the messages communicated by sentences and paragraphs.

* * * * *

Beginning to do social analysis is like learning how to read: you learn by doing.

[...] This chapter presents elements of the grammar of social literacy, some of the building blocks and workings of social analysis.

Four of these building blocks are symptoms, commodification, social costs, and structures. [...]

SYMPTOMS

Pain or malaise is often all too obvious. Good medical practice begins with a thorough description of the ailment, so we don't merely treat the symptoms with painkillers, but instead discover and remove the cause of the sickness. Anatomy and physiology provide an ideal picture of the whole body. The diagnostician can compare this picture with what has broken down and what is functioning properly.

Social malaise is also there on the surface for people to see: witness Canadians suffering from lack of access to adequate health care, affordable homes, nourishing food, or wages to pay for the necessities of life. Sometimes the malady, though perfectly obvious to those suffering from it, is hidden from those others who are well provided for. To note carefully, describe, categorize, and finally explore the symptoms—that is one task of social analysis.

Yet another link exists between medical diagnosis and social analysis. Bodily illness itself can be a symptom of social injustice. Infant mortality, reduced life expectancy, malnutrition, and many diseases are often symptoms of a social malaise, economic injustice, or political or cultural oppression. Moreover, these medical problems can be documented and quantified as proof that people's rights are being violated.

COMMODIFICATION

The tendency to reduce a person or relationship to an object of economic value, a commodity to be bought and sold in the marketplace, is called commodification. Reification is the first step in this process. The word reification comes from the Latin word *res,* meaning thing or object. It refers here to the tendency to reduce a person or a relationship to the status of an object. Commodification is the next step, the step that transforms the object into an item of economic exchange, something whose purpose is to be bought and sold.

[…] People who say Canadians have the "right to choose" where to spend their "after-tax dollars" often use arguments that shift health care away from its position as a basic human right and into the realm of a commodity. "Healthy people might choose to purchase a new car. Those who need diagnosis and treatment for illness should be able to spend their money to secure it," one writer says—thus comparing health care to going out and buying a car.[4] Similarly, having decent, affordable shelter, which is a basic need and human right, has been commodified into a market-driven product, a consumer item available to those who can afford it.

* * * * *

Social analysis tries to make clear how basic necessities of life are transformed into commodities. It tries to show where a market mentality is intruding on relationships—with other people, with nature—that reflect respect for such fundamental rights as the right to adequate nutrition, health care, housing, and useful work. And it tries to indicate the responsibility of various social groups (government, investors, employers, labour, consumers) to protect these rights.

SOCIAL COSTS

When big players in the food industry put small local producers and retailers out of business, the social costs often go unrecognized and end up being paid by the community at large, now or later. When developers choose to shift their money from housing to seemingly more lucrative shopping malls and office towers, their profits—and their losses—are not balanced by any accounting of the losses that Canadian taxpayers, tenants, and would-be tenants incur through this decision.

By themselves, profit-and-loss and other business categories fail to take long-term questions of health, aesthetics, culture, justice, or even jobs into account. Social analysis does take illness, pollution, and injustice into account, on the debit side. On the credit side it attends to human health and well-being, the flourishing of communities and their individual members. It analyzes these conditions as social costs and benefits that otherwise go unreckoned. Using this kind of analysis, citizens can see to it that the people who profit also repair the damages they cause, or pay for their repair, and that costs are not imposed on workers and communities without their knowledge and consent.

STRUCTURES

The word "structure" is familiar enough when it is being used as a reference to buildings—the Peace Tower, the Regina parliament buildings, a local hockey arena, or a high-rise apartment building. These become structures because a lot of parts—foundations, stairways, windows, rooftops—get set up in a certain pattern to form a whole.

It is the same with social structures. They are not so visible to the naked eye, but they are just as real as the prominent mass of the Château Frontenac or a grain elevator. We can identify social structures when we consider relationships, such as those involving:

- patient, health worker, doctor, hospital;
- consumer (tenant or buyer), landlord, developer;
- citizen, industry, regulator, newspaper.

Social analysis takes common relationships and considers them not as separate, isolated units but as parts of a whole, as parts of a structure. It unveils the more general structures that define and shape these common relationships, that construct the meaning and set the limits of our daily activities.

The structures can be beneficial or harmful in their effects on people. Too frequently they favour a few and damage the many. They may be invisible to the eye, but they are just as much "always there"—and apparently just as much

beyond the power of the individual citizen to move as the Halifax Citadel.

There are structures of different kinds: social, economic, cultural, political, religious. Social analysis has to adapt its approach to each issue, to find out what kind of structures are most important in a given situation. In the case of the medical profession, financial interests (which are part of certain economic structures) play a decisive role. But cultural and political considerations also serve to determine the nature of the relationship between doctors and patients or attitudes towards pay-as-you-go services.

The word "structure," as it is used in social analysis, suggests that root causes are not individual, but rather institutional; not transitory, but solid and long-lasting. Social analysis involves discovering, describing, explaining, and ultimately challenging the structures that define social existence in Canada—dismantling the destructive structures and rebuilding according to sounder principles of social justice.

WAYS OF READING

Learning to read is a fairly complex activity that can be broken down into a number of simpler components, like sounding out the letters in each word, recognizing whole words, recognizing how they work together with punctuation in phrases, sentences, and larger grammatical structures like paragraphs or even chapters. The activities of social reading and interpretation can also be broken down into a number of simpler processes, which are eventually brought together in the complex we call social analysis.

EXAMINING COMMONLY ACCEPTED BELIEFS

The economic and political structures of Canada are primarily—but not exclusively—responsible for giving the country its shape.

Patterns of thought and belief also influence the shape of society.

The belief that real estate developers have the right to do what they want with their earnings, or that a competitive marketplace always results in the best readily available goods for meeting human needs, leads society in certain directions. Canadians can quickly march down an unknown path, for instance, if they believe that science always means progress or that the slogan "buyer beware" is all the protection we need from food industry applications of developments in genetic engineering. Staying alert to possible dangers lying further down the road calls for vigilant attention to new scientific developments and a careful reading of how they are represented to the public. It also requires looking carefully for reports and scientific research that avoid the particular biases that come into play when the attention of government and industry research is distracted by the potential for national or private economic growth.

If commonly accepted understandings of issues were always accurate, there would be little need to embark on social analysis. In fact, common notions about society, Canada, and the world often tend to be based on scattered bits of information or even misinformation.

Opinions are promoted as facts, at times unwittingly yet quite vigorously, by radio, television, newspapers, and magazines. Problems with the labour market, for example, are more likely to be framed by discussions of supply (lack of trained workers) than of demand (lack of good jobs). The media are more likely to put forward already accepted, official, or established points of view than to report on critical or innovative viewpoints. A critical questioning of commonly accepted beliefs asks whose interests are served by their widespread acceptance. It explores the relationships between the social power of those whose interests are being served and the power that those beliefs have in society.

TRACING HISTORY

Nearly every issue has a long history and has been examined many times before. In a historical analysis, the object is to view the past not with nostalgia for the good old days, but critically, with an eye for the effect on the present.

Even in the short lifetime of Canadian medicare there have been periodic crises, with a remarkably consistent pattern of complaints by the medical associations and of responses by people who use the health-care system. That struggle is an essential thread in the process whereby medicare became part of the Canadian social fabric, and in which it continues to evolve.

* * * * *

If you were analyzing the relationships involved in the production of a cup of coffee, it would be important to consider what happened in the nineteenth century when indigenous peasants in Central America had their land taken away from them and turned into coffee estates—and what that means to today's coffee growers. Or, again, a great many of the problems posed by new technology today are similar to the ones that arose nearly two centuries ago. Most social issues have a history that contributes to the problem at hand—and, if understood, can help to explain that problem.

IDENTIFYING KEY PLAYERS AND PERSPECTIVES

* * * * *

It is clear that some players make decisions and benefit from the choices made. Others [...] have little say in what happens, even though they are often harmed in the process.

Perspective analysis is an important method of discovering how society divides into those with decision-making power and those who are powerless. Once the groups or classes have been identified, further questions help to sort them out. Who makes the decisions? Who benefits from the decisions? Who pays the cost of the decisions?[5] These questions clarify the social divisions that both surround an issue and are characteristic of society as a whole.

The questions of who the players are and how evenly the decision-making power is distributed apply easily to many issues besides housing. For example, what roles do the medical establishment, government, pharmaceutical companies, and investors in the growing private-sector "health-care industry" play in the structuring of Canada's health-care system? Who has a say in decisions about the regulation of the food industry? Who benefits from loose regulations?

* * * * *

MOVING BACK AND FORTH

We all experience a strong tendency to see individual problems as requiring individual solutions and to see social problems as insoluble. In response to this tendency, social analysis moves in two ways: from the individual case to the social structures in which that case is embedded, and back again; and from "someone's" vague problem to "everybody's" concrete social issue. [...]

- Illness at first appears to be a pre-eminently individual problem. Sick persons usually can't think of anything but their own misery. But going to a doctor would be difficult without medicare, which is a collective, social solution. At the widest social level, if government does not guarantee access to necessary health care or enforce (for instance) water pollution regulations, illness becomes an even more individual, apparently "private" matter.

- Housing is also a problem for every individual person or family. People with trouble finding housing they can afford may believe that they just need to get out and hustle for an appropriate apartment or house. Yet "the market" is not working for many of them. Any real solution to the problem of acquiring decent, affordable lodging must be sought on the social level—for example, by organizing an alternative structure such as a co-op to make housing available.

- The supermarket is a place to buy food for the family. The kind of in-store choices that shoppers can make are determined by market forces that they won't see unless they look beyond the supermarket shelves. At the same time, the choices they make have far-reaching implications for the lives of people who work in the production, processing, and sale of food products at home and all over the world.

- Unemployment can be one of the most socially isolating experiences a person can go through. Yet individual job losses are part of a much larger pattern. Looking at such patterns can raise new questions about how we think about work, how we use our time, energy, and skills, and how opportunities to contribute and to be rewarded for that contribution are distributed throughout society.

FOCUSING ON THE SYSTEM

Many symptoms, many players, many issues, and many structures are interconnected to form a functioning unity. The word "system" suggests how these elements fit together in a set pattern at a particular moment. "System" links apparently quite different issues and shows how very different groups are actually related.

* * * * *

A clearer focus on a system that ties a whole social issue together provides a greater sense of what makes Canada tick, of how its social, economic, political, and cultural structures interweave and overlap.

* * * * *

NOTES

1. "Coffee Cartel Shuts up Shop," BBC News (Oct. 19, 2001), <news.bbc.co.uk/hi/english/business> (July 12, 2002).

2. Liz Armstrong and Adrienne Scott, *Whitewash: Exposing Health and Environmental Dangers of Women's Sanitary Products and Disposable Diapers— What You Can Do About It* (Toronto: HarperPerennial, 1992), 9.

3. "Oxfam Paper on EU Common Agricultural Policy (CAP) Reform," Canadian Sugar Institute, Toronto, August 2000 <www.sugar.ca> (December 17, 2002).

4. Margaret Wente, "The Ridiculous $3-Million MRI Machine Problem," *The Globe and Mail* (December 5, 2002), A27.

5. J. Holland and P. Henriot, SJ, *Social Analysis: Linking Faith and Justice,* rev. ed. (Maryknoll: Orbis Books, 1983), 28.

CHAPTER 9

The Principles of Dialectics

DAVID HARVEY

Marx chose never to write out any principles of dialectics for a very good reason. The only way to understand his method is by following his practice. This suggests that the reduction of dialectics to a set of "principles" might be self-defeating. The dialectic is a process and not a thing and it is, furthermore, a process in which the Cartesian separations between mind and matter, between thought and action, between consciousness and materiality, between theory and practice, have no purchase. The long-standing debate, for example, over whether the dialectic is an ontological statement about the nature of reality or a convenient epistemology for understanding nature is, from this standpoint, as spurious as the Cartesian separation between mind and matter. Yet the debate does have significance. The debate over what constitutes a "dialectical mode of argumentation" is, Ollman argues, a debate over how to abstract from the phenomena we encounter in everyday life. Setting down the principles of dialectics provides an opening gambit for further enquiry, a preliminary discussion of how to formulate such abstractions. Marx, of course, had the example of Hegel's logic and method before him and without careful study of it, he probably could not have arrived at the dialectical practices embedded in *Capital,* the apparatus of conceptual abstractions that allowed him to understand the world in the way he did,

nor could he have formulated his political strategies and practices.

To write out "the principles of dialectical argumentation" is like going back to Hegel as a prelude to doing something much more Marxist. It is a necessary "going back" but only a means to go forward onto a terrain of action on which the principles themselves, in the fashion of Marx, disappear into a flow of theoretical and political practices. I shall not evoke Hegel's particular formulation here, but try to summarize as simply as I can some of the basic theses about dialectics that can be distilled not only from Marx's practices but also from those who have in recent years been drawn back to reflect on what dialectics might mean.

The principles of dialectics can be summarized in 11 propositions.

1. Dialectical thinking emphasizes the understanding of processes, flows, fluxes, and relations over the analysis of elements, things, structures, and organized systems. [...] There is a deep ontological principle involved here, for dialecticians in effect hold that elements, things, structures, and systems do not exist outside of or prior to the processes, flows, and relations that create, sustain, or undermine them. For example, in our contemporary world, flows of capital (goods, and money) and of people give rise to, sustain, or undermine

places such as factories, neighborhoods, and cities understood as things. Epistemologically, the process of enquiry usually inverts this emphasis: we get to understand processes by looking either at the attributes of what appear to us in the first instance to be self-evident things or at the relations between them. We typically investigate flows of goods, money, and people by examining relationships between existing entities like factories, neighborhoods, and cities. Newton, likewise, did not start with gravity, but with the apple, his head, the earth, and the moon. This method only really allows us, however, to compare the state of relations between such entities at different points in time (a confining method called "comparative statics"). On this basis we may infer something about the processes that have generated a change of state but the idea that the entities are unchanging in themselves quickly leads us to a causal and mechanistic way of thinking. Dialectical reasoning holds, however, that this epistemological condition should get reversed when it comes to formulating abstractions, concepts, and theories about the world. This transforms the self-evident world of things with which positivism and empiricism typically deals into a much more confusing world of relations and flows that are manifest as things. Consider, for example, the definition of "capital." In classical political economy and in neoclassical economics it is typically defined as a stock of productive assets of a certain value (a set of things) out of which a flow of services can be generated. But in Marx's definition, capital is constituted as *both* the process of circulation of value (a flow) *and* the stock of assets ("things" like commodities, money, production apparatus) implicated in those flows. In so far as workers become embedded in that process (as inputs to production and as consumers of finished products) so they too become "appendages" of and thereby a particular manifestation of "capital" ("variable capital" in Marx's

terminology). "Money" similarly takes on all manner of "thing-like" forms but those "things" (like coins or entries on a computer screen) only have meaning in terms of the processes of social production and exchange that validate them. Without the processes continually working to support it, money would be meaningless.

This way of thinking is rather more widespread than is generally realized. Quantum theory, for example, has the same entity (e.g., an electron) behaving "under one set of circumstances as a wave, and in another set of circumstances as a particle" (Bohm and Peat, 1987: 40). Since matter (thing-like substances) and energy (a flow) are interchangeable, neither one nor the other can be prioritized as an exclusive focus of enquiry without serious loss of insight and understanding. Electrons thus appear as both "things" and as "flows." Yet it took many years for physicists to recognize that these two conceptions were not incommensurable or mutually exclusive. Only when they overcame this barrier could modern quantum theory begin to take shape. It has likewise proven very difficult for social scientists to abandon what Ollman (1993: 34) calls the "common sense view"—erected into a philosophical system by Locke, Hume, and others—that "there are things and there are relations, and that neither can be subsumed in the other."

2. Elements or "things" (as I shall call them) are constituted out of flows, processes, and relations operating within bounded fields which constitute structured systems or wholes. A dialectical conception of both the individual *thing* and the *structured system* of which it is a part rests entirely on an understanding of the processes and relations by which thing and structured system are constituted. This idea is not intuitively self-evident since we are surrounded by "things" that seem to have such a permanent and solid character that

it is difficult to imagine them as somehow in flux. We cannot downplay, therefore, the significance of what Whitehead (1985: 137) calls "permanences"—the innumerable "practically indestructible objects" that we daily encounter in the world and without which physical and biological life would not and could not exist as we now know it. But, he went on to observe, even something as solid and long lasting as an Egyptian pyramid is constituted out of matter in motion. Dialectics forces us always to ask the question of every "thing" or "event" that we encounter by what process was it constituted and how is it sustained?

3. The "things" and systems which many researchers treat as irreducible and therefore unproblematic are seen in dialectical thought as internally contradictory by virtue of the multiple processes that constitute them. I am, for purposes of social theory, considered an individual within a social system and for certain restricted forms of enquiry such a supposition might appear entirely reasonable. But further inspection shows that I am a rather contradictory and problematic "thing" created by all sorts of processes. My body contains a variety of life-supporting organs such as the heart, lungs, liver, and digestive system "whose functioning is more or less automatic, and required by the fact that the body ... is involved in the perpetual process of internal self-reconstruction" (Ingold, 1986: 18). The metabolic processes which permit that internal self-reconstruction to proceed entail exchanges with my environment and a whole range of transformative processes which are necessary for the maintenance of my bodily individuality. If the processes change, then the body is either transformed or ceases to exist. My sociality (for example, the acquisition of language and symbolic skills) is likewise built up through my capturing of certain powers which reside in social processes. Continuous reconstitution of

those powers (with respect to mental faculties and symbolic skills, for example) is a process which is as perpetual as my life is long (we all know what it means to "keep sharp" or "get rusty" at what we do). To put the matter this way is not to view the "thing" (or the system) as a passive product of external processes (I certainly do not view myself that way). What is remarkable about living systems is the way they capture diffuse (and often high entropy) energy or information flows and assemble them into complex but well-ordered (low entropy) forms. Human individuals, furthermore, have a remarkable capacity to capture and reorganize energy and information flows in ways which are creative rather than passive. But the fact that they do so in no way challenges the ontological proposition that "things" and systems are perpetually constituted and reconstituted [...] out of processes.

4. "Things" are always assumed "to be internally heterogeneous [i.e., contradictory] at every level" (Levins and Lewontin, 1985: 272). This follows from the first two propositions but is worth stating explicitly. There are four major points to be made here:

(a) Any "thing" can be decomposed into a collection of other "things" which are in some relation to each other. For example, a city can be considered as a "thing" in interaction with other cities, but it can also be broken down into neighborhoods or zones which can in turn be broken down into people, houses, schools, factories, etc., which can in turn be broken down *ad infinitum*. The *ad infinitum* clause is very important because it says that there are no irreducible building blocks of "things" for any theoretical reconstruction of how the world works. It then follows that what looks like a system at one level of analysis (e.g., a city) becomes a part at another level, e.g., a global network of world cities. This idea has become very important in contemporary quantum physics where a fundamental guiding principle is that "whatever we say a thing or structure is, it isn't" because "there is always something more than what we say and something different" (Bohm and Peat, 1987: 141–142). There is, as Levins and Lewontin (1985: 278) put it, "no basement" since experience shows that "all previously proposed undecomposable 'basic units' have so far turned out to be decomposable, and the decomposition has opened up new domains for investigation and practice." It is legitimate to investigate "each level of organization without having to search for fundamental units." The other implication, taken seriously in the dialectics of deconstruction, is that all fixed and frozen categories are capable of dissolution. Critical practice in the humanities is very much guided these days, perhaps overly so, by concerns to dissolve fixed categories within conflicting fields and fluxes of socio-linguistic and representational practices.

(b) If all "things" are heterogeneous by virtue of the complex processes (or relations) which constitute them, then the only way we can understand the qualitative and quantitative attributes of "things" is by understanding the processes and relations they internalize. Ollman (1976) has been very explicit about this in constructing his arguments concerning internal relations. But such arguments are now advanced in much of the ecological literature (sec Eckersley, 1992: 49–55; Naess, 1989: 79; Zimmerman, 1988). The only way we can understand the (contradictory) qualitative and quantitative attributes of "things" is by understanding the processes and relationships which constitute them and which they internalize. I, as an individual, cannot be understood except by way of the metabolic, social, and other processes which I internalize. This implies, however, that I necessarily internalize heterogeneity and a bundle of associated contradictions. Contradiction is here understood in the sense given to the term by Ollman (1990: 49), as

"a union of two or more internally related processes that are simultaneously supporting and undermining one another." This is a sentiment that Whitehead (1985: 155), always preferring the word "event" to thing because it captures the dynamism involved, characterizes as follows:

> the concept of internal relations requires the concept of substance as the activity synthesising the relationships into its emergent character. The event is what it is, by reason of the unification in itself of a multiplicity of relationships.

(c) There is, however, a limitation to be put upon this argument. I as an individual, do not in practice internalize everything in the universe, but absorb mainly what is relevant to me through my relationships (metabolic, social, political, cultural, etc.) to processes operating over a relatively bounded field (my ecosystem, economy, culture, etc.). There is, however, no fixed or *a priori* boundary to this system. Where my relevant environment begins and ends is itself a function of the ecological, economic, and other processes which are relevant to me. Relevance is dependent, further-more, on my own actions (the atmosphere relevant to my breathing, to take a trivial example, depends on whether I stay indoors all day, take a hike in the country, or fly to Los Angeles).

(d) Setting boundaries with respect to space, time, scale, and environment then becomes a major strategic consideration in the development of concepts, abstractions, and theories. It is usually the case that any substantial change in these boundaries will radically change the nature of the concepts, abstractions, and theories. In geography we often encounter this problem in the form of the paradoxes generated by different scales of ecological correlation. We will frequently encounter this scale problem in what follows.

5. Space and time are neither absolute nor external to processes but are contingent and contained with them. There are multiple spaces and times (and space-times) implicated in different physical, biological, and social processes. The latter all *produce*—to use Lefebvre's (1991) terminology—their own forms of space and time. Processes do not operate *in* but *actively construct space* and time and in so doing define distinctive scales for their development. [...]

6. Parts and wholes are mutually constitutive of each other. "Part *makes* whole, and whole *makes* part" (Levins and Lewontin, 1985). This is a principle that Giddens (1984) promotes in some of his writings on structuration theory (agency makes structure and structure makes agency) and it is, of course, a fundamental principle which operates across the whole breadth and range of Marx's work. To say that parts and wholes are mutually constitutive of each other is to say much more than that there is a feedback loop between them. In the process of capturing the powers that reside in those ecological and economic systems which are relevant to me, I actively reconstitute or transform them within myself even before I project them back to reconstitute or transform the system from which those powers were initially derived. To take a couple of trivial but important examples: I breathe in, I reconstitute myself by virtue of the oxygen I gain but in the process transform the chemistry of the air within me, and I breathe out and in so doing transform the atmosphere around me or, I take in ideas and thoughts through listening and reading. I gain a sense of selfhood thereby but in the process reformulate and transform words and in projecting them back into society change the social world. Reductionist practices "typically ignore this relationship, isolating parts as preexisting units of which wholes are then composed" while some holistic practices reverse the preferential treatment.

7. The interdigitation of parts and wholes entails "the interchangeability of subject and object, of cause and effect" (Levins and Lewontin, 1985: 274). Organisms, for example, have to be looked at as both the subjects and the objects of evolution in exactly the same way that individuals have to be considered as both subjects and objects of processes of social change. The reversibility of cause and effect renders causally specified models (even when endowed with feedback loops) inappropriate. Precisely by virtue of its embeddedness in and representation of the flow of continuous processes, dialectics makes limited appeal to cause and effect argument and then only as a particular limiting case. Causal argumentation necessarily rests, for example, upon absolute, not relational, conceptions of space and time. There can be, argues Whitehead (1920: 53), "no explanation" of "nature as process" or the passing of time. "All that can be done is to use language which may speculatively demonstrate [them]."

8. Transformative behavior—"creativity"—arises out of the contradictions which attach both to the internalized heterogeneity of "things" and out of the more obvious heterogeneity present within systems. Heterogeneity, as Ollman and Levins and Lewontin (1985: 278) insist, means more than mere diversity: "the parts and processes confront each other as opposites, conditional on the wholes of which they are parts." Out of these oppositions, themselves constituted out of the flow of process, creative tensions and transformative behaviors arise. Becoming, to appropriate Hegel's language, arises out of the opposition between being and not-being. Or, to cite Whitehead (1969: 28), the "principle of process" is that "being is constituted by becoming." In the dialectical view, opposing forces, themselves constituted out of processes, in turn become particular nodal points for further patterns of transformative activity. Matter and not-matter, positive and

negative charges, repulsion and attraction, life and death, mind and matter, masculine and feminine, capital and labor, etc., are constituted as oppositions around which congeal a whole host of transformative activities that both reproduce the oppositions and restructure the physical, biological, and social world.

9. "Change is a characteristic of all systems and all aspects of systems" (Levins and Lewontin, 1985: 275). This is perhaps the most important of all dialectical principles and one which Ollman (1990, 1993) puts above all others. The implication is that change and instability are the norm and that the appearance of stability of "things" or systems is what has to be explained. In Ollman's (1990: 34) words, "given that change is always a part of what things are, [our] research problem [can] only be *how, when,* and *into what* [things or systems] change and why they sometimes appear not to change." Levins and Lewontin make a similar point:

> The dialectical view insists that persistence and equilibrium are not the natural state of things but require explanation, which must be sought in the actions of the opposing forces. The conditions under which the opposing forces balance and the system as a whole is in stable equilibrium are quite special. They require the simultaneous satisfaction of as many mathematical relations as there are variables in the system, usually expressed as inequalities among the parameters of that system.

Nature, says Whitehead (1969: 33) is always about the perpetual exploration of novelty. Since transformative action—and I here think primarily of creative rather than routine action—arises out of contradiction, it follows that it can in principle be found anywhere and everywhere in the physical, biological, and social world [...]. To put it this way does not

imply, however, that all moments within some continuous process are equally significant as creative points of transformative activity. The theoretical and empirical research task is to identify those characteristic "moments" and "forms" (i.e., "things") embedded within continuous flows which can produce radical transformations or where, conversely, "gatekeeping" or other mechanisms might be constructed so as to give a "thing" or a system (such as a person, a city, a region, a nation state) qualities of identity, integrity, and relative stability. If, as is intuitively obvious, the physical world around us appears to be constituted by what Whitehead (1969: 241–248) calls "permanences"—relatively stable configurations of matter and things—then the issue of how such permanences are maintained yet also integrated into a dynamic world of processes becomes a critical subject of analysis. Again, this tension is the focus of contradiction. "If the opposites, static and fluent," writes Whitehead (1969: 408), "have once been so explained separately to characterize diverse actualities, the interplay between the thing which is static and the things which are fluent involves contradiction at every step in its explanation." The question of "agency" in social and biological as well as in physical systems has to be formulated broadly in such terms.

10. Dialectical enquiry is itself a *process* that produces *permanences* such as concepts, abstractions, theories, and institutionalized structures of knowledge which stand to be supported or undermined by continuing processes of enquiry. A certain relationship is implied between the researcher and the researched, a relationship which is not construed in terms of an "outsider" (the researcher) looking in on the researched as an object, but one between two active subjects each of which necessarily internalizes something from the other by virtue of the

processes that connect them. Observation of the world is, Heisenberg argued, inevitably intervention in the world, in much the same way that deconstructionists will argue that the reading of a text is fundamental to its production. Marx similarly insists that only by transforming the world can we transform ourselves; that it is impossible to understand the world without simultaneously changing it as well as ourselves. Formal dialectical logic cannot, therefore, be presupposed as an ontological quality of nature: to do so would be to superimpose a particular mental logic on the world as an act of mind *over* matter. The dialectical unity of mental and material activities (expressed by Marx as the unity of theory and praxis) can never be broken, only attenuated or temporarily alienated.

11. The exploration of "possible worlds" is integral to dialectical thinking. In some ways this idea goes back to Aristotle, broadly rejected by seventeenth-century science, that "the becoming of a natural being is a constant process of actualization of its potentiality" (Leclerc, 1986: 21). The exploration of potentialities for change, for self-realization, for the construction of new collective identities and social orders, new totalities (e.g., social ecosystems), and the like is a fundamental motif in Marxian dialectical thinking. Bookchin likewise argues that *education* (the exploration of possibilities) rather than deduction (spinning out the implications of known truths) or induction (discovering the general laws regulating what already exists) is the central motif of dialectical praxis as well as the primary purpose of knowledge construction. When the location theorist August Losch (1954), in his opening argument, proposed that our task "is not to explain our sorry reality, but to improve it" and concluded with his vision of a science which "like architecture rather than architectural history, creates rather than describes," he was bringing to bear a dialectical (albeit Hegelian) sense of creative science as the exploration of more rational and equitable spatially ordered worlds. It is in this sense that his (infamous) statement that if "the model does not conform to reality then it is reality that is wrong" has to be understood.

Dialectical enquiry necessarily incorporates, therefore, the building of ethical, moral, and political choices (values) into its own process and sees the constructed knowledges that result as discourses situated in a play of power directed towards some goal or other. Values and goals (what we might call the "teleological" as well as the "utopian" moment of reflexive thought) are not imposed as universal abstractions from outside but arrived at through a living process (including intellectual enquiry) embedded in forms of praxis and plays of power attaching to the exploration of this or that potentiality (in ourselves as well as in the world we inhabit). The rise of a distinctively "green-value theory" in recent years, is an excellent case study of how an intersection of socio-ecological processes and plays of power can generate a new vision of possibilities. The search for *possibilities* was, of course, always central to Raymond Williams' work: recall how he repeatedly invokes that "sense of value which has won its way through different kinds of oppression of different forms ... [as] an ingrained and indestructible yet also changing embodiment of the possibilities of a common life" (Williams, 1989a: 321–322). The search for those possibilities is, given the dialectical rules of engagement, contained *within,* rather than articulated before or after social practices, including those of the research process. It is never, therefore, a matter of choosing between different applications of neutral knowledge, but always an embedded search for possibilities that lies at the very heart of dialectical argumentation.

* * * * *

REFERENCES

Bohm, D., and F. Peat. 1987. *Science, Order, and Creativity.* London: Routledge.

Bookchin, M. 1990a. *Remaking Society: Pathways to a Green Future.* Boston: South End Press.

_____. 1990b. *The Philosophy of Social Ecology: Essays on Dialectical Naturalism.* Montreal: Black Rose Books.

Booth, A., and H. Jacobs. 1990. "Ties That Bind: Native American Beliefs as a Foundation for Environmental Consciousness." *Environmental Ethics* 12: 27–43.

Borneman, E., ed. 1976. *The Psychoanalysis of Money.* London: Urizen Books.

Eckersley, R. 1992. *Environmentalism and Political Theory: Toward an Ecocentric Approach.* Albany, NY: State University of New York Press.

Giddens, A. 1984. *The Constitution of Society.* Cambridge: Polity Press.

Ingold, T. 1986. *The Appropriation of Nature: Essays on Human Ecology and Social Relations.* Manchester: Manchester University Press.

Leclerc, I. 1986. *The Philosophy of Nature.* Washington: Catholic University of America Press.

Lefebvre, H. 1991. *The Production of Space.* Oxford: Blackwell Press.

Levins, R., and R. Lewontin. 1985. *The Dialectical Biologist.* Cambridge: Harvard University Press.

Losch, A. 1954. *The Economics of Location.* New Haven.

Naess, A. 1989. *Ecology, Community and Lifestyle.* Cambridge: Cambridge University Press.

Ollman, B. 1976. *Alienation: Marx's Conception of Man in Capitalist Society.* Cambridge: Cambridge University Press.

_____. 1990. "Putting Dialectics to Work: The Process of Abstraction in Marx's Method." *Rethinking Marxism* 3(1): 26–74.

_____. 1993. *Dialectical Investigations.* New York: Routledge.

Whitehead, A. 1920. *The Concept of Nature.* Cambridge: Cambridge University Press.

_____. 1969. *Process and Reality.* New York.

_____. 1985. *Science and the Modern World.* London.

Williams, R. 1989a. *Resources of Hope.* London: Verso.

Zimmerman, M. 1988. "Quantum Theory, Intrinsic Value, and Panentheism." *Environmental Ethics* 10: 3–30.

Why Dialectics? Why Now? Or, How to Study the Communist Future inside the Capitalist Present

BERTELL OLLMAN

The law locks up the man or woman
Who steals a goose from off the common,
But leaves the greater villain loose
Who steals the common from under the
 goose.
—Anonymous, fifteenth century, English

1

The commons, of course, was the land owned by everyone in the village. By the late Middle Ages, feudal lords were claiming this land as their own private property. In universities today we can discern two opposing kinds of scholarship: that which studies the people who steal a goose from off the commons ("Goose from Off the Commons Studies," or GFOC for short) and that which studies those who steal the commons from under the goose ("Commons from Under the Goose Studies," or CFUG for short). If the "mainstream" in practically every discipline consists almost entirely of the former, Marxism is our leading example of the latter.

But whereas seeing someone steal a goose from off the commons is a relatively simple matter—you only have to be there, to open your eyes, and to look—seeing someone steal the commons from under the goose is not, neither then nor now (Russia today is a possible exception). Here, the theft is accomplished only gradually; the person acting is often an agent for someone else; force is used, but so

are laws and ideology. In short, to recognize a case of CFUG, one has to grasp the bigger picture and the longer time that it takes for it to come together. It's not easy, but nothing that we study is more important. [...]

Just how difficult it is to grasp the bigger picture was recently brought home to us when a group of astronomers announced that they had discovered what they called the "Great Attractor." This is a huge structure composed of many galaxies that is exerting a strong attraction on our galaxy and therefore on our solar system and on the planet on which we live. When questioned as to why something so big was not discovered earlier, one of the astronomers replied that its very size was responsible for the delay. These scientists had focused so intently on its parts that they couldn't see what they were parts of.

Capitalism is a huge structure very similar to the Great Attractor. It, too, has a major effect on everything going on inside it, but it is so big and so omnipresent that few see it. In capitalism, the system consists of a complex set of relations between all people, their activities (particularly material production), and products. But this interaction is also evolving, so the system includes the development of this interaction over time, stretching back to its origins and forward to whatever it is becoming. The problem people have in seeing capitalism, then—and recognizing instances of CFUG

Studies when they occur—comes from the difficulty of grasping such a complex set of relations that are developing in this way and on this scale.

No one will deny, of course, that everything in society is related in some way and that the whole of this is changing, again in some way and at some pace. Yet most people try to make sense of what is going on by viewing one part of society at a time, isolating and separating it from the rest and treating it as static. The connections between such parts, like their real history and potential for further development, are considered external to what each one really is and therefore not essential to a full or even adequate understanding of any of them. As a result, looking for these connections and their history becomes more difficult than it has to be. They are left for last or left out completely, and important aspects of them are missed, distorted, or trivialized. It's what might be called the Humpty Dumpty problem. After the fall, it was not only extremely hard to put the pieces of poor Humpty together again but even to see where they fit. This is what happens whenever the pieces of our everyday experience are taken as existing separate from their spatial and historical contexts, whenever the part is given an ontological status independent of the whole.

2

The alternative, the dialectical alternative, is to start by taking the whole as given, so that the interconnections and changes that make up the whole are viewed as inseparable from what anything is, internal to its being, and therefore essential to a full understanding of it. In the history of ideas, this has been called the "philosophy of internal relations." No new facts have been introduced. We have only recognized the complex relations and changes that everyone admits to being in the world in a way that highlights rather than dismisses or minimizes them in investigating any problem.

The world of independent and essentially dead "things" has been replaced in our thinking by a world of "processes in relations of mutual dependence." This is the first step in thinking dialectically. […]

* * * * *

So—why dialectics? Because that's the only sensible way to study a world composed of mutually dependent processes in constant evolution and also to interpret Marx, who is our leading investigator into this world. Dialectics is necessary just to see capitalism, given its vastness and complexity, and Marxism to help us understand it, to instruct us in how to do Commons from Under the Goose Studies, and to help us develop a political strategy to reclaim the commons. Capitalism is always and completely dialectical, so that Marxism will always be necessary to make sense of it, and dialectics to make correct sense of Marxism.

3

Why now? The current stage of capitalism is characterized by far greater complexity and much faster change and interaction than existed earlier. But if society has never been so imbued with dialectics, the efforts to keep us from grasping what is taking place have never been so systematic or so effective—all of which makes a dialectical understanding more indispensable now than ever before.

Socialism's sudden loss of credibility as a viable alternative to capitalism, however, a loss largely due to the collapse of the Soviet Union, has given Marxists still another important reason to devote more attention to dialectics, for many socialists, even some who had always been critical of the Soviet Union, have reacted to this recent turn of history by questioning whether any form of socialism is possible. Perhaps unsurprisingly, one result has been a kind of "future shyness" that has afflicted the writings of many on the Left today. What does a critical analysis of capitalism without any accompanying conception of socialism look like? It describes how capitalism works, shows who gets "screwed" and by how much, offers a moral condemnation of same, prescribes—*faute de mieux*—reformist solutions, and, because these no longer work, lapses into emotional despair and cynicism. Sound familiar?

Marx would not have been pleased, for, despite the absence of any single work on socialism/communism, there are no writings of his, no matter how small, where we are not given some indication of what such a future would be like. [...] This imaginative reconstruction of the future has been sharply attacked not only by his opponents but by many of Marx's followers, such as Edward Bernstein (1961: 204–205 and 209–211) and, more recently, Erik Olin Wright (1995), who view it as a lapse into utopianism that contaminates his otherwise scientific enterprise. But do all discussions of the future have to be "utopian"? With Rosa Luxemburg (1966: 40) and others, I do not think it is utopian to believe that a qualitatively better society is possible or to hope that it comes about. What is utopian is to construct this society out of such hopes, to believe, in other words, that such a society is possible without any other reason or evidence but that you desire it.

As opposed to this utopian approach, Marx insists that communism lies "concealed" inside capitalism and that he is able to uncover it by means of his analysis (1973: 159). And elsewhere he says, "we wish to find the new world through the critique of the old" (1967: 212). Rather than a moral condemnation, Marx's "critique of the old" shows that capitalism is having increasing difficulty in reproducing the conditions necessary for its own existence, that it is becoming impossible, while at the same time—and through the same developments—creating the conditions for the new society that will follow. The new world exists within the old in the form of a vast and untapped potential. Marx analyzes capitalism in a way that makes this unfolding potential for turning into its opposite (communism) stand out. As part of this, he is not averse to describing, if only in a general way, what the realization of this potential would look like.[1]

The central place of potential in dialectical thinking has been noted by a variety of thinkers. C.L.R. James refers to the internal relation between actuality and potentiality as "the entire secret" of Hegel's dialectics (meaning Marx's as well) (1992: 129). Marcuse claims to find an insoluble bond between the present and the future in the very meanings of the concepts with which Marx analyzes the present (1964: 295–296). [...] But this still doesn't explain how Marx does it. Where exactly is the future concealed in the present? And how does Marx's dialectical method help him to uncover it?

In brief: most of the evidence for the possibility of socialism/communism surrounds us on all sides and can be seen by everyone. It lies in conditions that already have a socialist edge to them, such as workers' and consumers' cooperatives, public education, municipal hospitals, political democracy, and—in our day—nationalized enterprises. However, it also lies in conditions that don't seem to have anything particularly socialist about them, such as our developed industries, enormous material wealth, high levels of science, occupational skills, organizational structures, education, and culture. Evidence for socialism can also be found in some of capitalism's worst problems, such as unemployment and worsening inequality. For Marx and his followers, it is clear that it is the capitalist context in which all these conditions are embedded that keeps them from fulfilling their potential and contributing to a truly human existence. Abstracting from this context, Marxists have no difficulty in looking at our enormous wealth and ability to produce more and seeing an end to material want, or looking at our limited and malfunctioning political democracy and seeing everyone democratically running all of society, or looking at rising unemployment and seeing the possibility of people sharing whatever work is to be done, working fewer hours and enjoying more free time, et cetera. Unfortunately, most others who encounter the same evidence don't see this potential, not even in the parts that have a socialist edge to them. And it is important to consider why they can't.

Investigating potential is taking the longer view, not only forward to what something can develop into but also backward to how it has developed up to now. This longer view, however, must be preceded by taking a broader view, since nothing and no one changes on its, his, or her own but only in close relationship with other people and things, that is, as part of an interactive system. Hence, however limited the immediate object of interest, investigating its potential requires that we project the evolution of the complex and integrated whole to which it belongs. The notion of potential is mystified whenever it is applied to a part that is separated from its encompassing system or that system is separated from its origins. When that happens, "potential" can only refer to possibility in the sense of chance, for all the necessity derived from the relational and processual character of reality has been removed, and there is no more reason to expect one outcome rather than another.

The crux of the problem most people have in seeing evidence for socialism inside capitalism, then, is that they operate with a conception of the present that is effectively sealed off from the future, at least any notion of the future that grows organically out of the present. There is no sense of the present as a moment through which life, and the rest of reality as the conditions of life, passes from somewhere on its way to somewhere. When someone is completely lost in the past or the future, we have little difficulty recognizing this as a mental illness. Yet, the present completely walled off from either the past or the future (or both) can also serve as a prison for thinking, though "alienation" is a more accurate label for this condition than "neurosis." Those persons affected by this condition simply take how something appears now for what it really is, what it is in full, and what it could only be. Hence, with the exception of the gadgetry found in science fiction, what most people call the "future" is occupied by all the usual social features only slightly modified from how they appear and function in the present.

With this mindset, there is no felt need to trace the relations any thing has with other things as part of a system—even while admitting that such a system exists—for, supposedly, there is nothing essential to be learned about it by doing so. Likewise, operating with narrow, independent parts that are also static, there is no difficulty in admitting that there was a past and will be a future while ignoring both when trying to understand anything in the present. If people can't see the evidence for socialism that exists all around them, therefore, it is not mainly because of an inability to abstract elements from capitalism and imaginatively project how they might function elsewhere. Rather, and more fundamentally, the conditions they see about them do not seem to belong to any social system at all, so there is no system to take them out of and, equally, no system to insert them into. The systemic and historical characters of both capitalism and socialism that would allow for such projections are simply missing.

4

The dialectic enters this picture as Marx's way of systematizing and historicizing all the conditions of capitalism so that they become internally related elements of an organic whole, which is itself but the most visible moment in how its components got that way and what they may yet become. With this move, the present ceases to be a prison for thinking and, like the past and the future, becomes a stage in a temporal process with necessary and discoverable relations to the rest of the process. It is by analyzing a present conceived in this way that Marx believes he can discern the broad outlines of the socialist and communist societies that lie ahead.

The dialectical method with which Marx studies this future inside the capitalist present consists of four main steps. (1) He looks for relations between the main capitalist features of our society at this moment in time. (2) He tries to find the necessary preconditions of just these relations—viewing them now as mutually dependent processes—in the past, treating the preconditions he uncovers as the start of an unfolding movement that led to the present. (3) He then projects these interrelated processes, reformulated as contradictions, from the past, through the present, and into the future. These projections move from the immediate future, to the probable resolution of these contradictions in an intermediate future, and on to the type of society that is likely to follow in the more distant future. (4) Marx then reverses himself and uses the socialist and communist stages of the future at which he has arrived as vantage points for reexamining the present, extended back in time to include its own past, now viewed as the sum of the necessary preconditions for such a future.

* * * * *

5

[...] The first step is to trace the main lines of the organic interaction that characterizes capitalist society—particularly as regards the accumulation of capital and the class struggle—at this moment of time. In order to focus on what is distinctively capitalist in our situation, Marx has to abstract out (omit) those

qualities—equally real, and, for different kinds of problems, equally important—that belong to our society as part of other systems, such as human society (which takes in the whole history of the species), or class society (which takes in the entire period of class history), or modern capitalist society (which only takes in the most recent stage of capitalism), or the unique society that exists at this time in this place (which only takes in what is here and now). Every society and everything in them are composed of qualities that fall on these different levels of generality. Taken together—which is how most people approach them—they constitute a confusing patchwork of ill-fitting pieces that makes the systemic connections that exist on any single level very difficult to perceive. By starting with the decision to exclude all noncapitalist levels of generality from his awareness, to focus provisionally on the capitalist character of the people, activities, and products before him, Marx avoids tripping on what human society or class history or the other levels mentioned have placed in his way in carrying out his work as our leading systematizer of capitalism.

The widespread view of capitalism as the sum of everything in our society rather than the capitalist "slice" of it has been responsible for repeated complaints, most recently from postmodernists and social movement theorists, that Marx ignores the role of race, gender, nation, and religion. He ignores them, at least in his systematic writings, because they all predate capitalism and consequently cannot be part of what is distinctive about capitalism. Though all of these conditions take on capitalist forms to go along with their forms as part of class society or the life of the species, their most important qualities fall on the latter levels of generality, and it is there (and on us, in so far as we are subject to these levels) that they have their greatest impact. Uncovering the laws of motion of the capitalist mode of production, however, which was the major goal of Marx's investigative effort, simply required a more restricted focus.

With the distinctive qualities of capitalism in focus, Marx proceeds to examine the most important interactions in the present from different vantage points, though economic processes, particularly in production, are privileged both as vantage points and as material to be studied. To avoid the overemphasis and trivialization that marks most one-sided studies, the relation between labor and capital is examined from each side in turn, and the same applies to all the major relations that Marx treats. Of equal significance is the fact that internal relations are taken to exist between all objective and subjective factors, so that conditions never come into Marx's study without umbilical ties to the people who affect and are affected by them, and the same applies to people—they are always grasped in context, with the essentials of this context taken as part of who and what they are. Capital, as Marx says, "is at the same time the capitalist" (1973: 412).

After reconstituting the capitalist present in this manner, the second step Marx takes in his quest to unlock the future is to examine the preconditions of this present in the past. If the dialectical study of the present treats its subject matter as so many Relations, a dialectical study of the past requires that we view these Relations as also processes. History comes to mean the constant, if uneven, evolution of mutually dependent conditions. The past, of course, takes place before the present, and in retelling the story one usually begins at the beginning and moves forward. But the correct order in inquiry is present first, and it is what Marx uncovers in his reconstruction of the present that guides him in his search into the past, helping him decide what to look for as well as how far back to go in looking for it. The question posed is: What had to happen in the past for the present to become what it did? This is not to suggest that what occurred

was preordained (though there may have been good reasons for it), only that it did in fact take place and that it had these results. It is in following this approach that Marx is led to late feudalism as the period when most of the important preconditions for capitalism are first laid down.

6

After reconstructing the organic interaction of the capitalist present and establishing its origins in the past, Marx is ready to project the main tendencies that he finds there into one or another stage of the future. As part of this third step in his method, Marx reabstracts (reorganizes, rethinks) these tendencies as "contradictions," which emphasizes their interaction as processes that are simultaneously mutually supporting and mutually undermining one another. Over time, it is the undermining aspects that prevail. The fundamental assumption that underlies Marx's practice here is that reality is an internally related whole with temporal as well as spatial dimensions. Things that are separate and independent (if this is how one conceives them) cannot be in contradiction, since contradiction implies that an important change in any part will produce changes of a comparable magnitude throughout the system, just as things that are static (again, if this is how one conceives them) cannot be in a contradiction, since contradiction implies there is a collision up ahead. [...]

Marx's contradictions organize the present state of affairs in capitalism, including the people involved in them, in a way that brings out how this cluster of relations has developed, the pressures that are undermining their existing equilibrium, and the likely changes up ahead. With contradictions, the present comes to contain both its real past and likely future in a manner that allows each historical stage to cast a helpful light upon the others. Early in his career, Marx compared problems in society with those in algebra, where the solution is given once a problem receives its proper formulation (1967: 106). The solution to capitalism's problems, he believed, would also become clear once they were reformulated in terms of contradictions. It is chiefly by projecting such contradictions forward to the point of their resolution and beyond, where the character of the resolution gives shape to the elements of what follows, that Marx is able to catch a glimpse of both socialism and communism. The resolution of a contradiction can be partial and temporary or complete and permanent. In the former, as exemplified in the typical capitalist crisis, the elements involved are simply reordered in a way that puts off the arrival of the latter. Our concern here is with the kind of resolution that completely and permanently transforms all of capitalism's major contradictions.

Marx sees capitalism as full of intersecting and overlapping contradictions (1963: 218). Among the more important of these are the contradictions between use-value and exchange-value, between capital and labor in the production process (and between capitalists and workers in the class struggle), between capitalist forces and capitalist relations of production, between competition and cooperation, between science and ideology, between political democracy and economic servitude, and—perhaps most decisively— between social production and private appropriation (or what some have recast as the "logic of production versus the logic of consumption"). In all of these contradictions, what I referred to earlier as the "evidence for socialism" inside capitalism can be found reorganized as so many mutually dependent tendencies evolving over time. Viewed as parts of capitalism's major contradictions, their current forms can only represent a passing moment in the unfolding of a larger potential.

Whatever necessity (best grasped as likelihood) is found in Marx's projection of a socialist revolution in what I referred to as the near future is the result of his demonstrating that the conditions underlying capitalism have become more and more difficult to reproduce, while the conditions that make socialism possible have developed apace. All this is contained in capitalism's main contradictions. According to Marx's analysis, these contradictions display capitalism as becoming increasingly destructive, inefficient, irrational, and eventually impossible, while at the same time socialism is presented as becoming increasingly practical, rational, conceivable, necessary, and even obvious— notwithstanding all the alienated life conditions and the enormous consciousness industry that work to distort such facts. Consequently, for Marx, it is only a matter of time and opportunity before the organization, consciousness, and tactics of the rising class bring about the expected transformation.

7

Marx's vision of what happens after the revolution is derived mainly from projecting the forms that the resolution of capitalism's major contradictions are likely to take in the hands of a new ruling class, the workers, who have already been significantly changed by their participation in a successful revolution and who are guided primarily by their class interests in making all major decisions. And the most important of these interests is to abolish their exploitation as a class along with all the conditions that underpin it. How quickly they could accomplish this, of course, is another matter. The question, then, is not "Why would the workers do this?" but "Why—given their interests—when they come to power would they do anything else?"

For class interests to bear the weight put on them by this account of future prospects, we need to place the relations between different classes in earlier times, including their interests, inside the main contradictions that link the present with the past and the future. Only by understanding how capitalist class interests determine the forms and functions of what I called the "evidence for socialism" inside capitalism (step one), and how, in response to these same interests, all this has evolved over time (step two) can we begin to grasp how quickly these forms and functions would change in response to the demands of a new ruling class with different interests (step three). In other words, when the capitalists (and the feudal aristocracy and slave owners before them) acquired the power to shape society according to their class interests, they did so, and the workers will do likewise. If the workers' assumption of power together with the material conditions bequeathed by capitalism provide us with the *possibility* for socialism, it is the workers' peculiar class interests together with the removal of whatever interfered with the recognition of them under capitalism that supplies us with most of its *necessity*.

While Marx's vision of socialism (or the middle future) is derived mainly from the contradictions of capitalism, his vision of communism (or the far future) is derived not only from these contradictions (that is, from projecting the resolution of these contradictions beyond the attainment of socialism) but also from the contradictions Marx sees in class history and even in socialism itself, in so far as it is a distinctive class formation. After socialism has developed to a certain point—in particular, when everyone becomes a worker, all means of production are socialized, and democracy is extended to all walks of life—the contradictions that have existed since the very beginning of classes (having to do with the general form of the division of labor, private property, the state, etc.) come gradually to resolution. At the same time and through the same processes, the contradictions that socialism still possesses as a class society (having to do with its own forms of the

division of labor, private property, and the state, which Marx sums up under "dictatorship of the proletariat") are also resolved. It is the resolution of the contradictions from all these overlapping periods—capitalism, class society, and socialism—together with the forms of alienation associated with them that marks the qualitative leap from socialism to communism and that makes the latter so hard for most people today to conceive.

To summarize: Marx begins to study the future by tracing the main organic interconnections in the capitalist present. He then looks for their preconditions in the past, and he concludes by projecting the chief tendencies found in both, abstracted now as contradictions, to their resolution and beyond for the stage of the future with which he is concerned. The order of the moves is present, past, and future (unlike most futurological attempts to peer ahead that move from the present directly to the future or, as in many utopian efforts, that go directly to the future, dispensing with the present altogether).

8

Marx's method for studying the future is still not complete. In a fourth and final step, Marx reverses himself and uses the socialist and communist stages of the future at which he has arrived as vantage points for reexamining the present, now viewed (together with its own past) as the necessary preconditions for such a future. This last step, though little understood, is the indispensable means by which Marx provides the "finishing touches" to his analysis of capitalism. It is also part of his method for studying the future, since the process I have described is an ongoing one. Building on what he learns from going through one series of steps, Marx begins the dance—the dance of the dialectic—all over again. For the work of reconstructing the present, finding its preconditions in the past, projecting its likely future, and seeking out the preconditions of this future in the present, now conceived of as an extension of the past, is never truly finished.

According to Marx, "The anatomy of the human being is the key to the anatomy of the ape" (1904: 300), and the same applies to the relations between later and earlier stages of society. In the same way that our present provides the key for understanding the past, the future (that is, the likely future, in so far as we can determine it) provides the key for understanding the present. It is Marx's grasp of communism, as unfinished as it is, for example, that helps him to see capitalism as the gateway to human history rather than its end and makes it easier to distinguish the capitalist-specific qualities of current society (those that serve as the preconditions of socialism) from the qualities it possesses as an instance of class and human societies. Communism also provides Marx with a standard by which the greater part of what exists today is found wanting as well as criteria for determining priorities for research and politics, distinguishing between the kind of changes capitalism can absorb from those that set transitional forces into motion.

* * * * *

But above and beyond all this, revisiting the present from the vantage point of its likely future concretizes and hence makes visible the potential that exists throughout the present for just such a future. To William Faulkner's supposed remark, "The past is not dead—it is not even in the past," Marx could have added, "And the future is not unborn—it is not even in the future." Potential is the form in which the future exists inside the present, but until now it has been a form without a particular content just because it was open to every conceivable content. Now, everywhere one looks, one sees not only what is but what could be, what really could be, not simply because one desires it but because the aforementioned analysis

has shown it to be so. Seeing the "facts" of capitalism as "evidence" of socialism becomes so many arguments for socialism. Furthermore, informing workers of and sensitizing them to the extraordinary possibilities that lie hidden inside their oppressive daily existence greatly increases their power to act politically by indicating how and with whom to act (all those who would benefit immediately from the enactment of these possibilities), just as it enhances their self-confidence that they can succeed. In sum, by enriching capitalism with the addition of communism, Marx's dialectical analysis "liberates" potential to play its indispensable role in helping to liberate us.

Taken altogether, the future proves to be as important in understanding the present and past as they are in understanding the future. And always, the return to the present from the future instigates another series of steps from the present to the past to the future, using what has just been learned to broaden and deepen the analysis at every stage.

9

Before concluding, it needs to be stressed that the projections of the future obtained through the use of the method outlined here are only highly probable, and even then the pace and exact forms through which such change occurs owes too much to the specificity of a particular place, the vagaries of class struggle, and also to accident to be fully knowable beforehand. Marx, as we know, recognized "barbarism" as a possible successor to capitalism, though he thought it very unlikely and devoted much less attention to this possibility than we need to after the blood-curdling events of the past century.

To avoid other possible misunderstandings of what I have tried to do in this chapter, I would like to add that my account of Marx's method is not meant to be either complete or final but rather—in keeping with Marx's own approach to exposition—a first approximation to its subject matter. Further, I do not believe that Marx's use of contradiction to project existing potential is the only means he uses to uncover the socialist/communist future inside the capitalist present; it is simply the main one. [...]

Once Marx constructed the chief elements of what came to be called "Marxism," however, projecting capitalism's main contradictions forward became his preferred approach for studying the future, providing that future with just the degree of clarity and necessity needed for him to use it in elaborating his analysis of the present (in doing his version of Commons from Under the Goose Studies). It is also the best way that we today can learn about a socialist future that is more than wishful thinking. Only then, too, can the vision of socialism, which has been so battered by recent events, fulfill its own potential as one of our most effective weapons in the class struggle. Putting this weapon in the hands of workers and other oppressed peoples, teaching them how to use it—to do this against all the pressures of the age—is largely why we need dialectics and, with the world that capitalism has made teetering on the brink, why we need dialectics now more than ever.

NOTE

1. For an attempt to reconstruct Marx's vision of socialism and communism from his scattered comments on this subject, see my book *Social and Sexual Revolution* (1979: Chapter 3).

REFERENCES

Bernstein, Edward. 1961. *Evolutionary Socialism*, translated by Edith Harvey. New York: Schocken Books.

James, C.L.R. 1992. *The C.L.R. James Reader*, edited by Anna Grimshaw. Oxford: Basil Blackwell.

Luxemburg, Rosa. 1966. *Reform or Revolution*. Columbo: Young Socialist Publications.

Marcuse, Herbert. 1964. *Reason and Revolution*. Boston: Beacon.

Marx, Karl. 1904. *A Contribution to the Critique of Political Economy*, translated by N.I. Stone. Chicago: Charles H. Kerr.

_____. 1963. *Theories of Surplus Value*, part 1, translated by Emile Burns. Moscow: Progress Publishers.

_____. 1967. "Toward the Critique of Hegel's Philosophy of Law: Introduction." In *Writings of the Young Marx on Philosophy and Science*, edited and translated by Lloyd D. Easton and Kurt H. Guddat, 249–264. Garden City: Anchor.

_____. 1973. *Grundisse: Foundations of the Critique of Political Economy*. Hammondsworth: Penguin.

Ollman, Bertell. 1979. *Social and Sexual Revolution: Essays on Marx and Reich*. Boston: South End Press.

Rubel, Maximilien. 1987. "Non-market Socialism in the Twentieth Century." In *Non-Market Socialism in the Nineteenth and Twentieth Centuries*, edited by Maximilien Rubel and John Krump, 10–34. London: Macmillan.

Wright, Erik Olin. 1995. "Class Analysis and Historical Materialism." Tape-recorded talk at the New York Marxist School, February 23.

Figure 10.1: Dance of the Dialect

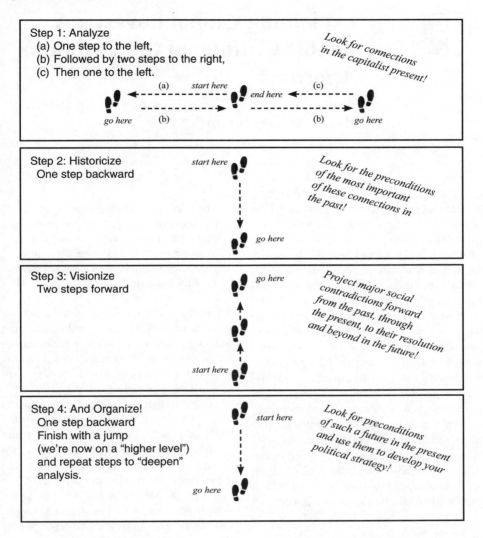

Step 1: Analyze
(a) One step to the left,
(b) Followed by two steps to the right,
(c) Then one to the left.

Look for connections in the capitalist present!

(a) *start here* (c)

go here (b) (b) *go here*

end here

Step 2: Historicize
One step backward

start here

Look for the preconditions of the most important of these connections in the past!

go here

Step 3: Visionize
Two steps forward

go here

Project major social contradictions forward from the past, through the present, to their resolution and beyond in the future!

start here

Step 4: And Organize!
One step backward
Finish with a jump
(we're now on a "higher level")
and repeat steps to "deepen"
analysis.

start here

Look for preconditions of such a future in the present and use them to develop your political strategy!

go here

CHAPTER 11

Explaining Global Poverty: A Realist Critique of the Orthodox Approach[1]

BRANWEN GRUFFYDD JONES

The global poverty crisis hits the headlines regularly these days, along with increasingly fervent statements of commitment to meet internationally agreed targets, to battle, fight, and eradicate poverty—once and for all, it sometimes seems.[2] Such assertions are characteristically made in moralistic language. Poverty is typically referred to as an anonymous, external threat or evil force, against which the whole world—governments north and south, citizens rich and poor, even the private sector—are united in fighting. Campaigns for debt relief are couched in terms designed to appeal to the "generosity" of rich countries; and in a similar fashion non-governmental organisations (NGOs) such as Oxfam appeal to the compassion and generosity of individuals in the West.[3] A recent report compiled by the UN, World Bank, IMF, and OECD finds (with apparent surprise) that

> the number living on less than $1 a day has actually grown, to 1.2bn from about lbn in 1995. The World Bank admits that the number will not fall in the next eight years unless something is done. (Elliott and Brittain, 2000: 13)

So what is to be done? Kofi Annan, the UN Secretary General, urges that

> The world's richest states must open their markets and show greater generosity in debt relief to help revitalise the global drive to beat poverty [...] developed countries must recommit themselves to battle against human misery. (ibid)

What is the understanding of the causes of poverty underlying this overtly moral and passionate discourse? What is the nature of its social analysis? The aim of this chapter is to provide a critique of the orthodox approach to explaining poverty from the perspective of critical realism. In doing so, it attempts to respond to Julian Saurin's assertion that the study of global poverty requires a distinct approach which draws on critical realism (Saurin, 1996: 662). It is argued here that a particular, dominant conception of the condition of poverty prevails today, to the extent that it can be seen as an *orthodoxy* (cf. Bourdieu, 1977: 168). The chapter begins by characterising this orthodoxy. It examines the way in which social phenomena are conceptualised and explained, and identifies the unexamined but implicit assumptions underlying the orthodoxy. Having identified these assumptions—namely empiricism and social atomism—and having sketched out the alternative and more adequate ontology and epistemology of critical realism, the chapter addresses the question: what difference does a critical realist approach make to explaining global poverty?

CHARACTERISING THE ORTHODOXY

There is a particular way of producing knowledge about the social world that is dominant, within academia and beyond. It can be seen clearly when examining society's ideas about poverty—ideas about poverty within societies, and more specifically ideas about the phenomenon of global poverty. An examination of the way in which the orthodoxy conceives of and explains poverty reveals the basic assumptions about the world upon which the orthodoxy rests. The claim to have identified an orthodoxy refers to the level of method, and the assumptions about the world implied by this method (cf. Lawson, 1999: 3–4).

The analysis of global poverty undertaken by the World Bank is an exemplar of the orthodox approach. The World Bank is particularly important and its analyses are characteristic of an approach that is prevalent on a much wider scale. The World Bank is the world's hegemonic development institution, and the agenda and advice of the World Bank is central to any orthodox understanding of poverty and attempts at poverty alleviation. [...]

* * * * *

Since the early 1990s, the Bank has reintroduced poverty as a central concern (Williams, 1994: 119); indeed, the World Bank Group has adopted the slogan "Our dream is a world free of poverty." The theme of the 1990 *World Development Report* (World Bank, 1990) was poverty. Examination of this key document reveals features which are definitive of the Bank's methodological approach, and of the orthodoxy more broadly.

The World Bank's Analysis of Poverty

Chapter 2 of the 1990 *World Development Report* on poverty is entitled "What do we know about the poor?" It begins as follows:

> Reducing poverty is the fundamental objective of economic development. It is estimated that in 1985 more than one billion people in the developing world lived in absolute poverty. Clearly, economic development has a long way to go. Knowledge about the poor is essential if governments are to adopt sound development strategies and more effective policies for attacking poverty. How many poor are there? Where do they live? What are their precise economic circumstances? Answering these questions is the first step toward understanding the impact of economic policies on the poor [...] Lifting them out of poverty will depend to a large extent on a better understanding of how many poor there are, where they live, and, above all, *why they are poor.* None of these questions turns out to be straightforward. (World Bank, 1990: 24, 25; emphasis added)

So, why are they poor? How does the World Bank try to explain poverty? The next section of the report presents an extended analysis under the heading "The characteristics of the poor," which examines data taken from detailed household surveys, conducted in different countries, "to estimate the number of poor people and to establish what is known about them" (1990: 24). The characteristics examined include geographic location, type, and quality of the physical environment; "demographic characteristics" such as gender, and size and composition of the household; ownership of "assets" such as land and "human capital" (education, health); occupational activities and main source of income; position in the surrounding society; and how the poor spend their incomes. This exercise in data analysis produces findings such as those listed below:

- Poverty as measured by low income tends to be at its worst in rural areas [...] The problems of malnutrition, lack of education, low life expectancy, and substandard housing are also, as a rule, more severe in rural areas.
- Households with the lowest income per person tend to be large, with many children or other economically dependent members.
- The poor usually lack assets as well as income.
- Poverty is highly correlated with landlessness [...] when the poor do own land, it is often unproductive and frequently lies outside irrigated areas.
- The poor are usually unable to improve such plots, since they lack income and access to credit.
- Agriculture is still the main source of income for the world's poor. We have seen that the greatest numbers of the poor, including the very poorest, are found overwhelmingly in rural areas. Their livelihoods are linked to farming, whether or not they earn their incomes directly from it.
- In many countries poverty is correlated with race and ethnic background.

(1990: 29, 30, 31, 32, 33, 37)

Thus, a detailed *description* of poverty is built up from empirical data taken from a variety of countries. On this basis, the report concludes by identifying "two overwhelmingly important determinants of poverty: access to income-earning opportunities and the capacity to respond" (1990: 38). According to this

approach, then, the common empirical aspects or characteristics of the condition of poverty constitute the "determinants" of poverty, and explanation consists of identifying these characteristics by means of the examination of empirical data.

The above extracts reveal defining methodological features of the orthodox approach, and the underlying assumptions about the nature of the world and how it can be known. The model of society implicit within this analysis is a society consisting of individuals and households, within the bounded unit of the nation-state. Poverty is seen as a condition which is distributed among a quantifiable proportion of the overall aggregate collection of people who constitute society. The notion of *individuals* being poor is clear: "[t]he income shortfall [...] measures the transfer that would bring *the income of every poor person* exactly up to the poverty line, thereby eliminating poverty" (1990: 27–28; emphasis added).

According to this approach, in order to explain why some people are poor it is necessary to identify patterns of correlation within the set of data about different empirical characteristics of the poor. Data about all sorts of characteristics of people and their environment are gathered, in different places, and compared in order to identify regularly recurring patterns of correlation. This procedure allows conclusions of the form: "[a]griculture is still the main source of income for the world's poor [...] the greatest numbers of the poor, including the very poorest, are found overwhelmingly in rural areas" (1990: 33).

The only things referred to in this exercise are things which can be observed and measured. The only way to explain the existence of certain observable characteristics, or variables, is by reference to other such characteristics. In short, this approach is characterised by empiricism. It is assumed that what exists consists only of what is knowable empirically. Causation, and consequently explanation, is thus conceived of as the constant conjunction of empirical variables.

What's Wrong with the Orthodoxy?

Recent realist theorising takes issue with such an empiricist account of causality and explanation. This realist critique started with a critique of empiricism in the natural sciences, before moving on to apply the alternative realist model of natural science to social science. At the forefront of such work is Roy Bhaskar. Roy Bhaskar's realist theory of science results from a transcendental inquiry into the ontological and epistemological presuppositions of the possibility and necessity of experiment in the practice of natural science (Bhaskar, 1997). It reveals the flaws in empiricism and provides an alternative and more adequate theory of ontology and epistemology. For experiments to be both possible and necessary, the world has to be structured, stratified, and open, consisting of structured entities with causal mechanisms that combine to generate the phenomena available to experience. Normally, these structures operate in contingent combination with other structures and are influenced by various prevailing conditions, to the extent that actual outcomes are not the straightforward result of the operation of any single mechanism. Hence normal, everyday observation of the world does not enable identification of the causes of experienced events because of the disjuncture between real structures, the actual events produced, and the restricted range of the events available to experience (that is, the empirical evidence). In other words, if real casual mechanisms were directly observable, then science would be redundant.

* * * * *

As we have seen, orthodox social analysis consists of gathering data—atomistic facts about individuals, events, and states of affairs—

and identifying patterns of covariance among variables in the data set. The identification of regularly recurring patterns is seen as constituting an explanation: events—either antecedent or coexisting—and states of affairs are seen as the "determinants" of a particular outcome. There is no notion of natural necessity or real, causally efficacious but non-empirical structures because of the implicit assumption that what exists is confined solely to that which appears, that is, to the empirical. In contrast, realism distinguishes between, on the one hand, structures and their causal powers, which are real and have the powers they do independently of particular instantiations, and which are the object of theory; and, on the other, events—actual outcomes—which are produced by the interaction of many different mechanisms in particular, contingent circumstances. A realist approach explains by reference to structures and generative mechanisms; it is concerned, as Bhaskar emphasises, with structures, not events.

Critical realism identifies social relations as a condition of any intentional action (Bhaskar, 1998). People can only ever achieve any end they may wish to pursue in the context of society, using material and social resources that are the product of social activity, current and past. It is therefore to structures of social relations that we must look in order to explain social phenomena, including poverty. Structures of social relations are analogous to the structures in nature by virtue of which entities have particular causal powers or tendencies. Structures of social relations and their causal powers and tendencies, however, are only relatively enduring, subject to (and the unintended outcome of) continual reproduction and occasional transformation by the practices of people. They are therefore historically specific and potentially transient; and historical outcomes are the result of different sets of structures conditioning outcomes in particular, contingent circumstances. Thus there are two related but distinct moments to a social explanation of historical processes: a theoretical knowledge of structures and their tendencies; and a historical analysis of the particular circumstances and combinations in which they exist (Bhaskar, 1986: 108; Manicas, 1987; Sayer, 1983: Part II).

Having outlined a realist approach to causality and social ontology—an approach predicated upon a critique of the flaws inherent within the empiricist assumptions pertaining to causality and explanation and which underlie the orthodoxy—we may now move on to explore the difference critical realism makes to substantive explanation. [...]

* * * * *

[...] How does an account of substantive phenomena grounded in realist principles differ from an empiricist account?

Fortunately, it is not necessary to try to work this out by beginning from scratch, because various examples of social science developed according to realist methodological principles already exist. Most notable, perhaps, is the work of Karl Marx. One can argue that Marx was the first implicit critical realist.[4] However, he himself did not explicitly set out at the philosophical level the principles and justification of his method. After "settling accounts" with the idealists, his explicit treatment of his own methodology and philosophy of science is confined to relatively few brief statements and remarks scattered throughout his works (see Bhaskar, 1991: 163; 1989: 133). But careful attention to his actual practice of inquiry—in *Capital* and the *Grundrisse* at least—reveals clearly its realist grounding. Thus it is with some justification that Bhaskar has hailed Marx as the "comet" of the tradition of critical realism. He observes, commenting upon the relationship between Marxism and critical realism, that "Marx's work at its best illustrates critical realism; and

critical realism is the absent methodological fulcrum of Marx's work" (Bhaskar, 1991: 143).

Marx is not the only social theorist whose work accords with the principles of realism; and realist social science is not necessarily Marxist/ historical materialist. But Marx's realist social science has discovered the properties and tendencies of the specific real social relations and generative mechanisms that produce global poverty. His theoretical elaboration of the necessary tendencies of the real, transfactually efficacious structures constitutive of the capitalist mode of production is arguably the existing social theory most adequate to the task of explaining global poverty.

What Difference Does Critical Realism Make?

The realist theory of social ontology shows that it is necessary to examine social relations in order to explain social phenomena (Bhaskar, 1998). Society consists of sets of social relations through which social practices are carried out. What particular social relations should be examined in order to explain poverty? In order to answer this question it is necessary first to consider what is understood by the notion of poverty.

What—if anything—is wrong with the orthodox understanding of poverty? The World Bank report defined poverty as being "concerned with the absolute standard of living of a part of society—the poor [...] poverty [... is] the inability to attain a minimal standard of living" (World Bank, 1990: 26). Thus, according to the orthodox interpretation, poverty can be conceived of as the non-fulfilment of human needs. This in itself is a satisfactory conception of poverty. The problem is that this orthodox notion rests on an atomistic social ontology, and an empiricism which *identifies empirically manifest wants with needs*. Because an empiricist approach reduces what exists to what is empirically knowable, it necessarily equates needs with wants as manifest in behaviour (consumption), and so behaviour directly reveals preferences. It is then argued that the market, in automatically allocating resources according to expressed preferences as revealed through demand in the market place, is the most efficient way of ensuring that maximum utility or welfare (as defined by people's free choice) is derived from available resources (Ramsay, 1992).

The orthodoxy correctly identifies the poor in contemporary society (whether in Africa or in Britain) as those who fail to earn enough money to buy the things necessary for a minimally reasonable existence. The orthodox solution is therefore to raise the incomes of the poor. In the case of Africa, the majority of the poor live in rural areas and farm for a living. Raising rural incomes therefore necessitates improving the productivity of the farmers' agriculture (for example, by increasing use of chemical inputs and improved seeds); and by encouraging (through incentives provided by a competitive market) a shift from subsistence farming to the production of "cash-crops" (predominantly export crops), which fetch a higher price on the market. In this way, it is suggested by the orthodoxy, the farmers' agricultural output will become more "profitable." To put it very simply, the orthodoxy reaches the following conclusion: that people satisfy their needs by spending money to buy what they require on the market. The poor are unable to satisfy all their needs because they lack money; therefore they need to earn more money so that they will be able to satisfy their needs.

The orthodoxy is accurate at the descriptive level of surface appearances, but is blind to the real, non-empirical relations that generate empirical appearances (cf. Marx, 1993 [1858]). A realist approach reveals the flaws in this orthodox conceptualisation of needs, and of how they are met. Human beings are complex, stratified natural beings. They have a range of

causal powers or potentials by virtue of their structured nature. In common with all natural beings, various conditions are required for the realisation of their potentials. These conditions can be seen as the objects of human need (Collier, 1979, 1989; Ramsay, 1992). Natural beings meet their needs in ways determined by their structured nature—thus the biological nature of a plant determines the way in which it absorbs nutrients from the soil and converts sunlight into energy. Human beings have emergent powers rooted in the social strata, and meet their needs through production in society. Unlike the instinctual activities of animals, human beings self-consciously create the objects that satisfy their needs. This difference is at the root of human history and notions of development and progress, and the historicity of human needs. Human production is a self-conscious, intentional process involving planning, reflection, and learning. It constitutes causal transformative interaction with material nature, and is an irreducibly social process that takes place through cooperation and the coordination of different activities (the division of labour). Knowledge about nature and techniques of production, as well as tools and other created means of production, are acquired and accumulated and passed on. The ways in which it is possible for humans to meet their needs are therefore not static and unchanging, as they are for animals; rather, they change and develop.

Poverty can be conceived of as a condition in which human needs are not adequately met and the realisation of various human powers is restricted or prevented. Any attempt to account for the existence of such a condition must start by identifying what sorts of things determine whether or not needs are met. The possibilities for satisfying human needs, the ways in which they are satisfied and the distribution of such possibilities in society, are determined by the social relations that govern the activities of producing the objects of human needs. In order to explain the historical phenomenon of widespread poverty—a condition in which historically satisfiable human needs are systematically not met for a significant proportion of society, or are met in inadequate ways, in the midst of enormous wealth and material abundance and unsurpassed development of productive capabilities—it is therefore necessary to examine the social relations that determine production and the distribution of social powers in society. In the current era, these are the relations of the capitalist mode of production.

Human Needs and the Capitalist Mode of Production

All production consists of producing objects with particular concrete features and properties by virtue of which they satisfy distinct purposes. All products, therefore, have a *use-value*. In non-capitalist modes of production, production is organised according to, and motivated by, use-values, driven by the ultimate aim of reproducing society by means of the use-values produced. Marx's analysis of the commodity reveals one of the fundamental characteristics that distinguish capitalism from other historically existing modes of production. Under generalised commodity production the aim of production is exchange rather than use. Commodities are exchanged not on the basis of their particular, useful qualities in accordance with human needs, but on the basis of their *exchange-value*—the amount of abstract, socially necessary labour-time embodied within them. The aim of production is not the reproduction of society, but the reproduction and expansion of capital. The private property relations and competition constitutive of capitalist relations of production necessitate the continuous accumulation of capital, by means of increasing the productivity of labour such that more commodities (and hence more surplus value) are produced in a given period of time. In order for capital to return

to its original money form, thus realising the surplus-value and enabling reinvestment in production, commodities have to be sold.

Under capitalism, production and distribution are governed by the law of value, and driven by the need for capital accumulation. Objects produced in society are exchanged on the basis of exchange-value. Money is the universal equivalent commodity, the universal representative of value that can be exchanged for any commodity. This means that an individual's ability to satisfy their needs, by acquiring certain objects, is determined by the amount of money they have. This in itself is determined by their position in society, because money is an expression of value, determined by the social relations of production. If they are a wage labourer, it will depend on the socially determined value of their labour power, and whether or not they are able to sell it; if they are a direct producer, it will depend on the socially determined value of the labour-time realised in their products, and whether or not they can sell them. The ability to do things, to meet needs, is determined by social relations that manifest themselves in, or take the form of, money. Thus the distribution of social power in society, which is determined by social relations, is manifest in *things* and the relations between things—money and commodities. As Marx puts it,

The reciprocal and all-sided dependence of individuals who are indifferent to one another forms their social connection. This social bond is expressed in *exchange-value*, by means of which alone each individual's own activity or his product becomes an activity and a product for him; he must produce a general product—*exchange-value*, or, the latter isolated for itself and individualized, *money*. On the other side, the power which each individual exercises over the activity of others or over social wealth exists in him as the owner of *exchange-values,* of *money.* The individual carries his social power, as well as his bond with society, in his pocket. [...] In exchange-value, the social connection between persons is transformed into a social relation between things; personal capacity into objective wealth. (Marx, 1993 [1858]: 157)

Generalised commodity production and capital accumulation is predicated upon the division of society into a class of property owners—capitalists—and a class of workers who are propertyless and therefore dependent on selling their labour power in order to attain the means of survival. Capitalists own concentrated means of production capable of putting large numbers of individuals to work in such a way as to achieve high levels of productivity (by means of the division and organisation of labour, and highly developed technology). Productivity has to be such that the value produced by labour is more than the value contained within the products necessary for its own reproduction. The labourers are dependent on selling their labour power to the capitalists for a wage, with which they buy the objects required to meet their needs.

In advanced capitalist societies the majority of the population are dependent on selling their labour power in order to meet their needs. An understanding of the specific nature of capitalist social relations is therefore important (though not sufficient) when explaining conditions of inadequate need satisfaction in capitalist societies. But throughout much of Africa society does not consist of a class of wage labourers and a class of capitalists. The majority of the population are not an urban proletariat solely dependent on selling their labour power in order to meet their needs. Yet, it is argued here, conditions of poverty in the African countryside are an outcome of the historical expansion of capitalism and the development of the world

market to the same extent, though in different ways, as they are in advanced capitalist societies. In order to substantiate this claim, a theoretical knowledge of the structural properties and necessary tendencies of the capitalist mode of production is important, but by itself is not sufficient. An explanation of actual social outcomes—whether in Britain or in Mozambique—necessitates an examination of the particular historical conditions and circumstances in which combinations of structures operate. As emphasised above, the elaboration of the structural properties and causal powers of relatively enduring social relations, and the analysis of concrete historical outcomes, are related but different moments of social inquiry. The next section attempts to consider briefly the particular historical outcomes of the inherently expansionary and global nature of the capitalist mode of production.

Human Needs, Global Poverty, and Global Production Relations

It has been argued that poverty can be conceived of as a condition in which human needs are not satisfied, and that the objects created to satisfy human needs vary according to the way in which they are produced, which is determined by historically specific social relations of production. It is possible, therefore, to argue for a notion of poverty as inadequate need satisfaction defined according to the possibilities prevailing in the particular societal context under examination. So, for example, an understanding of the concrete form and experience of poverty in Britain in the year 2002 would be very different from that of poverty in Britain in 1738. The "possibilities prevailing in society" are historically specific; and they are *social* possibilities. They are the product of society, available only by virtue of social labour, past and present. They do not and could not result from the actions of an isolated individual.

But if the notion of poverty is defined to some extent according to the possibilities prevailing in society at any one period, what is meant by "society"? How are the boundaries to be drawn, for the purposes of assessing the prevailing possibilities of meeting needs? Is "society" equal to the nation-state? If so, what can be said about differences between countries? The statistics in Table 11.1 provide a clear indication of the enormous difference in possibilities of need satisfaction that exist in Britain and Mozambique today.[5]

Is this pattern natural, just the way things are? Is it up to each individual nation-state to ensure the provision of resources in order to meet the needs of its population? This is the implication of the orthodoxy, which sees the economies of each nation-state as only externally, atomistically related to other economies. The suggestion is that differences between the capabilities within rich and poor nation-states can only be redressed through the generous donation of aid from rich to poor. Such a conclusion is only conceivable from a perspective blind to the existence of global production relations.

Is there a sense, however, in which existing possibilities of satisfying human needs are *global* possibilities; that "society" extends throughout the world? It has been argued that meeting human needs is only possible in society, because the objects necessary to meet needs result from social labour, including that of previous generations. Does this argument only apply within the confines of a nation-state, or does it transcend the nation-state?

Table 11.1: Contrasting Human Development Indicators for Mozambique and the United Kingdom

Human Development Indicator	Mozambique	United Kingdom
Life expectancy at birth (years)	43.8	77.3
Adult literacy rate (%)	42.3	99.0
Joint gross enrolment ratio (%)	25	105
GDP per capita (PPP$)	$782	$20,336
Population not expected to survive to age 40 (%)	41.9	9.6 (not expected to reach age 60)
Adult illiteracy rate (%)	57.7	21.8 ("functionally illiterate")
Population without access to safe water (%)	54%	*
Population without access to health services (%)	70%	
Population without access to sanitation (%)	66%	*
Children under age 5 underweight (%)	26%	*
Maternal mortality rate per 100,000 births	1,100	7
Infant mortality rate per 1,000 births	129	6
Under age 5 mortality rate per 1,000 births	206	6

Source: UNDP, *Human Development Report* (Oxford: Oxford University Press, 2000).
* Data not given; presumably negligent

This question can be illuminated by returning to examine further the realist understanding of society. The brief sketch of a realist ontology given above emphasised the social relations that constitute society. Different sets of relations exist, such as those between parent and child, teacher and student, employer and worker, landlord and tenant, and state and citizen, structurally linking different roles and practices. These sets of relations themselves are to greater or lesser extents overlapping and interconnected. Society consists in the whole network of different interconnected sets of social relations. Marx's description remains perhaps the most clear: "society does not consist of individuals, but expresses the sum of the interrelations, the relations within which these individuals stand" (Marx, 1993 [1858]: 265). On this basis, the extent to which different sets of relations may be considered as bounded is a *historical* question; and the particular social relations of interest depend on the question being considered. [...]

* * * * *

As far as poverty and human needs are concerned, the social relations of most importance are those that determine how needs are actually met and how social power is distributed—relations of production. Production has been social production on a global scale, to a greater or lesser extent and in different ways but increasingly so, at least for the past three hundred years. That is, resources which are the result of social labour in one place provide the necessary condition for processes of production and development in another. [...]

* * * * *

The resources that go together to provide possibilities for meeting human needs result from global social production. Ultimately, then, in the contemporary era it is the global sets of relations that determine how the social powers, made possible by virtue of produced resources, are distributed throughout the world; and so it is these relations—global production relations and the interstate structure through which capitalist accumulation is currently organised and regulated—that constitute the object of inquiry when considering global poverty.

Collier articulates the global nature of the social relations characteristic of the contemporary historical era, but which have not always existed. He asserts that today, unlike in previous eras, we live in a shared world:

> [...] Today [...] we have become one world in two ways: economically, in that we are all massively dependent on goods produced all over the world; and ecologically, in that we are *all* threatened by the ecological irresponsibility of *all*. The whole planet has become a shared world, even for those who never leave their village. Thus, a tie which is both real and universal has arrived; not yet in the form of a real collectivity embracing humankind, but of real relations of mutual dependence through the sharing of the world. (Collier, 1992: 87)

This has not always been the case. The era of "world history" results from the specific nature of the capitalist mode of production, its inherently expansionary character, and its tendency to bring about, necessarily, the continual revolution of productive forces and the augmentation of productive powers, a development that structurally connects geographically disparate peoples through globally organised production. As Marx and Engels explain:

> The further the separate spheres, which act on one another, extend in the course of

this development and the more the original isolation of the separate nationalities is destroyed by the advanced mode of production, by intercourse and by the natural division of labour between various nations arising as a result, the more history becomes world history. Thus, for instance, if in England a machine is invented which deprives countless workers of bread in India and China, and overturns the whole form of existence of these empires, this invention becomes a world-historical fact [....] From this it follows that this transformation of history into world history is [...] a quite material, empirically verifiable act, an act the proof of which every individual furnishes as he comes and goes, eats, drinks and clothes himself. (Marx and Engels, 1998 [1845]: 58–59)

* * * * *

The inherently and necessarily expansionary nature of capitalism has led both to its increasing penetration into ever more spheres of life, which previously remained outside the sphere of market relations, and to increasing geographical expansion throughout the world. Already-existing local modes of production and social formations around the world have been, and continue to be, to greater and lesser degrees, transformed by the penetration of capitalist relations and the development of commodity production. In different ways and different circumstances, all around the world, local modes of production organised on the basis of production for *use,* with the reproduction of society as the goal, have been transformed into the production of commodities, producing for exchange, with production subordinated to the requirements of capital accumulation. The particular ways in which this has occurred vary according to context in space and time, and are determined by the nature of local conditions and social

and political relations, as well as the historical phases of capitalist development as a whole. It is these relations and conditions that must be examined in order to explain, for example, the predominantly rural structure of societies in Africa today and the "rurality" of poverty, which the orthodoxy can describe but cannot explain. The historical tendency to move towards the transformation of production relations and commodification has not always led to industrial capitalism and generalised commodity production based on wage labour. In much of the Third World there is no mass urban industrial proletariat; "much of the population in many third world societies have not been divorced entirely from the land and basic means of production."

This does not mean, however, that such societies consist partly of autonomous pre-capitalist havens, untouched by capitalism. The conditions of the lives of peasants in Africa today are of course very different from those of the European working class, for example. But they are also very different from conditions prevailing in Africa five hundred years ago, and even two hundred years ago. Contemporary social conditions and relations in the African countryside and in industrial urban areas in Western Europe, though very different, must both be seen as products of *the* historical development of capitalism.[6] As Derek Sayer argues:

> Capitalism embraces far more than what is normally taken to be "modernity" [....] Wage labour may well be the basis upon which commodity production can alone be generalised, but given such a generalisation it is not *the* sole source of profits to be made from buying and selling commodities. On the contrary, the global dominance of the capitalist market breathes new life into (transforms) a variety of other modes of production, which adapt themselves to and become integral elements of the "modern"

world. The latter is thus a world whose modernity many of its inhabitants, strategic as they might be to the circuits of capital, have yet to experience. Plain slavery, serfdom, indentured labour, convict labour, sharecropping, and cash-crop peasant production have all at one time or another been component parts of the international capitalist order. (Sayer, 1991: 48)

A realist approach thus reveals the profoundly historical nature of global poverty. The orthodoxy, focusing on events rather than structures, sees history as an inert backdrop to the present, a chronological past in the linear sequence of atomistic, externally connected events whose juxtaposition, for it at least, make up "history." There is no notion of historical necessity, asymmetry or irreversibility. The frequent references to "catching up" (or, in the case of Africa, getting "left behind") typical of orthodox thinking about development reveal a complete lack of understanding of the structural determinants and interconnections of world history. For the orthodoxy, if something happened in one place and time, then it can happen in another place and time.

A realist approach, in contrast, distinguishes between, on the one hand, relatively enduring structures and, on the other, their combinations and interactions in particular circumstances that produce historical outcomes. The outcome of the orthodoxy's *ahistorical* analysis is that historically specific and potentially transient social forms become naturalised and therefore are seen to be eternal. The flawed empiricist assumptions underlying the orthodoxy render it capable of description but not explanation.

The importance of this is not simply that the orthodoxy is wrong. It is not the case that global poverty has not yet been eliminated simply because of the weaknesses in existing analyses. The realist theory of social ontology and epistemology shows that ideas matter

because in informing practice ideas are causally efficacious, making a real difference to social outcomes. The outcome—usually unintended and unacknowledged—of social practices is the reproduction of specific sets of social relations (Bhaskar, 1998). The orthodoxy prevents identification of the social relations that systematically generate the outcome of poverty. It takes as given historically specific features of existing society, portraying them as natural and eternal. Practice informed by such an understanding therefore does not explicitly challenge or see the need to transform existing social relations—indeed, it denies the existence of such relations.

The outcome is to secure the reproduction of these social structures: analysis informed by empiricism is inherently conservative. As such, the orthodoxy is ideological: its errors "are not just mistakes, but ones which function in the interest of a particular social system" (Collier, 1994: 104). It consists of a set of false ideas about society, which necessarily arise within and serve to reproduce the structure of that society. A full examination of the ideological status of the orthodoxy would reveal how the atomistic assumptions at its core arise spontaneously from the appearance and experience of capitalist society. This is a task in itself that lies beyond the scope of this chapter. However, it is important to emphasise that, while orthodox ideas about poverty and other social phenomena that serve to secure the reproduction of existing social relations may be to some extent intentionally propagated for that reason, this is not sufficient to account for their hegemonic status and efficacy. This is not to dismiss the fact that the institutions of the powerful consciously promote certain ideas and quite consciously attempt to quash others. Recognition and examination of the ways such ideas are promoted is certainly important.

However, the existence and nature of the orthodoxy cannot be accounted for solely because of its function in serving the interests of the powerful. The success of such intentionally promoted ideologies relies upon, and is parasitic upon, already existing "common-sense" ideologies. People are not dupes. Ideas, and more broadly consciousness, are internally related to an individual's practical experience of the world. This means that the notion of "false consciousness"—of people ordinarily being mistaken about the things they see—is misleading. Ideas will—and indeed must—have some measure of practical adequacy, even if they do not provide a fully adequate explanatory account of the phenomena in question. They must be adequate to the extent that they enable successful intentional action in the world. It is not necessary to understand why something works in the way that it does in order to interact successfully with it—it is not necessary, for example, to know how an internal combustion engine works in order to drive a car. This means that there must be some phenomenal grounding to common-sense ideologies such as atomism. An explanatory critique of the orthodoxy would therefore necessitate identifying the particular characteristics of contemporary society that give rise to such common-sense understandings (Collier, 1989: 56; Sayer, 1983: 8).

CONCLUSION

An examination of the orthodoxy shows it to be underpinned by an atomistic social ontology. This is because empiricism is blind to social structures and sees only individuals. The result is ahistorical: the status quo of a global capitalist market economy is taken entirely as given, as a natural state of affairs. Poverty is seen to be a problem to be tackled by private charity. The solutions offered represent at most the amelioration of affairs, or symptom suppression. This empiricist approach sticks to surface appearances and denies the existence of real but non-empirical structures and causal

mechanisms. It is ideological and ultimately amounts to a refinement of common-sense understanding based on everyday experience of the world. In contrast, realism identifies the real but non-empirical structures of social relations that generate the phenomena of experience as the necessary focus of an explanation of social phenomena. This chapter has sketched the difference critical realism makes to explaining global poverty.

The satisfaction of human needs demands material resources in order to enable people to develop their powers and capacities; furthermore, it demands social control over production, that is, socially organised and controlled production guided and determined by use values. Production for exchange, characterised as it is by private property relations in a competitive world market and hugely augmented productive powers mainly (increasingly) under control of large, concentrated transnational capital, is fundamentally contradictory to this end. A realist analysis, which replaces the atomism of the orthodoxy with a focus on the social relations of global capitalism, therefore leads to the conclusion that problems of poverty and inequality demand a transformation in the social relations through which production is organised and which determine the distribution of powers in society. As Andrew Collier has argued, scientific analysis of capitalism reveals the "case for socialism as *increasingly* relevant and indeed urgent in the modern world" (Collier, 1990: x). The realist conclusion contradicts the overtly voluntaristic appeals to generosity typical of the orthodoxy, which issue directly from empiricism and social atomism. While appealing to popular concern about the existence of extreme inequality and widespread poverty, it prevents comprehension of the cause of this phenomenon, and in so doing serves to secure the reproduction of the social structures causally responsible.

NOTES

1. This chapter is an outcome of doctoral research funded by an ESRC grant, which is gratefully acknowledged. I would like to thank Julian Saurin, Andrew Collier, Justin Cruickshank, Mervyn Hartwig, Mark Lacy, and Justin Rosenberg for their helpful comments.

2. Clare Short, in the 1997 Government White Paper on development and poverty, emphasised that the goal was poverty *elimination.*

3. Some organisations campaigning about issues such as poverty do provide incisive critical analyses. This chapter focuses on the mainstream approach.

4. There are of course various interpretations of Marx's work, many of which are themselves inconsistent with realist principles, leading to historicist, actualist, or idealist understandings of historical materialism. In this respect, critical realism "makes a difference" to historical materialism too. That is, it enables an explicit articulation and defence of Marx's method, grounded in a transcendental inquiry into the conditions of possibility of the given practice of scientific experiment (see in particular Collier, 1989, 1979). This reveals clearly the ways in which Marx's method is superior both to the methods of the classical and vulgar economists of his time and to those of subsequent mainstream social science, all of which are grounded in empiricism.

5. The statistics in this table serve only to emphasise the different conditions and possibilities that exist in different parts of the world. They are averages or percentages for two nation-states, and as such can be misleading because they give no indication of inequality within the two societies, nor of the different quality of poverty. There is considerable wealth in Mozambique, although the majority of the population are very poor. Furthermore, such figures should not be taken to suggest that there is little poverty in the U.K. (on this subject see, for example, Davies, 1998).

6. Much European writing on modernity and postmodernity appears to exhibit an almost total ignorance of the situation of many millions of people now living in the modern/postmodern globalising world. To this extent, such analyses are inexcusably Eurocentric. Derek Sayer makes this point eloquently:

> Typologies and theories grounded in the presumed radical distinctiveness of modernity continue to be the stock-in-trade of sociological thought. A century later Anthony Giddens, ardent critic of nineteenth-century evolutionism though he is, remains in no doubt at all that "the world in which we live today certainly differs more from that in which human beings have lived for the vast bulk of their history than whatever differences have separated human societies at any previous period" [...] a stupendous piece of modernist hubris (*and one which begs the obvious question of who are the "we" of and for who he speaks*). But where Marx is singular is in his insistence that what makes modernity modern is, first and foremost, capitalism itself. (Sayer, 1991: 12; emphasis added)

REFERENCES

Bhaskar, R. 1986. *Scientific Realism and Human Emancipation.* London: Verso.

_____. 1989. *Reclaiming Reality.* London: Verso.

_____. 1991. *Philosophy and the Idea of Freedom.* Oxford: Blackwell.

_____. 1997. *A Realist Theory of Science,* 3rd ed. London: Verso.

_____. 1998. *The Possibility of Naturalism: A Philosophical Critique of the Contemporary Human Sciences,* 3rd ed. London: Routledge.

Bourdieu, P. 1977. *Outline of a Theory of Practice.* Cambridge: Cambridge University Press.

Collier, A. 1979. "Materialism and Explanation in the Human Sciences." In *Issues in Marxist Philosophy,* vol. II, edited by J. Mepham and D.H. Ruben. Brighton: Harvester Press.

_____. 1989. *Scientific Realism and Socialist Thought.* Hemel Hempstead: Harvester Wheatsheaf.

_____. 1990. *Socialist Reasoning: An Inquiry into the Political Philosophy of Scientific Socialism.* London: Pluto Press.

_____. 1992. "Marxism and Universalism: Group Interests or a Shared World?" In *International Justice and the Third World,* edited by R. Attfield and B. Wilkins. London: Routledge.

_____. 1994. *Critical Realism: An Introduction to Roy Bhaskar's Philosophy.* London: Verso.

Davies, N. 1998. *Dark Heart: The Shocking Truth about Hidden Britain.* London: Vintage.

Elliott, L., and V. Brittain. 2000. "Annan Urges New Push to End Poverty." *Guardian* (June 27).

Isaac, J.C. 1987. *Power and Marxist Theory: A Realist View.* Ithaca: Cornell University Press.

Lawson, T. 1999. "Developments in Economics as Realist Social Theory." In *Critical Realism in Economics: Development and Debate,* edited by S. Fleetwood. London: Routledge.

Manicas, P.T. 1987. *A History and Philosophy of the Social Sciences.* Oxford: Blackwell.

Marx, K. 1993 [1858]. *Grundrisse.* London: Penguin.

Marx, K., and F. Engels. 1998 [1845]. *The German Ideology.* New York: Prometheus Books.

Ramsay, M. 1992. *Human Needs and the Market.* Aldershot: Avebury.

Saurin, J. 1996. "Globalisation, Poverty, and the Promises of Modernity." *Millennium: Journal of International Studies* 25(3): 657–80.

Sayer, D. 1983. *Marx's Method: Ideology, Science and Critique in Capital,* 2nd ed. Brighton: Harvester Press.

_____. 1991. *Capitalism, and Modernity: An Excursus on Marx and Weber.* London: Routledge.

UNDP. 2000. *Human Development Report 2000.* Oxford: Oxford University Press.

Williams, M. 1994. *International Economic Organisations and the Third World.* London: Harvester Wheatsheaf.

World Bank. 1990. *World Development Report: Poverty.* Washington, DC: World Bank.

Rethinking Part 2A: Making Connections, Unmasking Relations: Dialectical Social Analysis

CRITICAL THINKING QUESTIONS

Chapter 8: Getting Started on Social Analysis in Canada

1. If the alternative to critical social analysis is to accept "surface-meanings," what is so problematic about that? Why should we assume that there is any deeper meaning beneath the surface of our lives?

2. Czerny and his coauthors suggest that social analysis is *diagnostic*: to note, describe and explore the symptoms of social malaise so that the cause of the problem can be discovered and removed. What kinds of assumptions about the social world, and its potential for change, are made in this medical analogy?

3. Social analysis considers relationships not as isolated units but as a whole, as parts of larger structures that define and delimit our daily activities. Beginning from a particular relationship, perhaps between yourself and your teacher, try mapping out the larger structures in which that relation is embedded. Can you reach any conclusions as to how these structures define the meaning and set the limits of the activity that you and your teacher share?

Chapter 9: The Principles of Dialectics

1. Harvey maintains that there is a "deep ontological principle" involved in dialectical thinking. What is it, and why is it important in understanding social phenomena such as capital or money?

2. "Transformative action" arises out of contradiction, and can in principle be found anywhere in the physical, biological, and social world. Can you think of examples from each of these domains of transformative action; that is, action that creates novelty rather than reproducing sameness?

3. What are the implications of placing the "search for *possibilities*" at the very heart of dialectical argumentation, rather than relegating it to a separate, "applied" field of knowledge?

Chapter 10: Why Dialectics? Why Now? Or, How to Study the Communist Future inside the Capitalist Present

1. What analytical point is Ollman making when he contrasts Goose from Off the Commons Studies (GFOC) with Commons from Under the Goose Studies (CFUG)? Why is the latter such an important form of inquiry?

2. Ollman writes, "The crux of the problem most people have in seeing evidence for socialism inside capitalism … is that they operate with a conception of

the present that is effectively sealed off from the future" (p. 136). How does dialectical social analysis challenge this reified way of thinking?

3. "The widespread view of capitalism as the sum of everything in our society rather than the capitalist 'slice' of it has been responsible for repeated complaints, most recently from postmodernists and social movement theorists, that Marx ignores the role of race, gender, nation, and religion" (p. 137). How does Ollman defend Marx's analysis on this point?

Chapter 11: Explaining Global Poverty: A Realist Critique of the Orthodox Approach

1. How does Jones's explanation of poverty in terms of "the social relations that determine production and the distribution of social powers in society" (p. 150) differ from the explanation that has been provided by the World Bank?

2. Jones insists that "society" now extends throughout the world in the global sets of relations that determine how social powers are distributed throughout the world. What are the implications of this global reach for the conduct of critical social inquiry?

3. According to Jones, the orthodox explanation of poverty serves an ideological function in portraying as natural what are really historically specific features of existing society, and in preventing identification of the social relations that actually generate poverty as an outcome. Despite the fact that the orthodox explanation is *accurate* at the descriptive level (p. 149), it "consists of a set of false ideas about society" (p. 155). What is Jones getting at here?

GLOSSARY TERMS

Contradiction: A union of two or more internally related processes that are simultaneously mutually supporting and mutually undermining one another. In a capitalist system, for instance, wage workers depend on capitalists for employment and thus wages, and capitalists depend on workers for the agency that creates their own capital, yet these classes have diametrically opposed interests as capital is driven to find more and more effective means of exploiting labour while labour is driven to resist its exploitation.

Dance of the dialectic: A mode of open-ended analysis in which one reconstructs the present in its current relationality, then finds its preconditions in the past, next projects its likely future, and finally seeks out the preconditions for this future in the present, now conceived as an extension of the past.

Dialectical thinking: A form of thought that emphasizes the inherently dynamic, emergent, and relational character of reality. This means putting emphasis upon comprehension of flows, processes, and relations over the analysis of elements, structures, and organized systems (these latter being constituted out of flows and processes).

Empiricism: The view that what exists is confined solely to that which appears, i.e., to the empirical. Thus, causation and explanation are conceived as the constant conjunction of empirical variables, as in correlational analysis.

Permanences: Relatively stable configurations of matter and things, including institutionalized structures of knowledge, which appear to have a permanent character. This appearance should always be challenged. "Dialectics forces us to ask the question of every 'thing' or 'event' that we encounter: by what process was it constituted and how is it sustained?" (p. 127).

Philosophy of internal relations: The position, basic to dialectical analysis, that the interconnections and changes that make up the whole are inseparable from what anything is, and thus essential to a full understanding of it. A view that replaces a world of independent and static *things* with a world of "*processes in relations of mutual dependence.*"

Poverty: A condition in which human needs are not adequately met and the realization of human powers is restricted or prevented, relative to the possibilities prevailing in the particular societal context under examination.

Reification: The tendency to reduce a human relationship to a thing, i.e., to naturalize it so that its socially constructed and contingent character is denied. Dialectical social analysis strives to de-reify social relations, a precondition for any conscious process of social change.

Social atomism: An approach that reduces society to individuals and explains events by predicting them from the behaviour of individuals and the description of their situation. Example: the orthodox explanation of poverty, offered by the World Bank.

Social illiteracy: The condition of being unable to interpret events that are going on in one's society. This prevents one from participating in society, and the lack of participation can further reinforce social illiteracy.

System: The entire collection of structures, issues, actors, and symptoms as they fit together in a certain pattern at a given moment. The fact that they are interconnected means that groups and issues that may seem quite separate are actually related in mediated ways.

Transformative activity: Processes that are "creative" in producing change in the physical, biological, or social world.

FURTHER READING

Barndt, Deborah. 2002. *Tangled Routes: Women, Work and Globalization on the Tomato Trail*. Toronto: Garamond Press.

An excellent example of dialectical social analysis, the book traces the full relationality of tomato production and consumption in North America. It weaves together details on labour processes, production relations, corporate control, and globalization with ethnographic narratives from workers, consumers, and other participants on the tomato trail. The result is an impressive holistic analysis of class and gender, culture and economics, local and global.

Harvey, David. 1996. *Justice, Nature and the Geography of Difference*. Oxford: Blackwell.

A *tour de force* of dialectical social and ecological analysis.

Ollman, Bertell. 2003. *Dance of the Dialectic: Steps in Marx's Method*. Urbana-Champagne: University of Illinois Press.

Ollman's essays, collected from various journal publications, comprise perhaps the most helpful discussion of dialectical method for the social sciences.

Paolucci, Paul. 2001. "Assumptions of the Dialectical Method." *Critical Sociology* 27(3): 117–146.

This article clarifies certain assumptions (e.g., those of totality, essentialism, organicism, and evolutionism) that are often misunderstood by interpreters of Marx, but that Paolucci sees as integral to dialectical method.

Sayer, Andrew. 2000. *Realism and Social Science*. London: Sage.

A very clear introduction to the variant of dialectical social analysis known as critical realism, replete with excellent methodological advice.

Sherman, Howard. 1995. *Reinventing Marxism*. Baltimore: Johns Hopkins University Press.

This book shows how the decline of the old, official Soviet Marxian perspective has led to a new Marxism, which is "unofficial, independent, profoundly critical of all existing societies, and critical of all old, rigid ideas" (3). Methodologically, Sherman features historical and relational approaches and insists that the thrust of dialectical method lies in posing questions, not specific answers.

RELEVANT WEB SITES

Dialectical Marxism: The Writings of Bertell Ollman
http://www.nyu.edu/projects/ollman/index.php

Ollman's Web site contains a number of his writings as well as a good set of links to other sites of relevance to those interested in dialectical social analysis.

Illuminations: The Critical Theory Website
http://www.gseis.ucla.edu/faculty/kellner/Illumina%20Folder/index.html

A research resource for those interested in the Critical Theory project. Firmly based in Frankfurt School of thought, this site maintains a collection of articles, excerpts, and chapters from many contemporary writers of and about Critical Theory.

The Marxism Mailing List
http://www.marxmail.org/index.htm

A worldwide, moderated forum for activists and scholars in the Marxist tradition who favour a non-sectarian and non-dogmatic approach. Includes links to other sites, FAQs, and even an art gallery.

Marxists Internet Archive
http://www.marxists.org

A massive site containing many works by Marx, Engels, and subsequent scholars and political leaders working within Marxian frameworks. Includes an encyclopedia and a separate archive of "reference writers" relevant to understanding Marxism, such as Adam Smith, Helen Keller, Simone de Beauvoir, and Albert Einstein.

The Web Site for Critical Realism (WSCR)
http://www.raggedclaws.com/criticalrealism/index.php?sitesig=WSCR
A site established in 1997 as an independent space for the study and promotion of critical realism. Contains a glossary of terms and an archive of articles, papers, interviews, and books by critical realists.

2B PROBLEMATIZING THE EVERYDAY WORLD: INSTITUTIONAL ETHNOGRAPHY

We saw, above, in dialectical social analysis a concern to show the practical and relational character of the social ("connections"), and to "unmask" both the bases of injustice and the ideologies that conceal those bases. The latter aspect of unmasking is sometimes called ideology critique, and one of the key concepts developed for this purpose is *reification*, a term given extensive treatment by the political and cultural theorist Georg Lukács in 1923 and subsequently incorporated into the Critical Theory of the Frankfurt School (Jay, 1973). Lukács (1971) noted that capitalism, with its tendency to commodify any and all practices and objects in the service of private profit, brings a mode of *quantitative, calculative rationality* to an increasing array of human endeavours—the bureaucratic, the legal, the political, the cultural. Lukács referred to this phenomenon, which affects both "objective" social relations and "subjective" human consciousness, as reification. With reification, human practices and relations take on a thing-like, natural character that denies their own historicity—as in the notion of "the economy" as a mechanism whose movement can be measured and whose logic dictates social outcomes. Not only is "the whole of society" subjected "to unified economic laws" (1971: 81–82), but people participating in society tend to take on a characteristic mentality. Rather than question and attempt to transcend a problematic way of life, the reified mind accepts the *immediacy* of existing arrangements and their essential immutability. With reification, social processes take on the appearance of "a nature-like quality beyond human control" (Kellner, 1985: 92). Lukács noted further that the reified mind is particularly characteristic of the standpoint of the bourgeoisie, whose interests lie precisely in the immediacies of investment and management that their dominant position in the existing social order presents to them.[1]

In Lukács's concept of reification we find a strand of thought that explicates and critiques the *facticity* of contemporary realities—how an emergent and changing world takes on a settled, immediate, thing-like appearance in the minds of its participants. In good part, "unmasking" challenges this facticity—this sense that the social world is composed of obdurate "facts" rather than contingent and emergent practices. The challenge extends to a critique of the facticity that is produced by positivist social science, which accepts a reified conception of social reality.

Dorothy Smith has long shared these concerns, and institutional ethnography (IE), the critical strategy she has pioneered, owes much to Marx and Lukács. In 1972, she presented her paper, "Women's Perspective as a Radical Critique of Sociology," at the meetings of the American Academy for Political Science (Smith, 1992). The ensuing corpus of sociological analysis—from Smith herself, from her students, from students of her students, and so on—comprises a distinctive approach to inquiry that enables the researcher to make social relations visible as people actively constitute them, while critiquing the facticity of ruling relations and perspectives.

IE places the practical *accomplishment* of social life at the centre of analysis, in accordance with Marx's view of social reality as always under construction. But it offers a distinctive way of explicating how extra-local "ruling relations" reach into and organize everyday life, and thereby provides resources for challenging the reified categories of what Smith calls "textually mediated social organization." With these concepts—ruling relations and textually mediated social organization—IE builds upon Marxist and also Weberian views of power and knowledge in contemporary societies:

> By the "ruling relations," I mean that internally coordinated complex of administrative, managerial, professional, and discursive organization that regulates, organizes, governs, and otherwise controls our societies. It is not yet monolithic, but it is pervasive and pervasively interconnected. It is a mode of organizing society that is truly new for it is organized in abstraction from local settings, extra-locally, and its textually mediated character is essential (it couldn't operate without texts, whether written, printed, televised, or computerized) and characteristic (its distinctive forms of organizing and its capacity to create relations both independent and regulative of local setting depends on texts) .... To explore the ruling relations is to explore those peculiar forms of power that are diffused through complexes of text-mediated social relations constituting subjectivity and agency. It is the relations that rule, and people rule and are ruled through them. (Smith, 1999: 49, 82)

Smith's approach does more than follow the Marxist thread of ideology-critique. She incorporates lessons from feminist politics about the need to begin inquiry with lived experience and to preserve the presence of active subjects in our sociological accounts; indeed, Smith may be said to have pioneered the "methods from the margins" that Kirby and McKenna introduced in an earlier reading. From ethnomethodology (Garfinkel, 1967) she derives a democratic conception of people as knowledgeable practitioners of their lives, and of practice as a site-specific concerting of activity.

IE is not only a critical analysis of how ruling relations shape everyday life; it is also a critique of conventional sociology's complicity with those relations, i.e., of the ideological practices of conventional sociology. In a particularly incisive study Smith demonstrated how texts such as Emile Durkheim's *Rules of Sociological Method* transfer human agency "from actual subjects to the virtual entities of the sociological text" (Smith, 1989: 45). Conventional methods such as Durkheim's "construct an objectified standpoint situating their readers and writers in the relations of ruling and subduing particular local positions, perspectives, and experiences" (Smith, 1989: 43). Much as for Lukács liberal economics takes the standpoint of the bourgeoisie in presenting capitalism as a reified entity, for Smith conventional sociology takes the standpoint of ruling in producing a generalizing, objectified knowledge of the social that is well suited to the practices of surveillance, management, and administration.

To recover the active agent, to explore the actualities of her life, and to create awareness of possibilities for alternative organization, Smith begins her sociology in the everyday—not as descriptive ethnography but as institutional ethnography. In the article that launched IE as a method, she described it as a research strategy whose "aim is to explicate the actual social processes and practices organizing people's everyday experience ... a sociology in which we do not transform people into objects but preserve their presence as subjects" (Smith, 1986: 6). To *problematize* the everyday world is to explore how it is articulated to the social relations of the larger social and economic process (1986: 6)—how the actualities of the everyday are shaped by extra-local relations that people take up, and often take for granted, as they accomplish their lives.[2]

Smith's approach to social inquiry is grounded in feminist activism, one of whose aspects in the late 1960s and early 1970s was consciousness-raising, "a method by which, in coming together and talking about our lives we could elucidate the common grounds of our oppression" (Smith, 1987: 176). IE is itself a form of consciousness-raising "aiming to find the objective correlates of what had seemed a private experience of oppression" (1986: 7). To do this the researcher needs to take a standpoint outside the relations of ruling; she needs to begin with the actualities of the everyday and to problematize them. The institutional ethnographer is thereby able to develop empirically grounded sociological insight that escapes the logic and priorities of entrenched power, and that shows how those priorities are instantiated and inscribed in texts and extra-local relations that reach into everyday life. Taking the side of those excluded from ruling does not mean cheerleading for the oppressed; nor does it compromise the scientific character of the project. After all, as Howard Becker noted in one of our first readings, there is no possibility for detachment in social science: we must begin from some position in the world. Social inquiry that begins from locations of management, administration, and power tends to create knowledge that is useful for the purposes of ruling, and that reinforces the hierarchies of credibility and the common-sense facticities of the dominant social order. Institutional ethnography offers an escape-hatch from that closed circuit. The hatch is for both the researcher and the people whose side she takes. In fact, for Smith the crucial moment is not that of writing sociological texts in a new way, but of developing *ethical-political connections* such that "we who are doing the technical work of research and explication are responsible in what we write to those for whom we write" (Smith, 1987: 224). In this sense, IE is a form of *activist* sociology.

The four chapters that follow, written by colleagues and former students of Dorothy Smith, give an overview of this research strategy. In a selection from their "primer in institutional ethnography," Marie Campbell and Frances Gregor introduce us to the perspective, terminology, and approach basic to IE. The goal of IE, explicating how things are socially organized or "put together so that they happen as they do," directs us to two sites of interest: the local setting of lived actualities and the extra-local that is outside the boundaries of direct experience. The former can be investigated through ethnography; the latter requires special procedures that enable us to probe "the social organization that extends from elsewhere into people's lives and back outside again" (p. 170). Given that texts (including not only printed documents but forms, photographs, video, software, and money) are almost always implicated in ruling, these procedures include the analysis of texts as components of social relations. To conduct an institutional ethnography, the ruling relations that texts help organize must be discovered and the connections across sites in which the texts are "activated" must be described. The idea of the "active text" is an important one. It counsels us to keep our analysis subject-centred by recognizing that people *participate* in discursive activity. Ruling is accomplished as people activate the texts that organize their lives, whether they are the texts of the market, the state, professional discourses, or mass media. It is through their active participation that people are "brought into line with ruling ideas"—as in the way that the ideology of child-centred teaching organizes mothers' work around their children's schooling, a good example of how ideas from elsewhere may penetrate and shape everyday life.

Peter Grahame explains how three tasks centring respectively on ideology, work, and social relations define IE as a research strategy: (1) addressing the ideological practices that are used to make an institution's processes accountable; (2) studying the work processes through which people produce the world they experience in everyday life; and (3) discovering the ways in which a localized work organization operates as part of a broader set of social relations that link multiple sites of activity. He provides an extended example of how in IE the tasks related to ideology, work, and social relations are woven into an analytic narrative. Grahame also helps clarify the concepts of institution and standpoint as they are employed within IE. Institutions are seen as "functional complexes such as education, health care, and law, in which several forms of organization are interwoven" (p. 184). The relations of ruling are embedded in these complexes, as institutional processes transform concrete, local, particular actions into "standard forms of organizational action," thus imposing a generalized form upon local activities. As for standpoint, Grahame emphasizes that within IE this term does not signify a subjective perspective or specific world view but refers instead to the discovery, in how knowledge is socially organized, of a strategic entry point into the various "forms of coordination" that shape the everyday and hook it into broader forms of organization.

Marjorie Devault and Liza McCoy, in a comprehensive discussion of the use of interviews in IE (only part of which has been excerpted here), point out that IE strives not to generalize about a group under study (as in conventional survey research) but to "find and describe social processes that have generalizing effects" (p. 193); that is, "to disclose features of ruling that operate across many local settings" (p. 193). IE interviewing is an open-ended inquiry, a conversation in which researcher and informants explore "how things work" in a given institutional complex. Interviews are also useful in discovering how specific texts organize local activity: how they come into play, how they are activated by readers and used within work processes, where they go after the informant is done with them, etc. In this way, IE produces a sort of "map" that can guide researchers, and those for whom they write, through a complex ruling apparatus. Devault and McCoy conclude that "IE approaches offer distinctive advantages for researchers seeking to unmask the relations of ruling that shape everyday life" (p. 201).

In our final selection, Marie Campbell's study of a specific moment in the implementation of a Total Quality Management (TQM) system in a long-term care facility affords us a detailed example of IE in action. This case study illuminates how a "management technology" actually *works* as a ruling practice to reshape nursing care and how in the process market forces penetrate the consciousness of caregivers. Campbell discovers that the concept of "customer"—central to TQM as a discourse—operates in contradictory ways but subordinates nurses' caring work to concerns related to the market. She concludes that taking the standpoint of those subject to ruling relations—in this case a group of nursing assistants—enables the researcher to anchor her account in actual experiences, but does not consider experience itself as authoritative knowledge. An institutional ethnography is *trustworthy* to the extent that it accounts for the experiences of those whose standpoint it takes. In so doing, IE creates knowledge that can help those subject to ruling make effective choices about how to act. The knowledge that IE creates entails an important ethical-political commitment, to which I referred earlier:

> There is a commitment to making the conditions of people's everyday lives known and knowable as the basis for action. Rather than supporting a ruling perspective and approach, the new institutional ethnographic knowledge should help to form a subject's political consciousness related to equitable decision making, undermining subordination, and so on .... Our responsibility is to make texts that express the standpoint of people and to help make them available to those who will use the work's subversive capacity in their own struggles. (Campbell and Gregor, 2002: 128)

NOTES

1.   "For the bourgeoisie, method arises directly from its social existence and this means that mere immediacy adheres to its thought, constituting its outermost barrier, one that can not be crossed. In contrast to this the proletariat is confronted by the need to break through this barrier, to overcome it inwardly *from the very start* by adopting its own point of view" (Lukács, 1971: 164).
2.   At this point we can note another parallel between IE and dialectical social analysis. As presented by Swift et al. in this book, the latter begins with a seemingly simple object or practice (e.g., a cup or coffee) and explores its full relationality—a move similar to problematizing the everyday world. As the readings below demonstrate, IE has developed procedures for "mapping social relations" (Campbell and Gregor, 2002) that complement dialectical social analysis as a critical research strategy.

REFERENCES

Campbell, Marie, and Frances Gregor. 2002. *Mapping Social Relations*. Toronto: Garamond Press.
Garfinkel, Harold. 1967. *Studies in Ethnomethodology*. Englewood Cliffs, NJ: Prentice-Hall, Inc.
Jay, Martin. 1973. *The Dialectical Imagination*. Toronto: Little, Brown and Company.
Kellner, Douglas. 1985. "Critical Theory, Max Weber, and the Dialectics of Domination." In *A Weber-Marx Dialogue*, edited by Robert J. Antonio and Ronald M. Glassman, 89–116. Lawrence: University of Kansas Press.
Lukács, Georg. 1971. *History and Class Consciousness: Studies in Marxist Dialectics*. Cambridge: MIT Press.
Smith, Dorothy E. 1986. "Institutional Ethnography: A Feminist Method." *Resources for Feminist Research* 15(10): 6–13.
_____. 1987. *The Everyday World as Problematic: A Feminist Sociology*. Toronto: University of Toronto Press.
_____. 1989. "Sociological Theory: Methods of Writing Patriarchy." In *Feminism and Sociological Theory*, edited by Ruth A. Wallace, 89–116. London: Sage.

_____. 1992. "Remaking a Life, Remaking Sociology: Reflections of a Feminist." In *Fragile Truths*, edited by William K. Carroll et al., 125–134. Ottawa: Carleton University Press.
_____. 1999. *Writing the Social: Critique, Theory, and Investigations*. Toronto: University of Toronto Press.

CHAPTER 12

Theory "in" Everyday Life

MARIE CAMPBELL AND FRANCES GREGOR

SOCIAL ORGANIZATION AND SOCIAL RELATIONS

Institutional ethnographers believe that the world is invariably social and that the only way we can be in the world is as social beings. As Dorothy Smith conceives of it, the social arises in people's activities and through the ongoing and purposeful concerting and coordinating of those activities. Social life is not chaotic but is instead organized to happen as it does. What Smith calls the social relations of everyday life actually organize what goes on. People's own decisions and actions and how they are coordinated with outside events are part of social relations. It is the interplay of social relations, of people's ordinary activities being concerted and coordinated purposefully, that constitutes "social organization."

Institutional ethnography makes use of the forms of social organization that occur routinely in people's lives. These are the forms we take for granted in such mundane activities as buying groceries, borrowing a library book, eating in a restaurant. We also encounter social organization when we engage with the state or large bureaucracies in requesting services or reporting information about ourselves—submitting details of our income to the Tax Department, for example, or of our motor vehicle for insurance purposes. The point to understand about socially organized activities is that we all play a part in generating the phenomena that seem to occur independently.

* * * * *

Institutional ethnography makes use of the socially organized character of everyday life to explore its puzzles. The questions that institutional ethnographers delve into are about how things are socially organized, or put together so that they happen as they do. Analytically, there are two sites of interest— the local setting where life is lived and experienced by actual people and the extra- or trans-local that is outside the boundaries of one's everyday experience. The latter must be investigated in special procedures that allow access to the social organization that extends from elsewhere into people's lives and back outside again. In modern society, texts of all kinds are a ubiquitous feature of social organization and they are accessible to research. Smith coined the term "textually-mediated social organization" to express the notion that engagement with texts concerts and coordinates the actions of people. The following is an example of textual coordination observed in a local site and offering access to discovery of trans-local activities.

When Fran Gregor lived for a short time in a city in Western Canada, she often rode the bus to the local university. Every day, she observed the same thing: lines of young men and women gathered at bus stops along the route, apparently waiting for the bus. When it came along, they would board one by one, each of them showing a small plastic card to the driver. Some would hold it aloft at the end of an extended arm, others would momentarily flip open their wallet, exposing the card it contained. Each card looked the same. In large letters above a small photo of the person who held the card was the name of the university to which Fran, too, was travelling. The year date was also clearly visible on the face of the card. These symbols Fran interpreted as meaning the cardholders were university students. As each student moved by the driver, he looked at the card and nodded his head. No words were exchanged, each student moved down the bus to a seat, and, after all the passengers had boarded, the bus driver drove to the next stop. The same dance was repeated at each stop along the route. The driver would glance at the card held aloft by each passing student cardholder. Having displayed the card, the student would take a seat on the bus.

This example reveals a commonplace form of textually mediated social organization. The actions of the bus driver are coordinated with those of the students who first wait for, then board, the bus. Their actions are coordinated with his and take place around the bus pass, which is a piece of text. It authorizes the entry of the student on to the bus to ride apparently without paying fare. This is an instance like countless others that make up students' daily lives when their actions are coordinated with those of others and a piece of text does the coordinating. Furthermore, this sort of thing happens without much notice on anybody's part because we learn (at least in urban Canada) from a very young age to participate in a textually organized world. It is only when new forms of text enter our daily lives that we become conscious of textual organization. Consider how the smooth and timely progress

of the bus along the route depends on both driver and students acting competently in the situation. Both must understand how to treat the card as relevant to the authority being enacted. The driver plays his part by looking at and acknowledging the propriety of the card. The student's part is to display the card at the very moment she passes by the driver. We can imagine what might happen when a student with no prior experience of this form of access to bus travel enters the bus—explicit instructions would have to be given for the proper compliance to be enacted.

The moment between the bus driver and the student(s), while it displays their actions being concerted through a text, is just the first layer of what there is to know about the social organization of student bus travel in the city. There are all sorts of questions to ask, the answers to which are not obvious to someone watching a student boarding a bus. How does a student acquire the pass? Are all students eligible? On which routes is a pass valid? How is the transit company reimbursed for the travel that the bus pass allows? In asking these questions we are seeking a sense of the complex interweaving of action and text that connects the university, its student enrolment lists, its financial accounting system, and so on, to the transit company and its employee practices. For explication of these arrangements, more research would need to be done.

Because of all those questions that are not answerable by simply observing the exchange between the driver and student, we know that university student travel does not begin and end with this routine exchange. If we have the concept "social organization" we are able to use it to recognize that people's actions are coordinated and concerted by something beyond their own motivations and intentions. Using the concept "social relations" is another step in understanding concerted action. Smith proposes that social relations are actual practices and activities through which people's lives are socially organized. Think again of the bus driver and students. The driver looks for the pass; the students display their passes. These are actual actions being carried out by people in real time and an observer can witness this level of activity. But the social relation that is occurring brings in more than that activity. Social relations are *extended* courses of action that take place across social settings. The bus driver and students participate in the social relations but what we witness between driver and student is merely a segment of the social relation that begins elsewhere and continues on after they do their part.

The concept of social relations is being used here as a technical term in institutional ethnography (Smith, 1987: 183). Used in this context, it means something different from the way we usually talk about relationships between people—for instance, when referencing the relationship between a teacher and student, or a parent and child. Social relations are not done to people, nor do they just happen to people. Rather, people actively constitute social relations. People participate in social relations, often unknowingly, as they act competently and knowledgeably to concert and coordinate their own actions with professional standards or family expectations or organizational rules. We draw on what we know. This is how we are able to move competently through our days in workplaces or at home, taking up one action after another, in a more or less unselfconscious manner. As competent adults, we know how to get dressed, have breakfast, take a bus, and get to work on time. Or we know how to shop, pay for purchases and get from the mall to our homes, responding to traffic lights correctly, and so on. The social relations of this series of actions are invisible, and being part of them does not require the exercise of much, if any, conscious thought. It is only when something goes unaccountably wrong that we stop and notice the organized complexity of our lives that we otherwise navigate so easily.

Smith saw the benefits of being able to make visible *as social relations* the complex practices that coordinate people's actions across separations of time and space, often without their conscious knowledge. This theorizing of connections makes it possible for analysts to explore and clarify what are otherwise mysterious aspects of people's lives. As social analysts, having the concept of social relations makes it possible to recognize and investigate such everyday/everynight puzzles. Social relations may be a conceptualization, but the inquiry it supports is of material things. Something is actually connecting what happens here to what happens there. The analysis shows social relations being realized in people's practices and, as discussed in the next section, in texts.

TEXTS AND THE RELATIONS OF RULING

We have been considering how people take up a piece of action and move it forward—by showing a bus pass, for instance. We have made explicit that there is social organization "behind" this seemingly effortless and automatic concerting of actions. Texts are essential to this form of social organization. The organization of social life across geographic sites normally works smoothly because of the proliferation of texts of all kinds and how embedded text-based communication is in social relations. People who have basic literacy skills can go about their daily activities in ways that make a bus pass a useful instrument, or that make a bus schedule "work" as it is written, without ever being aware of the layers of activity that intervene. One actor in a social relation never needs to know the other actors. The text functions to make such invisible connections work.

Smith's approach to understanding texts as components of social relations is enormously useful. It opens up to empirical investigation aspects of power operating in social life that otherwise lie hidden and mysterious. This approach to analyzing texts as part of social relations allows researchers to discover how people are related to each other in pre-determined ways, even if they do not know each other and never even meet. If people handle and process the same texts, they find their actions coordinated by the requirements of working with the text. That is how a text has the power to coordinate and concert—to hold people to acting in particular ways. On the other hand, people who do meet face-to-face and think they are relating to each other as individuals may not recognize how, without their knowing it, their actions are also being shaped by texts. "Ruling" is the concept that Smith uses to name the socially organized exercise of power that shapes people's actions and their lives. Texts are nearly always implicated in ruling, at least in contemporary societies. Think of how prevalent paper, computers, and information systems are in our own everyday worlds. Texts carry the determinations of many of our actions.

* * * * *

ACTIVATING TEXTS AS RULING RELATIONS

People routinely conduct their work through texts, forms, and reports. This is particularly true for occupations in the human services where people are processed. Texts are likely to be important and taken for-granted-instruments for the work. Smith talks about texts being *activated* by the people who handle and use them (Smith, 1999: 148–151). The notion of activation expresses the human involvement in the capacity of texts to coordinate action and get things done in specific ways. The capacity to rule depends upon carrying messages across sites, coordinating someone's action *here* with someone else's *there,* for instance. […] Some observational data from a study by

Campbell, Copeland, and Tate (1999) show a case manager (a nurse) working within a regional health authority in British Columbia. […] This nurse uses an assessment form that is a particular kind of official *text.* Her job […] requires her to interview applicants for long-term care services and to gather information about them and their family members and about the health issues that have led to a request for help from a community health program. Here, in an assessment interview, we look more closely at the text-mediated relation being established. Working with the text is the occasion for *activating the assessment firm* to establish the applicant's appropriate level of public subsidy for whatever services might be deemed necessary. It turns out this is not a neutral undertaking, but one in which organizational policy and a variety of taken-for-granted assumptions are brought into the helping interaction. In that sense, the activation of the text in question is a procedure both for conducting a health care program and for exercising organizational power.

To speak about this scenario in the theoretical terms we have already introduced, texts and their activation constitute definite forms of social relations between the people involved. Mapping those relations allows analysts to identify how things are organized, how people's lives are ruled. The following excerpt from the transcription of an observed interview shows what kind of relation the activation of the assessment form organized between the case manager and the man who was applying for community health services. Far from being "a servant of the client"—how the nursing case manager understood her relation to her clients—Campbell et al. suggest that this relationship was conducted "in the service of the organization." Moreover, the analysis suggests that the priorities of the organization are very different from those of the applicant for services or even those of any particular case manager. As the assessment interview proceeds, we will see that activation of the assessment form dictates a work process that constitutes a *ruling relation*. We pick up the story as the case manager is interviewing the applicant and has already worked her way through some of the form's categories.

She proceeds to ask questions—the answers to which will provide her with the information that she needs to complete the categories of the assessment form. The text carries an administrative relation that determines what the case manager can be interested in. It makes her act in an unhelpful manner. For instance, the case manager's interest in collecting certain kinds of data means that she does not "hear" the applicant's experiences, including his current state of emotional turmoil about his medical condition and his trouble with pain. The following excerpt offers a glimpse of how this happens:

> Case manager: *Can I see that bottle? I'd just like to get the correct spelling and the correct dosage off the bottles. [...] When do you take these ... at night?*
>
> Applicant: *One a night, yup.*
>
> Applicant: *I just started that one yesterday, I take one a week ... And I take Ibuprofen at night time.*
>
> CM: *Now does this hold the pain for you?*
>
> Applicant: *Not really, um, I just stopped taking that.*
>
> CM: *You've stopped, OK I will not put that down. You're not taking it anymore.*
>
> Applicant: *I do not know, I thought Advil did more for me than these things. See I was taking it for knee pain in the middle of the night, I'm getting pain in the elbows, and knees and hips. I'm getting pain everywhere where there's a joint.*
>
> CM: *Do you smoke?* (Campbell et al., 1999: 41)

The situation that we glimpse here is of a case manager recording information and following the categories of an agency form. She finishes recording the applicant's medications and moves on to the next category on the assessment form. We are interested in the abrupt change in topic at the end of the excerpt. Here we can see vividly that the assessment form is dictating the flow of her attention. Of course, the form has actually dictated the whole interview, although in a less dramatic way. The applicant has been trying to explain his situation to the case manager. He is in pain and it is poorly controlled by his current medication. He has already explained that he has trouble getting around the house. He is worried about his future and needs information in order to make plans. The case manager is attending to both the applicant's story and to the assessment form's demands for information. She acts both as a professional caregiver—"a servant of the client"—and as a representative of the health care organization that administers the long-term care program.

This example of activating an assessment form allows us to see how her activation work structures the case manager's choices about how to act. The assessment form structures the assessment interview. The form requires that information be collected so that a valid determination of eligibility for public services can be made. The questions that the case manager asks relate to the form's categories, and that is how the organization's interests in determining needs and eligibility, etc., are advanced over any other interests. As you have already come to understand, the social relation of which the applicant and the case manager are part originates outside the room where the interview takes place. The assessment form carries the organizational aspect of the relation into the interaction. No matter how much the case manager hopes to act as the servant of the client, serving the client is not everything that is happening in this interaction. The text organizes this social relation as administrative, making administrative decisions the primary order of business. (As an aside, it should be noted that this is the feature of organizational forms on which management practice depends. Thus we are identifying and speaking not of an aberration, but of established good organizational practice.)

The text-mediation of any professional relationship is a commonplace and normally unquestioned occurrence. Human service provision is routinely organized through records, forms, and reports. Text-mediation regularizes and makes efficient and accountable the delivery of health care, social services, education, and all other human services. As such, it would usually be accepted as not only legitimate but unquestionably of benefit to the client, at least in the long run. But the analysis segment of the assessment interview reviewed here illustrates how contradictions for service provision arise in this commonplace practice. Priorities and interests that are not those of either the health care workers or their clients come to permeate systematically the work of service provision. A text has the capacity to carry a particular idea or meaning across sites and perpetuate it. But to have that effect, people who know how to do so must activate the text. The case manager had the skills, motivation, and authorization to activate the assessment text and to engage with it in the manner that advanced a ruling relation.

OBJECTIFIED KNOWLEDGE AND RULING

Smith uses the notion of ruling as a way of understanding how power is exercised in local settings to accomplish extra-local interests. Ruling takes place when the interests of those who rule dominate the actions of those in local settings. Some forms of knowledge are specialized as technologies for ruling. For instance, in the long-term health care setting being discussed, we saw how the

case manager's work made it possible for the information needs of organizational decision making to subordinate the interests of the man who thought he needed services. Smith has written extensively on the importance and ubiquity of text-mediated ruling practices (for example, Smith, 1990b: 209–224).

An important shift in knowing occurs when one moves from knowing at first hand to knowing in text-mediated ways. As this case manager worked, she was constructing an objective version of the applicant using a specialized text. It guided her work in a manner that had immediate effects in the setting and as part of a complex organizational process, it would have had extended effects. Here, a ruling practice is being rendered routine, through the use of a text that objectifies the person being acted on, organizationally. Standard questions are asked, categories are filled, and so on. A knowledgeable reader of the assessment form would be able to identify this process and its result as providing the basis for determining eligibility for, and level of, service. What we did not see in that excerpt of data was how this became a ruling practice, although we did begin to form an idea of how the case manager's interest in the client was guided away from the applicant and towards the categories of the form. She is creating a particular description of the client. We can assume that the text organizes her interest towards certain information because some facts are relevant to the organizational decision making and as they are made available there is no further need to address the particulars of the applicant as a person. It is this textual work-up that accomplishes objectification of the client.

Clearly the text-related work of case managers is administratively useful. The goals of administration are coordination and control of the paid effort of employees in the interest of organizational and program objectives. If the text is to work well it must structure the whole interview and subsequent interaction for such organizational purposes. As the example demonstrated, the case manager's interview generated for organizational decision making exactly the information needed to support the decisions that were to be made. On that basis, those decisions could be made not only efficiently, but also equitably and rationally— just as organizational mandates dictate. Besides that, the text of the assessment form created this particular interview as a close copy of other assessment interviews being conducted by other case managers in an administrative area, thus coordinating the effort and attention of all towards the organization's mission.

Institutional ethnographers' theorizing of text-mediated decision making tells them that such decisions will reflect organizational interests that are ruling interests. Even though the categories of the community health assessment form relate to the client's interests—getting help, for instance—that text-mediated process subordinates the client's interests to the organization's. The distinction is fine but vital. As we saw in this excerpt of observational data, the client's interests are transformed into a particular textual version. When the interviewer activates the assessment form, she determines what information "fits" the categories. That selection will appear in and to organizational readers simply as the textual presentation of the client's interests. It creates a version that tells the client's story by removing him as its subject. The objectivity created in this work-up is useful organizationally, especially under conditions where tough decisions have to be made. Agencies face situations where certain apparently eligible applicants have to be screened out on a rational and equitable basis. Categorizing accounts constructs stories into commensurable versions that allow for easier differentiation among people. In situations like this, the interests of people are subordinated.

To clarify this point, we might pursue some of the ways that ruling interests subordinate people's interests in the community health field. The information that a case manager collects makes it possible for her employer to manage scarce resources more effectively, offering services to categories of clients whose needs are more acute, for example. In a health care system like Canada's, acute care is privileged over long-term care through the Canada Health Act and subsequent policy and programs. At issue for the client in the example we have been considering were his plans for managing how to live, increasingly disabled with a degenerative illness. Some health care is publicly provided, while some is not. The objective formulation of his story within the assessment text builds in the policy-relevant categories of information. Let's assume that the categories are there to speak of the acuity of his condition and that the particular decisions about his application for services are to be influenced by the acuity of his needs relative to other applicants.

Even though the professional has constructed it by subordinating the client's story to her views on how to fill out the text's categories, the textual version may appear convincingly objective to her. She will become committed to this version. Smith would call such an account "ideological" owing to the socially organized practices of its construction (Smith, 1990a: 32–45). An ideological account has a ruling conceptual structure that makes it especially useful for organizational decisions. The categories that describe the client express organizational interests—around the questions of how a client's need for service is defined, for example. Case managers may find their own professional views of clients' needs shift as health budgets are tightened to reduce government deficit. When managers must reduce the amount of service provided, cuts can be made, rationally, by considering the texts. People as subjects with individual needs and claims disappear. That is one of the administrative benefits of an objectified account. Case managers become convinced by the apparent objectivity of their textual involvement in the rationing work that an organizational view provides the right way, perhaps even the only fair way, to act. What disappears from their view is the whole question of whose interests are being met and whose interests are being subjugated by a ruling practice. While text-based decisions might appear objective they are not necessarily disinterested or fair.

One of the debates that research in the area of disabilities encourages is about the legitimacy of citizens' claims for long-term health care in a culture that privileges acute care treatments. There is no question that organizational decisions to save money by screening out some clients may favour some over others. Working objectively may not be the right approach. An argument about the influence by proponents of so-called high-tech medicine on health policy could be inserted here, for instance, showing that ruling interests can be put in place objectively through administration, policy-making, and program implementation.

A shift in conceptualizing the case manager's work from simply conducting an assessment to activating a text-based ruling relation is analytically subtle, but significant. This language identifies how the everyday exercise of power may be identified and studied. And importantly, it introduces the concept of ruling, where ordinarily a health care professional would see this work as being "in the interests of the people." Having a method of inquiry that examines how ruling takes place in routine administrative practices is a very valuable contribution to understanding the troubles that emerge in everyday life. Smith's concept of ruling originates with Marx. However, she names practices of domination and subordination that are specific to contemporary times and not to Marx's (Smith, 1990b: 6–8). For example,

management practices of information-based and automated decision processes would not have been available in Marx's time. Smith claims that ruling practices operate and are operated to coordinate us all with the interests of capital in ways that are quite different from Marxist analyses of class oppression in nineteenth-century capitalism. Class and class interests still exist but capitalist business practices, management, and governance have changed, and so have relations of ruling. Texts, language, and expertise of all sorts are now central to the technologies of ruling practices. Technologies for knowing objectively—as illustrated in the community health case—are the basis of contemporary practices of ruling.

While it may not be comfortable for those involved, it is important to recognize that well-intentioned work may be part of oppressive relations of ruling. We can see how this would have been the case in the health care setting examined here. Working within an administratively framed organization, a nurse's interaction with her clients may be at odds with her own intentions to be caring. People positioned on either side of the relation can participate in ruling practices without their knowledge or consent. Texts and text-mediated practices are central features of this kind of exercise of power. As seen above, the long-term care client becomes, for organizational purposes, the object that the agency account describes. As a subject, he recedes out of sight, while the objectified version carries on into the organization as a "case," a "client," etc. Accounts such as this assessment determine how an organization knows a person, officially, and how the organization's employees can interact with him. The power of an officially mandated organization overrules personal or professional intentions and experiences. In the objectified and ideological version of knowledge being created in organizational records, there is no way back to the client's, or the professional's, own experience. The official objectified version dominates. Any experiential account that the professional makes is neither useful to the organization's action nor likely to be believed. The text replaces and "trumps" competing versions. Officially, the person exists as an object, just as he appears in organizational documents.

EXPERIENCE, DISCOURSE, AND SOCIAL RELATIONS

Smith's approach to understanding everyday life and how it is organized and ruled keeps the subject at the centre of the analysis. This is why institutional ethnography is said to begin in personal experience. Maintaining a standpoint in the everyday world offers the institutional ethnographer a stance from which to conduct an inquiry into its social organization. The inquiry is always about how the subject's experience is organized. As discussed above, institutional ethnographers work with a theory of contemporary social organization that is centred on the explication of ruling practices and their associated text-based discourses and objectified forms of knowledge. Here we want to focus on how to see discourse as an organizer of experience while maintaining one's analytic interest in the subject, the knower. [...]

* * * * *

The texts of interest to institutional ethnographers are those that are part of institutional or social relationships. These texts, we suggest, are features of discursive organization that relate people purposively to each other, and to events, organizations, and resources. To discover how ideas carried in texts actually affect people's lives, Smith wants us to understand that people *participate* in discursive activity. They participate in discourse as they carry out their everyday lives just as surely as they participate in nutrition and metabolism through eating their meals. What Foucault

(1984) conceptualized as knowledge/power is for Smith a social relation that comes into play as actual people participate in knowing and acting knowledgeably. Smith's view is that it is through their active participation and in contributing their own knowledge of how to go about things that people are brought into line with ruling ideas. Some elements of ruling arise formally and explicitly through legally binding discourses. Often ruling happens less explicitly as people consult their own understandings of prevailing and dominant discourses and act accordingly.

A helpful example of discourse as an enacted feature of social organization is found in some research that Smith conducted with Alison Griffith (Griffith, 1995; Smith, 1987). We have drawn on Griffith's (1995) analysis to illustrate how discourse powerfully organizes mothers' work around their children's schooling and its child-centred ideology. Child-centred teaching focuses on the child in a particular way and to accomplish it, the public school needs the active involvement of mothers. Griffith's interviews with mothers and teachers suggest how more or less easily and successfully mothers take up the work of becoming partners in the educational project (of child-centred education). Schools have come to rely on mothers being ready, willing, and able to produce their children as learning-ready and to work along with the teacher in specific ways. Mothers are incorporated into the schooling project through the school personnel's use of ideas (from discourses) about good mothering that all mothers are expected to know and share. Griffith writes:

A mothering discourse, now taken for granted, is the textual presentation of the dyadic mother-child interaction in terms that have been structured by the child development discourse. It includes (but is not limited to) the advice literature to mothers in magazines and newspapers, portrayals of "good" and "bad" mothers on television and radio, the academic discourse on families and the educational literature telling mothers how to improve their child's success at school. (Griffith, 1995: 112–114).

Teachers and their teaching processes rely on mothers accepting these responsibilities regarding their child's learning—mothers are expected to work on their children to advance the skills and personal habits that teachers evaluate in the classroom.

* * * * *

Griffith's study gives one example of how ideas from elsewhere may penetrate daily life, organizing people's relation to their own families, and affecting their everyday choices about how to act with them. What we are calling discourse sets a mother up to feel that either she is, or more often that she is not, doing a good enough job of helping her child succeed in school. The teachers' and schools' structuring of the relations among children, mothers, and teachers relies on mothers accepting the validity of their responsibility. Teachers and schools build authority into this view. There may be some discord, judgement, resentment, anxiety, or guilt in this organization of a mother-child-teacher relation. Yet it is unlikely that someone living the ordinary life of a mother will make the analytic connections that Griffith has done. One's experiential knowledge does not offer insights into discursive organization of everyday life. *Knowing* that the school is downloading educational work on her and that it *requires* her to act in a particular way with her child might bring a mother a sense of relief. But that kind of analysis requires a specialized inquiry.

As its procedure for inquiry, institutional ethnography would not import a theory of schooling and the state into such an analysis. The analysis would rely on a theorized way of exploring power and knowledge—as people's organized activities. The inquiry would attempt to uncover, explore, and describe how people's everyday lives may be organized without their explicit awareness but still with their active involvement. Conceptualizing the operation of power such that it can be discovered in people's everyday actions is a crucial theoretical feature of institutional ethnography. This kind of inquiry begins with a description of what research subjects are actually doing. As in Griffith's work, the analysis brings together an account of people's everyday experiences and actions with a matching exploration of how those experiences and actions are framed through discourses.

Smith's concept of social relations names the sequences of social action that may begin with an individual's activities in local settings but that extend beyond the local, into sites where power is held (see Smith, 1990b: 94–95). The concept of social relations also informs a methodological procedure. When the researcher assumes people's actions are undertaken methodically, an inquiry into what happens addresses an actor's (subject's) own procedures. As institutional ethnographers, we know that what the subject is doing is part of the more extended social relation. There will be clues in the informant's account to what informs his actions and where that message comes from. If power enters into what she does, we will need to find out how. In this chapter, we have looked at the coordination of mothers' work with teachers', and earlier, at the interaction of a bus driver and students getting on the bus, and a health care worker with a prospective client. The actions—of teachers, mothers and children, health care workers and clients, or of bus drivers and students—are socially organized. They are coordinated, ruled, put together as part of the social relations of their respective settings.

To study these settings means to figure out how each works, how the people we "take the side of" are implicated in social organization that extends beyond them. We have been suggesting how everyday life is discursively organized and how its analysis renders people's lives more understandable. It is possible to discover how the teachers, mothers, health care workers, clients, students, and bus drivers involved take up their particular part in a social relation. Theirs is only a piece of the whole. To understand more fully what is happening the researcher must discover and map in the missing pieces of the social relation.

REFERENCES

Campbell, Marie. 2001. "Textual Accounts, Ruling Action: The Intersection of Power and Knowledge in the Routine Conduct of Community Nursing Work." *Studies in Cultures, Organizations and Societies*, 7(2): 231–250.

Campbell, Marie, Brenda Copeland, and Betty Tate, with the Research Team. 1999. *Project Inter-Seed: Learning From the Health Care Experiences of People with Disabilities*, Final Research Report, November 30. Victoria: University of Victoria.

Foucault, Michel. 1970. *The Order of Things: An Archeology of the Human Sciences*. London: Tavistock.

_____. 1984. *Power/Knowledge: Selected Interviews and Other Writings, 1972–1977*. New York: Pantheon Books.

Griffith, Alison. 1995. "Mothering, Schooling, and Children's Development." In *Knowledge, Experience and Ruling Relations: Studies in the Social Organization of Knowledge*, edited by M. Campbell and Ann Manicom, 108–121. Toronto: University of Toronto Press.

Smith, Dorothy E. 1987. *The Everyday World as Problematic: A Feminist Sociology*. Toronto: University of Toronto Press and Northeastern Press.

_____. 1990a. *The Conceptual Practices of Power: A Feminist Sociology of Knowledge*. Toronto: University of Toronto Press.

_____. 1990b. *Texts, Facts and Femininity: Exploring the Relations of Ruling*. London: Routledge.

_____. 1999. *Writing the Social: Critique, Theory and Investigations*. Toronto: University of Toronto Press.

CHAPTER 13

Ethnography, Institutions, and the Problematic of the Everyday World

Peter R. Grahame

INTRODUCTION

A few years ago at the annual meetings of the American Sociological Association, I heard a prominent researcher protest, "don't find the everyday world problematic, the way Dorothy Smith does!" He had just been the target of an unsparing commentary by Smith. While his agitation was perhaps understandable, I still found the remark puzzling, and wondered how it was possible *not* to find the everyday world "problematic." After all, a critical examination of the troubles and issues affecting ordinary people has been central to the sociological enterprise from Marx through C. Wright Mills to the present. Anyone who has considered the forms of disadvantage and irrationality generated by the dominant arrangements in advanced capitalist societies should be in a position to acknowledge that everyday life is "full of problems." Was the researcher professing indifference towards this critical perspective on social life? But the difficulty lay deeper, for his remark betrayed a misreading of Smith. Her point is not simply that everyday life *is* problematic (troublesome, perplexing, difficult, etc.), but rather that we can treat the world of everyday *life as* sociology's problematic (the complex of concerns, issues, and questions which generate a horizon of possible investigations). Smith's work both draws attention to neglected features of how

everyday activities are coordinated and calls for research strategies suitable for grasping how those activities are tied into dominant forms of social organization.

* * * * *

THE EVERYDAY WORLD AS PROBLEMATIC

Smith's approach to sociological inquiry is formulated as a challenge to standard or mainstream forms of sociology. Two points are of immediate concern here. The first has to do with objectification, and the second has to do with ruling. As Mann and Kelly point out, a "critique of objectified forms of knowledge" is central to Smith's project (1997: 396). They point to the tendency of traditional sociology to favor the constructed realities of privileged experts over the lived realities of its subjects. However, Smith goes beyond a critique of the expert role to consider the institutional complex within which sociological research is produced and applied. She points out that the phenomena which conventional sociology addresses—for example, delinquency, poverty, unemployment, and mental illness—have their origin in bureaucratic, legal, and professional operations. Through categories like "delinquency," the activities of individuals appear in an objectified form, grasped in a way which defines those activities in terms of the imperatives and procedures of the institutions concerned (e.g., the police and the courts). In this way, sociology has routinely concerned itself with objectified constructs tied to practices of formal organization rather than expressions which originate in the actualities of everyday life. Further, standard sociological discourse represents the social world in terms of formal relations between properties of these conceptual constructs, typically relying on quantitative[1] strategies to express these relations. The result, Smith argues, is that the presence of active subjects who are knowers of their everyday worlds is eliminated in favor of an abstracted mode of knowledge constituted in terms of the relevancies of a ruling apparatus (Smith, 1987: 152–153). I suggest that an explanation of the researcher's protest to Smith reported above may lie here, in the trained incapacity to inhabit a standpoint outside of the standard conventions of the discourse.

To be sure, other theorists have critically examined the relation of the social sciences and the ruling institutions of the society. In recent decades, Habermas has pointed out that in their positivist forms, social sciences become part of the administrative system of modern societies, producing knowledge oriented to control over objectifed processes, and contributing to a "colonization of the lifeworld" (Habermas, 1971; Habermas, 1984). And Foucault has shown that the fields of discourse commonly referred to as the social sciences emerged as part of the disciplinary apparatus through which contemporary societies are governed (Foucault, 1977; Foucault, 1978). These critiques take the form, respectively, of a rational reconstruction of the human sciences and a history of discursive formations. In contrast, Smith develops her critique of sociology's role in processes of ruling through an analysis of how institutions and professional discourses exclude the standpoint of persons living and acting in the everyday world.[2] She argues that sociology's

standard ways of knowing the world operate within the framework of the society's dominant institutions. Taken together, management, the professions, government, the media, and the academy are seen as a complex of extended social relations that accomplish "ruling" in the sense that they organize, coordinate, and regulate what happens in contemporary societies (Smith, 1987: 56; Smith, 1990a: 14). This complex of ruling relations includes specialized scientific, technical, and cultural discourses which operate through a wide variety of textual formats as constituents of the process of ruling (Smith, 1987: 152; Smith, 1990b: 6). For example, Smith and Griffith's research shows how the concept "single parent" makes the mothering-schooling relation accountable in terms of institutional perspectives and priorities, identifying a family form seen as a source of problems for the conduct of classroom work processes, while glossing over the actual work organization through which women participate in the coordination of mothering and schooling, and obscuring the role of the state in reproducing social class (Griffith, 1984; Smith, 1987: 173–175).

Smith invites us to inquire into aspects of the everyday world ignored by conventional sociology. How can the everyday world be opened up for investigation? She explains that her approach departs from some of the familiar sociologies of everyday life which in different ways constitute the everyday world as an object for sociological study. For example, Goffman's dramaturgy provides a set of categories (impression management, definition of the situation, front and back regions, etc.) which makes certain elements of the everyday world available for study while presenting that world as a distinct and free-standing domain of inquiry (Goffman, 1959; Goffman, 1963). Following a different strategy ethnomethodologists have advocated a policy of treating social settings as self-organizing (Garfinkel, 1967: 33) and of properties produced and known within the local setting. […] Smith objects that these kinds of strategies assemble the everyday world as an object of investigation by isolating it from its context and making it appear self-contained. Thus the everyday world is turned into an object of study at the expense of severing it from its connections with broader forms of organization which are difficult to grasp from within the local setting yet which give that world its particular character.

The alternative for Smith is to approach everyday life as a site of a problematic open to sociological inquiry. Smith reverses the direction of conceptualization found in studies which approach everyday life from the standpoint of theory. She is careful to point out that she departs from the usual meaning of "problematic" as a set of theoretical questions and related concepts.[3] Instead of using the categories of conventional sociology as a point of departure, she proposes beginning with the everyday world as it is actually lived and proceeding from there to develop a conceptualization which clarifies the properties of that world. Smith uses the term "problematic" to direct attention to a domain of possible questions, questions which have not yet been formulated, but which are implicit in the way the everyday world is organized. The problematic is there prior to the application of concepts and theories; its development takes the form of an inquiry which begins to question how things are organized. Smith's argument is that the social organization which makes possible the daily scenes of life in contemporary societies isn't wholly contained within the local setting or its associated sensemaking practices.

Rather, this organization is generated by social relations which originate outside of the local setting and which can only be partially glimpsed within it (Smith, 1987: 92, 152–154).

While dramaturgy and ethnomethodology have focused on the local ordering of everyday activities, opening up the problematic of

the everyday world requires us to consider how the scenes of daily life are determined by an extended set of social relations. Generalized social relations, such as the relations of production and consumption, state administration, and managerial control, form part of the institutional order of contemporary societies, and reach beyond local settings to involve individuals often unknown to one another in extended sequences of social action. In Smith's account, a social relation is not an abstraction, but rather the actual linking and coordinating of activities and work processes in diverse sites: thus we can begin to grasp the anatomy of social relations as definite, extended forms of social organization which are both researchable but resistant to commonsense understandings. These extra-local forms of organization penetrate the local, but they are not easily grasped in terms of the everyday understandings through which we experience the local (Smith, 1987: 152–155). Indeed, Smith points out, we often experience the everyday world as disorganized. Events may seem disconnected, incoherent, or lacking in sense. For example, in the world described by Liebow in *Tally's Corner,* individuals referred to as streetcorner men often described their work as pointless and their relations with women as exploitative (Liebow, 1967). Smith points out that the disorganization which the men experienced had a source which did not lie in the local situation itself (the streetcorner and its environs), but rather in ways that the labor market and state agencies organized (and disorganized) the everyday worlds of these men and women (Smith, 1987: 95–96). Such experiences of disconnection and incoherence, perplexing in themselves, point to the need to rethink the everyday world as a problematic for sociological investigation.

INSTITUTIONAL ETHNOGRAPHY

While Smith has explored the possibilities of such inquiry on a number of fronts, including her explorations of women's experience of everyday/everynight social worlds (Smith, 1987; Smith, 1990a) and her recent work on texts and formal organization (Smith, 1990b; Smith, 1996; Smith, 1999), her conception of "institutional ethnography" has been particularly attractive to researchers with interests in field work and institutional processes. Institutional ethnography, as Smith defines it, is a specific approach which responds to the general challenges of taking up the problematic of the everyday world. According to a widely held view, often referred to as "naturalism," an ethnography is a field study of a particular group of people in their "natural" surroundings (as opposed to the artificial setting of the experiment); the ethnographer aims at an empathetic rendering of the perspective of both individual actors and the group as a whole, focussing on the meanings which events and relationships have for members of the group in their everyday lives.[4] The ways of the group are implicitly or explicitly viewed as alien; by careful attention to the culture of the group, the ethnographer produces a "translation" which explicates their way of life to an audience which shares the ethnographer's assumptions or background (cf. Hammersley and Atkinson, 1995). In contrast, Smith uses the term ethnography to emphasize the idea of exploring organization concretely by using the experience of some particular person or persons as the entry point into forms of social organization which shape local settings but originate outside of them. Understanding the localized social world of the individual or group is no longer treated as an end in itself, and inquiry is not restricted to observation and interviewing, as in conventional ethnographic approaches. Rather, actual practice—how things actually work—becomes the focus of investigation. The question of "how things work" is not confined to the conventional problem of describing an alien culture or subculture. Instead, the concrete experience of

individuals is treated as the key to discovering how the local organization of everyday worlds is connected with relations of ruling (Smith, 1987: 157–361). As a critical project, Smith's institutional ethnography shares a number of concerns with critical ethnographies which explore the relation of localized subcultures and the broader contradictions of class, race, and sexuality (Willis, 1977; MacLeod, 1995). However, Smith's approach to experience and institutions departs from the more conventional assumptions about the everyday world which characterize critical ethnography.

An institutional ethnography describes the social organization of everyday world from a standpoint outside of institutionalized discourses. In her writings on a sociology for women, Smith has sought to demonstrate that the standpoint of women has historically been excluded from professional discourses which supply the conceptual currency of ruling (managing, organizing, administering, etc.). The discovery of this excluded standpoint provides a point of departure for investigating how the everyday worlds in which we live and act are shaped by institutional processes. It is therefore crucial to grasp what Smith means by "institutions." Institutions are *not* viewed as singular forms of social organization, but rather as functional complexes such as education, health care, and law, in which several forms of organization are interwoven. Institutional processes transform local, concrete, and particular actions into "standard forms of organizational action"; in this way, local activities take on a generalized form. Here, Smith draws on Marx's discussion of commodity relations: when goods and services are exchanged in the market setting, their value appears in an abstract form, expressed through the medium of money. In a similar fashion, bureaucratic forms of organization make actions accountable in terms of abstract, generalized categories. The concrete experience of individuals can thus be viewed as a terrain structured by these generalizing relations but not wholly swallowed up by them. In this way, the experience of the individual presents itself not merely as "a case," but rather as an entry point into the actual workings of those institutions which produce the generalized and abstract character of contemporary societies (Smith, 1987: 157–158). A key dimension of the relation between individual experience and institutions lies in the use of institutional accounts of members' practices. Institutional accounts are "ideological" in the sense that local practices are to be made accountable in ways which express the functions of the institution. For example, schoolteachers learn to account for children's behavior in terms of "developmental stages," "learning styles," "attention deficits," and the like; such accounts narrow and transform what can be noticed and proposed about classroom activities. Through such procedures, institutional forms of discourse are made to stand in for the situated practices and reasoning of individuals, so that the latter appear only as psychological or social processes, if at all. Institutional ethnography, by beginning with the experience of individuals, seeks to break with these processes of institutional inscription (Smith, 1987: 157–161).

We have considered some of the ideas which make Smith's approach different from more conventional forms of ethnography, but what is actually involved in *doing* institutional ethnography? Smith singles out three tasks which define institutional ethnography as a research strategy. The first task centers on ideology, and involves addressing the ideological practices which are used to make an institution's processes accountable. The second task centers on work in a broad sense (not just paid employment), and involves studying the work activities through which people are themselves involved in producing the world they experience in daily life. The third task centers on social relations, and

involves discovering the ways in which a localized work organization operates as part of a broader set of social relations which link multiple sites of human activity (Smith, 1987: 166). To see how this strategy works in practice, it is helpful to follow the example Smith herself provides concerning the use of the expression "single parent." In the next section, I provide an outline of Smith's intricately wrought account.

EXAMPLE OF SCHOOLING AND THE "SINGLE PARENT"

Smith begins her investigation at a point of rupture between an institutional discourse and her own experience. She reports that while she lived for several years as a "single parent," her memories of her home, her children, and their school do not contain actual experiences of *being* a single parent. Instead, she sees that the expression "single parent" becomes operative in certain institutional contexts, for example, schooling and her child's problems with learning to read. While the term "single parent" doesn't explicate her own experiences, it provides school staff with a method for seeing the child as a problem and explaining the problem in terms of his home background. Here, Smith finds a disjuncture between her own experience of mothering and the institution's use of a professional discourse to account for its operations. What is left out of account are the work processes of mothering (Smith, 1987: 167–168).

Smith then turns to a consideration of what is involved in mothering. She notes that in the first place the school does not recognize that mothering itself consists of work performed under specific social and material conditions. For example, a government pamphlet offers a variety of suggestions about how mothers can promote reading skills in their children, such as developing language skills through art activities. The suggestions presuppose (but do not mention) a household organization featuring ample physical space and equipment, access to knowledge resources associated with a university-level education, and a division of labor which permits the mother to devote herself full-time to child rearing and housewifery. More generally, mothering involves a wide range of work activities in addition to routine housework, such as coordinating the schedules of family members, supervising homework, fostering participation in cultural activities, providing transportation to sports activities, volunteering at school, and dealing with emotional crises (Smith, 1987: 168–169). Smith continues her examination of the work process by pointing out that the work activities of mothering complement the work organization of the classroom. What mothers do in the home is consequential for what teachers do in the classroom, inasmuch as classroom activities call for a range of competences learned in the home. For example, what can be done in the context of art lessons depends on whether children have learned to handle paints and brushes without mixing up the colors until they all resemble mud. In this and other ways, teachers confront the outcomes of mothering work in the home as a condition of their own work in the classroom (Smith, 1987: 169–170). It should be noted that Smith does not categorize the work of teachers and other school staff as a species of formal rationality distinct from the lived experiences of women located in the domestic world; her point is rather that mothering and teaching are complementary dimensions of a process in which multiple local sites of work are coordinated (Smith, 1997: 820–821; cf. Mann and Kelley, 1997: 400).

Smith next aims to move beyond the work process which produces the everyday world to an examination of the extended social relations which shape that work. These relations include the professional discourses which supply the ingredients for accounting for institutional processes in a conceptual mode,

the bureaucratic organization of education, and the wider activities of the state in regulating class relations. These are elements of an institutional nexus in which different forms of organization are coordinated, and in which different everyday worlds are implicated. In particular, Smith notes that the complementary mothering/schooling relation works differently in different class contexts. The formal credentials required for entry into middle-class careers mean that the continuity of middle-class status across generations has come to depend more on education and less on inheritance than in the past. Smith proposes that class-specific mothering practices play a crucial role in the work organization of classrooms and schools geared to reproducing the middle class. In middle-class contexts, mothers gain familiarity, through university courses and independent reading, with the conceptual practices used to make home-school relations accountable. In effect, they receive instruction in the same ideological currency which school staff use in making schooling and its outcomes accountable, and they learn how to apply the professional discourse to their own experience. Thus middle-class mothers help to coordinate the school-home relation in a way which is attuned to institutional definitions (Smith, 1987: 171–172).

Smith shows that the term "single parent" needs to be understood as operating in this wider context of the social relations of schooling and class. Within the institutional ideology, "single parent" identifies a family form which is defined as defective with regard to the complementary mothering/schooling relation on which the work organization of the classroom depends. Smith emphasizes that when the term "single parent" is applied, this defect is presumed to exist regardless of the actual practices of the mother involved. As Smith writes elsewhere, such "conceptual strategies ... obliterate women as active agents" (Smith, 1987: 164). What women actually do thus disappears, and what happens in the classroom is made accountable within a conceptual apparatus geared to the ruling relations of the society (Smith, 1987: 170–175). Note that Smith's account begins as a story about her own experience as a parent, but ends with insight into the general relations of schooling and class reproduction. The point of the analysis is not to tell about Smith (to cultivate autobiography), but to begin to pry open the operations of an institutional complex which others can investigate from different starting points and with different emphases.

In the example outlined above, the tasks related to ideology, work, and social relations are taken up and woven into an analytical narrative. An institutional ethnography must be responsive to all three of these tasks, but that doesn't mean that they have to be all developed fully in a given piece of work; some dimensions of the tasks may be handled in a more exploratory fashion. Further, the investigative process can be entered at any point, so it is not necessarily the case that one would perform the tasks in the order presented here.[5] It is also tempting, but misleading, to see the tasks in terms of distinct micro and macro levels of analysis. For example, McCall (1996: 364) sees institutional ethnography as an investigation which progresses through levels or layers, moving from single mother to classroom to school bureaucracy to state. And Burawoy reads Smith as contrasting the "microstructures of everyday life" directed by women with "macrostructures controlled by men" (1998: 6). But resorting to macro/micro distinctions misses Smith's point that social relations exist as extended sequences of action which link together individuals' experiences and institutional processes. They do not exist, nor can they be discovered, as self-sufficient phenomena or self-enclosed spheres of organization. I propose that it is more productive to see the three tasks which Smith sets forth as an agenda which directs attention to key ingredients of the problematic, rather than as a model which depicts stages or levels of analysis. Each task underscores in its own way the coordinated and organized character of the everyday world which conventional analysis has ignored or misconstrued.

SUBJECTS AND STANDPOINT

The projects opened up by treating the everyday world as problematic are intended to restore the presence of active subjects who are knowers of their everyday worlds. What has been excluded from much of standard sociology, according to Smith, is not just certain topics or phenomena, but the standpoint of subjects who know and experience their worlds, and who might begin to ask questions about these worlds. Who, then, are the subjects of institutional ethnographies? Conventional ethnographies[6] assume a separation between the subject who reads the ethnographic account and the individuals whose world is described by the ethnographer. The latter are "the other," those whose ways are unknown or baffling, requiring translation. In contrast, the subjects of institutional ethnography are conceived in terms of the standpoint of those who have been excluded from the institutional discourses, and the investigation begins with the bifurcation between their everyday experience and institutional practice. It is important to note that in Smith's writings, "standpoint" does not signify a subjective perspective or a concrete worldview, but rather the discovery, in how our knowledge of the world is organized, of a critical point of entry into the multiple forms of coordination which shape the everyday world and tie it into broader forms of social organization (Smith, 1987: 106–107; Smith, 1990a: 21–23). Thus Smith's sociology is emphatically not a subjectivist enterprise.

Inasmuch as institutional ethnography uses the experience of exclusion as its point of departure, seeking to account for experience in terms of a broader organization which is unnoticed in significant ways, the kind of analysis aimed at is also a sociology *for*: it produces an awareness which enables us to find our bearings, making it possible to begin to consolidate a knowledge outside the institutional discourse. In the key writings about these prospects, Smith has defined her project as a sociology for women. She treats women's exclusion from the relations of ruling (Smith, 1987; Smith, 1990a) as the key to understanding these new possibilities; in effect, the position of women vis-à-vis the relations of ruling provides the exemplary case, the singularly instructive starting point for her considerations. The result is a powerful contribution to feminist theory and feminist social science. However, the possibilities for investigation which Smith opens up are multiple, and go beyond the particular concerns often associated with feminist research. Smith is careful to point out that the sociology she advocates can raise consciousness about diverse forms of oppression and provide a method for anyone to gain insight into

the social organization which shapes their everyday world (Smith, 1987: 88, 107, 154). Thus the standpoint of women as such is not intended as the end point of analysis.[7] As Mann and Kelly propose, what is involved is not an identity politics. They suggest that significance of the standpoint lies rather in how it provides a point of entry: "it is the social location that holds the key to greater understanding of the relations of ruling, not the fact that the knowledge producer is a woman or a member of an oppressed group" (Mann and Kelly, 1997: 397). Thus in developing a feminist sociology, Smith opens up a more general prospect: "In arriving at the formulation of the everyday world as problematic, we find a sociological subject who may be anyone" (Smith, 1987: 98–99). This "anyone" is in fact *us,* for as Heap points out, "Smith is including herself and the reader in the field of inquiry"; the practices to be investigated are our practices (Heap, 1995).

* * * * *

NOTES

1. To be sure, some similar problems of representation arise when conventional qualitative research strategies are used.
2. Burawoy writes that Smith grounds her critique of sociology in the standpoint of women rather than in an alternative conception of science (1998: 6). However, this misconstrues the role of "standpoint" in her sociology. See the last section of this essay, in which I argue that Smith's approach is neither subjectivist nor particularistic (i.e., committed to an identity politics).
3. Compare this with the version offered in the *Penguin Dictionary of Sociology* (Abercrombie et al. 1984: 168) where "problematic" is defined as sociological concepts related to each other within a theoretical framework (my paraphrase). To

put it another way, in sociological theory a problematic is not a concrete problem to be solved, but rather an interrelated set of questions to be studied.
4. To be sure, newer approaches to ethnography have challenged the naturalist orientation, questioning both the rhetoric of realism which naturalistic accounts rely upon, as well as the political implications of the value-neutral stance typically associated with naturalism. For a discussion of these issues, see Hammersley and Atkinson (1995). In spite of these criticisms, the naturalistic approach is still widely influential, and it is arguably the best point of departure for considering what is distinctive about Smith's proposals for ethnographic investigation.

5. In her own illustration, Smith does not treat ideology, work organization, and social relations as three separate steps of analysis. Instead, remarks about ideology are woven into her treatment of work organization and social relations.

6. Here I am thinking of both naturalistic ethnographies such as *Tally's Corner* (Liebow, 1967) and critical ethnographies such as *Learning to Labor* (Willis, 1977) and *Ain't No Makin' It* (MacLeod, 1995).

7. In Smith's words, the standpoint of women should be viewed as "a 'transformer' rather than a final position" (1987: 98).

REFERENCES

Abercrombie, Nicholas, Stephen Hill, and Bryan S. Turner. 1984. *The Penguin Dictionary of Sociology.* Harmondsworth: Penguin.

Burawoy, Michael. 1998. "The Extended Case Method." *Sociological Theory* 16(1): 4–33.

Foucault, Michel. 1977. *Discipline and Punish.* New York: Basic Books.

_____. 1978. *The History of Sexuality, Volume 1. An Introduction.* New York: Random House.

Garfinkel, Harold. 1967. *Studies in Ethnomethodology.* Englewood Cliffs: Prentice-Hall.

Goffman, Erving. 1959. *The Presentation of Self in Everyday Life.* New York: Anchor Books.

_____. 1963. *Interaction Ritual.* New York: Anchor Books.

Griffith, Alison I. 1984. "Ideology, Education, and Single Parent Families: The Normative Ordering of Families through Schooling." Unpublished Ph.D. thesis, University of Toronto.

Habermas, Jürgen. 1971. *Knowledge and Human Interests.* Boston: Beacon Press.

_____. 1984. *The Theory of Communicative Action, Volume I. Reason and the Rationalization of Society.* Boston: Beacon Press.

Hammersley, Martin, and Paul Atkinson. 1995. *Ethnography: Principles in Practice,* 2nd ed. London: Routledge.

Heap, James L. 1995. "Foreword." In *Knowledge, Experience, and Ruling Relations: Studies in the Social Organization of Knowledge,* edited by Marie Campbell and Ann Manicom. Toronto: University of Toronto Press.

Liebow, Elliot. 1967. *Tally's Corner: A Study of Negro Streetcorner Men.* Boston: Little, Brown.

MacLeod, Jay. 1995. *Ain't No Makin' It: Aspirations and Attainment in a Low-Income Neighborhood.* Boulder: Westview Press.

McCall, Michal M. 1996. "Postmodernism and Social Inquiry." *Symbolic Interaction* 19(4): 363–365.

Mann, Susan A., and Lori R. Kelley. 1997. "Standing at the Crossroads of Modernist Thought: Collins, Smith, and the New Feminist Epistemologies." *Gender & Society* 11(4): 391–408.

Smith, Dorothy E. 1987. *The Everyday World as Problematic: A Feminist Sociology.* Toronto: University of Toronto Press.

_____. 1990a. *The Conceptual Practices of Power: A Feminist Sociology of Knowledge.* Toronto: University of Toronto Press.

_____. 1990b. *Texts, Facts, and Femininity: Exploring the Relations of Ruling.* London: Routledge.

_____. 1996. "Telling the Truth after Postmodernism." *Symbolic Interaction* 19(3): 171–202.

_____. 1997. "Response to Susan Mann and Lori Kelley." *Gender & Society* 11(6): 819–821.

_____. 1999. *Writing the Social: Critique, Theory, Investigations.* Toronto: University of Toronto Press.

Willis, Paul. 1977. *Learning to Labor.* Westmead: Saxon House.

CHAPTER 14

Institutional Ethnography: Using Interviews to Investigate Ruling Relations

Marjorie L. DeVault and Liza McCoy

Social researchers use interviews in various ways, but they usually think of interviews as sources for learning about individual experience. In this chapter we discuss interviewing as part of an approach designed for the investigation of organizational and institutional process. [...] In this alternative to conventional forms of interview research, investigators use informants' accounts not as windows on the informants' inner experience but in order to reveal the "relations of ruling" that shape experiences (Smith, 1996).

We use the term *institutional ethnography* (IE), following Canadian sociologist Dorothy E. Smith, to refer to the empirical investigation of linkages among local settings of everyday life, organizations, and translocal processes of administration and governance. These linkages constitute a complex field of coordination and control that Smith (1999) identifies as "the ruling relations"; these increasingly textual forms of coordination are "the forms in which power is generated and held in contemporary societies" (79).

Smith (1987) introduced the term *institutional ethnography* in writing about a "sociology for women," illustrating with her studies of mothers' work at home in relation to their children's schooling, but she understands the approach as having wide application. Those who have followed Smith in developing IE have investigated many different social processes,

including the regulation of sexuality (Smith, 1998; Khayatt, 1995; Kinsman, 1996); the organization of health care (Campbell, 1988, 1995, 1999; Diamond, 1992; Mykhalovskiy, 2000; Mykhalovskiy and Smith, 1994; Smith, 1995), education (Griffith, 1984, 1992; Andre Bechely, 1999; Stock, 2000), and social work practice (de Montigny, 1995; Parada, 1998); police and judicial processing of violence against women (Pence, 1997); employment and job training (Grahame, 1998); economic restructuring (McCoy, 1999); international development regimes (Mueller, 1995); planning and environmental policy (Turner, 1995; Eastwood, 2000); the organization of home and community life (DeVault, 1991; Luken and Vaughan, 1991, 1996; Naples, 1997); and various kinds of activism (Walker, 1990; Ng, 1996).

Over the past two decades, a loosely organized network of IE researchers has emerged in North America, the members of which meet regularly to share developing projects and refinements of these methods.[1] This chapter surveys the work of that network. In preparing the discussion that follows, we have examined published examples of IE research, interviewed practitioners (individually and in small groups), and collected accounts of research practices and reflections via e-mail. We understand IE as an emergent mode of inquiry, always subject to revision and the improvisation required by new applications. […]

In the following section, we provide an introduction to this research approach and consider various uses of interviewing in IE projects. Next, we discuss the conduct of interviews. The subsequent section foregrounds the key role of texts and institutional discourses in IE research, showing how interviews can be oriented toward these aspects of social organization. We then turn to analysis and writing in relation to IE interviews.

INSTITUTIONAL ETHNOGRAPHY AS A MODE OF INQUIRY

Dorothy Smith proposes IE as part of an "alternative sociology," an approach she describes as combining Marx's materialist method and Garfinkel's ethnomethodology with insights from the feminist practice of consciousness-raising. "In different ways, all of these ground inquiry in the ongoing activities of actual individuals" (Smith, 1999: 232, n. 5). Analytically fundamental to this approach is an ontology that views the social as the concerting of people's activities. This is an ontology shared by phenomenologists, symbolic interactionists, and ethnomethodologists. Smith expands this through the concept of social relations, which, as in Marx, refers to the coordinating of people's activities on a large scale, as this occurs in and across multiple sites, involving the activities of people who are not known to each other and who do not meet face-to-face.

In contemporary global capitalist society, the "everyday world" (the material context of each embodied subject) is organized in powerful ways by translocal social relations that pass through local settings and shape them according to a dynamic of transformation that begins and gathers speed somewhere else (e.g., if the local hospital closes, the explanation will not be wholly local). Smith (1990) refers to these translocal social relations that carry and accomplish organization and control as "relations of ruling":

They are those forms that we know as bureaucracy, administration, management, professional organization, and the media. They include also the complex of discourses, scientific, technical, and cultural, that intersect, interpenetrate, and coordinate the multiple sites of ruling. (6)

A central feature of ruling practice in contemporary society is its reliance on text-based discourses and forms of knowledge, and these are central in IE inquiries (a topic we return to later).[2]

Building on this conception of ruling, Smith's notion of institution points to clusters of text-mediated relations organized around specific ruling functions, such as education or health care. *Institution,* in this usage, does not refer to a particular type of organization; rather, it is meant to inform a project of empirical inquiry, directing the researcher's attention to coordinated and intersecting work processes taking place in multiple sites. For example, when health care is considered as an institution, what comes into view is a vast nexus of coordinated work processes and courses of action—in sites as diverse as hospitals, homes, doctors' offices, community clinics, elementary schools, workplaces, pharmacies, pharmaceutical companies, advertising agencies, insurance companies, government ministries and departments, mass media, and medical and nursing schools. Obviously, institutions cannot be studied and mapped out in their totality, and such is not the objective of institutional ethnography. Rather, the aim of the IE researcher is to explore particular corners or strands within a specific institutional complex, in ways that make visible their points of connection with other sites and courses of action. […]

Institutional ethnography takes for its entry point the experiences of specific individuals whose everyday activities are in some way hooked into, shaped by, and constituent of the institutional relations under exploration. The term *ethnography* highlights the importance of research methods that can discover and explore these everyday activities and their positioning within extended sequences of action. When interviews are used in this approach, they are used not to reveal subjective states, but to locate and trace the points of connection among individuals working in different parts of institutional complexes of activity. The interviewer's goal is to elicit talk that will not only illuminate a particular circumstance but also point toward next steps in an ongoing, cumulative inquiry into translocal processes. [...]

The researcher's purpose in an IE investigation is not to generalize about the group of people interviewed, but to find and describe social processes that have generalizing effects. Thus interviewees located somewhat differently are understood to be subject, in various ways, to discursive and organizational processes that shape their activities. These institutional processes may produce similarities of experience, or they may organize various settings to sustain broader inequalities (as explored in DeVault, 1999: Chapter 5); in either case, these generalizing consequences show the lineaments of ruling relations. For example, George W. Smith (1998) treated the gay young men he interviewed not as a population of subjects, but as informants knowledgeable about school life for gay youth. He explains:

> The interviews opened various windows on different aspects of the organization of this regime. Each informant provides a partial view; the work of institutional ethnography is to put together an integrated view based on these otherwise truncated accounts of schools. (310)

The general relevance of the inquiry comes, then, not from a claim that local settings are similar, but from the capacity of the research to disclose features of ruling that operate across many local settings.

IE studies can "fit together"—much like the squares of a quilt (Smith, 1987)—because they share the same organizing ontology and the same focus on generalizing processes of ruling. Thus Janet Rankin's (1998) study of nurses' work and administrative categories in a British Columbia hospital extends the analysis in Eric Mykhalovskiy's (2000) study of health services research and hospital restructuring in Ontario, and both extend the analysis in Liza McCoy's (1999) study of accounting texts and restructuring in another area of the public sector in Canada. This does not mean that the three studies consciously locate their analyses in relation to one another, but that through the analytic frame they share they can be seen to be describing different moments and aspects of the same generalizing set of relations.

Dorothy Smith's work on the social organization of knowledge predates the emergence of feminist sociology, but her formulations gained increasing power as she situated them within a community of activist feminist scholars seeking a transformative method of inquiry (DeVault, 1999). IE researchers generally have critical or liberatory goals; they undertake research in order to reveal the ideological and social processes that produce experiences of subordination. For example, in Smith's classic feminist text *The Everyday World as Problematic* (1987), the idea is to "begin from women's experiences" and to take as the problematic for the research the question of how such experiences are produced. This notion shares with much feminist writing an interest in women's previously excluded views, but it uses women's accounts only as a point of entry to a broader investigation [....] The idea is to shift from a focus on women themselves (as in a sociology "of women") to a kind of investigation that could be useful in efforts to change the social relations that subordinate women (and others).

IE researchers aim at specific analyses of social coordination; the liberatory potential of the approach comes from its specification of possible "levers" or targets for activist intervention. Some IE research has emerged directly from the researcher's position as activist (G.W. Smith, 1990; Pence, 1997); these projects may be driven and targeted directly toward questions arising from activist work. Some academic researchers work collaboratively with activists: Roxana Ng with garment workers' unions, Marie Campbell with people who have disabilities, and Mykhalovskiy and McCoy with AIDS activists, for example. And some academics (and other professionals) research processes that shape their own work settings, often exploring the peculiar ways in which they themselves are implicated in ruling relations despite their intentions (de Montigny, 1995; Parada, 1998). Whatever the position of the researcher, the transformative potential of IE research comes from the character of the analysis it produces; it is like a "map" that can serve as a guide through a complex ruling apparatus.

Possible Shapes of IE Projects

Institutional ethnography is driven by the search to discover "how it happens," with the underlying assumptions that (a) social "happening" consists in the concerted activities of people and (b) in contemporary society, local practices and experiences are tied into extended social relations or chains of action, many of which are mediated by documentary forms of knowledge. IE researchers set out to provide analytic descriptions of such processes in actual settings.

There is no "one way" to conduct an IE investigation; rather, there is an analytic project that can be realized in diverse ways. IE investigations are rarely planned out fully in advance. Instead, the process of inquiry is rather like grabbing a ball of string, finding a thread, and then pulling it out; that is why it

is difficult to specify in advance exactly what the research will consist of. IE researchers know what they want to explain, but only step by step can they discover whom they need to interview or what texts and discourses they need to examine. In the discussion that follows, we describe some common "shapes" or trajectories of IE research.

Beginning with Experience

A common—even a "classic"—IE approach (recommended by Dorothy Smith, 1987) begins with the identification of an experience or area of everyday practice that is taken as the experience whose determinants are to be explored. The researcher seeks to "take the standpoint" of the people whose experience provides the starting point of investigation. For example, George Smith (1988) begins from the experience of gay men who were arrested by police in a series of sweeping raids on gay bathhouses; Didi Khayatt (1995) begins from the experience of young lesbian women in high school; Campbell and her associates begin from the experience of people attempting to live independently with physical disabilities (see Campbell, 1998; 1999); Diamond (1992) begins from the experience of people, mostly women, who work as nursing assistants in nursing homes for the elderly; and Susan Turner (1995) begins from the experience of community residents seeking to stop a developer from destroying a wooded ravine. In all of these studies, the researchers go on to investigate the institutional processes that are shaping that experience (e.g., the work of policing, the work of teaching and school administration, the organization of home-care services, the administration of Medicare and nursing homes, the organization of municipal land-use planning). The research follows a sequence: (a) identify an experience, (b) identify some of the institutional processes that are shaping that experience, and (c) investigate those processes in order to describe analytically how they operate as the grounds of the experience.

Some IE researchers spend considerable time at this point of entry (for it can take time to understand the complexity of an experience, and data from this exploration can provide material with much analytic potential). In other cases, a researcher may begin from an experience that he or she knows something about, or where the problematic is already clear (e.g., G.W. Smith, 1990; Walker, 1990). Eventually, however, the researcher will usually need to shift the investigation to begin examining those institutional processes that he or she has discovered to be shaping the experience but that are not wholly known to the original informants. Thus a second stage of research commonly follows that usually involves a shift in research site, although not in standpoint. Often, this shift carries the investigation into organizational and professional work sites. At this stage, other forms of research and analysis may come to be used. The researcher may employ observation and the analysis of naturally occurring language data to examine institutional work processes, for example. Or the researcher may use text and discourse analysis to examine the textual forms and practices of knowledge that organize those work processes. But interviews continue to play an important role here as well, whether as the primary form of investigation or as a way of filling in the gaps of what the researcher can learn through observation and document analysis.

A common aspect of IE research at this second stage involves the researcher's investigating institutional work processes by following a chain of action, typically organized around and through a set of documents, because it is texts that coordinate people's activity across time and place within institutional relations. For example, Turner (1995) traced the trajectory of a developer's planning proposal as it passed through a review process involving the city planning office, the local conservation authority, the railroad company, and a meeting of the city council.

Research Focused on "Ruling" Processes

In some IE research, the point of entry is in organizational work processes and the activities of the people who perform them. Rather than arriving at these processes through an exploration of the experience of people who are the objects of that work or who are in some way affected by it, the researcher in this type of IE jumps right into the examination of organizational work sites. The researcher knows about a set of administrative or professional practices and sets about studying how they are carried out, how they are discursively shaped, how they organize other settings. For example, Mykhalovskiy (2000) investigated health services research and its use in health care restructuring. Dorothy Smith and George Smith (1990) researched the organization of skills training in the plastics industry. Elizabeth Townsend (1998) studied the work of professionals in the mental health system and the contradictions between their professional goal of empowering people and system processes organized to control deviance. And Alison Griffith (1998) investigated the legislative and policy bases for educational restructuring in Ontario. This type of IE emphasizes the detailed examination of administrative and professional work processes.

Conceptualization and Place of Interviewing

Interviewing is present in some form in just about all IE studies. But "interviewing" in IE is perhaps better described as "talking with people," and IE uses of interviewing should be understood in this wide sense, as stretching across a range of approaches to talk with informants. At one end of the continuum are planned interviews, where the researcher makes an appointment with someone for the purpose of doing a research interview. Then there is the kind of "talking with people" that occurs during field observation, when the researcher is watching someone do his work and asks him to explain what he is doing, why he did what he just did, what he has to think about to do the work, where this particular document goes, and so on. "Informal," on-the-spot interviews can be combined with later "formal" or planned interviews, in which the researcher brings to the longer interview a set of questions or topics based the earlier observation-and-talk. [...]

Further, "talking with people" is not necessarily done one-to-one. At the planned end of the continuum, a number of recent IE studies have used focus groups to generate group conversations about shared experiences (Smith et al., 1995; Campbell, 1999; Stock, 2000 [...]). And Tim Diamond reports that his research into health insurance draws on collective interviews he holds with his students during class, in which participants collaborate in developing an account of how health care is covered in the news and on television (focus group, August 1999). Such an approach works in IE because institutional processes are standardized across local settings, so any group of informants encounters those processes in some way.

CONDUCTING IE INTERVIEWS

IE interviewing is open-ended inquiry, and IE interviewers are always oriented to sequences of interconnected activities. They talk with people located throughout these institutional complexes in order to learn "how things work." In many investigations, informants are chosen as the research progresses, as the researcher learns more about the social relations involved and begins to see avenues that need exploration. Given that the purpose of interviewing is to build up an understanding

of the coordination of activity in multiple sites, the interviews need not be standardized. Rather, each interview provides an opportunity for the researcher to learn about a particular piece of the extended relational chain, to check the developing picture of the coordinative process, and to become aware of additional questions that need attention.

Dorothy Smith reports that when she conducted interviews jointly with George Smith, in their study of the organization of job training (Smith and Smith, 1990), they thought of their talk with informants as a way to build "piece by piece" a view of an extended organizational process. Rather than using a standard set of questions, they based each interview in part on what they had learned from previous ones. She explains: "You have a sense of what you're after, although you sometimes don't know what you're after until you hear people telling you things .... Discovering what you don't know—and don't know you don't know—is an important aspect of the process" (interview, September 1999). As in any qualitative interviewing, there is a balance to be achieved between directing the interview toward the researcher's goals and encouraging informants to talk in ways that reflect the contours of their activity [....] The distinctiveness of IE interviews is produced by the researcher's developing knowledge of institutional processes, which allows a kind of listening and probing oriented toward institutional connections. Again, Smith explains, "The important thing is to think organizationally, recognizing you won't know at the beginning which threads to follow, knowing you won't follow all possible threads, but noting them along the way."

IE researchers often think of interviewing as "coinvestigation." Such an approach is evident in Gary Kinsman and Patrizia Gentile's (1998) discussion of the oral history narratives they collected from gay men and lesbians affected by Canadian national security campaigns of the late 1950s and early 1960s. They see the first-person narratives as both a "form of resistance to the official security documents" (8) and a basis from which to build a critical analysis of those documents. Because people were affected differently, the narratives took different shapes, and the researchers found that their providing some historical context often helped informants remember and reconstruct their experiences. They describe their interviewing as "a fully reflexive process in which both the participant and the interviewer construct knowledge together" (58).

INTERVIEWING ABOUT TEXTUAL PRACTICES

A prominent aspect of institutional ethnography is the recognition that text-based forms of knowledge and discursive practices are central to large-scale organization and relations of ruling in contemporary society. To use an organic metaphor, textual processes in institutional relations are like a central nervous system running through and coordinating different sites. To find out how things work and how they happen the way they do, a researcher needs to find the texts and text-based knowledge forms in operation. Thus IE investigation often involves close attention to textual practices, and interviewing is an important strategy in this regard.

When IE researchers talk about texts, they usually mean some kind of document or representation that has a relatively fixed and replicable character, for it is that aspect of texts—that they can be stored, transferred, copied, produced in bulk, and distributed widely, allowing them to be activated by users at different times and in different places—that allows them to play a standardizing and mediating role. In this view, a text can be any kind of document, on paper, on computer screens, or in computer files; it can also be a drawing, a photograph, a printed instrument

reading, a video or sound recording, and so on.

Much IE research has focused on standardized texts used in professional and bureaucratic settings, such as care pathway forms in hospitals (Mykhalovskiy, 2000), intake forms and applications at an employment agency (Ng, 1996), patients' charts (Diamond, 1992), nursing worksheets (Rankin, 1998), forms for calculating teachers' workloads (McCoy, 1999), course information sheets used in competency-based education reform (Jackson, 1995), and safety assessment forms used by child protection workers (Parada, 1998). Other bureaucratic texts studied have included job descriptions (Reimer, 1995) and developers' maps used in land-use planning (Turner, 1995). Griffith (1998) and Ng (1995) have examined legislative texts. Sometimes IE researchers look at the creation or generation of texts, such as the work of producing a newsletter for doctors (Mykhalovskiy, 2000), creating materials for job skills training (Smith and Smith 1990), or taking wedding photographs (McCoy, 1987; 1995).

IE researchers are also interested in the text-mediated discourses that frame issues, establish terms and concepts, and in various ways serve as resources that people draw into their everyday work processes, for example, health services research (Mykhalovskiy, 2000), the literature on child development (Griffith, 1984; 1995), the literature on "deviant" sexuality as an aspect of the policing of gay men (Kinsman, 1989), the terms of an international development regime (Mueller, 1995), and popular cultural discourses of femininity (D.E. Smith, 1990: Chapter 6). Whatever the text or textual process, in IE research it is examined for the ways it mediates relations of ruling and organizes what can be said and done.

Listening for Texts

At the early stages of research, when researchers are just beginning to learn about the institutional processes that shape the relations they are studying, they are alert to catch informants' references to texts or text-mediated processes. Sometimes these are fairly easy to catch, as when an informant mentions a specific document and how it functions. In the following extract, for example, a college administrator talks about a bureaucratic "D form":

> Well, that's the problem. We mounted programs and the last thing that's looked at is the return. Because the ministry—when we mount a program—has a little clause at the bottom of the D form, that simply says, you've got to make this work, we're not going to give you any more money than the funding units for it. So, if you want to put it on, fine. It's a disclaimer by the ministry of any acceptance of any debts that this program mounting creates.

At this point, or perhaps later in the interview, the researcher might ask to see a copy of the D form and, if possible, get one to take away with her. She will also want to learn more about how the D form is used: When is it filled out? By whom? What resources and future activities depend on the D form? In this way, the researcher begins to see how local settings are tied into extended institutional relations and at the same time lays the groundwork for future interviews ("Who could I talk to about that?").

Sometimes the researcher suspects that a textual process lies behind the description an informant is giving. It is not uncommon for informants who work in bureaucratic settings to use glosses and metaphors, as in the following example, where a college administrator is describing the work of a committee that recommends "per diem prices":

> And they report to the College Committee presidents who agree or disagree with their recommendation. And then that's sent on

to the Ministry of Skills Development who again have to nod their approval. And finally to the federal government who have to pay the per diem. And they nod their approval or whatever.

Experience suggests that this "nodding" occurs textually, and an IE researcher interested in this process might go on to ask explicitly what form the reporting and the approval take. She might also want to discover which office or person does the approving on behalf of the ministry.

Not all the texts mentioned will become focal in the analysis, but in the early stages of studies some researchers like to map out the main textual processes at work in an institutional setting. In some cases, "mapping" might precede the initial interviews. Pence explains:

> We get together a prep work of documents and legislation. We used to start by going out and blindly interviewing. Now we prepare. But we do find out things [about texts] when we interview that we didn't know were there. (focus group, August 1999)

Asking about Texts

However texts come to be identified as central to the relations under study—whether through exploratory interviews, through prep work, or through the researcher's prior knowledge—the research at some stage may involve interviews with people who can talk in detail about a text or those aspects of a textual process they know. One effective way for an interviewer to structure such an interview is to sit down with the informant and the text in question and talk very concretely about what is in the text and how the informant works with it. Diamond reports: "I ask people to bring a pay stub to the interview, so we can look at that text. We explore together: Where is health care in this pay stub?" (focus group, August 1999).

If the document in question is a standardized form, some researchers like to do the interview around a form that has been completed, rather than a blank one, as that will result in more concrete description. For example, when Dorothy Smith was interviewing a probation officer about a presentencing investigation form, she worked from an actual, completed form to ask about the sources of information (predominantly textual) and the practices of judgment that went into filling it out (interview, September 1999). [...]

In other cases, the text in question is not one the informant creates or completes, but one he or she activates in some way, such as a report or a memo. Here the interviewer might focus on practices of reading to learn how the text is taken up in an actual setting, within an accountable work process. [...]

What the researcher wants to learn about the text and the practices of making or using it will vary, depending on the nature of the text and the focus of the investigation, but in general IE researchers are after the following:

1. How the text comes to this informant and where it goes after the informant is done with it.
2. What the informant needs to know in order to use the text (create it, respond to it, fill it out, and so on).
3. What the informant does with, for, and on account of the text.
4. How this text intersects with and depends on other texts and textual processes as sources of information, generators of conceptual frames, authorizing texts, and so on.
5. The conceptual schema that organizes the text and its competent reading.

The Problem and Resource of Institutional Language

Institutional work processes are organized by conceptual schemes and distinctive categories. These are the terms in which the accountability of the work is produced, and procedures of accountability provide one of the main ways that various local settings are pulled into translocal relations. IE therefore pays strong attention to institutional categories and the interpretive schemata that connect them.

In interviews, it is common—and understandable—that people in an institutional setting describe their work using the language of the institution. This is especially the case with people who have been taught a professional discourse as part of their training or people whose work requires them to provide regular accounts of institutional processes. [...] The challenge for the institutional ethnographer is to recognize when the informant is using institutional language. Not to do so is to risk conducting interviews that contain little usable data beyond the expression of institutional ideology in action, because institutional language conceals the very practices IE aims to discover and describe. Dorothy Smith elaborates:

> These terms are extraordinarily empty. They rely on your being able to fill out what they could be talking about. During the interview, you do that filling in while you listen, but when you look at the transcript afterward, the description isn't there. (interview, September 1999)

As an example, Ann Manicom reports:

> One challenge I've faced in interviewing professionals is ... to get them beyond saying something like, "Well, I have a lot of ADHD kids" to getting them to actually describe day-to-day work processes. The discourses are of course also interesting and an important piece of the analysis, but shifting them out of the discourse is important for actual descriptions of the work process. (E-mail communication, September 1999)

An informant's comment that she has "a lot of ADHD kids" would not be treated by an IE researcher as a straightforward description of her work, although it does show the teacher using institutional concepts to make sense of and to talk about her day-to-day actuality. [...] An alert IE researcher [...] would try to get the teacher to describe, for example, what these "ADHD kids" are like: what they do or need, and in what ways their needs complicate or add to her teaching work. The researcher would try to learn how the teacher uses the ADHD concept to organize her work with the children and her conferences with their parents. Furthermore, the researcher might try to learn how ADHD as a category operates in the administration of schooling: for example, in some school districts, classroom assistants and other resources are allocated through a procedure that takes into account the number of students in a class who are entered in school records as having "special needs," such as ADHD. An IE researcher encountering institutional language has thus a twofold objective: to obtain a description of the actuality that is assumed by, but not revealed in, the institutional terms, and, at the same time, to learn how such terms and the discourses they carry operate in the institutional setting.

ANALYSIS AND PRESENTATION

Just as projects have different shapes, IE researchers aim toward different kinds of analyses. Some use their data to map out complex institutional chains of action; others describe the mechanics of text-based forms of knowledge, elaborate the conceptual schemata of ruling discourses, or explicate how people's lived experience takes shape within institutional relations. John McKendy (1999), who interviewed men incarcerated for violent crimes, focuses his analysis on the informants' stories and the interview itself as a conversation, but in a way that makes visible the juxtaposition of primary narratives and ideological, institutionally oriented accounts:

In doing the analysis now ... I am on the lookout for segments of the interviews where "fault lines" can be detected, as the two modes of telling—the narrative and the ideological—rub up against each other. I want to examine how such junctures are occasioned within the flow of the interview, what kinds of narrative problems they pose for the speakers, and what methods speakers improvise to handle (overcome, resist, circumvent) these problems. (9)

* * * * *

In general, IE analysts look at interview data as raising questions; according to Khayatt, the key is to ask, "How is it that these people are saying what they're saying?" She adds, "This methodology allows you to go back to a political-economic context for the answer" (focus group, October 1999). Ng and Griffith agree that analysis is always a matter of moving back and forth between collected speech and the context that produced it. For Ng (1996, 1999), whose research explores the work experiences of immigrant women, the analytic focus is how these women are drawn into institutional processes. She believes that conventional analyses of immigrants' lives often "produce ethnicity" through particular kinds of analytic work on interview data, linking informants' comments back to their "home cultures." Her goal, instead, is to find clues to "how things happen" for the people identified as immigrants in Canadian institutions. Griffith says of analysis: "It's never instances, it's always processes and coordination. It's all these little hooks. To make sense of it, you have to understand not just the speech of the moment, but what it's hooked into" (focus group, October 1999).

* * * * *

Writing Strategies

* * * * *

Institutional ethnographers try to maintain a focus on institutional relations not just during interviews, but in analysis and writing as well. This can be a challenge, because apparently minor features of presentation format, such as the identification of speakers, can support or interrupt that focus. For example, writing procedures that tag all quotes, regardless of topic, with the gender, race, and class status of the speaker risk inviting an individualizing line of analysis, in which class and ethnicity are treated as inherent in individuals rather than produced through coordinative social processes. Consequently, some IE writers suppress personal information about informants in order to keep the focus on the institutional processes they are describing; they identify quoted speakers only by their location in the institutional work process of which they speak (e.g., nurse, client, teacher, administrator). On the other hand, IE writers using life stories to examine an experience and elaborate a problematic usually find it analytically important to include biographical details and to distinguish speakers from each other through the use of pseudonyms. [...]

* * * * *

As in most aspects of IE, there is no fixed writing format to which all practitioners adhere; instead, writers have the goal of keeping the institution in view and different ways of realizing that goal.

CONCLUSION

[...] We believe that IE approaches offer distinctive advantages for researchers seeking to unmask the relations of ruling that shape everyday life.

Dorothy Smith's writing has been taken up in sociology as critique and revision of core theoretical concerns of the discipline, but the IE approach to empirical investigation has fit less comfortably within academic sociology, because its focus is not on theory building but on "what actually happens."[3] Much of the work we have discussed here, and much development of IE approaches, has occurred among professionals concerned with their relations to clients and the forces shaping their work or among activists working to understand the institutions they confront and seek to change. In addition, many IE researchers have found that the approach is a powerful teaching tool, because it can provide anyone with a strategy for investigating the lineaments of ruling (Naples, forthcoming).

Institutional ethnography is one of the new modes of inquiry that have grown from the cracks in monolithic notions of "objective" social science, as women of all backgrounds, people of color, and others previously excluded from knowledge production have found space and "voice" to explore their experiences and pose questions relevant to their lives. In this context, the distinctiveness of IE lies in its commitment to going beyond the goal of simply "giving voice."

Ann Manicom reports that her feminist students—sensitized to the occlusion and misrepresentation of women's experience in so much traditional social science—sometimes worry about "imposing" extended analyses:

So the work to be done is to help them think more deeply, first about the notion of "women's voices," and secondly about the notion of going "beyond" voice. The first process makes problematic any simplistic notion of "experience" arising in any one of us as individuals; the second brings into view how the traces of social relations are already in women's accounts of their experience. Thus, what is called for in IE is not so much "going beyond" as it is tracing more intently what is already there to be heard. (E-mail communication, September 1999)

Such analyses are directed toward ruling processes that are pervasive, consequential, and not easily understood from the perspective of any local experience. But the IE approach suggests that an understanding grounded in such a vantage point is possible, and necessary, if we are to build upon excluded perspectives the kind of "map" of institutional processes that might be used in making changes to benefit those subject to ruling regimes.

NOTES

1. The group includes several generations of Smith's students from the University of British Columbia and the Ontario Institute for Studies in Education (University of Toronto) and has attracted increasing numbers of other scholars.

    During the past decade, informal meetings have evolved into more regular conferences at York University and OISE, including a 1996 workshop sponsored by the American Sociological Association's Sex and Gender Section. Members of the group have collected exemplars of the approach in publications such as Campbell and Manicom's (1995) edited collection; a special symposium in *Human Studies* titled "Institutions, Ethnography, and Social Organization" (1998); and a forthcoming special issue of *Studies in Cultures, Organizations and Societies* on institutional ethnography (Smith, forthcoming).

2. Although this approach shares with Foucault an interest in texts, power, and governance, there are some central differences that are particularly significant for empirical research. In Foucault's work and in work taking up his approach, for example, the notion of discourse designates a kind of large-scale conversation in and through texts; Smith works with a wider notion of discourse that is consistent with her social ontology and her commitment to grounding inquiry in the activities of actual individuals. For Smith, *discourse* refers to a field of relations that includes not only texts and their intertextual conversation, but the activities of people in actual sites who produce them and use them and take up the conceptual frames they circulate. This notion of discourse never loses the presence of the subject who activates the text in any local moment of its use.

3. Smith's critique involves seeing the enterprise of theory building as implicated in ruling relations. The revision it calls for is one of orientation: Rather than building theory, the researcher seeks to explicate how the categories of social theory work, in concert with related institutional processes, to regulate activities in local sites.

REFERENCES

Andre Bechely, L.N. 1999. "To Know Otherwise: A Study of the Social Organization of Parents' Work for Public School Choice." Ph.D. dissertation, University of California, Los Angeles.

Campbell, M. 1988. "Management as 'Ruling': A Class Phenomenon in Nursing." *Studies in Political Economy* 27: 29–51.

_____. 1995. "Teaching Accountability: What Counts as Nursing Education?"

In *Knowledge, Experience, and Ruling Relations,* edited by M. Campbell and A. Manicom, 221–233. Toronto: University of Toronto Press.

_____. 1998. "Research on Health Care Experiences of People with Disabilities: Exploring the Everyday Problematic of Service Delivery." Presented at the conference "Exploring the Restructuring and Transformation of Institutional Processes: Applications of Institutional Ethnography," October, York University, Toronto.

_____. 1999. "Home Support: What We've Learned about Continuity and Client Choice." Discussion paper, Project Inter-Seed: Learning from the Health Care Experiences of People with Disabilities, University of Victoria and South Vancouver Island Resource Centre for Independent Living, Victoria, BC.

Campbell, M., and A. Manicom, eds. 1995. *Knowledge, Experience, and Ruling Relations.* Toronto: University of Toronto Press.

de Montigny, G. 1995. *Social Working: An Ethnography of Front-Line Practice.* Toronto: University of Toronto Press.

DeVault, M.L. 1991. *Feeding the Family: The Social Organization of Caring as Gendered Work.* Chicago: University of Chicago Press.

_____. 1999. *Liberating Method: Feminism and Social Research.* Philadelphia: Temple University Press.

Diamond, T. 1992. *Making Gray Gold: Narratives of Nursing Home Care.* Chicago: University of Chicago Press.

Eastwood, L. 2000. "Textual Mediation in the International Forest Policy Negotiation Process." Presented at the conference "Making Links: New Research in Institutional Ethnography," May, Ontario Institute for Studies in Education, Toronto.

Grahame, K.M. 1998. "Asian Women, Job Training, and the Social Organization of

Immigrant Labor Markets." *Qualitative Sociology* 21: 75–90.

Griffith, A.I. 1984. "Ideology, Education, and Single Parent Families: The Normative Ordering of Families through Schooling." Ph.D. dissertation, University of Toronto.

_____. 1992. "Educational Policy as Text and Action." *Educational Policy* 6: 415–428.

_____. 1995. "Mothering, Schooling, and Children's Development." In *Knowledge, Experience, and Ruling Relations,* edited by M. Campbell and A. Manicom, 108–121. Toronto: University of Toronto Press.

_____. 1998. "Educational Restructuring in Ontario." Presented at the conference "Exploring the Restructuring and Transformation of Institutional Processes: Applications of Institutional Ethnography," October, York University, Toronto.

"Institutions, Ethnography, and Social Organization" (symposium). 1998. *Human Studies* 21: 347–436.

Jackson, N. 1995. " 'These Things Just Happen': Talk, Text, and Curriculum Reform." In *Knowledge, Experience, and Ruling Relations,* edited by M. Campbell and A. Manicom, 108–121. Toronto: University of Toronto Press.

Khayatt, D. 1995. "Compulsory Heterosexuality: Schools and Lesbian Students." In *Knowledge, Experience, and Ruling Relations,* edited by M. Campbell and A. Manicom, 108–121. Toronto: University of Toronto Press.

Kinsman, G. 1989. "Official Discourse as Sexual Regulation: The Social Organization of the Sexual Policing of Gay Men." Ph.D. dissertation, University of Toronto.

_____. 1996. *The Regulation of Desire: Homo and Hetero Sexualities.* Montreal: Black Rose.

Kinsman, G., and P. Gentile. 1998. "'In the Interests of the State': The Anti-gay, Anti-lesbian National Security Campaign in

Canada." Preliminary research report, Laurentian University, Sudbury, Ontario.

Luken, P.C., and S. Vaughan. 1991. "Elderly Women Living Alone: Theoretical and Methodological Considerations from a Feminist Perspective." *Housing and Society* 18: 37–48.

_____. 1996. "Narratives of Living Alone: Elderly Women's Experiences and the Textual Discourse on Housing." Presented at the annual meeting of the Society for the Study of Social Problems, New York.

McCoy, L. 1987. "Looking at Wedding Pictures: A Study in the Social Organization of Knowledge." M.A. thesis, University of Toronto.

_____. 1995. "Activating the Photographic Text." In *Knowledge, Experience, and Ruling Relations,* edited by M. Campbell and A. Manicom, 181–192. Toronto: University of Toronto Press.

_____. 1999. "Accounting Discourse and Textual Practices of Ruling: A Study of Institutional Transformation and Restructuring in Higher Education." Ph.D. dissertation, University of Toronto.

McKendy, J. 1999. "Bringing Stories Back in: Agency and Responsibility of Men Incarcerated for Violent Offences." Unpublished manuscript.

Mueller, A. 1995. "Beginning in the Standpoint of Women: An Investigation of the Gap between *Cholas* and 'Women of Peru.'" In *Knowledge, Experience, and Ruling Relations,* edited by M. Campbell and A. Manicom, 96–107. Toronto: University of Toronto Press.

Mykhalovskiy, E. 2000. "Knowing Health Care/ Governing Health Care: Exploring Health Services Research as Social Practice." Ph.D. dissertation, York University.

Mykhalovskiy, E., and G.W. Smith. 1994. *Getting Hooked Up: A Report on the Barriers People Living with HIV/AIDS Face Accessing Social Services.* Toronto: Ontario Institute for Studies in Education.

Naples, N. 1997. "Contested Needs: Shifting the Standpoint on Rural Economic Development." *Feminist Economics* 3: 63–98.

_____. Forthcoming. "Negotiating the Politics of Experiential Learning in Women's Studies: Lessons from the Community Action Project." In *Locating Feminism,* edited by R. Wiegman. Durham: Duke University Press.

Ng, R. 1995. "Multiculturalism as Ideology: A Textual Analysis." In *Knowledge, Experience, and Ruling Relations,* edited by M. Campbell and A. Manicom, 35–48. Toronto: University of Toronto Press.

_____. 1996. *The Politics of Community Services: Immigrant Women, Class and State.* Halifax: Fernwood.

_____. 1999. "Homeworking: Dream Realized or Freedom Constrained? The Globalized Reality of Immigrant Garment Workers." *Canadian Woman Studies* 19(3): 110–114.

Parada, H. 1998. "Restructuring Families and Children in the Child Welfare Bureaucracy." Presented at the conference "Exploring the Restructuring and Transformation of Institutional Processes: Applications of Institutional Ethnography," October, York University, Toronto.

Pence, E. 1997. "Safety for Battered Women in a Textually Mediated Legal System." Ph.D. dissertation, University of Toronto.

Rankin, J. 1998. "Health Care Reform and the Restructuring of Nursing in British Columbia." Presented at the conference "Exploring the Restructuring and Transformation of Institutional Processes: Applications of Institutional Ethnography," October, York University, Toronto.

Reimer, M. 1995. "Downgrading Clerical Work in a Textually Mediated Labour Process." In *Knowledge, Experience, and Ruling Relations,* edited by M. Campbell and A. Manicom, 193–208. Toronto: University of Toronto Press.

Smith, D.E. 1987. *The Everyday World as Problematic: A Feminist Sociology.* Boston: Northeastern University Press.

_____. 1990. *Texts, Facts and Femininity: Exploring the Relations of Ruling.* New York: Routledge.

_____. 1996. "The Relations of Ruling: A Feminist Inquiry." *Studies in Cultures, Organizations and Societies* 2: 171–190.

_____. 1999. *Writing the Social: Theory, Critique, Investigations.* Toronto: University of Toronto Press.

Smith, D.E., ed. 2002. "Institutional Ethnography" (special issue). *Studies in Cultures, Organizations and Societies* 7 (2).

Smith, D.E., and G. Smith. 1990. "Re-organizing the Jobs Skills Training Relation: From 'Human Capital' to 'Human Resources.'" In *Education for Work, Education as Work: Canada's Changing Community Colleges,* edited by J. Muller, 171–196. Toronto: Garamond.

Smith, D.E., L. McCoy, and P. Bourne. 1995. "Girls and Schooling: Their Own Critique." Gender and Schooling Paper No. 2, Centre for Women's Studies in Education, Ontario Institute for Studies in Education.

Smith, G.W. 1988. "Policing the Gay Community: An Inquiry into Textually-Mediated Social Relations. *International Journal of the Sociology of Law* 16: 163–183.

_____. 1990. "Political Activist as Ethnographer." *Social Problems* 37: 629–648.

_____. 1995. "Accessing Treatments: Managing the AIDS Epidemic in Ontario." In *Knowledge, Experience, and Ruling Relations,* edited by M. Campbell and A. Manicom, 18–34. Toronto: University of Toronto Press.

_____. 1998. "The Ideology of 'Fag': The School Experience of Gay Students." *Sociological Quarterly* 39: 309–355.

Stock, A. 2000. "An Ethnography of Assessment in Elementary Schools." Ph.D. dissertation, University of Toronto.

_____. 1998. *Good Intentions Overruled: A Critique of Empowerment in the Routine Organization of Mental Health Services.* Toronto: University of Toronto Press.

Turner, S.M. 1995. "Rendering the Site Developable: Texts and Local Government Decision Making in Land Use Planning." In *Knowledge, Experience, and Ruling Relations,* edited by M. Campbell and A. Manicom, 234–248. Toronto: University of Toronto Press.

Walker, G.A. 1990. *Family Violence and the Women's Movement: The Conceptual Politics of Struggle.* Toronto: University of Toronto Press.

CHAPTER 15

Institutional Ethnography and Experience as Data[1]

MARIE L. CAMPBELL

INSTITUTIONAL ETHNOGRAPHY AND "EXPERIENCE"

This paper discusses how, in institutional ethnography, a researcher goes about exploring and understanding her own or someone else's everyday/everynight life in a methodical way. In the theoretical approach known as social organization of knowledge (where institutional ethnography is located as a research strategy), experience is the ground zero of the analysis (Smith, 1987, 1990a, 1990b). The analysis begins in experience and returns to it, having explicated how the experience came to happen as it did. The objective of making the analysis is to open up possibilities for people who live these experiences to have more room to move and act, on the basis of more knowledge about them. Dorothy E. Smith, long ago, called her work as sociology "for women"; more recently, she and other researchers who use this approach (e.g., Campbell and Manicom, 1995: 7–12) have claimed that this form of analysis offers something for all those whose lives are subject to ruling relations.

Recently, questions have been raised by postmodernists and poststructuralists about feminists' use of "experience" as a basis of knowing, in the context of a broader re-examination of earlier feminist scholarship. Some have usefully argued against the notion of a "unitary subject" of women's experience and against white, heterosexual, middle-class feminists' appropriation of women's experience as normative or exclusionary (e.g., Alarcon, 1994). A related critique of feminist analysis shows up the inadequacy of explanations that ground feminist knowledge claims in something essential or ideal arising from "women's experience" and for which authorizing women's voices might seem to be a solution (Bar On, 1993). Another set of important postmodernist/structuralist concerns (e.g., Scott, 1991) I take to be about the questionable status of experiential accounts produced by people whose knowing is discursively organized. Experience is one of the concepts, along with agency, subjectivity, discourse, and identity whose contestation has generated within feminism a fruitful rethinking of some of the traditional disciplinary methods in which feminist scholars have been trained and through which their conversations still take place.[2]

While these debates have motivated this paper, my goal here is not to add to the theoretical discussions around the possibility of knowing from experience. Rather, I am making a demonstration of what Dorothy Smith means when she enjoins us to "begin from the actualities of people's lives" if we want to understand what is happening to them. Smith is one of the feminist scholars for whom women's experience remains of key methodological importance, even as it has become contentious in postmodern/poststructural circles.[3] The aim of this paper is to show how to put personal experience into the center of a trustworthy analysis. I want to illustrate how the use and status of experience as data in an institutional ethnography sets it apart from "the authority of experience" that Scott (1991) challenges, and from Clough's (1993) view that experience is a construction of sociological conventions.

Institutional ethnography, like other forms of ethnography, relies on interviewing, observation, and documents as data.[4] Institutional ethnography departs from other ethnographic approaches by treating those data not as the topic or object of interest, but as "entry" into the social relations of the setting. The idea is to tap into people's expertise in the conduct of their everyday lives—their "work," as Smith wants us to think of it [....] The conceptual framing of everyday experiences heard or read about, or observed, constitutes one of the distinctive features of an institutional ethnography; another is its political nature. Exploring how people's lives are bound up in ruling relations that tie individuals into institutional action arising outside their knowing, "institutional ethnography allows one to disclose (to the people studied) how matters come about as they do in their experience and to provide methods of making their working experience accountable to themselves ... rather than to the ruling apparatus of which institutions are part" (Smith, 1987: 178).

THE STUDY

The setting of the study I discuss here to illustrate my argument about experience as data is a long-term care hospital[5] in Victoria, Canada. The experiences analyzed are those of some nurses observed and recorded by a researcher in the context of a study of the implementation of a "Service Quality Initiative"[6] management strategy in an institution that I call Dogwood

Villa. Using one story from several months of observational fieldwork, I argue that this particular management initiative has the capacity to alter staff-client relations at the most intimate level. Contrary to the democratic-sounding explanations of the strategy, it attempted to enforce a different and more rule-bound kind of practice, as it also revised the hospital's ideology of care that previously had been organized around being "home-like." The new ideological accomplishment of the quality improvement strategy, I concluded, would be a creeping colonization of the minds and hearts of the caregivers with the goals and values of the market—in which competitiveness, productivity, and cost-efficiency, etc., are paramount. Here, the methodology of that analysis is discussed, and I argue that experiential data offer a secure and methodical basis for my conclusions about the quality improvement strategy. [...]

Dogwood Villa's Service Quality Initiative is one of the family of Total Quality Management techniques that is altering the health care system significantly. This study gave me an opportunity to examine the dailiness of organizational change processes to discover how such efforts—to improve management and make decisions more rationally—affect caregivers and their clients. Elsewhere (Campbell, 1988, 1992a, 1992b; Campbell and Jackson, 1992) I have studied and written critically about the methods that organizations implement to try to make more efficient and effective use of caring labor and other costly resources. These undertakings are urged on health care managers by the difficult fiscal constraints under which health care is provided. I have watched with concern as a managerialist approach to service provision spreads with little critical appraisal throughout the social health and service sector in Canada.

So in looking at what was actually happening in this research site, I was not entering it as a naive observer working in naturalist mode, nor was I looking for theory to arise out of the data, as a grounded theorist might. As an institutional ethnographer, I was informed by prior analysis of the Canadian health care system and its increasingly rationalist stance towards management. I was also informed by a social organization of knowledge approach, about which I need to say a bit more now.

SOCIAL ORGANIZATION OF KNOWLEDGE AND RESEARCH ASSUMPTIONS

Dorothy Smith's (1987, 1990a, 1990b) writings on the social organization of knowledge provide the conceptual framework of this study and its grounding assumptions about how my research assistants[7] and I would think about what we were seeing in our fieldwork. Our first working assumption was that organizational knowledge is text-mediated in contemporary organizations in post-industrial society and that the nursing work that we were observing and hearing about was organized through text-based practices that coordinated it, made it accountable, and so on.[8] We knew that these practices build their own textual realities. This meant that as we gathered observational and interview data, we operated on the assumption that we would find different versions of what was understood, even of what was actually happening, as people we talked to spoke from different ways of knowing the workplace and the work.[9] Implicit in this assumption is our understanding of the discursively organized character of everyday life in organizations (Smith, 1990b: 209–224).[10] However, we also accepted that while people understand their experiences in organizations through discursive mediations, they remain bodily present and are active experiencers of the everyday/ everynight world from their various locations in it. Indeed, where one stands determines what one experiences, shaping to an important

extent what can be known.[11] "A setting known through special texts may appear to be different from how it is known experientially, and ... this may create problems" (Campbell and Manicom, 1995: 11) both for managers who rely heavily on textual accounts and for nursing personnel, whose work keeps them tied to local settings where knowing has a kind of bodily immediacy that also affects it. Managers who rely on texts for their knowing also experience their work, their human interactions, their environment, etc., but in this paper I draw out for research attention the experiences of front-line workers. I want to attend in my analysis to differences in the possibility of knowing that relate to the knower's location and everyday/ everynight work as well as to how such local experiences are ruled discursively, and thus constructed ideologically as the same across knowers.[12]

The notion of bifurcated consciousness that Smith (1987: 6) discusses with references to herself as a mother and an academic seems helpful here. She noted how, as a graduate student, it was possible and necessary to learn how to move between the world of babies and tending their bodies and the discursively organized university, entering each in its own (distinctive) terms. She made the move in both space and time: daytime here, nighttime there, and noted the disjuncture between the two. For nurses who work in a similarly bifurcated mode on the job, things are not so clearly demarcated spatially. In the workplace, they are immersed in the everyday/everynight world of bodies and at the same time their own work of recording and translating their nursing into organizational texts articulates those bodily concerns and tasks to the conceptual order of the institution (Campbell, 1984, 1988; Campbell and Jackson, 1992). They construct their knowing of bodies into discursive mode, bifurcating their own consciousness. In other words, they know their patients in two distinctive, and often contradictory, ways—as real people with bodily needs and as text-based objects of professional attention. The latter may, and under modern managerial technologies often does, mean that the bodily knowing is subordinated to the text-based or discursive.

This brings me to the next grounding assumption that my research team and I carried into the research setting: that the power of subordinating local experiential knowing to the discursive is the basis of textually mediated management and of what Smith calls ruling. As researchers, my team was always being attentive in our fieldwork to how the written word organizes what gets known and how it authorizes that version of it. We accepted that in those kinds of text-mediated procedures in the nursing setting, management works as a ruling practice.[13]

These are intrinsic features of Smith's social organization of knowledge that are also the premises of institutional ethnography and without which institutional ethnographic procedures and analyses don't make sense. Given these premises that Smith (1987: 117–135) argues are not theoretical in the ordinary sense, but are conceptual reflections of *actual relations* among people, the researcher goes into any new setting to see "how it works." It is not to test a hypothesis, but to examine the way that the social organization is put together such that people experience it as they do. In this approach, the researcher learns the standpoint or "takes the side" of those being ruled. The research explores and exposes how ruling affects people whose everyday/everynight lives come under the influence of specific ruling practice. One cannot know about their lives without their showing or telling it in one way or another. Thus, the researcher's attention to their voices.[14]

To carry out such an inquiry, the researcher begins with actual people involved actively in a social process, speaking from their experience. Writing fieldnotes is always a located social practice. Both the informant's account, and eventually the researcher's, are methodical in that they both rely on the relation to the located social process to discipline what is (can be) said. Insofar as the informant is speaking with the terms and relevances of her own life, she brings into the researcher's presence the actual social organization of that experience.[15]

Similarly to interview data, observations of everyday life, where the researcher captures the language used by participants, can be used to gain entry for analytic purposes into its social organization. The researcher is searching for traces of how the participants' actions and talk are conditioned. The researcher relies on the methodical nature of participants' behavior. Drawing on ethnomethodology, Smith (1987: 161–167) has written about people performing their everyday activities as "work" that they sensibly and expertly organize, coordinated in relation to the local social organization and also coordinating it. Experiential data, whether from interviews or observations, thus inform a method, allowing researchers an entry to social organization for the purpose of explicating the experiences; by explication I mean to write back into the account of experiences the social organization that is immanent, but invisible, in them.

"HARMONIE BRIEFS": THE STORY

For an instance of the kind of explicative analysis I am referring to, I want to turn now to a story from my study—an incident observed at Dogwood Villa involving nursing staff. I use it to analyse and illustrate the social relations of the Service Quality Initiative operating in the hospital and altering the care of the residents. Here I want to show how the voices of nurses in this story (their methodical telling of their experiences) allowed me to recover and display the meaning of this management strategy and make the argument about it that I have made. I also illustrate how to make analytic use of people's speaking of their everyday lives in ways that have the social relations "in" the talk. [...]

The analysis begins with some excerpts of observational data collected by a research assistant as she observed, on different days, the work of two nurses, one a clinical teacher, the other a nurse manager. The topic that the data excerpts address is the nursing staff's use of disposable diapers (called by their trade name Harmonie Briefs) for residents who are incontinent of urine, especially at night. The fieldnotes are presented with a minimum of explanatory comment (in square brackets). In the fieldnotes we see people in the setting talking about, puzzling over some questions about costs, the hospital's money, nursing plans, etc., as the researcher observed it; this provides the empirical ground for the analysis that follows.

A Clinical Resource Nurse [a nurse employed as a teacher within the hospital] was presenting an inservice education class on the use of the Harmonie Brief to a group of nursing assistants. [These are the staff who actually change people's beds, make the decisions about diapering people and using cotton pads under them, repair the damage done by a leaking brief, etc.] The class was being held because concern about recent stats on laundry costs had been brought to the educator's attention by her immediate supervisor.

The problem was that instead of reducing their linen [laundry] costs ... many units were actually increasing these costs in spite of the use of the disposable product. The Harmonie Brief policy had been in place for about six months when the Clinical Resource Nurse reported that on [the] unit [in question], the cost of Harmonie Briefs was $651.00 per month. She explained [in her class to the nursing assistants] that the organization had budgeted $60,000 for costs of Harmonie

Briefs across the whole hospital for the period in question and therefore, there was a need to recover $60,000 from the linen budget in the same period. She wrote these figures on a flipchart for the staff to see.

The nursing assistants then discussed what this was going to mean to them. They saw that they either had to use less linen for bed changes or they had to keep the bed linens from being so soaked, since the cost of the contracted-out laundry service was calculated by weight.

This rather muddled explanation of the management concern about Harmonie Brief usage was not the end of the story. Fieldnotes made by the same researcher on the same unit a week later show the Director of Resident Care (a nurse manager) discussing Harmonie Briefs with her Nursing Team Leaders (Registered Nurses). At this meeting, they are deciding how the nursing assistants who do the hands-on care are going to be required to manage the laundry cost problem.

One of the items discussed [at the Team Leaders' meeting] was linens and diapering. The general focus was on how it is "necessary to break even," according to the Director of Resident Care. Hence, she and the Team Leaders discussed cutting back on pads that are used underneath the resident at night. It was decided that those residents with Harmonie Briefs on should not require more than one pad underneath them. A Team Leader was concerned that if the brief were put on too early [in the evening shift] that more than one [of the disposable products] might be used at night. It was decided that only one Harmonie Brief should be used per night. If a wet brief were discovered during the night, the resident should be padded, as using two briefs per night per resident would escalate costs.

It is important to note that this discussion is taking place among Team Leaders who work days and who will be leaving messages for evening and night staff.

ANALYSIS: SOCIAL RELATIONS AS METHOD

I begin analysing these data by assuming that a specific social organization coordinates what the participant observer saw and heard happening and what she made notes on. Through her notes, I as analyst can see how these nurses are engaged in bringing that social organization into new sites—through the class where nursing assistants are told about the impact on the hospital budget of the expenditures on the new disposable briefs, how that relates to the laundry budget, and specifically that this is *the nursing assistants'* problem to solve. And later, I can see the nurse manager and RN team leaders developing new rules that will hold other nurses to the same routines that offer more economical use of the disposable briefs. My analysis begins in those experiences.

It is my task as institutional ethnographer to search out, come to understand, and describe the connections among these sites of experience and social organization. […] The procedure is to make problematic (or a topic for inquiry) those everyday experiences to which the observer makes us privy. Being able to count on using social relations to discover the concerting of action across time and space is what makes the inquiry methodical. The research relies on the embeddedness of social relations in the talk and action of the participants to direct the inquiry. The question to be explored is "What are the social relations coordinating those experiences?" I needed to discover, for instance, how ideas about "breaking even" and "recovering $60,000 from the linen budget" had made their way into a clinical teaching session for nursing assistants

and how, or if, those ideas were related to the hospital's Service Quality Initiative. What was concerting all these actions?

AUTHORITY RELATIONS RE-ORGANIZED THROUGH THE SERVICE QUALITY INITIATIVE

The authority relations operating among the nurses in this setting are easily identifiable in the fieldnotes. Hospitals rely on a distinctive mode of managing in which authority is vested in certain categories of employees. In the fieldnotes one can catch glimpses of traditional authority relations in the Clinical Resource Nurse teaching the nursing assistants about their role in "breaking even." It appears that she has been instructed by her superior to make the work associated with "breaking even" a topic for the nursing assistants. Nursing assistants take heed because they are required to, as part of their jobs. Another authority relation has the Director of Resident Services involving the Team Leaders, who are RNs, in planning how to pass on a new set of rules to their subordinates, the evening and night nurses. The nursing assistants, while occupying the lowest rung on the nursing authority ladder, still have power over the residents. They exercise a certain kind of authority with regard to caring work, and that is why these employees are being instructed in the economics of disposable briefs. These are all matters that can be empirically substantiated.

An interview I conducted with a Clinical Nurse Specialist (a Master's prepared nurse with a part-time university faculty appointment) showed that beyond the official authority relations, action in the hospital was being coordinated in a new manner. Her account of the work that went into the decision to purchase Harmonie Briefs offers a glimpse into the background of the experiences described in the fieldnotes. My research task at this point was to inquire into the discursive organization of these events. I was looking for the practical basis of (what I came to see as) the re-structuring of relations among managers, nurses, and residents at Dogwood Villa. According to the Clinical Nurse Specialist the decision to use Harmonie Briefs to supplement or replace entirely washable cotton pads had been made through a new process encouraging managers to work together across traditional department and disciplinary boundaries. According to her, this was the first time she had ever been part of such a multidisciplinary decision-making team. She was very proud of her own involvement, which had been to conduct clinical trials of a range of competing products and recommend one to the cross-department project group. This (Harmonie Brief) group also included the managers who made the hospital's purchasing and laundry decisions and were responsible for the budgets in these areas. The Clinical Nurse Specialist's clinical trials had identified which product would keep residents drier and thus protect their skin from breaking down. She had wanted to see if the disposable briefs made the residents more comfortable at night; there was some suggestion that changing wet beds during the night upset the residents and sometimes resulted in residents hitting nurses. The Harmonie Brief project thus brought her interest in resident comfort and staff safety together with other group members' different responsibilities. Working together influenced everybody's practices. For instance, she told me that she was surprised to learn that the manager of the Purchasing Department, as a result of her clinical trials, had had to alter his regular (equity-oriented across-the-board) purchasing practices, in order to buy the product she recommended.

The Clinical Nurse Specialist's story of the Harmonie Brief project contained recursive elements (see G. Smith, 1990) that I now want to highlight to illustrate the textual coordination of the organizational action of interest in this inquiry. Recurring in the interview were some of the Service Quality

Initiative principles that I had previously seen in the management documents describing the project. When I returned to the management documents, I found these phrases: "managers were instructed to change their values as managers, to value and trust their staff, whose intelligence is to be incorporated, as well as their caring; ... managers were expected to focus on process (how people interact to get the work done) and to work across departments, providing the social system and resources for employees to do their jobs." The idea was to bypass customary management practices where authority to act was entrenched in traditional practices of hospital management and supervision. Looking at the Harmonic Brief project as the Clinical Nurse Specialist described it, I could see that the way that this project group worked was consistent with new principles being taught to members of Dogwood staff in Service Quality workshops, etc. For example, the Clinical Nurse Specialist spoke enthusiastically about how a "communication workshop" she had attended as part of the Quality Initiative had helped her to work across the hospital's traditional disciplinary boundaries, avoiding barriers of status, hierarchy, and discipline that interfered with discussing and implementing better solutions.

The new authority, according to the Service Quality Initiative documents, was to be found in reference to meeting the customer's needs. Before I could understand how that idea was translated into nurses' action in different hospital sites, I needed to explore further the notion of "customer" as it was being introduced through the Service Quality Initiative.

CUSTOMERS AND SUPPLIERS: MEETING EACH OTHER'S NEEDS = QUALITY

The new system, an internal Quality Initiative document explains, requires staff to act as "suppliers of service as well as customers receiving service." The implementers of the Service Quality Initiative put great emphasis on everyone using the term "customer" at Dogwood Villa. This training began with the formal definition of the Service Quality Initiative emphasizing customer, as follows:

Service Quality determines the way we work. It is achieved through processes that meet or exceed the expectations of our internal and external customers. The Service Quality processes focus on identifying customer-supplier needs and expectations, meeting these expectations, team work, doing the right things the right way, continuous review of our performance and feedback to customer-supplier. (internal memo, April 15, 1993)

It seemed that talking about "customer" was supposed to engage employees' involvement in thinking about their work differently, following the new principles. But "customer" was a contested notion. [...]

* * * * *

In retrospect, I see that there were two incongruent and competing formulations of "customer" in use; the one was defined in the internal document, where employees were to be suppliers of service as well as customers receiving service, and the other was the commonsense one that staff operated with, where the resident was the customer. In practice, the distinctions were often blurred. The latter, the resident as customer, held positive implications for the nursing staff even when they objected to the language, because it was in line with well-established values of the hospital. In this interpretation what was good for the resident was an acceptable rationale for any change in work processes. Staff liked the suggestion (set out, for instance, by the CEO to the management group, January 4, 1994) that

"those most closely involved with a particular work process would be empowered to help design the work system to be used." Staff could identify with changes when the customer (the resident) was to be considered first. This came to be understood as "decision-making pushed down in the organization to those most closely involved with the work being done," which became a popular slogan used by Service Quality implementers. The slogan made the initiative seem to be a method of democratizing decision-making, allowing workers more individual discretion, in the name of resident satisfaction. And yet, in the Harmonie Brief story, we saw a high-profile project in which the suggested changes in the work processes were not designed by those closest to where the work was being done. Nor were they straight-forwardly "good for the resident."

As the fieldwork progressed, I saw that the flexible or squishy interpretations of "customer" were not simply a different choice of words. Rather, the Service Quality Initiative introduced a new ruling relation. "Employees as customers of each other's work," the version of customer that competed with "the resident as customer," legitimated an officially sanctioned approach to the work that organized employees' discretion in line with new organizational priorities. The new practices that the Service Quality Initiative legitimizes found their authority, not in established management hierarchies and professional practices, but in being consistent with the hospital's economic priorities. (At the time of the study, cutbacks, restructuring, and budget deficits were on everybody's minds.) The new social relations that coordinate work practices carry values organized around budget and cost-efficiency. In the fieldnotes examined, one moment becomes visible in which these changing values penetrate nursing work plans. This is an important moment because it lets us in on how individual caregivers are incorporated into a changing value system, in an enforceable way. The clinical teaching session introduced a new kind of thinking about what was important in the work.

Much has been written on "quality management" strategies about which as Price (1994: 69) says "consent to market values (is) strongly reproduced throughout the workplace." The critique made is that group discussion and input into re-design of work processes aim at intensifying individual worker commitment to the work group, to the productive task, and to the product. Central to Total Quality Management and other quality management strategies is the idea of employees being part of a chain of suppliers of products to both internal and external customers, with everybody's attention being focused on how each can satisfy their own customer's needs. ("Products" are here being understood as whatever it is that their work produces, even if, as in a hospital, it is changing bed linens.) Employees are asked to think about themselves as a link in this chain of relations extending throughout the whole work process. This strategy and the work organization that supports it is supposed to make individually relevant the issues of quality and productivity standards that each worker must be responsible for, to facilitate just-in-time delivery of products, satisfied customers, maximum valued added to the product, etc. In my analysis, the hospital's Service Quality Initiative attempts to bring these features of the hospital's problems with budgets (or the capacity to compete) to the individual worker and into his/her local decision-making and action.

SERVICE QUALITY INITIATIVE AND THE RE-ORGANIZATION OF CARING WORK

Using my conceptual framework, I see the Harmonie Brief story as an extension of the social relations of ruling into the individual effort of caregivers in the hospital workplace.[16] I now want to discuss briefly some effects of this new form of authority on those being ruled, especially the nursing assistants and the residents they care for. Returning to the fragments of data examined, I think that readers can begin to see how the cost-benefit plan that justifies the purchase of the disposable product is organizing actions that will be taken by nursing assistants. The requirement to "break even" on this project means not just that use of the Harmonie Briefs is to be rationed to match what would have been spent on laundry, but that decisions about how to nurse, decisions normally taken at the bedside on the basis of empirical data (and nursing knowledge) are to be replaced by general rules that relate nursing decisions directly to the hospital's fiscal concerns. While efficient management of resources is, of course, an important goal here as in all organizations, I contend that it is being accomplished in a process that fundamentally alters the caregiving.

That is why to make sense of the Harmonie Brief situation, it must not be understood simply commonsensically—as an instance where the nursing assistants are working for the resident as customer. This story is clearly not an instance where everyone focuses on how best to serve the resident. Nursing assistants, in the instance, stand in a particular consumer or customer relation to suppliers of other hospital services—those who are responsible for the contracted-out laundry services paid for by weight, to others who purchase disposable briefs, and to still others who must balance budgets. Nursing assistants' work creates varying levels of demand for those services and products. Because the overall goal for the Harmonie Brief project within the new competitive environment is to "break even," the officially legitimized customer-supplier response is for nurses to curtail their use of the (scarce) services and resources. The analysis that began in the nurses' experience of a clinical in-service class when the budget for disposal diapers was related to a need to reduce the laundry costs thus comes back to illuminate and make sense of that experience.

These nurses are learning how to carry out their work in terms of its cost-efficiency, learning how to make clinical decisions that are coordinated in relation to the hospital's budget. Their own everyday/everynight thinking is dominated by the market relations that are penetrating the long-term care hospital and the caring relation. To hospital managers, this is the successful outcome of the Service Quality Initiative. But the story has deeper implications. Given the delicate balance nurses must maintain between adequacy of care for the hospitalized elderly and the conservation of hospital supplies, moving decision-making over the use of disposable briefs further away from the bedside is a matter with serious clinical consequences. Decisions about the use of the Harmonie Brief are being established by people several levels above the nursing assistants in the organizational hierarchy. The new rules that are meaningful within the context discursively organized by the Harmonie Brief group (e.g., clinical trials, cost-benefit analysis of disposable vs. washable pads) will look completely arbitrary in the context of the night nurses' experiential knowledge. Nurses are left in an ambiguous position. It seems that the hospital is sanctioning a less stringent attention to resident care. Should caregivers try to work around these rules for the good of the resident?

Checking back a year later, I found that the nursing staff, left with the responsibility of keeping the residents' skin intact within the constraints set by the new rules for use of resources, have learned how to adjust their efforts to the new demands. They are happy with the nursing results of using the disposable product. However, most interesting for this analysis is how this hospital has adapted to its concerns about "breaking even": it has financed the extra costs of the disposable briefs by asking individual families to pay for them. When a resident's sensitive skin requires nurses to use more briefs then the rules allow, they must be paid for privately. Of course, not all residents have families, nor the money to pay extra charges; this is how inequity creeps into long-term care.

CONCLUSION

My analytic interest in this incident is of two kinds. I have examined how management strategies are helping health care institutions accommodate to the demands of fiscal restraint in a globalizing economy (Price, 1994) and I have demonstrated a method of analysis that moves from the particular (experiences) to a general analysis. In regards to the former, I have shown how a strategy of "quality improvement" works as a means of transforming institutional governance, making nurses' individual professional action accountable to a set of goals and objectives formulated externally to it, in this case a cost-benefit calculation. Nurses are being taught to see the sense of these rules and to bring their thinking and actions into line with them. They are being expected to take up the ruling actions and perpetuate them. This, I argue, is much more than training in economical use of resources. The new relations undermine the integrity of care-giving and professional practice.

The Service Quality strategy examined helps to organize the authority relations that pre-empt local nursing expertise, suggesting how organizational action in a long-term care facility can be made accountable to a political agenda of deficit reduction and reduced social spending. Here is (a piece of) the very complex business of bringing a new cost awareness into the everyday decision-making of health care workers. This Service Quality Initiative helps to insinuate ruling ideas into local settings where workers themselves will carry them forward.

The paper also makes a methodological argument about the use of people's experiences as data. Responding to the voices of nurses as they went about their work, I explicated the social relations that organize these nurses' thinking and acting. This is the way that institutional ethnography "makes sense" of people's experiences and draws broader implications from methodical analysis of local experiences. I can claim that what was happening amongst the nurses was part of something generalizable about "quality management" in that setting and indeed in the management of health care more broadly. This facility's Service Quality principles, the need to "break even" and so on, apply across the organization, not just to the nurses observed and interviewed. To further enlarge the claim, researchers could look for similar features of health care organization in other hospitals. So, while this incident may be specific to one time and place, and one set of actors and their experiences, the relations that organize those experiences can be demonstrated to be general.

Understanding how a management technology "works" as a ruling practice to influence nurses and nursing care helps to de-mystify this management practice, showing some of the ways that market forces penetrate the consciousness of caregivers. Here I made the empirical discovery that "customer" is a concept that operates in different and contradictory ways, its effects being to subordinate nurses' caring to concerns related to the market. This kind of knowledge may be crucial to the struggles that will need to take place over health care in Canada, as public policy shifts to subtly incorporate a market orientation.

The relations of ruling do not disappear by learning about them, however, nor can they be shaken off by individuals themselves. They are ever-present in our lives, like the water that fish swim in. Knowing more about how our lives are tangled in ruling relations can help to reduce the frustration we feel about living and working in societies such as ours where things seem to get decided behind our backs, or at least outside of our control. For health care workers who find themselves in these kinds of situations, knowing how one's work setting and one's own decisions are being influenced may help them make useful choices about how to act.

But what does this article say about experience? It is certainly not that experience is authoritative. And it is not "pure" in any essential way. One of the analytic points being made is how nursing assistants' lives (at least those experiences to which we are privy through field observations recorded here) are being discursively organized. In the analysis, those rather puzzling observations (of events that were perhaps just as puzzling to the participants) were the "entry" to understanding the manner in which a particular management discourse ruled the nurses' work lives. What was done and said in that work setting offered the clues, the traces of the social relations, that could be followed by the researcher, to be fleshed out and related back to the original field setting. Only then could that moment's experiences be read as the concerting by organizational actors of their local everyday work lives with ruling institutional arrangements. In the setting where this study was conducted, there were many contending versions of what was happening: some people said that the Service Quality Initiative was a participatory project to improve care; others said it was simply a management fad; others disagreed about whether or not it was a money-saving scheme. My analysis relies on experience to anchor what can be said to the actualities of nursing assistants' lives. Theirs is the standpoint from which the analysis is made. It is trustworthy to the extent that it accounts for their experiences. Perhaps the most important thing about experience as data is that, in institutional ethnography, it makes an analysis accountable to the everyday/everynight world as people live it.

NOTES

1. Earlier versions of this paper was presented at the 13th Qualitative Analysis Conference "Studying Social Life Ethnographically," McMaster University, May 28–31, 1996; and at the Society for Studies in Social Problems Conference, New York, August 17–19, 1996. Support for the research is gratefully acknowledged from Industrial Adjustment Services, Human Resources Management Canada, on a cost-sharing basis with the research hospital, Sept. 1993–March, 1995; and from Social Sciences and Humanities Research Council of Canada Grant #816-94-0003 that funds a research network, "Understanding and Changing the Conditions of Caring Labor," 1993–1997. I also want to thank Rosanna Hertz and the paper's four reviewers for comments that, while I have responded to them in my own way, have certainly strengthened the paper.

2. e.g., Canning (1994) in social history; Code (1991) in philosophy; Nicholson (1990) in literary criticism, among many others.

3. See Smith (1996) specifically.

4. For some lively examples of published institutional ethnography, see Ng (1996), Diamond (1992), Walker (1990), Swift (1995).

5. American readers may be more familiar with the term "nursing home" used to describe the same kind of facility.

6. The Service Quality Initiative was a locally developed and implemented strategy that owed much to the ideas and literature of Total Quality Management. Total Quality Management and Continuous Quality Improvement are popular management strategies employed in both industrial and human service organizations to improve organizational functioning. For a strongly optimistic account of how quality improvement strategies work in health care agencies, see Phillip Hassen's *Rx for Hospitals*.

7. Bev Miller, MSW, and Pat Larson, MN, graduate students at the time, were research assistants on this project and conducted much of the field research with great sensitivity; my analysis owes much to their grasp of the conceptual framework of the study and resulting attention to detail.

8. Ng (1996) shows how accountability relations influence an organization's goals and activities.

9. Diamond (1992) shows "reality" experienced and understood differently, from different sites in an organization.

10. A good deal of the work in any organization consists of turning events, experiences, transactions of the people whose lives are its concerns into text and acting on the basis of those textural accounts. Smith (1990b) has argued that this form of text-based interaction is ubiquitous in contemporary western societies, discursively organizing social relations in ways that can be investigated as practical activities.

11. DeMontigny (1995) provides a dramatic illustration and analysis of how this happens.

12. In Walker (1990), "discursive organization" is shown to be practical activities of policy-making and governing.

13. For a fuller discussion of this, see Campbell (1988 or 1992b).

14. As one reviewer of this article points out, the residents are also being ruled and the study might have used their voices, as Diamond's (1992) research did. It should be noted that the social relations organizing any setting are consistent, no matter whose standpoint is used to explicate them.

15. This paragraph paraphrases an e-mail communication between D. Smith and B. Lloyd, and responsibility for its interpretation is mine.

16. For Canadian readers, this analysis has special implications. Our public health care system has not until recently been directly subject to competitive capitalism. This paper shows how, within the non-profit (publicly funded and administered) Canadian hospital system, market relations are being established and are becoming the legitimate basis of care-giving decisions.

REFERENCES

Alarcon, N. 1994. "The Theoretical Subject(s) of This Bridge Called My Back and Anglo-American Feminism." In *The Postmodern Turn*, edited by S. Seidman, 140–152. Cambridge: Cambridge University Press.

Bar On, B. 1993. "Marginality and Epistemic Privilege." In *Feminist Epistemologies*, edited by L. Alcoff and E. Potter, 83–100. New York and London: Routledge.

Campbell, M. 1984. "Information Systems and Management of Hospital Nursing: A Study in Social Organization of Knowledge." Unpublished Ph.D. dissertation, University of Toronto.

_____. 1988. "Management as Ruling: A Class Phenomenon in Nursing." *Studies in Political Economy* 27: 29–51.

_____. 1992a. "Administering Child Protection: A Feminist Analysis of Conceptual Practices of Organization." *Canadian Public Administration* 34(4): 501–518.

_____. 1992b. "Canadian Nurses' Professionalism: A Labor Process Analysis." *International Journal of Health Services* 22: 751–765.

Campbell, M., and N. Jackson. 1992. "Learning to Nurse: Text, Accounts and Action." *Qualitative Health Research* 2(4): 475–496.

Campbell, M., and A. Manicom, eds. 1995. *Knowledge, Experience and Ruling Relations*. Toronto: University of Toronto Press.

Canning, K. 1994. "Feminist History after the Linguistic Turn: Historicizing Discourse and Experience." *Signs* 19(2): 368–414.

Clough, P. 1993. "On the Brink of Deconstructing Sociology: Critical Reading of Dorothy Smith's Standpoint Epistemology." *The Sociological Quarterly* 34(1): 169–182.

Code, L. 1991). *What Can She Know?* Ithaca: Cornell University Press.

DeMontigny, G. 1995. "The Power of Being Professional." In *Knowledge Experience and Ruling Relations,* edited by M. Campbell and A. Manicom, 209–220. Toronto: University of Toronto Press.

Diamond, T. 1992. *Making Grey Gold: Narratives of Nursing Home Care*. Chicago: University of Chicago Press.

Ng, R. 1996. *The Politics of Community Services: Immigrant Women, Class and State,* 2nd ed. Halifax: Fernwood.

Nicholson, L. 1990. *Feminism/Postmodernism.* New York: Routledge.

Price, J. 1994. "Lean Production at Suzuki and Toyota: A Historical Perspective." *Studies in Political Economy* 45(Fall): 66–99.

Scott, J. 1991. "The Evidence of Experience." *Critical Inquiry* 17(3): 773–797.

Smith, D.E. 1987. *The Everyday World as Problematic*. Boston: Northeastern University Press.

_____. 1990a. *The Conceptual Practices of Power.* Toronto: University of Toronto Press.

_____. 1990b. *Texts, Facts and Femininity.* New York and London: Routledge.

_____. 1996. "Telling the Truth after Postmodernism." *Symbolic Interaction* 19(3): 171–202.

Smith, G. 1990. "Political Activist as Ethnographer." *Social Problems* 37(4): 629–648.

Swift, Karen. 1995. *Manufacturing Bad Mothers: A Critical Perspective.* Toronto: University of Toronto Press.

Walker, G. 1990. *Family Violence and the Women's Movement: The Conceptual Politics of Struggle.* Toronto: University of Toronto Press.

Rethinking Part 2B: Problematizing the Everyday World: Institutional Ethnography

CRITICAL THINKING QUESTIONS

Chapter 12: Theory "in" Everyday Life

1. Institutional ethnography (IE) makes use of forms of social organization that are routine and mundane features of the everyday as a point of entry into its investigations of the social. What are the advantages of this strategy?
2. IE seeks to explicate how things are put together so that they happen as they do. It does not seek to explain social behaviour by resorting to variables or theoretical concepts. Why is the distinction between explication and explanation important?
3. Campbell and Gregor write of texts being activated by those who use them. In human services it is typical that the activation of organizational texts accomplishes objectification of the client. How does IE enable the researcher to explore and map out this process as an instance of extra-local ruling?

Chapter 13: Ethnography, Institutions, and the Problematic of the Everyday World

1. Peter Grahame notes that Dorothy Smith reverses the direction of conventional sociological inquiry, which approaches everyday life from the standpoint of theory. What difference does "problematizing the everyday world" make to the character of inquiry?
2. How do the three tasks that define IE as a research strategy—the analysis of ideological practices within institutional processes, the study of how people produce through their work activities the world they experience, and the discovery of ways in which localized organization operates as part of a set of social relations that span localities—fit together as a coherent whole?
3. Peter Grahame suggests that in IE "the standpoint of women as such is not intended as the end point of analysis" (p. 188). What is the relationship between taking up the standpoint of women and pursuing what Smith has more recently called a "sociology for people"?

Chapter 14: Institutional Ethnography: Using Interviews to Investigate Ruling Relations

1. The liberatory potential of IE "comes from its specification of possible 'levers' or targets for activist intervention" (p. 194). How does IE specify those levers and targets?
2. According to Devault and McCoy, in IE interviewing is perhaps better described as "talking with people." What are the various ways in which IE interviewing is done?

3. The distinctiveness of IE as a critical research strategy lies in "its commitment to going beyond the goal of simple 'giving voice'" (p. 201) to groups that have been excluded from knowledge production. In what ways does IE go beyond "giving voice"?

Chapter 15: Institutional Ethnography and Experience as Data

1. In IE, the researcher searches for *traces* of how people's talk and actions are conditioned. Compare this search to the work of a detective on the one hand and a psychoanalyst on the other.
2. How does Marie Campbell's case study clarify the role of ruling relations in undermining the integrity of caregiving while promoting the efficient management of resources?
3. IE rejects the claim that direct experience is *authoritative*. Rather, it makes use of experience as data that provides an *entry-point* for inquiry and an *anchor* for what can be said about the actualities of people's lives. How do you understand these three interpretations of experience?

GLOSSARY TERMS

Bifurcated consciousness: The tendency for people, as they participate in ruling relations, on the one hand, to take up the objectified forms of knowledge they require as they activate the texts that coordinate their work while, on the other hand, retaining in a subordinated way a more embodied, experientially based understanding of what they are doing. In the consciousness of hospital nurses, for instance, the fulfillment of administrative dictates jostles with the care for ill human beings.

Ethnography: A term that highlights the importance of methods of inquiry that can explore everyday activities and their positioning within more extended and extra-local sequences of action. Interviewing, field observation, and the analysis of actual texts and how they are used are all relevant research techniques in institutional ethnography.

Everyday world: The world as directly experienced—locally, physically, and socially—through the ongoing and purposeful concerting of people's activities.

Explicate: "to write back into the account of experiences the social organization that is immanent, but invisible, in them" (p. 209). Explication, as distinct from generalized causal explanation, is a prime goal of IE.

Generalization: In IE, a trustworthy explication, one that accounts for the experiences of those whose standpoint it takes, provides knowledge that is generalizable to that setting and quite likely to similar settings within the same institutional complex. That is, although the incident studied may be specific to one time and place and one set of people, the relations organizing their experiences can be shown to be general.

Institution: A cluster of text-mediated social relations organized around specific functions, such as health care or education. Each institution comprises a vast nexus of coordinated work processes and courses of action.

Objectified forms of knowledge: Knowledge of the social that abstracts from and overrides divergent localized perspectives, laying claim to an authority and objectivity based on its standing outside the world it claims to know. Typically constructed and used by privileged experts, such knowledge is favoured by traditional sociology over the lived realities of its subjects. Objectified forms of knowledge are an integral part of ruling relations, since they enable extra-local coordination of activity.

Problematic: A possible set of questions or puzzles latent in the actualities of everyday life and directing attention to the issue of how the particularities and patterns of daily life are shaped by an extended set of social relations.

Ruling relations: The internally coordinated complex of managerial, administrative, professional, and discursive organization that governs, regulates, and otherwise controls our societies. Ruling is the socially organized (and typically textually mediated) exercise of power that shapes people's actions and their lives.

Social relation: In IE, the actual linking and coordinating of activities and work processes in diverse sites. Social relations are often extra-local and textually mediated, in which case they may not be immediately evident to people who locally participate in them.

Text: A document or representation that has a relatively fixed and replicable character, enabling it, when activated by users at various times and places, to play a standardizing and mediating role. IE recognizes that our contemporary world is permeated by myriad texts in diverse media—paper, video, audio, Internet, and so on. A particularly important text in extra-local ruling relations is money, whether in paper or virtual (electronic) form.

Text-mediated social organization: Social organization that extends, via texts of various kinds, from elsewhere into people's lives and back outside again. In contemporary society, texts are "a ubiquitous feature of social organization" (p. 170); they have the power to coordinate people's actions, to direct people to act in particular ways.

FURTHER READING

Campbell, Marie, and Frances Gregor. 2002. *Mapping Social Relations*. Toronto: Garamond Press.
> A concise and highly accessible guide to doing institutional ethnography, featuring generous examples from a range of studies.

Campbell, Marie, and Ann Manicom, eds. 1995. *Knowledge, Experience, and Ruling Relations*. Toronto: University of Toronto Press.
> A collection of essays reporting results from various institutional ethnographies. Topics and themes are wide-ranging.

Ng, Roxana. 1996. *The Politics of Community Services: Immigrant Women, Class and State*. Halifax: Fernwood.
> A collection of mostly research-based essays that employ institutional ethnography, with a focus on the social organization and politics of community services.

Smith, Dorothy E. 1987. *The Everyday World as Problematic*. Toronto: University of Toronto Press.

These essays include some of Smith's most important work from the early 1970s through to the 1986 paper that introduced institutional ethnography as a feminist method.

Smith, Dorothy E. 1999. *Writing the Social: Critique, Theory, and Investigations*. Toronto: University of Toronto Press.

These are more recent essays from the early to mid-1990s, in which Smith develops some of her theoretical concepts (such as ruling relations) at length, presents a powerful critique of postmodernism, and offers a number of investigations into textually mediated social organization.

RELEVANT WEB SITES

Coordinating Family and School: Mothering for Schooling

http://epaa.asu.edu/epaa/v3n1.html

Alison Griffith, a student of Dorothy Smith, explores the relationship between mothering work in the family and the social organization of schooling in this very clearly written study, first published in 1995 in the Internet journal, *Education Policy Analysis Archives* (vol. 3, no. 1).

IE Newsletter

http://www.sssp1.org/extras/IE_SUMMER_NEWSLETTER.pdf

The newsletter of the Institutional Ethnography Division of the Society for the Study of Social Problems, in its second issue at the time of this writing. Note that the Internet address of subsequent issues will vary; a search engine is recommended.

Institutional Ethnography: A Tool for Merging Research and Practice

http://www.alumni-osu.org/midwest/midwest%20papers/Wright--Done.pdf

A refereed paper by Ursala T. Wright, presented in October 2003 at the Midwest Research to Practice Conference in Adult, Community and Continuing Education, at Columbus, Ohio. A good discussion of IE as a praxis-oriented research strategy.

Praxis International

http://data.ipharos.com/praxis/index.html

Praxis was organized in 1996 by activists in the battered women's movement to work with other social change activists to end violence against women. Praxis helps advocacy organizations and interagency collaborations analyze how institutions of social control can be challenged to adopt practices and philosophical approaches that promote autonomy, integrity, and safety for women and their children. In 1997, Ellen Pence, a researcher at Praxis, developed a method called the safety and accountability audit, which is used to analyze criminal justice and human service agency responses to women who are abused by their partners. The audit is based on the methodology of institutional ethnography.

Resources for Feminist Research
http://www.oise.utoronto.ca/rfr/
> The journal's objectives are to publish critical work addressing a broad range of issues relevant to feminist theory and activism, to provide an educational resource and a forum for the communication of ideas, news, and other information of interest to the community of feminist scholars, and to encourage research on gender, sexuality, race, ethnicity, nationality, and class, and how they inform and affect the conditions of women's lives. The site contains extensive Internet resources.

PART
2C SUBVERTING DOMINANT DISCOURSES: CRITICAL DISCOURSE ANALYSIS

In our readings in institutional ethnography (IE) we saw how textually mediated social organization plays a crucial role in sustaining contemporary structures of social domination. IE, in fact, provides an effective strategy for subverting dominant institutions and the discourses that legitimate them: look into how ruling relations, inscribed in texts, come to organize people's local practices, and use this knowledge in pressing for democratic and equitable social relations. Like IE, the strategies I present here as critical discourse analysis provide ways of *challenging systems of knowledge and power* by interrogating and contextualizing dominant discourses. "Discourse" refers to much more than simply printed text but to the full range of practices, structures, and media that saturate our world and our selves with meaning. Nancy Fraser has emphasized the importance of a conception of discourse for feminists, but clearly this way of thinking has value for emancipatory praxis of all sorts:

> ... a conception of discourse can help us understand at least four things. First, it can help us understand how people's social identities are fashioned and altered over time. Second, it can help us understand how, under conditions of inequality, social groups in the sense of collective agents are formed and unformed. Third, a conception of discourse can help illuminate how the cultural hegemony of dominant groups in society is secured and contested. Fourth and finally, it can shed light on the prospects for emancipatory social change and political practice. (1997: 152)

There is by now a wide range of approaches to the analysis of discourse within and between such (inter)disciplines as cultural studies, post-colonial studies, literary theory, and socio-linguistics (cf. Lakoff and Johnson, 1980; Hodge and Kress, 1988; Lee and Poynton, 2000; Loomba, 1998; Van Dijk, 1998; Barker and Galasiński, 2001; Wetherall et al., 2001). Phillips and Hardy (2002) provide a helpful two-dimensional typology of approaches to discourse analysis (see Figure 2C.1).

Figure 2C.1: Approaches to Discourse Analysis

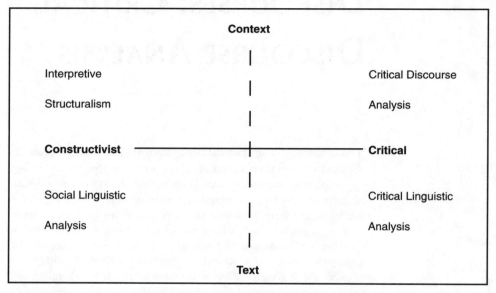

Source: Nelson Phillips and Cynthia Hardy, *Discourse Analysis: Investigating Processes of Social Construction* (London: Sage, 2002): 20.

Within this categorization, the approaches we feature here are *critical* in that they focus explicitly on dynamics of power, knowledge, and ideology as they surround and partially constitute discursive processes (not simply on the ways in which social reality is discursively *constructed*). For the most part, these approaches attend not only to "the text" but to its broad social *context*, although a good deal of deconstructive work does centre on particular pieces of text, as in the chapter by Norman Denzin in this book   `.

For our limited purposes we can further divide the field of critical discourse analysis into *post-structural* approaches and approaches grounded in the *critical realism* we encountered earlier (see Chapter 11). Post-structuralism shares IE's subversive skepticism toward dominant discourse. But post-structuralism's dispute is not with "facticity" and ideology; it is with "truth" and with Western modernity's regimes of truth. Post-structural social inquiry turns from the modernist search for truths underlying mystified forms to the undoing of hegemonic discourses and texts and the subversion of their authority. It also differs from institutional ethnography in its starting point. Post-structuralism begins not with practically constructed actualities but with discourse.[1] Indeed, for post-structuralists the subject is not a knowing agent but a product of discourse:

> Subjectivity is produced in a whole range of discursive practices—economic, social and political—the meanings of which are a constant site of struggle over power. Language is not

an expression of unique individuality; it constructs the individual's subjectivity in ways which are socially specific. Moreover for poststructuralism, subjectivity is neither unique nor fixed. (Weedon, 1987: 21)

There are many formulations that have been termed "post-structural." I will restrict our exploration to two strategies whose relevancies to critical research strategies are particularly strong. The first of these, deconstruction, subverts what is often taken for granted in the texts that form our cultural environment and that inform our selves. By showing the contradictions that are structured into the various dichotomies that enable the text to make its claims, deconstruction challenges the text's authority and coherence. As a method of inquiry, deconstruction not only destabilizes; it *creates openings* for transforming concepts as well as the social practices informed by the concepts. In "breaking the narrative open," it enables one to recognize "the construction of one's own subject position, to entertain the possibility that the 'I' that constitutes a speaking subject is a configuration always in process" (Ellis, 1989: 49). In these senses, deconstruction is a critical strategy of inquiry. As Ian Parker argues, "a deconstruction of a piece of text ... produces new meanings out of the texts it contacts. It changes what it studies" (1988: 189).

Deconstruction can be a powerful tool in efforts to overthrow dominant ideas. But as Parker goes on to point out, when one moves beyond philosophical texts into social texts, the final step in deconstructive work—the reinterpretation of oppositions, the production of new concepts and new social practices—inevitably raises questions of the researcher's own involvement in power and politics. Unlike the first steps in the analysis, which interrogate relations *within the text*, the final step can only be taken *outside the text*. This involves moral and political choices—a rewriting of the social. In a statement that recalls Marx's Thesis 11 (p. 22) Parker tells us that "without this step, which involves the construction of non-oppressive social relations, the hierarchies will simply be written and rewritten in the same old way" (1988: 197).

For Norman Denzin, deconstruction is a method, consistent with cultural studies' view of "human action as a text" (p. 242), that poses the central problem of "working from text to experiences" (p. 241)—a reversal of the strategy employed by institutional ethnography. Denzin introduces us to the post-structural philosophical analysis of Jacques Derrida and the social theory of Jean Baudrillard. Together, they offer resources for interpreting postmodern culture by interrogating the texts (filmic, televisual, musical, fictional, factual, social-scientific, etc.) "that purport to speak to the lived experiences of interacting individuals" (p. 234). The text that Denzin deconstructs—*The Morning After*, a film released in 1987—is organized as a melodrama in which a flawed protagonist finds her way in a man's world. Denzin's feminist deconstruction opens up the text, showing how its meanings rely on the play of sexual and racial differences, structured into the narrative, which reproduce cultural stereotypes. Drawing on the analysis introduced by Stuart Hall (1980 [1973]), Denzin moves from a hegemonic reading of the text (the reading preferred by the dominant ideology) to an oppositional reading that subverts the dominant perspective and its meanings.

The second post-structural strategy that merits our attention is what Michel Foucault, following Nietzsche, calls genealogy. Foucault holds that modern knowledge is structured around a division between the qualified and the disqualified, a division in which "local" forms of knowledge have become subject to global systems of scientific and professional thought. Qualified knowledge may be hegemonic in the modern era, but it is always vulnerable to criticism. Genealogical work provides such critique: an "insurrection of subjugated knowledge," as Foucault (1980) puts it, below.

Like deconstruction, genealogy is subversive: it destabilizes and unsettles what is otherwise taken for granted. Genealogy primarily contests the *normative* order that confines human possibilities within a narrow band of limits, as in the notion of "normality." For Foucault, the strategic question is how to organize resistance to normalization without setting up new technologies of domination, new discourses of power/knowledge. The basic strategy is to challenge established claims and identities by looking into their local formation—the contingent events, the complex struggles, the now-silenced voices that were active in the emergence and descent of a given institution or identity. "My role," Foucault said, "is to show people that they are much freer than they feel, that people accept as truth ... some themes which have been built up at a certain moment during history, and that this so-called evidence can be criticized and destroyed" (quoted in Best, 1995: 110).

Several excellent methodological discussions of genealogy are available (e.g., Kendall and Wickham, 1999; Tamboukou, 1999; Meadmore et al., 2000). I encourage readers interested in exploring this powerful approach to consult these works. Our selection on genealogy is perhaps the clearest statement from Michel Foucault himself. Given as a lecture on January 7, 1976, the essay describes genealogy as anti-science, waging struggle not so much against the methods, contents, or concepts of science but against the effects of the power of a discourse that is deemed scientific and that is inscribed within the institutions of contemporary society. It defines genealogy as "the union of erudite knowledge and local memories which allows us to establish a historical knowledge of struggles and to make use of this knowledge tactically today." The objective is to emancipate historical knowledge from the unified forms of subjection and discipline that established discourse imposes, to bring local and minor knowledges to life, to disrupt the commonly held conceptions that put us in our places.

Elsewhere, Foucault (in Dreyfus and Rabinow, 1982: 118) called genealogy a "history of the present." Meadmore and her colleagues refer to this as a "new kind of history" in which the present rather than the past becomes the object of inquiry. "Historical data are used to unsettle and destabilize the self-evidence of the conceptual bedrock of present understandings and analyses" (2000: 464). This strategy bears some similarity to that of dialectical social analysis (DSA) in that both approaches strive to pry open alternative futures by contesting the settled common sense of the present. Yet they differ in the use they make of social analysis as a spur to transformative agency. DSA views the *present as history* (Sweezy, 1953), that is, as history in the making, internally related to a future that is already imminent as a possibility here and now. Genealogy writes a *history of the present* that emphasizes the accidents, contingencies, and the "play of dominations" that have given birth to our way of life (Meadmore et al., 2000: 465). The former employs a dialectical analysis of past and present to point ahead toward a radically transformed future; the latter, in robbing the present of its claim to tradition and authority, "provides a useful way to transgress the boundaries that shape us" (Meadmore et al., 2000: 474).

As methods for critical discourse analysis, deconstruction and genealogy offer obvious advantages and seem to suit the temper of skeptical times. Yet despite the intentions of Foucault, Denzin, and others, post-structural approaches can degenerate into a "discourse idealism" that reduces social life to nothing but discourse (Chouliaraki and Fairclough, 1999: 28; cf. Reed, 2000; McNally, 2001; MacLennan and Thomas, 2003). Such a viewpoint also limits social critique to the realm of discourse, disabling researchers from making claims about the actualities of oppression, alienation, exploitation, and ecological devastation. This problem brings us to our second pair of readings in critical discourse analysis. Ian Parker and Lilie Chouliaraki and Norman Fairclough draw upon post-structuralist insights but locate their research strategies within a tradition of dialectical critical realism (Bhaskar, 1993). Together, these readings, which are excerpted from book-length works, take us some distance toward a practical approach to analyzing discourses in their full relationality.

Parker presents seven criteria as a series of "steps" in an analysis of discourse dynamics that draws on post-structuralist and related approaches. Along the way he clarifies how we might best approach the relations between discourses, texts, objects, subjects, meanings, other discourses, and history. Parker then introduces three "auxiliary criteria" that give discourse analysis a *critical* edge. These criteria alert the analyst to the relationships between discourses, institutions, power relations, and ideology. By identifying institutions that are reinforced or subverted when a discourse is used, by considering which categories of persons gain or lose from use of the discourse, and by showing how a discourse connects with other discourses that sanction oppression (and how discourse allows dominant groups to justify the present through narratives about the past), a critical analysis can challenge the ways in which discourses operate, and open spaces for resistance.

Chouliaraki and Fairclough build their framework for CDA partly from a detailed reanalysis of a case study presented by Dorothy Smith in her classic essay on "the active text." Their reanalysis suggests that the active text can also be a "hybrid text," assembling and combining a variety of genres and discourses. Drawing on Foucault, Chouliaraki and Fairclough define an *order of discourse* as the socially ordered set of discourses and genres associated with a particular social field. In this perspective, the social structuring of the semiotic is "a network of orders of discourse" (p. 264). Their framework for CDA attends to the structural and interactional dimensions of that network in relation to a given discourse-related problem in human affairs. These authors adopt Roy Bhaskar's (1986) method of "explanatory critique" as a way of identifying the problematic aspects of discursive practice, the barriers to resolving the problem, and possible ways past the barriers.

The starting point for this version of CDA is the perception of a discursive *problem*, either in a social practice itself (e.g., the failure to achieve authentic dialogue between participants) or in the reflexive construction of a practice (e.g., the misrepresentation of the actions of officials as always in accord with mandated procedures). Identification of *barriers* to resolving the problem requires three kinds of analysis. Analysis of the conjuncture locates the discursive problem in real time and within its overall context or frame of social practice. Analysis of the specific practice(s) of which the discursive problem is an aspect builds up a clear sense of how the discourse works in direct relation to "other things," including power struggles. Analysis of discourse itself focuses on both the structural issue of how the discourse draws selectively on the orders of discourse and the interactional issue of how the discourse "works the resource": how the voices, genres, and discourses that are drawn upon are worked together within specific textual processes. Having identified the problem and the barriers to change, the analysis shifts from explanation of what it is that makes a discursive practice problematic to an exploration of possible resources for change. This search needs to consider the range of what people can accomplish under given structural conditions as well as the gaps and contradictions in structures that render them vulnerable to transformative action.

It is evident from this brief survey of approaches to critical discourse analysis that the strategies of Parker and Chouliaraki and Fairclough are particularly sensitive to issues of power and domination that reside only partly "within" discourse, and thus to the need for fully contextualized study of discourses as they are taken up in practice. As I mentioned earlier, post-structuralism has a weakness in this regard. In making use of post-structural strategies, critical researchers need to remain grounded in a conception of the social as organized by practical relations—the kind of perspective we find in dialectical social analysis and institutional ethnography. In my view, post-structural methods can provide important leverage in what Marx in 1843 called "the self-clarification of the struggles and wishes of the age"—which includes deconstructing received views on what passes for "justice," "equality," or "democracy" in neo-liberal capitalism. But they achieve their most powerful impact when employed in ways that keep in view the practical, relational, material character of the human condition. One thing is certain. In a globalized world entirely saturated with mass-mediated, networked, and bureaucratic discourses, the approaches we have examined here will have continuing purchase in the conduct of critical inquiry.

NOTE

1.   For all these differences, however, there are important convergences and complementarities in the two strategies, which is why sociologists like Himani Bannerji (2000) and Nandita Sharma (2001) have been working quite effectively at their points of intersection. For a thoughtful critique of post-structuralism from the leading proponent of institutional ethnography, see Smith (1999: Chapter 6).

REFERENCES

Bannerji, Himani. 2000. *The Dark Side of the Nation: Essays on Multiculturalism, Nationalism and Gender*. Toronto: Canadian Scholars' Press.

Barker, Chris, and Dariusz Galasiński. 2001. *Cultural Studies and Discourse Analysis: A Dialogue on Language and Identity*. London: Sage.

Best, Stephen. 1995. *The Politics of Historical Vision*. New York: Guilford.

Bhaskar, Roy. 1986. *Reclaiming Reality*. London: Verso.

_____. 1993. *Dialectic: The Pulse of Freedom*. London: Verso.

Chouliaraki, Lilie, and Norman Fairclough. 1999. *Discourse in Late Modernity: Rethinking Critical Discourse Analysis*. Edinburgh: Edinburgh University Press.

Dreyfus, Hubert L., and Paul Rabinow. 1982. *Michel Foucault: Beyond Structuralism and Hermeneutics*. Chicago: University of Chicago Press.

Ellis, Kate. 1989. "Stories without Endings: Deconstructive Theory and Political Practice." *Socialist Review* 19(2): 37–52.

Fraser, Nancy. 1997. *Justice Interuptus*. London: Routledge.

Hall, Stuart. 1980 [1973]. "Encoding/Decoding." In *Culture, Media, Language: Working Papers in Cultural Studies, 1972–79*, edited by the Centre for Contemporary Cultural Studies, 128–138. London: Hutchinson.

Hodge, Robert, and Gunther Kress. 1988. *Social Semiotics*. Ithaca: Cornell University Press.

Kendall, Gavin, and Gary Wickham, 1999 *Using Foucault's Methods*. London: Sage.

Lakoff, George, and Mark Johnson. 1980. *Metaphors We Live By*. Chicago: University of Chicago Press.

Lee, Alison, and Cate Poynton. 2000. *Culture and Text: Discourse and Methodology in Social Research and Cultural Studies*. New York: Rowman & Littlefield.

Loomba, Ania. 1998. *Colonialism/Postcolonialism*. London: Routledge.

MacLennan, Gary, and Peter Thomas. 2003. "Cultural Studies: Towards a Realist Intervention." In *Critical Realism: The Difference It Makes*, edited by Justin Cruickshank, 161–177. New York: Routledge.

McNally, David. 2001. *Bodies of Meaning: Studies on Language, Labor and Liberation*. Albany: State University of New York Press.

Meadmore, Daphne, Caroline Hatcher, and Erica McWilliam. 2000. "Getting Tense about Genealogy." *International Journal of Qualitative Studies in Education* 13(5): 463–476.

Parker, Ian. 1988. "Deconstructing Accounts." In *Analysing Everyday Explanation*, edited by Charles Antaki, 184–198. London: Sage.

Phillips, Nelson, and Cynthia Hardy. 2002. *Discourse Analysis: Investigating Processes of Social Construction*. London: Sage.

Reed, Mike. 2000. "The Limits of Discourse Analysis in Organizational Analysis." *Organization* 7(3): 524–530.

Sharma, Nandita. 2001. "On Being *Not* Canadian: The Social Organization of 'Migrant Workers' in Canada." *Canadian Review of Sociology and Anthropology* 38(4): 415–439.

Smith, Dorothy E. 1999. *Writing the Social: Critique, Theory, and Investigations*. Toronto: University of Toronto Press.

Sweezy, Paul M. 1953. *The Present as History: Essays and Reviews on Capitalism and Socialism*. New York: Monthly Review Press.

Tamboukou, Maria. 1999. "Writing Genealogies: An Exploration of Foucault's Strategies for Doing Research." *Discourse: Studies in the Cultural Politics of Education* 20(2): 201–217.

Van Dijk, Teun A. 1998. *Ideology: A Multidisciplinary Approach*. London: Sage.

Weedon, Chris. 1987. *Feminist Practice and Poststructuralist Theory*. Oxford: Blackwell.

Wetherall, Margaret, Stephanie Taylor, and Simeon J. Yates, eds. 2001. *Discourse Theory and Practice: A Reader*. London: Sage.

CHAPTER 16

Postmodernism and Deconstructionism

NORMAN K. DENZIN

I went in search of *astral* America ... I looked for it in the speed of the screenplay, in the indifferent reflex of television ... in the marvelously affectless succession of signs, faces, and ritual acts on the road.
—Baudrillard (1988a: 5)[1]

My project is to show how deconstructionism may be employed as a postmodern research strategy for the interpretive study of contemporary society. In doing so, I draw upon my work on biographical method in the social sciences (Denzin, 1989a) as well as my ongoing research on film and the American alcoholic (Denzin, 1990a). I first discuss the definitions and assumptions of postmodernism and deconstructionism and then delineate various deconstructive strategies as they pertain to the critical, interpretive analysis of everyday life where biographies and selves circulate as differentially valued commodities (see Farberman, 1981).

I then provide a deconstructive reading of postmodernism through an analysis of a film, *The Morning After* (released in 1987),[2] which itself embodies the contemporary, postmodern moment. My deconstructive analysis of this film builds upon other approaches to film criticism, including recent feminist film theory (see De Lauretis, 1987; Gledhill, 1985, 1988; Mayne, 1990) to reveal how the postmodern and its representations contain their own

deconstructive features. Finally, I argue for a version of cultural studies (see Hall, 1980; Denzin, 1989c) that situates deconstructionism within the interpretive tradition.

A CULTURAL TEXT: *THE MORNING AFTER*

Nine o'clock A.M., Thursday, November 28, 1986, Thanksgiving Day, Los Angeles. Alex Sternbergen, an alcoholic actress who no longer gets parts, awakens with a hangover in a strange bed, in a loft apartment next to the body of a man. "Eye on L.A.," a local show featuring images of men and women working out (strikingly like those seen in Jane Fonda's exercise videos), is playing on the television. Bobby Korschak, a photographer known as "the King of Sleaze," is being interviewed. Laying her hand on the chest of the man beside her, Alex feels moisture and experiences a shock of recognition. It is blood. Fearfully crawling out of bed, away from the body, and quivering in the corner, she realizes that this is the "real" Bobby Korschack. A knife is sticking out of Bobby's chest ("Hey, what are you trying to pull? Is that one of those tricks?"), and he is dead. She walks out of the bedroom into a stark, lifeless, white studio with blue and orange shades on the windows. A cat cleaning its paws on a counter turns and looks at her. She pours a straight drink of vodka from a bottle sitting on the bar, grasps

232

her stomach, and runs to the bathroom. On her knees, hands around the toilet, she vomits, then gets up, washes her face, looks in the mirror, says "Congratulations," and finishes her drink. Thus begins Alex's morning after.

This movie, part film noir, part thriller, part "woman's film," part "alcoholism film," is a prime cultural text for a postmodern, deconstructionist reading. Its representations of "astral" woman, sexuality, violence, and the camera's reflective gaze connote key postmodern interpretations of conservative, patriarchal values, which turn on the treatment of women as sexual objects. The film's opening intertextual references to television, workout tapes, and Jane Fonda's offscreen personality point to two prominent features of contemporary life. Wherever one looks, the pervasive presence of the television screen as a gazing eye defines and shapes the contours of lived experience. And, the television screen is filled with popular culture figures who activate our filmic memories and connect our understandings of who we are to the values these public icons embody. We thus become everyday embodiments of these "astral" reflections.

The Morning After is focused on a single alcoholic woman and her attempt to set her life straight after she is framed for a murder. Alex is a complex figure, romantically involved with two men, one (Jackie) whose sexual identity is ambiguous and another (Turner) whose redneck, all-American values contradict her feminist beliefs. She requires both men to become whole again. In this, she embodies the androgynous gender ethics that circulated in 1980s popular culture. Also, the film is set in Los Angeles, the quintessential postmodern American city (see Baudrillard, 1988a). The film situates violence and the unpresentable within the immediate world of lived experience. These features no longer exist only as faraway images on the television screen. Finally, the film's time frame is the late 1980s. I will return to this text, and these features, after I have discussed postmodernism and deconstructionism.

DEFINING TERMS

Both terms in my title are complex and require clarification. *Postmodernism* refers to many things. In the arts, architecture, and humanities, it signifies recent aesthetic developments that challenge conventional modernist conceptions of structure, meaning, beauty, and truth (see Lyotard, 1984; Jencks, 1985). In the social sciences, it connotes a non-totalizing, antifoundational form of theorizing about the social world (see Denzin, 1986, 1991). [...] As a new historical era, postmodernism is most often defined theoretically in terms of the emergence of multinational forms of late capitalism, which have introduced a new cultural logic with new forms of communication and representation into the world system (see Jameson, 1984, 1991).

Most important, as the object of social inquiry, postmodernism refers to a new form of society, one that has been radically transformed by the invention of film and television into a visual, video culture. This transformation introduces a series of new cultural formations that impinge upon, shape, and redefine contemporary human group life. [...] In the sprawling urban shopping malls, in television soap operas, situation comedies, and evening news, in films like [...] *The Morning After*, at the computer terminal, and in the eye of the omnipresent camera, postmodernism, like the air we breathe, is everywhere around us.

The culture of postmodern society contains several contradictory features: an erasure of the boundary between past and present, often combined with a nostalgic longing for the past; an intense preoccupation with "the real" and its representations; a pornography of the visible; the commodification of sexuality and desire; celebration of a consumer life style that objectifies masculine cultural ideals; and emotional experiences shaped by anxiety, alienation, resentment, and detachment from others.

Deconstructionism is also a complex term. It is a concept most closely identified with the philosophical analyses of Jacques Derrida (see Lamont, 1987). Derrida's work may be read as a continuation of the attack on philosophy and social theory that traces its roots to Husserl's critique of the empiricist crisis in Western thought. It also builds on Saussure's structuralist theory of language, Nietzsche's radical attack on objective systems of truth and knowledge, Freud's critique of self-presence in consciousness, and Heidegger's critique of Western metaphysics. Because of its critical engagement with structuralist linguistics, deconstructionism is a prominent approach in the contemporary poststructuralist movement in philosophy and literary theory. [...]

Methodologically, deconstructionism is directed to the interrogation of texts. It involves the attempt to take apart and expose the underlying meanings, biases, and preconceptions that structure the way a text conceptualizes its relation to what it describes. This requires that traditional concepts, theory, and understanding surrounding a text be unraveled, including the assumption that an author's intentions and meanings can be easily determined.

The key strategies of deconstructionism include: a rupture of the formulas that equate written words with spoken words, spoken words with mental experience, and voice with mind; demonstrating the fundamental indeterminacy of meaning; the textual production of the subject as a system of differences; an attack on mimesis (the ability of a work to represent experience); and the development of what Derrida calls grammatology (a science or study of writing, speech, and texts) that entails rewriting the history of writing, developing a new theory of writing, and developing a set of

deconstructive grammatological practices (see Ulmer, 1985: 6; 1989).

Deconstructionism is an integral part of the postmodern project. It too aims to clear away the wreckage of a cluttered theoretical past, which clings to preconceptions that are regarded as no longer workable in the contemporary world. In this way, Derrida's project separates itself from sociologies that seek final, totalizing answers concerning the origins and causes of persons, structures, and intentions. It challenges sociology's desire to secure a fully centered human subject comfortably situated in a world of roles, statuses, norms, values, and structured social systems. It also intends to expose the underlying ideological presuppositions that organize contemporary research and theory, and thereby to lay the foundations for a profoundly humanistic social science. It is alive to the experiences of troubled individuals who find themselves in existentially problematic situations where history and choices are made behind their backs (Denzin, 1989b). As a way of knowing, the deconstructive strategy involves the analysis of social and cultural texts, including film, music, news, fiction, and social science writing, that purport to speak to the lived experiences of interacting individuals.

* * * * *

POSTMODERN TEXTS

Texts produced in the postmodern temper display a tendency to efface the boundaries between the past and the present in a way that situates the subject (and the viewer and the reader as well) in a perpetual present that is flooded with signifiers from the past.[3] This is postmodern nostalgia, which shows no respect for the integrity of the past. There is a parallel tendency in postmodern texts to bring the unpresentable (sexual violence, violent death, brutality, insanity, homosexuality, the degradation of women, sadomasochistic rituals, drug and alcohol abuse) before the viewer in ways that challenge "the boundaries that ordinarily separate private and public lives" (Denzin, 1988: 462). The wild sexuality, degradation, and violence that these texts depict represent modes of self-expression that are horrifying yet fascinating (Denzin, 1988; Baudrillard, 1983).

At the same time, postmodern texts frequently are organized under the rubric of the classic mortality tale (see Elbaz, 1987), where a subject is taken through three steps: seduction, corruption, and redemption. This biographical trajectory (Denzin, 1989a) is used as a vehicle for criticizing a corrupt, unethical society that has lost sight of traditional moral principles and values (see Denzin, 1990e). These texts narrate a fictional morality that underlies the postmodern age. They resort to the oedipal logic of competing father figures, one evil, the other good, and resolve ethical dilemmas through a nostalgia that returns the wayward subject to the traditional family setting (see Clough, forthcoming). Such tales have become valuable commodities in an age that has lost its footing, morally and aesthetically, recognizing only prestige and wealth (Baudrillard, 1981). Underneath, however, these texts keep alive the myth of the autonomous individual who, having fallen and been corrupted by immoral persons, returns to the values of family and individualism in the end. These works thus nostalgically create a sublimating fantasy for consumers of popular culture that represses the "real" destructive forces for a world gone wild.[4]

* * * * *

DECONSTRUCTION AND THE SOCIAL TEXT

For Baudrillard, the present age is defined by what he calls "the third order of the simulacrum" (1983: 11),[5] where a hyperreal logic of simulation organizes cultural experience. A thing is real if it appears real. Knowledge is true only to the extent that it conforms to simulated models of the real. This new situation produces a proliferation of social texts that purportedly map the world of concrete experience. Here nothing is ever outside a text (Derrida, 1976: 35), for "no thing is ever outside language, and hence incapable of being represented in a text." This being the case, the subject matter of postmodern interpretive studies must always be those texts that represent the social world.

Deconstructionism, specifically oriented to the analysis of texts, is a method that is particularly well suited for postmodern social inquiry. Focusing on the problematic nature of presence, intentionality, rationality, and causality in textual production, deconstruction critically reveals the ways in which social texts are organized.

The Logics of the Text

Conventional understandings have it that readers, writers, and speakers occupy concrete places in the here-and-now (e.g., on a page in a book). In these places and spaces, they enunciate and articulate thoughts, intentions, and meanings that are organized in terms of a logical, sequential, linear order. These intentions and meanings are seen as clearly understandable to anyone who speaks (or reads) the same language as the speaker or writer. Derrida deconstructs this belief.

According to Derrida, Western thought has been haunted by a metaphysics of presence, by the belief that the meaning of human experience can be most accurately rendered by a person who is fully present (and apparent) in speech or in a textual production. This is the heritage of the "logocentric," which is the argument that presence is the locus of truth. The foremost example of logocentrism is found in what Derrida calls "phonocentrism," the privileging of speech over voice and writing (see Dickens,

1990). Both logocentrism and phonocentrism assume that individuals have direct access to their thoughts through language. This access produces a perfect merger of voice and work, and of being and meaning. In ordinary language, what a person says is what she means. A person knows what she means because she knows what she thinks.

Consider the radical possibility that language does not facilitate this kind of understanding. Suppose that the signs that make up language can never function "without referring to another element which itself is simply not present" (Derrida, 1981: 27) and that this results in each element being constituted on the basis of the trace within it of other elements of the system. This interweaving "[yields] text produced only in the transformation of another *text* .... Nothing ... is anywhere ever simply present or absent. There are only, everywhere, differences and traces" (Derrida, 1981: 27).

This is Derrida's position. Language always entails a process of deferral and delay. Language does not permit speakers or writers to ever have full access to the meaning they are attempting to convey. Nor can they ever be fully present to themselves. As they reach forward or backward to catch a thought, that thought blurs with another, and that other thought (or word) blurs with another, until what they attempt to write or speak becomes something that bears the traces and meanings of everything that has come before.

Three important consequences follow from Derrida's position. First, speech and writing are not direct mirrors to thought. Second, speakers and writers are never fully present to themselves. Third, texts are always parts of other texts; there is never a pure text. The logocentric fallacy, which has been present since the Greeks, according to Derrida, is responsible for this false picture of speakers, writers, and texts. This being the case, texts must always be read in terms of the strategies

that writers convey as they consciously and unconsciously act as if they were fully present to themselves and their readers.

DOING A TEXT

Four general questions now appear. The first involves the deconstruction of the author's presence in the text. How, that is, are the author's presence, authority, knowledge, voice, and values evidenced in the text? Whose voice tells the story, and how do the various voices that combine to tell a story give different versions of the same narrative? In *The Morning After,* the story is told from four points of view: Alex's, Turner Kendall's (her new boyfriend), the detective's, and Jackie's (her husband). Each version is slightly different, revealing different values and different problems. Whose story is it? On the surface it is Alex's, but underneath it is also Jackie's, and Alex and Turner's together.

Second, how do the norms of logocentrism articulate with the phenomenon of intertextuality, where one text is seen to be part of another, even as this is hidden?[6] Return to Jane Fonda playing Alex Sternbergen in *The Morning After.* What viewer does not bring images of Jane Fonda doing aerobics to the film's opening scene, or recall her performance as Bree, the prostitute in *Klute* (1971), or her earlier image as a sex-doll in the 1968 film *Barbarella?* It is not possible to just see Fonda as Alex, for, as Williamson (1987: 23) observes, our filmic memory leads us to carry the images of a star from one film to another. [...] No film as a text is ever free from the effects of other texts. How this is the case must be shown.

The third problem is to identity how logocentrism leads to the production of a text that appears to unfold in a linear, rational manner, from point A in time through points B, C, and D, and so on, to an end. The metaphysics of presence permits no gaps in time. Otherwise there could be no "now," which is where presence makes itself known. The continuity of time, and hence of history, must always be fixed and certain and contained within the circle or logos of reason, which asserts that all that needs to be known can be known by logic and rationality (see Derrida, 1983; Harvey, 1985: 12).

Applied to a specific text, this problem concerns temporality and a text's construction of a reasonable, rational narrative that enunciates causes and effects, befores and afters, within an acceptable moral framework. Thus *The Morning After* takes Alex's alcoholism as a given at the outset of the film, suggesting first that it was caused when she and Jackie separated ten years earlier and her career began to slide downhill. But later the film reveals that she was an alcoholic even before she met Jackie, for there was an earlier marriage in which she attacked her ex-husband with a knife during a blackout. The "real" cause of her alcoholism is never answered, for the film keeps moving backward in time when it addresses this issue. She stops drinking only after she meets Turner. The effects of being framed for the murder, meeting Turner, and being confronted about her alcoholism by him, as well as his near death, are connected to her becoming sober. These effects (and causes) are presented in a natural, linear, sequential cause-and-effect order. Temporality becomes narrative causality (see Ricoeur, 1988). All that the viewer needs to know about Alex's case is given from inside this rational narrative. Yet the film falters in those key moments when it establishes these causal points, for it gives no reasons why Alex would choose this time to become sober.

The fourth issue relates to presence and is closely aligned with the concept of structure. Derrida challenges the notion of structure and the related idea of center. Recall his analysis of the sign. A sign is only made up of differences and has no stable center. Since structures can only be represented by signs, for example,

"society," then they too have neither fixed presences nor center points: "The center is at the center of the totality ... yet, since the center does not belong to the totality ... totality *has its center elsewhere*. The center is not a center" (Derrida, 1972: 248; italics in original). The center, like a structure, is merely a sign, a name for something that is not there. This carries several implications for the analysis of texts. How do writers get structures into their texts? How do they give their structures centers? How do they establish the presence, or absence, of a structure? How do they substitute one structure for another, and how do they connect authors and characters to structures and centers (in written works, films, and the like)?

The problem of presence and its representation is equally complex. It is a sociological and textual given that "presence" and "lived experience" are privileged terms. Their presence must be felt in a text. They must enter a text, express the person's point of view, and capture her experience. This is typically accomplished through particular forms of narrative, whether that be subjective sociological life histories, ethnographies, first-person voice in a novel, or a subjective camera in film (see Clough, forthcoming; Denzin, 1989a).

The problem of presence is not easily resolved, however, for as Derrida (1972) argues, nothing is ever just present. Presence is given only through difference, through the traces that connect this experience and that person to another experience and another subject, and so on.[7] At issue, then, is how a text gives the illusion of capturing presence and lived experience and connects these phenomena to recurring structures (society, culture), which presumably shape those experiences.

The Morning After takes up these problems in the following ways. Alex is a decentered character. She is an alcoholic who is outside marriage and work. Her life has become a series of one-night stands with strangers encountered at bars and parties. Her drinking, the memory of her films (which occasionally play on late-night television), Jackie, who bails her out of trouble, Charlie, her bartender friend, and Frankie, the drag queen, hold her together. Alex is constituted in these relationships, which are located in a variety of places throughout the city of Los Angeles, from seedy bars to art deco apartments, the quons et hut where Turner lives, and to Jackie's fashionable beauty salon. Alex is in all these places and relationships, yet she is not in them. Here presences and absences in the text serve to define who she is and who she is not. She is everywhere but nowhere, present only in the gaps and disjunctures that take her from place to place. She has no center. Yet her recurring presence on the screen, from scene to scene, serves to remind the viewer that this is her film, even if we do not know who she is or where she is going.

Centering his star in the fractured, desolate, lonely, L.A. landscape (his structure), shot "in exact pastiche of the Edward Hopper manner" (Milne, 1987: 181) in real time (9:00 A.M., Thursday, November 28, 1986), director Stanley Lumet goes to great lengths to tell a story about a world with empty streets devoid of human activity and meaning "where the powerless prey on each other, and ... [everybody] is a victim" (Edelstein, 1986: 74). The real star of the film is Los Angeles, which is made up of "great flat planes of cold pastels and threatening sunlit open spaces" (Ebert, 1986: 35), where empty lives are lived, and true darkness and real nightmares occur in the daytime.

Situated within this frame, the lives of Alex, Turner, and Jackie can now be read as decentered productions whose meanings lie in the differences that connect each to the other. There is no essential structure to the film, no center, no totality, only a sequence of fractured images that build on one another and together

create, in the end, a simple romantic thriller, a love story, about two recovering alcoholics (see Canby, 1986).

THE PATRIARCHAL BIAS

The four primary *logoi,* or logics, of presence, intentionality, reason, and causality structure the basic contours of *The Morning After* and make it intuitively understandable to the viewer. Yet, alongside these four logics rests another set of biases. They operate at the surface and deep levels, and represent values and meanings that are encoded into the text and then decoded by readers (Hall, 1980). They articulate values that circulate within the popular culture. I call these variants on the patriarchal bias (see De Lauretis, 1984, 1987), for they point to the text's treatment of the social identities attached to the circumstances and situations of age, gender, class, race, and ethnicity.

The textual presentation of these identity markers creates universes of appearance (Stone, 1970: 237) that immediately ascribe to any individual a self that is read through the biased lens of a white, middle-class patriarchal perspective. These identities and their meanings are embedded in the story and enacted in the performances of the various fictional characters who populate the text. This bias often relegates women's perspectives to the margins of the text, giving primary attention to the perspective of white, middle-class males. When a woman's perspective is presented, it is often filtered through dominant male eyes. These representations reproduce gender stratification systems within postmodern society. When race and ethnicity are added to the picture, similar biases are repeated. Minorities and members of the underclass are relegated to marginal places in the story, as are the very young and the elderly.

A feminist reading deconstructs the patriarchal biases that run throughout a text.[8] This again involves an application of the four deconstructive strategies outlined above (the critiques of presence, intentionality, rationality, and causality) to the social identities ascribed to a text's main and marginal characters. Such a reading moves through three steps. It identifies the preferred or hegemonic, the negotiated, and the oppositional readings that can be brought to bear on each character and level of the text (Hall, 1980). Paraphrasing Gledhill (1985: 827), these steps and strategies may be described as follows: the hegemonic reading takes the reading preferred by the dominant cultural ideology; the negotiated reading attempts to maintain the preferred reading in tandem with understandings drawn from a class or gender position; and the oppositional reading transforms the readings offered by the dominant ideology into what they mean for an oppositional discourse.

Phrased another way, the hegemonic and negotiated readings refer to "realist" readings that can be brought to a text. The oppositional reading is a subversive interpretation that challenges the dominant cultural perspective and its meanings in the text (see Hall, 1980; Denzin, 1989d: 51).

BACK TO THE TEXT

The Morning After cries out for an oppositional, feminist deconstruction. Consider the following dialogue, which takes place five minutes into the film. Alex has just met Turner at the L.A. airport. They are in his car. Alex immediately sizes Turner up as a redneck bigot:

Turner *(Driving, looking over his shoulder)*: A spade in a caddy ran into somebody.

Alex: Spade in a caddy. Is that anything like Jack in the Box?

Turner: I wish I had the caddy dealership in Watts. Spades, ah, they spend disproportionately on their transportation, also in dressing their young.

Alex: What are you, the Klan anthropologist?

Turner: You can learn a lot about a person by the car they drive.[9]

In this dialogue, the text criticizes Turner's racism through the two phrases "Jack in the Box," and "Klan anthropologist," thereby neutralizing the unpresentable through an appropriate moral stance. But the effacement of blacks stands.

Alex is caught between two men. Turner, a hick from Bakersfield with a streetwise encyclopedic collection of racist facts, is starkly contrasted to suave, debonair Jackie, a man with a sexually ambiguous name, a cultural outsider, a villain, and a victim. Turner has a heart of gold, "the raw material of Americanness" (Williamson, 1987: 23), but he is a racist and her savior at the same time.

Alex has two other friends, the aging Frankie ("Honey, I'm a drag queen, not a transvestite!") and Charlie, the fat, jovial bartender who gives her money and does not criticize her drinking. These two characters are situated on the fringes of her world. The audience is asked to play Frankie's open gayness off against Jackie's imputed (by the police and Turner) homosexuality. Thus subtext becomes a device for the film's reproduction of cultural stereotypes about homosexuality (in the closet and out of the closet, queens versus transvestites). At the same time, it allows the text to side against the homosexual in favor of the straight man (Turner over Jackie) and to favor the white racist male over the Hispanic gay. By folding both of the negative cultural characteristics into the same character (Jackie), the text negates Turner's racism in favor of his down-home good will toward Alex. This move is justified later by the fact that Jackie is discovered to be the one who framed Alex.

Now let's consider the figure of woman. Alex is a departure from the classic film noir icon of the flawed woman who is both good and evil but primarily evil (Williamson, 1987). Alex is not an evil woman. Rather, she is a flawed figure because of her alcoholism. By making her an alcoholic, the film is able to further erode the meanings brought to women. Alex is surrounded with all the negative signifiers that American culture has traditionally identified with the female alcoholic: low self-esteem, divorce, loss of work and family, loose sexuality, sexual degradation, hitting a sexual bottom, blackouts, and violence.

Alex is faced with the ambiguous choice of two flawed men. The film resolves this conflict by having her fall in love with Turner, the one who is not only helping her get sober but who also saved her life. This is what this film is all about: the choices women have in the late 1980s. The paths are not clearly marked, as this text demonstrates, but they are still framed from within a patriarchal structure that has men making the choices for women.

At the surface level, Lumet's film is a melodrama, a story of love and hope, of two human beings fearful of committing to one another. In this telling, at this level, Lumet is suggesting that American society can accept a female alcoholic as the heroine in a murder-mystery love story. He has transformed Alex from stigmatized alcoholic woman into woman-as-alcoholic who has stopped drinking and fallen in love with a man who has done the same. By inverting the signifiers of alcoholic and woman, Lumet turns Alex into a prototype of the single, modern woman who has lost and now found her way in a hostile, empty world, which tends, in the main, to make victims of all of us, but women more so.

This is the surface, hegemonic reading of the story. There also exists an equally hegemonic antigay, racist subtext, which is justified in terms of the happy ending. In allowing these hegemonic readings to stand, the viewer (and the critic) become willing accomplices in support of a conservative feminism that pleads (yet hides) its ideological biases in the name of a story which locates a woman in the company of a "good" man who has flaws.

A feminist deconstruction of these themes reveals that this text's meanings depend on the sexual and racial differences that are enunciated by Turner, differences that create the marginalized spaces Alex occupies. Their presence suggests that women, in order to find their place, have to go to the margins of society, where gays and drag queens will give them comfort, warmth, friendship, and support. But these relationships are not enough, hence Alex's decision to remain with Turner and the film's return to its comfortable, hegemonic position which asserts that gays and "spies" who, if not evil, are persons about whom jokes can be told.

DECONSTRUCTION AND CULTURAL STUDIES

The above analysis reveals how the deconstructionist method may be utilized in the reading of a contemporary cultural text. *The Morning After*, with its multiple meanings, is an apt text for postmodern deconstruction since America, like Alex Sterbergen, is in the long duree of an extended morning after. Hungover yet still intoxicated from too many images of the real and the hyperreal, the America that emerges from this reading longs for the day when things were really real, when men were men and women were women, with no ambiguity—a time when things are settled once and for all, when the unpresentable is no longer presented. In the extended nowness of this unbroken present, which constantly harks back to the past, even if by means of an irreverent nostalgia, there is the dream ("It's morning again in America") that the old myths and beliefs are true and still apply. In this way, *The Morning After* invokes nostalgia for the past as it weaves a pastiche visual structure through a conventional melodramatic narrative about a desperate woman lost and terrified in the big city.

At the same time, my deconstructionist reading of the film reveals other, more controversial features of postmodern society, such as sexism, racism, homophobia, and alcohol and drug addiction. These constitute the underside of astral America, where the signifier "America" is more problematic.

Conceived in this fashion, deconstructionism is also a postmodern, interpretive approach to the field of cultural studies.[10] This version of cultural studies is distinctly postmodern insofar as it is antifoundational. Each cultural reading begins anew, presuming only that all texts are constituted by an interminable play of differences. The structures of texts are scrutinized for their logocentric and patricentric biases. The intent is interventionist, to expose the underlying "structural" preconceptions that organize texts and to reveal the conditions of freedom that they suppress.

At the same time, deconstruction is an effort to penetrate the world of lived experience where cultural texts circulate and give meaning to everyday life. It is necessary to show the gap that separates the world of everyday meaning from the words that are inscribed about that world by various cultural authorities, including newsmakers, social scientists, novelists, and filmmakers. Also, the analyst turns to the social texts and narratives that persons tell one another, finding in these stories the textual foundations of meaning as it is lived in the current moment. The deconstructionist's agenda is always the same. How does any given text address the problems of presence and lived experience? How does it produce the intentional meanings that are ascribed to subjects? How does it center and anchor the subject and her experiences in a narrative text? How does it represent the "real" experiences of interacting individuals?

Cultural studies, so conceived, becomes a discipline that cuts across the social sciences. It knows no disciplinary boundaries. Its subject matter is everywhere. Its methods are interpretive and deconstructive. It is a project informed by the politics of liberation and freedom, by a post-Marxism with no guarantees (Hall, 1986: 48; also Sartre, 1976; Merleau-Ponty, 1973), firmly rooted in the tradition of critique and renewal that has historically given meaning to the "critical" approach in the human sciences (see Adorno, 1973).

As students of the postmodern moment, we have only texts and the stories people tell us. Our problem is working from text to experience. This means we read texts as narratives of experience and find in them recurring meanings that speak to the person-centered bias our culture instills in each of us. We read these texts as attempts to overcome the decentered presences that persons experience on a daily basis, seeing them for what they are: ideological efforts to find a common ground in a postmodern world that has neither a fixed center nor a coherent understanding of this thing called human.

NOTES

1. Baudrillard is after "astral" or "sidereal" America, the America revealed in reflections sent from the stars. In what follows, I argue that reflections sent from the stars (read Hollywood and film) embody a version of the "real" America that impinges directly in the lived experiences of ordinary people.

2. [...] See Denzin (1990a) for an extended discussion of this film. The story is simple. Alex is framed by her husband (a Mexican

hairdresser) and his girlfriend (whose father is a judge) for the murder of Korschack. Turner (an ex-policeman on disability who fixes broken things—cars, toasters, and people) helps Alex get back on her feet, but she keeps getting drunk. He suspects that she was framed and discovers that it was Jackie who framed her. In the climax, Jackie attempts to kill Alex. Turner saves her and is nearly killed by Jackie. Turner ends up in the hospital, Alex gets sober, and in a long good-bye scene where Turner reveals that he also used to be a drunk, they decide to stay together.

3. A text refers to "any printed, visual, oral or auditory statement that is available for reading, viewing or hearing" (Denzin, 1989b: 131). Texts always exist within systems of discourse, or discursive formations (see Foucault, 1970).

4. See Denzin (1990e) for a listing of contemporary films that perform this function.

5. Simulacrum means an image, the semblance of an image, make-believe, or that which conceals the truth (Baudrillard, 1981: 32–33). The present situation is defined by the power of the simulacrum, the power of images, and signs that stand for commodities, to become what they stand for. In the first order of the simulacrum, which Baudrillard locates in the Renaissance, signs began to be released from what they signified (i.e., in the fields of drama and religion). The second order was ushered in with the age of mechanical reproduction during the Industrial Revolution, where endless reproductions of the same thing could be made (i.e., photographs, mechanical objects, tools).

6. Intertextuality refers to the notion that boundaries of a text continually spill over into other texts (see Derrida, 1987a). Intertextuality operates in all texts, not just in films. This manuscript has by now been anchored in a half-dozen films, a century or more of European philosophy, contemporary American social theory, my previous works, the statements of the editors of this volume, the contributions of other authors in this volume, and even this footnote.

7. This raises the problem of the "other" in the text and how a particular work evokes an "other" whose presence and absence define the meaning of any given subject. Thus, Turner's self is defined in terms of his opposition to gays, "spics," and "spades." The presence of the deviant defines the essence of Turner's character. A text will create a set of oppositions between categories of selves (gay-straights, males-females, and so on). In so doing, it effaces the subjectivity of the "strange" other.

8. A feminist reading also introduces another level of interpretation dealing with the text's telling of the universal story of the gendered human relationships and the fear of forming and being contained within a bonded, loving, intimate relationship (see Lyman, 1987; Denzin, 1990a). Of course, not all texts tell this story, but few films escape its presence. Elsewhere (see Denzin, 1989c: 23; 1990a) I have outlined eight separate approaches to cultural studies. Here I focus only on the processual, subversive approach, which seeks to deconstruct the ideological biases and preconceptions that are routinely embedded in postmodern cultural texts.

9. This kind of dialogue goes on continually between the two of them, and it expands to include "spics," "Jews," and "gays." He becomes defined as a racist hick from Bakersfield, and she a sophisticated lady from L.A. "by way of the Big Apple." The plot thickens when he learns that Jackie, her husband, is a hairdresser and an immigrant from Mexico.

10. Cultural studies views "human action as a text" (Carey, 1988: 60) informed and shaped by the meanings persons bring to their

experiences. It takes as its subject matter the cultural texts that human beings produce, including popular entertainment (songs, films, stories), social science writings, myth, religion, and art. It examines the stories persons tell one another, moving from those contained in the daily news, to those given in weekly news magazines, to those appearing in popular drama and literature, to those told in social groups, to the cultural texts of groups, and to the texts and stories about society sociologists and other alleged experts tell (see Denzin, 1990b). Cultural studies attempt to make sense of the meanings that are embedded in these texts (Carey, 1988: 56), its task being one of making sense out of "the senses we make out of life" (Carey, 1988: 44).

REFERENCES

Adorno, Theodor W. 1973. *Negative Dialectics*, translated by John Ashton. New York: Seabury Press.

Baudrillard, Jean. 1981. *For a Critique of the Political Economy of the Sign*, translated by Charles Levin. St. Louis: Telos Press.

_____. 1983. *Simulations*, translated by Paul Foss, Paul Patton, and John Johnston. New York: Semiotext(e).

_____. 1988a. *America*, translated by Chris Turner. London: Verso.

Brown, Patricia Leigh. 1989. "A Stones Set of Steel and Magic." *The New York Times* (October 5): 15.

Canby, Vincent. 1986. "Review of *The Morning After.*" *The New York Times* (December 25): 22.

Carey, James W. 1988. *Communication as Culture: Essays on Media and Society*. Boston: Unwin Hyman.

Clough, Patricia Ticineto. Forthcoming. "The Rhetoric of Sexual Difference and the Narrative Construction of Ethnographic Authority." *Studies in Symbolic Interaction*.

Coleman, James S. 1968. "Review Symposium of Harold Garfinkel," *Studies in Ethnomethodology.*" *American Sociological Review* 33: 122–130.

Coser, Lewis A. 1975. "Two Methods in Search of a Substance." *American Sociological Review* 40: 691–700.

De Lauretis, Teresa. 1984. *Alice Doesn't: Feminism, Semiotics, Cinema*. Bloomington: Indiana University Press.

_____. 1987. *Technologies of Gender: Essays on Theory, Film and Fiction*. Bloomington: Indiana University Press.

Denzin, Norman K. 1986. "Postmodern Social Theory." *Sociological Theory* 4: 194–204.

_____. 1988. *"Blue Velvet:* Postmodern Contradictions." *Theory, Culture, and Society* 5: 461–473.

_____. 1989a. *Interpretive Biography*. Newbury Park: Sage.

_____. 1989b. *Interpretive Interactionism*. Newbury Park: Sage.

_____. 1989c. "Reading/Writing Culture: Interpreting the Postmodern Project." *Cultural Dynamics* 11: 9–27.

_____. 1989d. "Reading *Tender Mercies:* Two Interpretations." *Sociological Quarterly* 30: 37–57.

_____. 1990a. *Hollywood Shot by Shot: Alcoholism in American Cinema*. New York: Aldine de Gruyter.

_____. 1990b. "The Sociological Imagination Reconsidered." *Sociological Quarterly* 31: 1–22.

_____. 1990d. "Doing Cultural Studies." *Current Perspectives in Social Theory* 11: 17–39.

_____. 1990e. "Reading Wall Street: Postmodern Contradictions in the American Social

Structure." In *Theories of Modernism and Postmodernism,* edited by Bryan S. Turner, 31–44. London: Sage.

_____. 1991. *Images of Postmodernism: Social Theory and Contemporary Cinema.* London: Sage.

Derrida, Jacques. 1972. "Structure, Sign, and Play in the Discourse of the Human Sciences." In *The Structuralist Controversy: The Languages of Criticism and the Sciences of Man,* edited by Richard Macksey and Eugenio Donato, 247–264. Baltimore: Johns Hopkins University Press.

_____. 1973. *"Speech and Phenomena" and Other Essays on Husserl's Theory of Signs,* Evanston: Northwestern University Press.

_____. 1976. *Of Grammatology,* translated by Gayatri Chakravorty Spivak. Baltimore: Johns Hopkins University Press.

_____. 1978. *Writing and Difference,* translated by Alan Bass. Chicago: University of Chicago Press.

_____. 1981. *Positions,* translated by Alan Bass. Chicago: University of Chicago Press.

_____. 1983. "The Principle of Reason: The University in the Eyes of Its Pupils." *Diacritics* 12: 3–20.

_____. 1987a. *The Truth in Painting,* translated by Geoff Bennington and Jan McLeod. Chicago: University of Chicago Press.

_____. 1987b. *The Post Card: From Socrates to Freud and Beyond,* translated by Alan Bass. Chicago: University of Chicago Press.

Dickens, David. 1990. "Deconstructionism and Marxist Inquiry." *Sociological Perspectives* 33: 147–158.

Ebert, Roger. 1986. "Review of *The Morning After." New York Post* (December 26): 45.

Edelstein, David. 1986. "Review of *The Morning After." Village Voice* (December 30): 74.

Elbaz, Robert. 1987. *The Changing Nature of the Self: A Critical Study in Autobiographic Discourse.* Iowa City: University of Iowa Press.

Farberman, Harvey. 1981. "The Political Economy of Fantasy in Everyday Life." *Symbolic Interaction* 2: 1–18.

Featherstone, Mike. 1988. "In Pursuit of the Postmodern: An Introduction." *Theory, Culture, and Society* 5: 195–215.

Foucault, Michel. 1970. *The Order of Things.* New York: Vintage.

Garfinkel, Harold. 1967. *Studies in Ethnomethodology.* Englewood Cliffs: Prentice-Hall.

Gledhill, Christine. 1985. "Recent Developments in Feminist Criticism." In *Film Theory and Criticism,* edited by Gerald Mast and Marshall Cohen, 817–845. New York: Oxford University Press.

_____. 1988. "Pleasurable Negotiations." In *The Female Spectator: Looking at Film and Television,* edited by Deidre Pribam, 33–49. London: Verso.

Goffman, Erving. 1974. *Frame Analysis.* New York: Harper and Row.

Griswold, Charles L., Jr. 1989. "Letter on Deconstruction, the Nazis, and Paul de Man." *New York Review of Books* (October 12): 69.

Grossberg, Lawrence. 1989. *It's a Sin: Essays on Postmodern Politics and Culture.* Sidney: Power Publications.

Hall, Stuart, ed. 1980. *Culture, Media, Language.* London: Hutchinson.

_____. 1986. "On Postmodernism and Articulation: An Interview with Stuart Hall." *Journal of Communication Inquiry* 10: 45–60.

Harvey, Irene. 1985. *Derrida and the Economy of Difference.* Bloomington: Indiana University Press.

Huyssen, Andreas. 1984. "Mapping the Postmodern." *New German Critique* 33: 5–31.

Jameson, Frederic. 1983. "Postmodernism and Consumer Society." In *The Anti-Aesthetic: Essays on Postmodern Culture,* edited by

Hal Foster, 111–125. Port Townsend: Bay Press.

_____. 1984. "Postmodernism; or, The Cultural Logic of Late Capitalism." *New Left Review* 146: 53–72.

_____. 1990. *Signatures of the Visible.* New York: Routledge.

_____. 1991. *Postmodernism, or the Cultural Logic of Late Capitalism.* Durham: Duke University Press.

Jencks, Charles. 1985. *The Language of Postmodern Architecture.* New York: Basic Books.

Lamont, Michele. 1987. "How to Become a Dominant French Philosopher: The Case of Jacques Derrida." *American Journal of Sociology* 93: 584–622.

Lyman, Stanford. 1987. "From Matrimony to Malaise: Men and Women in the American Film, 1930–1980." *International Journal of Politics, Culture and Society* 1: 73–100.

Lyotard, Jean-Francois. 1984. *The Postmodern Condition: A Report on Knowledge*, translated by Geoff Benningston and Brian Massumi. Minneapolis: University of Minnesota Press.

Mayne, Judith. 1990. *The Woman at the Keyhole: Feminism and Women's Cinema.* Bloomington: Indiana University Press.

Merleau-Ponty, Maurice. 1973. *Adventures of the Dialectic*, translated by Joseph Bein. Evanston: Northwestern University Press.

Milne, Tom. 1987. Review of *The Morning After." Monthly Film Review* (June): 181.

Ricoeur, Paul. 1988. *Time and Narrative.* Chicago: University of Chicago Press.

Sartre, Jean-Paul. 1976. *Critique of Dialectical Reason*, translated by Hazel Barnes. London: New Left Books.

Spivak, Gayatri Chakravorty. 1976. Translator's "Preface." In *Of Grammatology* by Jacques Derrida, translated by Gayatri Chakravorty Spivak, ix–xc. Baltimore: Johns Hopkins University Press.

Stone, Gregory P. 1970. "Sex and Age as Universes of Appearance." In *Social Psychology through Symbolic Interaction,* edited by Gregory P. Stone and Harvey Farberman, 227–236. Waltham: Gin-Blaisdell.

Taylor, Mark, ed. 1986. *Deconstruction in Context.* Chicago: University of Chicago Press.

Ulmer, Gregory. 1985. *Applied Grammatology.* Baltimore: Johns Hopkins University Press.

_____. 1989. *Teletheory: Grammatology in the Age of Video.* New York: Routledge.

Williamson, Judith. 1987. "Review of *The Morning After*." *New Statesman* (June): 23.

CHAPTER 17

Two Lectures: Lecture One: January 7, 1976[*]

MICHEL FOUCAULT

LECTURE ONE: 7 JANUARY 1976

* * * * *

You will recall my work here, such as it has been: some brief notes on the history of penal procedure, a chapter or so on the evolution and institutionalisation of psychiatry in the nineteenth century, some observations on sophistry, on Greek money, on the medieval Inquisition. I have sketched a history of sexuality or at least a history of knowledge of sexuality on the basis of the confessional practice of the seventeenth century or the forms of control of infantile sexuality in the eighteenth to nineteenth century. I have sketched a genealogical history of the origins of a theory and a knowledge of anomaly and of the various techniques that relate to it. None of it does more than mark time. Repetitive and disconnected, it advances nowhere. Since indeed it never ceases to say the same thing, it perhaps says nothing. It is tangled up into an indecipherable, disorganised muddle. In a nutshell, it is inconclusive.

Still, I could claim that after all these were only trails to be followed, it mattered little where they led; indeed, it was important that they did not have a predetermined starting point and destination. They were merely lines laid down for you to pursue or to divert elsewhere, for me to extend upon or re-design as the case might be. They are, in the final analysis, just fragments, and it is up to you or me to see what we can make of them. [...]

After all, the fact that the character of the work I have presented to you has been at the same time fragmentary, repetitive, and discontinuous could well be a reflection of something one might describe as a febrile indolence—a typical affliction of those enamoured of libraries, documents, reference works, dusty tomes, texts that are never read, books that are no sooner printed than they are consigned to the shelves of libraries where they thereafter lie dormant to be taken up only some centuries later. [...] It would accord with all those who feel themselves to be associates of one of the more ancient or more typical secret societies of the West, those oddly indestructible societies unknown it would seem to Antiquity, which came into being with Christianity, most likely at the time of the first monasteries, at the periphery of the invasions, the fires and the

---

[*] This is a condensed version of the first of Foucault's two lectures. Both lectures are available in full in Michel Foucault, *Power/Knowledge*, edited by Colin Gordon (New York: Pantheon Books): 78–108. —Ed.

forests: I mean to speak of the great warm and tender Freemasonry of useless erudition.

However, it is not simply a taste for such Freemasonry that has inspired my course of action. It seems to me that the work we have done could be justified by the claim that it is adequate to a restricted period, that of the last ten, fifteen, at most twenty years, a period notable for two events which for all they may not be really important are nonetheless to my mind quite interesting.

On the one hand, it has been a period characterised by what one might term the efficacy of dispersed and discontinuous offensives. There are a number of things I have in mind here. I am thinking, for example, where it was a case of undermining the function of psychiatric institutions, of that curious efficacy of localised anti-psychiatric discourses. These are discourses which you are well aware lacked and still lack any systematic principles of coordination of the kind that would have provided or might today provide a system of reference for them. I am thinking of the original reference towards existential analysis or of certain directions inspired in a general way by Marxism, such as Reichian theory. Again, I have in mind that strange efficacy of the attacks that have been directed against traditional morality and hierarchy, attacks which again have no reference except perhaps in a vague and fairly distant way to Reich and Marcuse. On the other hand there is also the efficacy of the attacks upon the legal and penal system, some of which had a very tenuous connection with the general and in any case pretty dubious notion of class justice, while others had a rather more precisely defined affinity with anarchist themes. Equally, I am thinking of the efficacy of a book such as *L'Anti-Oedipe,* which really has no other source of reference than its own prodigious theoretical inventiveness: a book, or rather a thing, an event, which has managed, even at the most mundane level of psychoanalytic practice, to introduce a note of shrillness into that murmured exchange that has for so long continued uninterrupted between couch and armchair.

I would say, then, that what has emerged in the course of the last ten or fifteen years is a sense of the increasing vulnerability to criticism of things, institutions, practices, discourses. A certain fragility has been discovered in the very bedrock of existence—even, and perhaps above all, in those aspects of it that are most familiar, most solid, and most intimately related to our bodies and to our everyday behaviour. But together with this sense of instability and this amazing efficacy of discontinuous, particular, and local criticism, one in fact also discovers something that perhaps was not initially foreseen, something one might describe as precisely the inhibiting effect of global, *totalitarian theories.* It is not that these global theories have not provided nor continue to provide in a fairly consistent fashion useful tools for local research: Marxism and psychoanalysis are proofs of this. But I believe these tools have only been provided on the condition that the theoretical unity of these discourses was in some sense put in abeyance, or at least curtailed, divided, overthrown, caricatured, theatricalised, or what you will. In each case, the attempt to think in terms of a totality has in fact proved a hindrance to research.

So, the main point to be gleaned from these events of the last fifteen years, their predominant feature, is the *local* character of criticism. That should not, I believe, be taken to mean that its qualities are those of an obtuse, naive, or primitive empiricism; nor is it a soggy eclecticism, an opportunism that laps up any and every kind of theoretical approach; nor does it mean a self-imposed ascetism which taken by itself would reduce to the worst kind of theoretical impoverishment. I believe that what this essentially local character of criticism indicates in reality is an autonomous, non-centralised kind of theoretical production, one that is to say whose validity is not dependent on the approval of the established regimes of thought.

It is here that we touch upon another feature of these events that has been manifest for some time now: it seems to me that this local criticism has proceeded by means of what one might term "a return of knowledge." What I mean by that phrase is this: it is a fact that we have repeatedly encountered, at least at a superficial level, in the course of most recent times, an entire thematic to the effect that it is not theory but life that matters, not knowledge but reality, not books but money, etc.; but it also seems to me that over and above, and arising out of this thematic, there is something else to which we are witness, and which we might describe as an *insurrection of subjugated knowledges.*

By subjugated knowledges I mean two things: on the one hand, I am referring to the historical contents that have been buried and disguised in a functionalist coherence or formal systemisation. Concretely, it is not a semiology of the life of the asylum, it is not even a sociology of delinquency, that has made it possible to produce an effective criticism of the asylum and likewise of the prison, but rather the immediate emergence of historical contents. And this is simply because only the historical contents allow us to rediscover the ruptural effects of conflict and struggle that the order imposed by functionalist or systematising thought is designed to mask. Subjugated knowledges are thus those blocs of historical knowledge which were present but disguised within the body of functionalist and systematising theory and which criticism—which obviously draws upon scholarship—has been able to reveal.

On the other hand, I believe that by subjugated knowledges one should understand something else, something which in a sense is altogether different, namely, a whole set of knowledges that have been disqualified

as inadequate to their task or insufficiently elaborated: naive knowledges, located low down on the hierarchy, beneath the required level of cognition or scientificity. I also believe that it is through the re-emergence of these low-ranking knowledges, these unqualified, even directly disqualified knowledges (such as that of the psychiatric patient, of the ill person, of the nurse, of the doctor—parallel and marginal as they are to the knowledge of medicine—that of the delinquent, etc.), and which involve what I would call a popular knowledge *(le savoir des gens)* though it is far from being a general commonsense knowledge, but is on the contrary a particular, local, regional knowledge, a differential knowledge incapable of unanimity and which owes its force only to the harshness with which it is opposed by everything surrounding it—that it is through the re-appearance of this knowledge, of these local popular knowledges, these disqualified knowledges, that criticism performs its work.

However, there is a strange kind of paradox in the desire to assign to this same category of subjugated knowledges what are on the one hand the products of meticulous, erudite, exact historical knowledge, and on the other hand local and specific knowledges which have no common meaning and which are in some fashion allowed to fall into disuse whenever they are not effectively and explicitly maintained in themselves. Well, it seems to me that our critical discourses of the last fifteen years have in effect discovered their essential force in this association between the buried knowledges of erudition and those disqualified from the hierarchy of knowledges and sciences.

In the two cases—in the case of the erudite as in that of the disqualified knowledges—with what in fact were these buried, subjugated knowledges really concerned? They were concerned with a *historical knowledge of struggles.* In the specialised areas of erudition as in the disqualified, popular knowledge there lay the memory of hostile encounters which even up to this day have been confined to the margins of knowledge.

What emerges out of this is something one might call a genealogy, or rather a multiplicity of genealogical researches, a painstaking rediscovery of struggles together with the rude memory of their conflicts. And these genealogies, that are the combined product of an erudite knowledge and a popular knowledge, were not possible and could not even have been attempted except on one condition, namely that the tyranny of globalising discourses with their hierarchy and all their privileges of a theoretical *avant-garde* was eliminated.

Let us give the term *genealogy* to the union of erudite knowledge and local memories which allows us to establish a historical knowledge of struggles and to make use of this knowledge tactically today. This then will be a provisional definition of the genealogies which I have attempted to compile with you over the last few years.

You are well aware that this research activity, which one can thus call genealogical, has nothing at all to do with an opposition between the abstract unity of theory and the concrete multiplicity of facts. It has nothing at all to do with a disqualification of the speculative dimension which opposes to it, in the name of some kind of scientism, the rigour of well established knowledges. It is not therefore via an empiricism that the genealogical project unfolds, nor even via a positivism in the ordinary sense of that term. What it really does is to entertain the claims to attention of local, discontinuous, disqualified, illegitimate knowledges against the claims of a unitary body of theory which would filter, hierarchise, and order them in the name of some true knowledge and some arbitrary idea of what constitutes a science and its objects. Genealogies are therefore not positivistic returns to a more careful or exact form of science. They are precisely anti-sciences. Not that they vindicate a lyrical right to ignorance

or non-knowledge: it is not that they are concerned to deny knowledge or that they esteem the virtues of direct cognition and base their practice upon an immediate experience that escapes encapsulation in knowledge. It is not that with which we are concerned. We are concerned, rather, with the insurrection of knowledges that are opposed primarily not to the contents, methods, or concepts of a science, but to the effects of the centralising powers which are linked to the institution and functioning of an organised scientific discourse within a society such as ours. Nor does it basically matter all that much that this institutionalisation of scientific discourse is embodied in a university, or, more generally, in an educational apparatus, in a theoretical-commercial institution such as psychoanalysis or within the framework of reference that is provided by a political system such as Marxism; for it is really against the effects of the power of a discourse that is considered to be scientific that the genealogy must wage its struggle.

To be more precise, I would remind you how numerous have been those who for many years now, probably for more than half a century, have questioned whether Marxism was, or was not, a science. One might say that the same issue has been posed, and continues to be posed, in the case of psychoanalysis, or even worse, in that of the semiology of literary texts. But to all these demands of: "Is it or is it not a science?" the genealogies or the genealogists would reply: "If you really want to know, the fault lies in your very determination to make a science out of Marxism or psychoanalysis or this or that study." If we have any objection against Marxism, it lies in the fact that it could effectively be a science. In more detailed terms, I would say that even before we can know the extent to which something such as Marxism or psychoanalysis can be compared to a scientific practice in its everyday functioning, its rules of construction, its working concepts, that even before we can pose the question of a formal and structural analogy between Marxist or psychoanalytic discourse, it is surely necessary to question ourselves about our aspirations to the kind of power that is presumed to accompany such a science. It is surely the following kinds of question that would need to be posed: What types of knowledge do you want to disqualify in the very instant of your demand: "Is it a science?" Which speaking, discoursing subjects—which subjects of experience and knowledge—do you then want to "diminish" when you say: "I who conduct this discourse am conducting a scientific discourse, and I am a scientist?" Which theoretical-political *avant garde* do you want to enthrone in order to isolate it from all the discontinuous forms of knowledge that circulate about it? When I see you straining to establish the scientificity of Marxism I do not really think that you are demonstrating once and for all that Marxism has a rational structure and that therefore its propositions are the outcome of verifiable procedures; for me you are doing something altogether different, you are investing Marxist discourses and those who uphold them with the effects of a power which the West since Medieval times has attributed to science and has reserved for those engaged in scientific discourse.

By comparison, then, and in contrast to the various projects which aim to inscribe knowledges in the hierarchical order of power associated with science, a genealogy should be seen as a kind of attempt to emancipate historical knowledges from that subjection, to render them, that is, capable of opposition and of struggle against the coercion of a theoretical, unitary, formal, and scientific discourse. It is based on a reactivation of local knowledges—of minor knowledges, as Deleuze might call them—in opposition to the scientific hierarchisation of knowledges and the effects intrinsic to their power: this, then, is the project of these disordered and fragmentary genealogies. If we were to characterise it in two terms, then "archaeology" would be the

appropriate methodology of this analysis of local discursivities, and "genealogy" would be the tactics whereby, on the basis of the descriptions of these local discursivities, the subjected knowledges which were thus released would be brought into play.

So much can be said by way of establishing the nature of the project as a whole. I would have you consider all these fragments of research, all these discourses, which are simultaneously both superimposed and discontinuous, which I have continued obstinately to pursue for some four or five years now, as elements of these genealogies which have been composed—and by no means by myself alone—in the course of the last fifteen years. At this point, however, a problem arises, and a question: why not continue to pursue a theory which in its discontinuity is so attractive and plausible, albeit so little verifiable? Why not continue to settle upon some aspect of psychiatry or of the theory of sexuality, etc.? It is true, one could continue (and in a certain sense I shall try to do so) if it were not for a certain number of changes in the current situation. By this I mean that it could be that in the course of the last five, ten, or even fifteen years, things have assumed a different complexion—the contest could be said to present a different physiognomy. Is the relation of forces today still such as to allow these disinterred knowledges some kind of autonomous life? Can they be isolated by these means from every subjugating relationship? What force do they have taken in themselves? And, after all, is it not perhaps the case that these fragments of genealogies are no sooner brought to light, that the particular elements of the knowledge that one seeks to disinter are no sooner accredited and put into circulation, than they run the risk of re-codification, re-colonisation? In fact, those unitary discourses, which first disqualified and then ignored them when they made their appearance, are, it seems, quite ready now to annex them, to take them back within the fold of their own discourse, and to invest them with everything this implies in terms of their effects of knowledge and power. And if we want to protect these only lately liberated fragments, are we not in danger of ourselves constructing, with our own hands, that unitary discourse to which we are invited, perhaps to lure us into a trap, by those who say to us: "All this is fine, but where are you heading? What kind of unity are you after?" The temptation, up to a certain point, is to reply: "Well, we just go on, in a cumulative fashion; after all, the moment at which we risk colonisation has not yet arrived." One could even attempt to throw out a challenge: "Just try to colonize us then!" Or one might say, for example, "Has there been, from the time when anti-psychiatry or the genealogy of psychiatric institutions were launched—and it is now a good fifteen years ago—a single Marxist, or a single psychiatrist, who has gone over the same ground in his own terms and shown that these genealogies that we produced were false, inadequately elaborated, poorly articulated, and ill-founded?" In fact, as things stand in reality, these collected fragments of a genealogy remain as they have always been, surrounded by a prudent silence. At most, the only arguments that we have heard against them have been of the kind I believe were voiced by Monsieur Juquin:[1] "All this is all very well, but Soviet psychiatry nonetheless remains the foremost in the world." To which I would reply: "How right you are; Soviet psychiatry is indeed the foremost in the world and it is precisely that which one would hold against it."

The silence, or rather the prudence, with which the unitary theories avoid the genealogy of knowledges might therefore be a good reason to continue to pursue it. Then at least one could proceed to multiply the genealogical fragments in the form of so many traps, demands, challenges, what you will. But in the long run, it is probably over-optimistic, if we are thinking in terms of a contest—that of knowledge against the effects of the power of scientific discourse—to regard the silence of one's adversaries as indicative of a fear we have inspired in them. For perhaps the silence of the enemy—and here at the very least we have a methodological or tactical principle that it is always useful to bear in mind—can also be the index of our failure to produce any such fear at all. At all events, we must proceed just as if we had not alarmed them at all, in which case it will be no part of our concern to provide a solid and homogeneous theoretical terrain for all these dispersed genealogies, nor to descend upon them from on high with some kind of halo of theory that would unite them. Our task, on the contrary, will be to expose and specify the issue at stake in this opposition, this struggle, this insurrection of knowledges against the institutions and against effects of the knowledge and power that invests scientific discourse.

What is at stake in all these genealogies is the nature of this power which has surged into view in all its violence, aggression, and absurdity in the course of the last forty years, contemporaneously, that is, with the collapse of Fascism and the decline of Stalinism. What, we must ask, is this power—or rather, since that is to give a formulation to the question that invites the kind of theoretical coronation of the whole which I am so keen to avoid—what are these various contrivances of power, whose operations extend to such differing levels and sectors of society and are possessed of such manifold ramifications? What are their mechanisms, their effects, and their relations? [...]

* * * * *

NOTE

1.   A deputy of the French Communist Party.

CHAPTER 18

Discovering Discourses, Tackling Texts

IAN PARKER

* * * * *

What is a "discourse"? This chapter is concerned with the task of defining discourses. [...]

My main focus will be on the practical problems which confront a researcher attempting to carry out a discourse analysis. However, each practical problem raises broader issues about the nature of language, discourse, and texts. I will also argue, towards the end of the chapter, that discourse analytic research should go beyond seven necessary criteria for the identification of discourses, and consider the role of institutions, power, and ideology.

Discourse research strikes a critical distance from language, and one useful aspect of the approach is the reflexivity urged upon a researcher, and reader. When discourse analysts read texts they are continually putting what they read into quotation marks: "Why was this said, and not that? Why these words, and where do the connotations of the words fit with different ways of talking about the world?" I want to argue, however, that this reflexivity needs to be grounded if it is to have progressive effects, and that work in the post-structuralist tradition can ground discourse and reflection historically in a useful way. [...]

* * * * *

A number of issues arise from the history of discourse. Discourses do not simply describe the social world, but categorise it, they bring phenomena into sight. A strong form of the argument would be that discourses allow us to see things that are not "really" there, and that once an object has been elaborated in a discourse it is difficult *not* to refer to it as if it were real. Discourses provide frameworks for debating the value of one way of talking about reality over other ways. Types of person are also being referred to as the objects of the discourses. When we look at discourses in their historical context, it becomes clear that they are quite coherent, and that as they are elaborated by academics and in everyday life they become more carefully systematised. Discourse analysis *deliberately* systematises different ways of talking so we can understand them better. A study of discourse dynamics takes off from this to look at the tensions within discourses and the way they reproduce and transform the world.

A good working definition of a discourse should be that it is a *system of statements which constructs an object*. However, this definition needs to be supported by a number of conditions. In the main section of this chapter, then, I will set out seven criteria, the system of statements that should be used to identify *our* object, to enable us to engage with, and in, discourse analysis. [...]

SEVEN CRITERIA FOR DISTINGUISHING DISCOURSES

These seven criteria deal with different levels of discourse analysis. There is a degree of conceptual work that needs to go into the analysis before the material is touched, and then, as the analysis proceeds, it is necessary to step back a number of times to make sense of the statements that have been picked out. Each criterion raises questions about the theoretical framework the researcher is using. Along the way I will mark some "steps" in an analysis of discourse dynamics (and you will have to imagine quotation marks around the word "steps" from now on).

1. A Discourse Is Realised in Texts

First, though, where do we find discourses? It would be misleading to say that we ever find discourses as such. We actually find pieces of discourse. I want to open up the field of meanings to which discourse analysis could be applied beyond spoken interaction and written forms by saying that we find discourses at work in *texts*. Texts are delimited tissues of meaning reproduced in *any* form that can be given an interpretative gloss.

* * * * *

It is useful, as a first step, to consider all tissues of meaning as texts and to specify which texts will be studied. All of the world, when it has become a world understood by us and so given meaning by us, can be described as being textual. [...] Speech writing, non-verbal behaviour, Braille, Morse code, semaphore, runes, advertisements, fashion systems, stained glass, architecture, tarot cards, and bus tickets are all forms of text. In some cases we could imagine an "author" lying behind the text as source and arbiter of a true meaning. But the lessons to draw from this list are, first, that, as Barthes (1977) argued, there need not be

an author, and, second, that once we start to describe what texts mean we are elaborating meanings that go beyond individual intentions, discourses that are transindividual. The second step in a discourse analysis, then, should be a process of exploring the connotations, allusions, and implications which the texts evoke. [...] Discourse analysis, then, involves two preliminary steps:

1. Treating our objects of study as texts which are described, put into words; and
2. Exploring connotations through some sort of free association, which is best done with other people.

2. A Discourse Is about Objects

"Analysis" necessarily entails some degree of objectification, and in studies of discourse there are at least two layers of objectification. The first is the layer of "reality" that the discourse refers to. It is a commonplace in the sociology of knowledge (e.g., Berger and Luckmann, 1971) that language brings into being phenomena, and that the reference to something, the simple use of a noun, comes to give that object a reality. Discourses are the sets of meanings which constitute objects, and a discourse, then, is indeed a "representational practice" (Woolgar, 1988: 93). The representation of the object occurs as previous uses of the discourse and other related discourses are alluded to, and the object *as defined in the discourses* is referred to. Some local councils have had to close off sewer entrances to stop young children from going down to look for ninja turtles. The turtle discourse constitutes these beings as objects for children, and when the children refer to turtles they are referring to the objects of the discourse. They think, as most of us do when we talk about things, that they are talking about real objects in the world. Discourses are, according to one post-structuralist writer, "practices that systematically form the objects of which they speak" (Foucault, 1972: 49)

* * * * *

The second layer of reality, of objectification that a discourse sometimes refers to, is that of the discourse itself. One example is a badge given away at the Commonwealth Institute in London in 1988 with "Dialogue on Diarrhoea" printed around the top. It says "international newsletter" around the bottom, and these phrases frame a picture of a woman feeding an infant with a spoon. There were also huge posters around the cafeteria with the same message blazoned across them. At the first level of meaning, we have the object "diarrhoea," and the badge is a text which reproduces the object in particular ways: (i) we know that "diarrhoea" is, among other things, a medical description, and so we can identify a medical discourse; (ii) we assume that the woman feeding the infant is the mother, and so a familialist discourse also touches the text; and (iii) we understand the image and message as located in an appeal, located in a discourse of charity. The *second* layer of reality, then, is that of the "dialogue," and here there is a reflection in the text on a discourse, and the text says that there is another "object," which is the set of statements about diarrhoea. A discourse is about objects, and discourse analysis is about *discourses* as objects. This criterion, then, takes us into a third and a fourth step of analysis:

3. Asking what objects are referred to, and describing them (turtles, diseases, ghosts, etc.); and
4. Talking about the talk as if it were an object, a discourse.

3. A Discourse Contains Subjects

The object that a discourse refers to may have an independent reality outside discourse, but is given *another* reality by discourse. An example of such an object is the subject who speaks, writes, hears, or reads the texts discourses inhabit. I will stick with this rather abstract and dehumanising jargon a moment longer and say that a subject, a sense of self, is a location constructed within the expressive sphere which finds its voice through the cluster of attributes and responsibilities assigned to it as a variety of object. [...] A discourse makes available a space for particular types of self to step in. It addresses us in a particular way. When we discourse analyse a text, we need to ask in what ways, as Althusser (1971) put it when he was talking about the appeal of ideology, the discourse is hailing us, shouting "hey you there" and making us listen as a certain type of person.

It has been said that discourses are "ways of perceiving and articulating relationships" (Banton et al., 1985: 16). This is right, but it is more than that, for we cannot avoid the perceptions of ourselves and others that discourses invite. There are two ways in which this works, and discourse analysis both attends to and intensifies each of these. First, there is the relation between the addressor (which we should think of here as being the text rather than the author who may have originated it) and the addressee. When a badge says "Dialogue on Diarrhoea," who is it addressing? To put it crudely, and to employ an old social-psychological discourse, what "role" are we having to adopt to hear this message? (i) a medical discourse could draw us in as a carer, but merely to supplement the work of those who are medically qualified; (ii) the familialist discourse draws us in as protector (with different subject effects depending on the gender position we have in other discourses); and (iii) the charity discourse draws us in as benefactor, "millionaire philanthropist in stately Wayne Manor," say, and the "dialogue" is about listening, understanding, and giving.

The second way in which we are positioned as a subject in discourse flows from that last point about what we are expected to do when addressed. What rights do we have to speak in a discourse? The medical discourse, for example, is one in which we adopt the position of nonmedic, and, while we may use a medical vocabulary in some situations, there are others in which it is inappropriate. [...] This brings us to fifth and sixth steps in analysis:

5. Specifying what types of person are talked about in this discourse, some of which may already have been identified as objects (turtles, doctors, mothers, benefactors, etc.); and
6. Speculating about what they can say in the discourse, what you could say if you identified with them (what rights to speak in that way of speaking).

4. A Discourse Is a Coherent System of Meanings

The metaphors, analogies, and pictures discourses paint of a reality can be distilled into statements about that reality. It is only then that it becomes possible to say that a discourse is "any regulated system of statements" (Henriques et al., 1984: 105). This notion of discourse explicitly draws on Foucault's work. The statements in a discourse can be grouped, and given a certain coherence, insofar as they refer to the same topic. We have to employ culturally available understanding as to what constitutes a topic or theme, here making a virtue of the fact that there are different competing cultures which will give different slants on the discourse, ranging from those whom the discourse benefits (and who may not even want to recognise it as a discourse) to those whom it oppresses (who are already angry about that way of talking about things and categorising people in that way). [...]

* * * * *

To return to the problem of how to recognise one discourse when faced with a mass of text, how do we employ this notion of coherence? Take the example of Dan Quayle, [former] American vice-president, speaking at a Thanksgiving festival:

> I suppose three important things certainly come to my mind that we want to say thank you [for]. The first would be our family. Your family, my family—which is composed of an immediate family of a wife and three children, a larger family with grandparents and aunts and uncles. We all have our family, whichever that may be .... The family ... which goes back to the nucleus of civilisation. And the very beginnings of civilisation, the very beginnings of this country, goes back to the family. And time and time again, I'm often reminded, especially in this presidential campaign, of the importance of the family, and what a family means to this country. And so when you pay thanks I suppose the first thing that would come to mind would be to thank the Lord for the family.
>
> *(Guardian,* November 8, 1988)

Quayle attempts to define the "family," but what I want to draw attention to here is the way we have to bring our own sense of what "the family" is to this text in order to make it coherent, to string these repeated references to "the family" together so we recognise it as a discourse with an object (the family) and with subjects (mothers, fathers, children). In this case we are able to do this because there is such a strong "familialist discourse" in our culture: "society has been familiarized" (Barrett and McIntosh, 1982: 31). But we also have to bring a knowledge of discourses from outside, our awareness in this case that this is not the only way of talking about relationships, to bear on any example or fragment of discourse for it to become part of a coherent system in our analysis. A seventh and an eighth step can be taken here, in which we are:

7. Mapping a picture of the world this discourse presents (running in accordance with God's plans, through the operation of discourses, at the mercy of hidden conspiracies, etc.); and

8. Working out how a text using this discourse would deal with objections to the terminology [....]

5. A Discourse Refers to Other Discourses

Post-structuralists contend that thought is bound up with language, and that reflexivity is continually captured, and distorted, by language (Descombes, 1980). If they are right then reflexivity itself should be understood to be merely the employment of available discourses. At the very least, to take a weaker line on this, the *articulation* of our reflections on discourse must require the use of discourses. A critical reflection on a discourse will often involve the use of other discourses. [...]

Discourses embed, entail, and presuppose other discourses to the extent that the contradictions *within* a discourse open up questions about what other discourses are at work. For example, my children wanted to see the Mona Lisa when we went to Paris because it was painted by Leonardo, who is one of the ninja turtles. The turtle discourse, which constituted the painting as one type of object, can be understood as "just" a discourse by a competing discourse of artistic genius, one which captures most of the Louvre visitors in its vice-like grip as they admire the picture.

It is in this sense that it is right to argue that "[t]he systematic character of a discourse includes its systematic articulation with other discourses. In practice, discourses delimit what can be said, whilst providing the spaces—the concepts, metaphors, models, analogies—for making new statements within any specific discourse" (Henriques et al., 1984: 105–106). This point raises, in turn, two further issues.

First, metaphors and analogies are always available from other discourses, and the space this gives a speaker to find a voice from another discourse, and even within a discourse they oppose, is theoretically limitless. (It is not limitless in practice. I will take up this point when I discuss the role of institutions, power, and ideology in the next section of this chapter.)

Second, analysis is facilitated by identifying contradictions between different ways of describing something. The examples I have referred to so far include familialist discourse and Christian discourse, and these interrelate in various paradoxical ways with racist discourses. It is possible to imagine ways in which each of these can contradict the others. The metaphors of family used to describe the human race used alongside the currently popular liberal-humanist discourse could characterise Christian doctrine and racism as coterminous and equally dangerous (Barthes, 1973). Alternatively, some versions of liberation theology include conceptions of community which are suspicious of the nuclear family and are committed to anti-racism (Löwy, 1988). Then again, racist discourses which appeal to mysticism take forms hostile to the modern family and liberal Christianity (Trotsky, 1975 [1933]).

Now, I am *not* intending to imply that each of these discourses is discrete in practice. You may have to stretch your imagination to accept some of the combinations I suggested. At the moment, it could be argued that the discourses draw metaphors and institutional support from each other, and the process of distinguishing them is purely conceptual. Well, this is precisely the point, for we need to understand the *interrelationship,* the interrelationship between *different* discourses in an analysis. In the ninth and tenth steps of an analysis, then, we can start:

9. Setting contrasting ways of speaking, discourses, against each other and

looking at the different objects they constitute (brains, souls, epiphenomena, etc.); and

10. Identifying points where they overlap, where they constitute what look like the "same" objects in different ways (secretions of neural matter, immortal spiritual essences, rhetorical devices, etc.).

6. A Discourse Reflects on Its Own Way of Speaking

Not every text contains a reflection on the terms chosen, and not every speaker is self-conscious about the language they use. However, a condition which applies to each discourse taken as a whole is that it is possible to find instances where the terms chosen are commented upon. At these points, the discourse itself folds around and reflects on its own way of speaking. The devices employed to bring about this reflection range from the uneasy phrase "for the want of a better word" through disingenuous denials of a position being advocated—"don't get me wrong"—to full-blown agonising as to the moral implications of a world-view.

This raises the issue of "intuition" in the research, for the analyst needs to be able to step into the discourse at points to get a sense of what it feels like as a coherent whole. How are the contradictions in the discourse referred to, and how would another person or text employing this discourse refer to the contradictions within the discourse? When these questions are answered, other instances of a discourse can be identified, and it is important here not only to articulate instances of a discourse into a coherent pattern, but also to take it back where possible to the speaker, an interviewee perhaps, or to relate it to other texts.

A related point has been made by the authors of *Ideological Dilemmas* that it is necessary to attend to different layers of meaning. Working on the assumption that assertions in a discourse also pose an opposing position, by virtue of the "dilemmatic" nature of language and thought, they argue that we should attend to "hidden meanings": "discourse can contain its own negations, and these are part of its implicit, rather than explicit meaning" (Billig et al., 1988: 23). [...] What we can take from this is the idea that analysis should bring in other readers and listeners, and use their understanding of a discourse to bring out the implicit meanings, the views which are rarely voiced but which are part of that way of talking about things.

For the discourse analyst, the reflexivity of a discourse is found at points which will probably be found in other texts when it folds around to note its own nature as an argument or theory. Finding these points can be useful as a marker that the discourse analyst is actually picking up a discrete discourse. We can also think of this part of the research as proceeding through an eleventh and a twelfth step in which we are:

11. Referring to other texts to elaborate the discourse as it occurs, perhaps implicitly, and addresses different audiences (in children's books, advertisements, jokes, etc.) and;

12. Reflecting on the term used to describe the discourse, a matter which involves moral/political choices on the part of the analyst (describing discourses about "race" as "racist" discourses, for example).

7. A Discourse Is Historically Located

Discourses are not static. I have already pointed to the relationship between different discourses, and the ways in which discourses change and develop different layers and connections to other discourses through the process of reflection. [...] Discourses are located in time, in history, for the objects they refer to are objects constituted in the past by the discourse or related discourses. A discourse refers to past references to those objects.

For discourse analysts, the structure and force of particular discourses can only be described by showing other instances of that discourse, and explaining how it arose. The familialist discourse, for example, includes a history of the family and the way that history is reinterpreted to legitimate the Western nuclear family form. The way the metaphors of family are used are not only to describe other forms of life, but also often to reinforce the notion of the family as natural, as going back to the beginnings of civilisation. When we analyse the discourse of the family, we are disconnecting ourselves from that history. Similarly, discourse analysis of religion and racism switches back and forward from the elaboration of coherent systems of statements out of the texts it studies to look at what those discourses meant as they emerged, and so what the present allusions actually "refer" to.

It then becomes possible to use our knowledge of the historical weight of racist and religious discourses, say, to understand occasions when they combine. One reflection on the importance of language comes together with these themes in a statement made in 1986 by a supporter of a campaign in Southern California against the use of Spanish as a second language in the state. It ran: "If English was good enough for Jesus Christ, it's good enough for me." Of course, a reading of this phrase needs not only an understanding of what discourses there are and how they arose. It also calls for a study of the types of texts within which those discourses became dominant in the last fifty years or so. (My guess in this case would be that Hollywood films would be powerful texts in which these discourses fused and altered each other.) This prompts two further steps for the analyst in which she is:

13. Looking at how and where the discourses emerged; and
14. Describing how they have changed, and told a story, usually about how they refer to things which were always there to be discovered.

We have arrived, through these criteria and steps, at a sense of discourse as something dynamic and changing, but we need to go a little further to make the analysis politically useful.

THREE AUXILIARY CRITERIA

Although the seven criteria I have outlined are necessary and sufficient for marking out particular discourses, I want to draw attention to three more aspects of discourse that research *should* focus upon. The three further aspects of discourse are concerned with institutions, power, and ideology. I will go through each in turn, and indicate why each is important and why these final three should be worked through in an analysis.

8. Discourses Support Institutions

The most interesting discourses are those which are implicated in some way with the structure of institutions. The medical discourse, for example, exists in a variety of texts—medical journals and books, research reports, lectures, General Medical Council decisions, and popular medicine programmes, as well as the speech in every consultation with a doctor. In cases such as these, the employment of a discourse is also often a practice which reproduces the material basis of the institution. Feeling an abdomen, giving an injection, or cutting a body are *discursive practices*. For Foucault (1972), discourses and practices should be treated as if they were the same thing, and it is true both that material practices are always invested with meaning (they have the status of a text) and that speaking or writing is a "practice." Foucault's

(1977) work on discipline and power is concerned with the ways in which the physical organisation of space and bodies developed.

However, it is also possible, and more useful, to identify a distinction between physical order and meanings in his work, and it is helpful to hold onto a conceptual distinction between meanings, the expressive, and physical changes, the practical order (Harré, 1979). "Discursive practices," then, would be those that reproduce institutions, among other things. An academic Discourse Group could operate as an institution, for example, if it could validate or prevent certain styles of discourse analysis. Happily, at the moment discourse analysts reproduce a discourse about discourse which operates in a contradictory way in relation to institutions. Radical analysts could start by:

15. Identifying institutions which are reinforced when this or that discourse is used; and

16. Identifying institutions that are attacked or subverted when this or that discourse appears.

9. Discourses Reproduce Power Relations

We *should* talk about discourse and power in the same breath. Institutions, for example, are structured around and reproduce power relations. The giving and taking away of rights to speak in medical discourse and the powerlessness patients feel when in the grip of medical technology are examples of the intimate link between power and knowledge (Turner, 1987). [...]

Foucault (1980) and his followers popularised the couplet "power/knowledge," but the two terms are not the same thing. It is important to distinguish discourse from power. Discourses often do reproduce power relations, but this is a different claim from one which proposes that a criterion for recognising a discourse is that there is power. If this criterion

were to be adopted, we would fall into the trap of saying that "power is everywhere" and that, if power is everywhere, it would be both pointless to refer to it and politically fruitless to attack it (Poulantzas, 1978). There are three good reasons why we should not talk about discourse and power as *necessarily* entailing one another: (i) we would lose a sense of the relationship between power and resistance, lose the distinction between power as coercive and resistance as a refusal of dominant meanings; (ii) we would lose sight of the ways in which discourses that challenge power are often tangled in oppressive discourses, but are no less valuable to our understanding of relationships and possible future relationships for that; and (iii) it would be difficult, as researchers, to support the empowerment of those at the sharp end of dominant discourses and discursive practices. The further steps an analyst could take here include:

17. Looking at which categories of person gain and lose from the employment of the discourse; and

18. Looking at who would want to promote and who would want to dissolve the discourse.

10. Discourses Have Ideological Effects

Lying behind each of the objections to confusing discourse and power, of course, is a political position. This has to be even more explicitly marked when we talk about ideology. One deleterious effect of the rise of discourse analysis has been that the category of ideology virtually disappeared. In part, this has been a result of Foucault's (1980) insistence that the term ideology presupposes truth, and that we should instead, speak of "regimes of truth" in which one regime is no more correct than any other. It is right, I think, to say that discourse analysis need not necessarily be concerned with ideology, but it would be wrong to avoid it altogether. The use of the category of ideology has progressive political effects, and it is not necessary to buy the whole package of "mystification" and "false consciousness" that Foucauldians caricature (e.g., Henriques et al., 1984). However, if we are to hold onto the term "ideology," there are two theoretical traps we do need to avoid.

The first trap is to say that *all* discourses are ideological, and thus to follow in the steps of some sociologists who claim that "ideology" is equivalent to a belief system (e.g., Bell, 1965). As with the category of power, this position sees ideology everywhere and makes the term redundant. It neatly folds into the discourse which claims that the ideas of those who resist existing power relations are as ideological as those who support them, and it has similar political effects. This relativism either evacuates politics of any meaning (other than leaving things as they are) or confines politics to the sphere of individual moral choice. Both these positions are ideological positions. The second danger is that we try and distinguish between discourses which are ideological and those which tell the truth. For those who want to defend the use of the category of ideology, this is the simpler and more attractive trap.

The mistake being made in both these cases is that ideology is being treated as a thing, or is being evaluated according to its content. We should see ideology, rather, as a description of *relationships* and *effects,* and the category should be employed to describe relationships at a particular place and historical period. It could be, for example, that Christian discourse functions in an ideological way when it buttresses racism as a dominant world-view. But it is also *possible* that such a discourse can be empowering, and that even claims that it is a "subjugated knowledge," in Foucauldian jargon, could be well founded (Mudge, 1987). If discourse analysis is to be informed by descriptions of institutions, power, and ideology, then the history of discourses

becomes even more important. The final "radical steps," then, would involve:

19. Showing how a discourse connects with other discourses which sanction oppression; and
20. Showing how the discourses allow dominant groups to tell their narratives about the past in order to justify the present, and prevent those who use subjugated discourses from making history.

* * * * *

CONCLUSIONS AND REFLECTIONS

* * * * *

[...] We cannot escape systematising when we research into discourse. However, discourse analysis should bring about an understanding of the way things *were,* not the way things are. Another way of putting this is to say that when we strike a critical distance from a discourse we, in a sense, put it behind us, consign it to the past. If we adopt the three auxiliary criteria, we describe, educate, and change the way discourse is used. Discourse analysis should become a variety of action research, in which the internal system of any discourse and its relation to others is challenged. It alters, and so permits different spaces for manoeuvre and resistance.

* * * * *

A [...] final point relates to the politics of discourse analysis and to the importance of contradiction. Politics here is bound up with history, both in the sense that we have discourse now at this point in history (here we feel the weight of the past), and in the sense that politics and power are about the ability to push history in particular ways (there we construct a hope for the future). The difference between discourses is aggravated as one discourse is employed to supersede the other. When progress and change are notions built into contemporary political discourse, and things are changing so fast, it is hardly surprising that this dynamic should be reflected in our everyday experience of language. In political debate, the dynamics of resistance are of this discursive kind, and we have to have a sense of where discourses are coming from and where they are going to understand which are the progressive and which the reactionary ideas at different times and places. [...]

* * * * *

[...] The advantage of discourse analysis is that it reframes the object and allows us to treat it not as truth, but as one "truth" held in place by language and power. [...] The point we need to bear in mind is that in order to analyse institutions, power, and ideology, we need to stop the slide into relativism which much discourse theory, and post-structuralism generally, encourages. We need some sense of the real to anchor our understanding of the dynamics of discourse.

REFERENCES

Althusser, L. 1971. *Lenin and Philosophy and Other Essays.* London: New Left Books.

Banton, R., P. Clifford, S. Frosh, J. Lousada, and J. Rosenthall. 1985. *The Politics of Mental Health.* London: Macmillan.

Barrett, M., and M. McIntosh. 1982. *The Anti-Social Family.* London: Verso.

Barthes, R. 1973. *Mythologies.* London: Paladin.

_____. 1977. *Image-Music-Text.* London: Fontana.

Bell, D. 1965. *The End of Ideology: On the Exhaustion of Political Ideas in the Fifties.* New York: Free Press.

Berger, P.L., and T. Luckmann. 1971. *The Social Construction of Reality: A Treatise in the Sociology of Knowledge.* Harmondsworth: Penguin.

Billig, M., S. Condor, D. Edwards, M. Gane, D. Middleton, and A. Radley. 1988. *Ideological Dilemmas: A Social Psychology of Everyday Thinking.* London: Sage.

Descombes, V. 1980. *Modern French Philosophy.* Cambridge: Cambridge University Press.

Foucault, M. 1972. *The Archaeology of Knowledge.* London: Tavistock.

_____. 1977. *Discipline and Punish.* London: Allen Lane.

_____. 1980. *Power/Knowledge: Selected Interviews and Other Writings 1972–1977.* Hassocks: Harvester.

Harré, R. 1979. *Social Being: A Theory for Social Psychology.* Oxford: Basil Blackwell.

Henriques, J., W. Hollway, C. Urwin, C. Venn, and V. Walkerdine. 1984. *Changing the Subject: Psychology, Social Regulation and Subjectivity.* London: Methuen.

Löwy, M. 1988. "Marxism and Liberation Theology." *Notebooks for Study and Research/Cahiers d'Etude et de Recherche* 10.

Mudge, L.S. 1987. "Thinking in the Community of Faith: Toward an Ecclesial Hermeneutic." In *Formation and Reflection: The Promise of Practical Theology,* edited by L.S. Mudge and J.N. Poling. Philadelphia: Fortress Press.

Poulantzas, N. 1978. *State, Power, Socialism.* London: New Left Books.

Turner, B.S. 1987. *Medical Power and Social Knowledge.* London and New York: Sage.

Woolgar, S. 1988. *Science: The Very Idea.* London: Ellis Horwood/Tavistock.

CHAPTER 19

The Critical Analysis of Discourse

Lilie Chouliaraki and Norman Fairclough

THE "ACTIVE TEXT" AND THE HYBRID TEXT

In a paper entitled "The Active Text" Smith sets out to show how texts are active in organising the social relations that they mediate—in this case the relations of "public opinion" or "mass communications" (Smith, 1990). The conjuncture Smith's texts belong to is a dispute over the behaviour of police at a political demonstration in California in the 1960s—the texts are part of a public dialogue between a university professor and the Mayor of a city on the arrest of a young man in the course of a demonstration. The example is on the edge between mediated interaction and mediated quasi-interaction. The Professor witnesses police behaving violently towards people at a political demonstration and writes a letter to the Chief of Police with a copy to the Mayor (mediated interaction). He also "as an afterthought" sends a copy to the local "underground" press who publish it (mediated quasi-interaction). In response the Mayor distributes a statement which includes an extract from the Professor's letter and his own reply to the Professor. [...] Smith's analysis centres upon how the Mayor's reply revises the Professor's account of the events he witnessed so as to construct everything that happened as in accordance with what Smith calls a "mandated course of action," hence

legitimate policing. The "mandated course of action" is a sequence of steps which define proper police procedure: there is (the suspicion of) an offence; the police take action to make an arrest; if they are successful, the individual is charged; the individual is taken to court and, if found guilty, convicted.

The use of force by the police is legitimate provided it is tied to the mandated course of action. The Mayor's reply "rewrites" the Professor's account so that this appears to be the case in each incident. For instance, the incident described as follows in the Professor's letter:

> I was standing just below the corner of Haste and Telegraph opposite Cody's and I saw a boy, 16 or 17 years old, walking up Haste and past two policeman.
>
> Suddenly a young policeman in his early twenties, with a cigar he had just lit in his mouth, grabbed this young man, rudely spun him around, pinned him against his patrol car, tore at his clothes and pockets as though searching for something, without so much as saying one word of explanation. Then he pushed him roughly up the street yelling at him to get moving.

is rewritten in the Mayor's reply as:

You referred to four incidents which you were able to at least partially observe. The first concerned a young man who was frisked and who appeared to be then released. In fact this man was a juvenile who was arrested and charged with being a minor in possession of alcoholic beverages. He pleaded guilty and the court suspended judgement.

There are a number of interesting contrasts [....] The modality of the Professor's account is categorical: it is a series of unqualified statements. The modality of the statements in the Mayor's reply which refer to the "incident" is more complex. A contrast is set up with what "appeared" to happen and what "in fact" happened. And referring to the "incidents" the Professor described in terms of his "ability" to ("partially") observe them implies his "inability" to observe other "parts."

The Professor's account is full of actions ("material" processes) in which the policeman is the agent and the "boy" the patient, whereas actions are in the "agentless" passive voice in the Mayor's reply (for example, *a young man who was frisked*) and no policeman figures as an agent. In contrast to the Professor's action-based account, the Mayor's is partly about classifications, about the (official) category the "young man" belonged to, using attributes together with "relational" processes: *this man was a juvenile ... charged with being a minor.* Finally, the vocabulary of the Mayor's letter serves to reclassify what happened as part of normal police procedure—identifying what happened in an official way as an "incident," reclassifying the "boy" (a term which resonates with the Professor's construction of a case of wanton violence) as a "young man" who is moreover in official terms a "juvenile" and "minor," and introducing an institutional vocabulary of action which assimilates the event to the mandated course of action

(including "stages" from it which do not figure in the professor's account): *frisked, released, arrested, charged, pleaded (guilty).* [...]

Smith's argument is that the mandated course of action involves a particular mode of interpretation, what Garfinkel called the "documentary method interpretation": "treating actual appearances as 'the document of,' as 'pointing to,' as 'standing on behalf of' a presupposed underlying pattern" (Garfinkel, 1967: 78), which remains inexplicit in the process of reading: the mandated course of action as part of an official discourse of policing is taken for granted—actually in both letters, as Smith argues—as an interpretative principle but not made textually explicit:

Not only is the underlying pattern derived from its individual documentary evidences, but the individual documentary evidences, in their turn, are interpreted on the basis of "what is known" about the underlying pattern. Each is used to elaborate the other. (Garfinkel, 1967: 78)

There is a general point here: one way in which interactions may be shaped by system discourses is through implicit interpretative principles which shape how people contribute and interpret the contributions of others.

Smith's analysis effectively shows the textually mediated character of social life in this instance, but we want to suggest that the analysis can be developed and enhanced by drawing upon CDA [Critical Discourse Analysis]. We approach this argument by looking at a rather striking feature of the Professor's letter which Smith's analysis does not refer to: its hybridity.

The extract from the Professor's letter reproduced above consists of two paragraphs. [...]

* * * * *

[...] The two paragraphs differ in the sort of detail they focus: in the first it is place, position, number; in the second it is the manner in which actions were performed. [...]

The hybridity of the Professor's letter is illustrated by the different things that are going on in these paragraphs. [...] Let us say that these linguistic differences "realise" different "genres" (a genre is a type of language used in the performance of a particular social practice). We might call the first paragraph an example of the genre of witness accounts. The label we use is not so important (there is no closed "list" of genres or discourses, and there are relatively few that have stable names either for analysts or for participants); the important point is that it is recognisable as the type of language used in domains like the law for giving "objective," "factual" accounts of first-hand experiences which can be taken as evidence. The second paragraph, by contrast, is an example of what we might call the genre of story-telling. It is story-telling with a roughly "literary" quality which comes from the manifest ways in which it is worked up as a story, the effort that has manifestly been put into the texture of the text to make it work as a story. So one contrast here is between a broadly "factual" discourse in paragraph 1 and a broadly "fictional" discourse in paragraph 2.

* * * * *

Where is this analysis leading? What we are trying to establish is that the Professor's letter is considerably more hybrid than Smith's analysis suggests, and that indeed his strategy in writing the letter seems to be to assemble and combine a substantial variety of different genres and discourses. In short, that the active text is also a hybrid text, and that understanding its hybridity is the key to understanding its activeness. [...]

* * * * *

What we are arguing is that just as in sociological analysis it is necessary to envisage a "middle-range" level of social structuring between the overall structure of a society and social action which applies to specific social "fields" and their interconnections (Bourdieu, 1984) so in semiotic analysis it is necessary to recognise a social structuring of the semiotic into what we call (adapting Foucault's term—Foucault, 1971) orders of discourse and their interconnections. An order of discourse is the socially ordered *set* of genres and discourses associated with a particular social field, characterised in terms of the shifting boundaries and flows between them. [...] In this case there is a conjuncture at the intersection of the political and legal fields which includes an encounter between the practices of what is on the one hand ambivalently an even-handed exercise of citizenship and the conduct of oppositional politics, and on the other hand official reaction to public protest. The Professor's letter purports to be the letter of a concerned citizen to relevant authorities which appeared in the press as an "afterthought," but the hybridity we have identified is more consistent with it being part of a political campaign taking on the appearance of a gesture of civic concern. The hybridity of the letter shows that the network of orders of discourse is not a simple positioning device but a resource in interaction which can be drawn upon more or less creatively in ways which themselves depend on positioning within that network—this example shows for instance that letters to the press give more space for creative rearticulation of the resource than letters from officials. [...]

Analysis of any discourse in contemporary societies with their complex intersections of different forms and types of discourse should include an "interdiscursive" analysis of how different discursive types are mixed together (Fairclough, 1992). The claim is that such hybridity is an irreducible characteristic of complex modern discourse, and that the concepts of "order of discourse" and "interdiscursivity" constitute a powerful resource for researching what Smith calls the textually mediated character of contemporary social life [....] Moreover, analysis of all forms and types of discourse should include a "structural" dimension as well as an interactional dimension—the irreducible hybridity of modern communicative interaction is a matter of it being inevitably and always framed by and oriented to (structured by, but capable of structuring) the social structuring of the semiotic as a network of orders of discourse. The structural dimension attends to how interaction is constrained by the network of orders of discourse, while the interactional dimension attends to how that network is interactionally worked and potentially restructured through a rearticulation of resources (and so the interactional dimension feeds back into the structural dimension).

CRITICAL DISCOURSE ANALYSIS: A FRAMEWORK

Our aim in this section is to sketch out a framework for critical discourse analysis [....]

This framework gives a view of what is involved in actually doing a critical discourse analysis. The main headings can be seen as stages in CDA, though they are not necessarily all carried out in the order in which they are listed. [...]

The framework we have summarised below is modelled on Bhaskar's "explanatory critique" [1986].

1. A problem (activity, reflexivity).
2. Obstacles to its being tackled:
   (a) analysis of the conjuncture;
   (b) analysis of the practice re: its discourse moment:
       (i) relevant practice(s)?
       (ii) relation of discourse to other moments?
   • discourse as part of the activity
   • discourse and reflexivity;
   (c) analysis of the discourse:
       (i) structural analysis: the order of discourse
       (ii) interactional analysis
           • interdiscursive analysis
           • linguistic and semiotic analysis
3. Function of the problem in the practice.
4. Possible ways past the obstacles.
5. Reflection on the analysis.

We briefly comment on each stage in turn.

Problem

CDA begins from some perception of a discourse-related problem in some part of social life. Problems may be in the activities of a social practice—in the social practice per se, so to speak—or in the reflexive construction of a social practice. The former may involve [...] the ideational, interpersonal, and/or textual functions of discourse, whereas the latter are ideational problems, problems of representations, and miscognition. The former are needs-based—they relate to discursive facets of unmet needs of one sort or another. Illustrations of the two types of problem in the Smith example might be first, the failure of this sort of encounter as a public sphere, i.e., its typical failure to achieve real dialogue between the participants, and second, the tendency in official circles to represent everything officials (for example, police) do as in line with proper procedures. Although these problems are stated in a general way, they can be addressed with reference to detailed features of the discourse.

Obstacles to Its Being Tackled

We comment first on the three sorts of analysis subsumed under this heading, and then come back to a discussion of how they can jointly specify the obstacles to a problem being tackled. The first type of analysis here is *analysis of the conjuncture*—i.e., a specification of the configuration of practices which the discourse in focus is located within. The focus here is on the configuration of practices associated with specific occasioned social goings-on. Such a conjuncture represents a particular path through the network of social practices which constitutes the social structure. Conjunctures can be more or less complex in terms of the number and range of practices they link together, more or less extended in time and in social space. Smith does not contextualise the texts enough to give a full picture of the conjuncture, but one would think that the more immediate conjuncture the texts are located within is the public contention over police behaviour. As this implies, conjunctures can be identified at different levels of specificity—for instance, we might say that the contention over police behaviour is located within the more extended conjuncture of political protest in the 1960s—and there is no clear cut-off between conjuncture and structure. These are not matters for discourse analysts to decide—the point here is to have at least a broad sense of the overall frame of social practice which the discourse in focus is located within. One aspect of the analysis of more immediate conjunctures is to locate the discourse in focus in real time in a way which links it to its circumstances and processes of production and its circumstances and processes of consumption, which brings the question of how the discourse is interpreted (and the diversity of interpretations) into the analysis.

The second type of analysis here is *analysis of the particular practice or practices* which the discourse in focus is a moment of, with particular regard to the dialectic between discourse and other moments. What is at issue may be either discourse as part of the activity, or discourse in the reflexive construction of the

practice, or both. We can identify four main moments of a social practice: material activity (specifically non-semiotic, in that semiosis also has a material aspect, for example, voice or marks on paper); social relations and processes (social relations, power, institutions); mental phenomena (beliefs, values, desires); and discourse. We have arrived at just four moments by combining three of those distinguished by Harvey (1996) under "social relations and processes" (Harvey's categories are listed in the brackets). The objective here is to specify relationships between discourse and these other moments—how much of a part and what sort of a part discourse plays in the practice (for instance, some practices, for example, in education, consist of little but discourse, while in others, for example, some parts of industry, discourse may be relatively marginal), and what relations of internalisation there are between moments. In the case of the exchange of letters analysed by Smith, for example, one wants to know what went on "behind" the letters, how they came to be written, who was involved, what else was done on either side—the example illustrates how difficult it can sometimes be to "reconstruct" the practice some discourse is located within and to get a proper sense of how the discourse figures in the practice, if all one has is (in this case) the letters.

This is why discourse analytical research should be seen as only one aspect of research into social practices working together with other social scientific methods, particularly ethnography [....] The combination can be useful for both. Ethnography requires the systematic presence of the researcher in the context of the practice under study, usually for an extended period of time (fieldwork), and can therefore establish precisely the sort of knowledge that CDA often extrapolates from text, that is, knowledge about the different moments of a social practice: its material aspects (for example, locational arrangements in space), its social relationships and processes, as well as the beliefs, values, and desires of its participants. Depending on the research design and its methods (field notes, video and audio recordings, interviews, document selection, archive research, etc.), ethnography can illuminate multiple aspects of a practice, both synchronically (at the time of the fieldwork) and historically. It also provides an invaluable context for assessing the articulatory process in the practice and the specific function of discourse in it (see Bourne, 1992; Chouliaraki, 1995; Wodak, 1996; Iedema, 1997). Ethnography can benefit from CDA in the direction of reflexivity: data material should not be regarded as faithful descriptions of the external world but as themselves discursive formations that are assembled together to construct a particular perspective on the social world; neither do participants' accounts transparently reflect the social process in which they are embedded. In other words, there is a need to critically reflect upon and analyse both the ethnographer's and the informant's discursive practices (Clifford, 1986).

But the general objective here is to have as clear a sense as possible of how the discourse works in relation to "other things." In terms of internalisation, it is noteworthy that people quite normally "read off" other moments of social practice—social relations, power, beliefs, values, etc.—from written texts like letters (given that these may be all they have to go on). One issue [...] is the question of "empty words": a concern in this part of the analysis in specifying relations of internalisation between discourse and other moments is to identify cases where internalisation is absent— where the discourse remains external to other moments. Discourse has social force and effect not inherently, but to the extent that it comes to be integrated within practices.

Problem-oriented explanatory critique inevitably raises questions about power.

This is partly a matter of specifying relations between the social and discourse moments of the social practice. In the case of the Smith texts, for instance, the monological official discourse of the Mayor's letter is a discourse which has internalised the power relations between officials and citizens, rulers and ruled, and whose internal features are shaped by these power relations. In a reasonable sense discourse is power in this case—writing this letter is enacting power. Looking at such relations of domination historically, we can say that power has tended on balance to migrate from material activity to discourse—it is still internalised in both, but its internalisation in discourse has become more pervasive. One consequence is that discourse more pervasively gives rise to questions of power (as well as other questions, such as questions of belief or desire). The Professor's letter reminds us that power relations are relations of struggle—that power is not simply exercised, it is also fought over, and fought over in discourse, and that the interdiscursive articulation of different genres and discourses is (amongst other things) a strategy of power struggle—a way in which power struggle is internalised in discourse (it is quite differently internalized in material activities). Power and power struggle also arise in the analysis of the conjuncture, for the question of which practices are to be brought together, and how, is itself a potential focus of power struggle. Questions of power link with questions of ideology, which are best treated in terms of relations between the discourse moments of different practices and different orders of discourse. For instance, what Smith calls the "mandated course of action" is a discourse that constructs the practice of policing, which is generated within practices of police work but extended, as the example illustrates, into other practices where it functions ideologically.

The *analysis of discourse* proper is simultaneously oriented to structure and to interaction—to the social resource (orders of discourse) which enables and constrains interaction, and to the way that resource is interactively worked, i.e., to interdiscourse, and its realisation in language and other semiotics. (For a detailed explanation of analysis of discourse, see Fairclough, 1992, 1995.) Realisation itself involves the same double orientation—to semiotic systems, and to how selections from the potential of semiotic systems are worked in textual processes. From the structural perspective, the first concern is to locate the discourse in its relation to the network of orders of discourse, to specify how the discourse draws selectively upon the potential of that network, i.e., which genres, discourses, and voices, from which orders of discourse, it articulates together. (We use the term "genre" for the sort of language (and other semiosis) tied to a particular social activity, such as interview; "discourse" for the sort of language used to construct some aspect of reality from a particular perspective, for example, the liberal discourse of politics; and "voice" for the sort of language used by a particular category of people and closely linked to their identity, for example, the medical voice, i.e., the voice of doctors and other medical professionals.) The assumption here is that the relationship between the discourse and the social network of orders of discourse depends upon the nature of the social practice and conjuncture of social practices it is located within, and on how it figures within them. [...] From the perspective of interaction, the concern is with how the discourse works the resource—how the genres and discourses which are drawn upon are worked together in the textual process of the discourse, and what articulatory work, is done in the text. [...]

* * * * *

How then do these three types of analysis specify the obstacles to a problem being tackled? Let us take as an example the failure of this exchange of letters (and of such exchanges of letters) as a public sphere. The objective here is to understand structural obstacles to change, so at this point we are looking at the particular example as "typical." That of course would need to be established—in a real project using CDA, the analysis should be based on a substantial body of material which can be seen as representing a particular domain of practice (Wodak, 1996; and see the criticisms in Stubbs, 1997). What constitutes a successful public sphere? The issue is a complex one, but for present purposes we cut through its complexity to propose key properties of a successful public sphere: that it provides a place and a practice in which people as citizens (i.e., outside government and other institutional systems) can address together (maybe with those in government, etc.) issues of social and political concern in a way that gives access to all those with an interest, constitutes real dialogue between those involved, and leads to action (see Habermas, 1989; Calhoun, 1995; Fairclough, 1999). The notion of "real dialogue" is complex and contentious, but we might say that it involves first, a symmetry between participants in their capacity to contribute to discussion, second, a freedom for all to represent their particular perspectives, and third, a simultaneous orientation to alliance and to developing a new shared voice on the issue in question. A question that arises about the conjuncture is whether practices are so ordered together that dialogue can indeed lead to action: in most cases they are not, i.e., this sort of public exchange "leads nowhere," there are no channels to turn it into policy changes. So in that sense the nature of the conjuncture can be an obstacle. So too can the relationship between discourse and other moments of the social practice—for instance, it is questionable in such exchanges how sincere the discourse is, what its relationship is to beliefs and values, and whether the letters are strategically (and even cynically) designed to achieve certain outcomes rather than being properly communicative (Habermas, 1984). A successful public sphere depends upon sincere engagement. Furthermore, the selection and articulation of genres and discourses can also be an obstacle—manifestly, for example, the monological translation of the Professor's letter into official discourse by the Mayor, a strategy which excludes the emergence of any new, shared voice.

Function of the Problem in the Practice

The issue here is to look at whether and how the problematic aspect of the discourse which is in focus has a particular function within the practice. This may seem to be just focusing one aspect of the analysis above of obstacles to tackling the problem, but in fact in Bhaskar's account of explanatory critique this stage marks the shift from "is" to "ought"—the shift from explanation of what it is about a practice that leads to a problem, to evaluation of the practice in terms of its problematic results. Of course in actual analysis it may be difficult to keep the two rigidly apart, but the distinction is clear nevertheless. In the case of the Mayor's letter, for instance, it is one thing to explain its construction of everything the police do as in accordance with procedure as a (typical) consequence of the network of practices and reflexive self-constructions which constitute official life in local government, but it is another thing to develop a critique of local government on the lines that it is the flawed character of local government that causes such problematic constructions—that such constructions have, for instance, an ideological function in local government which makes them indispensable, that therefore the only way to overcome the problem is to change the practices.

Possible Ways Past the Obstacles

This is also part of the shift from "is" to "ought"—if the practices are flawed, then we ought to change them. The objective here is to discern possible resources for changing things in the way they currently are. [...] Whereas the previous two stages entail a focus on the relational logic of social scientific analysis, this stage involves a shift to the dialectical logic. The focus in the previous two stages was on how structural relations explain ("obstacles") and are responsible for ("functions") the problem at issue. It involves seeing the example as typical, and focusing upon its reproductive effects. For this stage by contrast, it is important that the data should fully represent the full range of variation within the practice in focus—in this case, the full range of variation in public debates and contestations between citizens and/or social movements and officialdom. The focus here is not so much reproduced structures but diversity of conjunctures, the range of what people can do in given structural conditions. This focus does still lead back to structures, but to an aspect of structures which does not get foregrounded in a relational analysis—their incompleteness, their contradictoriness, their gaps, i.e., the properties which keep systems open and make them amenable to transformative action. These properties manifest themselves in the variability of a practice, but also in tensions and contradictions within particular cases. Let us take an example from the Mayor's letter.

The third incident to which you referred involved another woman. To the best of my knowledge, you are referring to a young woman who was attempting to interfere with the arrest of a man who had attacked a police officer, punching him and ripping the officer's holster in a strenuous effort to seize his gun. Throughout the struggle involving this man and the police officer, this woman kept screaming and attempting to grab the man away from the officers. She was on the ground next to him when he was subdued but she was, to the best of my investigation, never struck with a baton or hit with a fist ....

There is a tension in the Mayor's letter around modality, i.e., around the Mayor's commitment to the claims he is making. Many are made as simple matters of fact without modal qualification, whereas others are modally qualified. In this extract, there is a mixture of the two: two claims are modally qualified (with *to the best of my knowledge* and *to the best of my investigation*—the latter seems to be a blend of the former and something like *on the evidence of my investigation*), the others are made as matters of fact. The issue is, whose voice is this? The Mayor has to speak for himself—he is putting his authority behind claims about what happened, and he has to "own" those claims, otherwise he will be damagingly seen as insincere. Yet they are not his claims—he has no personal evidence of what happened. Presumably they are claims made to the Mayor by the police, but although the Mayor's letter refers throughout to his "investigation," these claims are never attributed to anyone. Mostly they are made as the Mayor's own claims, but certain (perhaps the more contentious?) are modally qualified in a way which implies they belong elsewhere without saying where. The contradiction here is between the Mayor as a public individual who engages in public debate, and the Mayor as one link in an organisational chain. One might see the nature of such organisations as a reason why such exchanges fail as public spheres—the Mayor simulates being available for real dialogue, but the nature of the organisation means that he is not.

Reflexion on the Analysis

Critical social research should be reflexive, so part of any analysis should be a reflexion on the position from which it is carried out. One issue here [...] is the relationship between the theoretical practice of the analyst and the practical practices which are analysed. Our reanalysis of the Smith texts has been purely an exercise in theoretical practice, i.e., we have obviously not had contact with the people concerned, used their perspectives to help determine what was problematic, nor produced an analysis designed in terms of its possible uptake within the practice. We recognise these as limitations. Moreover, we are coming from a particular position within the theoretical field, a particular knowledge interest, entailing a perspective [...] which [...] is oriented to problems, to power, to ideology, and so forth. There are of course other things to say about any discourse which are likely to arise from various other perspectives. We do not see the specificity of our perspective as a negative one-sidedness (as Toolan, 1997, for instance, suggests)—providing that specificity is made clear, and providing that other perspectives are recognised, focusing on problems, power, and so forth is not a problem.

REFERENCES

Bhaskar, R. 1986. *Scientific Realism and Human Emancipation.* London: Verso.

Bourdieu, P. 1984. *Distinction: A Social Critique of the Judgement of Taste.* London: Routledge.

Bourne, J. 1992. Unpublished Ph.D. thesis, University of Southampton.

Calhoun, C. 1995. *Critical Social Theory.* London: Blackwell.

Chouliaraki, L. 1995. "Regulation and Heteroglossia in One Institutional Context: The Case of 'Progressivist' English Classroom." Unpublished Ph.D. thesis. University of Lancaster.

Clifford, J. 1986. "Introduction: Partial Truths." In *Writing Culture: The Poetics and Politics of Ethnography*, edited by J. Clifford and G. Marcus. Berkeley: University of California Press.

Fairclough, N. 1992. *Discourse and Social Change*. Cambridge: Polity Press.

_____. 1995b. *Critical Discourse Analysis: The Critical Study of Language*. London: Longman.

_____. 1999. "Democracy and the Public Sphere in Critical Research on Discourse." In *Challenges in a Changing World*, edited by R. Wodak et al. Vienna: Passagen.

Foucault, M. 1971. *L'ordre du discours*. Paris: Gallimard.

Garfinkel, H. 1967. *Studies in Ethnomethodology*. Englewood Cliffs: Prentice-Hall.

Habermas, J. 1979. *Communication and the Evolution of Society*. Boston: Beacon Press.

_____. 1984. *The Theory of Communicative Action, vol. 2: Reason and the Rationalization of Society*. London: Heinemann.

_____. 1989. *The Structural Transformation of the Public Sphere*. Cambridge: Polity Press.

Harvey, D. 1996. *Justice, Nature and the Geography of Difference*. London: Blackwell.

Iedema, R. 1997. "The Language of Administration: Organizing Human Activity in Formal Institutions." In *Genre and Institutions: Social Processes in the Workplace and School*, edited by F. Christie and J.R. Martin. London: Cassell.

Smith, D. 1990. *Texts, Facts and Femininity: Exploring Relations of Ruling*. London: Routledge.

Stubbs, M. 1997. "Whorf's Children: Critical Comments on CDA." In *Evolving Models of Language*, edited by A. Ryan and A. Wray. Papers from the 1996 Annual Meeting of BAAL. Milton Keynes: Multilingual Matters.

Toolan, M. 1997. "What Is Critical Discourse Analysis and Why Are People Saying Such Terrible Things about It?" *Language and Literature* 6.

Wodak, R. 1996. *Disorders of Discourse*. London: Longman.

Rethinking Part 2C: Subverting Dominant Discourses: Critical Discourse Analysis

CRITICAL THINKING QUESTIONS

Chapter 16: Postmodernism and Deconstructionism

1. What are the implications of Derrida's critique of logocentrism for how we read texts?
2. How can a deconstruction of the logics of presence, intentionality, reason, and causality that organize a text subvert its authority?
3. Norman Denzin maintains that "as students of the postmodern moment, we have only texts and stories people tell us" (p. 241). Do you agree, or has Denzin left some important elements out of the picture?

Chapter 17: Two Lectures: Lecture One: January 7, 1976

1. Michel Foucault viewed genealogy as an insurrection of subordinated knowledges, waging struggle against the power of a unitary discourse that is considered to be scientific. What are the strengths and possible weaknesses of this radical-pluralist strategy for critical inquiry?
2. Writing in the mid-1970s, Foucault observed the emergence, in the previous 15 years, of criticism of an "essentially local character," not dependent on validation by established regimes of thought. He described this criticism as an autonomous, non-centralized kind of theoretical production (p. 247). How does genealogy contribute to this sort of theoretical production?
3. The claim that knowledge is *scientific* entails an aspiration to a kind of power that is characteristic of modernity. As Foucault puts it, "What types of knowledge do you want to disqualify in the very instant of your demand: 'Is it a science'?" (p. 250). Are there certain types of knowledge—e.g., biological-determinist theories of racial difference—that a critical, reflexive science of the social might very well disqualify, or should all knowledges have equal footing in the postmodern marketplace of ideas that Foucault seems to have in mind?

Chapter 18: Discovering Discourses, Tackling Texts

1. A discourse addresses us in a particular way that creates a space for a certain type of person or subject. What are the implications of this "subjectification" for critical analysis of discourse?
2. Why is it important that critical analysis locate discourses in history?
3. Ian Parker argues that a critical discourse analysis should "bring about an understanding of the way things *were*, not the way things *are*" (p. 260). What is he getting at here?

Chapter 19: The Critical Analysis of Discourse

1. Chouliaraki and Fairclough suggest that the starting point for critical discourse analysis should be a discourse-related problem in some aspect of social life. How does this compare to the starting point of institutional ethnography, i.e., the problematization of the everyday world?

2. Why is an analysis of the conjuncture—of the configuration of practices in which the discourse is located—crucial in a critical discourse analysis?

3. In attempting to discern viable strategies for removing obstacles to change, Chouliaraki and Fairclough recommend a shift to dialectical logic—considering the incompleteness, gaps, and contradictions in discursive and other structures that keep systems open to transformative action. How does this approach compare with our earlier look at dialectical social analysis?

GLOSSARY TERMS

Deconstruction: An interrogation of a text that takes apart and exposes the assumptions on which it is based, often revealing hidden or marginalized meanings and demonstrating that meaning is not singular or fixed but rather multiple and contested.

Discourse: A system of meaning that provides a way of interpreting or understanding a set of objects in the world. For post-structuralists a discourse does more than provide an interpretive frame; it brings objects into being. Discourses are organized, maintained, and resisted by talk and action.

Explanatory critique: A method that first identifies a problem in some aspect of social life (which may involve misrepresentation or an unmet need), next identifies obstacles to resolving the problem, then considers what function is served by the problem (misrepresentation or unmet need) in maintaining extant social arrangements, and finally explores possible ways of removing the obstacles. One way to make a discourse analysis *critical* is to formulate it in terms of an explanatory critique.

Genealogy: A "history of the present" in which the union of scholarly knowledge and local memories "allows us to establish a historical knowledge of struggles and to make use of this knowledge tactically today" (Foucault, p. 249). As a form of critical discourse analysis, genealogy strives to "emancipate historical knowledges" as discourses "capable of opposition and of struggle against the coercion of a theoretical, unitary, formal, and scientific discourse" (p. 250).

Hybrid text: The condition in which a given text combines multiple discourses and genres (e.g., "fictional" and "factual"). Chouliaraki and Fairclough submit that such hybridity is "an irreducible characteristic of complex modern discourse" (p. 264).

Intertextuality: The inter-relations and references that cut across texts. "Discourses embed, entail and presuppose other discourses" (Parker, p. 256), and the resulting tensions and contradictions open spaces for making new statements.

They also oblige the discourse analyst to consider, as an aspect of the examination of a given discourse, its interrelationships with other discourses.

Logocentrism: The assumption, prevalent in Western thought, that individuals have direct access to their thoughts through language, so that they control the meaning of what they say. This assumption is rejected by post-structuralism.

Order of discourse: The socially ordered set of discourses and genres associated with a particular social field.

Post-structuralism: A loose grouping of analytical approaches that developed from structuralist theories of language and that view language or discourse as constitutive of subjectivity, social organization, and the world. Post-structural modes of critical discourse analysis include deconstruction and genealogy.

Relativism: An ontological stance that asserts the impossibility of ever knowing the true nature of the world, or of progressively coming closer to a veridical understanding. Relativism holds that there is in principle no way of privileging one account of reality over another. It is celebrated by post-structuralists, but is a concern for critical realists, who seek solid foundations for political practice.

Subject positions: The particular types of positions that are offered by discourse and that people (subjects) take up, or resist, as they participate in discourse. The positioning of subjects within discourse also can delimit their rights to speak and way of speaking; thus power is inscribed in subject positions.

Subjugated knowledges: Knowledges that have been disqualified as inadequate or insufficiently rationalized; "naïve" knowledges subordinated beneath scientific knowledge on the modern epistemic hierarchy.

FURTHER READING

Fairclough, Norman. 2001. *Language and Power,* 2nd ed. Don Mills: Longman.
A quite accessible introduction to "critical language study," a broad field within which critical discourse analysis occupies a space.

Kendall, Gavin, and Gary Wickham. 1999. *Using Foucault's Methods*. London: Sage.
A user-friendly introduction to genealogy and archaeology, replete with various exercises for students.

Meadmore, Daphne, Caroline Hatcher, and Erica McWilliam. 2000. "Getting Tense about Genealogy." *International Journal of Qualitative Studies in Education* 13(5): 463–476
The authors relate their respective experiences in attempting to carry out genealogical research in the field of education.

Søndergaard, Dorte Marie. 2002. "Poststructuralist Approaches to Empirical Analysis." *International Journal of Qualitative Studies in Education* 15(2): 187–204.
A useful discussion that highlights the value of deconstruction as an approach to discourse analysis.

Tamboukou, Maria. 1999. "Writing Genealogies: An Exploration of Foucault's Strategies for Doing Research." *Discourse: Studies in the Cultural Politics of Education* 20(2): 201–217.

This essay provides a reflective overview of Foucault's work from the 1970s and early 1980s. It is helpful both as an account of genealogy and as a digest of Foucault's contribution to social studies.

Wetherall, Margaret, Stephanie Taylor, and Simeon J. Yates, eds. 2001. *Discourse Theory and Practice: A Reader.* London: Sage.

A comprehensive reader in discourse theory and research, intended for the upper-level undergraduate student.

RELEVANT WEB SITES

Adbusters Culture Jammers Headquarters
http://www.adbusters.org/home/

A global network of artists, activists, writers, pranksters, students, educators, and entrepreneurs who seek to advance the "new social activist movement of the information age." The site holds that culture jamming can be to the present era what civil rights was to the 1960s, what feminism was to the 1970s, what environmental activism was to the 1980s. It will alter the way we live and think. It will change the way information flows; the way institutions wield power; the way TV stations are run; the way the food, fashion, automobile, sports, music, and culture industries set their agendas. Above all, it will change the way meaning is produced in our society.

Critical Discourse Analysis: A Primer
http://www.kon.org/archives/forum/15-1/mcgregorcda.html

In this article in the on-line journal *Kappa Omicron Nu Forum*, Sue McGregor presents a very clear introduction to the version of critical discourse analysis developed by Norman Fairclough.

The Foucault Pages at CSUN
http://www.csun.edu/~hfspc002/foucault.home.html

Contains many writings by Michel Foucault as well as a genealogy of influences upon him, plus links to other Foucault Web sites.

An Introduction to Poststructuralists and Deconstructionists
http://mesastate.edu/~blaga/deconstruction/deconstructiox.html

A small site, maintained by Barry Laga of Mesa State College, containing a very clear account of post-structural method and links to other useful material, particularly relating to deconstruction.

MCS: Media and Communication Site
http://www.aber.ac.uk/media/medmenu.html

Portal to very extensive Internet-based resources useful in the academic study of media and communication. The section on Textual Analysis is particularly helpful. Highly recommended.

PART 2D

INQUIRY AS EMPOWERMENT: PARTICIPATORY ACTION RESEARCH

Of the five research strategies this book considers in depth, participatory action research (PAR) is perhaps the most praxis-oriented. In PAR, research is only one of three elements, with inclusive participation and action to create change being of equal import. PAR is in effect a form of radical pedagogy. In Paulo Freire's (1970) original formulation of the pedagogy of the oppressed, Marx's dialectic of understanding the world in order to participate in its transformation figured heavily. Freire recognized that the oppressed must be active participants in their own emancipation, and that this requires them to critically recognize oppression's causes, "so that through transforming action they can create a new situation, one which makes possible the pursuit of a fuller humanity" (1970: 32). But given the "existential duality" of the oppressed—the fact that oppression is not only experienced as such but is internalized as both prescribed conduct and self-loathing—the oppressed are often fearful of freedom (Freire, 1970: 31). What Freire called "conscientization," and what participatory action researchers call "empowerment" is a movement from passive acceptance of circumstances "beyond one's control" to active participation in democratically controlled social change, founded on a sense of autonomy and responsibility. As a form of radical pedagogy, PAR works against the dualism that Marx in his third thesis on Feuerbach (p. 21) problematized: between the educator and those in need of education, a division that forgets that "it is essential to educate the educator himself." While recognizing the practical need to create an awareness and capacity among subaltern groups as to how they can liberate themselves, PAR insists on a two-way dialogue between professional researchers with their expert knowledge and lay communities with their local knowledge.

With roots in both the second Euro-North American wave of feminism and in the politics of decolonization that writers like Franz Fanon (1961) and Kwame Nkrumah (1964) represented in the 1960s, the notion of consciousness-raising as a shedding of internalized elements of oppression and a creation of personal and cultural autonomy has multiple lineages in social-justice struggles. PAR also has a mixed lineage, and a somewhat ambiguous relationship to critical social inquiry. Its historical precedents include not only the likes of Freire and Fanon but quality of work life programs through which large corporations have attempted to increase productivity and loyalty on the shop floor. Many action research projects, particularly those initiated and funded by corporate or state management, are obviously co-optative, or geared instrumentally toward realizing more effective service delivery (Stringer, 1996: 37). Without a firm and practical commitment to democratic empowerment, participatory action research becomes little more than a sophisticated form of social control. Even so, as Joe Feagin and Hernán Vera (2001: 177) point out, once effectively launched by extensive community participation, action research is difficult to contain, and local people, once organized, may move their organization in the direction of more radical goals than were initially intended.

This dynamic character is one of participatory action research's great virtues. It is a strategy that puts people in motion in what Budd Hall (1979) describes as a three-pronged initiative: as a method of research involving full participation of the community, as a dialogical educational process, and as a means of taking action for change. This allows "people to rediscover the realities of their lives and their potential capabilities"—to build self-reliance and re-humanize their worlds (Smith, 1997). In this sense, PAR complements initiatives like human social development (HSD), which share the same values and the same origins in struggles for justice on world capitalism's periphery. HSD rejects the dominant paradigm of development as a top-down process of economic growth that sacrifices human well-being and reinforces inequality; it emphasizes grassroots participation, empowerment, self-reliance, and capacity building as developmental practices; it values locality and local ways of knowing in pursuing structural reforms to achieve social justice. Likewise, PAR rejects the dominant paradigm of positivist research, which gives the researcher sovereignty over knowledge and objectifies the subjects of study; it recognizes that if the aim is human-centred development, then the inquiry must be organized around horizontal relationships among participants and shared decision making that promotes empowerment as both the means of knowledge creation and the end; it respects local knowledge and personal experience and challenges practices that unjustly constrain opportunity or oppress specific groups (Kondrat and Julia, 1997).

But can the coincidence of action and inquiry in the service of enhancing social justice be considered really "research" at all? Stephen Toulmin (1996) suggests that positivist critiques of action research are based in a Platonic conception of the universe and knowledge according to which there are universal forms to be discovered. In this perspective, which typically takes Newtonian physics as its standard, science requires a single, universal method. Action research, however, is based in an Aristotelian perspective according to which various kinds of knowledge require different methodologies. In this perspective, research with an interest in local, timely knowledge of concrete situations is not devalued, nor is research that explicitly poses value questions—to make clear the kinds of change that are desirable outcomes of the inquiry. Indeed, if the goal is to improve our practices (as in the pursuit of social justice) PAR may be seen as a particularly effective research strategy that produces knowledge relevant to the democratization of social life (Toulmin, 1996). "In PAR the question 'Is it rigorous?' is complemented by the equally important question 'Is it empowering?'" (Kondrat and Julia, 1997: 44).

The four readings that follow give us a sense of the logic, method, and politics of participatory action research.[1] Davydd Greenwood and Morten Levin present a conceptual analysis of action research as a dialogical process that bridges the two worlds of practical reasoning and scientifically constructed knowledge by integrating practitioners ("insiders") and professionals ("outsiders") in the same knowledge-generating process. As a measure of its success, action research generates both valid knowledge and effective social action by embodying democratic ideals in its basic practices. Successful action research involves a double democratization. The *research process* is democratized through full participation and colearning between outside facilitators and insiders, with power shifting to insiders over the course of the project. Moreover, the project yields as its *output* knowledge that increases participants' ability to control their own situation.

In Greenwood and Levin's "cogenerative" model, the process of action research entails at least two phases. The initial dialogue between insiders and outsiders achieves a working definition of the problem and an agreement on procedures for democratic conversation. These advances enable the coresearchers to construct, in the second phase, *arenas for communication* about problems of significance to the local participants. It is in these arenas, which may take various forms, that colearning, research, and reflection occur, all of which can lead to action that addresses the initial problem and also to reconceptualization of the problem itself. For action research to work, the project must resist both model monopoly (in which the authority of outsiders' theoretical knowledge is privileged) and insider monopoly (in which the authority of insiders' experience is privileged), and over time the process must be taken over by the participants, as they gain the skills and information to control their own knowledge production and action.

Verna St. Denis's presentation of community-based participatory research complements Greenwood and Levin's schematic analysis with a detailed account of the practice of PAR, based on a review of literature as well as her own experiences as a Cree/Métis participatory researcher in Alaska. In view of the extremely oppressive conditions facing Indigenous communities, a style of research that considers the welfare of the people and community needs and that is committed to social change, social justice, and self-determination is of great moment. When successful, community-based participatory research enables the community "to act upon its members' lives in an informed collaborative manner," but the challenges are many. St. Denis notes that in fostering participation within communities that are never homogeneous, researchers need to be self-reflective, diplomatic, and flexible in adapting to the cultural context. The research results are not necessarily straightforward, as they often reflect the multiple realities lived by the parties to the study. Use of the results is an indelibly political process in which the community must remain actively involved if the project is to fulfill its promise. The 14 summary guidelines that appear near the end of St. Denis's chapter are wise counsel to researchers interested in PAR. It is instructive to note how many of them refer to *the need to build healthy human relations* within the practice of action research. Community-based participatory research is indeed "like a community development project" (p. 300).

The concern with human relations and healthy communities is shared by Marge Reitsma-Street and Leslie Brown, who, in our third reading, introduce community action research (CAR) as a value-based approach to research that strives to promote individual self-discovery, to build communities, and to act as a catalyst for social change. Conceptualizing community as a diverse ensemble of overlapping lifeworlds, Reitsma-Street and Brown present CAR as a method for protecting and enhancing the "common grounds" that enable people to meet their needs and make humane choices. CAR is *useful* research for communities,[2] a *political* social work practice that combines community development with activism.

Using the image of CAR as a "wheel" of praxis, these authors place the values of community connectedness, social justice, agency, and critical curiosity at its hub. With social justice and collective agency among its core values, CAR is "a visibly political act" in which its practitioners consider themselves activists as much as researchers. Continuing with the metaphor, the wheel has as its spokes ten processes that illuminate the communicative, political, and research dimensions of CAR as a critical strategy. In the life of a CAR project, processes such as developing decision-making procedures; devising common principles; negotiating allies, resources, and access; and experimenting with change-oriented action are not sequential but are revisited as the work proceeds, making this approach highly dynamic and reflexive. Finally, the wheel is rimmed by social relationships among participants that connect the processes together and make CAR possible. Reitsma-Street and Brown illustrate these components of CAR with an extended example from Brown's study in an Aboriginal community, and conclude their essay with some searching questions on the promise and limits of their approach.

In our final selection, John Gaventa and Andrea Cornwall continue in a reflective mode as they theorize the relations between power and knowledge in PAR. They discuss four ways of conceptualizing power as knowledge, with differing implications for our understanding of empowerment *through* knowledge. Power might be said to inhere in the unequal distribution of resources (including knowledge), in the capacity to set agendas for discussion and to exclude certain voices from it, and in the mechanisms of socialization that organize mass consent to domination—all of which focus on the repressive side of power. A fourth, genealogical view emphasizes the ubiquity of power in "framing the boundaries of possibility that govern action" (p. 322). Variants of PAR have tended to embrace one or another of these understandings of power (and thus empowerment) to the exclusion of others. This has limited the practice of PAR, since in reality the four kinds of power are intertwined. Nevertheless, the various approaches to PAR share a critique of how power is inscribed within the dominant, positivist knowledge-production system as well as a commitment to producing a different form of knowledge. Gaventa and Cornwall discuss a wide range of literature that clarifies how participatory research may be used to challenge power in its multiplicity, in a nuanced way that facilitates change at multiple levels and among multiple actors.

Such a strategy becomes all the more relevant as PAR itself moves from the margins to the mainstream. In the 1990s, organizations such as the World Bank began to use participatory research methods to bring "popular" voices and "civil society" into their analyses. Gaventa and Cornwall call for a sober, ongoing assessment of both the co-optative dangers and the opportunities that emerge when PAR is "scaled up" to the macro-level and incorporated as "policy."[3] The five lessons that they delineate from the experience so far suggest that certain "enabling factors" (such as the presence of social movements that can fill new public spaces with voices and actions from below) can maximize the potential for empowering results.

NOTES

1. For simplicity's sake I sometimes use PAR to refer summarily to the slightly different approaches discussed in the four readings. Greenwood and Levin call their approach "action research"; St. Denis discusses "community-based participatory research"; Reitsma-Street and Brown advocate "community action research"; Gaventa and Cornwall use the terms "participatory research," "participatory action research," and "participatory rural appraisal."

2. As these authors note, communities are not necessarily geographically centred or bounded, nor is their membership fixed. CAR can be applied, for instance, to social movements, which are

diverse ensemble of overlapping lifeworlds, often held together by Internet and other extra-local means of communication.

3. A good example is the Community-University Research Alliances (CURA) program launched by the Social Sciences and Humanities Research Council of Canada in 1999. As the Council states on its CURA Web page, "alliances between community organizations and universities will foster new knowledge, tools and methods to develop the best strategies for diverse aspects of intervention, action research, program delivery and policy development that will be appropriate for our rapidly changing times." Go to http://www.sshrc.ca/web/apply/program_descriptions/cura_e.asp.

REFERENCES

Fanon, Franz. 1961. *The Wretched of the Earth*. New York: Grove Press.

Feagin, Joe, and Hernan Vera. 2001. *Liberation Sociology*. Boulder: Westview.

Freire, Paulo. 1970. *Pedagogy of the Oppressed*. New York: Seabury Press.

Hall, Budd L. 1979. "Knowledge as a Commodity and Participatory Research." *Prospects* 9(4): 393–408.

Kondrat, Mary Ellen, and Mari Julia. 1997. "Participatory Action Research: Self-Reliant Research Strategies for Human Development." *Social Development Issues* 19(1): 32–49.

Nkrumah, Kwame. 1964. *Consciencism: Philosophy and Ideology for De-Colonization*. New York: Monthly Review Press.

Smith, Susan E. 1997. "Introduction." In *Nurtured by Knowledge: Learning to Do Participatory Action-Research*, edited by Susan E. Smith, Dennis G. Willms, and Nancy A. Johnson, 1–7. Ottawa: International Development Research Centre.

Stringer, Ernest T. 1996. *Action Research: A Handbook for Practitioners*. London: Sage.

Toulmin, Stephen. 1996. "Is Action Research Really 'Research'?" *Concepts and Transformation* 1(1): 51–61.

CHAPTER 20

Local Knowledge, Cogenerative Research, and Narrativity

Davydd J. Greenwood and Morten Levin

In action research (AR), professional social researchers and insider community or organization members are cosubjects and coresearchers in the research process. Both contribute many kinds of knowledge and actions to their joint enterprise. The conventional social sciences have no difficulty with the idea of expert social researchers, but they reject the idea that local people, untrained in the theories and methods of academic social science, can make valuable contributions to both the form and the substance of a social research process.

* * * * *

AR centers on an encounter between the worlds of practical reasoning and the worlds of scientifically constructed knowledge. We do not assert the superiority of either type of knowledge. AR processes bridge these worlds by integrating practitioners and professionals in the same knowledge generation process. We call this *cogenerative learning*. Through these collaborative processes, the quality of the research can be enhanced because the insiders are able to contribute crucial local knowledge and analysis to the research, and can comment effectively on external interpretive frameworks as well. By the same token, the practical reasoning guiding the insiders' actions can be enhanced and reformulated through accessing

and transforming scientific knowledge for use in dealing with everyday problems.

We believe that local people often act skillfully on the basis of appropriate valid knowledge. We believe that local knowledge systems are complex, differentiated, and dynamic, and we believe that, without formal training, it is possible for people to develop warrants for action based on good analyses. We therefore believe that local people are essential partners in any social research activity. Action researchers do not believe in the idea of scientific, cosmopolitan knowledge that is valid everywhere, and we reject the notion that valid knowledge can be produced only by "objective" outsiders using formal methods that supposedly eliminate bias and error.

* * * * *

LOCAL KNOWLEDGE AND PROFESSIONAL SOCIAL RESEARCH KNOWLEDGE

Despite the importance of local knowledge, the AR literature does not offer many clear statements about it. [...]

For some action researchers, local knowledge simply means insider knowledge, the knowledge that people in the community or organization have. For others, local knowledge is understood to be detailed knowledge of local situations. In the second view, local knowledge belongs to insiders, but outsiders can also develop varieties of local knowledge through ethnographic research based on participant observation. Probably the most common view of local knowledge is that it is true knowledge, in opposition to the false and class-interested knowledge imposed by hegemonic outsiders. Each of these views carries very different consequences, both ideologically and methodologically.

Our own understanding of local knowledge centers on viewing it as practical reasoning in action and local reflections by participants on their actions. This conception of knowledge can be traced back to Aristotle's concept of *phronesis:* "the ability to spot the action called for in any situation" (Toulmin, 1996: 207). As Eikeland (1992) and Schwandt (1997) point out, this is a different type of knowledge from that used to develop scientific theories. For us, one of the aims of AR is to create a research process that reveals the combination of practical reasoning and socially constructed meaning (Berger and Luckmann, 1966) held by local people. AR becomes the process of bridging local knowledge and scientific knowledge, a process that will create both new local knowledge and new scientific understandings. For us, AR centers on the communication between locals and professionals in cogenerating new knowledge.

No matter which view of local knowledge an action researcher has, it is clear that local knowledge in AR is generally understood differently from the same knowledge in conventional social science. Although there have been a number of recent moves toward constructivism and discourse analysis, and there is a gradual return to qualitative research approaches, the dominant social science traditions still generally reserve to the researcher the right and power to create the structures into which knowledge is put, ostensibly to create separable units of objective knowledge that

can be intercorrelated, subjected to formal manipulations and comparison, hypothesized, and synthesized outside of the local context. Even when the conventional social scientist is not a positivist of this sort, he or she generally reserves the right to formulate and express what the subjects think, how they think it, and what import it has. What is valid, interesting, important, and trivial is treated as the professional researcher's decision.

This conception of the generation of social research knowledge makes social science research production and local knowledge production antithetical to each other because local knowledge is built in and conveyed through a wide variety of context-bound formats and often has a complex narrative structure. From ethnographic fieldwork and from AR experiences, we know that the narrative structures of local knowledge are often key components in the way it is constructed, learned, conveyed, and applied. Because AR privileges local knowledge, AR necessarily works with the role of narrative in the research process, as well as in the write up of the results.

A key question in dealing with local knowledge is validity [....] This validity question is capable of generating some very extreme and unproductive positions. Many conventional social scientists equate local knowledge with invalid or at least subjective information. They want to believe that untrained people cannot produce valid knowledge because they lack the methods, training, and commitment to transcend bias and self-interest in their interpretive processes. By contrast, a few action researchers equate local knowledge with valid information, believing that only those natives uncontaminated by the capitalist system are able to see things clearly.

We find neither position persuasive. [...] We think it is more important to examine the extent and ways local knowledge can be mobilized, relied on, acted on, and interpreted, and to learn how research results based in part on local knowledge can be communicated and contextualized effectively beyond the local situations where it was generated.

Co-researchers

We argue that AR, in addition to generating valid knowledge and effective social action, embodies democratic ideals in its core practices. This democracy is involved in both the research process and the outcomes of the research. In AR, the research process must be democratic in the sense that it is open, participatory, and fair to the participants. In addition, the outcome of AR should support the participants' interests so that the knowledge produced increases their ability to control their own situation. We summarize this double meaning of democratization by referring to AR as *cogenerative research*.[1]

Central to the effort to democratize research is changing the roles of the researched and the researcher. Democracy in inquiry cannot be promoted unless the local participants, however selected, are enabled to take charge of the meaning construction process. At the same time, trained researchers cannot make sense of local social life without secure communication links to these local participants. The dynamic tension between insider and outsider knowledge is the basis for this cogenerative process.

In AR, we believe that the whole can be greater than the sum of the parts. The outside researcher is assisted enormously in learning things she or he does not know or immediately perceive through dialogue with insiders and through experiencing and understanding actions. The insiders reformulate and revalue their own knowledge in response to queries from the outsider. Both sides gain understanding from their interactions. And both sides have a complex web of intentions and interpretations of the structures and processes they are engaged in. These two can

be made available, at least in part, to each other through the cogenerative process.

Trustworthiness

A key challenge in any social research centers on claims about the trustworthiness of the results. AR holds that validity and reliability can emerge only from a discursive process where participants and researchers negotiate the meanings created by their experiences during the research process. Thus, AR affirms that communication processes themselves are a vital component in creating trustworthy knowledge, linking AR directly to pragmatism and democratic theory [....] Accordingly, a central design challenge in any AR process is structuring arenas for communication that will effectively support an open and inclusive meaning construction process. Cogenerative learning is not merely a methodology or a set of techniques; it is a way of framing an AR process that aims to clarify social positions, communication processes, learning, and action options.

AR Takes Time

Any AR process builds on communications and actions between involved parties. From the research literature and from everyday experience, we all know that engaging in mutually interesting dialogues demands time for learning about each other and the creation of a language that is mutually accessible. AR processes accordingly demand time investments in the form of sustained communications and interactions that shape a common ground of understanding. There are no meaningful "drive-by," one-shot AR processes. Any AR approach that promises quick results should be treated with suspicion.

One Size Does Not Fit All in AR

As important as the cogenerative approach is, it is not a blueprint for designing an AR process. The knowledge produced in AR is linked to the actual context of the work. Methodological approaches are chosen to fit the problem focus of a particular context. The cogenerative view thus is a framework for thinking through how to choose appropriate methods and actions, not a recipe. It is fully and necessarily compatible with the deployment of a wide variety of research techniques and agendas.

The design of these communicative arenas and the use of particular group processes must always result from an assessment of the particular situation. Thus, where a neighborhood has an overriding common interest in economic and social survival, techniques based on consensus building might be appropriate. [...] By contrast, in a situation where opposing groups have manifest and latent conflicts, for example, regarding the use of natural resources, a conflict-bridging strategy might be more useful. A skillful AR practitioner must be able to read and make sense of specific situations and use this insight to suggest ways to design the AR process.

We are emphatic in rejecting a one-size-fits-all approach to AR. Doing AR means engaging in a process of mutual action and reflection. The skillful professional practitioner must continually reflect on experiences from the field, seeking what is necessary to keep a change process moving and tracking what is being learned. This is reflection-in-action and on-action and it is a core feature of the praxis of AR.

OUR COGENERATIVE AR MODEL

AR can be thought of as a process consisting of at least two analytically distinct phases. The first involves the clarification of an initial research question, whereas the second involves the initiation and continuation of a social change and meaning construction process. This does not mean that the problem definition process is ever final; in fact, a good sign of the learning taking place in an AR project is when the initial questions are reshaped to include newly discovered dimensions.

We can visualize the cogenerative model as shown in Figure 20.1.

The cogenerative model identifies two main groups of actors. The insiders are the focal point of every AR project. They are the "owners" of the problem, but they are not homogeneous, egalitarian, or in any way an ideal group. They simply "own" the problem. Outsiders are the professional researchers who seek to facilitate a colearning process aimed at solving local problems. Insiders and outsiders are both equal and different. They are different because most insiders have to live directly with the results of any change activity in a project, whereas most outsiders can leave. Another difference is the insiders have the central influence on what the focus of the research activity should be.

Problem Definition

The question to be researched must be of major importance to the participants or the process will go nowhere. Once it is established, we can gain additional leverage by using relevant bodies of professional knowledge in the field [....]

We have argued that an AR process deals with solving pertinent problems for the participants. In this respect, the whole research process emerges from demands arising outside the academy. This contrasts with conventional social science, where research problems are defined as much by developments within the disciplines as by external social forces. Yet AR professionals do not just blindly accept any problem formulation forwarded by the local participants. We view the problem definition process as the first step in a mutual learning process between insiders and outsiders. To facilitate a process where insider knowledge is clarified in relation to outsider professional knowledge, communication procedures must permit the development of a mutually agreed-on problem focus. These procedures include

Figure 20.1: The Cogenerative Action Research Model

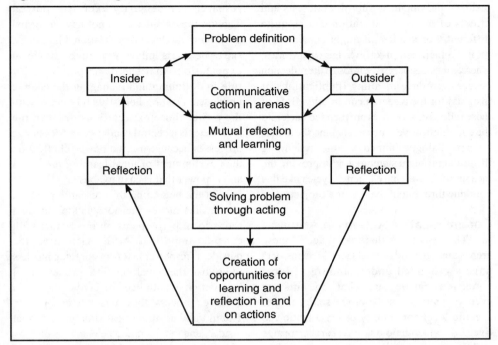

rules of democratic dialogue, which involve openness, mutual support, and shared "air time." A first working definition of the problem under study comes out of a discourse where knowledge held by insiders and outsiders cogenerates a new, mutual understanding through their communication with each other.

Communication Arenas

Central to the cogenerative process is its ability to create room for learning processes resulting in meanings that participants trust. To this end, the ground for communication between the groups of actors must be properly configured. This is what we refer to in Figure 20.1 as the arena. Arenas simply are locations where the involved actors encounter each other in a material setting for the purpose of carrying on AR. They can involve a meeting

between two and more people, a team building session, a search conference, a task force meeting, a leadership group meeting, or a public community meeting. The key point is that an arena allows communicative actions to take place.

* * * * *

In arenas, communication between insiders and outsiders can produce learning and open up a process of reflection for the involved parties. These discussions and reflections are the engine for an upward learning spiral. The initial problem focus suggests a design for an arena for discourse. The subsequent communication produces understandings that help move toward problem solutions, creating new experiences to reflect on for both the insiders and the professional researchers.

The feedback loops are similar for both insiders and outsiders, but the interests and effects of the communication can be quite different. For insiders, it might be central to improve their action-knowledge capabilities, whereas the outsiders may, through the reflection process, produce meaning (publications or insights) for the research community. Both of these reflective processes are then fed back into the communicative process, shaping the arenas for new dialogues aimed at either redefining the initial problem statement or improving the local problem-solving capacity. Cycles like this continue throughout the life of a project.

Communicative Actions in Arenas

The discourses that take place in these arenas are inherently unbalanced. The insiders have a grounded understanding of local conditions far beyond what any outsider ever can gain, unless he or she settles in that specific local community or organization to live. Likewise, the outside researcher brings with him or her skills and perspectives often not present in the local context, including knowledge about how to design and run learning and reflection processes. The asymmetry in skills and local knowledge can be an important force in cogenerating new understandings. The parties engage each other to make sense out of the situation. The democratic ideals of AR research mandate a process, however, whereby the outsider gradually lets go of control so that the insiders can learn how to control and guide their own developmental processes. These ideals also aim to develop the insiders' capacities for sustaining more complex internal dialogues with a more diverse set of participants than would have been the case without this value commitment.

This asymmetrical situation (Markova and Foppa, 1991) thus becomes the root of complex social exchanges. The outsider designs training sessions that make transfer of knowledge possible and uses his or her influence to direct

the developmental process. The professional researcher necessarily exercises power. Though the outsider does not have a formal position in the local organizational hierarchy, she or he exerts influence through participant expectations that she or he play a major role in designing and managing the change processes. Dealing honestly and openly with the power those expectations grant to the researcher is a central challenge in AR change processes because it has a powerful effect on the development of local learning processes and is power that is easy to abuse.

At the beginning of a research process, the outsider makes decisions and teaches and trains local participants on topics that both consider important. At the same time, the outsider is responsible for encouraging insiders to control the developmental process. [...] For participants to become active players in a change process, they must exercise power. The initially asymmetrical situation between insiders and outsiders can be balanced only by the transfer of skills and knowledge from the professional researcher to the participants and the transfer of information and skills from the local participants to the outside researcher. In the end, though, the process must be taken over by the participants. The AR process cannot fulfill its democratic obligations unless the main thrust of the process is toward increasing the participants' control over knowledge production and action. Standard training in conventional social science research and the whole academic reward system focus strongly on control over both the design and the execution of research activities, treating them as a hallmark of professional competence.

The struggle to solve important local problems shapes the ground for new understandings, hence the double feedback loops in Figure 20.1. That is to say that, through actions taken as a result of the cogenerative processes, the participants learn new things about the problems they are facing, often revising their understandings in fundamental ways. The outcomes of this collective process, action, and reflection support the creation of new shared understandings. The larger this shared ground is, the more fruitful the communication has been and the greater the likelihood is that further insights can be developed through reflection and actions based on this shared knowledge. This in turn can open up new ways of formulating the AR problems, and thus result in ongoing learning for all parties.

Model Monopoly

A major challenge in AR is to find a good first question that is at least partly shared among the involved parties, particularly at the outset. There are several obstacles to overcome. The conventional training of academic researchers generally makes them experienced debaters with lots of practice in managing conceptual models. This can create a situation of communicative domination that undermines the cogenerative process. This situation has been called "model monopoly" by Brathen (1973). He identifies and analyzes situations where one side dominates and, through skills in communication and the handling of certain kinds of conceptual models, constantly increases the distance between insiders and outsiders. In addition, the professional's social prestige and years of formal training may convince people to accept a particular point of view too easily. When this happens, it is a serious threat to the AR process because it distracts attention from local points of view, which are central to the initiation of any AR process. Skilled action researchers develop the ability to help articulate and make sense of local models and are sure they are well articulated in the communicative process.

Insider Monopoly

Another important trap in the initial problem formulation phase is getting locked into the initial insider formulation. This is a pseudo-democratic position based on the assumption that the participants are always right. Believing this creates another kind of constrained situation. In this case, the value of outside knowledge is rejected. We believe the best possible understandings are those negotiated between professional researchers and participants who search together for the best arguments and understandings of a situation. This is a dialogical process, with arguments shifting back and forth in productive tension.

How Good Is Good Enough?

We want to be careful not to overstate the case and make it appear that transcendentally high standards must be met in AR. It is possible and often necessary to start a project with an initially quite limited problem statement and without all the relevant parties at the table. The key is in designing and sustaining a process where important reflections can emerge through communication and some good practical problem solving. Over time, the initial problem can be refined and reformulated, just as hypotheses are reformulated and refined in laboratory science [...] and the composition of the initial group can be changed to reflect the full set of problem owners more adequately. But iteration of this process is limited by the resources, energy, and other elements of the situation in which AR is taking place.

Maintaining Differences

The insiders and outsiders are considered to be equal in integrity because both are expected to behave in accordance with their backgrounds and knowledge base. They have an equal right to be heard. It is important that the AR professional not try to play the game of pretending to become an insider. A professional researcher will always be an outsider situated in an institutional and professional setting that creates particular demands on the professional praxis and ethical standards of behavior. The cogenerative challenge in this unbalanced situation is to take advantage of the differences between the parties. Together, insiders and outsiders can create the ground for new learning for all participants, their differences being one of the main contributions they bring to the process. .

When Is It Research?

AR is not just participatory action; it is also research. Doing good things for communities and organizations is laudable, but is not a sufficient justification for calling a process AR. [...] For a process to be called AR, it must be systematic and oriented around posing questions whose answers require the gathering and analysis of data and the generation of interpretations directly tested in the field of action.

These research questions can be of different sorts. Research can refer to the production of knowledge (in the form of papers, reports, books, and Ph.D. theses) that communicates insights to an audience beyond the coresearchers in a particular project. That is, AR can contribute to social science learning.

AR can also refer to untangling and interpreting the complexities of a particular set of local conditions that lie at the center of the project. Whether it is the former kind of generalizing research activity or a more particular and local kind of research, it is not AR unless the knowledge is expressed, analyzed, and tested in action by the participants.

Another difference between AR and most conventional social science is that, in AR, the research activity is based on long-term and personal engagement with a case through living with and acting to solve practical problems. The personal experiences the professional action researcher acquires differentiate this research process radically from single-shot interventions and standard social science research.

Publications

Conventional research publications can result from AR when the researcher learns something of relatively little interest to the local participants but that may address a major issue in the research literature. We believe, however, that even these conventional research results are formulated on a much more solid basis than most conventional social science results because of the long-term engagement and shared understandings developed with insiders in AR.

Communications to the scientific community can be produced jointly by insiders and outsiders in AR projects (see [...] Levin, 1988; Levin et al., 1980a, 1980b). Although this process is complex and creates a variety of new issues about authorship, intellectual property, and so on, it is undeniable that insiders and outsiders together can communicate effectively with the professional research community.

Insider's Reflection

Coproducing reports with outside researchers is one way of introducing lay people to the tool of writing as a form of reflective learning. This writing process, which includes most of the tools of scientific reflection (working with data, analysis, and conclusions), can bring new dimensions to local knowledge production. Although this way of structuring the reflection process is no substitute for everyday practical reasoning, it can be a very useful tool for local organizations and communities to have at their disposal. The insiders also enhance their practical reasoning through sharing experiences and learning from the actions they take as members of the AR team. Such processes often run independently of the outside researcher's efforts, and yet are part of the AR process.

NARRATIVITY

The interaction between local knowledge and expert knowledge through a cogenerative process is a core feature of AR. One consequence of this is that most accounts of AR, trying to be true to the process that constructed them, are rendered in narrative form. They often take the form of case studies, with detailed discussions of the processes that the group went through in generating the knowledge that is being communicated and acted on. As a result, most AR follows many of the rhetorical conventions of narrative writing.

This runs directly against the style and wishes of conventional social scientists for whom narrativity (until the all-out attack on positivism by deconstructivists and postmodernists) is supposedly an evil, a source of confusion and co-optation to be overcome. To parody the conventional researchers, it is as if their practice is contained in the following syllogism:

- AR is storytelling.
- Storytelling is not science.
- AR is not science.

This is a widespread view. Most conventional social scientists are, in practice, positivists with a narrow view of what constitutes meaningful professional standards. Their commitment to objectification causes them to go through painful gyrations as they try to speak in nonnarrative forms about things they learned in contextualized discourse. It is sad to watch neophyte social scientists learning how to take their normal speech and writing habits and convert them into what Richard Lanham (1992) calls "the official style": "It is hypothesized that . . ." "The dependent variable is scalar while the independent variable is ..." "The hypothesis is confirmed at the .001 level." The passive voice dominates. Verbs are weak and the actors are invisible. These conventions not only turn normal speech into "officialese" but alienate the results of the work from all but another group of scientists who have learned to speak and write this way.

By contrast, the AR syllogism is quite different:

- All general laws must apply to all particular cases.
- AR develops detailed stories of particular cases.
- Therefore AR tests the validity of general laws.

AR gains much of its power through narratives because narratives are inherently particular. Though they may fall into broad types, each narrative refers to a specific situation and a specific set of connections between elements (people, organizations, and events). Thus, if the narrative developed in a particular AR project tells a story that is deemed at variance with a major generalization, the major generalization is either wrong or must somehow be modified to cover the case.

For example, the dominant generalization among economic theorists is that cooperatives cannot compete successfully with noncooperative businesses. The study of Mondragón (Greenwood et al., 1992) demonstrates that the cooperatives are considerably more successful than their direct competitors. Subsequent events have amply confirmed this. Thus, the narrative of Mondragón means that the generalization about the noncompetitiveness of cooperatives, as stated, is wrong—it is invalid!

Not long ago, this would have seemed an outrageous, wooly minded approach and would have been dismissed. But the conventional social sciences have been undergoing a variety of crises of their own making. Most of the general public has lost faith in most of what passes for academic social science, finding it unintelligible, self-serving, and, where it is understandable, either banal or wrong. The dream that the social sciences were building an edifice like that of the basic sciences is a thing of the past, living among the outdated practitioners and the conservative granting agencies that support nonthreatening social research.

* * * * *

CONCLUSIONS

These considerations bring us full circle. We began with local knowledge, which is largely narrative in form and expressed through action in context. We built a view of the cogenerative research process that characterizes AR when it is practiced, and we closed with a defense of narrativity as a reliable and meaningful form of knowledge with the power to force all generalizations to the test.

What, then, do conventional social scientists have to fear from AR? Only that their theories will have to meet the test of analysis in which local knowledge and action play a definitive role. This is not good news for them because it undermines both their epistemological project and their comfortable social distance from the world they study.

For us, this is the attractiveness of AR. This form of research most closely approximates the epistemology and methodology of a social science that links the local and cosmopolitan discourses in a reasoned framework that remains open to testing and modification through social action. AR is the high road to warrants for action and an authentic social science.

NOTE

1. One significant source of vagueness in our discussion here is just who the participants are and who they represent. That an AR process is participatory and cogenerative does not solve local issues of inclusion, hierarchy, gender oppression, and so on. When an AR process is begun, some local community or organizational group of stakeholders opens up a set of issues to be examined. Often, it takes the AR professional a long time to discover who these people are, how they were selected, who is not present, and how their actions may affect larger local collectives. This is inevitable. AR is not a silver bullet producing democracy everywhere in its wake. The obligation of the AR professional is to attempt to discover who is present and who is not, to understand the effect of this on the process and the actions stemming from it, and to advocate regularly for discussions about inclusion and for greater inclusiveness. Of course, the scope of such actions cannot be known in advance.

REFERENCES

Berger, P., and T. Luckmann. 1966. *The Social Construction of Reality.* Garden City: Doubleday.

Brathen, S. 1973. "Model Monopoly and Communication Systems: Theoretical Notes on Democratization." *Acta Sociologica* 16(2): 98–107.

Eikeland, O. 1992. *Erfaring, dialogikk og politikk* [Experience, Dialogue, and Politics]. Oslo: Work Research Institute.

Greenwood, D., et al. 1992. *Industrial Democracy as Process: Participatory Action Research in the Fagor Cooperative Group of Mondragón.* Assen-Maastricht: Van Gorcum.

Lanham, R. 1992. *Revising Prose.* New York: Macmillan.

Levin, M. 1988. *Lokal mobilisering* [Local Mobilization]. Trondheim: IFIM.

Levin, M., et al. 1980a. *Teknisk utvikling og arbeidsforhold i aluminiumselektrolyse* [Technical Development and Quality of Working Life in Aluminum Smelting]. Trondheim: IFIM.

Levin, M., et al. 1980b. *Hittervceringer vi kan vil vi?* [Citizens of Hitra We Can, But Will We?]. Trondheim: IFIM.

Markova, I., and K. Foppa. 1991. *Asymmetries in Dialogue.* Herfordshire: Harvester Wheatsheaf.

Schwandt, T. 1997. "Towards a New Science of Action Research." Paper presented at the Tavistock conference "Is Action Research Real Research," London.

Toulmin, S. 1996. "Concluding Methodological Reflection: Elitism and Democracy among the Sciences." In *Beyond Theory*, edited by S. Toulmin & B. Gustavsen, 203–225. Amsterdam: John Benjamins.

CHAPTER 21

Community-Based Participatory Research: Aspects of the Concept Relevant for Practice

Verna St. Denis

INTRODUCTION

I am a Cree/Métis woman who grew up in rural Saskatchewan, Canada. Throughout my "growing up" years, I experienced many of the painful effects of racial and class discrimination, which was fuelled, in part, by "knowledge" and policies generated from social science research. This experience is common to most people of colour, women, the underclass, and other groups who do not have access to powerful decision-making positions in society. Therefore, as a First Nations woman who grew up "dirt poor," I have searched for a way to do social science research that would be more responsive to the needs of First Nations communities and disempowered communities in general.

Knowledge produced by social science research is a powerful and effective means to influence decisions about people's everyday lives (Guyette, 1983; Hall, 1979; Reinharz, 1979). Whether this influence is detrimental or supportive to a group of people often depends on who controls the research process (Hall, 1979; Huizer, 1978). Although there are some examples of research that directly benefit Native communities, research is more commonly a negative experience (Laframboise and Plake, 1983). Yet research is not inherently bad. It is those who pay for it, conduct it, and decide what "good" research is who

have contributed to the negative attitude that First Nations people have towards research (Churchill, 1988; Deloria, 1984; Laframboise and Plake, 1983). This is the perspective from which I began to search to understand how to do research with and for First Nations communities.

"Community-based participatory research" suggests a way in which communities without socio-political power can use social science research to support their struggle for self-determination by gaining control of information that can influence decisions about their lives (Bopp and Bopp, 1985; Guyette, 1983; Hall, 1979; Stull and Schensul, 1987). Community-based participatory research proceeds differently from the way research is usually done, particularly because of its emphasis and respect for human interaction. Doing such research is a very different experience both for the researchers and for the communities who have been the "target" of other forms of research. Given the nature of human relationships and the politics of communities, the dynamics of community-based participatory research can be very complex.

I had an opportunity to engage in community-based participatory research while living in Alaska (St. Denis, 1989). The research, involving a needs assessment with a Native organization, brought home the everyday realities of *doing* community-based participatory research—including its strengths and weaknesses. I realized that, though this type of community-based research is difficult, frustrating, and time-consuming, it is worth the effort, because in that effort the community becomes empowered. Research can therefore become more liberating than manipulative.

* * * * *

FOUR ASPECTS OF COMMUNITY-BASED PARTICIPATORY RESEARCH

I have identified four aspects of community-based research that are central to its practice: first, the intent and purpose of the research; second, the nature of human relationships in the research process; third, data analysis and interpretation; and fourth, the use of the findings/results. The *experience* of doing community-based participatory research, which is sometimes described in the research literature, indicates the complexity of that research effort and the frequently unseen consequences that develop as a result of its implementation. Community-based participatory research is not a simple matter of going from theory into practice.

1. Intent and Purpose of Community-Based Participatory Research

What is the purpose of the research? Who will benefit from the research? Why is the research being conducted? The answers to these kinds of questions are of significant importance in the practice of community-based participatory research.

Community-based participatory research sees social science research as in a state of flux and therefore ripe for making changes (Lather, 1986). Community-based participatory research argues that research undertaken just for sake of knowing is pointless (Stokes, 1985), as well as asocial and immoral (Huizer, 1978), particularly in those communities that are experiencing socio-economic crises. The effort must be directed towards a merging of theory and practice in the service of those who are affected (Huizer, 1978; Hall, 1979).

Social science research must be committed to social change, "to critiquing the status quo and building a more just society" (Lather, 1986: 258), especially if in the course of doing research "you see that there are victims" (Huizer, 1978: 7). Research must consider the welfare of the people (Stokes, 1985; Lafromboise and Plake, 1983) and must be related to community needs (Bopp and Bopp, 1985; Laframboise and Plake, 1983; Light and Kleiber, 1981). Typically, social scientists have studied those who have not had the power to resist being studied or at times have lacked the perception of such power (Hamnett et al., 1984); therefore research has only served to enhance the researcher's agenda and career (Hall, 1979; Laframboise and Plake, 1983; Stokes, 1985). Researchers are challenged to do research for and with the people rather than on or about people (Light and Kleiber, 1981). Huizer (1978) suggests that research become "service work."

Given the deplorable socio-economic conditions of those communities that are often the target of study, research must address and promote social change, program development, and development of appropriate policies (Laframboise and Plake, 1983; Stokes, 1985; Hall, 1979). For example, researchers must seek to "increase the compatibility between research and Indian ways of life, ... and ultimately promote a better understanding of the forces that restrict the Indian environment" (Laframboise and Plake, 1983: 46). Guyette (1983: xvi) attributes the "roots" of community-based research on Native American reserves to "the idea of self-determination," asserting that research that "comes from within the community is an invaluable tool for community development."

If the community is not involved in the entire research process, the result is often misinformation and the perpetuation of negative stereotypes (Laframboise and Plake, 1983; Stokes, 1985). The research ends up serving the needs of those who paid for the research rather than those who are participating in the research (Hall, 1979). Instead, research must actively and meaningfully involve those who are participating in the research. Light and Kleiber (1981) found that early consultation helped the researcher avoid inappropriate decisions, improved input from various perspectives, and ensured that the research was relevant. Participation and collaboration between the researcher and communities is possible, as shown in the examples of Bopp and Bopp (1985), Brown and Kaplan (1981), Elden (1981), Light and Kleiber (1981), and Murchie (1984).

The term "community-based participatory research" is used by Bopp to describe a research process employed in his Ph.D. research (Bopp, 1985; Bopp and Bopp, 1985). He was committed to developing a research process that enabled Native communities to use the "knowledge which is an essential part of their culture to develop community programs appropriate to the community" (Bopp and Bopp, 1985: l). Bopp and Bopp (1985: l) characterize community-based participatory research as having the following capabilities: first, it can "help create a mirror by which a community can see its own eyes, that is, its own wisdom and knowledge"; and second, it can help a "community integrate cultural wisdom with academic knowledge." Community-based participatory research then becomes a tool through which the community is able to act upon its members' lives in an informed collaborative manner.

* * * * *

2. The Nature of Human Relationships in Community-Based Participatory Research

The nature of human relationships in community-based participatory research has received the most attention in the research literature. A large part of this discussion pertains to the role of the researcher. Another area that receives attention regards the complexity of working with communities that have diverse and sometimes opposing groups. Central to the relationship between the researcher and the research context are the issues of "power and control."

In community-based participatory research, new roles are emerging both within the community and especially for the researcher (VioGrossi, 1981; Elden, 1981). The researcher's roles are very complex because he or she must be sensitive to so many aspects of human interaction. Reinharz (1981) believes that researchers' main instruments are their own self-awareness. Researchers are advised to examine their underlying assumptions and ideological perspectives in regards to the research situation (Hamnett et al., 1984; Huizer, 1978), because their personal values will affect decision-making in the research process (Reinharz, 1979; Brown and Kaplan, 1981).

Since community-based participatory researchers are active participants, they must become subjects of their own investigation (Reinharz, 1979; Torbet, 1981b), which in turn facilitates the development of a sense of solidarity with those who are studied (Huizer, 1978). Given the intimate nature of this research, Reinharz (1979) and Rowan and Reason (1981) advise researchers to choose research issues that coincide with personal concerns, so that one engages in "unalienated labour" (Reinharz, 1979: 216). On the one hand, researchers are encouraged to foster self-awareness and a personal commitment to the research situation, but, on the other hand, they are cautioned not to project or impose their particular ideology (Guyette, 1983; Hall, 1979; Lather, 1986). Rather than projecting one's own ideas about development and change, the researcher is urged to acknowledge and respect community leadership (VioGrossi, 1981: 44). In this respect it becomes important to choose a community whose concerns mirror the personal concerns of the researcher, although one cannot expect homogeneity in any community on important concerns.

Researchers are also advised to involve and collaborate with as many people as possible and to make use of diverse groups within the community (Brown and Kaplan, 1981; Guyette, 1983; Swantz, 1981). The aim is for so called "subjects" to become co-researchers. Inevitably, community-based participatory research becomes a much "messier" process because it "brings together parties whose inquiry objectives, research methodologies, and conceptual frameworks are very different, and the result may be misunderstanding, ambiguity, or conflict" (Brown and Kaplan, 1981: 312). "It may be quite different for persons of different backgrounds and experiences to perceive a situation in sufficiently common terms to permit agreement of the existence of a problem" (Schensul et al., 1987: 29). A researcher will require the insight and diplomatic skills needed to hold together collaborators who differ in ideological, disciplinary, and cultural orientations (Hamnett et al., 1984). Finally, the researcher must be capable of developing "participatory techniques" that are compatible with the cultural context (Guyette, 1983; Torbet, 1981b). The researcher must have these interpersonal sensitivities because it is inevitable that some members of the community may question aspects of the research.

Participation is not easily achieved (Campbell, 1987). The effort required to facilitate collaboration requires appropriate organization (Brown and Kaplan, 1981) and determination not to compromise the principles of collaboration, despite probable pressure to do so (Torbet, 1981a), particularly in politically polarized situations (Brown and Kaplan, 1981). An option may include encouraging the various interest groups to agree on certain goals of the research as a prelude to the research (Judi Bopp, 1987; personal communication). In regards to addressing "controversial issues," Torbet (1981b) recommends early exchanges between groups and efforts to establish support from the administration or appropriate leadership. He suggests that the researcher must "try simultaneously to model and advocate a process of self-disclosure, support others' efforts to express themselves, and [maintain] openness to confrontation" (Torbet, 1981a: 336–337). Consensus between a community and its leadership becomes important because sometimes the leadership, unbeknown to itself, will use the research to maintain its control.

* * * * *

For Elden (1981) the concept of "being open" revealed another aspect of social research. Subsequent to doing his research, Elden realized that his role was one of "co-producer of learning," which meant that he had "to be open to deep [i.e., initially frameless] learning, [that] he could not assume that his framework [would] dominate or remain unchanged" (Elden, 1981: 263). This also meant being able to "distinguish between and draw the line between not directing the process and being completely non-directive" (Elden, 1981: 256–257).

Community-based participatory research entails an acceptance of "vulnerability" on the part of the researcher; this helps the researcher maintain "openness" to one's limitations and the community's direction of the research process. The researcher in community-based participatory research "is more dependent on those from whom data come, has less unilateral control over the research process, and has more pressure to work from other people's definition of the situation" (Elden, 1981: 261). It is suggested by Katz that if one can risk the experience of vulnerability—defined as a "radical questioning of one's worldview"—then researchers will be able to "better gain access to a different framework and therefore a deeper understanding" (Katz, 1987: 27).

* * * * *

3. Interaction with Data in Community-Based Participatory Research

The issues of concern in this aspect of community-based participatory research are related to the development of research instruments and the collection and analysis of data. Kushner and Norris (1980–1981) have written specifically on the need to collaborate with the people in the research context on the interpretation of data. They believe that the task of understanding can only be successfully pursued when provisions are made for people to "move from merely articulating what they know (i.e., providing us with data) to theorizing about what they know (i.e., creating meanings)" (Kushner and Norris, 1980–1981: 27).

Inviting participants to engage in data analysis can be quite difficult for a number of reasons. For Elden (1981: 260), it was difficult because in this process he realized "that the more [he] understood things from their point of view, the less meaning [his] own categories had"—it was difficult to give up his own interpretations! Elden makes a really important admission because researchers must realize that different people and cultures will have contrasting attitudes to knowledge, and as Stokes (1985: 6) states, there are "other dimensions to the value of knowledge." For example, the Maori have different concepts of private, community, and

public knowledge, which makes it imperative that Maori communities are involved in the interpretation of data collected in and on their communities (Stokes, 1985: 8). Stokes points out the need for the "interpretation of Maori data to be perceived in Maori terms, not forced into preconceived European methodologies or systems of categorizing knowledge" (1985: 7). Hall also has illustrated the need for collaboration in the analysis of data. He is concerned that, despite "all the best intentions in the world, the [researchers were] never going to fully comprehend, much less intuitively grasp, the conditions and priorities of survival and growth in the villages .... By virtue of the fact of our class positions and our class interests, the knowledge we created about their lives was bound to be in error" (Hall, 1979: 398). Bopp and Bopp (1985) and Kushner and Norris (1980–1981) provide excellent examples of research where data were analyzed collaboratively and the final version approved by the people.

The outcome of community-based participatory research reveals complex perspectives on social realities. This kind of research often produces ambiguous and inconclusive statements about behaviour. Brown and Kaplan (1981) found that, even when parties agreed on the general outcome of inquiry, specific emphases and interpretations might vary. Community-based participatory research does not produce unambiguous explanations of a reality; on the contrary it often produces competing explanations that reflect the multiple realities experienced by different parties to the inquiry (Brown and Kaplan, 1981: 314). Furthermore, it is possible—even likely—that the research will alter the reality it seeks to explore. Light and Kleiber (1981) found that this could work to their benefit. By feeding their data back into the research context, they were able to study how this feedback influenced further action, thus enabling them to test the validity and the significance of the social knowledge they were generating.

Research participants are invaluable in identifying sources of data, as well as helping to develop the appropriate questions to ask. Stull and Schensul (1987) found that collecting data in a community in a rigorous, predetermined manner can be difficult. They found there must be agreement reached through some form of consensus with community members regarding collection of data. Collaborators in the research process must see the collection of information as being in their best interests; otherwise, further problems can develop when the various audiences for research have different views of the role of research and the information to be collected (Stull and Schensul, 1987). In their research, Stull and Schensul found that negotiations with community members and the research team broke down and irreconcilable positions developed concerning group articulation and clarification of the theory or theories of action underlying explanations of the problem. The problem was then resolved through political means rather than in the scientific arena (Stull and Schensul, 1987). This kind of outcome is highly likely because in community-based participatory research scientific discourse is not extracted from its political context.

4. Use of Findings in Community-Based Participatory Research

In community-based participatory research, the use of research results is a political process (Schensul et al., 1987) Cassell (1980: 32) warns that serious harm is done when findings are disseminated or published and "only the conduct not the consequences of fieldwork are discussed." Some of the harm can be prevented if the research results are reviewed by the group or community prior to publication (Guyette, 1983).

Although the researchers may see themselves producing products for the collaborators, the collaborators may see these same products as belonging to the researchers; consequently, the products will not be used by collaborators to their full potential (Stull et al., 1987). Light and Kleiber were challenged on the ownership of research information, and they found that "openness helped resolve questions of ownership" (1981: 175). If the community is actively involved in developing recommendations that they see arising from the research, then it is more likely that the research will have an impact on the community (Murchie, 1984; Bopp and Bopp, 1985) and that the material will be used for the development of the community (Bopp and Bopp, 1985; Stokes, 1985). It is important to make sure that the information in the research report is written in a form understandable to all, which means writing it in the language understandable to the people (Guyette, 1983; Murchie, 1984; Elden, 1981).

* * * * *

SELECTED DIMENSIONS OF PRACTICE

My doing community-based participatory research confirmed points raised in the literature, and expanded upon them, revealing more of the everyday and at times ironic obstacles to this kind of research. The pragmatics of practice, it turns out, provide a formidable challenge.

Effects of Interpersonal Dynamics

Like Brown and Kaplan's (1981) factory research, community-based participatory research is described as being "messier" than "conventional" research. Community-based participatory research does not follow a standard formula; instead it depends on the interpersonal dynamics of all the research participants. Dependence on community dynamics makes it difficult to predetermine transpiring events that may influence the outcome of the research (Brown and Kaplan, 1981). For example, the research process can be affected by unforeseen community dynamics and organizational change in the sponsoring agency.

Part of the "messiness" of community-based participatory research comes from the process of facilitating the participation of diverse and possibly polarized groups of people. Community-based participatory research depends on the interpersonal dynamics of all research participants, including both the researchers and collaborators. Community-based participatory research "brings together parties whose inquiry objectives, research methodologies, and conceptual frameworks are very different; and the result may be misunderstanding, ambiguity, or conflict" (Brown and Kaplan, 1981: 312). It is unrealistic to expect homogeneity in any community or group. Inevitably there will be diverse opinions, likely including opposing views. The issue of how to accommodate the participation and involvement of diverse groups of people is difficult. The key is to facilitate an open discussion of people's expectations and to negotiate common grounds.

The researcher must first acknowledge the inevitability of working with diverse groups of people when doing a community-based project and then attempt to build a relationship of trust and respect between groups. The researcher needs the insight and diplomatic skills to bring together collaborators who differ in ideological, disciplinary, and cultural orientations (Hamnett et al., 1984). It is also helpful to have some skill in conflict resolution or, at least, a willingness to discuss disagreements. The goal is to assist the various groups in developing a commitment to the project through the negotiation of common goals. Commitment is fostered by facilitating open discussions about the research in the language of the people and involving the people in decisions regarding the research. More than likely, some common ground will develop. [...]

Research Participants Learn New Roles

Community-based participatory research requires that both the researchers and the collaborators learn new roles as research participants. In the literature, the nature of human relationships, particularly as they affect the role of the researcher, is addressed extensively. Both the researchers and the collaborators must learn new ways of relating and interacting with each other as their respective new roles and responsibilities emerge. As Carr-Hill (1984) found in his research, the collaborators did not know how to participate as equals in the research he was conducting. This is also particularly relevant for First Nations communities who have for so long been led to believe and forced to accept that members of the colonial society can and should act on their behalf.

It is the responsibility of the researchers to initiate modes of collaboration with community people, though the ways in which people are actually able to participate will vary from community to community. This initiation of collaboration needs to be done in a way that respects leadership and cultural traditions. The researchers must do a lot of groundwork before the work—the formal research project—even begins.

Participation Is Not Easily Achieved

The literature on community-based participatory research points out that participation in research is not easily achieved (Campbell, 1987); it cannot be assumed nor taken for granted. For example, participation depends on the quality of relationship that the sponsoring organization of the research has with the community. Effort and time are always needed to convey to potential collaborators that their involvement is sincerely desired and that the invitation is more than just "lip service."

If people do not understand the research and/or do not have the opportunity to negotiate a direction for the research to take, they will be reluctant to participate in that research. It is important to remember that community people are not academicians, and they will not take seriously or get involved in a research project that they do not understand. People want to know how the project will practically and concretely be helpful and/or useful. The purpose and intent of the research must be negotiated and communicated with these considerations in mind. Researchers and collaborators must come to some common agreement about the nature of the research before proceeding, or at least early on in the research process. To facilitate collaboration requires appropriate organization and the determination not to compromise the principles of collaboration despite pressure to do so, particularly in politically polarized situations. [...] Facilitating community-based participatory research requires consistent, clear, and common-sense communication.

In this paper, I have tried to extract implications for practice from my own experience and from the literature. Making community-based participatory research a reality in and for people's lives is the aim of that approach; therefore attention must be devoted to the often mundane specifics of practice. With that in mind, I would now like to summarize some possible guidelines to practice.

Summary Guidelines for Doing Community-Based Participatory Research

A. Community-based participatory research takes time. It should not be seen as an efficient way of doing research. For example, time needs to be set aside for everyone in the research process, researchers and community people alike, to get to know each other; and time is needed to allow all opinions, some in conflict with each other, to be heard.

B. Community-based participatory research is more an interpersonal than a technical process because of its emphasis on involving people and eliciting their opinions. Community-based participatory research is a human exchange.

C. In community-based participatory research it is important to have regularly scheduled research meetings because then all participants can know when and how they can give input over the life of the entire research process. The meetings must be well publicized.

D. Community-based participatory research is very much about developing trustworthy relationships between all participants in the process.

E. In community-based participatory research the process of doing the research is more important than the research product because the emphasis is on the relationships between people. Community participation emphasizes connecting people and encouraging mutual learning. Whether something is written that is appropriate for publication is a separate consideration, though publication, when effective, becomes an integral part of the process.

F. In community-based participatory research one must be sensitive to the leadership in the community, and ensure that all the appropriate people are properly involved.

G. Participation cannot be taken for granted. For a variety of reasons, people may be unwilling or unable to participate. For example, community participants may feel they lack the expertise. Others may assume that, since community-based participatory research is still "research," it is the researcher's job to do it. And others may just be too busy.

H. When a sponsoring or funding agency is involved, it must be sincere about and committed to the idea of community-based participatory research. However, this commitment creates a dilemma because the agency is not likely to fully understand the implications of community-based participatory research, such as involving potential critics of the agency.

I. If there are professional researchers with primary responsibilities, they must be aware of their own limitations. For example, a philosophical understanding of community-based participatory research is not enough; some experience in facilitating group discussions and the open flow of information is necessary.

J. Power and control are central to the process of doing community-based participatory research. Decision-making must be shared. For example, professional researchers, if they are involved, must give up their assumed control over the research. Power and control must be constantly negotiated between all participants, but power and control are abstract notions and are often identified only after the fact.

K. All must be willing to examine their assumptions about each other. For example, researchers must examine their assumptions about the community. Do they really trust the community? Is the community capable of interpreting data? Likewise, community participants must examine their assumptions about what the researcher can or will do, and their assumptions about their role in the research.

L. Professional research language—research "jargon"—should be avoided. This is not a sign of disrespecting the community's intelligence but rather a way to facilitate understanding.

M. Since the community is probably the participant least familiar with doing research—though they have had research done "on them"—community participants in particular need to know what is expected of them and what they can contribute to the research process.

N. Community-based participatory research is like a community development project. For example, it takes time, must be responsive to a variety of voices, and must be sensitive to those outside the immediate research team and research establishment. It is a process of facilitating communication and understanding about the needs of the community.

* * * * *

CONCLUSION

Doing community-based participatory research has helped me as a First Nations person to understand in a practical sense the importance of community collaboration in the analysis and presentation of the data. We must ask ourselves: What role do the collaborators play in structuring the final report? Do they edit parts? Do they direct revisions? Or will they only participate in the analysis of the data?

I feel uncomfortable with the obvious power and control I would have if I were solely—or even primarily—deciding what data to present and how to present the results. I do not want the presentation to offend the community or my research colleagues. I want and need their assistance in deciding what data would become public and how it would be presented.

I also grapple with doubts about whether or not this type of research is "scientific." It is easy to doubt whether or not one is following the "right" procedures. I think this is exacerbated by the unpredictability and the ambiguity of doing community-based participatory research. However, as a First Nations person, I feel the responsibility to do research that is applied and, more specifically, useful. Given the conditions of our communities, research must benefit the community in practical ways. I believe that community-based participatory research offers a way for people who have been denied access to the control of research to regain that control. With a community-based participatory research approach, we can determine what happens in our communities through our collaboration and participation in research affecting our communities.

NOTE

This article is a revision of several sections from the author's master's thesis (St. Denis, 1989), which presents an in-depth discussion and analysis of the author's own experience in doing community-based participatory research.

REFERENCES

Bopp, M. 1985. "Education for Human Development." Unpublished doctoral dissertation, University of Alberta, Edmonton, Alberta.

Bopp, J., and M. Bopp. 1985. *Taking Time to Listen: Using Community-Based Research to Build Programs.* Lethbridge: University of Lethbridge, Four Worlds Development Press.

Brown, D.L., and R.E. Kaplan. 1981. "Participative Research in a Factory." In *Human Inquiry: A Sourcebook of New Paradigm Research*, edited by P. Reason and J. Rowan, 303–314. New York: John Wiley & Sons.

Campbell, D.J. 1987. "Participation of a Community in Social Science Research: A Case Study from Kenya Maasailand." *Human Organization* 46(2): 160–167.

Carr-Hill, R.A. 1984. "Radicalizing Survey Methodology." *Quality and Quantity* 18: 275–292.

Cassell, J. 1980. "Ethical Principles for Conducting Field Work." *American Anthropologist* 82: 28–40.

Churchill, W. 1988. "Sam Gill's Mother Earth: Colonialism, Genocide and the Appropriation of Indigenous Spiritual Tradition in Contemporary Academia." *American Indian Culture and Research Journal* 12(3): 49–67.

Deloria, V.C. 1984. *The Nations within: The Past and Future of American Indian Sovereignty.* Pantheon Books.

Elden, M. 1981. "Sharing the Research Work: Participative Research and Its Role Demands." In *Human Inquiry: A Source Book of New Paradigm Research*, edited by P. Reason and J. Rowan, 253–266. New York: John Wiley & Sons.

Guyette, S. 1983. *Community-Based Research.* Los Angeles: University of California American Indian Studies Center.

Hall, B. 1979. "Knowledge as a Commodity and Participatory Research." *Prospects* 9(4): 393–408.

Hamnett, M., D. Porter, A. Singh, and K. Kumar. 1984. *Ethics, Politics, and International Social Science Research* (An East-West Center book). Honolulu: University of Hawaii Press.

Huizer, G. 1978. "Anthropology and Multinational Power: Some Ethical Considerations on Social Research in the Underdeveloped Countries." In *The World as a Company Town*, edited by A. Idris-Soven and E. Idris-Soven, 175–187. The Hague: Mouton Publishers.

Katz, R. 1987. "Hearing Healers: The Contribution of Vulnerability to Fieldwork." In *The Healing of Knowledge* (German language edition), edited by A. Schenk and H. Kalweit, 288–317. Munich: Wilhem Goldman Verlag.

Kushner, S., and N. Norris. 1980–1981. "Interpretation, Negotiation, and Validity in Naturalistic Research." *Interchange* ii(4): 26–36.

LaFramboise, T., and B. Plake. 1983. "Toward Meeting the Research Needs of American Indians." *Harvard Educational Review* 55(1): 4551.

Lather, P. 1986. "Research as Praxis." *Harvard Educational Review* 56(3): 257–277.

Light, L., and N. Kleiber. 1981. "Interactive Research in a Feminist Setting: The Vancouver Women's Health Collective." In *Anthropologists at Home in North America*, edited by D.A. Messerschmidt, 167–182. Cambridge: Cambridge University Press.

Murchie, B. 1984. *Rapuora Health and Maori Women*. Wellington: The Maori Women's Welfare League.

Reinharz, S. 1979. *On Becoming a Social Scientist*. New Brunswick: Transaction Books.

_____. 1981. "Implementing New Paradigm Research: A Model for Training and Practice." In *Human Inquiry: A Sourcebook of New Paradigm Research*, edited by P. Reason and J. Rowan, 415–436. New York: John Wiley & Sons.

Rowan, J., and P. Reason. 1981. "On Making Sense." In *Human Inquiry: A Sourcebook of New Paradigm Research*, edited by P. Reason and J. Rowan, 113–137. New York: John Wiley & Sons.

Schensul, J.J., D. Denelli-Hess, M.G. Borrero, and M. Prem Bhavati. 1987. "Urban Comadronas: Maternal and Child Health Research and Policy Formulation in a Puerto Rican Community." In *Collaborative Research and Social Change: Applied Anthropology in action*, edited by D.D. Stull and J.J. Schensul, 9–31. Boulder: Westview Press.

St. Denis, V. 1989. "A Process of Community-Based Participatory Research: A Case Study." Unpublished master's thesis, University of Alaska/Fairbanks, Fairbanks, Alaska.

Stokes, E. 1985. "Maori Research and Development." Discussion paper prepared for the University of Waikato Social Science Committee of the National Research Advisory Council, February.

Stull, D.D., and J.J. Schensul, eds. 1987. *Collaborative Research and Social Change: Applied Anthropology in Action*. Boulder: Westview Press.

Stull, D.D., J.A. Schultz, and K. Cadue, Sr. 1987. "In the People's Service: The Kansas Kickapoo Technical Assistance Project." In *Collaborative Research and Social Change: Applied Anthropology in Action*, edited by D.D. Stull and J.J. Schensul, 33–54. Boulder: Westview Press.

Swantz, M. 1981. "Culture and Development in the Bagamoyo District of Tanzania." In *Human Inquiry: A Sourcebook of New Paradigm Research*, edited by P. Reason and J. Rowan, 283–291). New York: John Wiley & Sons.

Torbet, W.R. 1981a. "A Collaborative Inquiry into Voluntary Metropolitan Desegregation." In *Human Inquiry: A Sourcebook of New Paradigm Research*, edited by P. Reason and J. Rowan, 333–347). New York: John Wiley & Sons.

_____. 1981b. "Empirical, Behavioral, Theoretical, and Attentional Skills Necessary for Collaborative Inquiry." In *Human Inquiry: A Sourcebook of New Paradigm Research*, edited by P. Reason and J. Rowan, 437–46. New York: John Wiley & Sons.

VioGrossi, F. 1981. "Socio-political Implications of Participatory Research." *Convergence: An International Journal of Adult Education* 14(3): 43–51.

CHAPTER 22

Community Action Research

Marge Reitsma-Street and Leslie Brown

Understanding how and why we engage in research is an important place to start the story of our journey. Early on in our respective journeys we realized that our enjoyment in thinking about ideas and solving puzzles increased if they were useful to people. People have to be in the "absolute centre of the useful action," we said in our June conversations. The context for our research was people in relationships with one another who wanted to think creatively about concerns and do things that were useful for themselves and their communities. Doing good science and good community works, therefore, are connected to one another, both situated within relationships and reflective practice. [...]

* * * * *

THE POLITICAL NATURE OF RESEARCH

As we each traveled through different experiences with people-centred, useful research for communities, we learned to leave the certainty of traditional methodologies behind. Each of us in our own way had to challenge the authority of who knows best (Becker, 1970). By displacing authoritative accounts (Lather, 1991) and the centrality of scientific expertise, there emerged space for the experiences, knowledges, concerns, and expertise of many people, especially those most vulnerable to exclusion and oppression. We both gravitated to doing research with peoples pushed to the margins of our society—Leslie with Aboriginal communities and Marge with people living on low incomes or in marginalized communities. The political nature of our social work research began to emerge.

Fundamental to the politics of research is the careful and continuous negotiation about whose voice one emphasizes, what research strategies are selected, and on whose behalf one engages in research. It also is a political act to examine who benefits from particular information and how. In the example presented later in this chapter, Leslie clearly chose, and contracted, not to work for the federal Department of Indian Affairs, which funded the project, but reported to and was held accountable by the Aboriginal community.

* * * * *

Our journey is not over. Feminist scholarship and current work in multicultural and Aboriginal communities continue to challenge us to explore what is good, useful research for a community. [...]

* * * * *

The next part of this chapter explains the common research approach that underpins our individual work. We have chosen to name it Community Action Research. It is not a new name, as others speak of community-based action research (Stringer, 1999) and community action-research (Banks and Mangan, 1999). What is unique is our naming the following characteristics, values, and processes of CAR.

WHAT IS COMMUNITY ACTION RESEARCH?

The interest in naming and debating this approach to research draws from an appreciation of the congruence between social work values and the values of participation, reflectivity, empowerment, relationships, and change espoused in action-oriented, community-based research traditions. The interest also stems from a need to sharpen the possibilities of CAR, to share specific strategies, and to examine the difficulties. CAR is a useful, action-oriented, community-based approach for change. It is a value-based approach inspired by the emancipatory work of education activists like Paulo Freire (1993) and bell hooks (1994); the feminist social work scholarship of Patti Lather (1991) and Janice Ristock and Joan Pennell (1996); the critical analysis of everyday living in a globally restructured world by writers like Linda Tuhwai Smith (1999) and Sheila Neysmith (2000); and the practical social action work of community organizers conceptualized by Marie Mies and Vandana Shiva (1993), Joan Kuyek (1990), and Nancy Naples (1998). CAR is an approach to research that can promote the self-discovery of individuals, build communities, and serve as a catalyst for social change. We have come to use the term CAR as a way to reflect the importance of the community building and the political activism in our research. As critical curiosity and self-discovery are promoted for all those engaged in CAR, we, too, continue to reflect on the meaning and limits of CAR and are critical of the naming of it.

The "Community" in Community Action Research

Community is the context for the work of CAR. Community well-being is its purpose. The lifeworlds of a community are its focus (Banks and Mangan, 1999). Lifeworlds are the collection of traditions, networks, and material realities created in part by interrelated individuals, but existing apart and beyond them. Community is often, but not necessarily, situated in a geographical local space. We do not assume community is made up of permanent members. Transient membership, lukewarm allegiance, and volatile living situations are common patterns in poor communities, in the virtual-cyberspace communities of youth, and in the marginalized communities of workers disconnected from regular jobs or isolated in their work spaces. Also, there are not one, but several lifeworlds in any community. We assume that in most communities there are sharp differences in the lifeworlds and futures of its members, shaped by gender, race, class, and ability. CAR, along with community organizing and other social justice initiatives, aims to make visible the inequities in these differences and to work toward a more just distribution of the resources needed for adequate lifeworlds for all citizens in a community.

Within the complex and diverse lifeworlds of a community, the contribution of CAR is to focus on understanding and changing that that enhances and that that destroys the *common grounds*. The common grounds is a metaphor for the necessities of life that all people need in order to survive and to make humane choices. The grounds must be protected and cared for in common through collective means, whether laws, customs, or relationships. The common grounds could be the land, air, and water that have become the foci of the work of public health activists and the Aboriginal land rights and environmental movements (e.g., Barndt, 1999; Krauss, 1998). The common grounds could be the legal and political freedoms sought by the slavery abolitionists of the nineteenth century and the economic rights sought by the unionists and unemployed workers of the twentieth century. Those participating in a CAR initiative choose to work with, for, and on behalf of not only themselves and their families, but also those outside their homes and places of work. It is this other-regarding character toward people (Milroy and Wismer, 1994) and toward the common grounds that is crucial to shaping the strategies of CAR and to evaluating their impact.

The "Action" in Community Action Research

The focus on action is inherent in any action research. This action could be nurturing growth in people and community relationships, abolishing unjust policies, or constructing new ideas and structures. What may be unique to CAR is its intentional, strategic actions that aim to include the active contributions of many participants and the reactions of multiple audiences. The action in CAR is geared to the present and to the future. Each step of the research project encourages participation of those interested in or affected by the project's focus. Opportunities for active engagement are a key part of the work in designing CAR activities. The researchers do not reserve for themselves the funds or the tasks of thinking about ideas, gathering and interpreting data, or strategizing dissemination. Thus, the immediate foci for action are the research processes themselves. Other related but longer-term foci for action include changes in relationships, ideas, and structures.

As in other empowering types of action-oriented research approaches (e.g., Reason, 1988; Park et al., 1993), a central site for action is the self of those who participate most

directly in a CAR project. Changes in the confidence and skills of individuals occur in part because members of the CAR initiative nurture a broader web of respectful relationships. The nurturing of relationships builds on specific, immediate research and change tasks, as well as the ongoing, daily, informal work of centre people and activist mothers in a community. The work of building research and other relationships spirals out to include family members, neighbours, and selected allies in positions of power (Naples, 1998).

Changing ideas is another site of intentional action in CAR. In each step of CAR, rather than only at the end of a project, conversations and tasks help to break the frames of accepted, unitary ideas of why people are poor, for example, or the unquestioned beliefs about the responsibilities of parents. Broadcasting results does not just happen at the end of a CAR venture. Our assumption is that the new ideas spawned by CAR activities are needed to solve practical problems. New ideas are also needed to challenge the distortions and *veils* that enslave imagination and ensnare people into thinking crazy, unhealthy ideas (Comstock and Fox, 1993). Furthermore, we search in CAR for what Mathiesen (1974) calls unfinished, competing, and contradictory ideas. The contradictory ideas help to abolish the certainty of current practices and open up spaces for community members to imagine other possibilities. Thinking about competing, but not finished, alternatives supports the opportunities for people to go beyond reaction and into creation, to take control of their own destiny.

Changes in people and ideas may be short-lived unless action is taken to embody the changes in practice, policies, laws, and institutions (Banks and Mangan, 1999; Chambers, 1997; Reinharz, 1992), This is the strongest reason for doing CAR. It is also very difficult to achieve. LeCompte (1993) argues that successfully embedding change in institutions can be obscured by our own rhetoric and thwarted by the real difficulty in moving beyond awareness to activism. She warns that "bringing about change is not a quiet academic pursuit; to empower is to get into trouble" (1993: 15). Nonetheless, we also argue that knowledge about an institution, an unjust law, and the nature of power may only come through the struggles to change them. As Mies states, one "comes to know the naked face of aggression through struggles versus it" (1993: 40). Thus, there are risks in CAR and in other forms of empowering action research. CAR practitioners learn to be strategic. They engage in realistic, and often modest, change activities that build momentum and feed the commitment to action. At the same time, they select tasks to serve as steps toward more fundamental change.

The "Research" in Community Action Research

A hallmark of CAR is its use of a variety of methods for a variety of audiences. Using several methods and sources of information increases the possibility of understanding complex phenomenon. Multiple methods and triangulation also help to uncover evidence that may convince different audiences (Moss, 1995).

Three sets of multiple methods are used in CAR. The first set is the now-common set of qualitative and quantitative methods, each with their own disciplines and standards of rigour. Examples include life-history narratives of people living in poverty (e.g., Banks and Mangan, 1999) and statistical analysis of the numbers of people in a community living below national poverty lines (Reitsma-Street et al., 2000). The second set of research methods is sustained, democratic dialogue on one hand and on the other, shorter research activities, such as community mapping, that fit with procedures people are comfortable with.

The democratic dialogue is geared to small but changing groups of people, including the researchers, who help to facilitate CAR and take responsibility for ensuring momentum and productivity (Maguire, 1987; Reason, 1988). By way of contrast, informal, speedy methods are introduced into CAR in order to invite more people to participate in a project, to contribute their unique pieces of local knowledge to the larger puzzle, and to gather evidence useful to different audiences (Chambers, 1997; Mavalankar et al., 1996; Riley, 1997).

The third set of methods deals with the theorizing work in research. There is the local, public process of interpretation and making sense of the data through democratic dialogue, with provisional hypotheses and multiple explanations relevant to different audiences. Hours of private thinking and writing by the researchers and others are needed to interpret, for example, the statistical analysis of the specific impact of toxic materials on people's health (Merrifield, 1993) or the deconstructive analysis used by Ristock and Pennell (1996) in their empowerment, community-based research project on unionization drives among workers in shelters for battered women.

As in all research, CAR uses methods that can account for how conclusions are reached. This account needs to be accessible to public scrutiny. Good research also includes standards against which information can be compared and evaluated. Standards used in CAR include subjective interpretations of relevance and authenticity; evaluations comparing results to community principles or to international covenants of rights; qualitative research standards of trustworthiness and congruence; and quantitative statistical standards of reliability, validity, and generalizability. What is more unique to CAR is the strategic attention to broadcasting and dissemination of what is happening, what has been learned, and what the implications are. As developed in the next section on values and processes of

CAR, results are presented in various styles and forums, carefully selected to reach specific audiences who can make decisions or apply pressure for change.

THE VALUES AND PROCESSES OF COMMUNITY ACTION RESEARCH

This section presents the values of CAR and a brief summary of key processes common to CAR initiatives. We have selected a wheel as a symbol, with the centre hub of values, the ten spokes of processes, and the rim of relationships that connects the activities together and to the hub. A wheel also captures the dynamic and nonlinear nature of CAR. The hub, spokes, and rim are all necessary for the wheel to turn and for the project to move forward. The hub of values is the centre circle to which the CAR processes are attached. All the processes are necessary for the wheel to turn, but they are not initiated in any fixed order and can be conducted simultaneously. The rim of relationships among people connects the processes together and makes CAR possible.

The Centre: Values of Community Action Research

CAR is a value-driven activity. The values that underlie it are not a discrete list of attributes, but rather they are an integrated set of concepts that, taken together, provide direction for the planning, implementation, and utilization of CAR (Figure 22.1). A circle, with four directions to it, is illustrative of how each value of social justice, agency, community connectedness, and critical curiosity come together to inform the work of CAR.

Social Justice

To begin understanding the values, start with the concept of social justice. CAR is undertaken in the pursuit of social justice. It is not a neutral activity. Rather it is research that has a very overt political intention. This means that those involved in a CAR project are deliberately taking a particular stand on the topic of interest. Whether it is poverty research that aims to reduce poverty in a community or health research that intends to improve the lives

Figure 22.1: The Values of Community Action Research

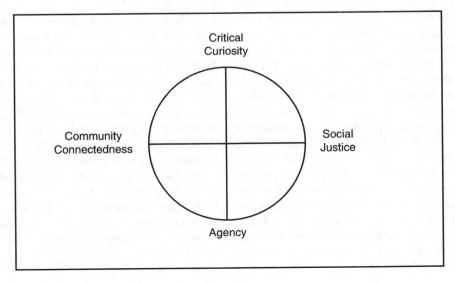

of persons with HIV, there is a clear agenda that is understood by those participating. [...] CAR is research for social change. It is not about simply any kind of change, however; it is change that seeks to work for the elimination of injustice and oppression. This distinguishes CAR from other types of action research that desire to change organizational behaviour or to have participants involved in the exploration of a topic of academic interest. CAR is a visibly political act.

Agency

CAR is about the doing; it is not only about reflecting or theorizing. In order for social justice to be pursued, there needs to be an action component to any CAR project. Agency refers to the ability to act. Again, the action that takes place in a CAR project is informed by the values of social justice and therefore manifests itself as activism. CAR is politically active, and many CAR practitioners consider themselves activists as much as they consider themselves researchers. We differ from Stringer's (1999) view that the researcher should not be an activist, but rather a facilitator. Facilitation is a key role for a Community Action Researcher. Yet activism to us means supporting the philosophical and political beliefs of those one works for and with while engaging in such facilitation roles. It is action with a social justice agenda.

There is a fundamental belief in the agency of the community. Researchers respect the abilities of communities to define and answer questions of importance. There is individual expertise within communities of all kinds, and CAR attempts to utilize the strengths within communities. The value of agency goes beyond simple participation. It is the recognition of the agency and the power of the participants to act. As argued earlier in this paper, having a commitment to action means more than simply making recommendations for change. It means engaging in action at all stages of the research process. As such, agency is a value that motivates one to look continually for opportunities to act, to engage others, and to advocate for justice.

Community Connectedness

A primary strategy to maximize a community's capacity to act on its own behalf is to develop collective expertise and connections. The power of coalitions in community collectivity is respected. CAR values relationships and the connections that are built and maintained within a community as part of a CAR project. This value necessitates participation by a community in the action research. Participation is not sought only for the provision of data. Rather, the social justice value that interacts with community connectedness and participation means there is a team approach to the research that respects the contributions of all participants and pays attention to the power relationships between participants, which includes the researchers. A feature of CAR is the democratic dialogue based on participation and relationships.

* * * * *

Critical Curiosity

Finally, there is the value of critical curiosity. CAR is about research, and research aims to discover, explore, and explain. Research is often undertaken in response to a curiosity or puzzlement. Curiosity also motivates CAR. In addition to being a political tool, it is an academic pursuit in that it seeks to respond to a curiosity. The interaction of the other values makes this curiosity a critical curiosity. Understanding power and injustice is part of the academic and personal reflections that accompany CAR. CAR, while aiming to contribute to social science knowledge, is firmly grounded in the daily experiences of people and communities. As such, it is a reflexive practice.

The Spokes: Processes of Community Action Research

At first glance, the work processes of CAR are similar to those in other research approaches presented as stages or components of a project, including clarification of a research question and review of the literature, establishment of the method, collection, and interpretation of data, and writing and sharing results. However, the work of CAR makes visible other processes, such as the decision to join together to address a community concern and the work of broadcasting results to engage people in change actions. CAR also features visiting research principles and developing relationships among people who participate in the action research processes. Throughout each of the CAR processes, attention is paid to designing opportunities so that those committed to the community concern are invited and helped to participate when they wish to in the research activities and decisions. We have found that the CAR processes are not necessarily efficient research procedures, although they can be inexpensive and speedy. [...] The processes are, however, intended to sponsor action while implementing the values of social justice, agency, community connectedness, and critical curiosity. How the processes of CAR are conducted, we argue, is an essential part of building momentum to create new ideas, new relationships, and new institutional changes. We have identified ten processes. They are not numbered, as that would give the illusion of linearity. [...] The processes are

- decide to join together to address a community concern
- enter the experiences and expertise of those concerned
- devise, revisit, and reinvent principles
- develop decision-making procedures

- negotiate resources, access, and allies
- design research procedures
- gather and inspect data
- analyze data and debate interpretations
- broadcast results to engage multiple audiences
- experiment with actions

Decide to Join Others to Address a Community Concern

This process is almost invisible, yet fundamental to CAR. Without at least two or three people deciding to spend time thinking about a concern and addressing it, there would be no CAR. The concern that prompts the decision to begin may be an unjust practice, such as a welfare snitch line, or a pressing decision, such as the site for a new community. The concern may also be vague, huge, and complex, such as poverty or racism in a neighbourhood. It may take a few weeks, months, or even years to gain sufficient momentum for a few people to decide to engage in CAR processes around a community concern. Deciding to begin is a process that continues throughout the life of a CAR project, as new people decide to join and others need to leave. Usually, the original few people decide also to form an organizing or steering group made up of interested people who vary in skills but have a common commitment and willingness to work together on the community concern. The organizing group makes initial decisions to facilitate several of the CAR processes; it can expand, shrink, evolve, divide, or disband as the needs of the CAR change. One of the many tasks that are embedded in this decision to address a community concern is negotiations around the specific research foci, purpose, and questions.

Enter the Experiences and Expertise of Those Concerned

Before the research questions and action tasks can be clarified, we argue it is important to enter the experiences and appreciate the expertise of the original few and the organizing group who decide to make a concern something they want to address. Why are people concerned? What do they know? What motivates people to learn more and to take action? People need to take time to discuss and explore their experiences and expertise and to invite interested others to join in this exploration. Particular attention is paid in this process to the knowledge and reality of those most affected by a concern. The academic and popular literature on ways of understanding the concern and responses to it are also reviewed. Entering the experiences and knowledge needs to be revisited several times throughout the course of a CAR, especially as new people join or another round of data gathering or sharing results is launched.

Devise, Revisit, and Reinvent Principles

People decide to work on a community concern for different reasons and with varying energy, skills, and time. It is essential that common principles are negotiated early on in a CAR venture and as new people join, whether as community citizens, agency representatives, or researchers in a university position. [...] These principles will guide the activities of those engaged in this value-based approach to doing action research in a community. The values of CAR regarding social justice, agency, community connectedness, and critical curiosity are the centre from which specific principles are debated, negotiated, and agreed to. Perhaps only a few principles can be agreed to early on, such as "care for members of the project by providing mutual support, learning, and personal development opportunities" and "do research in a way to help build skills that we can carry with us."

[...] Other principles emerge or old ones are reinterpreted when specific work is needed, as relationships develop, or after unanticipated situations necessitate a change in direction. So, for example, in a poverty project, the principle of "accurate, comprehensive data will be made available and accessible at minimal cost" was agreed to early on. Two years later, however, this principle was revisited and interpreted to mean that the final report had to be made free, and fund-raising efforts had to be launched to raise money for the report (Reitsma-Street et al., 2000).

Develop Decision-Making Procedures

Although decision-making is a part of each of the processes of CAR, one of the readers of the first draft of this chapter, a community development social worker, brought to our attention that it deserves to be articulated as a process in and of itself. Initially, decisions are needed about who joins the project and what are the project purposes and principles. These types of decisions are revisited as the project moves through time and encounters new or unexpected situations. Also, other decisions must be made: about research design, interpretation and ownership of data, and use of the research results for specific actions. If there are funds and people to hire, personnel and accounting decisions are needed.

There is no preferred mode of decision-making. We have participated in designing procedures that make decisions by consensus, by majority votes, and by executive fiat. What is necessary for CAR, however, is developing and revisiting decision-making procedures that are congruent with the values of social justice, agency, connectedness, and critical curiosity. Decision-making also needs to respect the cultural norms of the community, as well as be congruent with the specific principles that the community devises for a particular research project. That is, because connections within the community is one of the core values in CAR, decision-making procedures must include ways and time for people to sort out how best to develop relationships with their chosen community and to determine how to maintain authentic representation and accountability. Or, if participation is a key principle of a project, then procedures about determining the research direction, personnel hiring or firing, and the release of results must promote opportunities for people to participate in those decisions. Furthermore, as the unexpected is expected, and as serious differences of opinion are inevitable, when researching complex topics that evoke strong feelings, it is also necessary to design procedures for conflict resolution, healing of tensions, and revisiting key decisions. For instance, if the participants have chosen to make decisions by consensus, then a procedure is needed for when consensus breaks down. If voting is used to make decisions, there need to be procedures to revisit decisions in the event of a vote that alienates a large minority of participants or threatens the credibility of the project. [...]

Negotiate Allies, Resources, and Access

CAR ventures may be funded in part or for a time period. Much of CAR, however, is unfunded. The preparatory work leading to the decision of people to join together to address a concern, the work of building relationships and gaining access to information, and the work of communicating results and initiating actions depend heavily on existing resources, the time of people with paid jobs, and the volunteer energies of many people. These negotiations cannot be rushed. Principles emerge from these negotiations; these principles in turn become a guide to further the CAR work. In addition, each negotiation over resources and access with an individual, with an Aboriginal government, or with an agency's board of directors becomes an opportunity for developing allies. Allies are key players who may play small roles in a CAR venture and larger roles when research results are communicated and actions are debated.

Design Research Procedures

In this process we find the familiar research steps of sample selection, design of instruments, development of responses to ethical and organizational requirements, and pilot work to test feasibility of procedures. In CAR, however, there is awareness that the strategic selection of methods can enhance the possibility of people listening to the findings and taking subsequent action. As multiple methods are a hallmark of CAR projects, it is not uncommon to invite those with expertise in qualitative and quantitative procedures to join or teach members of the organizing group. Using multiple methods means that nearly everyone will learn something new. An atmosphere of sharing and learning new procedures enhances critical curiosity. Various procedures are needed to answer complex questions and convince different audiences.

Gather and Inspect Information

This process is also familiar. As in other community-based or action-oriented research projects, so, too, in CAR ventures particular attention is paid to creating opportunities for people to participate in gathering data and inspecting it. The opportunities can include activities as varied as collecting water samples, conducting interviews, distributing questionnaires, participating in focus groups, and debating the collected numbers, words, and ideas spread over the ground or on the walls. We have found that the more people who have the "data inside them," the stronger their interest in owning the results. As different individuals or groups figure out a piece of the results for themselves, they are more likely to translate data into action. For theoretical purposes, it is important at this stage to develop procedures so that the provisional hypotheses, hunches, and early analytical insights of those engaged in gathering and inspecting data are recorded and made available for additional analysis.

Analyze Data and Debate the Interpretations

This process begins early on and is visited several times as people join the CAR venture and try to make sense of the information—how much to believe, what is missing, and what is biased or incomplete. We have learned to seek out the most sophisticated technical assistance necessary to help analyze certain data at the same time as we develop opportunities for simple ways of analyzing information. Part of the analytical process is to place the information continuously in context of the experiences of the people most affected by a community concern and in the context of what openings there are for change. More problematic to this process is figuring out what the information means to individuals personally or as a group and what responsibility flows from what people have learned.

Broadcast Results to Engage Multiple Audiences

As mentioned previously, unique to CAR is the strategic attention to broadcasting and dissemination of results. Nearly from the beginning of a project and parallel to the process of gathering and inspecting information, a strategic plan is developed and revisited on how to present results and how to encourage debates on implications. The intent is to think about specific audiences who can make decisions or apply pressure for change. Printed or electronic fact sheets and community forums are strategically designed, as are reports, speeches, workshops, press releases, curriculum readers, popular plays, and academic articles.

The audiences for the results are often multiple, as a community concern is usually complex and many actions are needed to respond. Thus careful time is spent understanding how politicians, the public, grassroots advocacy groups, and business organizations hear information and respond to it. Up to one-third, and sometimes more,

of funds and energy in the CAR projects we have completed were dedicated to publicizing results, including, for example: discussions in kitchens, presentations in agency board rooms, long conversations with allies, press conferences, and academic speeches. Broadcasting results does not just happen at the end of a CAR venture. This process can begin early on in a CAR, when a few simple preliminary results are shared to help the original organizing group reach out to expand their core group and to develop connections to potential allies and sympathetic decision-makers. Broadcasting results to indifferent or unsympathetic decision-makers takes place, but later in a CAR venture, once solid relationships have been built and strong data analyzed. The first audience that needs to hear and debate results, however, includes people closest to the information and to the processes of gathering and analyzing it. Although we have sensed the impatience of academics and bureaucrats needing the finished products for their use, we argue that the values of CAR, especially those of community connectedness, imply that a community needs to digest the results first, to figure out responses and possible action. [...]

Experiment with Actions

This process is not the last one in a CAR initiative. As with the other CAR processes, work begins early on thinking about actions: what changes in research procedures, relationships, ideas, and institutions would be helpful to address the community concern. If, for example, the presence and magnitude of poverty is denied among some leaders in a community or is invisible to its policy-makers, one action could be the construction of a strong coalition of influential groups, including popular media, who could give legitimacy to a solid statistical analysis of the extent of poverty in the community. To address the causes of poverty will need many more actions, such as abolition of punitive government regulations that limit combining welfare and job payments or revisions to municipal zoning that restricts renovating homes to include affordable suites. The following example illustrates the values and processes of CAR, including the successful completion of an action.

CAR IN AN ABORIGINAL COMMUNITY: WHERE TO MOVE THE COMMUNITY?

An Aboriginal community requested Leslie's assistance in conducting a survey of their membership to determine the location of a new village site. The existing village site had been forced on them by the Canadian federal government about forty years prior and had not proven to be a healthy place. Many people had moved away due to the lack of space, the poor environment (due to a location next to a pulp mill that polluted their air and water), and other social and political reasons. They had talked on and off for years about moving the village site, but the current administrative and political leadership of the community was ready to push once again for such an initiative. They saw the move as not only a way to get away from an environmentally unsafe location, but as an opportunity to rebuild a community. They wanted a survey of the community members to determine where the new village should be located. The research team, consisting of Leslie, a non-Aboriginal woman, and an Aboriginal man from another Nation, responded to the request of the Band Chief and Council with a CAR approach to the proposed survey. The researchers had previous relationships with people in this community and knew from many discussions with people there that moving the village was only one of many interrelated problems that faced this community. Administrators were frustrated with the apathy, infighting, and general negative attitudes that permeated the community. They thought that moving the village would be a

catalyst to improving the overall well-being of the community. They were hopeful that the proposed research approach would motivate the community to work together to make the move possible.

This CAR project was owned and operated by the people in the community. As such, there is a tension for the researcher in writing or talking about it for purposes outside the community, such as this chapter. The data belong to them, not to the researchers. Knowing that Leslie is an academic, they had given permission for her to talk about the process for educational purposes, but they expect that the relationship established between them and the researcher will be honoured in choosing how to do this. With respect, this illustration is offered in order to demonstrate the potential of CAR to facilitate social change and justice. After commenting on the use of CAR values in this venture, the major activities engaged in are listed. These activities illustrate the CAR processes, although not all ten are specifically addressed.

The Values

This project was framed by the values of CAR. Social justice was an ongoing motivator of the project. This community had been forced to live in an environmentally unhealthy place. They had subsequently become unhealthy socially and culturally as well. The intent of the project was to facilitate empowerment through consciousness raising about health status and the possibilities for the future. The collection of data from individuals was also an opportunity to engage in dialogue with people about their lives, their hopes, and their fears. As Freire (1993) characterizes such work, the researchers are educators who come to know with the participants about the reality of their lives.

The value of agency was a conscious one that had to be constantly rekindled. From the initiation of the project, the community was pushed to be involved and to take real ownership of the process and outcome. After years of dependency, community members often just wanted the researchers to do the work and to simply make a recommendation on their behalf to the federal government. The researchers had to work hard to resist this and work actively at every step to keep the ownership of the project in the community. Consciousness raising occurred at the individual, family, and community levels through personal discussions, regular meetings with administrators and politicians, community meetings, and so on. As the project progressed, the responsibility for maintaining the action shifted from the researchers to others in the community.

The belief in the capacity of the community to act and determine its future was a fundamental belief. Outsiders could not fix the problems for the community. The community members had to take hold of the issues and solutions, and then they were able to negotiate with outsiders such as the federal government for what they had decided was needed. The potential power of the community was a fundamental value that was often challenged by apathy and internalized oppression and dominance among the community members. Maintaining this value of agency was strengthened by the other values of social justice and connectedness. The role of the researcher really was one of activist.

Rebuilding this community necessitated a commitment to connecting community members with each other in the visioning of a new community. Valuing the connections despite family feuds and long geographic or time distances did not make it easy. However, through using processes that encouraged interactions between people, the community members developed a collective understanding of their health and social issues. Community members were also made aware of the resources within their community that could be utilized as they rebuilt their cultural, social, and economic society.

Finally, the value of critical curiosity was ever present. There had been rumors about the poor health and living conditions, but no studies had been done to substantiate them. The community had complained for years to the government, which had minimized the effects on the entire community. Once the health status for all was compiled, the community was amazed at the results. They were outraged, but now they had the data upon which to act. They also now knew the people's beliefs about moving were not as divisive and controversial as people had feared. They saw in the data the potential to come together as a community and act.

The Processes

The community members owned the research. This meant that the researchers had to do a lot of talking and listening in the community about the proposed research so that people committed themselves to participating as owners of the research and not as passive subjects. Whenever the research was referred to, it was as community research—the researchers' names were not attached. The Band Council and others were consulted at every step, from designing the questions to planning how to conduct interviews. The process was transparent, including being referred to continually at band meetings, in newsletters, and on the local community television station.

The commitment of the researchers went beyond a contractual commitment to conduct a survey. The community made it clear that the researchers had a relationship with them and that conducting research this way meant that the researchers, too, were a part of their future. Developing new personal associations with people is often a part of doing research. A social relationship among researchers and participants was a particular feature of this CAR project. The researchers have a connection with those people forever.

Every band member, on and off reserve, was involved. Because building community connectedness was important, the researchers had to track down people who had left the local area and invite them to participate. Individual interviews of about three hours each were conducted with more than 300 adults. Forums for youth and children were also held several times. Involving band members from all over the region was important to the rebuilding enterprise. As one person said, "It's hard to be scattered and a family."

The survey instrument was designed to elicit information on community health and social issues, as well as to get indicators of what would be important to people in choosing a new site for the village. The instrument aimed to set the tone of community building, not only the selection of a physical site. People interviewed offered three levels of information to the researchers. The survey questions were discussed and, together with a researcher, the respondents would decide what would be written down as their responses to the formal questions (i.e., the official responses that would appear in a report that could be submitted to outside agencies such as the Department of Indian Affairs). Also written down were other points that the respondent wanted the community to know but that should not go outside the community. Respondents had control over what was written. Some chose to do the writing themselves; others reviewed what the researcher had written. In many cases it was a cooperative task. Finally, there were comments that the respondents wanted the researchers to keep confidential. All interviews were tape recorded, with the control of the on/off button in the hands of the respondent. Tapes were the property of the respondent, not of the community or the researcher.

As data were collected, workshops and meetings were held to present the data and engage the community in analysis. This not only enabled the construction of the analysis and recommendations in the research, but it also galvanized the community members to take ownership and action. They were angered by what they had discovered—that their people were unhealthy and that they had to do something about it.

As community ownership of the project increased, the role of the researchers diminished. Eventually, the researchers were not needed as researchers. The data had been collected and presented in various forms and forums. Subsequent meetings, reports, and strategy papers were conducted and written without the researchers having to initiate them or even be present.

The Aboriginal reserve community in this project agreed on the need to move to a new village site and took the necessary steps for this to be realized a few years later. Four years after the relocation was realized, at the time of writing this chapter, the commitment to building a healthy community that was sparked in part by the values and processes of the CAR venture remains. The relationships that rimmed the project continue to be the glue that holds this ongoing community work together.

CONTINUING THE CONVERSATION

Community Action Research is the name we have given to a value-based approach to politicized research processes that address community concerns. Based on experiences and the literature, we have conceptualized values and processes of this dynamic approach that are responsive to the need for useful community-based research. We continue to debate the limits of CAR and to experiment with its promise in order to understand how research can on one hand build and empower communities, and on the other, examine the hidden, messy, fundamental forces that destroy the common grounds and lifeworlds required by diverse people to live in community with each other.

From our experience and reflections, we suggest there is a need to understand and debate the implications of dualities and contradictions in the core values and specific work processes within empowerment types of research, such as CAR. We are debating what these dualities are, what tensions they provoke, and how much they are inevitable, necessary, or problematic. Is it possible that the obvious tension between action and research, for example, or between too much information and not enough, or between making opportunities for individuals to participate within a CAR project and the needs of research to be rigorous and legitimate can help to clarify what tasks are most important, when, and for whom? We contend that attention needs to be given to these types of debates and consideration given to both poles of a duality in them. [...]

* * * * *

The contradictions and the dualities, however, add a complexity to what may already be a difficult, unwieldy endeavour. [...] We need to debate when a CAR project would make sense and for whom. When, for example, is a community development initiative, not a CAR project, needed? Or when would a top-down, science-driven research approach be appropriate, without the additional CAR processes that pay attention to relationships, principles, opportunities for participation, broadcasting results, and strategizing change? Are the critical curiosity value of CAR and the rigorous research activities added primarily to legitimate an initiative for the sake of academics? Budd Hall (1993) argues that university researchers, and probably social workers, are not necessary to participatory research.

Countless groups make use of processes which resemble participatory research every day without naming it or certainly without asking for outside validation of the knowledge which is produced. (xx)

Another debate we have is about resources. To conduct CAR in a substantial and not token manner takes time, skill, and funds. Too often it depends on professionals adding something to their already full days or community members giving volunteer time. Our experience is that people, even those with limited incomes and minimal energies, will give a great deal and far more than expected when they feel they can negotiate freely what to give and when, and if they feel they can withdraw their contributions without shame or retribution (Reitsma-Street and Neysmith, 2000). Nonetheless, CAR is not possible without material resources, especially time. There also is an injustice or imbalance in paying funds and honouring the expertise of academic, technical skills while expecting those with other expertise, in the experience of poverty or Aboriginal traditions, for instance, to give it freely.

Further debate and clarity on such issues are needed as the popularity of action-research and community-based research traditions grows (Brown, 1994; Fetterman et al., 1996; Fleming and Ward, 1999; King, 1995; Levin, 1999). With the legitimization of such research approaches, there is an accompanying worry that CAR will be coopted for the benefit of those already holding privilege and power. Accompanying popularity are attempts to transform community research for change into an unrealistic, depoliticized service. There is also the pressure to simplify the processes, making them into technical prescriptions focusing, for instance, on people as clients and beneficiaries, not as citizens. More insidious are claims of authentic collaboration when only token or restricted participation of the community in action research is possible or desired (Smith, 1999; VanderPlaat, 1997). Just as there is the strong possibility for CAR to be

a strategy for liberation, it also has the potential to be used to further oppress. Research is a political tool.

NOTE

The authors wish to acknowledge with deep appreciation the teachings, patience, and encouragement of our many teachers, in particular

Pat Rogerson, Harry Street, Mabel Jean Rawlins-Brannon, Bobby Joseph, and Bruce Parisian.

REFERENCES

Banks, C.K., and J.M. Mangan. 1999. *The Company of Neighbours: Revitalizing Community through Action-Research.* Toronto: University of Toronto Press.

Barndt, D., ed. 1999. *Women Working the NAFTA Food Chain: Women, Food & Globalization.* Toronto: Second Story Press.

Becker, H.S. 1970. "Whose Side Are We on?" In *The Relevance of Sociology*, edited by J.D. Douglas, 99–111. New York: Appleton-Century Crofts.

Brown, P.A. 1994. "Participatory Research: A New Paradigm for Social Work." In *Education and Research for Empowerment Practice*, edited by L. Gutierrez and P. Nurius, 293–303. Seattle: University of Washington, Center for Policy and Practice Research, School of Social Work.

Chambers, R. 1997. *Whose Reality Counts? Putting the Last First.* London: Intermediate Technology Publications.

Comstock, D.E., and R. Fox. 1993. "Participatory Research as Critical Theory: The North Bonneville, USA, Experience." In *Voices of Change*, edited by P. Park, M. Brydon-Miller, B. Hall, and T. Jackson, 103–124. Toronto: Ontario Institute for Studies in Education Press.

Fetterman, D.M., S.J. Kaftarian, and A. Wandersmand, eds. 1996. *Empowerment Evaluation: Knowledge and Tools for Self-Assessment and Accountability.* Thousand Oaks: Sage.

Fleming, J., and D. Ward. 1999. "Research as Empowerment: The Social Action Approach." In *Empowerment Practice in Social Work: Developing Richer Conceptual Foundations*, edited by W. Shera and L.M. Wells, 370–389. Toronto: Canadian Scholars' Press.

Freire, P. 1993. *Pedagogy of the Oppressed*, rev. ed., translated by M.B. Ramos. New York: Continuum.

Hall, B. 1993. "Introduction." In *Voices of Change*, edited by P. Park, M. Brydon-Miller, B. Hall, and T. Jackson, xii–xxii. Toronto: Ontario Institute for Studies in Education Press.

hooks, b. 1994. *Teaching to Transgress: Education as the Practice of Freedom.* New York: Routledge.

King, J.A. 1995. "Bringing Research to Life through Action Research Methods." *Canadian Journal on Aging* 14(Suppl. 1): 165–176.

Kuyek, J. 1990. *Fight for Hope: Organizing to Realize Our Dreams.* Montreal: Black Rose Books.

Krauss, C. 1998. "Challenging Power: Toxic Waste Protests and the Politicization of White, Working-Class Women." In *Community Activism and Feminist Politics,* edited by N.A. Naples, 129–150. London: Routledge.

Lather, P. 1991. *Getting Smart: Feminist Research and Pedagogy within the Postmodern*. New York: Routledge.

LeCompte, M.D. 1993. "A Framework for Hearing Silence: What Does Telling Stories Mean When We Are Supposed to Be Doing Science?" In *Naming Silences Lives: Personal Narratives and Process of Educational Change*, edited by D. McLaughlin and W.G. Tierney, 9–27. New York: Routledge.

Levin, M. 1999. "Action Research Paradigms." In *Action Research*, edited by D.J. Greenwood, 25–38. Amsterdam: John Benjamins.

Maguire, P. 1987. *Doing Participatory Research: A Feminist Approach*. Amherst: University of Massachusetts, Center for International Education, School of Education.

Mathiesen, T. 1974. *The Politics of Abolition*. Oslo: Universitagaet.

Mavalankar, D.V., J.K. Satia, and B. Sharma. 1996. "Experiences and Issues in Institutionalizing Qualitative and Participatory Research Approaches in a Government Health Programme." In *Participatory Research in Health*, edited by K. de Koning and M. Marton, 216–228. London: Zed Books.

Merrifield, J. 1993. "Putting Scientists in Their Place: Participatory Research in Environmental and Occupational Health." In *Voices of Change*, edited by P. Park, M. Brydon-Miller, B. Hall, and T. Jackson, 65–84. Toronto: Ontario Institute for Studies in Education Press.

Mies, M. 1993. "Feminist Research: Science, Violence, and Responsibility." In *Ecofeminism*, edited by M. Mies and V. Shiva, 36–54. Halifax: Fernwood.

Milroy, B.M., and S. Wismer. 1994. "Communities, Work and Public/Private Sphere Models." *Gender, Place and Culture* 1(1): 71–90.

Moss, P. 1995. "Embeddedness in Practice, Numbers in Context: The Policies of Knowing and Doing." *The Professional Geographer* 47(4): 442–449.

Naples, N.A. 1998. *Community Activism and Feminist Politics: Organizing across Race, Class, and Gender*. New York: Routledge.

Neysmith, S., ed. 2000. *Restructuring Caring Work: Power, Discourse and Everyday Life*. Toronto: Oxford University Press.

Park, P., M. Brydon-Miller, B. Hall, and T. Jackson, eds. 1993. *Voices of Change: Participatory Research in the United States and Canada*. Toronto: Institute for Studies in Education Press.

Reason, P., ed. 1988. *Human Inquiry in Action: Developments in New Paradigm Research*. London: Sage.

Reinharz, S. 1992. *Feminism Methods in Social Research*. Toronto: Oxford University Press.

Reitsma-Street, M., and R. Arnold. 1994. "Community-Based Action Research in a Multi-site Prevention Project: Challenges and Resolutions." *Canadian Journal of Community Mental Health* 13(2): 229–240.

Reitsma-Street, M., A. Hopper, and J. Seright, eds. 2000. *Poverty and Inequality in the Capital Region of British Columbia*. Victoria: University of Victoria.

Reitsma-Street, M., and S. Neysmith. 2000. "Restructuring and Community Work: The Case of Community Resource Centres for Families in Poor Urban Neighbourhoods." In *Restructuring Caring Labour: Power, Discourse and Everyday Life*, edited by S. Neysmith, 142–163. Toronto: Oxford University Press.

Riley, D.A. 1997. "Using Local Research to Change 100 Communities for Children and Families." *American Psychologist* 52(4): 424–433.

Ristock, J.L., and R. Pennell. 1996. *Community Research as Empowerment: Feminist Links, Postmodern Interruptions*. Toronto: Oxford University Press.

Smith, L.T. 1999. *Decolonizing Methodologies: Research and Indigenous Peoples.* London: Zed Books.

Stringer, E.T. 1999. *Action Research,* 2nd ed. Thousand Oaks: Sage.

Vanderplaat, M. 1997. "Emancipatory Politics, Critical Evaluation and Government Policy." *Canadian Journal of Program Evaluation* 12(2): 143–162.

CHAPTER 23

Power and Knowledge

JOHN GAVENTA AND ANDREA CORNWALL

Participatory research has long held within it implicit notions of the relationships between power and knowledge. Advocates of participatory action research have focused their critique of conventional research strategies on structural relationships of power and the ways through which they are maintained by monopolies of knowledge, arguing that participatory knowledge strategies can challenge deep-rooted power inequities. [...]

* * * * *

In more recent years, the uses and understandings of participatory research have broadened considerably. Rather than being seen as an instrument only of the powerless, the language and methods of participatory research are being adopted by large and powerful institutions. The new legitimacy and acceptance of participatory research raises critical questions. What aspects of participatory practice are institutions like national governments and the World Bank taking up? Does this new incorporation represent co-optation, or does it represent new spaces for larger and more effective action? How are power relations mediated across agencies and actors as participatory practice moves to larger scale? What are the interrelationships of the uses of participatory research for social, institutional, and individual change?

POWER AS KNOWLEDGE

Power and knowledge are inextricably intertwined. A starting point for situating our analysis of power and knowledge in participatory research is to map out some of the different ways in which power is conceptualized and their implications for research. [...] We take as our starting point the three dimensions of power elaborated by Lukes (1974) and built upon in Gaventa's analysis.[1] Adding a fourth dimension, the relational view of power emerging from the work of Foucault (1977, 1979) and his followers, we explore questions of power, knowledge, and participation.

Lukes (1974) begins his argument by challenging the traditional view in which power is understood as a relationship of "A over B": that is, power is the ability of A (the relatively powerful person or agency) to get B (the relatively powerless person or agency) to do what B might not otherwise do (Dahl, 1969). In this approach, power is understood as a product of conflicts between actors to determine who wins and who loses on key, clearly recognized issues, in a relatively open system in which there are established decision-making arenas. [...]

Within this first dimension of power, knowledge or research may be conceived as resources to be mobilized to influence public debates. Practically, with this view, approaches to policy influence, knowledge, and action relate largely to countering expertise with other expertise. The assumption is that "better" (objective, rational, highly credible) knowledge will have greater influence. Expertise often takes the form of policy analysis or advocacy, both of which involve speaking "for" others, based not on lived experience of a given problem, but on a study of it that claims to be "objective." Little attention is paid in this view to those whose voices or whose knowledge were not represented in the decision-making process, nor on how forms of power affected the ways in which certain problems come to be framed.

This pluralist vision of an open society, in which power is exercised through informed debate among competing interests, continues to affect many of our understandings of how power affects policy. However, this view has been widely challenged. Political scientists such as Bachrach and Baratz (1970) put forward a second understanding of power. They argued that the hidden face of power was not about who won and who lost on key issues, but was also about keeping issues and actors from getting to the table in the first place. [...] The study of politics, Bachrach and Baratz argued, must focus "both on who gets what, when and how and who gets left out and how" (1970: 105).

In this view knowledge, and the processes of its production, contribute very strongly to the mobilization of bias. Scientific rules are used to declare the knowledge of some groups more valid than others, for example "experts" over "lay people," etc. Asymmetries and inequalities in research funding mean that certain issues and certain groups receive more attention than others; clearly established "methods" or rules of the game can be used to allow some voices to enter the process and to discredit the legitimacy of others.

From the second dimensional view, empowerment through knowledge means not

only challenging expertise with expertise, but it means expanding who participates in the knowledge production process in the first place. It involves a concern with mobilization, or action, to overcome the prevailing mobilization of bias (see Gaventa, 1993). When the process is opened to include new voices, and new perspectives, the assumption is that policy deliberations will be more democratic, and less skewed by the resources and knowledge of the more powerful.

While the second dimension of power contributed to our understanding of the ways in which power operates to prevent grievances from entering the political arenas, it maintained the idea that the exercise or power must involve conflict between the powerful and the powerless over clearly recognized grievances. This approach was then challenged by others such as Steven Lukes, who suggested that perhaps "the most effective and insidious use of power is to prevent such conflict from arising in the first place" (1974: 24). The powerful may do so not only by influencing who acts upon recognized grievances, but also through influencing consciousness and awareness of such grievances in the first place.

In this approach, the control of knowledge as a way of influencing consciousness is critical to the exercise of power. Knowledge mechanisms such as socialization, education, media, secrecy, information control, and the shaping of political beliefs and ideologies, all become important to the understanding of power and how it operates. In this approach, power begins to resemble Gramscian notions of "hegemony" (Entwistle, 1979) or Freirean ideas (1981) of the ways in which knowledge is internalized to develop a "culture of silence" of the oppressed.

Countering power involves using and producing knowledge in a way that affects popular awareness and consciousness of the issues which affect their lives, a purpose that has often been put forward by advocates of participatory research. Here the discussions of research and knowledge become those involving strategies of awareness building, liberating education, promotion of a critical consciousness, overcoming internalized oppressions, and developing indigenous or popular knowledge. [...]

Each of these approaches to power carry with them implicit or more explicit conceptions of knowledge, and how it relates to power, as well as to strategies of empowerment. In the first view, knowledge is a resource, used and mobilized to inform decision-making on key public issues—issues of who produces knowledge, or its impact on the awareness and capacity of the powerless are less important. In the second view, the powerful use control over the production of knowledge as a way of setting the public agenda, and for including or excluding certain voices and participants in action upon it. In response, mobilization of the relatively powerless to act upon their grievances and to participate in public affairs becomes the strategy—one in which action research is an important tool. In the third dimension, the emphasis is more upon the ways in which production of knowledge shapes consciousness of the agenda in the first place, and participation in knowledge production becomes a method for building greater awareness and more authentic self-consciousness of one's issues and capacities for action.

BEYOND THE THREE-DIMENSIONAL VIEW

While over the years this three-dimensional framework has provided a useful way of understanding power and knowledge in research, it has also been critiqued from a number of differing perspectives. [...]

All three dimensions of power focus on the repressive side of power, and conceptualize power as a resource that individuals gain, hold, and wield. Building on work by Foucault,

others have come to see power more as productive and relational. In this view, power becomes "a multiplicity of force relations" (Foucault, 1979: 92) that constitute social relationships; it exists only through action and is immanent in all spheres, rather than being exerted by one individual or group over another. For Foucault, power works through discourses, institutions, and practices that are productive of power effects, framing the boundaries of possibility that govern action. Knowledge is power: "power and knowledge directly imply one another ... there is no power relation without the correlative constitution of a field of knowledge, nor any knowledge that does not presuppose and constitute at the same time power relations" (1977: 27).

* * * * *

Recent work by Hayward draws on Foucault to argue for "de-facing power" by reconceptualizing it as "a network of social boundaries that constrain and enable action for all actors" (1998: 2).[2] She argues that freedom is the capacity to act on these boundaries "to participate effectively in shaping the boundaries that define for them the field of what is possible" (1998: 12). This has a number of important implications for thinking about power and knowledge in participatory research. First, it shifts the analysis of power only from resources that "A" holds or uses, to include other broader ways in which spheres of action and possibility are delimited. If power is shaped by discourse, then questions of how discourses are formed, and how they shape the fields of action, become critical for changing and affecting power relations.

Secondly, this approach recognizes that no human relationship is exempt from a power component. In so far as power affects the field of what is possible, then power affects both the relatively powerful and the relatively powerless. From this perspective, power involves "any relationship involving two or more actors positioned such that one can act within or upon power's mechanisms to shape the field of action of the other" (Hayward, 1998: 15). Power can exist in the micro-politics of the relationship of the researcher to the researched, as well as in broader social and political relationships; power affects actors at every level of organizational and institutional relationships, not just those who are excluded or at the bottom of such relationships.

Finally, this broader approach to power includes the more positive aspects through which power enables action, as well as how it delimits it. Power in this sense may not be a zero-sum relationship, in which for B to acquire power may mean the necessity of A giving up some of it. Rather, if power is the capacity to act upon boundaries that affect one's life, to broaden those boundaries does not always mean to de-limit those of others. In this sense power may have a synergistic element, such that action by some enables more action by others. [...]

KNOWLEDGE AS POWER

If, in this expanded view, freedom "is the capacity to participate effectively in shaping the social limits that define what is possible" (Hayward, 1998: 21), then we can also more clearly situate knowledge as one resource in the power field. Knowledge, as much as any resource, determines definitions of what is conceived as important, as possible, for and by whom. Through access to knowledge, and participation in its production, use, and dissemination, actors can affect the boundaries and indeed the conceptualization of the possible. In some situations, the asymmetrical control of knowledge productions of others can severely limit the possibilities which can be either imagined or acted upon; in other situations, agency in the process of knowledge production, or co-production with others, can broaden these boundaries enormously.

Throughout the literature on participatory action research, we find various theories and approaches which to some degree or another are premised upon the claim that democratic participation in knowledge production can expand the boundaries of human action. [...]

Below we illustrate and explore some commonalities and differences that draw especially (but not exclusively) from the approaches which have influenced our thinking the most. These are those associated with the Freirean tradition of participatory action research, and those associated with more/recent work around participatory rural appraisal [PRA], an approach which has spread very quickly in the 1990s with an enormous impact on development thinking and practice.[3]

The Nature and Locations of Power

For those early writers on participatory action research (PAR), power is understood as relation of domination in which the control of knowledge and its production was as important as material and other social relations. [...]

The knowledge that affects people's lives is seen as being in the hands of a "monopoly" of expert knowledge producers, who exercise *power over* others through their expertise. The role of participatory action research is to empower people through the construction of their own knowledge, in a process of action and reflection, or "conscientization," to use Freire's term. Such action against power over relations implies conflict in which the power of the dominant classes is challenged, as the relatively powerless begin to develop their new awareness of their reality, and to act for themselves (Selener, 1997: 23).

While in this earlier view of PAR, power is located in broad social and political relations, later work by Chambers, more often associated with PRA, puts more emphasis on domination in personal and interpersonal terms. Starting with a focus on "hierarchies of power and weakness, of dominance and subordination"

(1997: 58), Chambers outlines two categories: "uppers," who occupy positions of dominance, and "lowers," who reside in positions of subordination or weakness. In his account of "uppers" and "lowers," power is less fixed in persons than in the positions they inhabit *vis-à-vis* others: people can occupy more than one position as "upper," and may occupy both "upper" and "lower" positions depending on context. [...]

* * * * *

Departing from a "power over" perspective, PRA is characterized as a means through which a zero-sum conceptualization of power can be transcended: "lowers" speak, analyse, and act, in concert with each other and with newly sympathetic and enabling professionals who have become aware of the power effects of their positions as "uppers." Through analysis and action, "lowers" are able to lay claim to their own distinctive versions and visions, acquiring the "power to" and "power within" that restores their agency as active subjects. By listening and learning, "uppers" shed the mantle of dominance:

> From planning, issuing orders, transferring technology and supervising, they shift from convening, facilitating, searching for what people need and supporting. From being teachers they become facilitators of learning. They seek out the poorer and weaker, bring them together, and enable them to conduct their own appraisal and analysis, and take their own action. The dominant uppers "hand over the stick," sit down, listen, and themselves learn. (Chambers, 1995: 34)

While offering an optimistic view of the possibilities of individual change, this view has also been critiqued for failing to analyse broader sources of oppression (e.g., Crawley,

1998). At the same time, those involved with PAR have also been critiqued for offering a broad analysis of social power relations, without clear starting points for change at the micro and personal level. [...]

Part of the difference in views here is found in the level of analysis. Rather than thinking about these approaches as necessarily competing, it is perhaps more useful to think of them of as complementary, each with a differing starting point in addressing mutually re-enforcing levels of power. [...] If freedom, as defined earlier, is the capacity to address the boundaries of possibility which are drawn in multiple ways and relationships, then surely the multiple levels of change are each important.

Power and the Nature of Knowledge

While differing approaches to action research may have differing understandings of the location of power, they all share an epistemological critique about the ways in which power is embedded and reinforced in the dominant (i.e., positivist) knowledge production system. The critique here is several-fold. First, there is the argument that the positivist method itself distorts reality, by distancing those who study reality (the expert) from those who experience it through their own lived, subjectivity (Gaventa, 1993). Second is the argument that traditional methods of research—especially surveys and questionnaires—may reinforce passivity of powerless groups, through making them the objects of another's inquiry, rather than subjects of their own. Moreover, empirical, quantitative forms of knowing may reduce the complexity of human experience in a way that denies its very meaning, or which reinforces the status quo by focusing on what is, rather than on historical processes of change. Third is the critique that in so far as "legitimate" knowledge [...] [remains] largely within the hands of privileged experts, dominant knowledge obscures or under-privileges other forms of knowing, and the voices of other knowers.

Against this epistemological critique, participatory action research attempts to put forth a different form of knowledge. On the one hand, such research argues that those who are directly affected by the research problem at hand must participate in the research process, thus democratizing or recovering the power of experts. Secondly, participatory action research recognizes that knowledge is socially constructed and embedded, and therefore research approaches that "allow for social, group or collective analysis of life experiences of power and knowledge are most appropriate" (Hall, 1992: 22).

Thirdly, participatory action research recognizes differing forms of knowing, and that feeling and action are as important as cognition and rationality in the knowledge creation process. While participatory research often starts with the importance of indigenous or popular knowledge (Selener, 1997: 25), such knowledge is deepened through a dialectical process of people acting, with others, upon reality in order both to change and to understand it.

Resonating with the feminist critique of objectivity (see Harding, 1986 [...]) writing on participatory research emphasizes the importance of listening to and for different versions and voices. "Truths" become products of a process in which people come together to share experiences through a dynamic process of action, reflection, and collective investigation. At the same time, they remain firmly rooted in participants' own conceptual worlds and in the interactions between them.

KNOWLEDGE, SOCIAL CHANGE, AND EMPOWERMENT

While there is thus a certain amount of commonality in the various approaches in terms of their critique of positivist knowledge, and the liberating possibilities of a different approach to knowledge production, there are important differences across views as to what about participatory research actually contributes to the process of change. That is, what is it in participatory research that is empowering?

In our earlier analysis of three approaches to power, we saw that each carried with it a distinctive approach to knowledge, and how it affects power relations. Participatory research makes claims to challenge power relations in each of its dimensions through addressing the need for:

- knowledge—as a resource which affects decisions;
- action—which looks at who is involved in the production of such knowledge; and
- consciousness—which looks at how the production of knowledge changes the awareness or worldview of those involved.

However, in much of the literature, and indeed in the practical politics of participatory research, processes of empowerment, or of overcoming unequal power relations, tend to emphasize one or the other of the above approaches. To do so, as we shall discuss below, is limiting, for it fails to understand how each dimension of change is in fact related to the other, as Figure 23.1 illustrates.

Participatory Research as an Alternative Form of Knowledge

Undeniably one of the most important contributions of participatory action research to empowerment and social change is in fact in the knowledge dimension. Through a more open and democratic process new categories of knowledge, based on local realities, are framed and given voice. As Nelson and Wright suggest,

Figure 23.1: Dimensions of Participatory Research

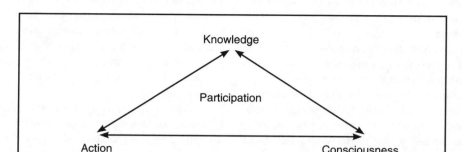

based on an analysis of PRA approaches, the change process here involves "an ability to recognize the expertise of local farmers as against that of professional experts; to find more empowering ways of communicating with local experts; and to develop decision-making procedures which respond to ideas from below, rather than imposing policies and projects from above" (1995: 57).

* * * * *

The importance of using participatory methods to surface more democratic and inclusive forms of knowledge, as a basis of decision-making, cannot be denied. At the same time, by itself, this approach to using participatory research for altering the boundaries of knowledge is fraught with challenges for several reasons. First, there is the danger that knowledge which is at first blush perceived to be more "participatory," because it came from "the community" or the "people" rather than the professional researcher, may in fact serve to disguise or minimize other axes of difference (see critiques by Maguire, 1987, 1996 on PAR; Guijt and Shah, 1998 on PRA). In the general focus on the "community," an emphasis on consensus becomes pervasive. Yet consensus can all too easily masquerade as common

vision and purpose, blotting out difference and with it the possibility of more pluralist and equitable solutions (Mouffe, 1992). By reifying local knowledge and treating it as singular (Cornwall et al., 1993), the possibility is rarely acknowledged that what is expressed as "their knowledge" may simply replicate dominant discourses, rather than challenge them. Little attention is generally given to the positionality of those who participate, and what this might mean in terms of the versions they present. Great care must be taken not to replace one set of dominant voices with another—all in the name of participation.

Moreover, even where differing people and groups are involved, there is the question of the extent to which the voices are authentic. As we know from the work by Freire (1970), Scott (1986, 1990), and others on consciousness, relatively powerless groups may simply speak in a way that "echoes" the voices of the powerful, either as a conscious way of appearing to comply with the more powerful parties' wishes, or as a result of the internalization of dominant views and values. In either case, participatory research implies the necessity for further investigation of reality, in order to change it, not simply to reflect the reality of the moment. [...]

The dangers of using participatory processes in ways that gloss over differences among those who participate, or to mirror dominant knowledge in the name of challenging it, are not without consequence. To the extent that participatory processes can be seen to have taken place, and that the relatively powerless have had the opportunity to voice their grievances and priorities in what is portrayed as an otherwise open system, then the danger will be that existing power relations may simply be reinforced, without leading to substantive change in policies or structures which perpetuate the problems being addressed. In this sense, participation without a change in power relations may simply reinforce the status quo, simply adding to the mobilization of bias the claim to a more "democratic" face. […]

Participatory Research as Popular Action

For this reason, to fulfil its liberating potential, participatory research must also address the second aspect of power, through encouraging mobilization and action over time in a way that reinforces the alternative forms and categories of knowledge which might not have been produced.

Though the action component of the participatory action research process is developed in all schools, it has particular prominence in the work of Lewin, and those organizational action researchers who have followed in his tradition. Action research focuses first on problem-solving, and more secondarily on the knowledge generated from the process. The emphasis of the process is not knowledge for knowledge sake, but knowledge which will lead to improvement, usually, for the action researcher, taken to mean in terms of organizational improvement or for the solution of practical problems.

At the same time, while knowledge is not for its own sake, neither is action; rather, the process is an iterative one. Through action, knowledge is created, and analyses

of that knowledge may lead to new forms of action. By involving people in gathering information, knowledge production itself may become a form of mobilization; new solutions or actions are identified, tested, and then tried again. Thus, in action research, knowledge must be embedded in cycles of action-reflection—action over time (Rahman, 1991). It is through such a process that the nature of action can be deepened, moving from practical problem-solving to more fundamental social transformation (Hall, 1981: 12). The ultimate goal of research in this perspective is not simply to communicate new voices or categories, but

> the radical transformation of social reality and improvement in the lives of the people involved ... Solutions are viewed as processes through which subjects become social actors, participation, by means of grassroots mobilizations, in actions intended to transform society. (Selener, 1997: 19–21)

Participatory Research as Awareness Building

Just as expressing voice through consultation may risk the expression of voice-as-echo, so too action itself may represent blind action, rather than action which is informed by self-conscious awareness and analysis of one's own reality. For this reason, the third key element of participatory action research sees research as a process of reflection, learning, and development of critical consciousness. […]

Here again, however, it is important to recognize that reflection itself is embedded in praxis, not separate from it. Through action upon reality, and analyses of that learning, awareness of the nature of problems, and the sources of oppression, may also change. For this reason, participatory research which becomes only "consultation" with excluded groups at one point in time is limited, for it prevents the possibility that investigation and action over time may lead to a change in the knowledge of people themselves, and therefore a change in understanding of one's own interests and priorities. Not only must production of alternative knowledge be complemented by action upon it, but the participants in the knowledge process must equally find spaces for self-critical investigation and analysis of their own reality, in order to gain more authentic knowledge as a basis for action or representation to others. Such critical self-learning is important not only for the weak and powerless, but also for the more powerful actors who may themselves be trapped in received versions of their own situation. For this reason, we need to understand both the "pedagogy of the oppressed" (Freire, 1970) and the "pedagogy of the oppressor," and the relation between the two.

The important point is to recognize that the approaches are synergistic pieces of the same puzzle. From this perspective, what is empowering about participatory research is the extent to which it is able to link the three, to create more democratic forms of knowledge, through action and mobilization of relatively powerless groups on their own affairs, in a way that also involves their own critical reflection and learning.

THE NEW CONTEXT: FROM MARGINS TO MAINSTREAM AND FROM MICRO TO MACRO

In much of the literature on action research in the past, the assumption has been that this process of participatory action research was used primarily at the micro level, and often with or on behalf of relatively marginalized groups. Participatory action research was often associated with social movements, various forms of participatory rural appraisal with local planning and development projects, and forms of action research with organizational change.

As we have seen, the links between knowledge, power, and empowerment are complex and difficult, even at these levels.

During the 1990s, however, participatory research has faced a new challenge. Rather than being used only at the micro level, it has been scaled up and incorporated in projects or programmes working at regional, national, or even global levels. Rather than being used by social movements or marginalized groups, its rhetoric and practice have been adopted by large and powerful institutions, including governments, development agencies, universities, and multinationals.[4]

There are many examples. One is the "Consultations with the Poor" project, commissioned by the World Bank in 1999, in preparation for the World Development Report on Poverty 2000/2001. [...] This represented the first time the World Bank had sought a report based on hearing from "popular" voices, rather than on analysis by its in-house experts.[5] Now, the World Bank and the IMF are even beginning to use participation as a new "conditionality." In order to receive debt relief under the new Highly Indebted Poor Countries programme, representing a key success of the global Jubilee 2000 Campaign, national governments will have to demonstrate not only that the funds will go towards poverty alleviation, but also that the poverty plan is "participatory" in its approach.

In a number of countries, similar processes have been used for some time at the national level. In Uganda, for instance, a national Participatory Poverty Assessment Process involving government officials, NGOs, and local communities is using participatory research approaches to gain information about the expressed priorities and needs of poor people, as well as for local action planning at the district level. [...]

There are changes at the local level as well. In a number of countries such as India, the Philippines, and Bolivia, new local government legislation institutionalizes processes of participatory action planning, and of participatory monitoring through local vigilance committees. In other countries, such as the U.S. and the U.K., processes for direct consultation, such as citizens' juries, are seen as new forms of direct democracy, supplementing past forms of representative democracy (Gaventa and Valderrama, 1999).

These and other examples raise new challenges for participatory action research and questions of power. How do we understand the dynamics of power when participatory methods are employed by the powerful? What happens when participatory research becomes incorporated as "policy"? Whose voices are raised and whose are heard? And how are these voices mediated as issues of representation become more complex with the use of participatory methods in larger-scale planning and consultation exercises?

Here there are at least two possible positions, each of which has its proponents. On the one hand, there are those who argue that such adoption of participatory processes from above represents co-optation of its core concept and principles. And, the evidence is abundant that even if this is not the intent, the problems associated with rapidly taking participatory approaches to scale are abundant. Flexible approaches give way to blueprints; participation has been rushed and superficial; methods and techniques have been overly stressed, rather than the purposes for which they are used, or the behaviours and attitudes which must also be present; hopes are raised, and follow-up has often been weak. The rapidly developing misuse and abuse of participatory approaches has raised serious questions of quality, and of the ethics of what constitutes good practice (see Chambers, 1998a: 12).

On the other hand, there is the argument that under such conditions new policies and programmes for participatory approaches create opportunities for change, and at a much more far-reaching and significant level than

could be reached through local, micro action alone. Even if there are cases of misuse, the hope is that large-scale programmes create "spaces" which can legitimate local action, through which relatively powerless groups can find new voice and gain capacity and leverage resources for more effective change. [...]

The fact is that we know relatively little about what happens when participatory approaches are adopted on a large scale, or about the degree to which they are used to co-opt resistance and reinforce existing power relations, or the degree to which they provide new spaces and opportunities that strengthen change from below. At the Institute of Development Studies, several exploratory studies are beginning to pursue this question. While the answers are not yet fully conclusive, we can begin to suggest certain enabling factors which will help to maximize the change potential for participatory processes. Early lessons include:

• *The importance of organizational and institutional change:* Scaling-up of participatory approaches must mean more than simply adding a new set of tools and methods to existing institutions, which themselves may be hierarchical, inflexible, and non-participatory. As those working with action research in organizations have perhaps realized for some time, effective promotion and use of participatory methods at the "grassroots" by large organizations means changing the organizations themselves—addressing issues of organizational culture, procedure, incentives, and learning. [...] Such organizational change is most effective when there are high-level "participation champions" who will support the process, who encourage middle managers to take risks and behave differently, who can interpret the new way of working for others.

• *The importance of personal attitudes and behaviour change:* Closely related to the importance of organizational change is the importance of personal attitude and behaviour change. [...] Approaches to training and dissemination must be found which also focus on changing personal values, ethics, and commitments by those who are using the tools, again at all levels.

• *Taking time to go slow:* There is [a] tendency when participatory approaches are adopted on a large scale to rush them into place quickly. Targets are adopted. Mass training must be done. Funds must be dispersed. The risk of course is that the bureaucratic needs will drive the process rather than allowing a slower more deliberate participatory process to take its course. Those programmes which have gone to scale most effectively, in fact, have done so horizontally—rather than vertically. That is, they have included processes of peer-to-peer sharing, of building demonstration projects which then spread to other areas, and of including time for learning, testing, and continuous improvement in the process.

• *Links to social movements and local capacity:* Even if openings for change are created from above, such spaces must be filled by simultaneous movements and actions from below which can occupy the new spaces with different voices. [...] Where there are social movements in place which have helped to "conscientize" and mobilize local voices, this is more likely to occur. Where there is no prior organizational and mobilization experience of those "at the bottom," it is unlikely that these new public spaces will be filled, though the new opportunities may help to stimulate and catalyse new local demands.

• *Creating vertical alliances and networks:* If a prior level of social capital is important for encouraging local groups to mobilize and to occupy political spaces created above, so too is there a need for new forms of trust

and collaboration across levels of power. By definition, large-scale change must happen at multiple levels—changing global actors will not be done by the villagers, nor will village-level change be created by a staff person in a global organization. But change at both levels is important, for large-scale and meaningful change to occur. Such change processes can best be aligned, to create new synergies with one another, to the extent that actors at differing levels learn to engage critically across power differences. For this to happen, mediating organizations, processes, and networks that vertically cut across hierarchies are critical—but so too are processes of meaningful representation and voice from one level to the other. [...]

• *The importance of monitoring for quality and accountability:* Finally, it is clear that to do participatory research on a large scale also means constantly monitoring and holding to account the nature and degree of participation which is occurring. This argues for the need to evolve new concepts of validity in participatory research, ones which measure the quality of participation, as well as the quality of knowledge. [...] How to evolve such quality standards, and how to use them to hold differing actors and institutions to account, represents one of the most important challenges facing participatory research today.

Such approaches to large-scale change begin to recognize, with Hayward and others, that power relations occur at every level and sphere, affecting the powerful as well as the powerless. Rather than seeing participatory research as only a tool for mobilizing the powerless against the powerful, this approach takes a more nuanced view, to explore how participatory methods can facilitate change at multiple levels, among multiple actors. Such an approach is not to wish away conflict—for conflict of interests and views will also be present within and between levels—but it is to suggest that to change the boundaries of the possible, especially in a highly globalized world in which actors and issues are so interrelated, means to bring about change in multiple spaces and arenas, and to link those processes of change through new and accountable forms of interconnection. This approach also argues that the potential for large-scale change through participatory research is determined as much by the quality of the relationships of one set of actors to another, and the extent to which they each address power relations, as by the capacity or strength of any one set of actors in the process.

Ultimately, developing and using new forms of participatory knowledge on a large scale is a question of promoting and creating new forms of participatory democracy, in which ordinary citizens use their knowledge and experience to construct a more just and equitable society. In a time in which inequality between the rich and the poor is greater than ever before, in which globalization threatens even the limited democracy of nation states, the challenges of going to broader scale with participatory research are enormous, but so also are the risks of failing to do so.

NOTES

Our thanks to Kate Hamilton and Mel Speight for research assistance on this chapter.

1. This section draws heavily on Gaventa (1999).
2. Among the most interesting recent empirical studies of power we have seen, the study is based upon her dissertation on power in the schools in New Haven (Hayward, 2000). [...]
3. PRA evolved through innovation and application in the South in the late 1980s and early 1990s, influenced by Rapid Rural Appraisal (RRA), applied anthropology, participatory action research, feminist research, and agro-ecosystems analysis (Chambers, 1992; Guijt and Shah, 1998).

Core methodological principles include iterative, group-based, learning, and analysis, the use of visualization methods to broaden the inclusiveness of the process and enable people to represent their knowledge using their own categories and concepts, and an explicit concern with the quality of interaction, including a stress on personal values, attitudes, and behaviour.

4. For reviews of some of these experiences of scaling up, see Blackburn et al. (1999), Gaventa (1998), and Chambers (1998b).
5. Further information on this project can be found on the World Bank web page at http://www.worldbank.org/poverty/voices/conspoor/index.htm

REFERENCES

Bachrach, P., and M.S. Baratz. 1970. *Power and Poverty: Theory and Practice*. New York: Oxford University Press.

Blackburn, J., R. Chambers, and J. Gaventa. 1999. "Learning to Take Time and Go Slow: Mainstreaming Participation in Development and the Comprehensive Development Framework (CDF)." Paper prepared for Operations Evaluation Department, World Bank. Brighton: Institute of Development Studies.

Chambers, R. 1992. "Rural Appraisal: Rapid, Relaxed and Participatory." *IDS Discussion Paper, 311.* Brighton: Institute of Development Studies.

_____. 1995. "Paradigm Shifts and the Practice of Participatory Research and Development." In *Power and Participatory Development: Theory and Practice,* edited by N. Nelson and S. Wright, 30–42. London: Intermediate Technology Publications.

_____. 1997. *Whose Reality Counts? Putting the First Last.* London: Intermediate Technology Publications.

_____. 1998a. "Foreword." In *The Myth of Community: Gender Issues in Participatory Development,* edited by I. Guijt and M.K. Shah, xvii. London: Intermediate Technology Publications.

_____. 1998b. "Beyond 'Whose Reality Counts?' New Methods We Now Need." In *People's Participation: Challenges Ahead,* edited by O. Fals Borda, 105–130. Bogota: Terrier Mundo SA.

Cornwall, A., I. Guijt, and A. Welbourn. 1993. "Acknowledging Process: Challenges for Agricultural Research and Methodology." *IDS Discussion Paper, 333.* Brighton: Institute of Development Studies.

Crawley, H. 1998. "Living Up to the Empowerment Claim? The Potential of PRA." In *The Myth of Community: Gender Issues in Participatory Development,* edited by I. Guijt and M.K. Shah, 24–34. London: Intermediate Technology Publications.

Dahl, R.A. 1969. "The Concept of Power." In *Political Power: A Reader in Theory and Research,* edited by R. Bell, D.M. Edwards and R. Harrison Wagner, 80. New York: Free Press. Reprinted from *Behavioral Science 2* (1957): 201–205.

Entwistle, H. 1979. *Antonio Gramsci.* London: Routledge and Kegan Paul.

Foucault, M. 1977. *Discipline and Punishment.* London: Allen Lane.

_____. 1979. *The History of Sexuality, Part 1.* London: Allen Lane.

Freire, P. 1970. *Pedagogy of the Oppressed.* New York: Seabury Press.

_____. 1981. *Education for Critical Consciousness. New* York: Continuum.

Gaventa, J. 1993. "The Powerful, the Powerless, and the Experts." In *Voices of Change: Participatory Research in the United States and Canada,* edited by P. Park, M. Brydon-Miller, B. Hall and T. Jackson, 21–40. Westport: Bergin and Garvey and Toronto: OISE Press.

_____. 1998. "The Scaling-Up and Institutionalization of PRA: Lessons and Challenges." In *Who Changes? Institutionalizing Participation in Development,* edited by J. Blackburn with J. Holland, 153–166. London: Intermediate Technology Publications.

_____. 1999. "Citizenship Knowledge, Citizen Competence, and Democracy Building." In *Citizen Competence and Democratic Institutions,* edited by S.L. Elkin and K.E. Soltan, 49–66. University Park: The Pennsylvania State University Press.

Gaventa, J., and C. Valderrama. 1999. "Participation, Citizenship and Local Governance. Background note prepared for workshop on Strengthening Participation in Local Governance." IDS, Brighton, June 21–24.

Guijt, I., and M.K. Shah. 1998. "Waking Up to Power, Process and Conflict." In *The Myth of Community: Gender Issues in Participatory Development,* edited by I. Guijt and M.K. Shah, 1–23. London: Intermediate Technology Publications.

Hall, B.L. 1981. "Participatory Research, Popular Knowledge and Power: A Personal Reflection." *Convergence* XIV(3): 6–17.

_____. 1992. "From Margins to Center? The Development and Purpose of Participatory Research." *The American Sociologist* 23(4): 15–28.

Harding, S. 1986. *Feminism and Methodology.* Bloomington: Indiana University Press.

Hayward, C.R. 1998. "De-facing Power." *Polity* 31(1): 1–22.

_____. 2000. *De-facing Power*. New York : Cambridge University Press

Lukes, S. 1974. *Power: A Radical View*. London: Macmillan.

Maguire, P. 1987. 'Towards a Feminist Participatory Framework: Challenging the Patriarchy." In *Doing Participatory Research: A Feminist Approach*. Amherst: Centre for International Education, University of Massachusetts.

_____. 1996. "Proposing a More Feminist Participatory Research: Knowing and Being Embraced Openly." In *Participatory Research in Health: Issues and Experiences*, edited by K. de Koning and M. Martin, 27–39. London: Zed Books.

Mouffe, C. 1992. "Feminism, Citizenship and Radical Democratic Politics." In *Feminists Theorize the Political*, edited by J. Butler and J. Scott, 369–384. New York: Routledge.

Nelson, N., and S. Wright. 1995. "Participation and Power." In *Power and Participatory Development: Theory and Practice*, edited by N. Nelson and S. Wright, 1–12. London: Intermediate Technology Publications.

Rahman, M.A. 1991. "The Theoretical Standpoint of PAR." In *Action and Knowledge: Breaking the Monopoly with Participatory Action-Research*, edited by O. Fals Borda and M.A. Rahman, 13–23. New York: The Apex Press and London: Intermediate Technology Publications.

Scott, J.C. 1986. *Weapons of the Weak*. New Haven: Yale University Press.

_____. 1990. *Domination and the Arts of Resistance*. New Haven: Yale University Press.

Selener, D. 1997. *Participatory Action Research and Social Change*. New York: The Cornell Participatory Action Research Network, Cornell University.

Rethinking Part 2D: Inquiry as Empowerment: Participatory Action Research

CRITICAL THINKING QUESTIONS

Chapter 20: Local Knowledge, Cogenerative Research, and Narrativity

1. How does cogenerative research bridge the gap between local knowledge and scientific knowledge?
2. How is action research, when successful, democratic in both process and outcome?
3. Davydd Greenwood and Morten Levin argue that "most of the general public has lost faith in most of what passes for academic social science, finding it unintelligible, self-serving, and, where it is understandable, either banal or wrong" (p. 289). How can action research provide a way out of this crisis?

Chapter 21: Community-Based Participatory Research: Aspects of the Concept Relevant for Practice

1. Verna St. Denis observes that community-based participatory research entails an acceptance on the part of the researcher of "vulnerability." How can this acceptance, and the reflection on it, be a resource for gaining trustworthy knowledge?
2. In community-based participatory research the use of findings is a political process. What are some of the challenges in this process for researchers and collaborators?
3. In reviewing the guidelines that St. Denis presents before her conclusion, consider what they imply about the kind of human relations that are necessary if participatory research is to be successful.

Chapter 22: Community Action Research

1. How do the values of community connectedness, social justice, agency, and critical curiosity inform the practice of community action research?
2. What are the different senses in which "action" forms part of community action research?
3. Community action research places considerable strategic emphasis upon broadcasting results to engage multiple audiences. Why is this important and how can it be accomplished?

Chapter 23: Power and Knowledge

1. What are the implications of Gaventa and Cornwall's fourfold conceptualization of power for our understanding of empowerment through knowledge?
2. How are knowledge, action, and consciousness interrelated in participatory action research?
3. All four of our readings in PAR emphasize that the process requires time and cannot be rushed without subverting its democratizing and empowering potential. Why is "taking time to go slow" such an important consideration, and what threats can large-scale institutional funding pose in this regard?

GLOSSARY TERMS

Agency: The ability to act. Community action research promotes agency in conjunction with the pursuit of changes to eliminate injustice and oppression. It is a form of activist research.

Cogenerative learning: A dialogical communicative and research process in which local participants and trained researchers pose a problem and strive to solve it through research, action, and reflection. Both sides gain understanding from their interactions, but local participants must have the central influence in defining the focus of research activity, and over time they should gain the skills and information to control their own knowledge production and action.

Common grounds: The necessities of life that people need in order to survive and to make humane choices in their lives. These can include ecological conditions and material resources, legal and political freedoms, economic rights for working people, and cultural resources for communities. Community action research takes the side of communities in endeavouring, through research and action, to protect and enhance the common grounds.

Communication arena: A site, constructed within an action research project, where cogenerative learning can occur. This could be a public community meeting, a team building session, a task force meeting, and so on.

Community: A diverse ensemble of overlapping lifeworlds often but not necessarily sharing a local space.

Community-based participatory research: A process of inquiry and action through which a community lacking socio-political power can use social science research to support its struggle for self-determination by gaining control of information and acting upon its members' lives in an informed collaborative manner.

Empowerment: Gaining the capacity for self-determination in actions and thoughts. Empowerment is always a social process (pertaining, e.g., to social relations, groups, communities, institutions, and socially defined categories of people), although it entails changes for both individuals and collectivities.

Freedom: The capacity to participate in shaping the social limits that affect one's life and that define the field of what is possible. PAR is premised on the claim that democratic participation in knowledge production can expand these boundaries.

Mobilization of bias: A concept of power and knowledge that highlights the way that entrenched interests are able to control the agenda in ways that keep issues and actors from even getting to the table for debate. On this account, empowerment means expanding who participates in the knowledge production process.

Model monopoly and insider monopoly: Distortions in the communicative relation between between local participants and trained researchers that threaten the trustworthiness of action research. In the former instance, trained researchers dominate the project and, in asserting the authority of their conceptual models and professional expertise, undermine dialogue; in the latter local participants dominate the project and assert the authority of their experience, with a similar impact.

Multiple realities: The different, even divergent, experiences of the world that variously situated parties to social inquiry have. Part of the "messiness" of action research lies in how its dialogical processes yield competing accounts that reflect multiple realities.

Scaling up: The recent move by mainstream organizations such as the World Bank to incorporate PAR into their policies and programs. When this occurs, PAR is transformed from a local process identified with specific communities and social movements to a large-scale undertaking embedded in hierarchical institutions, posing new challenges for PAR and new questions of power.

FURTHER READING

Banks, C.K., and J.M. Mangan. 1999. *The Company of Neighbours: Revitalizing Community through Action-Research*. Toronto: University of Toronto Press. This book tells the story of an action research project as it unfolded between 1992 and 1995 in the town of Hespeler, Ontario. The project attempted, with some success, to revitalize an ethic of participatory citizenship and community spirit.

Feagan, Joe R., and Hernán Vera. 2001. *Liberation Sociology*. Boulder: Westview. Feagan and Vera place action research at the centre of their vision of a sociology that is committed to social justice, empowerment of the oppressed, and democratic practice. This book is very accessible to a wide range of readers.

Reason, Peter, and Hilary Bradbury, eds. 2001. *Handbook of Action Research*. London: Sage. A comprehensive collection of essays: the definitive reference work to date on action research.

Hall, Budd L. 1992. "From Margins to Center? The Development and Purpose of Participatory Research." *American Sociologist* 23(4): 15–28. A highly insightful account of the development of participatory research, beginning with developments in Tanzania in the early 1970s, in which Hall played a formative role, and continuing into the early 1990s.

Stringer, Ernest T. 1999. *Action Research: A Handbook for Practitioners*, 2nd ed. London: Sage.

A very clearly written and practical text, emphasizing specific techniques and issues of project design.

RELEVANT WEB SITES

COMM-ORG: The On-Line Conference on Community Organizing and Development

http://comm-org.utoledo.edu/

An extensive site that strives to link activists and academics and to bridge theory and practice. Its Resources pages contain extensive links to action-research Web sites and databases.

CPEPR: Center for Popular Education and Participatory Research

http://cpepr.net/

CPEPR, pronounced "sea-pepper," is a student-initiated centre created in January 2000 in the University of California at Berkeley's Graduate School of Education. CPEPR's mission is to promote and support popular education and participatory research in order to strengthen the participation of ordinary people—especially the poor, youth, immigrants, and people of colour—in efforts for social justice. Useful articles and links.

PARnet: An Interactive Community on Action Research

http://www.parnet.org/

PARnet aims to create a self-monitored, community-managed knowledge base and gateway to action research resources, connecting practitioners and scholars with each other, the literature, and other educational opportunities. It seeks to reflect the broad spectrum of approaches that characterize the international action research community.

WEB Links to Participatory Action Research Sites

http://www.goshen.edu/soan/soan96p.htm

An action research resource for both students and practitioners. Contains links to 30-odd sites.

SOCIAL INQUIRY AS COMMUNICATIVE REASON: TOWARD A PUBLIC SOCIOLOGY

The final strategy of inquiry I want us to consider was enunciated very clearly by C. Wright Mills in *The Sociological Imagination* and has been elaborated most convincingly by Jürgen Habermas. I am referring to what Steve Seidman calls a reflexive, engaged "public sociology" (2004: 98)—a sociology that provides "critical perspectives on the present which citizens would draw on to understand their social conditions" (2004: 103). Expressing a Gramscian sensibility that all people are intellectuals, Mills envisaged the sociological imagination as a critical capacity for social analysis that could be spread among democratic publics rather than jealously guarded as an expert knowledge. For Mills, the sociological imagination enables us to grasp history, biography, and the relations between the two within society. It affords a particularly fruitful "self-consciousness" by means of which people can understand what is going on in the world and in their own lives. That Mills saw cultivating the sociological imagination as the task and promise of social science recalls Marx's earlier conception of critical social analysis as "the self-clarification of the struggles and the wishes of the age" (Marx, 1975: 209).

Mills's concern that social study help delineate the major *issues* for publics and the key *troubles* for individuals was motivated in part by his observation that indifference and uneasiness—the vague sense that all is not well—had become "the signal feature of our period" (p. 349). For those who, like Mills, accept the Enlightenment values of reason and freedom, "it is the uneasiness itself that is the trouble; it is the indifference itself that is the issue" (p. 349). By means of a public sociology, "the personal uneasiness of individuals is focused upon explicit troubles and the indifference of publics is transformed into involvement with public issues" (p. 345). For Mills, critical social inquiry has a democratizing mission: it can facilitate a transition from a culture of political passivity to one of activism. In the introductory chapter to *The Sociological Imagination*, our first reading, Mills invites us to be public intellectuals, to write an engaged sociology that speaks to publics about public issues and their links to personal troubles.[1]

In the early 1960s Habermas (1989 [1962]) went on to develop an account of the public sphere's[2] rise in the urban zones of 17th-century Europe, and its later degeneration with the advent of expert cultures, the commercialization of mass media, the conversion of political debate into instrumental electoral mobilization, and the decline of the public intellectual. Two decades later, in his Theory of Communicative Action, this degeneration was characterized as a colonization of the lifeworld by the system (Habermas, 1987). In our second reading, Stephen Kemmis explores the implications of Habermas's theory for critical social inquiry and action research in particular. The theory understands system and lifeworld as "dialectically related aspects of social formation in late modernity" (p. 360). From a systems perspective modern society appears as an ensemble of formalized structures, centred upon the capitalist economy and the state, whose functioning is oriented toward efficient goal attainment, as in private profits and cost-effective administration. From a lifeworld perspective, the same society appears in the communicative practices and relations that secure individual identity, social order, and cultural meaning.

In Habermas's critical-modernist framework, the social evolution that has eventuated in this bifurcated reality has been a multifaceted learning process of *rationalization* releasing new emancipatory potential for both lifeworld (via cognitive-moral learning) and system (via scientific and technical innovation) (Ray, 1993: 39–41). However, in the making of modernity capitalism's expansive reach has given dominance to system rationality over the communicative rationality imminent in the lifeworld; indeed, lifeworld rationalization has been hampered by colonization by the system, a process in which "the imperatives of the economic and political-legal systems dislodge the internal communicative action which underpins the formation and reproduction of lifeworlds" (p. 355). Such colonization is evident in the predominant roles that the system makes available to most people—those of subordinated worker, consumer, and client—which contrast sharply with the idea of an engaged citizenry.

Yet if system rationalization has outpaced and inhibited the rationalization of the lifeworld, the logic of development does not foreclose the possibility of further lifeworld rationalization, which Habermas takes to be the unredeemed promise of modernity. For him, such rationalization takes the form of advances in communicative rationality. These provide the basis for a democratic way of life, subjecting unexamined normative consensuses and legitimations of power to argumentative doubt. Social norms previously invested with incontestable authority become subject to the argumentative power of language, as social action becomes regulated less by background consensus and increasingly open to critical reason, that is, communicative rationality. As I have stated elsewhere, "a rationalized lifeworld entails a distinctive morality based not upon hierarchical authority and fixed traditions but upon self-reflexive individuals able to take the standpoint of others, aware of the relativity of personal values, and committed in their interactions to free and open discussion of issues" (Carroll, 1997: 20). Lifeworld rationalization, then, increases the scope of communicative action in human affairs. It means decolonization, and particularly a *revitalization of the public sphere*, which "makes it possible for ideas to circulate freely and to be explored sufficiently for them to attain legitimacy" (Kemmis, p. 358).

As an advocate of critical action research, Stephen Kemmis is well aware that communicative action not only involves its parties in a quest for *mutual understanding* and *unforced consensus about what to do*; it also *brings people together* around shared issues and troubles. Kemmis holds that before people can work together to achieve mutual understanding and consensus they must constitute a communicative space—in meetings, through media, in conversations—for the mutual examination of issues and troubles. With Kemmis, we can readily see action research as an important form of communicative action, whose task is partly to open communicative space in a way that allows participants to achieve mutual understanding and consensus about what to do. But the communicative space opened up by a participatory research project serves not only as a vehicle for the participating community; it becomes a "self-constituting public sphere." Likewise, as they pursue a program of research, dialogical education, and action, the participants become "engaged citizens committed to local action but with a wider critical and emancipatory vision for their work" (p. 359). In this way, participatory action research contributes to lifeworld rationalization and revitalization of the public sphere, particularly as conversations reach beyond the immediate community of participants to wider processes of social movement.

Kemmis notes, however, that participants' perspectives are shaped by the contrasting imperatives of the lifeworlds and systems they inhabit. Social inquiry that simply proceeds from the interpretive perspectives of participants will tend to elide the significance of lifeworld/system relations, the understanding of which is crucial to effective action.[3] For Kemmis the task of critical social inquiry becomes the exploration and address of "*the interconnections and tensions between system and lifeworld aspects of a setting as they are lived out in practice*" (p. 357). It is in and through such exploration that the scope for further democratization of human relations can be discerned.

Graham Scambler builds on this last insight of Kemmis, arguing in our third selection that sociological inquiry needs to shift away from what has been its primary allegiance—to system rationalization—and become geared to the further rationalization of the lifeworld. Scambler's argument parallels Abigail Fuller's critique, in Part 1B, of the tendency in peace research to focus on issues of relevance to dominant groups—thereby circumscribing peace research within the dominant standpoint. Scambler points out that a sociology concerned primarily with system needs and oriented to the system-based intellectuals who administer to those needs tends to promote further lifeworld colonization. Using examples from British medical sociology, he shows that the research agenda has been driven by state-defined issues that depoliticize health by emphasizing personal behaviour and responsibility. Although the reality of system dominance cannot be ignored, practitioners of a critical sociology should engage primarily with the lifeworld, and particularly the public sphere. Not only do critical researchers, following Mills, need to *speak to democratic publics* to enter public discourse; they need to *build alliances* with activists promoting more democratic ways of life, since these are crucial agents of a potentially reconstituted public sphere. Such alliances need not involve actual collaboration, as in participatory action research, but must involve *dialogue* between sociologists and those addressed by sociology. Feminist and anti-racist studies provide many examples of social inquiries that serve as conversations between activists and academics striving for mutual self-clarification (cf. Lund, 2003; Mohanty, 2003).

Whatever form the relation between critical sociological practice and the lifeworld might take, the commitment to a more democratic lifeworld and a revitalized public sphere places the study of the actual *processes* of lifeworld colonization high on the agenda of critical social inquiry. As Andrew Parkin suggests,

> Applied researchers have been led to investigate the circumstances surrounding the communicative interactions undertaken in a wide variety of spaces, such as in the workplace, within the public sphere, in the classroom, within state bureaucracies, in the home and within

the family, and in the market place. Not only has the theory of communicative action allowed applied researchers to appreciate the richness and complexity of the interaction within these spaces, it has also sensitized them to the fact that such interaction is prone to distortion due to interference from a crisis-prone economic and administrative system. The applied research has directed itself to the task of exposing and analyzing the causes of specific instances of such distortions, thereby endeavoring to pinpoint and critique those developments that threaten the integrity and health of lifeworlds (1996: 429).

Much of this work has centred on education, where Michael Welton (1995) has argued that critical adult education practice should strive not only to preserve the lifeworld but to extend communicative action into systemic domains. The same mandate may be said to apply to critical social inquiry more generally. In addressing democratic publics, in building alliances with forms of democratic activism, and in explicating and criticizing actual processes of lifeworld colonization, a social science committed to revitalizing the public sphere not only *defends* the lifeworld against further systemic incursions while contributing to its rationalization. It provides elements for an *expansion* of democratic practice into fields that have been ceded to the alienated rationality of the market and hierarchical administration.

The alliances between critical social researchers and those committed to expanding the scope for communicative reason can very well reach into "the system," as Scambler intimates and as our final reading demonstrates. Madine VanderPlatt considers the problems and prospects of critical evaluation research as a strategy of emancipatory intervention in and around the state. Program evaluation has been a technique of applied research that emulates the experimental paradigm in assessing the effects of social programs on targeted populations (cf. Suchman, 1967; Weiss, 1972). In this, evaluation research followed the same system-rationality as the programs themselves. State programs have served primarily as tools for control and manipulation of the lifeworld. They have focused not on empowering people to become active *citizens* but on serving system-defined needs of *clients*. Emancipatory approaches to social programming reverse the priority of the system/lifeworld relation, and they require a different kind of evaluation research.

VanderPlatt's examination of the Canadian government's policy on program evaluation illustrates how the conventional approach to evaluation research is no more then a "strategic management tool." She advocates, instead, redirecting the evaluative gaze from lifeworld to system. With this shift in perspective the object of the evaluative inquiry changes. The worth of a program is not measured by changes in the behaviours and attitudes of users, but by relying on users as expert witnesses and by considering how well the intervention relates to their expressed needs and interests. As VanderPlatt put it in an earlier article, "relevant evaluation questions might be: Whose interests are being served by the intervention? How are these interests reflected in the intervention's statement of objectives, rationale, structure, content and process? What implications do these interests have for the intervention's emancipatory potential?" (1995: 93).

Questions such as these point us in the direction of a dialogical sociological practice that helps rebuild the public sphere by reflexively mediating between "expert" and "lay" knowledge in ways that promote democratic processes and outcomes. In Raymond McLain's view, this requires that lay-expert engagement meet three criteria:

First, engagement must be structured to foster mutual reflexivity so that both experts and lay participants are open to revising knowledge claims based on the other's view. Second, engagement must be democratically structured to provide equal access and full participation to lay publics who possess relevant knowledge. Third, engagement must be oriented toward transformative outcomes that reflexively reconstitute the realities in question, rather then toward instrumental or ideological outcomes. (2002: 262)

It is through these kinds of commitments—to dialogue, to publics, to participation, to social change—that critical inquiry becomes a crucial form of communicative reason in the struggle for a vibrant public sphere.

NOTES

1. Mills's advice on the practice of "intellectual craftsmanship," which we examined earlier in Part 1B, is worth revisiting at this point.
2. For a definition of the public sphere, see the Glossary (p. 381–2).
3. Here we can notice the parallel with institutional ethnography, whose problematization of the everyday world enables the analysis to go beyond strictly ethnographic concerns in exploring how local actualities are shaped by extra-local ruling relations.

REFERENCES

Carroll, William K. 1997. "Social Movements and Counterhegemony: Canadian Contexts and Social Theories." In *Organizing Dissent: Contemporary Social Movements in Theory and Practice*, 2nd ed., edited by William K. Carroll, 3–38. Toronto: Garamond Press.

Fraser, Nancy. 1989. *Unruly Practices: Power, Discourse and Gender in Contemporary Social Theory*. Minneapolis: University of Minnesota Press.

———. 1997. *Justice Interruptus*. New York: Routledge.

Habermas, Jürgen. 1987. *The Theory of Communicative Action*. Boston: Beacon Press.

———. 1989 [1962]. *The Structural Transformation of the Public Sphere*. Cambridge: MIT Press.

Lund, Darren E. 2003. "Educating for Social Justice: Making Sense of Multicultural and Antiracist Theory and Practice with Canadian Teacher Activists." *Intercultural Education* 14(1): 3–16.

Marx, Karl. 1975. "Letter to Arnold Ruge, September 1843." In *Early Writings: Karl Marx*, 206–209. London: New Left Books.

McLain, Raymond. 2002. "Reflexivity and the Sociology of Practice." *Sociological Practice* 4(4): 249–277.

Mohanty, Chandra Talpade. 2003. *Feminism without Borders: Decolonizing Theory, Practicing Solidarity*. Durham: Duke University Press.

Parkin, Andrew C. 1996. "On the Practical Relevance of Habermas's Theory of Communicative Action." *Social Theory & Practice* 22(3): 417–440.

Ray, Larry. 1993. *Rethinking Critical Theory*. London: Sage.

Seidman, Steven. 2004. *Contested Knowledge: Social Theory Today*, 3rd ed. Oxford: Blackwell.

Suchman, Edward Allen. 1967. *Evaluative Research*. New York: Russell Sage Foundation.

VanderPlatt, Madine. 1995. "Beyond Technique: Issues in Evaluating for Empowerment." *Evaluation* 1(1): 81–96.

Weiss, Carol H. 1972. *Evaluation Research: Methods for Assessing Program Effectiveness.* Englewood Cliffs: Prentice-Hall.

Welton, Michael R. 1995. "In Defense of the Lifeworld: A Habermasian Approach to Adult Learning." In *In Defense of the Lifeworld: Critical Perspectives on Adult Learning*, edited by Michael R. Welton, 127–156. Albany: State University of New York Press.

CHAPTER 24

The Promise

C. Wright Mills

Nowadays men often feel that their private lives are a series of traps. They sense that within their everyday worlds, they cannot overcome their troubles, and in this feeling, they are often quite correct: What ordinary men are directly aware of and what they try to do are bounded by the private orbits in which they live; their visions and their powers are limited to the close-up scenes of job, family, neighborhood; in other milieux, they move vicariously and remain spectators. And the more aware they become, however vaguely, of ambitions and of threats which transcend their immediate locales, the more trapped they seem to feel.

Underlying this sense of being trapped are seemingly impersonal changes in the very structure of continent-wide societies. The facts of contemporary history are also facts about the success and the failure of individual men and women. When a society is industrialized, a peasant becomes a worker; a feudal lord is liquidated or becomes a businessman. When classes rise or fall, a man is employed or unemployed; when the rate of investment goes up or down, a man takes new heart or goes broke. When wars happen, an insurance salesman becomes a rocket launcher; a store clerk, a radar man; a wife lives alone; a child grows up without a father. Neither the life of an individual nor the history of a society can be understood without understanding both.

Yet men do not usually define the troubles they endure in terms of historical change and institutional contradiction. The well-being they enjoy, they do not usually impute to the big ups and downs of the societies in which they live. Seldom aware of the intricate connection between the patterns of their own lives and the course of world history, ordinary men do not usually know what this connection means for the kinds of men they are becoming and for the kinds of history-making in which they might take part. They do not possess the quality of mind essential to grasp the interplay of man and society, of biography and history, of self and world. They cannot cope with their personal troubles in such ways as to control the structural transformations that usually lie behind them.

Surely it is no wonder. In what period have so many men been so totally exposed at so fast a pace to such earthquakes of change? [...] The history that now affects every man is world history. Within this scene and this period, in the course of a single generation, one sixth of mankind is transformed from all that is feudal and backward into all that is modern, advanced, and fearful. Political colonies are freed; new and less visible forms of imperialism installed. Revolutions occur; men feel the intimate grip of new kinds of authority. Totalitarian societies rise, and are smashed to bits—or succeed fabulously. After two centuries of ascendancy, capitalism is shown up as only one way to make society into an industrial apparatus. After two centuries of hope, even formal democracy is restricted to a quite small portion of mankind. Everywhere in the underdeveloped world, ancient ways of life are broken up and vague expectations become urgent demands. Everywhere in the overdeveloped world, the means of authority and of violence become total in scope and bureaucratic in form. [...]

The very shaping of history now outpaces the ability of men to orient themselves in accordance with cherished values. And which values? Even when they do not panic, men often sense that older ways of feeling and thinking have collapsed and that newer beginnings are ambiguous to the point of moral stasis. Is it any wonder that ordinary men feel they cannot cope with the larger worlds with which they are so suddenly confronted? That they cannot understand the meaning of their epoch for their own lives? That—in defense of selfhood—they become morally insensible, trying to remain altogether private men? Is it any wonder that they come to be possessed by a sense of the trap?

It is not only information that they need—in this Age of Fact, information often dominates their attention and overwhelms their capacities to assimilate it. It is not only the skills of reason that they need—although their struggles to acquire these often exhaust their limited moral energy.

What they need, and what they feel they need, is a quality of mind that will help them to use information and to develop reason in order to achieve lucid summations of what is going on in the world and of what may be happening within themselves. It is this quality, I am going to contend, that journalists and scholars, artists and publics, scientists and editors are coming to expect of what may be called the sociological imagination.

1

The sociological imagination enables its possessor to understand the larger historical scene in terms of its meaning for the inner life and the external career of a variety of individuals. It enables him to take into account how individuals, in the welter of their daily experience, often become falsely conscious of their social positions. Within that welter, the framework of modern society is sought, and within that framework the psychologies of a variety of men and women are formulated. By such means the personal uneasiness of individuals is focused upon explicit troubles and the indifference of publics is transformed into involvement with public issues.

The first fruit of this imagination—and the first lesson of the social science that embodies it—is the idea that the individual can understand his own experience and gauge his own fate only by locating himself within his period, that he can know his own chances in life only by becoming aware of those of all individuals in his circumstances. In many ways it is a terrible lesson; in many ways a magnificent one. We do not know the limits of man's capacities for supreme effort or willing degradation, for agony or glee, for pleasurable brutality or the sweetness of reason. But in our time we have come to know that the limits of "human nature" are frighteningly broad. We have come to know that every individual lives, from one generation to the next, in some society; that he lives out a biography, and that he lives it out within some historical sequence. By the fact of his living he contributes, however minutely, to the shaping of this society and to the course of its history, even as he is made by society and by its historical push and shove.

The sociological imagination enables us to grasp history and biography and the relations between the two within society. That is its task and its promise. To recognize this task and this promise is the mark of the classic social analyst. [...]

No social study that does not come back to the problems of biography, of history and of their intersections within a society has completed its intellectual journey. Whatever the specific problems of the classic social analysts, however limited or however broad the features of social reality they have examined, those who have been imaginatively aware of the promise of their work have consistently asked three sorts of questions:

(1) What is the structure of this particular society as a whole? What are its essential components, and how are they related to one another? How does it differ from other varieties of social order? Within it, what is the meaning of any particular feature for its continuance and for its change?

(2) Where does this society stand in human history? What are the mechanics by which it is changing? What is its place within and its meaning for the development of humanity as a whole? How does any particular feature we are examining affect, and how is it affected by, the historical period in which it moves? And this period—what are its essential features? How does it differ from other periods? What are its characteristic ways of history-making?

(3) What varieties of men and women now prevail in this society and in this period? And what varieties are coming to prevail? In what ways are they selected and formed, liberated and repressed, made sensitive and blunted? What kinds of "human nature" are revealed in the conduct and character we observe in this society in this period? And what is the meaning for "human nature" of each and every feature of the society we are examining?

Whether the point of interest is a great power state or a minor literary mood, a family, a prison, a creed—these are the kinds of questions the best social analysts have asked.

They are the intellectual pivots of classic studies of man in society—and they are the questions inevitably raised by any mind possessing the sociological imagination. For that imagination is the capacity to shift from one perspective to another—from the political to the psychological; from examination of a single family to comparative assessment of the national budgets of the world; from the theological school to the military establishment; from considerations of an oil industry to studies of contemporary poetry. It is the capacity to range from the most impersonal and remote transformations to the most intimate features of the human self—and to see the relations between the two. Back of its use there is always the urge to know the social and historical meaning of the individual in the society and in the period in which he has his quality and his being.

That, in brief, is why it is by means of the sociological imagination that men now hope to grasp what is going on in the world, and to understand what is happening in themselves as minute points of the intersections of biography and history within society. In large part, contemporary man's self-conscious view of himself as at least an outsider, if not a permanent stranger, rests upon an absorbed realization of social relativity and of the transformative power of history. The sociological imagination is the most fruitful form of this self-consciousness. By its use men whose mentalities have swept only a series of limited orbits often come to feel as if suddenly awakened in a house with which they had only supposed themselves to be familiar. Correctly or incorrectly, they often come to feel that they can now provide themselves with adequate summations, cohesive assessments, comprehensive orientations. Older decisions that once appeared sound now seem to them products of a mind unaccountably dense. Their capacity for astonishment is made lively again. They acquire a new way of thinking, they experience a transvaluation of values:

in a word, by their reflection and by their sensibility, they realize the cultural meaning of the social sciences.

2

Perhaps the most fruitful distinction with which the sociological imagination works is between "the personal troubles of milieu" and "the public issues of social structure." This distinction is an essential tool of the sociological imagination and a feature of all classic work in social science.

Troubles occur within the character of the individual and within the range of his immediate relations with others; they have to do with his self and with those limited areas of social life of which he is directly and personally aware. Accordingly, the statement and the resolution of troubles properly lie within the individual as a biographical entity and within the scope of his immediate milieu—the social setting that is directly open to his personal experience and to some extent his willful activity. A trouble is a private matter: values cherished by an individual are felt by him to be threatened.

Issues have to do with matters that transcend these local environments of the individual and the range of his inner life. They have to do with the organization of many such milieux into the institutions of an historical society as a whole, with the ways in which various milieux overlap and interpenetrate to form the larger structure of social and historical life. An issue is a public matter: some value cherished by publics is felt to be threatened. Often there is a debate about what that value really is and about what it is that really threatens it. This debate is often without focus if only because it is the very nature of an issue, unlike even widespread trouble, that it cannot very well be defined in terms of the immediate and everyday environments of ordinary men. An issue, in fact, often involves a crisis in institutional arrangements, and often too it

involves what Marxists call "contradictions" or "antagonisms."

In these terms, consider unemployment. When, in a city of 100,000, only one man is unemployed, that is his personal trouble, and for its relief we properly look to the character of the man, his skills, and his immediate opportunities. But when in a nation of 50 million employees, 15 million men are unemployed, that is an issue, and we may not hope to find its solution within the range of opportunities open to any one individual. The very structure of opportunities has collapsed. Both the correct statement of the problem and the range of possible solutions require us to consider the economic and political institutions of the society, and not merely the personal situation and character of a scatter of individuals.

Consider war. The personal problem of war, when it occurs, may be how to survive it or how to die in it with honor; how to make money out of it; how to climb into the higher safety of the military apparatus; or how to contribute to the war's termination. In short, according to one's values, to find a set of milieux and within it to survive the war or make one's death in it meaningful. But the structural issues of war have to do with its causes; with what types of men it throws up into command; with its effects upon economic and political, family and religious institutions, with the unorganized irresponsibility of a world of nation-states.

Consider marriage. Inside a marriage a man and a woman may experience personal troubles, but when the divorce rate during the first four years of marriage is 250 out of every 1,000 attempts, this is an indication of a structural issue having to do with the institutions of marriage and the family and other institutions that bear upon them.

Or consider the metropolis—the horrible, beautiful, ugly, magnificent sprawl of the great city. For many upper-class people, the personal solution to "the problem of the city" is to have an apartment with private garage under it in the heart of the city, and forty miles out, a house by Henry Hill, garden by Garrett Eckbo, on a hundred acres of private land. In these two controlled environments—with a small staff at each end and a private helicopter connection— most people could solve many of the problems of personal milieux caused by the facts of the city. But all this, however splendid, does not solve the public issues that the structural fact of the city poses. What should be done with this wonderful monstrosity? Break it all up into scattered units, combining residence and work? Refurbish it as it stands? Or, after evacuation, dynamite it and build new cities according to new plans in new places? What should those plans be? And who is to decide and to accomplish whatever choice is made? These are structural issues; to confront them and to solve them requires us to consider political and economic issues that affect innumerable milieux.

In so far as an economy is so arranged that slumps occur, the problem of unemployment becomes incapable of personal solution. In so far as war is inherent in the nation-state system and in the uneven industrialization of the world, the ordinary individual in his restricted milieu will be powerless—with or without psychiatric aid—to solve the troubles this system or lack of system imposes upon him. In so far as the family as an institution turns women into darling little slaves and men into their chief providers and unweaned dependants, the problem of a satisfactory marriage remains incapable of purely private solution. In so far as the overdeveloped megalopolis and the overdeveloped automobile are built-in features of the overdeveloped society, the issues of urban living will not be solved by personal ingenuity and private wealth.

What we experience in various and specific milieux, I have noted, is often caused by structural changes. Accordingly, to un-

derstand the changes of many personal milieux we are required to look beyond them. And the number and variety of such structural changes increase as the institutions within which we live become more embracing and more intricately connected with one another. To be aware of the idea of social structure and to use it with sensibility is to be capable of tracing such linkages among a great variety of milieux. To be able to do that is to possess the sociological imagination.

3

What are the major issues for publics and the key troubles of private individuals in our time? To formulate issues and troubles, we must ask what values are cherished yet threatened, and what values are cherished and supported, by the characterizing trends of our period. In the case both of threat and of support we must ask what salient contradictions of structure may be involved.

When people cherish some set of values and do not feel any threat to them, they experience well-being. When they cherish values but do feel them to be threatened, they experience a crisis—either as a personal trouble or as a public issue. And if all their values seem involved, they feel the total threat of panic.

But suppose people are neither aware of any cherished values nor experience any threat? That is the experience of indifference, which, if it seems to involve all their values, becomes apathy. Suppose, finally, they are unaware of any cherished values, but still are very much aware of a threat? That is the experience of uneasiness, of anxiety, which, if it is total enough, becomes a deadly unspecified malaise.

Ours is a time of uneasiness and indifference—not yet formulated in such ways as to permit the work of reason and the play of sensibility. Instead of troubles—defined in terms of values and threats—there is often the misery of vague uneasiness; instead of explicit issues there is often merely the beat feeling that all is somehow not right. Neither the values threatened nor whatever threatens them has been stated; in short, they have not been carried to the point of decision. Much less have they been formulated as problems of social science.

In the 'thirties there was little doubt—except among certain deluded business circles that there was an economic issue which was also a pack of personal troubles. In these arguments about "the crisis of capitalism," the formulations of Marx and the many unacknowledged re-formulations of his work probably set the leading terms of the issue, and some men came to understand their personal troubles in these terms. The values threatened were plain to see and cherished by all; the structural contradictions that threatened them also seemed plain. Both were widely and deeply experienced. It was a political age.

But the values threatened in the era after World War Two are often neither widely acknowledged as values nor widely felt to be threatened. Much private uneasiness goes unformulated; much public malaise and many decisions of enormous structural relevance never become public issues. For those who accept such inherited values as reason and freedom, it is the uneasiness itself that is the trouble; it is the indifference itself that is the issue. And it is this condition, of uneasiness and indifference, that is the signal feature of our period.

All this is so striking that it is often interpreted by observers as a shift in the very kinds of problems that need now to be formulated. We are frequently told that the problems of our decade, or even the crises of our period, have shifted from the external realm of economics and now have to do with the quality of individual life—in fact with the question of whether there is soon going to be anything that can properly be called individual life. Not child labor but comic books, not poverty but mass leisure, are at the center of concern. Many great public issues as well as many private troubles are described in terms of "the psychiatric"—often, it seems, in a pathetic attempt to avoid the large issues and problems of modern society. Often this statement seems to rest upon a provincial narrowing of interest to the Western societies, or even to the United States—thus ignoring two-thirds of mankind; often, too, it arbitrarily divorces the individual life from the larger institutions within which that life is enacted, and which on occasion bear upon it more grievously than do the intimate environments of childhood.

Problems of leisure, for example, cannot even be stated without considering problems of work. Family troubles over comic books cannot be formulated as problems without considering the plight of the contemporary family in its new relations with the newer institutions of the social structure. Neither leisure nor its debilitating uses can be understood as problems without recognition of the extent to which malaise and indifference now form the social and personal climate of contemporary American society. In this climate, no problems of "the private life" can be stated and solved without recognition of the crisis of ambition that is part of the very career of men at work in the incorporated economy.

It is true, as psychoanalysts continually point out, that people do often have "the increasing sense of being moved by obscure forces within themselves which they are unable to define." But it is not true, as Ernest Jones asserted, that "man's chief enemy and danger is his own unruly nature and the dark forces pent up within him." On the contrary: "Man's chief danger" today lies in the unruly forces of contemporary society itself, with its alienating methods of production, its enveloping techniques of political domination, its international anarchy—in a word, its pervasive transformations of the very "nature" of man and the conditions and aims of his life.

It is now the social scientist's foremost political and intellectual task—for here the two coincide—to make clear the elements of contemporary uneasiness and indifference. It is the central demand made upon him by other cultural workmen—by physical scientists and artists, by the intellectual community in general. It is because of this task and these demands, I believe, that the social sciences are becoming the common denominator of our cultural period, and the sociological imagination our most needed quality of mind.

4

In every intellectual age some one style of reflection tends to become a common denominator of cultural life.

* * * * *

The sociological imagination is becoming, I believe, the major common denominator of our cultural life and its signal feature. This quality of mind is found in the social and psychological sciences, but it goes far beyond these studies as we now know them. Its acquisition by individuals and by the cultural community at large is slow and often fumbling; many social scientists are themselves quite unaware of it. They do not seem to know that the use of this imagination is central to the best work that they might do, that by failing to develop and to use it they are failing to meet the cultural expectations that are coming to be demanded of them and that the classic traditions of their several disciplines make available to them.

Yet in factual and moral concerns, in literary work and in political analysis, the qualities of this imagination are regularly demanded. In a great variety of expressions, they have become central features of intellectual endeavor and cultural sensibility.

Leading critics exemplify these qualities as do serious journalists—in fact the work of both is often judged in these terms. Popular categories of criticism—high, middle, and low-brow, for example—are now at least as much sociological as aesthetic. Novelists—whose serious work embodies the most widespread definitions of human reality—frequently possess this imagination, and do much to meet the demand for it. By means of it, orientation to the present as history is sought. As images of "human nature" become more problematic, an increasing need is felt to pay closer yet more imaginative attention to the social routines and catastrophes which reveal (and which shape) man's nature in this time of civil unrest and ideological conflict. Although fashion is often revealed by attempts to use it, the sociological imagination is not merely a fashion. It is a quality of mind that seems most dramatically to promise an understanding of the intimate realities of ourselves in connection with larger social realities. It is not merely one quality of mind among the contemporary range of cultural sensibilities—it is the quality whose wider and more adroit use offers the promise that all such sensibilities—and in fact, human reason itself—will come to play a greater role in human affairs.

The cultural meaning of physical science— the major older common denominator—is becoming doubtful. As an intellectual, style, physical science is coming to be thought by many as somehow inadequate. [...] The obvious conquest of nature, the overcoming of scarcity, is felt by men of the overdeveloped societies to be virtually complete. And now in these societies, science—the chief instrument of this conquest—is felt to be footloose, aimless, and in need of re-appraisal.

The modern esteem for science has long been merely assumed, but now the technological ethos and the kind of engineering imagination associated with science are more likely to be frightening and ambiguous than hopeful and progressive. Of course this is not all there is to "science," but it is feared that this could become all that there is to it. The felt need to reappraise physical science reflects the need for a new common denominator. It is the human meaning and the social role of science, its military and commercial issue, its political significance that are undergoing confused reappraisal. [...]

* * * * *

But there are, in C.P. Snow's phrase, "two cultures": the scientific and the humanistic. Whether as history or drama, as biography, poetry, or fiction, the essence of the humanistic culture has been literature. Yet it is now frequently suggested that serious literature has in many ways become a minor art. If this is so, it is not merely because of the development of mass publics and mass media of communication, and all that these mean for serious literary production. It is also owing to the very quality of the history of our times and the kinds of need men of sensibility feel to grasp that quality.

What fiction, what journalism, what artistic endeavor can compete with the historical reality and political facts of our time? What dramatic vision of hell can compete with the events of twentieth-century war? What moral denunciations can measure up to the moral insensibility of men in the agonies of primary accumulation? It is social and historical reality that men want to know, and often they do not find contemporary literature an adequate means for knowing it. They yearn for facts, they search for their meanings, they want "a big picture" in which they can believe and within which they can come to understand themselves. They want orienting values too, and suitable ways of feeling and styles of emotion and vocabularies of motive. [...]

* * * * *

[...] In the absence of an adequate social science, critics and novelists, dramatists and poets have been the major, and often the only, formulators of private troubles and even of public issues. Art does express such feelings and often focuses them—at its best with dramatic sharpness—but still not with the intellectual clarity required for their understanding or relief today. Art does not and cannot formulate these feelings as problems containing the troubles and issues men must now confront if they are to overcome their uneasiness and indifference and the intractable miseries to which these lead. The artist, indeed, does not often try to do this. Moreover, the serious artist is himself in much trouble, and could well do with some intellectual and cultural aid from a social science made sprightly by the sociological imagination.

5

It is my aim in this [chapter] to define the meaning of the social sciences for the cultural tasks of our time. I want to specify the kinds of effort that lie behind the development of the sociological imagination; to indicate its implications for political as well as for cultural life; and perhaps to suggest something of what is required to possess it. In these ways, I want to make clear the nature and the uses of the social sciences today, and to give a limited account of their contemporary condition in the United States.

* * * * *

Of late the conception of social science I hold has not been ascendant. My conception stands opposed to social science as a set of bureaucratic techniques which inhibit social inquiry by "methodological" pretensions, which congest such work by obscurantist conceptions, or which trivialize it by concern with minor problems unconnected with publicly relevant issues. These inhibitions, obscurities, and trivialities have created a crisis in the social studies today without suggesting, in the least, a way out of that crisis.

* * * * *

[...] My biases are of course no more or no less biases than those I am going to examine. Let those who do not care for mine use their rejections of them to make their own as explicit and as acknowledged as I am going to try to make mine! Then the moral problems of social study—the problem of social science as a public issue—will be recognized, and discussion will become possible. Then there will be greater self-awareness all around—which is of course a pre-condition for objectivity in the enterprise of social science as a whole.

In brief, I believe that what may be called classic social analysis is a definable and usable set of traditions; that its essential feature is the concern with historical social structures; and that its problems are of direct relevance to urgent public issues and insistent human troubles. I also believe that there are now great obstacles in the way of this tradition's continuing—both within the social sciences and in their academic and political settings—but that nevertheless the qualities of mind that constitute it are becoming a common denominator of our general cultural life and that, however vaguely and in however a confusing variety of disguises, they are coming to be felt as a need.

Many practitioners of social science, especially in America, seem to me curiously reluctant to take up the challenge that now confronts them. Many in fact abdicate the intellectual and the political tasks of social analysis; others no doubt are simply not up to the role for which they are nevertheless being cast. At times they seem almost deliberately to have brought forth old ruses and developed new timidities. Yet despite this reluctance, intellectual as well as public attention is now so obviously upon the social worlds which they presumably study that it must be agreed that they are uniquely confronted with an opportunity. In this opportunity there is revealed the intellectual promise of the social sciences, the cultural uses of the sociological imagination, and the political meaning of studies of man and society.

* * * * *

CHAPTER 25

Exploring the Relevance of Critical Theory for Action Research: Emancipatory Action Research in the Footsteps of Jürgen Habermas

STEPHEN KEMMIS

In the mid-1970s, I first encountered Habermas's work through his books *Theory and Practice* (1974) and *Knowledge and Human Interests* (1972). These books seemed to offer a promising way through some of the debates I had encountered about explanation and understanding in the social sciences, about the relationship between objective and subjective perspectives, the relationship between the individual and the social realms of cognitive and cultural realities, and the relationship between theory and practice. [...]

With colleagues at Deakin University, where I was working by the end of the 1970s, I thus began a 20-year long exploration of the theory and practice of action research. Our Deakin action research group was firmly of the view that action research is first and foremost *research by practitioners*—something they do, not something done "on" or "to" them. This view gained widespread acceptance at a 1981 National Seminar on Action Research held at Deakin University (Brown et al., 1982). This conclusion had been forced upon me by Habermas's dictum that "in a process of enlightenment there can be only participants" (1974: 40). That is, others cannot do the enlightening for participants; in the end, they are or are not enlightened in their own terms. (This point also applies to "empowerment," another aspiration of many advocates of action research.)

* * * * *

THE THEORY OF KNOWLEDGE-CONSTITUTIVE INTERESTS

Influenced by Habermas's (1972) theory of knowledge-constitutive interests, our research group had begun to distinguish *empirical-analytic* (or *positivist*), *hermeneutic* (or *interpretive*), and *critical* approaches in research theory and practice. Each had its own basic *raison d'être* in terms of the interests which guided its quest for knowledge: a technical or instrumental (or means-ends) interest in the case of empirical-analytic research—that is, an interest in getting things done effectively; a practical interest in the case of interpretive research—that is, an interest in wise and prudent decision-making in practical situations; and an emancipatory interest in the case of critical research—that is, an interest in emancipating people from determination by habit, custom, illusion, and coercion which sometimes frame and constrain social and educational practice, and which sometimes produce effects contrary to those expected or desired by participants and other parties interested in or affected by particular social or educational practices.

* * * * *

In our action research work in the 1980s, we were powerfully compelled by the connection Habermas made between truth and justice—the notion that truth could only emerge in settings where all assertions are equally open to critical scrutiny, without fear or favour. This applied as much to the practices of social and educational research as to other processes of social and political debate and discussion. We were acutely aware that the processes of critical action research should aspire to be democratic in the sense that the requirement of authenticity (at the level of the individual) would be paralleled by a social and discursive criterion of validity—that participants should be committed to reaching mutual understanding and unforced consensus about what to do. Here, we steered in the light of Habermas's famous validity claims developed in his theory of communication in works including *Communication and the Evolution of Society* (1979). The four validity claims are questions which can be asked of any utterance, and which every utterance tacitly asserts (until challenged), and they provide a start for critical reflection by interlocutors. The four key questions are: "Is this utterance comprehensible?" "Is it true (in the sense of accurate)?" "Is it right and morally appropriate?" and "Is it sincerely (or truthfully) stated?" These questions help interlocutors to open critical doors on the nature, social and historical formation, and consequences of the ways they think and what they do. In short, the aim of the kind of critical social science we were developing was to help people to grasp the ways they are shaped by taken-for-granted assumptions, habit, custom, ideology, and tradition, and to see what kind of collaborative social action might be necessary to transform things for the better. [...]

THE THEORY OF COMMUNICATION ACTION AND THE THEORY OF SYSTEM AND LIFEWORLD

* * * * *

In *The Theory of Communicative Action*, Habermas considers the strengths and weaknesses of systems theory and theories of social action. He criticizes both, and arrives, through a reconstruction of earlier social theories, at a "two-level" social theory which explores the tensions and interconnections between system and lifeworld as two faces of the social world of modernity.

Seen from a systems perspective, modern society encompasses organizational and institutional structures (including roles and rules) and the functioning of these structures—in particular, their functioning as oriented towards the attainment of particular goals. Systems operate through rational-purposive action—that is, (instrumental, means-ends) action oriented towards success. They operate through definition of goals, the definition of criteria against which progress towards achieving the goals can be measured, the setting of targets for what will count as success (maximization of outcomes in relation to goals), and the monitoring of progress towards goals to evaluate and improve system efficiency defined in terms of the ratio of inputs to outcomes achieved. Since it is circumscribed by system structures and processes, and oriented towards achieving outcomes defined in terms of system goals, its central concerns are with systems functioning; hence it characteristically employs a form of reason which can be described as *functional rationality*.

Modern societies are characterized by advanced differentiation in a variety of dimensions, posing particular kinds of problems of social integration and system integration, with a variety of effects (including pathological effects) which the theory of communicative action aims to address. Habermas is particularly concerned with the nature, functioning, and interrelationships between economic and political-legal systems in modern societies (particularly capitalism and the state which have been linked together in particular mutually compensating ways in the modern welfare state).

Seen from a lifeworld perspective, modern society encompasses the dynamics by which culture, social order, and individual identity are secured. Drawing on a key insight from American sociologist George Herbert Mead that "no individuation is possible without socialization, and no socialization is possible without individuation" (Habermas, 1992: 26), Habermas develops a more extensive conceptualization of the social matrix of lifeworlds, identifying three "structural nuclei" of the lifeworld—culture, society, and person—which are "made possible" by three enduring and interacting sets of processes—cultural reproduction, social integration, and socialization.[1] [...]

* * * * *

(a) The Thesis of "Uncoupling" of System and Lifeworld

The thesis of the "uncoupling" of system and lifeworld refers to the development of "relative autonomy" in systems regulated by the distinctive steering media of money and administrative power. A principal line of argument in *The Theory of Communicative Action* is that modern societies are characterized by such an elaborate pattern of differentiation (for example, in contexts of production and the division of labour) that it is barely possible to secure collective social "anchoring" in a shared culture, shared social order, and shared social identity. The burden of maintaining such societies against fragmentation and dissolution

has been transferred from individuals and small face-to-face social groups to open social systems which provide co-ordination.

What is distinctive about late modernity, in Habermas's view, is that *steering media* characteristic of the economic and political-legal systems—money and administrative power, respectively—now do their work of co-ordination so smoothly that the systems have begun to operate "relatively autonomously," that is, "on their own terms." This relatively autonomous functioning of systems in societies characterized by advanced differentiation involves an "uncoupling" of system and lifeworld in the sense that systems appear to be "objects" (reified) to the people who inhabit them, as if (but only as if) they functioned according to their own rules and procedures, in a disinterested manner indifferent to the unique personalities and interests of the individuals inhabiting them, and thus, in a manner which appears to be indifferent to the dynamics of cultural reproduction, social integration, and socialization necessary for the development and reproduction of lifeworlds.

(b) The Thesis of Colonization of the Lifeworld

Habermas's second thesis follows from the first. In societies characterized by advanced differentiation and the relative autonomy of economic and political-legal systems, he argues, individuals and groups increasingly define themselves and their aspirations in systems terms—in particular, so that their "privatized hopes for self-actualization and self-determination are primarily located ... in the roles of consumer and client" (Habermas, 1987a: 356) in relation to the economic and political-legal systems respectively. This is "colonization" in the sense that the imperatives of the economic and political-legal systems dislodge the internal communicative action which underpins the formation and reproduction of lifeworlds, providing in its place an external framework of language, understandings, values, and norms based on systems and their functions. Under such circumstances, the symbolic reproduction processes of the lifeworld (cultural reproduction, social integration, and socialization) become saturated with a discourse of roles, functions, and functionality, reshaping individual and collective self-understandings, relationships, and practices. [...]

The effect of the colonization of the lifeworld by the imperatives of systems is that individuals and groups in late modernity increasingly identify themselves and their aspirations in systems terms. The theory of communicative action aims to offer a "stereoscopic vision" which allows the effects of uncoupling and colonization to come into perspective. In doing so, it allows us to

> become conscious of the difference between steering problems and problems of mutual understanding. We can see the difference between systemic disequilibria and lifeworld pathologies, between disturbances of material reproduction and deficiencies in the symbolic reproduction of the lifeworld. [...] Money and power can neither buy nor compel solidarity and meaning. In brief, the result of the process of disillusionment is a new state of consciousness in which the social-welfare-state project becomes reflexive to a certain extent and aims at taming not just the capitalist economy, but the state itself. (Habermas, 1987b: 363)

From this conclusion, Habermas proceeds to examine the possibilities for revitalizing a public political sphere which has side-lined mutual understanding in favour of system self-regulation through the steering media of money and power, and which is now paying a high price in terms of the withdrawal of motivation and legitimacy from those systems—as a result of "the intolerable imperatives of the occupational system [and] the penetrating side effects of the administrative provision for life" (1987b: 364). In short, the economic and political-legal systems have become insensitive to the imperatives of mutual understanding on which solidarity and the legitimacy of social orders depends. He suggests that a possible way forward is through the formation of autonomous, self-organized public spheres capable of asserting themselves with "a prudent combination of power and intelligent self-restraint" against the systemically integrating media of money and power.

> I call those public spheres autonomous which are neither bred nor kept by a political system for purposes of creating legitimation. Centres of concentrated communication that arise spontaneously out of microdomains of everyday practice can develop into autonomous public spheres and consolidate as self-supporting higher-level intersubjectivities only to the degree that the lifeworld potential for self-organization and for the self-organized means of communication are utilized. Forms of self-organization strengthen the collective capacity for action. [...] (Habermas, 1987b: 364–365)

It might be argued that grassroots movements and self-organized groups conducting participatory and collaborative action research in system settings (for example, in education, social welfare, and community development) are examples of such "autonomous public spheres" at the local level. It is certainly the case that, where they are successful in bringing about changes in institutional practices, it is generally through indirect rather than direct means, by sensitizing systems to previously unnoticed effects—especially when projects draw attention to circumstances under which participants withdraw motivation or legitimacy from system operations.

COMMUNICATIVE ACTION AND ACTION RESEARCH

The theory of system and lifeworld provides a theoretical discourse clarifying a significant shift in the social conditions of late modernity. It allows us to articulate problems which have emerged in late modernity as social systems have become more extensive, and as problems of integrating different kinds of social organizations and systems have emerged. It provides a useful framework from which to view changes in schooling—for example, the functional integration of schooling with political-legal and economic systems. It also provides a new perspective on action research.

Instead of taking the interpretive perspective according to which participants themselves are meant to be the sources of all theoretical categories arising in a research project (though usually with the mediating assistance of a researcher not indigenous to the setting), the theory of system and lifeworld offers a way of understanding participants' perspectives as structured by the contrasting and sometimes competing imperatives of social systems and the lifeworlds participants inhabit. As a co-researcher with others in an action research setting, one could, on the one hand, explore with participants how they were engaged in three kinds of lifeworld process in the settings they daily constituted and reconstituted through their practices:

- the process of individuation-socialization (by which practitioners' own identities and capacities are formed and developed);
- the process of social integration (by which legitimately ordered social relations among people as co-participants in a setting are formed and developed); and

- the process of cultural reproduction and transformation (by which shared cultures and discourses are formed and developed).

Alongside this exploration, one could also investigate how practices in the setting enmeshed participants in *systems functioning*—the exchanges and transformations taking place to yield outcomes of interest to those involved, to the systems of which they are part, and to the wider environment beyond. On this view, the overall task of a critical social science, including critical action research, *is to explore and address the interconnections and tensions between system and lifeworld aspects of a setting as they are lived out in practice.*

It seemed to me that critical action research could help to create the circumstances in which communicative action among those involved could be encouraged, enabled, sustained, and made generative in terms of personal, social, and cultural development in and around the setting. In particular, this communicative action could be focused on the boundary-crises which arise at the intersection of system and lifeworld aspects of the setting, as they are realised in the immediacy and under the exigencies of daily practice.

* * * * *

THE CRITIQUE OF THE PHILOSOPHY OF THE SUBJECT AND THE NOTION OF THE SOCIAL MACRO-SUBJECT

Habermas has continued to develop the theory of communicative action. In his *Between Facts and Norms* (1996) he [...] revisits the notion of the public sphere, to show how it is an open realm of intersecting discourses. But this realm (rooted in lifeworlds as much as in the organization of social systems) is crucial for legitimacy—for laws or policies or principles to be regarded as legitimate norms.

Laws and policies are endured as impositions rather than felt to be organic to the people to whom they are addressed unless they develop legitimacy; and they will only be regarded as legitimate when they gain authentic personal assent (the level of the person), are seen as morally right and socially integrative in their effects (at the level of the society), and are regarded as discursively valid in cultural and discursive terms (at the level of the culture). The democratic process of communicative action in the public sphere makes it possible for ideas to circulate freely and to be explored sufficiently for them to attain legitimacy. Just as the theory of communicative action transfers the category of truth from the individual cognitive subject to the domain of debate and discussion in which communicative action occurs, so it now transfers legitimacy from the social macro-subject (for example, the state) to the fluid communicative networks of the public sphere.

It might not be an exaggeration to say that in these developments, Habermas has identified a third feature of communicative action. Formerly, it was described as being oriented towards (first) mutual understanding and (second) unforced consensus about what to do. To these, a third feature has been added: making communicative space. A previously unnoticed aspect of communicative action was that it brings people together around shared topical concerns, problems, and issues with a shared orientation towards mutual understanding and consensus. To recognize that this as an element of communicative action is to acknowledge that the orientation to mutual understanding and consensus arises in all sorts of ways, around all sorts of practical problems and issues, and that people must constitute a communicative space (in meetings, in the media, in conversations with friends and colleagues, etc.) before they can work together to achieve mutual understanding and consensus. As Habermas shows, such

communicative spaces are open and fluid associations, in which each individual takes an in-principle stand to participate, but does so knowing that a variety of forms of participation are available—to use the meeting metaphor, as a speaker or listener, at the podium, or in the gallery, as an occasional participant or as a fully engaged advocate, or even as the person who finds the discussion irrelevant and slips away by a side door.

Much of my advocacy of action research had been premised upon the prior existence of groups of people (an action research group in a school or community, for example) willing to work together on shared concerns. Because when we met them in real circumstances, they were composed of some number of actual people—though they might aim to involve others interested in and affected by the social or educational practices of the group—we could think of them as "whole" and finite. A by-product of this way of thinking was that we began to see groups as self-organizing or potentially self-organizing social "wholes"—as social macro-subjects (as Habermas described them). So it seemed appropriate that strictures about democratic debate and decision should be binding on the whole group—even when the group was confronted by the evident lack of interest of some participants and potential participants. This contradiction was thrown into sharp relief in the light of Habermas's redefinition of the public sphere—"the group" turns out to be fluid (as action research project groups tend to be), and permits a range of different kinds of communicative role (speaker and listener, permanent and passing membership—as happens in most action research projects). The first step in action research turns out to be central: the formation of a communicative space which is embodied in networks of actual persons, though the group itself cannot and should not be treated as a totality (as an exclusive whole). A communicative space is constituted as issues or problems are opened up for discussion, and when participants experience their interaction as fostering the democratic expression of divergent views. Part of the task of an action research project, then, is to open communicative space, and to do so in a way that will permit people to achieve mutual understanding and consensus about what to do, in the knowledge that the legitimacy of any conclusions and decisions reached by participants will be proportional to the degree of authentic engagement of those concerned.

It seems to me helpful to think about action research without a "social macro-subject"—to think instead about how it constitutes a communicative space in which people can come together to explore problems and issues, always holding open the question of whether they will commit themselves to the authentic and binding work of mutual understanding and consensus. In the light of this insight, we may think differently about how rigorously to require that debate and decision-making be binding on all participants; instead, we may want to think more about how the debate itself can become more open and engaging, as a basis for arriving at perspectives and decisions where necessary, in the (overlapping) organizational and lifeworld settings in which people live and work together.

CONCLUDING COMMENT

In this chapter, I have described a broad journey through the territory of critical action research, informed by perspectives from the critical theory of Jürgen Habermas. In the first stage, my view of the action research group was of a "critical community," bound together to work on some common problems or issues in their own situation. I viewed each participant as an authentic person, whose own views were paramount in determining what a "problem" or an "issue" or a reasonable interpretation of reality might be. [...]

In the second stage, my view of the action research group was changing. It was defined less in geographical or local terms, and more in terms of shared engagement in communicative action. Nevertheless, the concrete image of a face-to-face group of "members" continued to inform my thinking, despite Habermas's critique of the possibility of a self-organizing "social macro-subject." During this stage, I had begun to view each individual participant as a conversation partner in communicative action, but I still regarded the conversation as principally internal to the group. [...]

In the third stage, the critique of the social macro-subject began to have real force in my thinking about the action research group. I have come to see a critical action research project as more open and fluid, as a "self-constituting public sphere," and to see those who participate in the shared project of a particular programme of action research as engaged citizens committed to local action but with a wider critical and emancipatory vision for their work. The critical action research group might thus be understood in relation to, and as a contribution to, wider processes of social movement. [...]

My reading in critical theory, and especially the work of Habermas, has been a programme of continuing study through most of my professional life. I believe that it is useful—that it is important—to show that theory is a powerful resource for developing insight and understanding, and that critical theory of the Habermasian kind is especially relevant to contemporary discussion and debate about the nature of action research. The point is not to claim credence for a view of critical action research by appeal to authority—in this case the authority of Habermas as a leading social theorist of our times. It is to show that some central problems of contemporary social theory have clear resonances for our work as action researchers. Problems about the nature of practice, the relationship between theory and practice, the relationship between systems theory and theories of social action, tensions and interconnections between system and lifeworld, the relationship between the critique of the philosophy of the subject and the critique of the social macro-subject (so crucial to praxis philosophy)—all these (and others) are highly relevant to a contemporary understanding of the potential and limitations of our theories and practices of action research.

These profound issues cannot be ignored as we develop our field of action research through our communicative action in the fluid communicative space constituted by our networks and communications in the international community of action researchers. Addressing such issues requires that we draw deep from the well of available theoretical resources.

NOTE

1. System and lifeworld are not separate realms of social existence in which the expansion of the one (system) threatens to obliterate the other (lifeworld), so that we are in danger of becoming social automatons whose lives are merely realizations of the functional requirements of systems. The Habermasian theses of the uncoupling of system and lifeworld, and the colonization of the lifeworld by systems perspectives and values, are based on no such bifurcation. On the contrary, system and lifeworld aspects of sociality continue to co-exist in interconnection, creating mutually constitutive conditions for one another, though admittedly with some rather one-sided (functionally integrative) effects as we live through the consequences of late modernity. System and lifeworld need to be understood as dialectically related aspects of social formation in late modernity, not as two separate entities at odds with one another.

REFERENCES

Brown, L., C. Henry, J. Henry, and R. McTaggart. 1982. "Action Research: Notes on the National Seminar." *Classroom Action Research Network Bulletin* 4(Summer): 1–6.

Habermas, J. 1972. *Knowledge and Human Interests*, translated by Jeremy J. Shapiro. London: Heinemann.

_____. 1974. *Theory and Practice*, translated by John Viertel. London: Heinemann.

_____. 1979. *Communication and the Evolution of Society*, translated by Thomas McCarthy. Boston: Beacon Press.

_____. 1987a. *The Theory of Communicative Action*, vol. 2: *Lifeworld and System: A Critique of Functionalist Reason*, translated by Thomas McCarthy. Boston: Beacon Press.

_____. 1987b. *The Philosophical Discourse of Modernity*, translated by Frederick Lawrence. Cambridge: MIT Press.

_____. 1992. *Postmetaphysical Thinking: Philosophical Essays*, translated by William Mark Hohengarten. Cambridge: MIT Press.

_____. 1996. *Between Facts and Norms*, translated by William Rehg. Cambridge: MIT Press.

The "Project of Modernity" and the Parameters for a Critical Sociology: An Argument with Illustrations from Medical Sociology

GRAHAM SCAMBLER

INTRODUCTION

It is a basic—orthodox but unfashionable —premise of this paper that much of the literature on postmodernity is of significance less because it offers a convincing analysis of some kind of epochal transition than because it is—in a generalised, diffuse way—reflective of change within modernity. Thus talk of the end of modernity is taken to be, at best, premature. It is argued that the recent work of Jürgen Habermas has established that the much-criticised Enlightenment legacy, the so-called "project of modernity," can and must be reconstructed, and requires to be viewed as incomplete, not abandoned. In the course of expounding this argument an outline of Habermas's own perspective on what will here be called, "high"—in preference to the more prejudicial "late"—modernity is incorporated. The paper goes on to utilise Habermas's studies of modernity and its reconstructed project to posit a series of metatheoretical theses which, it is suggested, might establish the parameters for a *fin-de-siècle* sociology which is both defensible and critical in orientation.

* * * * *

While there is no gainsaying either the continuing absence of the good society or the scale of the varied crises that have beset the

peoples of virtually all societies this century, it will be argued here, following Habermas, that the project of modernity should be regarded as "incomplete," not abandoned. Why has the project failed thus far? Building on Weber's analysis, Habermas approvingly notes that modernity has led to a threefold differentiation of cultural or "value spheres." Indeed, he accords this process pride of place in his definitions of the project of modernity:

> The project of modernity, formulated in the eighteenth century by the philosophers of the Enlightenment, consisted in their efforts to develop objective science, universal morality and law, and autonomous art according to their inner logic. At the same time, this project intended to release the cognitive potentials of each of these domains from their esoteric forms. The Enlightenment philosophers wanted to utilise this accumulation of specialized culture for the enrichment of everyday life—that is to say, for the rational organization of everyday life. (1981: 9)

There is a clear sense in which the entire corpus of Habermas's work can be interpreted as an insistent defence of a reconstructed version of this project, increasingly through the 1970s and 1980s against those he regards as the agents of counter-Enlightenment, inspired above all by Nietzsche, Heidegger, and Bataille (Best and Kellner, 1991).

For Habermas (1984), Weber's concepts of rationality and rationalization are too restricted and insufficiently abstract. This misled Weber in at least two related ways. First, distracted by the manifestly varying contents they afford, he underestimated the extent to which rationality and rationalisation in the different value spheres (and, indeed, in different cultures) possess the same formal or procedural properties. Second, he maintained that the different value spheres are not only inherently irreconcilable, but become more openly and explicitly so the further rationalisation progresses. Habermas, by contrast, espouses the universality of reason, and holds that the different value spheres have come to appear increasingly irreconcilable primarily because of "selective rationalization" due to the growth and dominance of the capitalistic and state bureaucracy (Brand, 1990).

* * * * *

In short, the dynamic of development has meant that system rationalisation has outstripped the rationalisation of the lifeworld, hence the reference to selective rationalisation. Rationalisation of the lifeworld here refers to an increase in the scope of communicative action and to a growth of communicative rationality. Distancing himself from the "iron cage" pessimism of Weber and others, Habermas insists that the logic of development allows for further rationalisation of the lifeworld through a reconstitution of its public sphere. Currently the most promising agents of such a reconstitution—and of a reconstructed project of modernity—are the "new" (as opposed to older class-based) social movements. Yet for all his reasoned preservation of hope, Habermas sees little immediate prospect of its fulfillment.

Habermas's reconstruction of the project of modernity can now be summarised.

Enlightenment thinking has had its (system) successes and its (lifeworld) failures, but any flaws in its philosophical grounding can be overcome, according to Habermas, by means of a reconstruction of the project of modernity. [...] The universality of reason, using Habermas's more expansive and abstract concept than Weber's, is implicit in communicative action. Rationalisation in the West has in fact been selective, leading to an uncoupling of system and lifeworld and the former's colonisation of the latter. Relatedly, overwhelming priority has been given to one of the triad of value spheres, that of objective knowledge (via science and technology), and an elitist culture of expertise has arisen in all three value spheres. But these developments were contingent rather than inevitable and are in principle open to change through political action. Effective action may be dependent on further rationalisation of the lifeworld—which Habermas admits seems far from imminent—but the formal or procedural concept of reason which "unites" the otherwise differentiated value spheres both grounds the reconstructed project of modernity and permits its description as incomplete, thus (re-) affirming the possibility of its completion (see Honneth et al., 1992a, 1992b).

* * * * *

PARAMETERS FOR A CRITICAL SOCIOLOGY

A strong case can be made for arguing that while much sociological work arising out of unreconstructed Enlightenment thinking has proved to be flawed (on theories of social change, for example, see Smart, 1992), and the idea of a postmodernist sociology is internally inconsistent, both reason and hope are to be found in a critically oriented sociology at once appropriate to high modernity and allied to Habermas's reconstructed project. Such a sociology would be geared to lifeworld rationalisation. This commitment to the further rationalisation of the lifeworld, grounded in Habermas's theory of communicative action, is of the essence of the critical sociology commended in what follows.

It is now possible to articulate a series of five metatheoretical theses, drawing on the preceding argument and discussion and most conspicuously on the work of Habermas. These concern and suggest some parameters for the discipline as a whole, although they are anchored occasionally in examples from medical sociology in Britain.

Thesis 1: The full ramifications of the reflexivity of high modernity for sociological practice have been insufficiently addressed.

Reflexivity has long been a strong theme in the work of Giddens (1990, 1991), linked as it is to his earlier concept of the double hermeneutic, but it has recently become central also to the theories of social change of other influential writers (see Beck et al., 1994). For Giddens (1990: 38) the reflexivity of modernity "consists in the fact that social practices are constantly examined and reformed in the light of incoming information about those very practices, thus constitutively altering their character." He argues that this reflexivity has become deeply unsettling in its subversion of early and outmoded Enlightenment ideals of certain knowledge: the world is thoroughly constituted through reflexively applied knowledge, but there is now no surety that "any given element of that knowledge will not be revised." Furthermore, the re-entry of sociological discourse into the contexts it analyses is pivotal; indeed, "modernity is itself deeply and intrinsically sociological" (Giddens, 1990: 43).

While the importance of reflexivity, as defined by Giddens, is now widely acknowledged by sociologists, it is less apparent that this acknowledgement translates into "appropriate" practices. This, as thesis 2

maintains, is principally because sociologists' system ties tend to outweigh their ties to the lifeworld.

Thesis 2: Sociology needs to more critically examine its primary allegiance to economy and state and, via the media of money and power, system rationalisation.

Given sociology's origins in, and subsequent affinity, with the unreconstructed Enlightenment project, it is not surprising that its history is one of abetting as much as resisting selective rationalisation and lifeworld colonisation. Two examples from medical sociology are pertinent here.

Consider, first, the debate on welfare statism and the potential for market-oriented or privatised health care. For all the intense political and academic (including mainstream social theoretic) interest in the "crisis of welfare statism," many British medical sociologists working in the field appear more responsive to short-term system needs than to the far-reaching effects of changes in U.K. welfare and health policy for the lifeworld. The multiplicity of system-driven, and increasingly commissioned, projects around the health reforms embodied in the NHS and Community Care Act of 1990 in general, and service audit and evaluation (incorporating much "quality of life" research) in particular, testify to this. The readily available funding for such projects is doubly significant given the return on fund-holding for the careers of academics adjusting to a creeping "McDonaldization" of academic (Ritzer, 1993). The point is not that these projects are intrinsically undesirable, but rather that their engineered and disproportionate pursuit now has to be understood in the context of an impetus to "economic privatism" and "statist authoritarianism" (Cohen and Arato, 1992).

* * * * *

The second example focuses on attempts to combat social class related health inequalities in the U.K. As the Black Report (Davey Smith et al., 1980) long ago attested, the key priority here is the reduction of material or structural deprivation, and especially child poverty: "Above all, the abolition of child poverty should be adopted as a national goal for the 1980s" (Townsend and Davidson, 1992: 206). One reason why an "anti-poverty strategy" along the lines of that preferred in the Black Report is as—or more—urgently required now as then is the government's pursuit since of what might be called a "pro-poverty strategy" resulting, for example, in a doubling of the number of children stricken by poverty: whereas in 1979, 12 per cent of all children were living in poverty (if poverty is defined as below 50 per cent average income), by 1987 this had risen to 26 per cent. Clearly most vulnerable are children in families experiencing unemployment or where there is a lone parent.

The evidence suggests that class-related health inequalities have increased since 1979 and are set to continue do to so (Davey Smith et al., 1990; Whitehead, 1992; Black, 1993). But the point of concern here is how readily many medical sociologists seem to have "adjusted" to the government's disinclination to accept established causal links between material or structural deprivation and health, and to its policy of "depoliticising health" (see *The Health of the Nation*, HMSO, 1992) by stressing cultural or behavioural factors like smoking and alcohol and drug consumption and presenting an individual's health as more or less exclusively a matter of personal behaviour and responsibility. Once again this is in large part a function of system-generated and monitored research and of changes in the institutions of academia. The study of the role of cultural and behavioural factors in accounting for class-related health inequalities is important, but less so than the neglect

or concealment of the potentialities of the economy to sustain and deepen class-related health inequalities, and of the state, in all but rhetoric, to tolerate them.

What these brief examples illustrate is a primary and disproportionate commitment to a pattern of enquiry and research consonant with, or at least not *effectively* opposed to, the imperatives of economy and state. Some of this work is undoubtedly defensible, but what of sociology's link with the lifeworld?

Thesis 3: Sociology's principal commitment is to the rationalisation of the lifeworld.

It is a core theme of this paper that the overriding commitment of a critical sociology is to the rationalisation of the lifeworld, and this is, of course, incompatible with a primary allegiance to system needs. The implications of this commitment for sociological practice can be considered in relation to the examples from British medical sociology just outlined. While the search for answers to questions deriving from system-driven projects around the health reforms and the salience of behavioural risk factors for class-related health inequalities may be defensible, what is not is either their systematic displacement of questions less compatible with system imperatives, or the control or containment of any answers made possible by an as yet unreconstituted public sphere of the lifeworld (see thesis 4 below).

There are solid grounds for maintaining that medical sociology's system ties are such that many of its exponents—by fine-tuning a cluster of health reforms leading inexorably to a service which will cost more to administer while reducing choice for most patients, by neglecting the prepotent material causes of class related health inequalities, or by communicating almost exclusively to system-based or "established intellectuals" (Eyerman and Jamison, 1991)—are either witting agents of "manipulation" in the lifeworld or unwitting agents of "systematically distorted communication"; either way, their work serves strategic action and lifeworld colonisation rather than communicative action and lifeworld rationalisation (Habermas, 1984, 1987; Scambler, 1987).

Thesis 4: The nature of sociology's commitment to lifeworld rationalisation requires its promotion of and engagement in a reconstituted public sphere.

According to Habermas, societies like Britain are characterised by "formal" democracy, namely, "a legitimation process that elicits generalized motives—that is, diffuse mass loyalty—but avoids participation" (1973: 36). Since social (and health) policy priorities are framed by private investment decisions in the subsystem of the economy, politics is democratic in form only; thus it is largely irrelevant which political party holds office since the state's commitment endures—administering the economy so that crises are avoided. Formal democracy may be contrasted with "substantive" democracy, which affords "genuine participation of citizens in processes of will-formation" (Habermas, 1973: 36). Substantive democracy, in effect, institutionalises in the public sphere the fundamental norms of rational speech (although Habermas here warns against utopianism and against equating substantive democracy with any particular form of organisation).

Substantive democracy entails further rationalisation of the lifeworld via the reconstitution of the public sphere out of the residue of a "bourgeois public sphere," once progressive and resistant to economy and state but long since '"collapsed into a sham world of image creation and opinion management in which the diffusion of media products is in the service of vested interests" (Thompson, 1995: 177; see Habermas, 1989). If practitioners of a critical sociology, fated to be actors in high modernity, are to realise an overriding commitment to lifeworld rationalisation, then they must of necessity engage with a reconstituted public sphere. And such engagement, of course, requires them to seek answers to the question:

> ... of whether, and to what extent, a public sphere dominated by mass media provides a realistic chance for the members of civil society, in their competition with the political and economic invaders' media power, to bring about changes in the spectrum of values, topics, and reasons channelled by external influences, to open it up in an innovative way, and to screen it critically. (Habermas, 1992b: 455)

Thompson has recently suggested that Habermas himself, perhaps over-indebted to his Frankfurt predecessors, is too pessimistic in this regard, that he tends to exaggerate the extent to which "the recipients of media products are relatively passive consumers who are enthralled by the spectacle and easily manipulated by media techniques" (1995: 74).

Thesis 5: If sociology is to be effective in promoting and engaging in a reconstituted public sphere, alliances must arguably be built with system-based and, especially, lifeworld-based activists.

As thesis 4 avers, the public sphere might be "the target as well as the terrain of contemporary collective action" (Cohen and Arato, 1992: 526). Consistently with the Michelsian iron law of oligarchy, in the absence of its reconstitution the goals of inclusion and participation will predictably lead to "cooptation, deradicalisation, professionalisation, bureaucratisation and centralisation," "success" amounting to failure to effect. As Cohen and Arato contend, however, inclusion and participation can be means to reconstitution. Thus they write of new social movements:

> While the democratization of civil society and the defence of its autonomy from economic or administrative "colonization" can be seen as the goal of these new movements, the creation of "sensors" within political and economic institutions (institutional reform) and the democratization of political society (the politics of influence and inclusion), which would open these institutions to the new identities and egalitarian norms articulated on the terrain of civil society, are the means to securing this goal. (1992: 526)

The subsystems of economy and state are not, of course, unitary phenomena and fruitful alliances between sociologists and system-based activists in these subsystems are not uncommon. But perhaps the alliances with the most potential for contemporary sociologists committed to lifeworld rationalisation through gains in substantive democracy are those with lifeworld-based activists or "movement intellectuals" from the new social movements (Eyerman and Jamison, 1991). Habermas sees these movements as provoked by the colonisation of the lifeworld, appearing "at the seam between the lifeworld and system in a kind of ongoing boundary dispute over the limits of systemic intrusion" (Ray, 1993: 60). He also sees in some of them a genuine potential for effecting a decolonisation of the lifeworld. Indeed, such movements might be prototypes for, and are associated with, "the development of new participatory-democratic institutions which would regulate markets, bureaucracies and technologies" (Ray, 1993: 62). However, although they may currently be the most likely agents of a reconstituted public sphere and of a further rationalisation of the lifeworld, having displaced the "old" class

movements in these respects, Habermas is—as any self-respecting critical sociologist would be—cautious and far from optimistic.

* * * * *

Axiomatically, the media of mass communication are crucial, and it is in relation to these that sociologists' potential alliances with system-based especially, lifeworld-based activists representing the new social movements could be most telling. As Garnham insists, there is a need to move beyond the orthodox liberal view of the free press which assumes either that "the market will provide appropriate institutions and processes of public communication to support a democratic polity" or that "only the market can ensure the necessary freedom from state control and coercion" (1992: 363). Garnham notes the evidence of the effects of a growing and globalising trend towards the commodification of public information, referring to "oligopoly control" and a "depoliticisation of content" far removed from the liberal concept of a free market of ideas. He commends Habermas's concept of the public sphere of the lifeworld:

> Habermas ... distinguishes the public sphere from both state and market and can pose the question of the threats to democracy and the public discourses upon which it depends coming from the development of an oligopolist capitalist market and from the development of the modern interventionist welfare state. (1992: 361)

CONCLUSION

This paper utilises the social theory of Habermas to argue that sociologists have yet to face up to the consequences of the reflexivity of high modernity for their own work. Often they are committed by their system ties to a blinkered or inappropriate pursuit of system rationalisation at the cost of an increasingly colonised lifeworld. Too many British medical sociologists, for example, have pulled their punches in relation to the government's flawed health reforms and refusal to countenance the salience of material deprivation as a cause of class-related health inequalities. Astonishingly, only a marginalised few have invested in theory or research on such alarming and vital current global threats to people's health as relative and absolute poverty, the trades in arms and dangerous substances, agribusiness, or, indeed, the ubiquitous "risk" in high modernity characterised so graphically by Beck (1989, 1992; Scambler and Goraya, 1994a, 1994b).

It has been intimated that reason, conceived formally or procedurally as universal, commits sociology to what Habermas has referred to as the reconstructed, and as yet incomplete, project of modernity; that this commitment requires that sociology be directed first and foremost to the decolonization and further rationalisation of the lifeworld; and that this, in turn, necessitates sociologists, fated to be actors in high modernity, acting consciously through alliances of interest with other system-based and lifeworld-based activists, perhaps most notably from the new social movements, to promote and engage with a reconstituted public sphere of the lifeworld.

Importantly, it is not being suggested that all system-driven sociology is undesirable, nor that all sociological work that might be defined in the context this paper as pre- or non-critical is without value or return. Moreover it should now be clear that, if sociology be committed to the completion of the project of modernity, there is no occasion either for Utopian prophecy or for much in the way of optimism. As Habermas explains in his recent interview with Haller:

> The "emancipated society" is an ideal construction that invites misunderstanding. I'd rather speak of the idea of the undisabled subject. In general, this idea can be derived from the analysis of the necessary conditions for reaching understanding—it describes something like the image of symmetric relations of the freely reciprocal recognition of communicatively interacting subjects. Of course, this idea can't be depicted as the totality of a reconciled form of life and cast into the future as a Utopia. It contains nothing more, but nothing less, than the formal characterization of necessary conditions for nonanticipatable forms of an undisabled life. (Habermas, 1994: 112–113)

REFERENCES

Beck, U. 1989. "On the Way to the Industrial Risk-Society? Outline of an Argument." *Thesis Eleven* 23: 86–103.

_____. 1992. *Risk Society: Towards a New Modernity*. London: Sage Publications.

Beck, U., A. Giddens, and S. Lash. 1994. *Reflexive Modernization: Politics, Tradition and Aesthetics in the Modern Social Order*. Cambridge: Polity Press.

Best, S., and D. Kellner. 1991. *Postmodern Theory: Critical Interrogations*. London: Macmillan.

Black, D. 1993. "Deprivation and Health." *British Medical Journal* 307: 163–164.

Brand, A. 1990. *The Force of Reason: An Introduction to Habermas' "Theory of Communicative Action."* London: Allen and Unwin.

Cohen, J., and A. Arato. 1992. *Civil Society and Political Theory*. Cambridge: MIT Press.

Davey Smith, G., M. Bartley, and D. Blane. 1990. "The Black Report on Socio-Economic Inequalities in Health 10 Years on." *British Medical Journal* 301: 373–377.

Department of Health and Social Security. 1980. "Inequalities in Health: Report of a Research Working Group Chaired by Sir Douglas Black." London: HMSO.

Eyerman, R., and A. Jamison. 1991. *Social Movements: A Cognitive Approach*. *Cambridge*: Polity Press.

Garnham, N. 1992. "The Media and the Public Sphere." In *Habermas and the Public Sphere*, edited by C. Calhoun. Cambridge: MIT Press.

Giddens, A. 1990. *The Consequences of Modernity*. Cambridge: Polity Press.

_____. 1991. *Modernity and Self-Identity: Self and Society in the Late Modern Age*. Cambridge: Polity Press.

Habermas, J. 1973. *Legitimation Crisis*. London: Heinemann Educational Books.

_____. 1981. "Modernity versus Postmodernity." *New German Critique* 22: 3–11.

_____. 1984. *Theory of Communicative Action, Vol. 1: Reason and the Rationalisation of Society*. London: Heinemann.

_____. 1987. *Theory of Communicative Action, Vol. 2: Lifeworld and System: A Critique of Functionalist Reason*. Cambridge: Polity Press.

_____. 1989. *The Structural Transformation of the Public Sphere: An Inquiry into a Category of Bourgeois Society*. Cambridge: Polity Press.

_____. 1992. "Further Reflections on the Public Sphere." In *Habermas and the Public Sphere*, edited by C. Calhoun. Cambridge: MIT Press.

_____. 1994. *The Past as Future*. London: Polity Press.

HMSO. 1992. "The Health of the Nation: A Strategy for Health in England." London: HMSO.

Honneth, A., T. McCarthy, C. Offe, and A. Wellmer, eds. 1992a. *Philosophical Interventions in the Unfinished Project of Enlightenment*. Cambridge: MIT Press.

Honneth, A., T. McCarthy, C. Offe, and A. Wellmer, eds. 1992b. *Cultural-Political Interventions in the Unfinished Project of Enlightenment*. Cambridge: MIT Press.

Ray, L. 1993. *Rethinking Critical Theory: Emancipation in the Age of Global Movements*. London: Sage.

Ritzer, G. 1993. *The McDonaldization of Society: An Investigation into the Changing Character of Contemporary Social Life*. Thousand Oaks: Pine Forge Press.

Scambler, G. 1987. "Habermas and the Power of Medical Expertise." In *Sociological Theory and Medical Sociology*, edited by G. Scambler. London: Tavistock.

Scambler, G., and A. Goraya. 1994a. "The People's Health: Habermas, the Public Sphere and the Role of Social Movements." *British Medical Anthropology Review* 2: 35–43.

Scambler, G., and A. Goraya. 1994b. "Movements for Change: The New Public Health Agenda." *Critical Public Health* 5: 4–10.

Smart, B. 1992. *Modern Conditions, Postmodern Controversies*. London: Routledge.

Thompson, J. 1995. *The Media and Modernity: A Social Theory of the Media*. Cambridge: Polity Press.

Townsend, P., and N. Davidson, eds. 1992. *The Black Report*. London: Penguin.

Whitehead, M. 1992. *The Health Divide*, 2nd ed. London: Penguin.

CHAPTER 27

Emancipatory Politics, Critical Evaluation, and Government Policy

MADINE VANDERPLAAT

Since the 1980s the language of empowerment has had a powerful influence on the development of interventionary strategies in the health, education, and social welfare sectors. Health Canada has been particularly committed to this philosophy, and has since 1986 based its programming strategies on the Ottawa Charter, an approach to health promotion that emphasizes increased public participation, network/coalition building, and community development.

The evaluation industry has generally recognized that the aspirations of this genre of intervention require a significant reconstruction of traditional evaluation practices. The pioneering work of Scriven (1973), Stake (1975), and Guba and Lincoln (1989) has provided much needed inspiration and the basis for considerable innovation. Fischer (1985), Kemmis (1993), Everitt (1996), and Fettermen et al. (1996), to name but a few, have made important contributions to the concept of "empowering" evaluation strategies.

Although I applaud the gains made by these endeavors, I would argue that we still have a long way to go in developing an approach to evaluation research that truly informs and supports empowerment-oriented aspirations. To date, most of the attention has focused on program participants and "empowering" methodologies. What is missing

is the recognition that social change emerges from the interplay between human agency and systemic structures. Evaluation practices guided by an emancipatory ethic must develop the capacity to address this dynamic. I would argue that such aspirations necessitate a dramatic shift in the institutional role of evaluation research and in the focus of the evaluative gaze.

This chapter provides a basis for rethinking the evaluation function given the demands of interventions governed by an emancipatory ethic. In doing so, I draw on Jürgen Habermas's concept of communicative action to provide a theoretical grounding for the shift in perspective.[1]

THE CONCEPT OF COMMUNICATIVE ACTION

Habermas's work is particularly useful for thinking critically about evaluation research because it offers a political location and context within which to examine the practice of social intervention and evaluation. Habermas's primary concern is the relationship between human agency and systemic structures. In his construction of modern society, he distinguishes two forms of "systemic" oppression, that is, oppression supported by the political, economic, and normative structures of the state's administrative apparatus. First, there is the oppression that results from the unequal distribution of and access to resources. This is what traditional approaches to intervention attempt to compensate for or ameliorate. The second form of systemic oppression derives from the over-reliance on scientific discourse and technocratic rationalization as the basis for instrumental decision making. This privileging of "scientism" not only justifies material and social disparities but also discursively disarms political challenges to the status quo. It is this form of oppression that interventions informed by emancipatory politics are intended to address.

Habermas (1971) alerts us to the relationship between actions and the interests that govern actions. *Communicative actions*, which are directed at achieving a sense of mutual understanding and collective will, are actions we pursue to satisfy our interest in social harmony, integration, and solidarity. *Instrumental actions* are those emerging from our technical interest in controlling nature and our environment. In the liberal model of capitalist society communicative actions are primarily pursued in the realm of everyday life—the "lifeworld" (Habermas, 1984: 70)—and technical interests have become systemically structured and formalized in economic institutions, state bureaucracies, and professional agencies—"the system." For Habermas, the differentiation between systemic and lifeworld interests is not problematic in and of itself, as long as the direction and content of systemic interests and instrumental capacities are grounded in everyday experience and guided by collective interests. As such, the only legitimate rationale for systemic action is one that is "communicatively secured" through public discussion and agreement.

In *The Theory of Communicative Action* Habermas (1984, 1987) argues that the reverse is occurring. Social and political issues emerging from everyday life are increasingly being recast as technical concerns subject to systemic intervention and the application of scientific and technocratic imperatives. Issues related to how we want to live together and to what end are framed and legitimated by systemic logistics and priorities rather than determined discursively within the public arena. Consequently, "public will," or collective agency, is being politically subverted by systemic discourses and institutional arrangements. Our capacity to engage in the production of social change is, thus, gradually undermined by the growing inability to collectively explore and debate the nature and direction of that change. For Habermas this constitutes one of the most fundamental threats to democracy in the modern world.

From Habermas's perspective, traditional approaches to social programming thus serve as a systemic tool for control and manipulation of the lifeworld. On the one hand, they offset serious political challenges to the status quo by providing compensation or ameliorative services to those dispossessed by the economic contradictions inherent in capitalism. On the other hand, they provide a means for penetrating the lifeworld and exposing the dimensions of everyday life to technocratic scrutiny, rationalization, and control. Within this context the social interventionary process may be seen as a means by which "the system," as opposed to "the collective," organizes and manages issues related to collective living and social integration. Social problems are increasingly the domain of the "professional," who dictates the understanding of discontent, the appropriate level of intervention, and the skills required to overcome the condition. The assumption is that "social change" is a process that requires the upgrading of the instrumental capacity of the dispossessed and that this ability is linked to the acquisition of specific skills.

Habermas asks us to think again about this approach. He points out that we need a wider structural analysis so that the acquisition of such skills makes experiential as well as systemic sense. He challenges us to recognize the need to harness the technocratic efficiency and scientific capacity of the modern state to communicatively secured interests, thereby ensuring that the actions of systemic agents are firmly grounded in the needs emerging from everyday life.

EMPOWERMENT-ORIENTED INTERVENTION AND EVALUATION

The critical imperative identified by Habermas is recognized, in varying degrees, in the rhetoric of empowerment-oriented intervention. Where previously the discourse of intervention had been strongly oriented to the positivistic elements in the social sciences, now the practice of social programming is increasingly influenced by the emancipatory language of critical adult educators (Carr and Kemmis, 1986; Collins, 1991; Fay, 1987; Freire, 1970; Giroux, 1988, 1991) feminist pedagogical theorists (Hart, 1990; Lather, 1991; Weiler, 1991) and social action researchers (Hall, 1981; Maguire, 1987; Reason and Rowan, 1981). Having rejected the conventional individualistic and behavioristic approach to intervention, these social activists attempt instead to develop strategies that will enhance the collective ability of the disempowered to affect social change on their own behalf. This discourse is characterized by a perspective that acknowledges the constraints imposed by our embeddedness in history, social struc-tures, and personal biographies while at the same time recognizing the potential to change both ourselves and society. Perhaps what distinguishes the discourse of empowerment most clearly from its predecessors is its acknowledgement and deep respect for people's capacity to create knowledge about, and solutions to, their own experiences. Within this discourse, the valid knowledge base from which to initiate social change originates in the collective everyday understandings and

experiences of participants rather than in the annals of the social scientific community.

In adhering to an emancipatory ethic social programmers shift their focus from increasing the instrumental abilities (skills) of program users to increasing their communicative capacities (political voice/agency) to inform instrumental actions. The key concern is with the agency of the political citizen, not the self-sufficiency of the client of state resources. What this means in practical terms is that program objectives are not framed in terms of helping participants to increase their knowledge and skills using available resources, within existing institutional arrangements. Instead, the focus is program intervention, as the creation of a communicative space, that affords participants the opportunity to collectively identify the skills, resources, and institutional organization they require to meet the needs emerging from their lifeworld locations (VanderPlaat, 1995b).

Emancipatory approaches move beyond conventional approaches to social programming. They envision a system/lifeworld relationship whereby the instrumental capacity of the former is directed by the communicatively secured needs and interests of the latter. Ideally, an emancipatory approach to social programming should provide systemic agents—academics, professionals, and bureaucrats—with the opportunity and knowledge to organize their resources and research efforts to better meet the demands of experiential need.

Evaluation, of course, plays an integral role in the development and subsequent formulation of social programs, including those guided by emancipatory interests. The desire to demonstrate effectiveness and the demand for accountability affect how a program is defined and the standards by which its "success" is judged. The discourse of evaluation research shapes what is publicly "known" or communicated about a social program. Program developers' awareness of the need to evaluate often affects how a program is documented. Program descriptions are limited not only by the discursive concepts available but also by the "credibility" of the discourse in which these concepts are embedded. What a program does and what it is or has the potential to be must "fit" within the discursive capacity and legitimating claims of systemic structures.

Empowerment-oriented interventions, therefore, require evaluation strategies that can reconcile the need to demonstrate effectiveness with the principles underscoring an emancipatory ethic. The initial reaction to this challenge was to incorporate more interpretive-oriented, qualitative methods into existing evaluation models (Guba and Lincoln, 1989). Later, and as is exemplified by the work of Fetterman et al. (1996), qualitative data collection techniques were combined with "participatory" approaches in an effort to make the evaluation process more consistent with the principles of empowerment-oriented social programming.

* * * * *

As I have argued elsewhere, the inclusion of empowering methods, in and of themselves, cannot effectively inform and support the political aspirations of emancipatory intervention (VanderPlaat, 1995a). In a recent review of more than 100 evaluation reports of Canadian health promotion activities (Castle and VanderPlaat, 1996) we found that the practice of participatory research is all too often reduced to a process whereby program users "contribute" within the confines of a predetermined evaluation research design. There is also the widespread assumption that only qualitative data can serve an empowering practice. This misconception regarding quantitative data collection seriously undermines the important contribution such data can make to emancipatory efforts. In addition, we found that the concern with

"voice" and the focus on story telling is often pursued without clear reference to an analytical context. As a result, the effectiveness of some programs becomes extremely difficult to substantiate.

What we have today, in terms of empowerment-oriented evaluation, is a solid body of literature that explores empowering evaluation methodologies and data collection strategies. However, a single-minded concern with technique tends to negate the political value of both the participatory approaches employed and the narratives generated through qualitative approaches. What we need is a careful consideration of how evaluation research, as a practice, can support emancipatory interests. The starting point for this endeavor is not methods, but a critical reconstruction of the role and focus of evaluation research.

To demonstrate what an emancipatory approach to evaluation would look like, I will now turn to an examination of the Canadian government's evaluation policy. Before doing so, however, I would like to stress the importance of retaining the conventional notion of evaluation as a form of assessment. The ideas of "accountability" and "program effectiveness" are not antithetical to emancipatory politics, and we must be careful to maintain the distinction between evaluation and action research (Reason, 1988; Reinharz, 1992). Action research constitutes an important part of an empowerment-based interventionary strategy. It provides the means through which collective interests are articulated and pursued. It emphasizes collaborative research to produce knowledge for the purposes of social change. Evaluation research is distinct. It focuses on the effectiveness of such efforts. Of course, action research may include an evaluation function, but the two are not, in principle, the same thing. Bearing this in mind, let us now look at the Treasury Board's guidelines to the evaluation function.

CRITICAL EVALUATION AND CANADIAN EVALUATION POLICY

The Canadian government's policy on program evaluation is that any project funded fully or partly by federal monies must participate in a periodic, formal evaluation process. Since 1981 it has been the responsibility of the Office of the Comptroller General to implement this policy, which it has done with varying degrees of success (Mayne, 1986). The role of program evaluation at the federal level is to serve as a systemic informant—"a strategic management tool" (Mayne, 1986: 35), "a source of information for resource allocation, program improvement and accountability in government" (Office of the Comptroller General [OCG], 1981: 4). According to Mayne, evaluation distinguishes itself from other information-gathering systems, such as audits, in that it has the capacity to determine "the influence of a program on the events

or conditions it is intended to affect" (1986: 33). Although relatively flexible in terms of methodology and data collection techniques used, the OCG does recommend that all program evaluations address the basic evaluation issues outlined in Table 27.1.

If we apply a Habermasian understanding to the OCG's conventional notion of evaluation-as-systemic-informant, we note that evaluation is perceived as an activity that assesses how well "the system" has penetrated and manipulated a problematic area within the lifeworld. Evaluation thus functions from a system to a lifeworld location. Projects initiated and/or sponsored by the system are consequently judged in light of systemically defined criteria of effectiveness. In essence, it is a self-monitoring process.

An emancipatory approach to intervention necessitates a reversal of this position. The evaluative gaze should be from lifeworld to

Table 27.1: Basic Program Evaluation Issues

A. CONTINUED RELEVANCE
Program Rationale
• To what extent are the objectives and the mandate of the program still relevant?
• Are the activities and outputs of the program consistent with its mandate and plausibly linked to the attainment of the objectives and intended impacts and effects?

B. PROGRAM RESULTS
Objectives Achievement
• In what manner and to what extent were appropriate objectives achieved as a result of the program?

Impacts and Effects
• What client benefits and broader outcomes, both intended and unintended, resulted from carrying out the program?
• In what manner and to what extent does the program complement, duplicate, overlap, or work at cross purposes with other programs?

C. COST-EFFECTIVENESS
Alternatives
• Are there more cost-effective alternative programs that might achieve the objectives and intended impacts and effects?
• Are there more cost-effective ways of delivering the existing program?

system. The focus should be on the extent to which communicative interference from the lifeworld has resulted in the effective organization and allocation of systemic resources. The role of emancipatory or critical evaluation is a bridging one between the administrative and professional apparatus of the state (system) and a program site (lifeworld). Evaluation acts as critical informant on behalf of the lifeworld. Its primary purpose is to assess how well the energies and resources of the state have been organized to meet the realities of everyday life. Evaluation becomes a self-conscious, as opposed to a self-monitoring, activity. This stance need not contradict the government's view of evaluation. Critical evaluation still functions to inform the system, but it does so based on the interests of the lifeworld.

* * * * *

The development of a critical approach to evaluation also requires a careful rethinking of who, or what, is the focus of an evaluation. The Office of the Comptroller General, in describing the evaluation function, defines the measurement of program impacts and effects in terms of "the resulting goods, services and regulations produced by others and the consequent chain of outcomes which occur in society and parts thereof (1981: 16, emphasis mine). Here again, the underlying assumption is that the direction of an interventionary act and the subsequent evaluation is system to lifeworld. Even in more participatory approaches to evaluation, the idea of "program effectiveness" is primarily constructed in terms of the relationship between the program and those for whom the program was designed, that is, its participants/users. This assumption underlies the basic evaluation criteria identified by the OCG and has a significant impact on both how the issue is understood and where we look for the answer.

Consider the evaluation issue regarding program sensibility. The research question posed is: "To what extent are the objectives and the mandate of the Program still relevant?" (Office of the Comptroller General, 1991: 1–4). The conventional approach would include, among other things, an examination of whether "the problem" still exists. Is the original, systemically defined and validated rationale for the program still relevant? [...] The issue of continued rationality is a question that "the system" asks itself, about its own original assumptions, and using its own discourse.

A critical approach requires that the question of program rationality be asked from the perspective of the lifeworld. The questions become: Does the program make sense given the needs emerging from lifeworld experience? Can we establish linkages between systemic assumptions, practical activities, and collective interests? The key point is not whether we can find lifeworld evidence to support systemic assumptions, but whether systemic assumptions (activities) support lifeworld realities.

The same argument applies to the basic evaluation issue concerning program consequences. In the words of the Comptroller General (Office of the Comptroller General, 1991: 1–4), "What client benefits and broader outcomes, both intended and unintended, resulted from carrying out the program?" Conventional approaches to this question look to the behaviors and attitudes of program users as the prime indicators of program effectiveness. However, there is a considerable body of critical literature that argues against the idea of an interventionary mindset focused exclusively on "the other" (Fine, 1994; Gore, 1992, hooks, 1990). This argument needs to be incorporated into a critical evaluation function. An emancipatory ethic requires that professional and technocratic "systemic agents" place themselves at the center of the evaluative gaze. The focus of attention should be on the effectiveness of systemic actions as they relate to the expressed (not assumed) needs and interests of program users. The worth of a program is not judged by how well program users respond to a systemically organized resource, but rather by how responsive systemic resources are to the realities of program users. In essence, a critical approach to evaluation necessitates a change in the object of the evaluative inquiry and puts systemic agents and their activities in the center of the assessment. Program users/ participants come to act as critical informants, or expert witnesses, to the process rather than as bearers of the indicators (e.g., behaviors and attitudes) by which the effectiveness of a program is judged. A critical approach thus requires an examination of the effects a program site, as a communicative space, has on the subsequent organization of resources and systemic responsiveness to everyday experience.

This shift in focus greatly expands the range of evaluation questions we might pose. For example, for public participation programs like DAWN-Ontario and the Self-Help Connection the concept of "participation" is almost always measured in terms of the number of people who join the network and remain actively involved (Castle and VanderPlaat, 1996). A critical approach would define participation in terms of the political input the network is allowed to have in public policy formation and the reorientation of health services. The question is not only how many political activities participants engage in, but also how these activities were responded to and incorporated by the system, the assumption being that one's involvement in an empowerment-oriented social program, which does not afford the capacity to influence social change, serves little more than a therapeutic function.

Likewise, if we look at Health Canada's parenting programs, such as Nobody's Perfect and CAPC, conventional evaluations are content with measuring the learning experiences of parents—little attention is given to the learnings that systemic agents could be deriving from these sites and applying to the reorganization of resources. For example, the opportunity for mutual support among participants has consistently been identified as the precursor to needs identification and a sense of collective identity. As such, it is often identified by parents as the catalyst for individual change and it is obviously the basis for potential collective action (VanderPlaat, 1998). Critical evaluation would demand that this finding be carried back into the system and incorporated into the way we (as systemic agents) organize resources and design and evaluate programs. Subsequent evaluation questions would focus on how well the system has supported the capacity for mutual support and allowed political energies to emerge. Instead, we continue to treat mutual support as one of the many, and often anecdotal, indicators of participant behavior, thereby effectively disarming its emancipatory potential.

As noted earlier, critical evaluation also requires that systemic agents become self-conscious or reflective about their interventionary efforts. In doing so they must seriously address the barriers imposed by their own political/disciplinary locations and the institutions that they help to maintain. This requires a willingness to address potentially difficult and politically sensitive questions. For example, what impact does the involvement of "professionals" have on the effectiveness of empowerment-oriented programs? What barriers are posed by professional assumptions and approaches? [...]

There is enough anecdotal evidence emerging from evaluations to warrant serious consideration of these types of questions. Whether or not they get asked depends on the extent to which we, as systemic agents, are willing to commit to an emancipatory ethic. To do so requires that we redirect the power inherent in our positions and act more like

Foucault's idea of a specific intellectual (1977: 126)—a person who uses their privilege as a weapon to dismantle, rather than guard, the structures of domination and oppression.

CONCLUSION

Evaluation activities informed by emancipatory politics retain the notions of "accountability" and "program effectiveness" but respond to these imperatives from the perspective of the lifeworld, not the system. As such, they require that a participatory, democratic ethos be restored to the concept of "public policy." The criteria by which a social program is judged should be validated by the public for which it was intended. The question of proof lies not in the behaviors and attitudes of program users but in the responsiveness of system agents and resources to the needs of everyday life.

Evaluation underscored by an emancipatory intent is also a process that must be judged by its catalytic validity (Reason and Rowan, 1981), "the degree to which the research process reorients, focuses and energizes participants toward knowing reality in order to transform it" (Lather, 1991: 68). Integral to this idea is the recognition that academics, professionals, and bureaucrats are often the participants in question. They (we) and their (our) activities become the foci of the evaluative gaze (dispelling the subject/object dichotomy so disdained by critical and feminist thinkers). The catalytic validity of an evaluation is thus judged by the extent to which it provides system agents with a precise picture of the systemic barriers that block the emergence of collective interests, political agency, and communicatively secured resource allocation. Key questions galvanize around the ways in which a program site has created an empowering space and whether emancipatory interests have been allowed to penetrate and influence the energies, resources, and policies of the system.

Those committed to emancipatory politics must also give careful consideration to the research practices that best support this position. Although quantitative methods, in particular the survey, have been less than adequate in reflecting lived experience and supporting emancipatory interests (Graham, 1983; Reinharz, 1992), the usefulness of empirical data cannot be denied (Finch, 1991; Harding, 1991; Jayaratne, 1983; Reinharz, 1992; Stanley and Wise, 1990). Harding (1987) and Smith (1987) note that it is not the methods or techniques themselves that are problematic, but rather the ways they are deployed to construct knowledge. We need to be conscious of and sensitive to the limitations and impositions presented by particular ways of collecting and analyzing information.

A critical approach to evaluation also raises questions about representation (Borland, 1991; Brodkey, 1987; Fine, 1994; Mascia-Lees et al., 1989). In traditional evaluations a research report is presented in the voice of the system or in a detached voice that claims to be representing the interests of all parties. Critical evaluation as a narrative form problematizes the writing of the voice(s) of others. Can complexity be presented without privileging a voice? Should the voice(s) of program users be presented in their own speech styles and grammatical structures or do we edit this narrative to give it greater "legitimacy" within the system? These questions are not easily answered. Although we may want to present the voices of the dispossessed as heard, this does not necessarily aid the process of systemic change. Indeed, there may be value in translating the voice(s) of the dispossessed so that, say, the implications for resource reallocations are clearly understood by the system in system terms.

Herein lie the very profound contradictions that face researchers who step out, who presume to want to make a difference, who are so bold or arrogant as to assume we might. Once out beyond the picket fence of illusory objectivity, we trespass all over the classed, raced, and otherwise stratified lines that have demarcated our social legitimacy for publicly telling their stories. And it is then that ethical questions boil. (Fine, 1994: 80)

The issue of representation leads directly to questions of validity, and these touch all areas of the evaluation process, including the validation of data collection instruments and procedures (Cronbach, 1980; House, 1980), the credibility of narratives and descriptions (Lather, 1991), and the legitimacy of conclusions and recommendations (Heron, 1988). At a minimum, most critical researchers require the considered reaction of the actors from whom the information was derived. Guba and Lincoln suggest that the process of establishing validity through member checks is

the single most crucial technique for establishing credibility. If the evaluator wants to establish that the multiple realities he or she presents are those that the stakeholders have provided, the most

certain test is verifying those multiple constructions with those who provided them. (1989: 239)

Lather (1991) puts forward the concept of maximum reciprocity where all concerned are actively engaged in the design of the research tool, and in the construction and validation of findings and conclusions. For Lather, it is the principle of maximum reciprocity that determines the potential usefulness of a data collection technique and the subsequent validity of the knowledge generated.

This, then, is the context for a critical approach to evaluation. Clearly, participatory strategies are not empowering if they are conducted within the confines of predetermined systemic mandates. Likewise, empowerment-oriented interventions are not emancipatory if the concept of social change begins and ends with the behaviors of program participants. As Habermas (1987) reminds us, social change requires interaction between human agency and social structures. Evaluation strategies that ignore this and focus only on the program user have little capacity to inform an emancipatory interest.

NOTE

1. Fischer (1980) and Ryan (1988) have also applied Habermasian concepts to evaluation research, particularly from his earlier work on knowledge and human interests (1971).

REFERENCES

Borland, K. 1991. "That's Not What I Said: Interpretive Conflict in Oral Narrative Research." In *Women's Words: The Feminist Practice of Oral History*, edited by S.B. Gluck and D. Patai, 63–76. New York: Routledge.

Brodkey, L. 1987. "Writing Critical Ethnographic Narratives." *Anthropology and Education Quarterly* 18(2): 67–76.

Carr, W., and S. Kemmis. 1986. *Becoming Critical*. London: The Falmer Press.

Castle, D., and M. VanderPlaat. 1996. *Issues in Measuring Effectiveness in Health Promotion Activities, Projects, Programs: A Collection of Canadian Examples*. Ottawa: Health Canada.

Collins, M. 1991. *Adult Education as Vocation*. New York: Routledge.

Cronbach, L. 1980. *Toward Reform of Program Evaluation*. San Francisco: Jossey Bass.

Everitt, A. 1996. "Developing Critical Evaluation." *Evaluation: International Journal of Theory, Research and Practice* 2(2): 173–188.

Fay, B. 1987. *Critical Social Science*. Ithaca: Cornell University Press.

Fetterman, D.M., S.J. Kaftarian, and A. Wandersman, eds. 1996. *Empowerment Evaluation*. Thousand Oaks: Sage.

Finch, J. 1991. "Feminist Research and Social Policy." In *Women's Issues in Social Policy*, edited by M. Maclean and D. Groves, 194–204. New York: Routledge, Chapman and Hall.

Fine, M. 1994. "Working the Hyphens: Reinventing Self and Other in Qualitative Research." In *Handbook of Qualitative Research*, edited by N. Denzin and Y. Lincoln, 70–82. Newbury Park: Sage.

Fischer, F. 1980. *Politics, Values and Public Policy: The Problem of Methodology*. Boulder: Westview Press.

_____. 1985. "Critical Evaluation of Public Policy: A Methodological Case Study." In *Critical Theory and Public Life*, edited by J. Forester, 231–257. Cambridge: MIT Press.

Foucault, M. 1977. *Power/Knowledge*, translated by C. Gordon. New York: Pantheon Books.

Freire, P. 1970. *Pedagogy of the Oppressed*. New York: Seabury Press.

Giroux, H.A. 1988. "Literacy and the Pedagogy of Voice and Political Empowerment." *Educational Theory* 38(1): 61–75.

_____. 1991. "Modernism, Postmodernism and Feminism: Rethinking the Boundaries of Educational Discourse." In *Postmodernism, Feminism, and Cultural Politics*, edited by H.A. Giroux, 1–59. New York: State University of New York Press.

Gore, J. 1992. "What We Can Do for You! What Can We Do for You? Struggling over Empowerment in Critical and Feminist Pedagogy." In *Feminisms and Critical Pedagogy*, edited by C. Luke and J. Gore, 55–73. New York: Routledge, Chapman & Hall.

Graham, H. 1983. "Do Her Answers Fit His Questions? Women and the Survey Method." In *The Public and the Private*, edited by E. Gamarnikow, D. Morgan, J. Purvis, and D. Taylorson, 132–146. London: Heinemann.

Guba, E., and Y.S. Lincoln. 1989. *Fourth Generation Evaluation*. Newbury Park: Sage.

Habermas, J. 1971. *Knowledge and Human Interests*. London: Heinemann.

_____. 1984. *The Theory of Communicative Action*, vol. 1. Boston: Beacon Press.

_____. 1987. *The Theory of Communicative Action*, vol. 2. Boston: Beacon Press.

Hall, B.L. 1981. "Participatory Research, Popular Knowledge, and Power: A Personal Reflection." *Convergence* 14(3): 6–19.

Haraway, D. 1988. "Situated Knowledges: The Science Question in Feminism and the Privilege of Partial Perspective." *Feminist Studies* 14(3): 575–599.

Harding, S. 1987. "Is There a Feminist Method?" In *Feminism and Methodology*, edited by S. Harding, 1–14. Milton Keynes: Open University Press.

_____. 1991. *Whose Science? Whose Knowledge?* Ithaca: Cornell University Press.

Hart, M. 1990. "Liberation through Consciousness Raising." In *Fostering Critical Reflection in Adulthood*, edited by J. Mezirow, 47–73. San Francisco: Jossey-Bass.

Heron, J. 1988. "Validity in Co-operative Inquiry." In *Human Inquiry in Action*, edited by P. Reason, 40–59. Newbury Park: Sage.

hooks, b. 1990. *Yearning: Race, Gender and Cultural Politics*. Boston: South End.

House, E.R. 1980. *Evaluating with Validity*. Beverly Hills: Sage.

Jayaratne, T.E. 1983. "The Value of Quantitative Methodology for Feminist Research." In *Theories of Women's Studies*, edited by G.

Bowles and R.D. Klein, 140–161). Boston: Routledge and Kegan Paul.

Kemmis, S. 1993. "Foucault, Habermas and Evaluation." *Curriculum Studies* 2(1): 35–54.

Lather, P. 1991. *Getting Smart: Feminist Research and Pedagogy with/in the Postmodern.* New York: Routledge.

Maguire, P. 1987. *Doing Participatory Research: A Feminist Approach.* Amherst: Centre for International Education.

Mascia-Lees, F.E., P. Sharpe, and C.B. Cohen. 1989. "The Postmodernist Turn in Anthropology: Cautions from a Feminist Perspective." *Signs* 15(1): 7–33.

Mayne, J. 1986. "Ongoing Program Performance Information Systems and Program Evaluation in the Canadian Federal Government." *Canadian Journal of Program Evaluation* 1(1): 29–38.

Office of the Comptroller General. 1981. *Guide on the Program Evaluation Function.* Ottawa: Supply and Services Canada.

_____. 1991. *Program Evaluation Methods.* Ottawa: Supply and Services Canada.

Reason, P., ed. 1988. *Human Inquiry in Action.* Newbury Park: Sage.

Reason, P., and J. Rowan, eds. 1981. *Human Inquiry: A Sourcebook of New Paradigm Research.* Chichester: Wiley.

Reinharz, S. 1992. *Feminist Methods in Social Research.* Don Mills: Oxford University Press Canada.

Ryan, A.G. 1988. "Program Evaluation within the Paradigms: Mapping the Territory." *Knowledge* 10(1): 25–47.

Scriven, M. 1973. "Goal-Free Evaluation." In *School Evaluation: The Politics and Process*, edited by E.R. House, 319–328. Berkeley: McCutchan.

Shields, V.R., and B. Durvi. 1993. "Sense-Making in Feminist Social Science." *Women's Studies International Forum* 16(1): 65–81.

Smith, D.E. 1987. *The Everyday World as Problematic.* Boston: Northeastern University Press.

_____. 1990. *The Conceptual Practices of Power.* Toronto: University of Toronto Press.

Stake, R.E. 1975. *Evaluating the Arts in Education: A Responsive Approach.* Columbus: Merrill.

Stanley, L., and S. Wise. 1990. "Method, Methodology and Epistemology in Feminist Research Processes." In *Feminist Praxis*, edited by L. Stanley, 20–62. London: Routledge.

VanderPlaat, M. 1995a. "Beyond Technique: Evaluating for Empowerment." *Evaluation: International Journal of Theory, Research and Practice* 1(1): 81–96.

_____. 1995b. "A Critical Perspective on Social Intervention and Evaluation in the Modern Welfare State." Doctoral dissertation, Dalhousie University, Halifax.

_____. 1998. "Empowerment, Emancipation and Health Promotion Policy." *Canadian Journal of Sociology* 23(1): 71–90.

Weiler, K. 1991. "Freire and a Feminist Pedagogy of Difference." *Harvard Educational Review* 61(4): 451–474.

Rethinking Part 2E: Social Inquiry as Communicative Reason: Toward a Public Sociology

CRITICAL THINKING QUESTIONS

Chapter 24: The Promise

1. Mills begins his analysis with the observation that many people feel their private lives are a series of traps. How does the sociological imagination provide a means of undoing these traps?

2. As you survey your own life or those of people you know well, what personal troubles of milieu come to mind and how can they be analytically linked to public issues of social structure?

3. Mills sees a social science made sprightly by the sociological imagination as a desirable alternative to both the technological ethos of modern science and artistic concerns of contemporary literature. How does his approach claim a space *between* the scientific and the humanistic?

Chapter 25: Exploring the Relevance of Critical Theory for Action Research: Emancipatory Action Research in the Footsteps of Jürgen Habermas

1. Stephen Kemmis argues that the theory of system and lifeworld provides a new perspective on action research. What are the key elements in that new perspective?

2. An effect of colonization of the lifeworld is that people "increasingly identify themselves and their aspirations in systems terms" (p. 356). What are the implications of this problem for critical research strategies?

3. At the close of his chapter, Kemmis describes three stages in his journey through the territory of critical action research and critical theory. How has his perspective on research changed over the course of these stages?

Chapter 26: The "Project of Modernity" and the Parameters for a Critical Sociology: An Argument with Illustrations from Medical Sociology

1. Graham Scambler agrees with Habermas that the project of modernity is not a failure but an unfinished project. How does he develop this argument and what are its ramifications for the practice of social inquiry?

2. What are the implications for critical research strategies of Scambler's claim that sociology's primary allegiance should be to the rationalization of the lifeworld?

3. What role and place do a revitalized public sphere and a vibrant field of critical social movements occupy in Scambler's vision of critical sociological practice?

Chapter 27: Emancipatory Politics, Critical Evaluation, and Government Policy

1. Madine VanderPlatt criticizes the literature on empowerment-oriented evaluation for its single-minded concern with technique. What is the gist of her critique?
2. Within the Canadian federal state apparatus, the role of program evaluation is to serve as a "system informant." How is this standpoint inscribed within the basic evaluation issues that the Office of the Comptroller General outlines?
3. VanderPlatt's shift from a systems to a lifeworld perspective "greatly expands the range of evaluation questions we might pose" (p. 375). What questions become important with this shift?

GLOSSARY TERMS

Colonization of lifeworld by system: A tendency in late modernity, stemming from selective rationalization, for the priorities and discourses of the political-economic system to be infused within the lifeworld, as in the commercialization and commodification of everyday life and the conversion of citizens into clients of state programs.

Communicative action: Action oriented toward achieving a sense of mutual understanding and collective will, through discussion and agreement. As communicative action becomes rationalized, it is regulated less by unexamined background consensus (as in the absolute authority of tradition) and is increasingly open to critical reason, providing a basis for a democratic way of life.

Critical evaluation: An approach to evaluating social programs that reposes the question of program rationality from the perspective of the lifeworld.

Lifeworld-based activists: Activists in the new social movements (e.g., environmentalism, feminism, human rights) that have emerged in resistance to the colonization of the lifeworld, or as agents of further lifeworld rationalization (i.e., communicative democracy and the restoration of a public sphere). A sociology for communicative reason needs to build alliances with such movements and activists as they promote democratic ways of life.

Lifeworld perspective: The perspective on modern society that emphasizes the communicative practices and relations that secure identity, social order, and cultural meaning. Lifeworld includes (inter)personal "everyday life" as well as the public sphere; lifeworld rationalization involves the increasing scope of communicative rationality based on the validity claims stated below.

Public sociology: A reflexive, engaged sociology that provides critical perspectives citizens can draw upon to understand their social conditions.

Public sphere: "A theater in modern societies in which political participation is enacted through the medium of talk. It is the space in which citizens deliberate about their common affairs, hence, an institutionalized arena of discursive interaction. This arena is conceptually distinct from the state; it is a site for the production and circulation of discourses that can in principle be critical of the state" (Fraser, 1997: 70).

Scientism: The over-reliance on scientific discourse and technocratic rationalization as the basis for instrumental decision making. Scientism disarms political challenges to the status quo by installing the authority of technical expertise as the precondition for participation and by misrepresenting the decision-making process as a purely technical matter.

Selective rationalization: The condition in the modern world in which system rationalization (within capitalist economics and bureaucratic administration) has outstripped the rationalization of the lifeworld.

Sociological imagination: A critical capacity for social analysis that enables us to grasp history, biography, and the relations between the two within society. Such a capacity enables us to put urgent public issues and insistent human troubles into context. When diffused widely among the citizenry, the sociological imagination promotes a democratic way of life.

Systems perspective: The perspective on modern society that emphasizes organizational and institutional structures and technologies as they are oriented toward the attainment of specific goals. A systems perspective incorporates a certain kind of instrumental rationality that emphasizes the efficiency of action oriented toward success, particularly in the domains of the market and state.

Validity claims: In Habermas's theory of communicative action, the four questions that can be posed of any utterance, providing a starting point for critical reflection on communicative action, are: Is the utterance comprehensible? Is it true (i.e., accurate)? Is it right and morally appropriate? Is it sincerely stated?

FURTHER READING

Blaug, R. 1997. "Between Fear and Disappointment: Critical, Empirical and Political Uses of Habermas." *Political Studies* 45(1): 100–117.

Blaug reviews three types of research inspired by Habermas's theory of communicative action: (1) work that uses the normative theory as an interpretive tool in generating cultural criticism; (2) studies that actually use the theory as an empirical tool to research the social world; and (3) attempts to use the theory in evaluating the democratic (or distorted) character of instances of communication.

Calavita, Kitty. 2002. "Engaged Research, 'Goose Bumps,' and the Role of the Public Intellectual." *Law and Society Review* 36(1): 5–20.

Calls for a renewed commitment to engaged research by intellectuals in law and society studies. This means "asking the big questions," distinguishing between engaged and policy-driven research, and identifying political obstacles that face the public intellectual and critical researcher, along with ways that these may be overcome.

Flyvbjerg, Bent. 2001. *Making Social Science Matter*. New York: Cambridge University Press.

Flyvbjerg draws on Habermas, Foucault, Bourdieu and other critical thinkers in developing "phronetic social science" as a methodological alternative to positivism. Flyvbjerg's approach emphasizes public deliberation and praxis rather than the vain emulation of natural science.

Forester, John, ed. 1985. *Critical Theory and Public Life*. Cambridge: MIT Press.

This collection applies Habermas's critical communications theory to explore issues of public life, with a focus on the research implications and empirical applicability of the theory.

Fraser, Nancy. 1997. "Rethinking the Public Sphere: A Contribution to Actually Existing Democracy." In Nancy Fraser, *Justice Interruptus*, 69–98. New York: Routledge.

A reformulation of Habermas's concept of the public sphere, breaking from the liberal model (Habermas's own starting point) and developing four tasks for "a critical theory of actually existing democracy" (92). Fraser's essay carries important lessons for any sociology committed to a vibrant public sphere.

McLain, Raymond. 2002. "Reflexivity and the Sociology of Practice." *Sociological Practice* 4(4): 249–277.

McLain advocates a reflexive perspective on sociological and lay knowledge and a model of lay-expert engagement that recentres sociological practice as a mutually reflexive, democratically structured, and transformatively oriented activity. His approach is influenced by Habermas and also by theorists of reflexive modernization, particularly Ulrich Beck.

RELEVANT WEB SITES

Canadian PIRG Listings
http://opirg.sa.utoronto.ca/links/pirgs.html

Links and addresses for public interest research groups that promote, through research activities, discussion, debate, and activism around social-justice and environmental issues. Also see the similar site in the United States: http://www.uspirg.org/.

Center for Communication and Civic Engagement
http://depts.washington.edu/ccce/Home.htm

Based at the University of Washington, the CCCE is dedicated to understanding and facilitating the uses of dynamic media systems and communication practices to promote citizen engagement and effective participation in local, national, and global affairs. Faculty and student affiliates of the center engage in research, policy analyses, educational programs, and the development of Web-based information and network resources for citizens, scholars, and journalists.

PIRG Power: Public Interest Research Groups in Canada Celebrate 25 Years of Student Activism

http://www.eya.ca/yaec/docs/pgpirg/PIRG%20Power.doc

An interesting article by Karen Farbridge and Peter Cameron, published also in *Alternatives* (Summer 1998). It recounts the history of Public Interest Research Groups in Canada. PIRGS have been important vehicles for rekindling public spheres in and around university campuses.

Public Knowledge

http://www.publicknowledge.org/

A Washington, D.C.-based public-interest advocacy organization dedicated to fortifying and defending a vibrant information commons. The group works with a "wide spectrum of stakeholders—libraries, educators, scientists, artists, musicians, journalists, consumers, software programmers, civic groups, and enlightened businesses—to promote the core conviction that some fundamental democratic principles and cultural values—openness, access, and the capacity to create and compete—must be given new embodiment in the digital age." Its Web site contains news and documents on the struggle to protect the information commons and links to various other sites, some of them research oriented.

Study Circles Resource Centre

http://www.studycircles.com/

Study circles—small-group, democratic, peer-led discussions—provide a simple way to involve community members in dialogue and action on important social and political issues. The Study Circles Resource Center is dedicated to finding ways for all kinds of people to engage in dialogue and problem solving on critical social and political issues. SCRC helps communities by giving them the tools to organize productive dialogue, recruit diverse participants, find solutions, and work for action and change.

Toda Institute for Global Peace and Policy Research

http://www.toda.org

Through research activities, conferences and seminars, and publications the Toda Institute promotes a "dialogue of civilizations for world citizenship." It brings three epistemic communities–peace researchers, policymakers, and community activists–into communication and collaboration on selected projects in conflict resolution. The Institute provides research, advisory, and educational services on policy issues that affect the world community.

Conclusion

Each of the five critical strategies I have featured in this collection offers resources for praxis-oriented researchers—those interested not only in understanding the world, but in changing it in emancipatory ways. The strategies are distinctive, yet they also intersect. But although they share a commitment to social critique and some vision of human emancipation, they are not without creative tension when juxtaposed against each other.

CONVERGENCES, COMPLEMENTARITIES, AND TENSIONS

To get a grip on the convergences, complementarities, and tensions among our critical strategies, we can briefly proceed through a series of paired comparisons, beginning with two strategies of broadest scope—dialectical social analysis (DSA) and social inquiry as communicative reason. In striving to draw out the relational, dynamic, emergent, and contingent character of the social, and to unmask underlying relations that generate social injustices and ecological maladies, DSA gives us a general strategy for critical investigations attuned to the possibilities in the present for "making history" in novel, liberatory ways. Any study of social life can benefit from adopting this strategy, which originates in Marx's critique of capitalism. When we view social inquiry as communicative reason we gain another vantage point, just as Habermas did when he reformulated historical materialism by placing communication—a dimension of practice undertheorized by Marx—at the centre of social life (Habermas, 1979). It is not enough to *unmask* what lies behind social experience and action if the communicative practice of inquiry itself falls short of its democratizing potential. This means fashioning inquiry so as to contribute to lifeworld rationalization, to the recovery of the public sphere, to the furtherance of democratic social relations within which people can discuss issues of common concern openly and with some reasonable sense of efficacy. More concretely, it might mean taking the side of critical social movements—themselves arenas for subaltern counterpublics[1]—in conducting research of value to their praxis (including constructive critiques of that praxis). It might mean investigating the actual *processes* of life world colonization, in a version of dialectical unmasking, or conducting evaluations of state programs and other system initiatives from the perspective of needs and interests rooted in the lifeworld. It certainly means fostering, through the research process and the communication of its results, the kind of sociological imagination in all of us that can inform a revitalized public sphere.

There are definite convergences between these two most general strategies on the one hand and institutional ethnography (IE) on the other. When we problematize the everyday world, when we take up the standpoint of the ruled, when we explicate the ways in which ruling relations reach into and colonize everyday life, we are very much practising a sociology for people and for the lifeworlds that they continually bring into existence. As Campbell and Gregor (2002) have suggested, the practice of IE entails an ethical-political commitment to the democratization of everyday life. Compared to the strategy we have called social inquiry for communicative reason, however, IE offers a specific methodology—the combination of fieldwork, interviewing, and textual analysis that stems from an initial problematization of the everyday. By explicating just how it is that ruling relations reach into local settings, IE can create veridical mappings of the social that can provide important leverage in the decolonization of lifeworlds and the rejuvenation of public spheres.

The congruencies between IE and DSA, noted earlier, are also worth recalling here. These strategies share an ontology that is explicitly historical materialist and a commitment to ideology critique, as in Dorothy Smith's analysis of the objectifying practices of conventional sociology (1989). In developing IE, Smith turned to Marx's critical analysis of capitalism as an extra-local complex of social relations, but her approach extends that critique to take in the characteristically textual mode through which ruling occurs in late modernity. IE can also be read as a critique of those interpreters of Marx who convert his analysis into an abstract theory disconnected from the lived realities of the everyday. IE, then, gives us a flexible yet richly detailed research strategy that resonates well with both dialectical social analysis and the project of a public, lifeworld-oriented sociology.

Much the same can be claimed for PAR, even though IE and PAR are not without some creative tensions. Centred upon the dialectical relation of theory and practice—understanding the world in order to participate in its transformation—PAR is praxis-oriented in precisely the way one would want in a fully dialectical social analysis. However, while DSA often focuses on social *structures* and on systemic problems such as poverty (see, e.g., Chapter 11) PAR's focal point is site-specific *agency*—the development of knowledge and action that can directly contribute to social justice for a specific group. PAR is both dialectical and *dialogical*: it requires democratic communicative relations among the practitioners and professionals engaged in a cogenerative learning process. Indeed, without a process of democratic empowerment, through which the local practitioners gain the capacity to control their own knowledge production and action, PAR degenerates into little more than a sophisticated exercise in social control: it becomes an instrument for system rationality, not a catalyst of lifeworld rationalization. PAR both requires and generates new communicative spaces and actions. Within its dialogues public intellectuals and communities can learn together and in the process contribute to "the formation of autonomous, self-organized public spheres capable of asserting themselves ... against the systematically integrating media of money and power" (Kemmis, p. 356).

However, if IE and PAR both resonate strongly with dialectical and public sphere-oriented strategies, they do so in distinctive ways. If IE is a sociology *for* people, PAR is a sociology *with* them. Marie Campbell and Frances Gregor point out that "institutional ethnography attempts something different from most participatory research" (2002: 67). The "radical potential" of IE is to rethink social settings taking power relations fully into account and on that basis "to produce an analysis in the interest of those about whom knowledge is being constructed" (2002: 68). This objective is quite distinct from the thrust of PAR, which in Campbell and Gregor's view is to democratize the interpersonal relations among researchers and researched. In this respect, IE is somewhat more inclined toward dialectical social analysis, which emphasizes the conflicting interests and standpoints in knowledge/power relations, while PAR highlights the practice of communicative democracy within the knowledge-generating process. In certain contexts it may be feasible to combine IE and PAR, as Campbell and her colleagues did in Project Inter-Seed, a collaborative research project on disability issues and health care in which the research team (which included people with disabilities) accepted IE as coherent with the values of the project. This meant that, as an aspect of the participatory research process, the entire research team had to learn how to take up the standpoint of people with disabilities (Campbell and Gregor, 2002: 117–119), a desirable result in itself. In other contexts, as I will argue below, one or the other of these critical strategies is probably preferable.

There is, finally, the question of how critical discourse analysis (CDA) might be placed within the context of our other four critical strategies. An eclectic bundle of approaches that share a commitment to analyzing discourse as an expression of knowledge/power, CDA can be differentiated into post-structural and critical-realist versions, as I did in introducing Part 2C of this book. The post-structural forms of discourse analysis we have examined—deconstruction and genealogy—are designed to disturb, subvert, and undo the coherence and persuasiveness of discourses. They are not primarily ways of reaching an understanding of a situation to enable effective action, but are political acts in their own right. This action-orientation aligns post-structural discourse analysis to some degree with action research. Fittingly, Jennings and Graham (1996) have argued that there needs to be *dialogue* between the two approaches. When PAR is placed in dialogue with deconstruction, two points of convergence become clear. The approaches share a critique of the interplay of knowledge and power, which implies that part of PAR's project is to deconstruct authoritative voices—those who speak for and on behalf of others. Moreover, in as much as action research is committed to reconstructing social relations, deconstructive method can be helpful in locating the contradictions in texts that open possibilities for reconstruction. Genealogy also has great relevance to action research, as is obvious when we re-read Tuhiwai Smith's discussion of 25 indigenous projects (see Chapter 6), many of which are at once genealogical initiatives to emancipate knowledges that have been repressed under the weight of colonization *and* action-research projects to empower and rejuvenate indigenous communities.

There are likewise some interesting parallels between IE and genealogy as both strategies begin by problematizing what is generally taken for granted. However, what IE problematizes are the lived actualities of people, considered as active, knowledgeable practitioners, whose everyday lives are shaped by ruling relations. What genealogy problematizes are the discourses that make us what we are. Centring on the endemic problems of subjectification and normalization, the genealogical project is one of self-overcoming and self-transformation, "to give new impetus, as far and as wide as possible, to the undefined work of freedom" (Foucault, 1984: 46). Yet despite the concern, shared by IE and post-structural analysis, to analyze discourse and textuality as an integral aspect of social practice, Dorothy Smith (1993, 1999) has registered some important criticisms of post-structural forms of discourse analysis. She asks "how can we take up post-structuralism's discovery of how discourse speaks through us and beyond our intended meaning while at the same time avoiding its solipsistic confinement to discourse?" (1999: 76). Smith's (1999: 96–130) own engagement with the praxis-oriented theories of language and meaning in the work of Mikhail Bakhtin and Valentin Vološinov, and David McNally's (2001) use of the same authors in critiquing the linguistic structuralism of Ferdinand de Saussure, which underwrites post-structural theory, are steps toward *theorizing* discourse on a sound footing. But our concern in these pages has been with strategies for *research*, and for these we have turned to recent developments in the critical-realist tradition that take up post-structuralism's key insights but broaden the analysis beyond discourse.

Overall, the critical-realist approaches we considered in our second pair of readings in CDA converge with IE since, along with dialectical social analysis, they share an ontological framework that explicitly recognizes the materiality of human practices and social relations. Parker's approach to "discourse dynamics" and Chouliaraki and Fairclough's use of "explanatory critique" in CDA provide us with the tools to conduct discourse analyses that are sensitive to *intertextuality*—the complex ways in which discourses intersect and intermingle—as well as *substantive relationality*—the relations among discourses, social institutions, structures, and struggles. These forms of critical discourse analysis obviously resonate with dialectical social analysis, but they also have important relevancies to the project of social inquiry as communicative reason. Using critical-realist CDA one can analyze precisely how system discourses colonize lifeworlds, a concern expressed by Andrew Parkin (1996); one can unpack *distortions* in communication that arise from power imbalances, whether in organized hierarchies, in the mass media, or in everyday life; one can explore possible resources for achieving authentic dialogue between participants in a discursive practice. Indeed, in their development of CDA as explanatory critique (p. 268), Chouliaraki and Fairclough are led to propose as the key properties of a "successful public sphere" that it provide a place and a practice in which people as citizens can address together issues of social and political concern, "in a way that gives access to all those with an interest, constitutes real dialogue between those involved, and leads to action."[2]

These critical-realist strategies accept that social reality—including our comprehension of it, which is part of social reality—is discursively saturated and discursively dependent, but they reject the claim, common among post-structuralists, that the social is discursively determined (cf. Sayer, 1982). This last claim creates the "solipsistic confinement" about which Smith and others complain. It limits social critique to the realm of discourse. As I mentioned in my earlier discussion of CDA, such a position rules out claims about the *actualities* of oppression, alienation, exploitation, and ecological devastation, since if one takes the nominalist view of language and meaning favoured by post-structuralism, all such claims can be no more than positions *within* discourse. In a world of profound material injustice and ecological crisis—our world—analyses of discourse need to avoid disabling retreats from the philosophy of praxis that Marx outlined in his "Theses on Feuerbach," our first reading. This means that for the most part, deconstructive and genealogical methods will have an *ancillary* status relative to the other critical strategies featured herein. Their great value to critical inquiry lies in the heightened reflexivity they bring to our understanding of language and power. After post-structuralism, it is no longer sufficient to treat language and discourse instrumentally as transparencies or neutral tools, either within social life or within the study of social life. Any discourse, including those we use in critical social science, can be opened up to reflexive scrutiny using deconstructive and genealogical techniques. The result will be greater self-clarification, always a virtue in itself, but never sufficient in the struggle for social justice.

GOALS, CONTEXTS, AND CRITICAL RESEARCH STRATEGIES

Our comparisons of critical strategies raise the question of *when* a given approach, or perhaps some combination, is most helpful to praxis-oriented inquiry. Both the *goals* of the project and the *context* in which it takes place should be kept in view in thinking through this issue. Space does not permit a thorough discussion, but let me gesture toward the kinds of considerations that seem relevant. In her discussion of social justice, Nancy Fraser (1997) has nicely framed one major aspect of the issue of goals. Our era is one of multiform social-justice struggles, pursuing a variety of goals. Some emphasize cultural issues of *recognition*, identity, and the like, as with multiculturalism and queer politics (on the latter, see Glick, 2000; Storr, 2000; Brookey and Miller, 2001); some emphasize material *redistribution*, as with class politics; some emphasize both recognition and redistribution, as with feminism, anti-racism, and Aboriginal politics.

These differing forms of emancipatory politics connect with our critical strategies in specific ways. Post-structural strategies of genealogy and deconstruction, in subverting the social construction of identity and meaning, are particularly helpful in assisting struggles for recognition. They provide intellectual resources to transform such struggles from an essentialistic politics of identity, which simply accords new respect to disparaged groups (as in "gay pride") to a radical politics of difference, which challenges the discursive distinctions that stabilize a system of identities (as in the queer critique of the hetero/homo binary).[3] When it comes to the politics of material redistribution, as in the struggle to end poverty or to democratize work relations, post-structural readings continue to have relevance, but they become ancillary to dialectical analyses of social relations, institutional ethnographies, and the like.[4] Viewed in this light, deconstruction and genealogy can be seen as resources for radical cultural politics; critical modernist analyses such as DSA can be seen to inform a politics of redistribution. Both are needed, perhaps in different degrees, by different movements and actors, and both are certainly needed in order to comprehend and critique the nationalist hegemonies that now mobilize popular desires for community and "security" and that structure so much of the formal political field, both within states and among them.

Differing socio-political *contexts* have also to be considered in selecting among possible research strategies. To illustrate, consider what we learn from Colleen Reid's (2000) attempt to implement a feminist action research (FAR) strategy at a YWCA employment-training program for low-income single mothers. Despite an official organizational discourse of empowerment, the hierarchical positions of service providers and clients were deeply inscribed within the formal organization of the YWCA. The service providers occupied positions of power and were wedded to a professionalized perspective on their relation to clients; the clients lacked the time and resources to really collaborate in the project, and were not entirely trusting of a researcher, aligned with the formal organization, who came from an affluent background. In this situation, so far removed from a community or "subaltern counterpublic," none of the conditions for successful participatory research was in place. Rather, Reid, a well-meaning researcher, took up a position within ruling relations and then attempted the Herculean feat of democratizing the interpersonal relations among research participants, with disappointing results:

> As I became more immersed in my research I began to question FAR's assumption that collaboration and negotiation were possible in a structured organizational setting. My location as a relatively privileged and educated researcher coupled with the limitations imposed by the research site became increasingly problematic. The growing awareness of my power challenged me to consistently document my assumptions and to confront the issue of voice appropriation. (2000: 179)

Reid's insightful account suggests that participatory action research is a strategy that is most appropriate in lifeworld settings where democratic, communicative action is already in play and can be drawn upon as a primary resource in building new communicative spaces and useful knowledge. In settings that are organized around system rationalities—as in the hierarchical relation between service providers and clients—or where power is otherwise entrenched, institutional ethnography is a more effective strategy, since it specifically addresses ruling relations.

CRITICAL STRATEGIES AND RESEARCH TECHNIQUES: THE QUESTION OF QUANTITATIVE METHOD

This is not a book on the techniques of research method. Yet it is worthwhile, in this conclusion, to consider briefly how our critical *strategies* for research pertain to actual research *techniques*. Institutional ethnography, the most procedurally well-defined strategy, employs the techniques of ethnographic and textual analysis. Other strategies, however, are less easily characterized in terms of techniques. It is fair to say that, on the whole, critical strategies lean in the direction of qualitative methods. However, this does not rule out the judicious and reflexive use of quantitative approaches. Just as there is nothing in quantification that renders an empirical analysis inherently more veridical, there is nothing inherent in the quantification of aspects of social practice that predestines such analysis to be a "tool of social control." Returning to Howard Becker's question, we must ask *whose side we take* when we conduct the research—a question that has telling implications from the moment of problem formulation clear through the analysis, interpretation, and dissemination of results.

The British-based Radical Statistics Group (whose Web site is described on page 106), an organization of politically progressive statisticians and researchers founded in 1975, takes a sensible position on the construction and use of social statistics:

> Members of Radstats are concerned at the extent to which official statistics reflect governmental rather than social purposes. Our particular concerns are:
> * The mystifying use of technical language to disguise social problems as technical ones;
> * The lack of control by the community over the aims of statistical investigations, the way these are conducted and the use of the information produced;
> * The power structures within which statistical and research workers are employed and which control the work and how it is used;
> * The fragmentation of social problems into specialist fields, obscuring connectedness.
>
> Radstats members believe that statistics can be used as part of campaigns for progressive social change—just as they were used to support measures that led to improvements in public health in the nineteenth century.[5]

What Radstats alerts us to is the need for critical researchers employing quantitative methods to do so in ways that are broadly consonant with the ontological and ethical commitments we have discussed under the rubrics of dialectical social analysis and social inquiry as communicative reason. The latter insists that quantitative research serve lifeworld needs (particularly those of subaltern groups and communities) and enhance the quality and inclusiveness of public discussion. The former insists that the *relationality* of the social (including deeply structured relations that may not be directly measurable or quantifiable) not be lost in a statistical welter of variables and their co-variances.

Andrew Sayer has presented some penetrating comments on the limitations of quantitative methods in social science. For Sayer, a critical realist, before we can quantify we must ask the ontological question, "what must objects be like for it to be possible to quantify them?" (1982: 159). Conventional social science has typically eschewed this question. Strictly speaking, the assignment of numbers (including ones and zeroes) to objects and processes is only appropriate if they are "qualitatively invariant," that is, "we can measure them at different times or places in different conditions and know that we are not measuring different things" (Sayer, 1982: 160). However, context-dependent entities, such as opinions and attitudes or, for that matter, social relations, do not satisfy this condition. The entities that compose the social—including people "making their own history"—are not only context-dependent; they are dynamic—they have "emergent powers" that bring qualitative change to what they are. As Sayer points out, if the entities referred to by the variables of an equation interact in ways that produce qualitative change (e.g., through a learning process), the variables will not be able to make stable reference (Sayer, 1982: 160). Typically, this is the case in social life, although single-slice quantitative studies of large populations may not bump up against this reality. Even if the assumption of qualitative invariance may be claimed for one set of variables in a quantitative model, since the social is an open system in which emergence and contingency are integral features, the model itself "will have to be fitted anew for each and every application, and hence parameters, coefficients and regression lines will vary from case to case" (Sayer, 1982: 167). Contrary to Hubert Blalock's (1961) claim that "regression equations are the laws of science," we must conclude that quantitative methods cannot, in principle, yield predictive and generalizable knowledge of the social.

Since the 1980s, insiders to quantitative method have produced important critiques that renounce grandiose claims such as Blalock's and that clarify the more modest role that quantitative method can play in social science (Lieberson, 1985; Marini and Singer, 1988; Freedman, 1991). Lieberson's remains the most insightful text in this literature. Using a form of sociological reasoning that is typically absent from quantitative analysis, Lieberson (1985) invites us to reflect on:

- The contingent processes of social selectivity that underlie measured "variables" and that confound attempts at quasi-experimental statistical control (18–37);
- The relationality of social life, which means that "the impact of an independent variable is not confined to the situations in which it is present" (50), and which generates an intractable "contamination problem" for quantitative analysts (50–61);
- The asymmetrical and irreversible character of many causal processes—the *historical* nature of social reality—which is not captured in the symmetrical mathematical notation of regression and related approaches (67–86);
- The power relations and strategies of social closure that generate many of the statistical relationships that are quantitative sociology's stock-in-trade (166–168);
- The distinction between "superficial causes" (typically featured in quantitative analysis) that appear to be responsible for a given outcome and the often unmeasurable "basic causes" that are actually generating the outcome (185–199);
- The related tendency in quantitative sociology to restrict our thinking about social causation to variables that are observable and measurable (223).

As Lieberson notes in his extended discussion of the relationship between race, education, and income in the United States, a complicated quantitative model showing that racial differences in income are, after appropriate statistical controls, attributable to racial differences in educational attainment:

> has not the causal value that one might have assumed. It describes the given set of events at a given time; it describes what a black person might well follow as a get-ahead strategy if he or she can assume that not many other blacks will follow the same strategy and hence the basic matrix will remain unaltered (1985: 192).

This is an unreasonable assumption in Lieberson's view.

Quantitative analyses, however elegant mathematically, give us no more then *descriptive* summations of social patterns and trends. As Lieberson concludes, "explanations of variation are not substitutes for explanations of the existence of the phenomena in itself" (1985: 223).

In the study of late modernity there is the additional complication that quantification is not only an analytic tool, but is part of the object of investigation. We see this most clearly in *commodification*, a specific historical reality of capitalism that is often misinterpreted as a human universality (see the earlier discussion of reification on page 161). Commodification assigns a number, on an apparently ratio scale, to every practice and object that enters into the market system, namely, its price. But prices and other quantifications created within capitalism—measures of labour productivity and the like—are not "natural" entities. They are social, discursive constructions. A critically scientific approach to comprehending aspects of our lives that come prepackaged in quantified forms—such as commodity prices, stock-market indices, and personal income—needs to interrogate *how quantification occurs as a social process*. This means digging beneath the surface appearances of market society to problematize the everyday world of a commodified social order. The refusal of mainstream economics to make this initial critical move, its appropriation of prices, and the like as self-evident "facts" is the key reason for the failure of the most quantitative of social sciences to generate knowledge of value beyond the narrow, generally short-term, and system-bound horizons of investors, corporate managers, and state officials.

In recent decades, quantitative indices that offer precise scores based on elaborate calculations, such as Gross Domestic Product (GDP) in economics, socio-economic status in sociology (Goldman and Tickamyer, 1984), and IQ in psychology (Kamin, 1974), have been subjected to critical scrutiny that has revealed them to be of limited scientific value but of some ideological use in bolstering entrenched power. In the case of GDP, progressive economists have not only delivered a devastating critique of this system-oriented measure of "economic health," they have developed an alternative "Genuine Progress Indicator" that comes at the issue of economic well-being from a lifeworld and ecological perspective (Venetoulis and Cobb, 2004).[6] The debunking of GDP and of other uncritical, reifying measures that have organized a great deal of positivist inquiry is entirely welcome, not only for its value as a catalyst to public debate on economic and social priorities but also as a reminder to critical researchers that they need to be particularly reflexive in their use of quantitative data.

What, then, can we conclude about the role of quantitative method in critical social research? I am again guided by Andrew Sayer's helpful discussion, and in particular the distinction he draws between "intensive" and "extensive" research designs. Extensive designs, such as large-scale surveys, search for regularities in large populations in the belief that many repeated observations will reveal significant relations. It is in these kinds of studies that quantification is a favoured technique for managing and analyzing massive amounts of data. Intensive designs investigate how a process works, what produces change, or what agents actually do in a particular case or small number of cases. Extensive research "seeks out mainly formal similarities and differences rather than substantial connections. Intensive research seeks out substantial relations of connection and situates practices within wider contexts, thereby illuminating part-whole relationships" (Sayer, 2000: 22). In Sayer's view, which I share, these approaches are complementary. Comprehension of social causation—of the relational dynamics that generate change (or stasis)—requires intensive investigation of relations in context. But extensive research can help map social conditions and practices at one time or over time. For all the reasons given above, the claims of some quantitative methodologists—that quantification and statistical analysis provide explanatory, generalizable, and predictive knowledge of the social—lack credibility. What we actually get from a quantitative analysis is a mapping of certain formal properties and relations that can be of descriptive and heuristic value, but that does not reveal the substantial relations of connection that comprise social causality.[7]

Still, the extensive representations of practice that issue from quantitative analysis can be useful to several forms of critical social research. In participatory action research, communities often undertake self-surveys as part of the project. The results of such endeavours can be tabulated and analyzed using quantitative methods, and then forwarded to public discussion, which can help clarify issues and contribute to the formation of action strategies (see Carr-Hill, 1984; Social Action Commission, 1987). Although some feminist researchers reject quantitative methods outright, Marjorie De Vault (1996) has argued that quantitative method can be effective in presenting "hard data" on policy issues, and that, against certain cultural traditions that oppress women, positive science can be a force for liberation. Researchers committed to dialectical social analysis have also made use of quantitative techniques in sketching the "big structures" and "large processes" that critical macro-sociological inquiry often entails (Tilly, 1984).[8] Even in the realm of discourse analysis, a modicum of quantification can sometimes be beneficial, as David Silverman (1985) has shown.

Notwithstanding its limitations, quantitative method thus remains highly relevant to sociology's interest in social justice. As I argued earlier, quantitative method may, if used unreflexively, objectify its subjects and reduce the many-sided relationality of the world to the bloodless language of variables and correlations. Yet quantitative data, when interpreted not as obdurate "facts" but as rough representations of practice, and when complemented by such distinctively sociological methods as network analysis, do provide maps of the social. Such representations can contribute both to the unmasking of social inequity and to the stimulation of public discussion.

CRITICAL STRATEGIES AS AN OPEN TOOLKIT

Together, the strategies I have surveyed in this book give researchers a methodological toolkit for social study that is critical—whether the critique take an oppositional, radical, or subversive form.[9] They enable inquiry grounded in the actualities of the past and present and alert to future possibilities. They prefigure a sociology allied not only with currents of social justice extending beyond academe but with other fields of knowledge: development studies, gender studies, labour studies, critical legal studies, political economy, cultural studies, environmental studies, social history. They provide resources for a critical social *science*, in the most defensible sense of the term: a systematic, disciplined inquiry into how the social world is put together, and how it can be remade to enhance well-rounded human development and ecological health. The metaphor of "toolkit," which I have borrowed from Foucault, leaves us with two final questions: (1) Can the toolkit be expanded—are the five strategies sufficient? and (2) Why a toolkit—with its implications of eclecticism—why not an integrated paradigm?

On the first question, it is best to view the toolkit as itself under construction. For the most part, the approaches I have featured here emerged out of the wave of activism that crested most visibly in 1968 but whose ramifications form part of the political and cultural environment for contemporary activism and dialogue. As humanity's condition and problems change, so do the proffered solutions, including critical strategies for social inquiry. By the same token, it is advisable to keep the toolkit unlocked and open to quantitative techniques, to network-analytic approaches that afford mappings of substantive and not simply formal relations, to psychoanalytic methods of dialogical self-clarification, and to other methods of social inquiry not pursued herein.

On the second question, there are, as we have seen, many overlaps and some creative tensions among the approaches we have considered. There is no doubt that a triangulation of these strategies, where feasible and appropriate, can enrich our work. But I do not think that a grand synthesis—a singular paradigm—is in the offing, nor is there any obvious reason why we should seek such integration. My hunch is that the manifold aspirations for social justice and ecological health in today's world can be best served by a diversity of scholarly and political interventions. What our survey of critical strategies shows is the value of a plurality of approaches, pursued in a reflexive manner sensitive to their epistemological and ontological entailments and ethical-political implications. If the point is not simply to *interpret* the world but to *change* it, these strategies give us a good deal of leverage.

NOTES

1.   In her illuminating discussion of Habermas's concept of the public sphere, Nancy Fraser defines subaltern counterpublics as "parallel discursive arenas where members of subordinated social groups invent and circulate counter-discourses, which in turn permit them to formulate oppositional interpretations of their identities, interests, and needs" (1997: 81).

2.   Similarly, Ian Parker (p. 260) draws a direct connection between PAR and his version of CDA: "discourse analysis should become a variety of action research, in which the internal system of any discourse and its relation to others is challenged."

3.   As Fraser puts it, "gay-identity politics treats homosexuality as a cultural positivity with its own substantive content, much like (the commonsense view of) an ethnicity. This positivity is assumed to subsist in and of itself and to need only additional recognition. Queer politics, in contrast, treats homosexuality as the constructed and devalued correlate of heterosexuality; both are reifications of sexual ambiguity and are codefined only in virtue of each other. The transformative aim is not to solidify a gay identity but to deconstruct the homo-hetero dichotomy so as to destabilize all fixed sexual identities. The point is not to dissolve all sexual difference in a single, universal human identity; it is, rather, to sustain a sexual field of multiple, debinarized, fluid, ever-shifting differences" (1997: 24).

4.   As Michael Ryan (1982) has argued, there was a deconstructive aspect to Marx's critique of political economy, yet the burden of Marx's project was an *unmasking* of capital's social relations, not a deconstruction of the liberal ideology that celebrates and naturalizes capitalism.

5. http://www.radstats.org.uk/about.htm, accessed April 12, 2004.

6. In their analysis of economic trends comparing the GDP and GPI in the United States from 1950 through 2002, Venetoulis and Cobb show that although GDP per capita rose from approximately $12,000 to $35,000, GPI per capita rose only slightly from its base of $6,000 to approximately $8,000 in 1970, and thereafter remained flat (figures are in 2000 dollars). As a household-centred measure of economic well-being, the GPI takes into account such factors as income inequality, the social costs of crime, and the depreciation of environmental assets and natural resources. Whereas GDP increases whenever the volume of monetized transactions grows—whether through the rapid expansion of the U.S. prison industry, through the unsustainable harvesting of nonrenewable resources, or through disasters such as the Exxon *Valdez* spill—the GPI is adjusted downward for these sorts of undesirable developments. Both measures, we should note, are value-laden, but the GDP takes the standpoint of capitalists in measuring the total quantity of commoditized exchange value, while the GPI takes a lifeworld-centred perspective in introducing concerns for the quality of life and environment.

7. Jones's critique (in Chapter 11) of the World Bank's "explanation" of global poverty is worth re-reading at this point. As Jones puts it, "the orthodoxy is accurate at the descriptive level of surface appearances, but is blind to the real, non-empirical relations that generate empirical appearances" (p. 149).

8. A good recent examplar is Beverly Silver's (2003) sweeping study of workers' movements and globalization since 1870, which uses quantitative data gleaned from a systematic study of newspaper reports on labour actions in various countries.

9. See the Introduction (p. 3) for a discussion of these three images of the critical edge in social inquiry.

REFERENCES

Blalock, Hubert M. 1961. *Causal Inferences in Non-Experimental Research*. Chapel Hill: University of North Carolina Press.

Brookey, Robert Alan, and Diane Helene Miller. 2001. "Changing Signs: The Political Pragmatism of Poststructuralism." *International Journal of Sexuality and Gender Studies* 6(1–2): 139–153.

Campbell, Marie, and Frances Gregor. 2002. *Mapping Social Relations*. Toronto: Garamond.

Carr-Hill, Roy A. 1984. "Radicalising Survey Methodology." *Quality and Quantity* 18: 275–292.

De Vault, Marjorie L. 1996. "Talking Back to Sociology: Distinctive Contributions of Feminist Methodology." *Annual Review of Sociology* 22: 29–50.

Foucault, Michel. 1984. "What Is Enlightenment?" In *The Foucault Reader*, edited by Paul Rabinow, 32–50. New York: Pantheon.

Fraser, Nancy. 1997. *Justice Interruptus*. New York: Routledge.

Freedman, David A. 1991. "Statistical Models and Shoe Leather." In *Sociological Methodology 1991*, vol. 21, edited by Peter V. Marsden, 291–314. Oxford: Blackwell.

Glick, Elisa. 2000. "Sex Positive: Feminism, Queer Theory, and the Politics of Transgression." *Feminist Review* 64: 19–45.

Goldman, Robert, and Ann Tickamyer. 1984. "Status Attainment and the Commodity Form: Stratification in Historical Perspective." *American Sociological Review* 49: 196–209.

Habermas, Jürgen. 1979. *Communication and the Evolution of Society*. London: Heinemann.

Jennings, Leonie E., and Anne P. Graham. 1996. "Postmodern Perspectives and Action Research: Reflecting on the Possibilities." *Educational Action Research* 4(2): 267–278.

Kamin, Leon J. 1974. *The Science and Politics of IQ*. Toronto: John Wiley & Sons.

Lieberson, Stanley. 1985. *Making It Count: The Improvement of Social Research and Theory*. Berkeley: University of California Press.

McNally, David. 2001. *Bodies of Meaning*. Albany: State University of New York Press.

Marini, M.M., and B. Singer. 1988. "Causality in the Social Sciences." In *Sociological Methodology 1988,* vol. 18, edited by C.C. Clogg, 347–409. Oxford: Blackwell.

Parkin, Andrew C. 1996. "On the Practical Relevance of Habermas's Theory of Communicative Action." *Social Theory & Practice* 22(3): 417–440.

Reid, Colleen. 2000. "Seduction and Enlightenment in Feminist Action Research." *Resources for Feminist Research* 28: 169188.

Ryan, Michael. 1982. *Marxism and Deconstruction*. Baltimore: Johns Hopkins University Press.

Sayer, Andrew. 1982. *Method in Social Science: A Realist Approach*. London: Hutchinson.

_____. 2000. *Realism and Social Science*. London: Sage.

Silver, Beverly J. 2003. *Forces of Labor: Workers' Movements and Globalization Since 1870*. New York: Cambridge University Press.

Silverman, David. 1985. *Qualitative Methodology: Describing the Social World*. Brookfield: Gower Publishing Co.

Smith, Dorothy E. 1989. "Sociological Theory: Writing Patriarchy into Feminist Texts." In *Feminism and Sociological Theory*, edited by Ruth Wallace, 34–64. Newbury Park: Sage.

_____. 1993. "High Noon in Textland: A Critique of Clough." *The Sociological Quarterly* 34: 183–192.

_____. 1999. *Writing the Social*. Toronto: University of Toronto Press.

Social Action Commission, Diocese of Charlottetown. 1987. *From the Grass Roots: A Critical Consciousness Approach to Social Justice in Prince Edward Island*. Chalottetown: Catholic Diocese of Charlottetown.

Storr, Merl. 2000. "Response to Elisa Glick." *Feminist Review* 64: 46–48.

Tilly, Charles. 1984. *Big Structures, Large Processes, Huge Comparisons*. New York: Russell Sage Foundation.

Venetoulis, Jason, and Clifton Cobb. 2004. "Genuine Progress Indicator (GPI): Measuring the Real State of the Economy." *Redefining Progress*. http://www.redefiningprogress.org/publications/gpi_march2004update.pdf, accessed April 13, 2004.

Workshops on Critical Research Strategies

NOTE TO INSTRUCTORS

The following workshops have proven quite effective in several classes. They are designed for seminar groups of 25 or less, and for discussion periods that run for one hour and 20 minutes, although with a few adaptations the same workshops could accommodate groups of different sizes and shorter or longer time frames.

Each workshop is closely linked to one or more readings in this book. Ideally, students should have worked through most of the material in a given part before the workshop is held. I have found that having students read and think about the assignment before the session improves the quality of discussion. Students enjoy writing up their reflections on the workshops in brief reports. (I ask each student to write five such reports over the course of the term, each weighted as five percent of the course grade.)

WORKSHOP 1: REDISCOVERING THE CRITICAL EDGE IN SOCIAL ANALYSIS

In this workshop we apply Howard Becker's idea of "taking sides" and Joe Feagin's notion of a "counter-system tradition" in social research to four scenarios of lived oppression.

The four scenarios are as follows:

Spades: Work at McDonald's is poorly paid, hard, and hectic. Pressure to keep profits high and wage costs low results in understaffing, so staff have to work harder and faster. Workers are often denied breaks or given shortened breaks, and required to stay late. In the reviews for pay raises, employees are marked on how often they smile. The majority of employees are people who have few job options; for many this is their first job. Two-thirds of employees are under 21. Staff turnover is high, making it virtually impossible to unionize. (http://www.mcspotlight.org)

Diamonds: Gays and lesbians in Canada have recently gained the right to marry and, in some provinces, to adopt children. But homophobia remains a strong current of prejudice. Many gays and lesbians spend their teen years closeted or ostracized from the heteronormative "straight" culture that renders them objects to be ridiculed and despised.

Clubs: Slavery is defined as work for no pay under the threat of violence. Siri was born in Thailand and sold into sex slavery by her parents when she was 14. Brutalized by her first client, she tried to run away, but was caught, beaten, and raped. Later that night she was forced to service a stream of customers until the early morning. The beatings and the work continued, eventually breaking her will. Now a teenager, she is convinced she is a bad person. As Kevin Bales writes: "When I commented on how pretty she looked in a photograph, how like a pop star, she replied, 'I'm no star; I'm just a whore. That's all.'" (http://www.iabolish.com/today/experience/mental.htm)

Hearts: In the United States, a series of government laws and policies since the 1970s has steadily targeted Arab and Muslim non-citizens for selective interrogation, detention, harassment, presumption of terrorist involvement, and removal from the country, The Patriot Act of 2002 and the Presidential Order to establish quasi-military "tribunals" exacerbated the selective targeting of Arab and Muslim non-citizens in a climate of fear that sanctions blatant racial profiling.

The workshop involves three steps:

1. Each member of the class will be dealt a card from a deck that has as many cards as students in the class. We will then divide into four groups according to suit, with each group assigned the corresponding scenario. Each group should discuss the following issues:
   - What kinds of *questions* might a critical social researcher, rooted in the counter-system tradition, pose in researching one or more of these scenarios, taking the side of the oppressed?
   - What kinds of *questions* might a researcher on the side of established power pose?
   - How might these differing questions lead the respective researchers to conduct rather different investigations, that is, to use different *styles or strategies of inquiry*?
   - How might the knowledge gained be *used* to empower or emancipate, or perhaps to deter such outcomes and to legitimate *status quo* arrangements? *Who* would the knowledge be useful for? (25 min.)
2. We will regroup according to card number (e.g., the Deuces will form a group of four). In a roundtable discussion, each group member will report the basic outcomes of the initial discussions. Each group can then distil its ideas on the four scenarios into some provisional conclusions. The key question is what a comparison of the four scenarios tells us about the difference that being critical makes in the kinds of research questions posed, the strategies of inquiry employed, the knowledge gained, and the uses to which that knowledge might be put. (25 min.)
3. In a final plenary session we will hear from the groups assembled in Step 2. Discussion can focus on differing *forms* of oppression and the possible *roles* of social research in facilitating social justice in different contexts of knowledge and power. (25 min.)

WORKSHOP 2: STEPS TOWARD CRITICAL INQUIRY

In the Appendix to *The Sociological Imagination*, C.Wright Mills conveys his approach to reflexive social inquiry. Mills keeps his life and his work closely integrated by the use of a "file." In first chapter of their book, *Experience, Research, Social Change*, Sandra Kirby and Kate

McKenna describe a three-step process for beginning a research project "from the margins," which resembles Mills's approach in some respects. The first step is to identify your *research interest*, to find a focus for your project, which usually has some connection to your experience, a community you identify with or support, or some other relevant issue in your lifeworld. The second step is to frame your *research question* clearly but in a flexible form that leaves possible lines of inquiry open. The third step is to unpack your *conceptual baggage*—to account for yourself as an active agent in the research process, and for the larger context in which the research is to occur.

In this workshop we will emphasize the second and third steps. I am providing you with the *research interest*, namely, *the conditions of life and learning among students at your institution or in your class.*

1. Break into groups of three. Appoint a note-taker who will report the results of your efforts back to the class. *Your first task is to move from the general research interest to a more specific **research question** that is framed in a way that can guide a social inquiry.*

   In making this move, keep in mind Kirby and McKenna's advice:
   - Choose a question that has enough scope but not so much that it cannot be answered.
   - Choose a question that you are able to gather information about.
   - Choose a question that is exciting or enticing—that will sustain your interest over the long haul.
   - Choose a question that comes from your experience, that is relevant to your biography or that is important to you.

   Spend some time discussing and refining the research question, and reflecting on why it might be worth pursuing in a research project. How might the knowledge gained speak to public issues, empower disadvantaged groups, release human potential, or otherwise advance social justice?

2. We will then hear brief reports from the groups and consider the questions that have been posed.

3. Reassemble into your original groups of three. *The next step is to examine, more thoroughly, the **conceptual baggage** you bring to this research.* "Doing" conceptual baggage resembles what Mills called keeping a file. "It is your way of keeping your own experience and process observable and accounted for in the investigation" (Kirby and McKenna, p. 51). Writing your conceptual baggage involves reflecting carefully on the research as an aspect of your life and of the larger social order—putting and keeping the project in its full context. It includes "both intellectual thinking and emotional comments," and it can help you recognize how the aspirations and concerns you bring to the project and the constraints that surround it may influence how the research develops. Conceptual baggage thus makes research *reflexive*. Such reflexivity is a prerequisite to critical inquiry.

   At this very preliminary stage, your conceptual baggage might include:
   - a self-description or an account of your world view;
   - a consideration of what in your experience leads you to be interested in the research question;
   - a reflection on how your experience contributes to or informs the research;

- an analysis of how "external parameters"—the historical and political context in which the project is situated—might organize and shape the research and the knowledge resulting from it.
4. The workshop concludes with brief reports from the groups and discussion.

WORKSHOP 3: DIALECTICAL SOCIAL ANALYSIS

In this session our objective is to explore the full relationality of an object. The course director should choose an object that forms part of our everyday world. (I have done this workshop very successfully with an athletic shoe, a can of soda pop, and a fast-food hamburger.) Use of the blackboard to map some of the relations revealed in steps 1 to 3 is helpful. The exercise works well with a minimum of introduction and a maximum of exploratory discussion.

Step 1: Description (to be done with the class circled around the object, enabling each individual to write observations and descriptions, followed by a brief general discussion)
Please observe the object very carefully. What is it? How would you describe it in detail? What do you call it? How is it referred to?

Step 2: Local Analysis (depending upon class size, this and the steps that follow can either be done via general discussion or by small groups that report back after brief discussion)
How does the object relate to other aspects of social life in our local milieu? How is it used, bought, sold? In what everyday context does it exist? How does it directly relate to your life?

Step 3: Diagnosis
Locate the object in its total time and space, and with its total human and ecological implications. The following questions may help guide your investigation.

- Where did it come from; how was it produced, by whom, and under what conditions?
- How is it consumed, and with what consequences for who we are and for the ecosystem?
- What is the history of this object and of objects of this sort?
- In what social relations and power structures is the object embedded locally and globally?
- What ways of life, ideologies, and kinds of human beings does it promote or discourage?
- What public issues or social problems are raised by this object?

Step 4: Reconstruction (you can complete this part at your leisure, if class time runs short)
How might this object, and the practices that make it what it is, be redesigned to serve people's and ecological needs better? What changes to our social relations and ways of life would be required in order to accomplish this?

The source for steps 1 to 3 of this workshop is: Ira Shor, "No More Teacher's Dirty Looks: Conceptual Teaching from the Bottom Up," in *Studies in Socialist Pedagogy*, edited by Theodore Mills Norton and Bertell Ollman (New York: Monthly Review Press, 1978): 177–195. See also

Peter Kaufman, "Michael Jordan Meets C. Wright Mills: Illustrating the Sociological Imagination with Objects from Everyday Life," *Teaching Sociology* 25 (1997): 309–314.

WORKSHOP 4: INSTITUTIONAL ETHNOGRAPHY

In *Doing Institutional Ethnography*, Marie Campbell and Frances Gregor note that institutional ethnographies are rarely planned out in fine detail—after all, the method is primarily exploratory in nature. None the less, one needs to begin on firm footing. "The notion of problematic and the work you do to discover the problematic helps you identify the place for inquiry to begin" (2002: 47).

This workshop is divided into two parts: (1) a set of parallel small-group discussions in which each group attempts to identify a possible problematic, and (2) a plenary session in which groups present their problematics and comment on each other's problematics.

As Campbell and Gregor emphasize, to identify a problematic you must become familiar with the experienced actualities of the group in question. Since as students you have in common the actuality of being part of this class, *I suggest that your problematics be developed from your experience in this class so far this term. (You could, if it proves helpful, extend the context to, say, the larger program you are in, but this is not necessary.)*

1. Identifying a Problematic

In groups of three, begin by appointing a note-taker/spokesperson. The person will have the task of presenting a report to the class as a whole. The report should have the following structure:

a. *What knowledge of lived actualities did your group mobilize in getting the ball rolling: what accounts of your experiences in this course were voiced and discussed?* I suggest that as an entry point you go round the group, sharing and comparing experiences in this course that you find relevant. As you provide these accounts to each other, look for clues about their *social organization*. Note these clues; they can be springboards into a problematic.

b. *What problematic did you identify on the basis of your critical reflections on that knowledge?* In developing a problematic, keep in mind the following points:

- By carefully examining an account of experience, you can make problematic what is ordinarily taken for granted—*how things happen as they do.*
- As a puzzle, a problematic arises *for someone* and makes a difference *for someone*. In identifying a problematic, you are taking sides and taking up the inquiry from a specific standpoint in the everyday world. Your problematic should not lead you into a "positionless account"; it should not cause you to lose your stance in the everyday world.
- The problematic should direct attention to questions that may not have been posed but are latent in the actualities of the experienced world.
- Sometimes a problematic can be inspired by analysis of something troubling in experience, or some sense of unease.
- Remember that a problematic for inquiry can emerge for a researcher only when the theoretical framework of institutional ethnography is used. This is a framework that emphasizes the relational, lived, practical, emergent character of the social world and the importance of ideological practices, extra-local relations, and ruling apparatuses in organizing the actualities of specific settings.

2. Plenary Discussion

Each group will make a presentation. Other members of the class will have the responsibility of active listening, which also means giving constructively critical feedback on how promising or viable the problematic might be as a way of organizing a possible inquiry from the standpoint of students in the class.

WORKSHOP 5: CRITICAL DISCOURSE ANALYSIS

In this workshop we will try to engage with *genealogy* as a critical research strategy. As Maria Tamboukou (1999) states in the conclusion to her essay, "Writing Genealogies: An Exploration of Foucault's Strategies for Doing Research":

> Rather than following methodological principles, Foucault's genealogies create a methodological rhythm of their own, weaving around a set of crucial questions .... What is happening now? What is this present of ours? How have we become what we are and what are the possibilities of becoming "other"? Such questions create unexplored and even unthought areas of investigation.

These questions, particularly the last one, guide genealogical inquiry toward developing "a historical ontology of ourselves." "It is significant that a genealogy should start with a major interrogation of what has been accepted as the 'truth,' any truth concerning the ways individuals understand themselves as subjects of this world. The genealogy is thus starting by shattering any certainties ..." (Tamboukou, 1999: 214).

The Assignment

Typically, genealogy requires extensive reading of the various texts that in part constitute a discursive formation—e.g., "the modern prison." Like deconstruction, there is no fixed methodological procedure in genealogy; in fact, the approach is inimical to methodological canonization. For pedagogical purposes, we will restrict ourselves to a single text, and we will divide our genealogical work into three steps.

The *text* consists of passages from books by Benjamin Franklin, published not long before the mid-18th century. These passages were presented by Max Weber in *The Protestant Ethic and the Spirit of Capitalism* (New York: Charles Scribner's Sons, 1958, 48–50). Franklin was an important figure in the American Revolution of the late 18th century, but for genealogy, which decentres the subject from the focal point of analysis, the key issues are not what may have motivated Franklin to write what he wrote, or what he intended to communicate. In your analysis you should approach the text not as the product of an author but as an element of discourse that, although put into circulation more than 250 years ago, still has "currency" (no pun intended) in contemporary discursive formations.

Step 1: Interrogate the *truth effects* of the text. On this issue, remember that for Foucault "... discourses are productive: medical discourses about 'folly' and 'unreason' produce the mentally ill person, penological discourses produce the criminal, discourses on sex produce sexuality ...." What does the text and the practices bundled along with it produce as "truths" about ourselves and our world? And how does it produce these truths—through what terms and devices?

Step 2: Genealogy interrogates not only the "truths" through which we constitute ourselves as subjects of knowledge, but also "the field of power through which we constitute ourselves as subjects acting on others" (Foucault, in Tamboukou, 1999: 211). Power, however, is not conceptualized as an entity to be possessed or used in a domination/subordination relationship. For Foucault, power is bound up in specific techniques for governing oneself and governing others: "technologies of power which determine the conduct of individuals and submit them to certain ends or domination, an objectivising of the subject" (quoted in Tamboukou, 1999: 212). In this step, you interrogate the text as to its *technologies of power*. How are certain human relations and identities "normalized"—made to appear universal or ethically pre-eminent? Such normalization constructs a hegemonic historical narrative—a comprehensive story that writes us into its script.

Step 3: We look into local, minor sequences of events that subvert hegemonic historical narratives. In this way it is possible to question the authority of the identities built upon those stories, and to question the global, systematic character of hegemonic discourses. This aspect of genealogy entails what Foucault called an "insurrection of subjugated knowledge," of local historical contents submerged within systematic modes of thought and disqualified from authority. (A good example is the "queering" of hegemonic discourses of sexuality by looking into events and practices on the margins of heterosexuality, nuclear families, and other constituents of normalized sexuality.) If Franklin's text can be said to claim a certain hegemony, what kinds of subjugated knowledges have been submerged and disqualified in securing it?

In the workshop the class divides into groups of three (each with a designated note-taker/speaker) and works through these three steps. In each step, students should feel free to bring in their own knowledge and understanding (historical or contemporary) in interrogating how the text produces truth, power, and normality, and what local historical contents get submerged and disqualified, but may still carry subversive implications. The workshop shuttles between small-group and plenary format, as follows:

Step 1	Truth effects:	15 minutes small group, 10 minutes plenary
Step 2	Power, normalization:	15 minutes small group, 10 minutes plenary
Step 3	Subjugated knowledge:	15 minutes small group, 10 minutes plenary

WORKSHOP 6: PARTICIPATORY ACTION RESEARCH

As I was casting about for a way of introducing participatory action research, I remembered an approach to popular education developed by the development-education group GATT-Fly in the 1970s and used extensively throughout Canada and other countries. Based on the radical pedagogy of Paulo Freire, the method is called Ah-Hah! The Ah-Hah seminar is:

> education for a particular purpose, for collective political action, not for greater understanding as an end in itself. The seminar aims to empower groups by reinforcing their confidence in their abilities to analyze their situations and develop strategies to change them. (GATT-Fly, 1983: 17)

Typically, the Ah-Hah seminar is used as a way of collectively pooling the experiences of a subordinate group to build a critical social analysis that leads toward strategies for action. It is a kind of rudimentary participatory research that does not involve "gathering data," but relies instead upon our own stocks of knowledge as practitioners of our everyday worlds. The workshop becomes a "communication arena" for sharing that knowledge with an eye toward possible action. Normally, Ah-Hah seminars take one or two full days, and involve a group whose shared interests are fairly self-evident (e.g., a community group or union local). To hold the seminar, the following conditions need to be met:

1. A *goal* for the seminar—clearly stated, practical, and action-oriented—must be agreed to by the group. To make the workshop relevant to the class as a group, it makes sense to build on any insights from earlier workshops (particularly #2 and #4), which already focused on conditions of life and learning among students in the class. The goal might involve a particular issue or problem that most of the class is experiencing. It should have a social-change element, and should be democratically adopted by the group.

2. Although leadership in an Ah-Hah seminar is a responsibility shared among group members, the *animator/recorder* facilitates discussion by asking questions, diagramming analyses, and taking direction from the group. "The overall process is an interaction between the group and the animator/recorder, the issues raised by the participants and the specific objectives of the seminar" (GATT-Fly, 1983: 25). The course director can serve as animator, although all participants should reflect on the power dynamics in such an arrangement.

3. It is important that the animator/recorder keep a *record of the key points* of the discussion. Try to fit this on one panel of the blackboard, and use another panel for diagramming analyses, visually representing the main aspects of the group's analysis.

4. Another important role is that of *observer*, for which you will need a volunteer. The observer keeps track of the progress of the seminar, drawing attention to problems such as the domination of the discussion by a few, divergence from the declared focus/agenda without a group decision to do so, or a contribution that has been passed over. The observer should interject any time a problem comes up that needs attention, and can give feedback at the end of the session on the group process.

5. The group should *evaluate periodically* how the seminar is progressing. Are we on track with the goal we set? Is the level of participation good? At the mid-point and the close of the session, we should take time to consider these issues.

6. It is sometimes helpful, at points, to *break the larger group into smaller parts* for some quick brainstorming. We may want to do this if we feel stymied at a certain point.

7. *The starting point* in an Ah-Hah seminar is the lived reality of participants. The seminar needs to begin with some observations that put its participants into the picture. From there, you can begin to draw out themes for discussion and sketch the bigger picture.

WORKSHOP 7: SOCIAL INQUIRY AS COMMUNICATIVE REASON

A good starting point for social inquiry as communicative reason is C. Wright Mills's distinction between private troubles and public issues. For Mills, the sociological imagination enables us to fathom the connections between the former and the latter, and healthy democracy—a vibrant public sphere—requires that such an imagination be widely cultivated in the general population. Listed below are several "troubles"; members of the class may want to add others to the list.

- Students in many universities and colleges have been subjected for years to heavy tuition increases, often accompanied by smaller available grants. Many students are obliged to work nearly full-time to make ends meet and to avoid heavy debt loads. Fees for non-affluent students, and especially for students from the global South, are becoming prohibitive.
- "You will be fighting not to conquer ... but to liberate," declared George W. Bush, addressing thousands of cheering American troops on January 3, 2003. The same *Globe and Mail* story quotes Bush stating "America seeks more than the defeat of terror. We seek the advance of human freedom in a world at peace." By May 2004, Iraqis lacking basic subsistence, employment, and security might have had doubts about the advance of their freedom under American power. "Imperialism" seems to describe their experience more closely than "liberation."
- How does it come to be that everything in our world has a price—whether a poor woman's spare kidney in India or a course featuring "critical research strategies"?
- My neighbour, now in her late 70s, fell and injured her ankle. She spent nearly a year on a waiting list before receiving treatment. Why is basic health care apparently becoming degraded and less accessible?
- In my study at home I have an *Adbusters* calendar. The graphic for January shows a running shoe divided into two unequal parts: Nike, $250 | Sweatshop, 83¢.

These are *troubles* in the sense that they threaten one or another cherished value. Perhaps they invite us to re-examine or reformulate those values, or to revise our ways of life. For critical social researchers, they raise a couple of questions, flagged by Mills:

- What are the structural and historical sources of these troubles; how are they, as social phenomena, embedded within larger social and historical relations and practices, whether economic, cultural, political, or social?
- What do these troubles, and the larger social issues they raise, tell us about the kinds of human beings that prevail, or that are coming to prevail, in our historical era?

The object of this exercise is to draw upon your own sociological imagination in moving from a private trouble to a *public issue*, and thus to a properly sociological research strategy. This workshop consists of six steps:

1. With a partner of your choice, choose any one of the above troubles, or make up your own alternative trouble.
2. Brainstorm with your partner some of the structural and historical *sources* and the human *implications* of this trouble. This means developing a list that may initially be quite lengthy and untidy. Your ideas need not be based in official "sociological" discourse; they may be based on your own experience or hunches, etc.
3. Edit your initial lists of sources and implications into a more concise form, perhaps collapsing some ideas together or eliminating ones that are quite tangential.

4. Look at your revised analysis and begin posing questions as to *what you need to find out* in order to take the analysis further. *What kind of research* will you need to do? What will be the sources of information?
5. What publics and lifeworld actors will your investigation speak to? How might your program of research help foster a more democratic lifeworld and a revitalized public sphere?
6. As many groups as time permits will make brief reports on points 3 to 5.

REFERENCES

GATT-Fly. 1983. *Ah-Hah! A New Approach to Popular Education*. Toronto: Between the Lines.

Kirby, Sandra, and Kate McKenna. 1989. *Experience, Research, Social Change: Methods from the Margins*. Toronto: Garamond.

Tamboukou, Maria. 1999. "Writing Genealogies: An Exploration of Foucault's Strategies for Doing Research." *Discourse: Studies in the Cultural Politics of Education* 20(2): 201–217.

Copyright Acknowledgments